Understanding Superher
Comic Books

Understanding Superhero Comic Books

A History of Key Elements, Creators, Events and Controversies

ALEX GRAND

Foreword by Jim Steranko

McFarland & Company, Inc., Publishers

Jefferson, North Carolina

ISBN (print) 978-1-4766-9039-1
ISBN (ebook) 978-1-4766-4861-3

LIBRARY OF CONGRESS AND BRITISH LIBRARY
CATALOGUING DATA ARE AVAILABLE

Library of Congress Control Number 2023006584

Front cover image © Youness Elh

Printed in the United States of America

*McFarland & Company, Inc., Publishers
Box 611, Jefferson, North Carolina 28640
www.mcfarlandpub.com*

For my parents, Natalie, and our beautiful kids.

Table of Contents

Part 4—Modern Superheroes

Part 5—Diversity and Aftermath

Acknowledgments

This book was a six-year project, compiled from a long series of endnotes and conversations with friends in the industry. The endnotes speak for themselves, but it's the conversations with friends that require some attention. First, I want to thank my fellow moderators on the Comic Book Historians Facebook group, David Armstrong and N. Scott Robinson, Ph.D. David, a former senior VP of MGM and Golden Age comic book collector, has become a friend with whom I attend conventions. I enjoy absorbing his stories about defunct comic book companies that he's visited and creators whom he's befriended since the 1960s. When I first showed him an initial draft of this book, he encouraged me to submit the work. N. Scott has become a colleague over the years and is a fellow editor on the Comic Book Historians Zines. His fellowship and advice have encouraged me to think academically, and he always pushes me to do better, which is demonstrated here by his graceful edit of this book. I also have to thank Layla Milholen at McFarland, with whom I began a dialogue with meaningful feedback that resulted in this book's publication.

I also spent the last few years listening to anecdotes from Comics and Comix cofounder Bud Plant, whose objective knowledge about the direct market and insight into classic illustrators, artists, and writers contributed to my understanding of how readers experienced old comic books in real time. I'm also grateful to comic artist Guy Dorian, Sr., who spent many hours discussing the ins and outs of the professional comic book industry with me. He is also responsible for publishing my first contribution to a comic book, the foreword to his trade paperback, *COR*.

It was Jim Steranko's *History of Comics* that first opened my eyes to the importance of interviewing creators and writing a history book that future scholars would refer to in their projects. Sitting with him at the Dallas Fantasy Fair and interviewing him for hours after the convention fueled my drive to interview other talented professionals. I'm also lucky to have established a fun and ongoing exchange with Roy Thomas, who published one of my interviews in his award-winning magazine, *Alter Ego*. Tom Palmer is another Silver Age artist who was kind enough to agree to an interview that provided insight into the importance of classic illustration. I should also mention Gary Groth and David Anthony Kraft, whose comic creator interviews over the decades influenced me to do something similar. I must also mention Jim Shooter, Paul Levitz, Tom DeFalco, Tom Brevoort, Alex Segura, Danny

Fingeroth, Carl Potts, Scott Shaw and Mort Todd, whose insights into the corporate and editorial aspects of the comic book industry shaped my practical view of its economics. Neal Adams was the first Silver Age artist I interviewed, and I'm still grateful to him for sharing his story with me in a manner that encouraged my dedication to comic history.

When I first encountered the comic book history pages on Facebook, there was a sequence of comic book historians who, in their own ways, took me under their wing. They taught me about various aspects of the field that shaped my approach to dissecting this material. Trina Robbins was critical in enhancing my understanding of women in comics, prompting me to review our interview and include it here. Thanks also to Professor William Foster III, whose tireless research into African American creators and characters continues to shed light on the necessity of inclusion in the comic book industry. J. David Spurlock and I have spent a great number of phone calls and conventions discussing the importance of Wally Wood, Carmine Infantino, and Frank Brunner. He wields a unique insight that converges history, art analysis, and publishing. Thanks also to Nicky Wheeler-Nicholson, whose illuminating book and anecdotes on her grandfather provided a necessary insight into the origins of DC Comics.

I didn't realize how influential Dr. Michael Vassallo would become when I met him at Comic Con International in San Diego some years ago, but his writings are informative in all things related to Timely-Atlas. His research in compiling every Stan Lee story was an invaluable resource that enabled me to analyze the creator's Marvel precursors. Our mutual friend, historian Barry Pearl, joined the Comic Book Historians Facebook Group in its early days, and he was kind enough to share some great inside information about Marvel in the 1960s. Ken Quattro, the comics detective, is a comics history tour de force whose determination in uncovering the truth became an example for many historians to live by. Thanks also to Anthony Tollin and Howard Chaykin, who both were kind enough to sit down for an interview, discussing their personal history into comics that gave me an appreciation for the key contributors from the Golden Age to the Bronze Age. Mike DeLisa could teach years of courses on comic strip history, and his recommendations shaped my research and selection of strip reprint books. I must also mention Arlen Schumer's group, The Silver Age of Comic Book Art, where he shares the importance of the artists of the late 1950s through the late 1960s who influenced the development of the modern superhero. Ger Appeldoorn is an accomplished editor and magazine contributor whose comic blog on the 1950s has artifacts that most people have never seen. His kindness and feedback are always enjoyed.

During my research into the Platinum Age, I spent a great deal of time talking about the topic with Robert Beerbohm, whose expertise in the field was invaluable. Although the romance genre is briefly mentioned here, I must mention comics historian Sydney Heifler, who is accomplished in studies of that genre. Peter Coogan is another scholar and friend of mine who established the definition of the superhero that I refer to in the beginning of this text. I should also share affection for my old fellow podcasters Bill Field and Jim Thompson, with whom I shared laughs and interview experience. Thanks to the good people of McFarland who saw something of value in my first draft and encouraged me to evolve the material.

Most importantly, I thank my wife, Natalie, whose love made this endeavor possible. Our children, Max, Nadja, Brodie, and Brooke, and my parents, Mehdi and Nazee, all of whom gave me the spiritual fuel to study comic book history.

Foreword

by Jim Steranko

Surprising as it may seem, across the spectrum of cultural history, there are only two authentic art forms indigenous to America—and, because there are only two, it seems incumbent that both should be lauded with similar and spirited dedication: jazz and comic books.

Obviously, the former has reached its apex, but the latter is still in transition. Over the past few decades, however, narrative art forms have matured significantly, from creation to assimilation—particularly showcasing the ultra-successful superhero genre in film, TV, and comics.

Vitality. Color. Movement. Irresistibly presented! I fell under their spell very early, learning to read at about two years of age from stacks of used, two-for-a-nickel comics—and my mother's guidance. Coincidentally, it may not be unreasonable to assume that the accompanying imagery had a profound impact on my youthful mentality and sense of perception—powerful enough to shape my destiny and generations of others like me.

The spawn of Kirby, Siegel, Crandall, Kubert, Wood—and numerous others who have subsequently faded from the cultural spotlight—have become icons in the American scene, and their importance must not be ignored or forgotten. To that end, I interviewed and interacted with hundreds of seminal, first-wave, four-color artists, writers, editors, and publishers—the good, the bad, the forgotten—ultimately generating the first two volumes of comic book history ever published.

Author Alex Grand interviewed me in much the same way in his quest to continue exploring the magic of the narrative arts and the generations of superheroes that emerged in its wake. We mutually confirm that the past is as important as the future and that the story of the American superhero deserves to be remembered, insightfully analyzed and preserved—and this volume continues in that tradition.

From cinema to comic books, STERANKO is synonymous with the American hero, and cited by Stan Lee as one of the prime architects of the Marvel Universe. As a filmmaker, he collaborated with Steven Spielberg, George Lucas, and Francis Ford Coppola on some of their hottest blockbuster films. His volumes of THE

STERANKO HISTORY OF COMICS *have sold more than 100,000 copies each. As an escape artist, his death-defying performances inspired the character Mister Miracle and more—designer, historian, magician, photographer, ad-agency art director, sideshow fire-eater, male model, typographer ... the list goes on. Steranko painted a multitude of movie posters, record albums, and book covers; and in 1975, created* RED TIDE, *the First Modern Graphic Novel. As the editor-publisher of the international entertainment magazine* PREVUE, *he conducted hundreds of superstar interviews and penned more than three million words.*

Preface

My personal history in comics started at age four when my parents bought me my first Mattel He-Man action figure in 1982. These action figures were introduced after the overwhelming commercial success of the *Star Wars* (1977) Kenner toys and their corresponding Marvel comic books. Mattel quickly figured out that the best way to give their He-Man toy line meaning was by telling their character backstories through minicomic books. I absorbed page after page of the first four *Masters of the Universe* minicomics (written by Donald Glut and drawn by Alfredo Alcala), realizing there was a whole other world hidden in between those covers. I asked my parents to read them to me again and again, until I could finally read them on my own. I also watched Christopher Reeve's *Superman* (1978) on TV whenever I could and begged my parents for any of the associated merchandise when we went shopping. Additionally, I watched reruns of Adam West's *Batman* (1966), which induced fantasies of me being Robin and fighting crime shoulder to shoulder with Bruce Wayne. Lynda Carter's *Wonder Woman* (1975) was so charming, daring, and beautiful that I often asked my mother to mimic her bullet-deflection moves with her bracelets. *Spider-Man and His Amazing Friends* (1981) and *The Incredible Hulk* (1982) were Saturday morning cartoons that I woke up early to watch, long before my parents got a chance to get out of bed to prepare breakfast. I was so fascinated by these characters with secret identities, abilities, costumes, and their mission to help people.

One day, my parents stopped at a local gas station. I walked in, noticing a newsstand full of comic books, and realized that they were the source of my favorite TV characters. It turned out that there were even more superheroes than I had thought possible. Not only that, but these heroes also interacted with one another in these stories. If I wanted to learn more about them and their adventures, all I had to do was buy them off the rack and read them. So, that's exactly what I did. Anytime we stopped at a gas station, I asked my parents for money that I had earned from doing odd jobs around the house. I bought, collected, and read comic after comic, even if they were out of order.

Growing up, I was a science geek. My parents worked all the time, so my grandparents raised me for a good portion of my comic-reading childhood. When I read *The Amazing Spider-Man*, I found that Peter Parker was raised by his Aunt May and Uncle Ben, and that he was a similar nerdy science student. Naturally, I organized my comics numerically, and then picked up *The Official Handbook of the Marvel Universe* (1982) and *Who's Who: The Definitive Directory of the DC Universe* (1985) to find out who these superheroes were and what powers they had.

When I entered my teenage years, comic book shops opened in our town and around the country. I asked my mom for a ride to our local shop every week to pick up new comics that I was dying to read. I also studied trade paperback reprints, including *Marvel Masterworks*, *Classic X-Men*, *Superman*, and *Batman* annuals, that introduced me to older material. Simultaneously, I was studying hard in high school to eventually go to medical school to become a doctor. During those high school years, I saw the industry rise and crash through iconic events such as the Image Revolution (1992), *The Death of Superman* (1993), and the Spider-Man *Clone Saga* (1994). As I entered university, my interest in comic books became peripheral so I could focus on my biochemistry major and visual arts minor.

As I continued through medical school, I created comics to organize my study notes in preparation for difficult courses and my medical residency. In a way, comics helped me become a neuro-ophthalmologist. At age thirty-three, I joined a medical practice and enjoyed helping my patients with their nerve-related visual problems. But somehow the intense studying of yesteryear and my obsession with comics came together, and I decided to conduct a series of interviews and study old comic books and comics history publications including books, articles, older interviews, and comic strip reprints. In the process, I re-created my medical school study routine with the history of comics, which led me to become a comic book historian. I was both learning from old discoveries and making my own using a systematic process of establishing historical cause and effect. I came across some amazing comics history online groups and eventually founded the official Comic Book Historians social media. I documented my findings on the Comic Book Historians YouTube channel and eventually mapped together disparate elements that connected the co-development of the comic book medium and the superhero genre. This is not meant as a complete history of comics, but rather a specific way of looking at the key events and players that influenced the development of modern superhero comic books.

Introduction

The modern comic book format started in the 1890s and evolved into its modern form by the 1980s. Prior to this period, visual sequential art had been used to construct linear stories that are referred to here as proto-comics. Proto-comics evolved into sequential panels with text that formed a narrative called comics. Comics began as strips published within a greater non-comic-based periodical such as a newspaper or magazine. Comic books are publications devoted solely to comics, which generally carry comic strip reprints or original material. Newspaper comic strips, pulp magazine proto-superheroes, Hollywood cinema, American illustration, and the mystique of early magicians combined traits that can be found in the initial superhero comic books. The standard superhero is a fictional being with extraordinary abilities, unique costumes and/or code names, and generally follows an internalized mission to make the world a better place by protecting the innocent.[1] The superhero genre started in the early 20th century within the comic book medium with such success that mainstream audiences tend to equate the two. Often, many fans refer to the later 1980s as the beginning of the modern age of comic books. That's both true and false. It's false because the industry still changes with fan demands as time moves forward. It's also true in that the comic book, graphic novel, and superhero have all incorporated their key characteristics by this point. Both comic books and graphic novels were finalized as commercial units, and the standard superhero evolved by incorporating relatability, imperfections, fear of death, modernization, and deconstructions. After this point, the industry crystallized into variations of the theme. This book discusses the history of the key elements, creators, events, and controversies that established the modern superhero comic book.

As far as terminology goes when referring to DC and Marvel, the names of the two major comic book companies will at times be simplified to express a greater point. Malcolm Wheeler-Nicholson formed National Allied Publications in 1934, which was purchased by Detective Comics Inc. in 1938. Detective Comics Inc. was created in 1937 but merged with All-American Publications and National Allied Publications to form National Periodical Publications in 1946, eventually becoming DC Comics in 1977. These entities will be referred to, for the most part, as DC Comics throughout this book. Martin Goodman's comics line used multiple sub-businesses. For the sake of simplicity, throughout this book these will be referred to as Timely Comics during the Golden Age, Atlas Comics for the 1950s, and Marvel Comics for the 1960s and after, unless when specifying something more specific. This simplification is because there are exceptions, such as the case of Marvel versus Timely versus Atlas. The name "Marvel Comic Group" was used by Goodman as a tryout label for his publishing line as far back as 1949, but it wasn't until 1963 that it maintained a notable market presence.[2] The Atlas logo was occasionally used to represent Goodman's publishing line in the 1940s on various covers such as *The Human Torch* #14 (1943) and *All Winners Squad* #11 (1943). However, historians still refer to those issues as part of the Timely period because it's more consistent. Also, the name Atlas was mainly used to describe Goodman's distribution company in the early 1950s, but he also used distributor Kable News briefly through 1952. Yet, historians still refer to the comics line of that period as Atlas Comics.

There are also references in this text made to comic book ages, and it's important to first define the Eight Ages of Comic Books. Defining an age can be tricky since there is no definition universally accepted by comic book historians. To be considered a historic age, there must first be a national comic book marketplace in which a popular trend is chased by the industry to appease an existing fanbase. The popular trend is generally defined by a dominant genre, including a writing and art style that attracts the most market share. In practicality, comic book ages tend to be distinguished by the presence or absence of superheroes, and what type of superhero is driving the marketplace. Defining ages by superhero can be problematic because it ignores other genres, but it creates a useful and recognizable framework that allows categorization into which comics fall in a particular era of history. This opens channels for better communication between casual fans, historians, and scholars alike, utilizing one common framework. Metals were initially used to name the early comic book ages, but as superhero comic books were developed and marketed in new ways, the names of the latter ages changed to be more descriptive.

Victorian Proto-Comics (1600–1896)

After the first printing press was developed by Johannes Gutenberg in what was later known as Germany in the 1400s, proto-comics started to be published in the early 1600s. In England from 1621 to 1635, an early recognized proto-comic series was *Triumphs of Gods Revenge and the Crying and Execrable Sin of (Wilful and Premeditated) Murther* by John Reynolds.[3] In 1837, Swiss writer-artist Rodolphe Töpffer published *Histoire de Mr. Vieux Bois*, a multipaneled visual sequential narrative in French that included captions and dialogue. This work was translated to English and published in New York City in the weekly newspaper supplement *Brother Jonathan Extra* #9 as a 40-page comic strip known as *The Adventures of Obadiah Oldbuck* (1842).[4] This era is not considered a part of the Eight Ages of Comic Books because its publications were not presented in a modern comic book format in an established national marketplace. *Oldbuck* was notable in the local New York area, where it "became a household character,"[5] but it did not appear to penetrate the national

Falling in the room of a sleepy citizen, Mr. Oldbuck opens a communication with his ladye-love by means of the window.

Making a rope of the cityzen's curtains, he descends without losing sight of his beloved.

Midway, Mr. Oldbuck, by a well-directed leap, lands himself exactly in the chamber of his ladye-love.

Rodolphe Töpffer's *The Adventures of Obadiah Oldbuck* was reprinted as a 40-page comic strip in a newspaper supplement, *Brother Jonathan Extra #9* (1842). Panel 1 caption: "Falling in the room of a sleepy citizen, Mr. Oldbuck opens a communication with his ladye-love by means of the window." Panel 2 caption: "Making a rope of the cityzen's [*sic*] curtains, he descends without losing sign of his beloved." Panel 3 caption: "Midway, Mr. Oldbuck, by a well-directed leap, lands himself exactly in the chamber of his ladye-love."

consciousness, nor does it seem to have been followed by a significant number of competitors seeking to copy its style. However, this comic strip is an interesting precursor from which modern commercial comic books would eventually be derived.

Platinum Age (1897–1937)

The Platinum Age of comic books consists of reprints of newspaper comic strips or pre-superhero original material. A popular consensus is that the first "real" comic book was produced in 1897, which was Richard Felton Outcault's *The Yellow Kid in McFadden's Flats*. This publication comprised mainly text, but with a title purely devoted to comic material, and pages that reprinted Sunday strips in black and white. Its presence proved to retailers that there was a potential marketplace that could thrive from the existing viability of the newspaper comic strip medium, which was repurposed into a comic book format that sold on magazine newsstands. Further reprints followed, including the 1911 reprint of the *Mutt and Jeff* newspaper strip, depicting the famous cartoon by Bud Fisher. Various comic books of reprinted material were sold to the public, including those by Cupples & Leon publications such as *Bringing Up Father* (1914–1934), *Tillie the Toiler* (1925),[6] and *Mickey Mouse Magazine* (1935).[7] The formats of these comics were not uniform; they were published in hardcover and softcover in various sizes and shapes.[8]

Richard Felton Outcault's *The Yellow Kid in McFadden's Flats* (1897) is considered by many to be the first published comic book with a title devoted to comic material with some pages that reprinted Sundays in black and white.

George Delacorte started Dell publishing and produced original material in a newspaper tabloid insert without staples called *The Funnies* #1–36 (1929–1930). What distinguished this from a comic book was its location in a greater periodical and its lack of stapled binding, preventing it from being presented independently on a newsstand. Eastern Color Printing published *Funnies on Parade* (1933), a small eight-page promotional comic book comprising reprinted comic strips, which did not sell on newsstands but instead was sent free to customers who mailed in coupons for Procter & Gamble products.[9] Later, a stapled 36-page comic book that consisted of reprint material and was called *Famous Funnies: A Carnival of Comics* (1933) was "distributed through the Woolworth's department store chain"[10] and made by Dell with help from former elementary school teacher Max Gaines.[11] A 68-page stapled comic book full of reprint material called *Famous Funnies: Series* #1 (1934) was published by Dell, printed by Eastern Color, and sold successfully on newsstands.[12] This was the first modern comic book for sale on newsstands and its success helped establish the comic book marketplace in the United States.[13]

A year later, Major Malcolm Wheeler Nicholson produced *New Fun Comics* #1 (1935), published by National Allied Publications. This is largely credited as the very first staple-bound comic book with original material sold on newsstands. Wheeler-Nicholson partnered with magazine distributor Harry Donnenfeld to create *Detective Comics* #1 (1937) under Detective Comics Inc., which later became DC Comics.[14] These early original-material comic books were generally anthologies, containing short stories largely based on westerns, crime, and mystery genres that were popular in preexisting pulp magazines. There were many attempts during the Platinum Age to reprint licensed newspaper strips or to create original material by inexpensive young artists and writers. Although the modern comic book format was established during this period, the marketplace was still struggling to find its footing.

Golden Age (1938–1947)

The Golden Age starts with the coming of superheroes—beings with superhuman abilities, costumes/code names, and a mission of justice.[15] Detective Comics Inc. published *Action Comics* #1 (1938) featuring Superman and established the first standard superhero in the American comic book marketplace. Superman defined the superhero by utilizing qualities that were successful in previous characters and media such as the crime-solving tendencies of *Nick Carter, Master Detective* (1886), the brute superiority of Bernarr Macfadden's *Physical Culture* (1899) magazine, John Carter's super jumping (1917), the caped heroism of Douglas Fairbanks' *The Mark of Zorro* (1920), the science fiction of Hugo Gernsback's *Amazing Stories* (1926), the resilience of *Popeye* (1929), the strength of Philip Wylie's *Gladiator* (1930), and the super mission of justice found in *Doc Savage Magazine* (1933).[16] The superhero concept quickly became popular, and formed its own new genre as artists, writers, and publishers began to create characters by copying this successful formula, firmly establishing the American comic book marketplace. Bob Kane and Bill Finger introduced Batman in *Detective Comics* #27 (1939) as a costumed extension of the crime genre. Bill Everett created Sub-Mariner, first published in *Marvel Comics* #1 (1939), which also premiered Carl Burgos's Human Torch for Timely Comics. Joe Simon and Jack Kirby's *Captain America Comics* #1 (1941) was published to capture a patriotic trend in the market. The next year, Wonder Woman was created by psychiatrist William Moulton Marson and artist Harry Peter in *All-Star Comics* #8 (1942). Other iconic Golden Age superheroes established during this time were the Flash, Green Lantern, Captain Marvel, Aquaman, and Hawkman.

Originally, superheroes were written to portray the violent temperament popular in pulp magazines. They were rudimentary beings that often vented their frustrations rather than demonstrated any serious humanity. For example, Sub-Mariner crushed the heads of onlooking divers in his first issue.[17] Batman punched a man into a vat of chemicals, killing him with the famous quote, "a fitting ending for his kind."[18] Superman even watched a villain choke to death from poison gas and sneered, "One less vulture!"[19] That changed in 1941 due to an edict from Editorial Director Whitney Ellsworth to the editors in DC Comics, forcing creators toward more family-friendly and patriotic storylines.[20] Ellsworth likely made this request for a couple of reasons. First, to elevate the storytelling to a higher standard, and second to escape harsh criticism of angry parental groups. The violence became subdued, and superhero challenges were focused on problem-solving and defending the helpless. Staying kid friendly proved to be successful, as did incorporating patriotism during the years of America's involvement in World War II.[21] Dell, Archie, Disney, and many other publishers also tailored their content toward children, selling millions of funny animal, teen, and humor comics called "Funny Books."

Atomic Age versus Television Age (1948–1955)

This era has been called the "Atomic Age," but based on the content produced, "Television Age" seems more appropriate. After World War II, superhero comics slowly faded out of the mainstream as the industry transitioned to other genres. Soldiers returned from the battlefield, newly married, and eager to forget the conflict of war. These readers instead sought out genres consistent with the variety format of developing black-and-white television shows such as *The Lone Ranger* (1949), *Stand By for Crime* (1949), and *Space Patrol* (1950). The rapid growth of television also paralleled a stark increase in comic books with licensed material of various genres such as Dell's *Roy Rogers* (1948), *Lone Ranger* (1948), and *Gang Busters* (1948). It seemed like comic books were now chasing television shows much like they had previously chased reprint newspaper comic strips and superheroes. The comic book industry thrived with genres such as romance, crime, westerns, war, science fiction, and the more risqué "good girl" titles pushing superhero content off the newsstands. Teen humor and funny animal genres also continued to thrive. Batman and Superman maintained a newsstand presence during this tenuous period, but other superheroes failed to stay relevant. For example, Green Lantern was removed from the cover of *All American Comics* #102 (1948) and the title changed in the next issue to *All American Western* #103. A similar demise occurred to the Human Torch, who was originally famous for being on the cover of *Marvel Comics* #1 but was phased out by issue #93 with the comic renamed to *Marvel Tales* (1949). Other comic book titles competing for an audience with shifting tastes did the same. *Sub-Mariner Comics* #32 (1949) was changed to a romance comic by its next issue, *Best Love* #33. The issue following *Captain America Comics* #73 (1949) became *Captain America's Weird Tales* #74 and by issue #75, the hero was removed from his own book. This once best-selling patriotic comic book character disappeared in the face of economic pressures. Publishers also faced another pressure in the form of rising paper costs, and in response, decreased their page count to avoid raising prices in an inflation-driven market. They used less paper to keep their comics affordable for as many people as possible. Readers who once got 52 pages for 10 cents were getting 32 pages for the same price.

As war comics solidified during the Korean War, Harvey Kurtzman made a name for himself writing *Two-Fisted Tales* (1950) and *Frontline Combat* (1951). He made commentary on war and the profound cultural intoxication and fear of the atomic bomb. His work with Wally Wood in *Two-Fisted Tales* is commonly celebrated by comic scholars, along with Wood's science-fiction titles, *Weird Fantasy* (1950) and *Weird Science* (1950), that generally provided thought-provoking suspense stories. Often, some historians call it the Atomic Age due to these critically successful comics; however, the overall era speaks more to a wider variety of other genres.

There was an increased popularity of horror comics by 1950, and the most successful publisher of this genre was Bill Gaines's EC Comics. Their most salacious stories, generally edited by Al Feldstein, depicted vicious crimes such as gun-related murder and beheading of women. Eventually, the graphic nature of their material received criticism from concerned parental groups and politicians who worried about their effects on the mental health of children. These horror and crime comics soon came under attack by Dr. Fredric Wertham, author of *Seduction of the Innocent* (1954), who claimed that comic books encouraged juvenile delinquency. While Dr. Wertham's claims were unfounded and untrue, the series of heated accusations were sufficient to initiate an oversight evaluation by Congress during the Kefauver hearings.[22] These hearings led to an initiative by the comic book industry to regulate itself with the implementation of the Comics Code Authority (CCA) in 1954. The CCA set up rules that created the framework for what could and couldn't be used in comic books[23] and, unfortunately, limited the subject matter that could be published. If a comic book failed to display the CCA seal on the cover, then it would not be sold at the local newsstand, which significantly impacted the publisher that financed the print run.

This led to a two-year period of stagnancy in the comic book industry as publishers struggled to figure out what they could and could not publish under the CCA's rules. Bill Gaines could no longer produce crime and horror comics, leaving EC Comics nonviable, but he continued *MAD* comics as a magazine where he circumvented the CCA's control.[24] Meanwhile, the comic book industry abandoned crime and horror genres, contributing to many publishers and distributors going out of business because they became unable to publish comics that were successfully tailored to their audience.

Silver Age (1956–1969)

The Silver Age is defined as a period when science fiction was used to retcon old superheroes or create new ones while incorporating relatability, a trait generally missing in their Golden Age counterparts. Carmine Infantino worked at DC Comics and contributed to science fiction and western titles. He was tasked by Editor Julius Schwartz to pencil a Comics Code–approved story written by Robert Kanigher about Barry Allen, a.k.a. the Flash,[25] an average guy who gained superpowers from a bizarre science-fiction event. This successful retcon of this Golden Age hero was presented in *Showcase* #4 (1956) and became a hit with mainstream readers. The Flash's uncertainty and human foibles provided a personal realism that contrasted well with discovering his superpowers. This concept and framework became the go-to template that other publishers used to create their characters, establishing the Silver Age of Comic Books. Schwartz applied this formula to re-creating another character with writer John Broome and artist Gil Kane. This was the new Green Lantern, a.k.a. Hal Jordan, for *Showcase* #22 (1959), a pilot who gained his superpowered ring from meeting a dying alien named Abin Sur. This bizarre science-fiction event worked well with audiences and Schwartz assembled his new heroes with Wonder Woman, Aquaman, and Martian Manhunter into DC's premiere superpowered team in *Justice League of America* #1 (1960). This was a classic era for DC Comics, as many of their heroes from this period are still prominently used today.[26]

Although the superhero genre demonstrated accelerated growth by 1960, there were world events that promised an era of progress. One company, soon to be called Marvel, was finding its footing when it released *Rawhide Kid* #17 (1960), which was Stan Lee and Jack Kirby's first-ever collaboration on an ongoing character. This western comic premiered the same year that The Beatles formed, Cassius Clay won the gold medal in boxing at the Olympics, and John F. Kennedy became president. The age of astronauts started the following year, in 1961, as Alan Shepard flew high above the atmosphere, becoming the first American in space. One year later, John Glenn became the first American to orbit Earth, and in 1969, Neil Armstrong took more than just one small step on the moon for all of mankind. Shepard, Glenn, and Armstrong were the real-life heroes of this decade, powered by scientific discovery as the entire world admired their almost superhuman accomplishments. Four months after Shepard's space mission and America's first foray into space, *The Fantastic Four* #1 (1961) by Stan Lee and Jack Kirby was published.[27] This story told the tale of four astronauts who became superheroes from exposure to cosmic rays, keeping in line with the Silver Age character template of ordinary humans obtaining powers through science-fiction events. Another famous character that Marvel created using this template was the widely known Spider-Man, created by Stan Lee and Steve Ditko for *Amazing Fantasy* #15 (1962). The wall-crawler premiered the same year as the Hulk, Thor, and Ant-Man. The Marvel superheroes generally had the science-fiction background and relatability of the DC characters but lacked their Eisenhower-era conformity and exhibited imperfections that made them more realistic to a changing 1960s audience. There is more discussed on that in later chapters. By 1969, DC and Marvel had both created successful mythologies of superheroes who gained powers and stories through scientific accidents.

Bronze Age (1970–1984)

The Bronze Age is defined by a shift in the industry to emphasize both antiheroes and social relevance, which were prompted by internal comic book industry events as well as external forces that changed the American cultural landscape. Marvel's sales overtook DC Comics,[28] and Jack Kirby left Marvel for DC and introduced New Gods in *Jimmy Olsen* #133 (1970). Mort Weisinger left DC Comics as the editor of the Superman comics with his final issue, *Superman* #231 (1970), and *Showcase* comics was put on hiatus with issue #93. Outside of comics, the Kent State massacre shocked the nation, Jimi Hendrix and Janis Joplin died, Paul McCartney announced the breakup of The Beatles, and NASA lost its funding for space travel due to declining public interest in space exploration.[29] The USA experienced an increasing series of disappointments; however, one positive aspect was present likely due to the previous decade of social consciousness, which was the decline of comics censorship at the CCA. The CCA's looser filter allowed the reappearance of violent storylines in comic books, signifying that the innocent naivete of the Silver Age was lost to a new and hardened reality, which focused on domestic concerns such as vengeance and social relevance. Instead of bizarre science-fiction superheroes, the Bronze Age demonstrated the creation of pulp-era vengeful antiheroes. This all occurred as *Conan the Barbarian* #1 (1970) by Roy Thomas and Barry Windsor-Smith was published by Marvel, emphasizing this trend. Conan was created by Robert E. Howard in 1932 as a Hyborian Tarzan–like warrior and animalistic survivor living in a kill-or-be-killed world. Many readers welcomed the violent antihero with open arms, as a fictional depiction of how the real world had changed around them. Conan became critically acclaimed and extremely successful, and was featured in two additional black-and-white magazines, *Savage Tales* (1971) and *The Savage Sword of Conan* (1974).[30] Names such as *Satana, Ghost Rider, Brother Voodoo*, and *The Son of Satan* captured the interest of audiences. The industry produced more antiheroes, including the Punisher, a Dirty Harry–type character who premiered in *The Amazing Spider-Man* #129 (1974),[31] and Wolverine, who first appeared in *The Incredible Hulk* #180–181 (1974). Both characters were keeping in line with the other antiheroes, as good-guy type of killers who got the job done.

Comic books also started to reflect the social consciousness of the times with stories highlighting racial and gender inequalities. The first *Friday Foster* strip (January 18, 1970) was introduced, giving an African American female front and center stage in an ongoing comic narrative.[32] *Green Lantern/Green Arrow* #76 (1970) premiered the collaborative work of Denny O'Neil and Neal Adams. This issue examined how superheroes overlooked the plight of Americans with African descent and started a series examining cracks within the United States' social system. *Superman's Girl Friend, Lois Lane* #106 (1970) by Bob Kanigher showcased the tale "I Am Curious (Black)!," where Lane turned into an African American female and observed how differently she was treated by society. During the same year over at Marvel, *The Invincible Iron Man* #21 (1970) had Eddie March as the first Black man wearing the Iron Man armor and *Hulk* #131 (1970) had the emerald behemoth take on the young Black sidekick, Jim Wilson. These storylines reflected the growing discussion around race in the United States. Feminism and women's liberation were also highlighted in *The Avengers* #83 (1970) in a story written by Roy Thomas that premiered "Valkyrie and her Lady Liberators" ready to take on "Male chauvinist pigs!"[33] This issue assembled various women from the super team and highlighted their concerns that they can function without being protected by the male members. As the decade progressed, some comics combined both civil rights movements, such as *Wonder Woman* #204 (1973) by Robert Kanigher and Don Heck, who introduced the superheroine's long-lost Black sister, who represented both African and female strength.

Priorities shifted in the early 1980s as local magazine stands and pharmacies ceased to display racks of comic books to sell, leading to a serious decline in newsstand distribution.[34] Independent comic book shops arose in neighborhoods around the country, creating a new marketplace called the direct market. DC and Marvel licensed properties from new source material such as films, toys, and video games, including *Star Wars*, *Atari Force*, *G.I. Joe*, and *Micronauts*. The direct market's birth led to new publishers and distributors who wanted a share of this new source of commerce, including Eclipse, Pacific, and First.[35] Simultaneously, the industry competed by using better paper quality, which increased cover prices. Adult content in comic books could not get CCA approval and stayed away from newsstands but could bypass this obstacle by going straight to direct-market comic book shops. The independent publishers pushed this material with titles such as *Sabre* #1 (1982) and *American Flagg!* (1983), both advancing the comic storytelling medium but also including sexually mature themes. DC started to compete in the direct market with comic books such as *Omega Men* #7 (1983), by artist Tod Smith and writer Roger Slifer, which depicted aliens called Psions clinically observing a woman getting repeatedly raped until she became pregnant. Longtime publishers of kid-friendly titles such as Gold Key, Harvey, and Charlton were forced to shut down as they were no longer publishing what shops wanted to order for their mature customers.[36]

Dark Age (1985–1990)

During the mid–1980s, comic creators emphasized new, dark, psychological content that broke the superhero into something angry and disappointed. The growth of the direct market was a pivotal part of this change, which did not require approval by the CCA, so independent creators and companies were free to create complex adult storylines with far more freedom than ever before.[37] DC had to suddenly deal with competition from independent publishers.[38] This approach to comics began to be considered normal, as one miniseries, *Crisis on Infinite Earths* (1985), created by Marv Wolfman and George Perez, formalized the overall industry trend to explore darker concepts with great success. This series shed the innocence of DC's past by killing Supergirl, Flash, and many others. Other stories continued to follow this pattern in the form of dark miniseries turned graphic novels, including *The Dark Knight Returns* (1986) by Frank Miller and *The Watchmen* (1986) by Alan Moore and Dave Gibbons.[39] Both deconstructed the superhero into a selfish and violent being. Even Superman was not immune to this trend. In 1988, John Byrne depicted him killing evil Kryptonians with a lead box of kryptonite to save other planets from their evil wave of genocide.

Marvel also shifted into this new direction with storylines such as the "Morlock Massacre" (1986) in the pages of *The Uncanny X-Men* and "Scourge" (1986) in the pages of *Captain America*. The Morlocks were a race of benevolent mutants killed by eugenics-crazed geneticist Mr. Sinister. Their underground massacre crossed over different series, including *The Mighty Thor* and *X-Factor*, both of which showcased the character Angel being crucified. Scourge was a vigilante who brought his gun into a bar and murdered many low-grade villains. With antiheroes such as Wolverine and Punisher now facing murderous sociopaths such as Sabretooth and Nuke, one could see how the tone of comic books shifted compared with the lighter super heroics of the 1960s. "Born Again" was Frank Miller's script for *Daredevil*, which demonstrated the hero's fall from grace, as he lost his job while his girlfriend became a heroin addict. Young children were less of a publisher's priority since audiences found in comic book shops tended to be older. Unsurprisingly, kids were also purchasing this darker material instead of reading the Dell funny books of their parents' childhoods.[40] These series crystallized modern superhero comic books, and stories of today are generally variations of these already pioneered themes.

Extreme Age (1991–1997)

The Extreme Age was the period when the industry featured over-the-top anatomy, weaponry, and sexuality combined with sales-driven gimmicks such as multiple covers, multi-issue crossovers, and polybagged comic cards to maximize sales at all costs. Despite this age technically starting in 1991, some comics produced in the late 1980s and early 1990s still transition into the Extreme Age. For example, Todd McFarlane's *Spider-Man* #1 (1990) premiered exaggerated poses and musculature and sold two and a half million copies. However, the industry shifted in a significant way when *X-Force* #1 (1991) by Rob Liefeld came to comic book shops in sealed bags for purchase by collectors. Readers bought a copy to read as well as multiple unopened copies for a speculative investment.[41] Teenage readers celebrated Liefeld's depiction of exaggerated muscles and extreme guns, helping push sales to five million copies. Jim Lee released *Uncanny X-Men* #1 (1991) with four different covers that connected into a larger quadriptych art piece, which sold eight million copies as the greatest-selling comic book of all time. Capitalized by their success, Rob Liefeld, Jim Lee, Todd McFarlane, and others departed from Marvel Comics to create Image Comics.[42] *X-Force* and *Youngblood* enjoyed blockbuster success that coincided with action films starring popular muscular figures like Arnold Schwarzenegger, Jean-Claude Van Damme, and Dolph Lundgren. The muscles on these action heroes, wearing tights and packing shoulder pads, guns, and ammo, ultimately sold just as well in theaters as they did in these extreme comic books.

It was around this time that the commercially successful *Death of Superman* story arc was started by DC Comics.[43] This storyline progressed over one year, showcasing an intense scenario where a physical confrontation by super monster Doomsday, who had extreme size and durability, eliminated the last son of Krypton and created a vacuum filled by a new wave of superheroes. Sales of the initial event were very high, followed by a blatantly obvious need by both DC and Marvel to feed into extreme, over-the-top aesthetics, combined with sensational multi-issue crossover stories to match revenue by maxing out consumption. The industry went so far with this trend that at times the plot or basic anatomy of the story didn't matter as much as the visual gimmicks, die-cut hologram covers, and swimsuit specials. Although these factors sold very well to the collectors' corner of the direct market, readers eventually became tired of this approach to comic books, bringing about a market dip that lasted from 1993 to 1997 as the Extreme Age went into decline.

Movie Age (1998–2023)

CGI and special effects provided the economic viability of superhero comic book films starting with *Blade* (1998). Despite previous successes such as *Superman* (1978) and *Batman* (1989), it wasn't until *Blade* that movie studios realized how lucrative comic book films can be. By using sophisticated computer and makeup effects, comic books translating into blockbuster films were described as a "gold mine."[44] Soon, Marvel franchise films premiered, including *X-Men*, *Spider-Man*, and *The Fantastic Four*, that did well at the box office. DC premiered the Christopher Nolan *Batman* trilogy, *Man of Steel*, and *Wonder Woman*. Even non-superhero comic books were being made into films, such as Max Allan Collins's *Road to Perdi-tion*, Alan Moore's *V for Vendetta,* and Frank Miller's *Sin City.*

Movie adaptations of the comic books generally require changes from the source material. As the films' financial success eclipsed that of the comic books, their characterization impacted some of the characters in the comics[45] when super-heroes took on traits from the actors portraying them. Tony Stark's dialogue from the later 2000s often matched the cadence and speech of Robert Downey, Jr., and after the success of Samuel L. Jackson's Nick Fury, the established Caucasian charac-ter from Marvel was written out to be replaced by his son, who resembled the Afri-can American film version. Screenplays and actors now affect the content in comic books, and many comic book writers create series that they hope get optioned into a highly profitable movie. The pulp magazine format went extinct in the wave of comic books in the 1940s, and comic books are dangerously close to doing the same in the 21st century, as kids and teenagers flock toward video games and online streaming. It appears that during the Movie Age, film and television provide a lifeline of rele-vancy to the comic book industry.[46]

This is a basic overview of the Eight Ages of Comic Books, which unavoidably carries generalizations. Not every superhero comic from a particular age fits the description. There have been many comics created during these ages that haven't been mentioned yet, and some are not always related to the theme of the era. How-ever, defining the Eight Ages by the lack or presence of superheroes and what drives the market helps form a lens through which one can view and categorize comic books throughout history. Several comic book companies will be referred to here, with a greater emphasis on DC and Marvel. These two companies employed creators including Jerry Siegel, Joe Shuster, Bob Kane, Bill Finger, Joe Simon, Jack Kirby, Stan Lee, Julius Schwartz, Steve Ditko, John Byrne, Jim Starlin, and Alan Moore who created and developed the superhero comic book by incorporating narrative tools, art styles, and the mystique present in comic strips, pulp magazines, cinema, clas-sic illustration, and classic magicians. These superhero comic books evolved due to legal obstacles, science-fiction tropes, genre focus changes, and market forces, while incorporating realistic aspects of human nature, including relatability, imperfec-tions, the fear of death, and selfishness. This occurred during the creation of crit-ically important characters such as Superman, Batman, Captain America, Flash, Fantastic Four, Doctor Doom, Spider-Man, Thor, X-Men, Black Panther, New Gods, Wolverine, Thanos, and the Watchmen. These comic books evolved alongside graphic novels that depicted the human condition, which evolved from the efforts of Frans Masereel, Milt Gross, Lynd Ward, Gayle Hoskins, and Georges Prosper Remi, among others. Before arriving at how superhero comic books and graphic novels crystallized in the 1980s, it's very important to start at the beginning of the comic book medium.

PART 1

Building Blocks

1

Early Comic Book Origins

European proto-comics from the 1600s started a literary trend of depicting stories in sequential visual and narrative form. These proto-comics evolved over a couple of hundred years, before arriving in America as early comic strips. Eventually, comic strips found a viable presence in syndicated newspapers, which in turn found significant commercial success in the 1890s. During this period, comic strips became a cheap form of visual entertainment for the masses, as strip creators and publishers pioneered the legal framework for copyrights, licensing, and merchandising. These strips were then reprinted into comic books that started the modern comic book industry. Indeed, many of the early techniques and surrounding business practices seen in the Golden Age were founded upon the history of comic strip publishing.

The history of America's comic storytelling is tied to Europe. One of the earliest examples of a proto-comic series, from England, is *Triumphs of Gods Revenge and the Crying and Execrable Sin of (Wilful and Premeditated) Murther* (1621–1635) by John Reynolds, which comprised his collected works of political comic pamphlets that eventually led to his imprisonment by the king of England.[1] These pamphlets had many pages of text with interspersed comic pages laid out in side view of three or four rows of horizontal panels containing a sequence of various events. Each panel depicted a sequence of human figures in action, separated by a gutter filled with text. Reynolds's comics used the gutter space as caption boxes but lacked the typical dialogue balloons of later comics. Dialogue balloons are not necessary for a publication to be classified as a comic, but it certainly helps.

Dialogue balloons were used roughly five decades later in Francis Barlow's *A True Narrative of the Horrid Hellish Popish Plot* (1682), which depicted the tale of the arrest of Titus Oates.[2] The Popish Plot was a conspiracy by Titus Oates to develop anti–Catholic sentiment through false accusations. Barlow illustrated this proto-comic with more detail than Reynolds did his, and utilized background and foreground in a three-dimensional manner, but the reader still viewed the story from a side view. There were three rows of four panels with captions and dialogue balloons and a larger text piece underneath explaining the story. Both of these British proto-comics were printed in black and white.

Another notable development came in 1837, when Rodolphe Töpffer, a Swiss

A True Narrative of the Horrid Hellish Popish Plot by Francis Barlow is an example of an early proto-comic with dialogue balloons.

writer and artist, published in Switzerland *Histoire de Mr. Vieux Bois*, a sequential multipaneled proto-comic of an unlucky suitor who failed numerous times before succeeding to marry his true love. Töpffer's work was originally written in French but was later reprinted in America in English in a weekly newspaper supplement, *Brother Jonathan Extra* #9 (1842), as a 40-page comic strip sold out of New York as *The Adventures of Obadiah Oldbuck*. This picturized story had captions, sequential actions, and reactions, and moved the medium one step closer toward books devoted to comics.[3] This new medium was also slowly budding in 1860s Germany when Wilhelm Busch created the notable proto-comic book of this era, *Max und Moritz* (1865),[4] about the practical jokes of two naughty German boys. This was more of a picture book with captions, made for children rather than a multipaneled comic book. However, this mischief-driven proto-comic had a wide reach influencing later comic strip artists.

American newspapers provided a commercial space for comic strips to develop over time. Joseph Pulitzer's *New York World* began publishing Richard Felton Outcault's cartoons in 1894, and a year later he created the character Mickey Dugan for the strip *Hogan's Alley* (1895). One year later, William Randolph Hearst bought the *New York Journal* and hired Pulitzer's publisher the same year. Hearst acquired a high-speed multicolor press, syndicated his material to other newspapers, and hired Outcault[5] to continue Mickey Dugan's adventures under a new name, *The Yellow Kid*.[6] It was during Outcault's time under Hearst that he created the iconic interaction between the main character and a parrot in *The Yellow Kid and His New Phonograph* (October 1896). This sequential interaction involved dialogue balloons that mimicked the tempo of a discussion that a reader could follow between two cartoon characters. It was well received, and many historians consider this a pivotal moment because comics ceased to be illustrated picture stories at this point and demonstrated prompt actions and reactions with dialogue. This strip began a post–Outcault period as other comics followed this pattern, establishing the style of modern comics.[7] Technically, this was not a new technique; however, it was the almost frictionless combination of characters, format, cheap production, fast printing presses, Hearst's syndication of the material to a national audience, and mass consumerism that penetrated the country's consciousness that popularized this initial era of newspaper comic strips.[8] All of this was the case with the commercial success of *The Yellow Kid*, which eventually had some of its Sunday comic art reprinted and repackaged into *The Yellow Kid in McFadden's Flats* (1897). This was the first comic book, mostly composed of text with interspersed comic pages, starting the Platinum Age of comic books. Other publishers sought to repeat the same success and hired cartoonists to create similar characters that could entice readers to buy more newspapers.

The success of *The Yellow Kid* under Hearst's *New York Journal* also introduced legal lessons that were about to be learned. In 1896, Outcault applied for a copyright by sending a letter with a copy of *The Yellow Kid* to the Library of Congress. Unfortunately, the copyright was not granted since Outcault had neglected to ascribe a copyright notice on *Hogan's Alley*. Since both newspapers did not own the copyright to the character, Joseph Pulitzer's *New York World* continued to publish *Hogan's Alley*, forcing Outcault to compete with a copycat artist.[9] Since Outcault did not own the character and competed with another version of his own idea, he lost interest in *The Yellow Kid* and left the strip in 1898. At the time, no one predicted the confusing legal challenges that would arise from Outcault creating two competing entities that included the same character. This competition justifiably confused the newspaper comic marketplace as customers bought either periodical.

In 1902, Outcault produced another comic strip, *Buster Brown*, for James Gordon Bennett's *New York Herald*. Later, he left the *Herald*, and Bennett hired another artist to continue his work. This artist was considered inferior to Outcault by the public, but despite this, the newspaper did not see a drop in sales. This outcome was largely due to the character's popularity, which established that fictional characters became the main selling point rather than the artist responsible for drawing them. The character was worth more than the creator, a lesson that publishers had quickly learned and were all too eager to teach artists. This seemed to become an overall pattern throughout the industry ever since it first happened to Outcault. In the end, both papers were legally granted the right to produce the character, with the sole requirement that they use a different name. The critical outcome of this legal quarrel was that Outcault significantly benefited by being given ancillary rights to the character.[10] Ultimately, Outcault made more money from merchandising than he did off his comic strips. His character's brand name was licensed to a shoe company, a watch manufacturer, toys, games, coffee, dolls, bread, and many more. He was the first creator to do this with a comic character, establishing the significant importance of merchandising comic characters.[11]

More legal challenges arose surrounding German cartoonist Rudolph Dirks. Dirks immigrated to New York as a young adult and found work as a cartoonist when *Hogan's Alley* was becoming popular, and publishers were ready to pay for more comic strip material. In response to this interest, Rudolph Dirks created the comic strip *Katzenjammer Kids* (1897) for Hearst's *New York Journal*. It told the tale of the mischievous Hans and Fritz, similar characters as Wilhelm Busch's *Max und Moritz* (1865). Dirks worked on *Katzenjammer Kids* for 15 years in total and eventually left Hearst for Joseph Pulitzer's *New York World*, causing both papers to carry their own versions of the German-hearted strip. Harold Knerr was the artist hired by Hearst to continue *Katzenjammer Kids*, but since the strip was published in two different newspapers, a court case eventually decided that Dirks would be allowed to draw his original characters under a different title, *Hans and Fritz*, for the *New York World*.[12] Hearst could keep the original title, which prevented Dirks from using that elsewhere.[13] Dirks later renamed his feature again to *Captain and the Kids* during World War I due to the rapidly declining goodwill toward German culture in the United States.

Despite the legal precedents, there was more opportunity to be found in licensing comic characters. A few years after *Katzenjammer Kids* started, another notable character appeared, an unlucky hobo by the name of *Happy Hooligan*, created in 1900 by Frederick Burr Opper for Hearst's *New York Journal*.[14] The *Happy Hooligan* comic strip ran until 1932, but in its early run was already turned into a movie of the same name by the Thomas Edison Film Company in 1900 and became one of the earliest examples of comics-based movies.[15]

Winsor McCay, an incredibly fast draftsman, was the next comic strip artist who developed new storytelling techniques, elevated their artistic quality, and pioneered a new medium in which characters could be licensed. His skill enabled him to create two comic strips during the same period, *Little Sammy Sneeze* and *Dream of the Rarebit Fiend*, both in 1904. McCay was known for his clever combination of comic illustration and satire. In 1905, he depicted Sammy Sneeze sneezing in a comic panel, shattering its gutters. This satire on the comic strip medium worked by depicting the title character as comedically aware that he existed in a comic. With this simple device, McCay created a groundbreaking milestone that, in the right hands, comics could be depicted as a clever visual art form. That same year, he created his signature comic strip, *Little Nemo in Slumberland* (1905), which first appeared in James Gordon Bennett's *New York Herald* and influenced both Jerry Siegel and Joe Shuster, who stated their love for the strip's imaginative fantasy.[16] McCay's Sunday strips depicting Slumberland are sublime, and his facility at high-speed and highly detailed comic art enabled him to draw sequential stills of characters in motion, pioneering two of the early animated short films, *Little Nemo* (1911) and *Gertie the Dinosaur* (1914).[17] He developed animation as a new medium in which to license his comic characters. McCay continued to develop *Nemo* at the *Herald* until 1911 and proceeded with a better offer from William Randolph Hearst's periodical, the *New York Journal*.[18] The *Herald* still owned the strip's trademark, and a lawsuit ensued that resolved in allowing him to continue using the characters he had created under a new title, *In the Land of Wonderful Dreams*. The *Herald* did not find a replacement artist who could match his talent, cementing McCay as the first truly irreplaceable superstar comics artist.[19]

There was another comic strip artist who applied these previous lessons in copyright law toward his own advantage. Harry Conway "Bud" Fisher created *A. Mutt* (1907), a character designed to gamble and play races in a sports cartoon for the *San Francisco Chronicle*. *Mutt* was received well by the public and Fisher found success in this recurring, comedic character. This comic was the first to be presented in the popular horizontal daily format that became everyday reading material syndicated in newspapers across America.[20] The strip eventually graduated into *Mutt and Jeff* when Fisher developed a fictional co-star. In the end, the "odd couple" style comic strip included fun situational humor, which worked very well in its plot template of a two-guy comedy style that mimicked similar acts in vaudeville and later depicted in television and films such as *Laurel and Hardy* and *Abbott and Costello*. Generally savvy and possibly learning from previous creators' mistakes, Fisher found a unique way to copyright his *A. Mutt* strip without the newspaper's awareness. Hearst was impressed with Fisher's skill and quality of work and offered him a job at the *San Francisco Examiner*, which put him in direct competition with his strip's initial home, the *Chronicle*. Fisher made sure to write "Copyright 1907 H.C. Fisher" on the very last strip he sent to the *Chronicle* as well as on the first two he drew for the *Examiner*. He then went on to register his copyright in Washington, D.C., a move that paid off tremendously for him. He thus made *A. Mutt* his personal legal property instead of releasing the rights to the publisher.

When the *San Francisco Chronicle* tried to replace him for their *A. Mutt* strip, Fisher rightfully challenged this legally. In 1908, the *Chronicle* ceased to publish the strip because they acknowledged that Fisher had been established as the full owner of the title and character.[21] The Fisher copyright scenario was certainly a lesson learned by many. Fisher went on to sign a five-year contract with Hearst, though later he signed a more profitable deal with the Wheeler Syndicate, leaving a rather furious Hearst behind. The newspaper mogul retaliated by attempting to copyright the title *Mutt and Jeff*. Hearst also filed an court order to stop the Wheeler group from using the strip or its characters. Wheeler then filed two lawsuits to prevent Hearst from producing any imitation of *Mutt and Jeff*.[22] The judge deemed Fisher's team the victor in all three lawsuits. This legal story did not end there, however. As stubborn as Hearst was, he took the issue before the U.S. Supreme Court, which in 1921 chose not to intervene in the previous case decision. This decision bestowed on the very clever Bud Fisher 100 percent ownership of the characters, film rights, titles, and merchandising rights, as well as a share of profits from the comic strip whenever it was reprinted.[23] The lesson of this story was that copyright equals money, a crucially important concept that likely made it harder for other creators and artists to do what Fisher had done. Fisher was also one of the earlier comic artists who depicted himself as a character in his own *Mutt and Jeff* comic strip (February 5, 1919), interacting with other characters. This strip portrayed a scene in which he complained there was no way that a comic artist could please all comic readers and remain funny. This was a very early reference to chronically unhappy fandom, as well as a precursor to modern times. This style is notably similar to later comic writers and artists including Stan Lee, John Byrne, Roy Thomas, and Jack Kirby, who would all later insert themselves into their own comics once they rose to fame in the comic book industry.

With many initial legal precedents set in the newspaper comic strip industry, many artists focused on expanding the art form. George Herriman was of mixed African American descent and created *Krazy Kat* (1913). Though his birth certificate dubbed him "colored," he was light skinned and able to ingratiate himself with the mostly Caucasian newspaper publishers when he started working in comics in 1897.[24] His coworkers thought him to be Greek because of his black curly hair. Before he created *Krazy Kat*, he created the strip *Musical Mose* (February 16, 1902) about a Black man who unsuccessfully tried to pass himself off as white. This strip put into perspective how much work needed to be done for African American equality and highlighted the constant struggle that mixed-race people with lighter skin tones had at the time fitting into society by denying their racial heritage. As a strip writer-artist, Herriman captured aspects of basic life and hooked readers by introducing the unfulfilled love triangle in the comic medium. The premise was that Krazy Kat was in love with Ignatz the Mouse, who did not return the same sentiment. However, Krazy Kat had an admirer, Officer Bull Pupp, who loved Kat, who in turn kept loving the mouse.[25] He successfully captured this tension, and kept readers interested in the daily struggles of the three funny animals. A similar love triangle occurred in publisher MLJ Magazines' *Pep Comics* in the 1940s, when Veronica was added to the Archie and Betty courtship. Archie was loved by Betty, but he loved Veronica, and Veronica loved herself. Stan Lee and John Romita, Sr., later created this same dynamic in *The Amazing Spider-Man*. Peter Parker's run-ins with Gwen Stacy and Mary Jane were welcome plot devices that added more sales to the monthly title.[26]

Krazy Kat also introduced some thought-provoking topics such as sexuality in 1915. "I don't know whether to take unto myself a wife or a husband," Kat confessed in the September 16, 1915, daily.[27] This was a whimsical approach to social commentary in popular culture in early 20th-century America. A decade after *Little Sammy Sneeze* playfully broke the fourth wall in comics, *Krazy Kat* did the same on August 5, 1915. A spilled inkblot covered the panel likely as a reference to the artist spilling ink all over the art page. A speech bubble from Kat read, "Daaa-Gunnit I knew it" as the spilled ink filled the panel and left Krazy Kat soaked.[28] This syndicated daily strip indicated that the character in the comic knew he was a drawing and saw the inkblot for what it was.

Political commentary was also present in Herriman's strip. The American presidential election of 1920 was the first one after both World War I and the 1918 flu pandemic. The results of that election in Ohio showed Democratic governor James M. Cox being defeated by Republican senator Warren G. Harding. *Krazy Kat* joined in on the political situation with humorous insights into political party fatigue during an April 25, 1920, Sunday strip where an elephant and donkey protested their respective causes, while Ignatz described the two political parties as "ancient" entities that "give me a pain."[29]

Cliff Sterrett also elevated comic storytelling in his newspaper strip, *Polly and Her Pals*, by intelligently inserting art that referred to abstract concepts. Sterrett penciled and wrote the strip for most of the first half of the 20th century beginning in 1912. By the mid–1920s, his artistic style underwent a huge transformation from the family situational comedy genre to surreal art experiments and expressions that took on a life of their own.[30] There was one strip from March 20, 1927, that told the story of an evening at Polly's house from a cat's perspective, which utilized abstract imagery that seemed to express something similar to the visuals found in the film *The Cabinet of Dr. Caligari* (1920). A Doctor Strange–like window was illustrated as part of the house's eerie background, demonstrating little visual regard for right angles. Through these panels, Sterrett expressed the high-art styles of cubism and surrealism in the "low" art form of comic strips.[31] This experimental art style in *Polly*'s newspaper strip went deeper and deeper into a Doctor Strange–style aesthetic as it began to depict emotions in the astral plane. There is a particular newspaper strip published on July 29, 1928, that showed Polly's father going to a dental appointment. Sterrett surrealistically depicted her father's fears and out-of-body psychological dissociation during the office procedure. What appeared to be his astral form escaped into darkness just as the dentist's arm and drill were seen through a small circle of light, piercing her father's consciousness. Another example was shown in the April 22, 1928, strip when Polly's father entered a nightmare dreamscape and visually confronted his own insecurity concerning his daughter's upper-class boyfriend. The boyfriend felt superior to him, and to better illustrate this, Polly's father was drawn as a caveman. To add to the surrealism, the background was constantly shifting with each panel, and nothing seemed certain as both symbolism and form were exaggerated to create this metaphysical effect. These visual techniques solidified Sterrett's reputation as one of the first comic strip artists who introduced high art into comic strips. His iterations of dreamland, the astral plane, or the nightmare world were well done and arguably just as fascinating as those depicted in the *Strange Tales* comics by Steve Ditko and the *Sandman* comics by Neil Gaiman—both published many decades later.

The early proto-comic format was advanced during the Victorian Age by pioneering European creators Barlow and Töpfer, who experimented with panels, gutters, and dialogue balloons. Töpfer's proto-comic was reprinted in New York as a comic strip in a weekly newspaper supplement. Eventually, comic strips found a commercially viable home in syndicated newspapers around the country, offering previously unheard-of opportunities to artists. Some of these comic strips were reprinted in comic books during the Platinum Age. Despite various legal challenges, artists and publishers enjoyed the monetary benefit of licensing, merchandising, and copyrights. The resulting financial security allowed the creators, George Herriman, Cliff Sterrett, amongst others to elevate the artistic storytelling quality of comic strips, using satire and abstract visuals. These creators established the medium, language, and legal foundations of the comic strip business, forming a strong lineage into the 1920s and 1930s, when the next generation of cartoonists developed more plot and character innovations that were critical to creating early superheroes.

2

Comic Strips' Legacy
in Modern Storytelling

The next generation of comic strip cartoonists advanced comic strip storytelling in new and unique ways with techniques that appeared in the works of Golden and Silver Age comic book creators. Two notable publishers—Joseph Medill Patterson and William Randolph Hearst—fostered comic strips that influenced superhero comic books. Patterson was initially manager and majority owner of the Chicago Tribune Syndicate and later the *Daily News*. Born into a newspaper family, he had an innate sense of what comic strips would sell to a mass readership.[1] Similar to Hearst, he knew that a faithful subscriber base depended on comic strips that depicted serialized and intelligent adventures that kept readers continually interested in more content. His success at the newspaper business eventually led to creating the Chicago Tribune-New York News Syndicate (1933). As a publisher, he approved and supervised comic strips such as *Little Orphan Annie* (1924), *Dick Tracy* (1931), and *Terry and the Pirates* (1934),[2] all of which have qualities that were used by Golden and Silver Age comic book creators. Patterson's competitor, Hearst, initially owned the *San Francisco Examiner* and the *New York Journal*, and later syndicated his periodicals' content to other newspapers using his early syndicate that eventually developed into King Features Syndicate.[3] He understood that customers bought newspapers with the best comics, so he hired the finest cartoonists. A King Features Syndicate comic strip that he fostered depicting one of the first antiheroes in comics was *Thimble Theatre*, featuring Popeye (1929).

Little Orphan Annie was created by cartoonist Harold Gray, who, like many young cartoonists in the 1920s, hoped to succeed in the newspaper comic strips. He submitted a tryout strip of a curly haired boy named Little Orphan Otto to Joseph Medill Patterson, who felt that the comic strip would resonate better with audiences if the main character was a girl. After appropriating the name from James Whitcomb Riley's poem "Little Orphant Annie" (1885), Gray created *Little Orphan Annie*.[4] Patterson was correct, and Annie became a mainstream success, proliferating beyond strips into much of American media such as comic books, big little books, radio shows, television, Broadway musicals, and movie productions. Gray's comic storytelling in *Annie* was ahead of its time due to three main qualities critical to later superhero comic books: dialogue with heart, politics in stories, and exploring the crime genre.

Harold Gray in the 1920s, similarly to Stan Lee in the 1960s, wrote dialogue that connected with readers by giving a genuine voice to his characters. Gray gave Annie monologues discussing how she felt about the day's events and had her process life's difficulties with dignity and grace. In her first daily strip on August 5, 1924, Annie was praying alone at her orphanage, "Please make me a real good little girl so some nice people will adopt me, then I can have a papa and a mama to love."[5] Her humility was her first feature, and in the next daily, Gray quickly made it clear that Annie found it challenging when others did not extend to her a similar courtesy. She dealt with these situations fairly and refused to be a pushover when a rich socialite wanted Annie to entertain her spoiled son, who said, "Where did you find those clothes? In a grab bag?"[6] Annie quickly punched him in the jaw with a quick retort, "I'll teach you some manners," showing the world she was strong-willed with a quick instinct for justice. These initial dailies established her core personality, which endured over 80 years of publication. Much of her dialogue focused on social justice, self-development, and continuity. The January 19, 1926, daily depicted an anti-racism lesson when a sly businessman said, "Why fool wit dem wops? … Lay off dem ferriners."[7] Annie was insulted by the man's casual xenophobia and immediately kicked him in the behind and yelled, "I'll wop yuh on th' nut I will!"[8] Annie later ran away from the orphanage and learned hard lessons on the road, while helping various people in her travels. Her challenges were met with perseverance and common-sense commentary, while surviving adversity was the key to her heartfelt storylines and mainstream success. Kids followed her adventures in the strip, hoping to learn more about her when they joined the *Radio Orphan Annie's Secret Society* (1934). This is similar to Stan Lee's *Merry Marvel Marching Society* (1964),[9] which gained attention from fans in a similar way, hoping to get a front-row seat to the new adventures of Spider-Man.[10]

Harold Gray infused politics into the strip mostly as mild lessons by Annie teaching individualism and hard work. However, at times, Gray's politics took a more potent form when told from the perspective of Daddy Warbucks, who echoed Gray's sentiments when he brought libertarianism into *Little Orphan Annie*. One example is the list of observations that Warbucks described at his wife's dinner party consisting of intellectuals, academics, and artists in the May 18, 1932, daily. The eclectic party crowd was depicted with various phrases shown above and around them such as "destroy capital," "to me poetry is religion," "the curse of gold," and "A hundred thousand for our cause."[11] Meanwhile, Warbucks stood back and proclaimed, "Geniuses, eh? Crack-pots if you ask me, what a shallow restless lot, jealous of success, yet too lazy or dull to attain it."[12] This is clearly a polarizing statement in any era, but Harold Gray, through Warbucks, made it clear that he found this crowd to be hypocritical liars. These moments with Warbucks are interesting for the same reason that Steve Ditko's Mr. A character (1967) is interesting. In a similar manner to Gray, Steve Ditko expressed Ayn Randian beliefs in his *Mr. A* comic books by illustrating and writing about his objectivist worldview. Some panels showed Mr. A next to diagrams explaining the difference between corruption and honesty, with a caption or dialogue balloon holding a stern moral lesson.[13] As disdainful as these opinions may be to some, it offered a unique and genuine insight into a comic creator who utilized the medium to mix entertainment with his politics.

Gray's politics in comics became more interesting when he directed his antagonism toward President Franklin Roosevelt, whose politics were generally seen as pro-social and anti-libertarian. In the August 18, 1933, daily, the New Deal appeared to deplete Daddy Warbucks's strength as he declared he was dying from a terminal disease. In 1945, however, Roosevelt's death seemed to reinvigorate Warbucks and his health was restored. It was situations such as this that revealed Daddy Warbucks as a fascinating capitalist character. First, he's very similar to other rich war-profiteering playboys, similar to Tony Stark but of an older era. He'd gained and lost his fortune due to reckless and risky decisions, and he was a terrible parental guardian who involuntarily and routinely abandoned Annie, then reclaimed her in a never-ending cycle for Gray to keep the comic fresh. His personal life always maintained the reader's interest, especially when he went on adventures in exotic countries. He went to Singapore and fought pirates in Africa during a sequence of dailies from March 4–8, 1930, living out his Jungle Jim–type role four years before Alex Raymond created *Jungle Jim*. His depiction of Africans was generally and unfortunately dehumanizing, and with the popularity of Edgar Rice Burroughs's *Tarzan*, that was a relatively common part of media at this time. The Great Depression caught up with Warbucks when Gray depicted him losing his fortune and getting into a truck driving accident that made him blind in the May 19, 1931, daily. He was depicted going through a series of rehabilitating and humanizing daily events to get himself back up and wealthy again. He eventually met a doctor who performed an experimental optic nerve surgery reviving his vision. This was an example of the illusion of change, when a "permanent" change occurred to a character but that eventually resolved itself to keep characters the same. However, Warbuck's character arc dealing with poverty and blindness pioneered the depiction of the stages of grief in comics, including depression, self-doubt, acceptance, coping, and adaptation.

Harold Gray also dealt with the gritty world of organized crime in the 1920s Chicago area. Gray delivered action sequences such as the August 31, 1927, daily when Annie ran for cover after mobsters shot bullets through a window to intimidate her for money.[14] The March 9, 1927, daily depicted an armed car pulling up next to a truck in which Annie was traveling. They pulled out their guns and murdered the driver, forcing her to jump out to escape.[15] Annie survived these situations by running to safety. Daddy Warbucks, however, faced his adversaries head-on, similar to the Kingpin from Marvel Comics, who first appeared in *The Amazing Spider-Man* #50 (1967) by Stan Lee and John Romita, Sr. Warbucks, just as the Kingpin, was a tall, bald, and robustly suited man, who often turned an attack on him into an opportunity to eliminate enemies. He delivered his own brand of justice rather than involve the police. In the September 7, 1928, daily, Warbucks and his henchmen broke into a gambling establishment, guns blazing, and physically dominated a corrupt political figure who withheld information.[16] In the September 25, 1928, daily, he was ambushed in a dark alleyway by two thieves, and emerged victorious with his clothes in tatters.[17] In the September 28, 1928, daily, he fell through a trapdoor, and by the next panel, six enemies escaped with their lives as Warbucks chased them with an ax.[18] In a sense, Warbucks fulfilled the role of a comic strip Kingpin, four decades before the more famous character was created by Lee and Romita.

Another comic strip that pioneered later comic book storytelling techniques was Chester Gould's *Dick Tracy*. *Dick Tracy* expanded the crime genre in comics, explored the use of forensics in detective work, and pioneered sadistic masked villains, which were plots and tropes that were later used in *Batman*. Chester Gould created "Plain-clothes Tracy" in 1931. After a few tryout comic strips, Gould's boss, Joseph Medill Patterson, changed Gould's name to "Dick Tracy"[19] and recommended he get Tracy's girlfriend's father killed by robbers to justify the starring character's war on crime.[20] Gould did so and utilized pulp-era violence with Elliott Ness-versus-Al Capone-inspired "law and order" storylines. Gould at times wrote Tracy to coordinate his enforcement of law and order with controversial FBI director J. Edgar Hoover, who portrayed the head of the comic strip's "Washington Bureau."[21] Hoover was relatively popular in the 1930s, and Gould proved to be his fan by using the FBI director's caricature to send Tracy off on the occasional federal case, away from his usual city police beat. Gould was also quick to show gruesome elements of criminal life by depicting the realistic violence committed by mobsters. In the early tryout strips that Gould turned over to Patterson, there was a mobster in the foreground, watching his henchman torture an informant by pulling his toenails out one by one.[22] These scenes depicted the harsh reality of humanity's underbelly that Gould included throughout his series to better portray Great Depression–era crime culture. For example, the February 23, 1938, daily strip depicted a storyline regarding the topic of human trafficking. Gould mastered the fascinating visual contradiction between his simple cartoon art style and the graphic content. Emaciated victims in the ship's hold were beaten down, covered in rotten fish, and snuck into the country,[23] proving that Gould depicted gritty realism in his strip, decades before Marvel was celebrated for doing the same thing. One example of keeping the strip linked to reality was fashioning Tracy's villains after famous criminals of the time. On March 3, 1934, John Dillinger publicly humiliated local law enforcement when he charmed his jailers and posed with them for newspaper photos while wearing a white shirt and black vest. Although the photos were all smiles, behind the scenes in his cell, he shaved down a fake wooden gun used to trick his jailers to free him. Dick Tracy faced a tricky villain named Arson who was a direct homage to Dillinger, wearing the same white shirt and black vest. In the March 19, 1935, daily, Arson escaped from jail using a fake gun made from a potato that was darkened with iodine, which humiliated the local police chief.[24]

Dick Tracy's villains eventually became more eccentric, which was showcased when Gould utilized the bald evil scientist trope in the strip well before Siegel and Shuster created the mad scientist Lex Luthor in *Action Comics* #23 (1940). One example was featured in the November 4, 1934, *Dick Tracy* daily, in which a mad scientist experimented on both humans and dogs to better understand germ warfare by infecting them with rabies. This vicious researcher injected tied-up victims with syringes full of the deadly virus to conquer their minds. Dick Tracy and company were soon disgusted when they uncovered this plot, watching through a window while the wicked fiend choked a dog and injected it with the maddening microbe. Gould demonstrated that crime did not pay when the germ warfare virologist got his throat torn out by the rabies-infected dog in front of Dick Tracy, who was tied up and powerless to save him.[25]

Gould eventually evolved Tracy's adversaries into masked sociopaths and developed a rogues' gallery of new masked villains with code names, years before comic books such as *Batman* or *Spider-Man*. The October 16, 1936, daily strip introduced the Purple Cross gang, who were ruthless and cruel similar to Tracy's previous enemies, but also wore domino masks while robbing banks. Donning the symbol of the purple cross on their foreheads, they used machine guns to unnecessarily kill unarmed witnesses.[26] After Tracy eliminated the Purple Cross gang, his villains became more theatrical two years before either Batman or his rogues' gallery were created. Gould introduced the Blank in the October 21, 1937, daily as *Dick Tracy*'s first fully costumed and masked mystery man. The Blank wore a faceless mask, a black top hat, and trench coat. Similar to the 1960s Steve Ditko character The Question and the 1980s Alan Moore character Rorschach, the Blank sadistically murdered criminals whom he felt deserved it. The Blank's real name was Frank Redrum, and he employed a brutality that was extreme for some readers to behold. The October 26, 1937, strip depicted him tying a criminal under a running car in a garage to die from carbon monoxide poisoning. In the November 6, 1937, strip, he threw another mobster out of a moving car going 50 miles per hour to break his neck, and in the November 14, 1937, strip, he threw another mobster out of a plane to fall to his death. The Blank was depicted laughing maniacally as his guilty victims all suffered and died. In another example, he made a sport of killing mobsters in the November 19, 1937, strip when he trapped a mobster in a moving car and jumped out as it drove into a train. The Blank felt a certain esteem with that last kill as he yelled, "Perfect!"[27] He mystified detectives when he disappeared in a puff of smoke the way that Batman later did in the pages of *Detective Comics*. In the January 9, 1938, daily, Gould revealed that the Blank's face was disfigured under the mask because his face was accidentally shot off a decade earlier. His fellow criminals rejected him for being too ugly, so he made a list of criminals to brutally kill. The Blank sneered as he explained, "And why not! Even my last name, Redrum, with the letters reversed spells M-U-R-D-E-R!"[28] Bob Kane referenced the Blank with his own faceless masked character in *Detective Comics* #34 (1939), and with cocreators Bill

Finger and Jerry Robinson, created a similar ominous, facially mutilated, and deadly serial killer, the Joker, in *Batman* #1 (1940).

Dick Tracy used forensic methods to track down criminals such as the Blank in a manner later seen by Batman, who was also known as "The World's Greatest Detective."[29] Forensics significantly advanced during the days of J. Edgar Hoover's FBI as they used innovative equipment such as the lie detector test in the August 29, 1935, daily strip.[30] The lie detector was pioneered by *Wonder Woman* creator Dr. William Moulton Marston, who in 1913 studied systolic blood pressure that increased during deception. In 1921, John Augustus Larson modified the sphygmograph, originally invented in 1854, to give a continuous blood pressure and pulse curve to study thousands of criminals.[31] Gould incorporated the lie detector into this daily strip to demonstrate its use in criminal investigations. Dick Tracy also applied the science of ballistics in the November 14–20, 1932, strip sequence to calculate where a bullet came from to rule out some of the suspects on his list. He spent a good portion of a continuity that year assessing distance, bullet fragments, and direction to determine who pulled the trigger of a gun.[32] Sequences such as this made Dick Tracy the world's greatest detective in comics, years before Batman.

Once those criminals were found, Dick Tracy's police force, similar to early Golden Age superheroes, Superman and Batman, showed little mercy. In the late 1930s, Batman punched a man into a vat of chemicals, killing him,[33] and Superman watched a villain choke to death from poison gas.[34] Tracy, a few years earlier, was no different. He did not send criminals to an ineffective asylum to risk them escaping and harming more innocent people. Instead, both Tracy and his squad were out for blood in various "kill or be killed" scenarios. In the March 16, 1934, daily, Tracy spotted an armed criminal and immediately shot him through the hands to disarm him. He wasted no time and shot him a second time through the chest, preventing him from lighting a nearby bomb.[35] The hazards were many, with cars exploding around him in scenes containing Chicago-style gang warfare. Regardless of the challengers, the punch line was always the same. In the March 21, 1938, daily, Tracy caught up to a sadistic human trafficker and quickly shot him between the eyes.[36] Gould made sure to assure his audiences that the villains deserved their punishment by depicting them torturing or killing innocent people. No matter what it took, Gould made sure Tracy gave criminals what they deserved, preferably death, including one of his adversaries in the October 27, 1938, daily who was mauled to death by a bear. Another helpless underworld prisoner was tied with chains under a house until he suffocated and died, with his body later discovered decomposed into dust and bones. These examples in the *Dick Tracy* strips demonstrated a trend of unforgiving violence that was also present in the early Golden Age superheroes.

Milton Caniff pioneered important storytelling techniques for long-form adventure comic strips, also utilized by later comic book creators, that depicted the human condition by aging characters in real time and emphasizing sexual tension, female empowerment, social awareness, death of a reoccurring character, artistic innovations, war, romance, and the realism of everyday struggles. His work inspired an overall trend by cartoonists to shift comic strip plots away from single-strip gags. Comic book creators such as Stan Lee,[37] Jack Kirby,[38] John Romita, Sr.,[39] Carmine Infantino,[40] and Bob Kane[41] have all referred to him as an influence.

Caniff was hired by the Chicago Tribune–New York News Syndicate to produce a new strip.[42] Joseph Medill Patterson, who acted previously as the *Tribune*'s foreign correspondent to the 1900 Boxer Rebellion in China, suggested the eastern country as a locale for Caniff.[43] However, Caniff knew next to nothing about China, but he researched the country's history, culture, and scenery and set it as the location of his strip, *Terry and the Pirates* (1934).[44] The story depicted the life of young boy, Terry Lee, who, similar to the later sidekick Robin, traveled as a ward of adult adventurer Pat Ryan. This dynamic duo was observed by Bob Kane, who patterned one of his pre–Batman comics on the *Terry* strip.[45] Pat was a tall, dark, and handsome hero who very much resembled the later Bruce Wayne; however, Caniff did not center the strip on him, but instead on the teenager, Terry. Compared with most strips that had a continuity that ended back at the initial status quo, Caniff depicted the human conditions of Terry growing up as a young boy sidekick, then a teenager who began to adventure on his own, and finally as a young man and World War II soldier. Up to this point in Caniff's career, it was generally agreed upon in the comics community that cartoonists should avoid aging their main protagonist to avoid damaging a strip's brand. However, Caniff aged Terry in real time over the span of 12 years from 1934 to 1946, as Terry grew to become the hero of the story. The ability for Caniff to portray Terry's growth while maintaining the high standard of the strip remained an invaluable reading experience that many current mainstream superhero comic book writers find difficult. However, Stan Lee, a fan of Caniff,[46] emphasized teenage superheroes and oversaw their aging in the pages of *The X-Men* (1963) and *The Amazing Spider-Man* (1963) in a similar manner to Caniff during his run as their script writer in the 1960s.

Caniff developed the influential Dragon Lady, a ruthless East Asian pirate and feminist figure, who felt a sexual tension with Pat Ryan. In a 1936 continuity, the Dragon Lady captured Pat as her prisoner and proclaimed that she will kill him with curare, reveling in the notion that his mind will be clear as his body shuts down. Pat asked to write a farewell letter to his friends. She provided him a pen, and he stabbed her hand with it, proclaiming, "From me to you, with love!"[47] He escaped briefly, but was captured again. However, this moment of conflict prompted a mutual attraction between the two enemies. Exhausted, he slept but didn't realize that the Dragon Lady took the opportunity to hold him tenderly during his slumber. In another game of cat and mouse, she threatened him with death unless he joined her, but instead he resisted and yelled, "You're a Goddess to the men, but...I'm going to break you."[48] She stared at him until he departed, but then smiled, expressing a profound sexual tension. Caniff used these scenarios to depict the Dragon Lady as a strong woman and feminist figure who would be commanded by no man yet was intrigued by the stubborn manhood of Pat Ryan. Bob Kane and Bill Finger did the same when they created Catwoman in *Batman* #1 (1940), a villainess who similarly can be thought of as attracted to crime to rebel against a male-dominated society. Similar to Dragon Lady, Catwoman propositioned Batman to join her in a life of crime,[49] but he resisted her advances, and she escaped, maintaining the possibility of both characters interacting as adversaries and sexual partners. Similar to Catwoman, Dragon Lady also rebelled against a patriarchal society through her role as a pirate who would rather live by her own rules than do what was expected of her as a woman in the 1930s. She was depicted as a firebrand who raised an army by commenting on the very real 1937 Rape of Nanking from March 30 to April 3, 1938: "I entreat you to follow me, China has borne the world's mockery and exploitation for centuries because our civilization was too ancient to be disturbed by petty passions. If this vast land is conquered, we will become a lost people! I ask you to die that your descendants may not lose face!"[50] To Caniff, she could at times function in the story as a useful antihero who rightfully sought revenge or as a villain who rose to challenge any man. Her character inspired various comic artists such as John Romita, Sr., who mentioned that he visually created the Kingpin's wife, Vanessa, as an older version of the Dragon Lady.[51]

Caniff also depicted social issues by introducing one of comics' first LGBTQ characters, the villainess Sanjak, who premiered on February 12, 1939. Sanjak was the name of a Greek island close to Lesbos, the root word for "lesbian." Sanjak was assigned female at birth, dressed as a man, and longed for Terry's girlfriend, April. This continuity was especially brave as Sanjak broke gender stereotypes by being depicted as the opposite of other characters from the strip that were born female: short hair, wore a business suit, hypnotizing monocle, with a thin masculine figure. In the March 16, 1939, daily, April resisted Sanjak's advances, but Sanjak replied, "[I] have found the so rare jewel, eendeed!"[52] Sanjak relentlessly pursued attention from April, who couldn't help but feel intrigued by the offer. Far from a simple villain, Sanjak was a complex figure, alone and sad, but also smart and cynical. This was probably the first time a transgender character was represented in conventional comics, and it wouldn't occur in mainstream comic books for another five decades in "A Game of You" by Neil Gaiman in *The Sandman* #32–37 (1991).

Caniff also touchingly represented the death of a reoccurring character in comic strips. In *Terry* strips dated October 13–19, 1941, Dude Henning and Terry processed the death of Dude's girlfriend, Raven Sherman. After a violent conflict, Raven lay dead with Dude holding her close in the October 16, 1941, daily, with no dialogue balloons, and four panels depicting his facial expression changing as he accepted her passing. The October 17, 1941, daily had a panoramic shot showing empty valleys in the background, and both Dude and Terry staring at her newly dug grave. The October 19, 1941, Sunday started with Dude asking for some time alone, and two more panels showed Terry walking away, depressed without saying a word.[53] This continuity is one of the most seminal moments in comics that demonstrated to readers that the comic strip medium could humanely portray death. Sherman's death was read by later *Spider-Man* artist John Romita, Sr., who mentioned it as an inspiration during plotting sessions concerning the death of Gwen Stacy in *The Amazing Spider-Man* #121 (1973).[54]

Caniff also pioneered artistic innovations that enhanced movement and drama in comics. Caniff brilliantly captured speed lines in a panel from October 29, 1939, depicting Pat Ryan's revenge on the villain Klang, who physically abused the captive Dragon Lady in a previous panel. He punched Klang repeatedly and at high speed, which Caniff presented as multiple fists in varying forceful positions.[55] He also had the villain's head showing multiple positions of recoil within the same panel, demonstrating with his penciling technique several high-speed punches that gave the villain the beating that he deserved. Movement such as this was depicted in the Modernist painting by Marcel Duchamp *Nude Descending a Staircase, No. 2* (1912). However, it was Caniff who captured the concept well in comics. In later years, several comic artists, including Carmine Infantino[56] and Mort Meskin,[57] used the same technique for speedsters such as the Flash and Johnny Quick. Caniff's visual sense of drama also changed in the strip as World War II evolved *Terry and the Pirates* from the 1930s East Asian pirate theme to a 1942 war epic. Caniff used the additional available space on the Sunday larger page format to represent all aspects of an armed battle in the skies and on land as soldiers were running from bombers. The June 3, 1942, daily displayed a similar drama with heavily shaded soldiers putting their lives at risk while storming oncoming tanks.[58] Caniff applied ink onto a whiteboard to simulate shadow and light and enhance the drama of these sequences while applying the technique of chiaroscuro that he learned from his friend and colleague Noel Sickles, who pioneered this method in comics in his 1930s strip, *Scorchy Smith*.[59] Caniff also depicted the tragedies of war in broad daylight, as families escaped from enemy soldiers who chased after them at gunpoint in the June 16, 1942, daily.[60] These scenes were cinema on paper that required a visionary, namely Caniff, to develop them into sequential panel form that properly depicted the war genre. Although the anatomical detail was missing from Caniff's strips, it didn't matter because he effectively depicted human drama. Romita referred to the influential cartoon realism portrayed by Caniff as getting "all the depth and all the convincability [*sic*] of every panel that he did without laboring over the art … giving the illusion of reality because this is genuine."[61]

Milton Caniff left *Terry and the Pirates* in 1946 to move on to his creator-owned strip, *Steve Canyon*, where he experimented with other genres and depicted his hero dealing with everyday problems.[62] Steve Canyon seemed to approximate a grown-up Terry, a war veteran with his own air-transport business. As a maverick and mercenary, he ran into a series of private enterprise adventures all over the world. Caniff used this strip to introduce a hero who was forced to deal with down-to-earth problems like paying bills. Canyon's secretary commented, "It would have been nice to have money to pay this office rent, but I guess it's bad form to get into regular habits like that."[63] Paying rent was what many believe Stan Lee brought to comic books in the early 1960s with *The Fantastic Four* and *The Amazing Spider-Man*,[64] but Caniff did that almost two decades earlier. Caniff also explored romance in the comic medium, which was concurrently being developed by Joe Simon and Jack Kirby for Prize Publications in *Young Romance* #1 (1947). The December 7, 1947, Sunday depicted Dr. Deen Wilderness, who was to leave soon and address global epidemics. She said her goodbyes and asked, "Can't you spare a kiss, pal?" Canyon responded in kind. The airplane in the back and the three consecutive panels dedicated to their kiss represented another cinema-inspired comic moment. Caniff's writing excelled here when Canyon revealed he would be escorting her, which shocked her, considering they just had a hearty goodbye kiss. She asked, "You mean you stood there and made love to me all that time ... before all those people, when you knew all along?" Canyon replied, "You said for me to kiss you, and I always follow my doctor's prescriptions to the letter."[65] Caniff was always pushing new directions in comic strips by mostly depicting human situations in cinematic ways.

While Caniff depicted the human condition in comics, E.C. Segar demonstrated the foibles of being superhuman in a human world in a strip featuring one of comics' first antiheroes. Segar created Popeye as a side character for his *Thimble Theatre* newspaper strip in 1929.[66] The strip began a decade earlier in 1919, created for Hearst's *New York Journal* as a relatively simple cartoon production. After years of improving his visual sequential pace of comedic timing, Segar presented a sailor for hire, Popeye, to help the strip's main protagonist, Castor Oyl, on adventures around the world. Eventually, Castor was written out of the strip and Popeye became the main star and one of the most prominent comic characters around the world. Segar's sailor was so famous that both Bob Kane and Stan Lee once competed on who could draw him the best.[67] Segar spent the last 10 years of his life creating and developing Popeye, who could be considered a proto-superhero, written with unique traits such as invulnerability, rage, heart of gold, super-strong arch-nemesis, frequenting bars, earned money by fighting, unattractive outward appearance, and self-defining catchphrase, which positioned him as one of comics' first antiheroes. These qualities were successful enough tropes or conventions in comics that they repeatedly appeared in later Silver and Bronze Age superheroes such as the Thing and Wolverine.

Antiheroes are central protagonists who generally lack idealism and have some unresolved dark side. In some cases, they have a mysterious backstory and anger issues. EC Segar's original Popeye, as opposed to the later cartoons, had these qualities in a comic strip before more well-known established comic book superheroes. Popeye's background was never clear, and it wasn't until he faced physical trauma that he discovered he was mostly invulnerable. In the September 28, 1930, daily, Popeye absorbed a huge hail of bullets from an armed villain, never flinching while stating triumphantly, "Bullets can't stop me now—I'm go'ner getcher!!"[68] Characters in the comic strip could not figure out why he didn't die. After he defeated the villain, the main protagonist and Popeye's friend, Castor, forced him to see a doctor. During the examination, the doctor expressed his sheer disbelief that Popeye was still walking despite several bullet holes in him and explained that the sailor will probably die, but despite the odds, arranged an entire team of surgeons to remove the slugs from his body. During surgery, they realized they could only remove a few bullets, but ended up accidentally leaving some tape inside his body.[69] Popeye healed quickly over the next few dailies and shocked everyone around him, including Castor Oyl. In strips from April 27–29, 1933, Popeye's near invulnerability was tested again when an assassin tried to cut the back of his neck with a saber, and later, a saw. Popeye continued his conversation unharmed as the assassin screamed, "I've been hacking away on it, and he doesn't even notice it.... The muscles in his neck are like wires!" His sturdy flesh and inhumanly metallic neck highlighted Popeye's body as stronger than it appeared to be. Wolverine, another character with a superhuman body, first appeared in *The Incredible Hulk* #181 (1974) with similar characteristics, a shadowy past, and was later revealed by writer Chris Claremont to have bones composed of unbreakable adamantium in *The Uncanny X-Men* #126 (1979). Wolverine's hidden abilities were revealed to readers over time in the same manner as Popeye.

Popeye shared similarities with Superman when his invulnerability was gauged in the desert. Stranded and thirsty, he found that the only water close by was a horrendous poison that killed every animal that drank it. E.C. Segar had done well to build up the tension over several panels, as he emphasized just how poisonous this water was to ingest in strips from February 23–28, 1931. Ignoring all common sense, Popeye took gulp after gulp of the deadly liquid. In the end, Popeye drank a gallon of the poison and despite having a bad stomachache, surprised readers and survived. The strip ended that sequence with a reference to Popeye as a "Super Man" due to his ability to persevere through this extreme physical challenge.[70] This reference appeared seven years before Superman's first appearance in *Action Comics* #1 (1938). Popeye's "abilities" did not stop there. A year later, strips from December 12–16, 1931, depicted Popeye as not only having superhuman durability and stamina, but also superhuman strength when he fought a giant Brazilian boa constrictor. As the snake wrapped around his body, Popeye entered a fit of rage and tore the snake to shreds.[71] All that was left of the snake was a bloody pulp next to his feet. This outburst of rage that was triggered when his life was in danger was also present in Wolverine, whose anger left his enemies beaten or torn to comparable bloody pulps.[72] In *X-Men* #96 (1975), an angry Wolverine slashed up a great red beast and then lamented, "Ten years o' psycho-training, o' hypnotism o' drug therapy, ten years o' prayin' and I cut him to pieces without a thought."[73]

Unfortunately, both characters' rage stemmed from unresolved violent issues in their past. In the August 31, 1930, Sunday, it became evident that Popeye carried deep psychological pain. Due to some comedic circumstance, he shared the same bed as Olive Oyl's father. While sleeping by his side, dream bubbles appeared, filled with dreadful memories of questionable men running at him with a gun. This flashback resulted in Popeye unconsciously and repeatedly punching Olive's dad. When he woke up, he immediately explained, "Oh, was I actin' out me dreams—I does that sometimes."[74] Wolverine also demonstrated similar unresolved anger in the first *X-Men* film (2000). His nightmares caused him to unknowingly stab Rogue with his claws, demonstrating that when he was asleep, he too, was an unintentional danger to those around him. Readers recognized that the antiheroic Popeye had a good heart despite his rough exterior. Popeye's shady past was partially revealed in the June 23, 1932, comic strip when he encountered the enigmatic Woo Fong. The daily strip mentioned how Popeye spent time in Singapore, where he used to deal with allies and enemies who referred to him as the "One-Eyed Satan."[75] This reference to Popeye having a past as a possible mercenary was intriguing and kept readers eager to learn more details of his former life. Wolverine carried the same allure with readers, when he traveled to the fictional Madripoor as the one-eyed shady adventurer "Patch." This side of his life was first depicted in *Wolverine* #1 (1988) by writer Chris Claremont and artist John Buscema.

Popeye encountered his super-strong arch-nemesis Bluto in the September 12, 1932, daily during the "Eight Sea Adventure." Popeye knew Bluto from his old days as a mercenary for hire in Singapore and dreaded his enemy's sociopathic and feral tendencies, which functioned as an evil analogue to the hero. He was first seen pushing his face through a ship's porthole, screaming, "Mister Popeye, I will see you and kill you tomorrow at daybreak."[76] Popeye represented the smaller, kinder seaman whereas Bluto was his opposite: the larger, stronger, and animalistic sailor who murdered innocent people. After some tense buildup in the dailies, they fought each other in the September 26, 1932, strip, when an onlooker commented, "They've been fighting for four hours! How can they stand it?" Another passerby called them "Supermen. I've never seen anything like this before!"[77] Modern comic book readers would see similar battles happen between Superman and Zod or Wolverine and Sabretooth. Sabretooth is an evil analogue to Wolverine: larger, bloodthirsty, and enjoys the pain he gives others. He first fought Wolverine in *Uncanny X-Men* #212 (1986), and, comparable with Popeye and Bluto, their history went back many years. A flashback in *Wolverine* #10 (1989) by writer Chris Claremont depicted a savage conflict with art by Bill Sienkiewicz that was similar to the way Popeye and Bluto's onlookers described their fight.

Despite Popeye's heart of gold, he occasionally vented his frustrations at bars in the same way as the Thing and Wolverine. Bars are typical visiting locations for many antiheroes that provide a location for bullies and bruisers to pick on them, providing a perfect excuse for gratuitous action sequences. An entire June 21, 1931, Sunday portrayed Popeye fighting a bar full of men in an unstoppable rage after they unjustly harassed him,[78] allowing him to release a little steam. In *Marvel Two-in-One* #86 (1982), the Thing and Sandman enjoyed a drink together after spending years as enemies and Wolverine had a similar scene in *Wolverine* #17 (1989), wearing his patch in a Madripoor pub and sparring with another heavy drinker.

Some antiheroes will get paid to fight people in arenas if they are short on money and Popeye was no different when he earned a living as a prizefighter. After winning a boxing match in a May 3, 1931, Sunday, he continued to appear in the ring with increasingly stronger opponents. He defeated one boxer, then a group of boxers, and eventually freakishly large boxers and always emerged as the victor, proving he was a natural in the ring. No matter how outmatched he seemed, he managed to obliterate anyone and everyone who dared challenge him, referee included. In another Sunday from May 1, 1932, he was drawn in the ring once again, facing off against a robotic "Iron Man," whom he broke into a pile of bolts, using his superhuman strength.[79] Wolverine did the same in the first *X-Men* movie (2000), appearing in a gated UFC-style ring. After shaking off some vicious punches, he flexed his mutant muscle and struck the fighter, knocking him down with relative ease. The Thing also was in the same situation as a wrestler in *The Thing* #28 (1985), physically competing for money and enjoyed the fame and bruises that came with it. These antiheroes knew that they could always count on violence to make a living.

Despite his super abilities, Popeye still had an "ugly mug" that carried the weight of years as a seafaring antihero, making it difficult to find a woman. A group of ladies in the March 1, 1931, Sunday were quickly disgusted when he tried to separate his nose from his chin to make room for a kiss. The horrified onlookers gasped, then raced to jump out of a nearby window.[80] Despite his rough exterior, he showed sensitivity and loyalty to Olive Oyl, whom he regularly defended with his life. She was also the one female who enjoyed being with him because she acknowledged his noble soul and valued how he protected her more than anything else. The Thing embraced a similar unconditional love for his girlfriend, Alicia Masters, who first appeared in *The Fantastic Four* #8 (1962), and Wolverine also acted as a guardian to his lover, Mariko Yashida, protecting her with his life in *Wolverine* #1 (1982). These antiheroes appeared to protect their love interests as ways of atoning for a lifetime of violence.

Similar to other antiheroes, Popeye eventually had a catchphrase that summed up his sense of self-identity, famously expressed as, "I yam what I yam an' tha's all I yam."[81] The incorrect spelling and poor pronunciation was the ultimate self-declaration of Popeye as an imperfect character, with both good and bad qualities. This is similar to other antihero catchphrases, such as Wolverine's, coined by writer Chris Claremont: "I'm the best there is at what I do, and what I do best isn't very nice."[82] In the same vein, Stan Lee had his orange rock monster call himself "the ever-lovin' Thing," which became his catchphrase in *Fantastic Four* #35 (1965). All three antiheroes accepted themselves just as they were.

Publishers such as Patterson and Hearst understood the value of hiring talented cartoonists, including Harold Gray, Chester Gould, Milton Caniff, and E.C. Segar, all of whom elevated comic storytelling by pioneering highly successful tropes and plot devices. Gray delivered humility, unique voices, political expression, and the illusion of change to readers. Gould explored crime, detective work, and sadistic masked villains. Caniff excelled in depicting sexual tension, death in comics, war, romance, and the realism of everyday struggles. Segar explored the concept of an antihero as a nigh invulnerable orphan and super man with a heart of gold. The first three comic auteurs wrote comics that engaged their fans for decades and formed a strong foundation of concepts utilized by Golden Age comic book writers and artists to create superheroes. The fourth auteur depicted an archetypal antihero with qualities that are present in modern superheroes. However, there are more concepts, characters, villains, costume designs, science-fiction plots, and panel ideas from a much wider variety of comic strips that were reused and present in the Golden and Silver Ages of superhero comic books.

3

Comic Strips That
Influenced Superheroes

Golden Age superhero comic book creators followed the work of newspaper strip cartoonists of the 1930s such as Chester Gould, Burne Hogarth, Lee Falk, Harold Gray, Hal Foster, Alex Raymond, Noel Sickles, Milton Caniff, Winsor McCay, and Dick Calkins. Although some of them have been previously discussed, it's important to tackle the larger scope of their influence. Under the pressure of a daily or weekly strip, these cartoonists innovated a significant number of concepts and characters to keep their work interesting. Once comic books with original material were being published under similar monthly pressures, writers and artists looked to the work of comic strip creators to utilize or swipe ideas. This led to many Golden or Silver Age comic books containing ideas that were previously seen in comic strips, such as orphan protagonists, villain designs, character types, poses, costumes, science-fiction gimmicks, crime-fighting techniques, and the illusion of change. Some comic book greats, including Jerry Siegel, Joe Shuster, Bob Kane, Jerry Robinson, Jack Kirby, Stan Lee, Steve Ditko, and Gardner Fox, were not above reusing old material.

A popular trend in the world of superhero comic books is giving a central character an orphan origin. Usually, these heroes lost both their parents, who either died or disappeared. This shaped the superhero into becoming self-aware and lonely, constantly measuring themselves against the world. This is evident with Superman, whose biological parents died when his home planet exploded in *Action Comics* #1 (1938). Batman's parents were killed in front of him in a dark alleyway when he was a child in *Detective Comics* #33 (1939). Spider-Man's parents also disappeared, leading him to be raised by his uncle Ben, who was also killed by a criminal in *Amazing Fantasy* #15 (1962). With no parents around, the orphan follows some internal code of justice, compelling readers to follow the narrative away from the situational comedy into a continuity of adventure in which they can become invested. In some cases, a dynamic duo formed when the main orphan, namely Batman, experienced an overwhelming compassion for a younger orphan such as Robin, prompting their adoption. Orphans often took on the role of a guardian to provide stability and direction to their wards. This superhero orphan trope extends back to comic strips that set up the same plot structure.

Superheroes are often orphans and follow an internal code of justice that is driven by trauma. In some cases, they will adopt other orphans who share a similar worldview. *Detective Comics #33* (1939) and *Detective Comics #38* (1940).

Little Orphan Annie (1924) ran away from an orphanage and adopted her trusty sidekick, Sandy, a dog whom she looked after, as he too, was an orphan who premiered in the January 5, 1925, daily. As an orphan, she made it clear that she did not want to disappoint her orphan dog. Holding Sandy close, she swore, "I know how you feel, little feller—I'm an orphan too—But don't you worry—I'll take care of you from now on."[1] This also occurred with *Dick Tracy* (1931), who was essentially orphaned after the murder and robbery of his fiancée's father in the October 16, 1931, daily that started off Tracy's decades-long war on mobsters: "Over the body of your father, Tess, I swear I'll find you and avenge this thing—I swear it!"[2] One year later, Dick Tracy met Junior, a homeless orphan, in the September 18, 1932, daily. Seeing potential, Tracy raised him as his ward to one day become a detective, with the boy swearing, "Someday, I'm goin' to be a detective like you."[3] His wish tragically came true after Junior watched his own recently discovered father gunned down by mobsters,[4] prompting Junior to quickly share Tracy's sentiment of vengeance toward crime. Gould's imagery of Junior reaching forward in shock, a smoking gun in the foreground, and the silhouette of his fallen father evoked a similar personal tragedy later shared by Batman.

Another orphan story, *Tarzan of the Apes* (1912) by Edgar Rice Burroughs, was adapted into the newspaper comic strip (1929) with non-stylized realistic art by Hal Foster. Non-stylized realism is the depiction of organic reality with no exaggerations, which was a great fit for the *Tarzan* strip because the jungle hero provided the opportunity for its artists to demonstrate the hero's anatomy and movement. This led Superman cocreators Siegel and Shuster to study the story and art of *Tarzan of the Apes*[5]; however, Tarzan's action was driven by a brutal origin. The proto-superhero's traits were molded by the death of his parents early in his childhood, which caused him to be brought up in the care of apes in an African jungle. In a December 24, 1939, Sunday strip by Foster's successor, Burne Hogarth, Tarzan picked up a short-lived sidekick in the form of an orphaned baboon called Bo-Dan, whose parents were shot and killed in front of him. This Sunday was titled "Orphan of the Veldt" (1939) and Bo-Dan "clung to Tarzan, his only comfort in a world grown dark with terror."[6]

Comedy strips also used the same orphan trope, namely Popeye, who was introduced as a side character in E.C. Segar's comic strip, *Thimble Theatre*, in 1929 as an orphan. In the August 24, 1931, daily, Popeye stated in his usual broken English that he had always been an orphan for as long as he could remember: "I ain't got no parinks. I has always been a orphink."[7] Similar to some of his comic strip colleagues, he adopted another orphan by the name of Sweet Pea on July 28, 1933, which became a foil for odd-parent comedy. Another orphan origin was written into Milton Caniff's *Terry and the Pirates* (1934) about dynamic duo Pat Ryan and Terry Lee. Caniff established that the younger sidekick, Terry, was also an orphan in the April 6, 1938, daily when lamenting, "If it weren't for him, I'd probably be parked in some orphan's home!"[8] He was adopted by the older, tall, dark, and handsome Pat Ryan, who took him on adventures in China. Comic strips such as those above influenced Bob Kane, who commented on the topic:

> Syndicated newspaper strips, and their creators, are the major leagues. I suppose my preference stems from having literally been weaned on newspaper comics at a very early age, before my introduction to comic books…. These newspaper strip artists were the first major influence on my becoming a cartoonist.[9]

In *Detective Comics* #38 (1940), Kane, Finger, and Robinson depicted Batman adopting Robin in the same manner as the previously mentioned comic strips. Batman started training the newly orphaned Dick Grayson as his sidekick using very bold dialogue: "My parents too were killed by a criminal. That's why I've devoted my life to exterminate them." Grayson replied, "Then I want to also!" Batman said, "I guess you and I were both victims of a similar trouble…. I'll make you my aid."[10] Over the years, Robin grew up into Nightwing and a second Robin was adopted by Batman following the same pattern. Writer Max Collins followed Chester Gould's strips and started scripting *Dick Tracy* in 1977 after the strip's creator retired. A decade later, Collins wrote the origin of Jason Todd in *Batman* #408 (1987), depicting a backstory similar to Junior's from *Dick Tracy*. Todd was also a homeless orphan who robbed people to survive, prompting him to try to steal Batman's tires. This brave attempt at theft induced Batman to adopt and train him as the new Robin in much the same way as Tarzan, Dick Tracy, and Orphan Annie, who all became a comfort for their respective young orphaned sidekicks.

Comic book artists and writers often creatively utilized villain designs from comic strips as either an homage or swipe from the original creator. Keeping with the topic of comics strips' influence on *Batman*, it's interesting to recognize that Batman enemy the Penguin premiered with a design that appeared before. The Penguin was created by Bill Finger, Jerry Robinson, and Bob Kane as a villain in *Detective Comics* #58 (1941). Dressed in black-and-white suit attire, top hat, monocle, and a walking cane, he was a caricature of a mafia boss scheming to control Gotham. Nine years earlier, there was a strikingly similar character in the *Dick Tracy* newspaper strip on May 5, 1932, created by Chester Gould and called Broadway Bates, depicted with the same stature, suit, monocle, top hat, and overall attire. Drawing another parallel, the *Dick Tracy* character the Blank was a blank-masked character with a trench coat and hat who appeared in the October 21, 1937, daily. His aesthetic was startling, with no eyes, mouth, or nose, and was likely the inspiration for the faceless man who dressed in the same manner from *Detective Comics* #34 (1939) by Bob Kane and Gardner Fox.

When it came to the look and feel of *Dick Tracy* strips, it is easy to draw a direct comparison to *Batman*. Both arise from the crime genre, and fortunately for historians, *Batman* writers Bob Kane and Al Schwartz commented on these similarities. Kane mentioned:

> I never wanted to make *Batman* too illustrative. I wanted it more like *Dick Tracy*, so my *Batman* art always had the flavor of semi-comic art…. I always kept a little bit of the *Dick Tracy* flavor in my comic strip…. Along with Chester Gould's *Dick Tracy*, *Batman* has the most bizarre and unique villains in comics. Indeed, it was *Dick Tracy* which inspired us to create an equally weird set of villains for *Batman*.[11]

As a writer who was directly involved in the creation of the Golden Age *Batman* newspaper strip, Al Schwartz described a literary connection between Batman and the preexisting Dick Tracy strip: "The reason I remember Pomade is because the idea for him really came out of the pomaded hair of a character in Dick Tracy. I wasn't too crazy about Pomade as a name, but Jack came up with it, he liked it, and so we went along with it."[12]

Bob Kane also swiped from comic strips to depict Batman's body language and fight choreography. For the cover of *Detective Comics* #27 (1939), Kane's depiction of Batman swinging into action toward armed criminals was swiped from Alex Raymond's *Flash Gordon* Sunday from January 12, 1937, whose hero swung on a jungle vine using the same right arm and body positioning. Six issues later, in *Detective Comics* #33 (1939), Batman was seen lingering on the edge of a building, arms flailed back with legs bent in a predatory pose. This was also swiped by Bob Kane from Edgar Rice Burrough's *The Illustrated Tarzan Book* No. 1 (1929) with art by Hal Foster, showing Tarzan standing in the jungle using the same stance. Bob Kane also swiped from Milton Caniff's *Terry and the Pirates* daily from November 5, 1936, depicting Pat Ryan giving a left cross while straddling his opponent, with right hand drawn back and prepared for the next punch. Kane drew Batman in the same pose knocking out a criminal in *Detective Comics* #36 (1940) whose head also flailed back in the same direction.

Sometimes a dramatic sequence in a comic book was also swiped from a comic strip. Kane, Finger, and Robinson depicted Batman pushing a statue on top of its worshippers in *Detective Comics* #39 (1940), providing thrilling action and excitement to readers, despite the hero probably killing a few people from the stone figure's crushing weight. However, this sequence had been portrayed before when it was presented in earlier comic strips by Foster and Raymond. Hal Foster previously demonstrated the same scenario in the *Tarzan* Sunday strip on March 5, 1933, when he depicted the statue of an Egyptian god crashing down the stairs upon cult-worshipping villains. Alex Raymond also presented Flash Gordon pushing a statue over onto Ming the Merciless's followers in his throne room in the March 11, 1934, Sunday. It's very likely that Kane also swiped from those comic strips.

Batman's method of using superstition to frighten his enemies was also depicted before in the comic strip *The Phantom* (1936). Bob Kane verified the Phantom as a heavy influence on the creation of Batman[13] and one example was the character's greatest strength: his use of superstition and symbolism to scare and confuse enemies by portraying himself as a supernatural being. His love interest commented, "That's why the natives think you're immortal! They think you're the phantom of 400 years ago!" In a daily from November 26, 1936, the Phantom hid and struck various criminals from unseen vantage points and quickly disappeared, causing each of them to consider that maybe he had supernatural powers of teleportation: "But he was just over there! How can you catch a man that's in three places at the same time!"[14] Bob Kane and Bill Finger routinely used similar tactics in their storytelling; for example, in *Detective Comics* #28 (1939), Batman similarly struck superstitious criminals from the shadows, as they cowardly interpreted his actions as part of a set of superhuman abilities. These methods worked against his adversaries because they were too frightened to shoot accurately.

Many other DC artists and writers also drew costume ideas from comic strips, including Alex Raymond's 1930s strip, *Flash Gordon*. This is not surprising since Raymond was a visually gifted pioneer of the science-fantasy genre and comic book artists couldn't help themselves from swiping or downright copying portions of his work since they desperately needed content to fill their pages of original stories. For example, Sheldon Moldoff, who later became Bob Kane's ghost artist, swiped Alex Raymond's *Flash Gordon* January 22, 1939, Sunday panel of Major Lingan for his cover of *All-American Comics* #16 (1940) depicting the first appearance of the Golden Age Green Lantern. Lingan was dressed in green with a domino mask, green cape, and boots with a circular symbol on his chest, which Moldoff seemingly traced, and only mildly modified. This is no character judgment against Moldoff but it was his usual modus operandi, which was confirmed by gifted designer and illustrator, Carmine Infantino, who once commented, "Sheldon used to copy Alex Raymond. Copy Foster, Caniff, anybody. Everybody."[15]

Bob Kane, Sheldon Moldoff, and Dave Wood created the villain Mr. Freeze, originally known as Mr. Zero, in *Batman* #121 (1959). Freeze needed to live in sub-zero temperatures, and his costume and helmet acted as a portable refrigerator while he used his powerful freeze gun to crack metal and rob banks. He was an innovative villain who seemed to be a derivation of Carmine Infantino and John Broome's Captain Cold from *Showcase* #8 (1957), who had his own freeze gun; however, this weapon may have its origin in comic strips. Infantino once commented, "I couldn't wait to get the newspapers to look at that stuff,"[16] so with himself, Kane, and Moldoff having read comic strips, it is no surprise that both freeze-ray characters were preceded by Alex Raymond's character and enemy of Flash Gordon, Count Malo of the Northlands, who had a similar ice gun in the April 16, 1939, Sunday that he used to treacherously freeze his adversaries.

DC's *Aquaman* also had visual sequences that were previously seen in Raymond's *Flash Gordon*. *Aquaman* was created by Mort Weisinger and Paul Norris in *More Fun Comics* #73 (1941), and many of the visuals match a continuity by Raymond where the blond Flash Gordon developed underwater breathing abilities and traveled to the oceanic civilization of Coralia to fight alongside an undersea race led by a royal couple, Triton and Undina. Similar to the later *Aquaman*, during the strips from April 12 to October 11, 1936, Gordon rode underwater seahorses, fought a tentacled octopus, and used transparent glass helmets filled with water to walk on land. These glass helmets full of water worn by Gordon's undersea Coralian armies were identical in concept to those worn by Sub-Mariner's Atlantean soldiers 25 years later in *The Fantastic Four Annual* #1 from Marvel Comics (1963) by Stan Lee and Jack Kirby. This similarity is consistent with Kirby once commenting on his study of classic comic strips, "My school was Alex Raymond and Milton Caniff."[17]

DC's Hawkman, created by Gardner Fox and Dennis Neville for *Flash Comics* #1 (1940), was very likely inspired from *Flash Gordon*'s Hawkmen, a winged warrior race that used their wings for coordinated attacks on Ming the Merciless. This aerial force first appeared in the July 8, 1934, Sunday and functioned as allies to the comic strip hero, whose Sundays were routinely swiped by artist Sheldon Moldoff. A few examples of this were evident when Moldoff swiped the June 18, July 13, and July 16, 1939, Sundays of *Flash Gordon* to depict Hawkman and Hawkgirl in *All-Star Comics* #3 (1940). Another DC property, Adam Strange, was created by Julius Schwartz and Murphy Anderson for *Showcase* #17 (1958) and appears based on Raymond's Flash Gordon. Anderson himself commented that in his early years, all colleagues around him during the Golden Age were "influenced by and copied from Raymond."[18] Both Gordon and Strange were blond masculine heroes with a brunette love interest, respectively, Dale Arden and Alanna. Both heroes traveled to planets far away from Earth to defend an unknown planet from oncoming hazards and carry out justice. "Power Men of Mongo" (June 23, 1940) was a storyline where Gordon donned an electrician's outfit bizarrely similar to the red-and-gold rebooted Flash costume that Carmine Infantino designed for the speedster in DC Comics' *Showcase* #4 (1956).

Both outfits had the yellow lightning bolt on the chest, yellow gloves and boots, and red full bodysuit with exposed lower face, and the same costume is credited for helping jump-start the superhero Silver Age. It is this Flash costume that is used in today's comics as well as the CW Network's TV show *The Flash* (2014).

Superman's physique and appearance also appear to have had a comic strip precursor. Malcolm Wheeler-Nicholson, Jerry Siegel, and Joe Shuster's character Slam Bradley premiered in *Detective Comics* #1 (1937) as a dark-haired tough private eye who went on a series of adventures with a diminutive sidekick named Shorty Morgan. Morgan was a short adult male with immature and boyish features, and the duo shared similarities with the two heroes from a comic strip that Joe Shuster followed, Roy Crane's *Wash Tubbs* (1924).[19] *Wash Tubbs* was a strip with daily gags about a short adult man with immature and boyish features similar to the later character, Shorty Morgan. The strip developed into an adventure series when Tubbs met the adventurer Captain Easy, a tall, hard-boiled, and dark-haired bruiser who premiered in the May 7, 1929, daily, and eventually became the main protagonist of the strip. Together, Easy and Tubbs, same as the later Bradley and Shorty, traveled in a series of global adventures, providing action and comedy to readers. Bradley appears to be based on Captain Easy, but with smoother facial features, and it was Bradley's physique that was reused by Siegel and Shuster to create the appearance of Superman in *Action Comics* #1 (1938).[20]

Jack Kirby produced many plots and characters for comic books, and evidence suggests that some of that material came from comic strips. Raymond was mentioned as part of Kirby's self-taught school; however, he also mentioned an influence from Hal Foster: "*Prince Valiant*, of course, it was astonishing to see beautiful illustration in the newspaper."[21] Foster left the *Tarzan* strip to create *Prince Valiant* in 1937 and one of his early adventures involved dressing up in a yellow demon mask to disguise himself in the December 25, 1937, Sunday. Kirby read this Sunday and later created *The Demon* #1 (1972) for DC Comics using the same aesthetic as an homage to his childhood love of Hal Foster's artwork.[22] Hal Foster later created another character in the *Prince Valiant* June 2, 1940, Sunday called "the Watcher," a tall, bald, robed figure. He was depicted as spying on Prince Valiant from the top of a mountain. The character's name, voyeuristic nature, and appearance were very similar to Stan Lee and Jack Kirby's Watcher, who premiered in *The Fantastic Four* #13 (1963). This Watcher was also a robed and bald figure, who used his cosmic senses to observe the universe's inhabitants from light-years away. Considering that Kirby paid close attention to Hal Foster's *Prince Valiant*,[23] the connection between the two Watchers is highly probable.

Jack Kirby created "the mad bomb" for *Captain America* #193 (1976), which activated a large group of humans to destroy everything around them. DC Comics had something similar in *Doom Patrol* #96 (1965), in which invisible waves caused populations to riot. Both ideas already existed in the *Flash Gordon* December 22, 1940, Sunday strip, which contained a science-fiction device called the "maddening riot-ray." When this ray was fired, everyone within its specific radius would become mad, causing significant amounts of property damage and human pain. Joe Simon and Jack Kirby seemed to also borrow fashion tips from Alex Raymond for Captain America's first appearance in *Captain America Comics* #1 (1941). The patriotic hero's distinct boots with ankle collars resemble the shoes worn by Gordon on the cover of the *Flash Gordon Strange Adventure* pulp magazine (1936). The colors are different, but the shoes are otherwise the same exact unique design.

Kirby mentioned that Milton Caniff was one of his chief schools in comic art. This could explain his cocreation of the Golden Age villain the Red Skull, who first appeared in *Captain America Comics* #1 (1941). The Red Skull was a vicious sociopath who snuck up to his victims and choked them to death while avoiding police capture and reveled in the fact that his bony visage was the last thing his victims saw. *Terry and the Pirates* by Milton Caniff had a similar villain called "the Skull" six years earlier in the March 24, 1935, Sunday. His similarly bony face and dark robe scared away superstitious natives while he murdered helpless victims. His sinister head glowed in the dark, and during his continuity, he was generally one step ahead of the strip's heroes.

Kirby also created adversaries for comic books that appear to already have been present in comic strips. He wrote and drew a science-fiction story called "The Last Enemy!" in *Alarming Tales* #1 (1957) about a scientist who entered a time cube to travel to the 26th century, a desolate future where humans were extinct and various types of upright and evolved animals engaged in war. Kirby expanded on this concept in his series *Kamandi* (1972), produced for DC Comics, about the last boy on Earth's distant future that contained a varied landscape of evolved animals and their fiefdoms. This reversal of the species' role in fiction made for an opportunity in social commentary regarding class distinctions. By making an animal the dominant species and humans as their slaves, it forces the reader to consider their own biases. Winsor McCay did this half a century earlier in a *Little Nemo in Slumberland* Sunday strip from August 8, 1909, when Little Nemo and Flip were captured by intelligent apes in the jungle, and humbly dealt with being caged by animals who were smarter and more organized.

Jack Kirby utilized classic science-fiction tropes that also appeared in older newspaper strips. One example is the flight to Mars seen in the space flight that gave the Fantastic Four their initial powers in their first issue. In *The Fantastic Four* #2 (1962), Reed Richards revealed, "It was my fault that our flight to Mars failed, and we nearly lost our lives when we crash-landed on Earth."[24] The Mars flight went back more than a hundred years in comic strips. First, it was present in the classic literature story *War of the Worlds* (1898) by H.G. Wells about Martians invading earth. However, comic strips first visually depicted travel to Mars before television and movies in *Little Nemo in Slumberland* (1909). Winsor McCay depicted Little Nemo and his friends traveling to Mars and encountering green aliens using an airship with advanced hot-air balloons.[25] Another "flight to mars" was depicted by Dick

Calkins in *Buck Rogers in the 25th Century*, which discussed interplanetary travel in the year 2430. The spaceship Rogers used was called "Satellite," which traveled from Earth "with no gravity or air friction to slow us down."[26] Another flight to Mars was depicted by Wally Wood for *Weird Fantasy* #9 (1951), titled "Spawn of Mars," about an astronaut team that left Earth to explore the red planet.

Some space- or radiation-based superheroes in comic books had a star logo on their chest, which was also preceded by comic strips. Jerry Robinson and Ken Crossen designed the character *Atoman* (1946), who wore a costume that had a multiple-pronged star on his chest. An almost identical chest logo was seen earlier, depicted by Alex Raymond on the chest of a costume worn by Flash Gordon 12 years earlier on February 4, 1934. Atoman's costume also influenced Captain Marvel's costume created by Roy Thomas and Gil Kane in 1969 for Marvel Comics. Roy Thomas wrote, "I based the look on a little-known 1946 superhero called Atoman with a multi-pronged star on the chest."[27] Joining the growing list of superheroes with stars on their chest was Nova. His costume was designed by Marv Wolfman and Len Wein for their fanzine *Super Adventures* #3 (1966) 10 years before his official Marvel comics appearance in *The Man Called Nova* #1 (1976). Although the star symbolized space travel or power, a *Little Nemo in Slumberland* (July 19, 1910) Sunday strip held a more interesting explanation. The star logo was used on the chest of a space policeman from Mars and explained as a symbol of galactic law enforcement.

Chiaroscuro was pioneered for comics in the strips, well before comic books. Frank Miller became famous for his use of black-and-white shadows that established a specific noir-style cinematography in his *Sin City* (1991) comic book series. This chiaroscuro technique described the method of drawing light coming from discreet angles and hitting an object to cast a stark shadow. This method added mood and tension, following in the footsteps of comic book pioneer Jim Steranko, who used chiaroscuro in his *Chandler: Red Tide* (1976) illustrated novel. The light source can be a window, cigarette lighter, or light bulb, etc., with each source casting a different emotional impression or tone for a panel. However, this technique goes back to Noel Sickles, who pioneered the addition of the chiaroscuro technique onto the comic strip medium in *Scorchy Smith*. Initially, Sickles started on the strip in 1933 mimicking the basic cartoon style of his predecessor, John Terry, but eventually made it into his own style, with shadows emphasizing the suspense. By the time he reached the October 10, 1936, daily with Scorchy in hand-to-hand combat in a dark room lit by a nearby open door, chiaroscuro had firmly made it into comics.

Comic strips utilized the illusion of change before comic books. The illusion of change is an issue that is generally considered when a writer carries a character's story arc over many years. Should they age the character and keep the stories fresh? Or do they preserve the brand by keeping the status quo? The answer is both. Most readers don't want to see their favorite superhero grow old. Even fewer would read Spider-Man as a geriatric patient, or Batman getting Alzheimer's disease, or Orphan Annie celebrating her 50th birthday. These changes would alienate younger

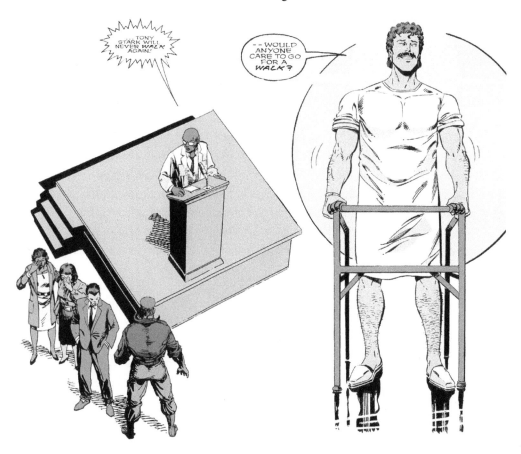

The illusion of change is a common method of maintaining a comic's brand while keeping the material interesting for ongoing readers. *Iron Man* **#243 and #248 (1989). Dialogue balloon 1: "...Tony Stark will never walk again!" Dialogue balloon 2: "—Would anyone care to go for a walk?"**

audiences and could dramatically impact a publisher's revenue. To carry on with the same characters for decades, cartoonists usually kept their star character the same age, but still push them through several short-term crises to keep the stories interesting. This is not change, but rather the illusion of change as the character returns to status quo, ready to start a new adventure in the next continuity. Occasionally a writer will refer to an old arc, but the character's appearance and overall status will generally never change. This illusion can have its painfully obvious moments—for example, story continuities about permanent, crippling spinal cord damage. Tony Stark was shot in the spine in *Iron Man* #243 (1989) and confined to a wheelchair and was told that he would never walk again, prompting a series of issues where the hero was depicted processing this event through a spectrum of emotions that ranged from self-pity to proactive coping. These issues were constructed well by Bob Layton and David Michelinie, but the grief was short-lived because an innovative surgery brought forth a full recovery by issue #248. What was depicted as a shocking and permanent status quo change quickly reversed to normal with the hero learning from the experience. This was mostly due to Stan Lee, who instituted a similar policy at Marvel Comics in 1970 when he advised editors that "superheroes should have only the 'illusion of change,' forever appearing to break new ground but always returning firmly to the status quo."[28] However, it's important to understand that the illusion of change wasn't new and comic strips utilized this first. For example, in the September 14, 1926, daily of *Little Orphan Annie*, Annie fell from a great height, sustaining spinal damage, and was unable to walk. The drama and helplessness experienced by Annie coping with her new lot in life was masterfully written by Harold Gray. However, by the November 20, 1926, daily, she received a miracle surgery and was able to walk again. The relief in Daddy Warbucks's face screaming, "ANNIE! You're WALKING!"[29] was emotional and well-written but demonstrated that writers of any ongoing comic character must eventually deal with the question of the illusion of change.

Syndicated newspaper comic strips developed plots, characters, costumes, tropes, and ideas over a forty-year period before original material comic books such as *New Fun* #1 (1935) were published. Many of the Golden Age comic book creators were fans of these comic strips and knew that strip cartoonists advanced comic storytelling in various genres such as crime, adventure, jungle, science fiction, war, and romance. This made it very convenient for comic book artists and writers, struggling to get published, to reuse these comic strip techniques and ideas for developing superhero comic books. However, there are also other key influences. Once superheroes manifested in comic books, they became a rapidly growing industry, and creators needed to meet their next issue's page count by going beyond strips to incorporate more story ideas and theatrical elements found in pulp magazines.

4

From Pulp Fiction
to Comic Books

Pulp magazines laid a strong foundation for the comic book industry. One important reason is that the two main comic book companies, DC Comics and Marvel, initially started out as pulp magazine publishers that utilized illustrations by artists who later contributed to Golden Age comic books. Pulp magazines also featured proto-superheroes who had characteristics that later comic books creators utilized to construct an effective superhero story. These proto-superheroes existed before the superhero genre and lack one or more traits that are needed to be called superheroes, such as a special ability, a distinctive costume, code name, or a mission of justice.[1] The first comic book superheroes were created by such young storytellers as Jerry Siegel, John Broome, Gardner Fox, Joe Simon, Jack Kirby, Joe Shuster, Gil Kane, Bob Kane, Mort Weisinger, Wally Wood, Jerry Robinson, Bill Finger, Joe Kubert, Carmine Infantino, Robert Kanigher, and Stan Lee. Their generation often found enjoyment reading pulp magazines from which they utilized ideas for creating superheroes such as Superman, Batman, Sub-Mariner, Ka-Zar, Suicide Squad, and Green Lantern, to name a few.

While literary ancestors or antecedents can go back thousands of years, it's pertinent to start in the 1800s with the emergence of two proto-superheroes from which later superheroes conceptually descend. First there is Super-Detective Nicholas Carter, who shares characteristics with and appears to be a literary ancestor to Superman. The second is the British bat-suited bogeyman Spring-Heeled Jack, who seems to have a strong lineage with Batman. The idea for Nicholas Carter, Master Detective originated from Ormond Smith and was expanded upon by John Russell Coryell for a 13-week serial, "The Old Detective's Pupil," starting in *New York Weekly* #46 (September 18, 1886). The character was successful enough to be given over to Frederick Van Rensselaer Dey to generate more plots and stories for publisher Street and Smith.[2] The protagonist was a private detective who was gifted with superior strength and super knowledge. He was a man of many disguises, solved crimes using expertise in all fields, and, similar to a later Street and Smith character, Doc Savage, was raised by his father, Sim Carter, to be a great man. Similar to several later heroes, including Doc Savage, he was orphaned, and his first job was to solve his father's murder. Carter also faced an ongoing archnemesis, Dr. Quartz,[3] an extremely intelligent sociopath premiering in *The Nick Carter Library* #13 (October 31, 1891) who shares manipulative characteristics with Doc Savage's enemy, John Sunlight (1938). Readers enjoyed Carter's heightened approach to detective work and his mission of justice against criminals.

The next incarnation of proto-superhero after Nick Carter in the line of Superman was John Carter, first appearing in *The All-Story* (February 1912) pulp magazine for a serial named "Under the Moons of Mars," written by Edgar Rice Burroughs. It was set on Mars, a planet correctly described in these adventures to have less gravity than earth, which allowed John Carter, with normal human physique, to leap across the red planet in great bounds. In a similar way, Superman, premiering in *Action Comics* #1 (1938) by Jerry Siegel and Joe Shuster, had the physique of a superhuman alien on earth and could jump an eighth of a mile in a single step with the aid of the lighter Earth gravity. Siegel was an avid reader of pulp magazines, evident in his letter to the editor in *Amazing Stories* (August 1929), listing stories that he recommended for other fans to read.[4] In regard to writing his early Superman plots, Siegel stated, "The John Carter stories did influence me. Carter was able to leap great distances.... I visualized the planet Krypton as a huge planet, much larger than Earth; so whoever came to Earth from that planet would be able to leap great distances and lift great weights."[5] The stories of John Carter also influenced Gardner Fox, a writer of superhero comic books during the Golden and Silver Ages, who commented that they "opened up a complete new world for me."[6]

Super abilities and other science-fiction principles from comics also previously appeared in Philip Wylie's books *Gladiator* (1930), *The Savage Gentleman* (1932), and *When World's Collide* (1933). After the stock market crash of 1929, the culture of the Great Depression demanded an urgent need for escapism. Science-fiction pulps and books provided a way to imagine a better world for tomorrow, fascinating the reader with hope and excitement. Philip Wylie used this opportunity to present his books as situational science fiction, which focused less on optimism and more on selfish human situations with exaggerated science principles. His characters were not superheroes, but rather survivalists who tried to understand and interact with a failing world; however, despite the differences, it is impossible to ignore the connection between the origins of Superman and *Gladiator*. The parallels are striking, causing many sources to link the two characters.[7] Both characters have scientist fathers who experimented on their son to increase their offspring's relative strength. In Superman's case, his father rocketed him to a planet with lower gravity in an experimental ship to avoid certain death, where he became Earth's strongest man. In *Gladiator*, the protagonist's father was Professor Abednego Danner, who experimented on his wife's fetus with an ant formula. His resulting son, Hugo Danner, wielded super strength and invulnerability and was able to lift cars the same as Superman, who was depicted on the cover of *Action Comics* #1 (1938). Other similarities between both characters include growing up in the American interior, with Superman from

Kansas and Gladiator from Colorado. Their parents taught them both to exercise humility by not showing off their powers in public and both had unbreakable skin, outran trains, and leaped 40 feet in the air in a single bound. This situation caused Danner, the super boy, to experience trouble fitting in with society in a significantly darker tale than that of Superman, containing no vigilantism or costumes. Super strength wasn't a gift, but rather a curse filled with consequences including accidental murder, social awkwardness, and distrust of humanity. Instead of becoming a hero, he was struck down and killed by lightning.

Danner as well as Superman both had super strength described through analogies of ants and grasshoppers.[8] Wylie wrote in *Gladiator*, "The ants. Strength a hundred times our own…. A man as strong as a grasshopper, and he'll be able to leap over a church."[9] Jerry Siegel wrote in *Action Comics* #1 that Superman, same as an ant, can "support weights hundreds of times its own" and also described that "the grasshopper leaps what to man would be the space of several city blocks."[10] The odds of both writers using the same analogies of ants and grasshoppers to describe their character's strength, independently, are incredibly low, suggesting that Siegel was familiar with the book. Despite the obvious similarities, there is no confirmed interview with Siegel or Shuster declaring Wylie as an influence. The opposite, however, does have some documentation. Phillip Wylie wrote to dime novel historian J. Randolph Cox in 1970:

> I even consulted my lawyer to see if I ought not to sue for plagiarism [*sic*]. He agreed I'd probably win but found the "creation" of "Superman" were two young kids getting $25 a week apiece, only, and that a corporation owned the strip so recovery of damages would be costly, long, difficult and maybe fail owing to that legal set-up…. We all borrow in ways from others, though. The first Superman wasn't my Gladiator but Hercules or Samson.[11]

Applying insect strength to superheroes was also repeated in the 1960s at Marvel for Spider-Man and Ant-Man, who both gained proportional insect strength.

Philip Wylie and Edwin Balmer wrote *When Worlds Collide* (1933) as a six-part series in *Blue Book* magazine from September 1932 to February 1933, which depicted a premise used to start off both Alex Raymond's *Flash Gordon* (1934) and *Action Comics* #1 featuring Superman. This novel told the story of chief scientist, Dr. Cole Hendron, who detected an incoming planet approaching Earth to eventually cause massive destruction. An athletic hero, David Randall, and his love interest, the nurse Eve, rode a spaceship to land on the planet to escape certain doom and assess a method to save the human race.[12] The character trio is the same as the team portrayed in *Flash Gordon* published one year later. Athletic Flash Gordon and his girlfriend, Dale Arden, ride a rocket to the incoming planet Mongo, first detected by the scientist Dr. Hans Zarkov. Their mission was to prevent Mongo's king, Ming the Merciless, from destroying Earth.[13] In Superman's origin story by Jerry Siegel, a similar premise was used when Jor-El sent his spaceship to Earth carrying his son, Kal-El, away from the doomed planet Krypton.

Wylie also created *The Savage Gentleman* (1932) using the same core premise later utilized by Lester Dent in *Doc Savage Magazine* #1 (1933) about a man who took his son, Henry Stone, away to a tropical island to train him to become the perfect human. Henry grew into a bronze-haired, mahogany-skinned, strong, and intelligent man. Similar to Doc Savage, Stone later returned to New York with his father's fortune but instead did not end up fighting crime because he would rather use his mind and body to better understand the opposite sex.[14] *Doc Savage* writer Lester Dent instilled a similar origin into his lead character, Clark Savage, Jr. Clark Savage, Sr., assembled a team of scientists to create the perfect son, Clark Savage, Jr., a physician, detective, psychologist, scientist, and engineer who used his unique abilities to solve crimes and fight criminals.[15] By making Savage mentally and physically flawless, Lester Dent intended to construct the ultimate hybrid "between Tarzan and Sherlock Holmes."[16] This origin story of both *The Savage Gentleman* and *Doc Savage*, both with professors who used eugenics to make their sons perfect in isolation, were used as the origin by Joe Simon and Jack Kirby for the comic book *Private Strong* #1 (1959).[17] Four decades later, Alan Moore and Chris Sprouse used the same origin in *Tom Strong* #1 (1999).[18] *The Savage Gentleman* should be considered a strong precursor to both *Strong* characters, Superman, and other superheroes that were influenced by Doc Savage.

Doc Savage appeared to combine qualities from Nick Carter, John Carter, Hugo Danner, and *The Savage Gentleman* in his first appearance in *Doc Savage Magazine* #1 (1933), created by Street & Smith's Henry W. Ralston, John L. Nanovic, and Lester Dent. Although he lacked a superhero costume, Clark Savage, Jr., had many qualities identical to Superman, Batman, the Fantastic Four and the X-Men. Savage was referred to as "The Man of Bronze"[19] that no warrior dared fight due to "his reputation of a superman,"[20] and lived in a fortress that was initially discussed in his first appearance and later illustrated as an impenetrable hemisphere or "strange blue dome" above the snow and ice.[21] He periodically retired there to study and train his awesome mind.[22] DC's Superman had the same first name, "Clark" Kent, and was referred to as the "Man of Steel," while also sharing a similar area of respite in an arctic "fortress of solitude," first appearing in *Superman* #58 (1949), which he built "in the polar wastes because the intense cold keeps away snoopers."[23] Similar to Superman, Doc Savage hid advanced weaponry there, confiscated during his career, to keep away from criminals who would abuse them.[24]

Doc Savage and Superman were both orphans who had only one family member left—their first cousins. Doc Savage's first cousin was Patricia Savage, created by Lester Dent, premiering in *Brand of the Werewolf* (1934).[25] She was younger, physically perfect, lusted for adventure, was quick on her feet, and every man wanted her. In the magazine series, she was reported as being tall with a slender form, tan skin, golden eyes, and dark bronze hair.[26] Patricia's counterpart in the Superman mythos was his Kryptonian cousin, Supergirl, created by Otto Binder and Al Plastino for *Action Comics* #252 (1959). Both sets of cousins share the tragic fact that they were the last survivors of the hero's family.

Despite influencing Superman, Doc Savage also had traits later found in Batman. Both Doc Savage and Batman were physically and mentally perfect human beings. In Bruce Wayne's origin, writers Bill Finger and Gardner Fox and artists Bob Kane and Sheldon Moldoff depicted the young Bruce Wayne as angry, saddened by his parents' death, and emboldened to become "a master scientist" who "trains his body to physical perfection until he is able to perform amazing athletic feats."[27] This is the same for Doc Savage, who isolated himself to exercise for two hours every day for an "intensive physical and mental drill."[28] Both men strove to be superior to their enemies by adopting a strict workout routine and adhering to it with great discipline. They used well-earned muscle to master diverse fighting styles offered in various countries around the world, allowing them to adapt to any overwhelming situation. In one fight scene, Savage dealt with multiple enemies at once when he "shook the two Mayans whose throats he held. He brought their heads together, knocking their senses out. The other two were tangled in the tapir-hide strands … using the two men in his hands as human clubs, Doc beat the others down."[29]

Both Savage and Batman inherited millions of their father's dollars used to fund their adventures. In his origin issue, Bruce Wayne sat in a luxurious room in front of a fireplace considering his possibilities as a crimefighter when he stated, "Dad's estate left me wealthy."[30] Similarly, Doc Savage inherited the cache of "great stacks of the raw, rich gold" described in his first adventure as "the legacy his father had left him. He was to use it in the cause to which his life was dedicated … punishing those who deserve it."[31] They used their wealth to fund secret hangars to store their vehicles. The Batcave stored those vehicles under Bruce Wayne's mansion—first demonstrated by Bob Kane and Bill Finger in *Batman* #12 (1942)—housing the Batplane, Batmobile, and repair workshop. Doc Savage also created a similar hangar, the Hidalgo Trading Company Warehouse, to house and store various transport vehicles he owned, varying from a zeppelin to an aircraft, and even a submarine.[32]

Both Doc Savage and Batman also utilized forensic skills as problem-solving detectives to analyze crime scenes. In various stories, Doc Savage used his knowledge in fields such as physics and chemistry to discover clues that assisted him in catching a story's villain. A classic situation has him "studying the hole in the safe door, noting particularly the angle at which the powerful bullet had entered…. Doc weighed the bullet in his palm… 'seven hundred and fifty grams … probably the gun that fired that shot was a double-barreled rifle.'"[33] Similarly, Batman was depicted as obsessively investigating a crime, "through the night he works in his secret laboratory … mixing … probing,"[34] at times using his utility belt that carried materials needed to solve problems. This device was first introduced in *Detective Comics* #29 (1939) by Gardner Fox and came in handy when Batman was shot and used a gas pellet, retrieved from his belt, on his assailant. His utility belt was equivalent to Doc Savage's utility vest created in 1933 by Lester Dent in his eighth magazine, "The Sargasso Ogre."[35] *Batman* cocreator Bill Finger was a reader of *Doc Savage* and corroborated the link between both figures' utility accessories.[36] The vest was described

Many early superheroes utilized tropes and mechanisms from pulp magazines, namely Batman's utility vest from *Detective Comics* #29 (1939), which was taken from Doc Savage's utility vest created by Lester Dent in *Doc Savage Magazine* (October 1933).

by Dent when it was clarified that "the bronze man carried no firearm … he did, however, wear a well-padded vest fashioned with many pockets, and worn under his outer clothing so that its presence was hardly noticeable … he delved into the concealed pockets."[37] Doc Savage's vest and Batman's belt both had gadgets for various hazardous situations.

Stan Lee stated that he "loved" reading *Doc Savage*, which carried traits later found in the 1960s Marvel books *The Fantastic Four* and *The X-Men*.[38] Doc Savage's loyal friends from World War I, the "Fabulous Five," consisted of Monk, Ham, Renny, Long Tom, and Johnny[39] with clashes seen between their unique personalities as early as their first issue, *Doc Savage Magazine* #1 (1933). This was also the case with Stan Lee and Jack Kirby's *Fantastic Four*, consisting of Reed, Ben, Johnny, and Susan. Members of both teams argued with each other to keep the reader interested; for example, the Human Torch (Johnny) and the Thing (Ben) generally played practical jokes on each other, which prompted quarrels. In one instance, the Thing confronted the Torch, "I don't believe in sendin' a kid to do a man's job!" To which the Torch responded, "Aw, shut up and let us think, will ya?"[40] The Human Torch and the Thing's interactions paralleled two of the "Fabulous Five," namely Monk Mayfair and Ham Brooks. Monk was an ape-like scientist, while Ham was the silver-tongued attorney. Together, they displayed some internal friction in the group but still succeeded in overcoming differences to solve mysteries. Monk was a chemistry genius despite his physical makeup: "a few inches over five feet tall, he weighed better than two hundred and sixty pounds … the build of a gorilla, arms six inches longer than his legs."[41] He resembled Hank McCoy, the Beast, created by Stan Lee and Jack Kirby for *The X-Men* #1 (1963) with the same ape-like body and high IQ.

Doc Savage and his Fabulous Five lived in their headquarters on the 86th floor of the Empire State Building,[42] resembling the Fantastic Four's living quarters in the Baxter Building—the fictional high-rise that first appeared in *The Fantastic Four* #3 (1962). Both are considered tall, multipurpose buildings in which the main team occupied the uppermost floor. This issue also premiered the Fantasti-car used by the team for fast transport, which appeared to be a newer derivation of the original Autogyro that Doc Savage and the Fabulous Five piloted to travel to their global missions.[43] Batman also had a similar device that he used to fly to missions called the Batgyro, created by Gardner Fox, found in his "secret hangar" and designed with a propeller and wings that could easily be steered.[44]

Jack Kirby also appears to have been influenced by Lester Dent. One of the more notable books that Dent wrote for the Doc Savage series was his sixth entry, *The Red Skull* (August 1933). In the Doc Savage universe, the "Red Skull" was a large geographic location where the story took place, but Kirby, a well-known pulp fan, used this same name when he cocreated the villain "Red Skull" in *Captain America Comics* #1 (1941) with Joe Simon and Ed Herron.[45] The Red Skull often took to sadistic methods when dealing with Cap and his sidekick, Bucky, and faked his death regularly to stay one step ahead of them.

Despite Batman sharing characteristics with Doc Savage, he had more in common with another line of wealthy, masked, and dark proto-superheroes descending from Spring-Heeled Jack. Spring-Heeled Jack started in 1838 as an English bogeyman,[46] a ghost or devil, and made appearances in the local literature of the time.[47] He was depicted wearing a skin coat with a horned mask in British penny dreadfuls,[48] and although his many appearances and backstories have been written about in various stories, the most detailed iteration of the character's motivations was presented in the one-penny magazine serial *Spring-Heeled Jack* (1904), written by Alfred Burrage. This series continued for 12 issues depicting the nobleman Bertram Wraydon, who was framed for conspiracy by his half brother, Hubert Sedgefield, who now controlled his estate. Spring-Heeled Jack helped Wraydon's effort, until the story was abruptly canceled with no resolution; however, this multipart saga is historically notable for containing specific paragraphs that are key descriptions of not only Burrage's Spring-Heeled Jack but also of the later Batman. Burrage wrote text that informed the reader of Spring-Heeled Jack's appearance as a vengeful antihero wearing a bat costume who delivered vengeance in a nobleman's war on crime. The coincidence alone makes Jack significant, but could one of the *Shadow* writers, specifically Theodore Tinsley, have read about this character? Theodore Tinsley's *Shadow* story "Partners of Peril" (1936) was swiped by Bill Finger for Batman's first appearance, "The Case of the Chemical Syndicate" (1939).[49] It's an intriguing question because Tinsley served in France during World War I[50] and may have been exposed to local one-penny magazines such as *Spring-Heeled Jack*, where Jack was referred to as "bat-like,"[51] a phrase that Tinsley repeatedly used in "Partners of Peril." Tinsley stated, "A black form slid 'batlike' to a narrow ledge" or "with the uncanny speed of a bat" or "over the dark outline of The Shadow's body, bats wheeled and squeaked."[52] Although Bill Finger received bat iconography from this *Shadow* story, it's possible that its writer, Tinsley, received it from *Spring-Heeled Jack*.

Similar to *Batman*, *Spring-Heeled Jack* is a costumed revenge saga, where the antihero gets payback against criminals in a long elaborate plot. For Jack and Batman alike, the best way to exact revenge is to have psychological power over the enemy. It is difficult to tell if Spring-Heeled Jack has any true mystical powers, but his victim's fear and superstition are used against them. One passage described him as "man or fiend, it dropped into the hall, leapt upwards, spreading out what appeared to the horror-stricken spectator a pair of bat-like wings."[53] It appeared to readers that Jack utilized illusion and trickery to depict himself as part man and part beast. Batman exhibited a similar ability to frighten superstitious criminals using his cape and cowl by pretending he wasn't fully human in his first appearance in *Detective Comics* #27 (1939) and invoked dread and fear in nearby enemies.[54] As Spring-Heeled Jack sightings continued in the series, his athletic prowess, mystique, and ability to camouflage into shadows gave criminals the impression that he was "gifted with the power of flying." When Jack "rose in the air," he tricked criminals into thinking he possessed "wonderful powers" and that he was not "mortal and can clear an obstacle twelve feet in height."[55] This frightening presence allowed Jack to maintain an element of surprise when he leaped out of the dark at armed criminals who shot at him but missed. "A form, dark and shadowy, coming from where no one could tell … the guard … fetched out a pistol and fired it at random."[56] He horrified onlookers with his "grinning mouth" and "brightly-glaring eyes" making villains too scared to shoot straight. Before villains could even use a pistol, the room was filled with flame and smoke that masked his escape: "weird figure … black, gruesome, and spreading what appeared to be a pair of wings from its shoulders … he went out of my sight just like a puff of smoke!"[57] However, Jack did not only threaten enemies with his appearance, because he expressed no qualms about terrorizing criminals with death.[58] He stared his prey in the eyes as they dropped to their knees and he described himself as the "Avenger of Wrong" when stating, "I am Spring-Heeled Jack…. Prepare to die!"

Batman had the same qualities listed above. He used smoke, darkness, and fear to surprise mobsters and avoid damage. One panel showed him hiding from his enemies and leaping out of nowhere to keep his enemies afraid to guess which horrors were coming next.[59] He used fear as a weapon against superstitious criminals to give a false impression that he was supernaturally powerful, which allowed a moment of confusion while he took each armed culprit down.[60] When another character turned to look at Batman, similar to Jack, he disappeared in a puff of smoke and vanished from meetings when colleagues momentarily looked away.[61] In his origin story

(1939), Batman was depicted staring at the city from a ledge, getting ready for an offensive attack as a caption described him as an "Avenger of Evil."[62] This was accurate in his early years since he occasionally avenged evil by killing people, which was seen with an early adversary, Dr. Death, who at one point ran from Batman, afraid for his life, only to burn in flames when the caped hero threw a gas container at a nearby fire. Batman's response was, "Death … to Doctor Death!"[63] Another adversary in Batman's first issue was punched into a tank of acid, and the hero's only response was, "A fitting ending for his kind."[64] Batman reveled in this because he believed that all criminals deserved to pay for what they had done.

Spring-Heeled Jack's backstory and supporting characters reveal more similarities to those of Batman. Jack was strongly suggested to be alter ego Bertram Wraydon, a young heir to his family's fortune. His motive was to avenge his wrongful conviction against his evil half brother, Hubert Sedgefield, who aimed to steal his estate.[65] With similar parallels in his origin, Batman also had his secret identity, Bruce Wayne, revealed at the end of Batman's first story. After Commissioner Gordon remarked that Bruce Wayne lived a boring life, Wayne manor's door opened, revealing the millionaire in the cape and cowl.[66] Batman, too, was a young heir to his family's fortune, and both antiheroes had the same initials, BW, for Bruce Wayne and Bertram Wraydon. Each also had a faithful servant. In Wraydon's case, his servant, Denis Stocks, wanted to see the young nobleman restored to his inheritance and overseeing Wraydon Manner. This is discussed in a scene at their secret headquarters, a graveyard crypt: "The only thing I hope for … is seeing you restored to the ownership of Wraydon House, and me your very humble and faithful servant."[67] Paralleling this, Bruce Wayne has Alfred Pennyworth, who was introduced in *Batman* #16 (1943) as his master's faithful butler at Wayne Manor. Pennyworth, same as Stocks, assisted Bruce Wayne in his war on crime. Alfred Burrage's depiction of Jack as a bat-like antihero who used fear and trickery to defeat his enemies, with a secret headquarters, a fortune, a butler servant, and a mission of vengeance, deserves to be recognized.

After *Spring-Heeled Jack*, there are two more proto-superheroes that carry traits later seen in Batman: *The Scarlet Pimpernel* (1905), a British story by Baroness Orczy, and "The Grey Seal" (1914) by Frank L. Packard. Orczy wrote the tale of an English nobleman, Sir Percy Blakeney, who pretended to be concerned with wealth and appearance but used a unique disguise as a masked adventurer to protect the innocent. After the hero made an appearance in costume, he routinely left behind a symbolic red flower during missions to save aristocrats from violent French revolutionaries in 1792.[68] Nine years later, Packard introduced the character Jimmie Dale with the code name "The Grey Seal" in *People's Magazine* (May 1914), which was about a wealthy playboy who donned a costume with gloves and domino mask. He often snuck around rooftops and left behind a gray paper seal that signified his conquests, after evenings of confronting organized crime.[69] The Grey Seal was an influence on comic strip creator Lee Falk, whose costumed adventurer The Phantom

(1936) was originally going to be called The Gray Ghost.[70] Deciding to call his character The Phantom worked to Falk's advantage, but there was an homage to the discarded name in "Beware the Gray Ghost," a childhood hero to a young Bruce Wayne in the November 4, 1992, episode of *Batman: The Animated Series*.

There are several pulp magazines in the 1930s that contain plots and characters found in early *Batman* stories, such as *The Shadow, Spicy Mystery Stories, The Whisperer, All-Detective Magazine*, and *Black Book Detective*. The Shadow was the voice narrator for *Detective Story Hour* (July 31, 1930) radio show and then a proto-superhero developed by Walter B. Gibson for Street and Smith publications for "The Living Shadow" in *The Shadow Magazine* #1 (April 1931). The Shadow was disguised as wealthy billionaire playboy Lamont Cranston[71] and used darkness and illusion to infiltrate evil organizations as well as torment and kill criminals using two large .45 automatics. Bill Finger, Batman's cocreator, mentioned in *The Steranko History of Comics* vol. 1 (1970) that he swiped a *Shadow* story and integrated it into the first Batman script, "The Case of the Chemical Syndicate," in 1939.[72] Comics historian Anthony Tollin identified that it was "Partners of Peril" (1936) by Theodore Tinsley that was taken scene for scene by Bill Finger for the 1939 Batman story.[73] Walter Gibson also wrote the story "Lingo" (1935) that included a *Shadow*-based boomerang that likely inspired Gardner Fox to create the Batarang in *Detective Comics* #31 (1939).[74] Batman's name also has pulp origins in Lew Merrill's short story titled "Batman" in *Spicy Mystery Stories* (February 1936) about a man whose brain had been transplanted into the body of a bat.[75] Batman's law enforcement ally, Commissioner James Gordon, who appeared in the hero's first issue, also appears to be rooted in the pulp magazine *The Whisperer* (October 1936), which featured an ongoing character, Commissioner James Gordon, who had the same name, job, clothing, and hairstyle.

There is a high likelihood that some of *Batman*'s rogues' gallery, the Joker, Dr. Death, and Two-Face, also took inspiration from the pulps. His chief villain is the Joker, who premiered as a grinning sociopath in *Batman* #1 (1940), created by Jerry Robinson, Bill Finger, and Bob Kane, and may be an imitation of Theodore Tinsley's "The Grim Joker," a clown-faced mob boss presented in a backup story in *The Whisperer* magazine (July 1937). *Batman*'s Joker lacked an origin story for years until Bill Finger eventually wrote "The Man Behind the Red Hood" in *Detective Comics* #168 (1951), describing the Joker's evolution from his earlier days as a small-time criminal dressed in a long tuxedo and red helmet. The Red Hood escaped Batman but fell into a vat of chemicals at the "Ace" Playing Card Company, which gave rise to the character resembling a disfigured clown. Coincidentally, Theodore Tinsley also wrote about the Scarlet "Ace," whose long tuxedo and red cowl is shown prominently on the cover of *All Detective Magazine* (February 1933), sharing a resemblance with the Joker's prior alter ego, the Red Hood. Perhaps Theodore Tinsley, the pulp writer, was the creative grandfather to the Joker. There is also a somewhat forgettable story, "Song of Death," published in *Amazing Stories* (November 1938) by writer Ed Earl

Repp that featured an illustration by Joseph Wirt Tillotson of a character who could certainly serve as a possible visual precursor to the comic book version of the Joker. The hair that points to the sides, pale skin, sneering smile, and oddly designed suit certainly appear related.

Doctor Death was a villainous head of a crime syndicate who first appeared in *All Detective Magazine* (August 1934) and entertained audiences enough to warrant his own periodical titled *Doctor Death* (1935) from Dell. The series was about a second Doctor Death, an occultist who left behind his former life as a college professor, and it is likely not a coincidence that the name was also used by Gardner Fox and Bob Kane for a villain in *Detective Comics* #29 (1939). DC Comics' Dr. Death was a bald mad scientist who developed a poisonous pollen extract for the purpose of blackmailing wealthy families into paying him a ransom. His scheme failed as Batman disarmed the mad doctor of his poison and tossed it into a nearby fire, which combusted into an inferno that burned his entire body.

Bob Kane and Bill Finger's popular *Batman* villain Two-Face debuted in *Detective Comics* #66 (1942) and was likely patterned after pulp character "The Face" from *The Shadow Magazine* story "Face of Doom" (March 15, 1938). Both the pulp and comic book characters have a normal right side of the face and an abnormally green left side, split straight down the middle. Two-Face was originally attorney Harvey Dent, who was scarred on that side of his face from a criminal's acid attack, which was a comic book origin that seems to stem from another pulp character, the Black Bat, created by writer Norman A. Daniels for Thrilling Publications' *Black Book Detective* (July 1939). Black Bat, same as Two-Face, was a district attorney who was blinded due to an acid attack to the face and used guns much like The Shadow. He also originated in a "detective" magazine and debuted around the same time as Batman. The two Bat characters premiering around the same time is thought to be an example of parallel thinking, and a legal event was needed to reconcile the two similar characters. DC editor Whitney Ellsworth mediated a deal whereby both companies could continue to use their characters simultaneously despite their striking similarities. There is a high probability that the agreement depended on the Black Bat staying a pulp and Batman staying a comic so that both companies didn't infringe on the copyright of the other's medium.[76] Black Bat, however, has more similarities to a later Marvel superhero. After his eyes were scarred from acid, the Black Bat found a surgeon who grafted a cadaver eye that gave him superhuman sight, prompting him to pretend to be blind during his day job as an attorney. This backstory is the same as Marvel's Silver Age *Daredevil* (1964), whose titular character was also known as attorney Matt Murdock, whose eyes were exposed to a radioactive substance that elevated his perception with a radar sense. It seems that Black Bat is a creative ancestor or antecedent to both Two-Face and Daredevil more so than Batman.

Outside of *Superman* and *Batman*, there are other comic books that have material previously seen by pulps, including *Sub-Mariner*, *Ka-Zar*, *Nighthawk*, *The X-Men*, *Ghost Rider*, *The Suicide Squad*, *Enemy Ace*, and *Green Lantern*. This preexisting material includes characters, genres, settings, concepts, titles, and story ideas. For example, Namor, the Sub-Mariner, created by Bill Everett in *Marvel Comics* #1 (1939) had pointy ears, dark black hair, stark eyebrows, and a deep widow's peak that are strikingly similar qualities to an antihero detective by the name of "Satan Hall." Satan Hall first appeared in Street & Smith's *Detective Story Magazine* (August 8, 1931) and eventually reoccurred in *Detective Fiction Weekly*. Hall was a policeman who was described to resemble the devil, and in a similar manner as other hard-boiled detectives of the time, showed no mercy toward criminals. He generally shot to kill, in a singular pursuit to eliminate wicked men in his city in early 1930s crime stories that aimed to appeal to angry victims of the Great Depression. Sub-Mariner was also merciless in his early adventures, crushing human heads and murdering his opponents. Despite their very different genres, abilities, and locations, their similarities in facial design and violent temperament are hard to miss.

Ka-Zar is a Marvel Comics jungle hero that probably descended from two stories by Edgar Rice Burroughs, *Tarzan of the Apes* and *The Land That Time Forgot*. *Tarzan of the Apes* premiered in *The All-Story* (October 1912) about a British orphan raised by apes in the African jungle. Burroughs later wrote *The Land That Time Forgot*, which premiered in *Blue Book Magazine* (August 1918) about an island off the coast of Antarctica where volcanic activity preserved a tropical island of dinosaurs. Tarzan was emulated by later Timely Comics publisher Martin Goodman for his own pulp magazine, *Ka-Zar* (October 1936), created by Bob Byrd. Ka-Zar was originally David Rand, whose parents died in the jungle, causing him to be raised by a local lion. This jungle adventurer was featured in his own ongoing comic book continuity three years later called "Adventures of Ka-Zar the Great" in *Marvel Comics* #1 (1939), which was a smart decision by Goodman to transfer this pulp character into comic books, which at the time was considered a newly popular and successful medium. Twenty years later, Stan Lee and Jack Kirby revamped Ka-Zar into a new Silver Age version with numerous modifications made to the character, including his name changing to Kevin Plunder for his first appearance in *Uncanny X-Men* #10 (1965) and setting the story in an Antarctic dinosaur preserve called the "Savage Land." This issue was titled "The World that Time Forgot" as an obvious homage to Burroughs's work. The Savage Land took on a life of its own as various Marvel superheroes visited the exotic locale over the decades.

The first flying armored proto-superhero by the name of Night Hawk first appeared in the English pulp magazine *The Nelson Lee Library* #11 (April 5, 1930) and appears to precede a few comic book superheroes. Wealthy son of a murdered scientist, Thurston Kyle built his mechanical winged suit to target his father's killers, the Benton Gang. His introductory issue referred to him as "The Winged Avenger" (1930), which was an accurate name since he threw the gang leader over a cliff to die. Winged heroes akin to Night Hawk were also present in later Marvel comic books; for example, Red Raven, who first appeared in *Red Raven Comics* #1 (1940), created by Joe Simon and Louis Cazeneuve. A plane crashed into an island of Bird People and killed two passengers—the parents of a young boy who was raised on the

The Marvel Comics jungle hero Ka-Zar premiered in *The X-Men* #10 (1965) while utilizing prehistoric features from Edgar Rice Burroughs's *The Land That Time Forgot* (1924) and the company's own pulp magazine from 1936.

island and given artificial "membranous" wings.[77] Another comic book hero similar to Night Hawk was the Marvel character Nighthawk premiering in *The Avengers* #69 (1969), a wealthy orphan named Kyle Richmond, created by Roy Thomas and Sal Buscema. Both characters have the same code name and the same personal name, Kyle. Another Timely–era pulp magazine featured a winged heroine with a scarlet helmet on the cover of *Marvel Tales* #6 (1939), in a short story called "Angel from Hell."[78] The art was drawn by J.W. Scott and was an indication that Martin Goodman tried out various winged characters during his time as publisher, including the mutant Angel, who premiered in *The X-Men* #1 (1963).

Marvel's superpowered mutant comic book series *The X-Men* appears to descend from the science-fiction novel *Odd John* (1935), written by Olaf Stapledon. John was a superhuman born with psychic gifts as the next genetic step in human evolution. Similar to Professor X from *The X-Men* (1963), John built a haven for fellow mutants that he protected from regular humans with his psionic abilities.[79] It is *Odd John* that first referred to mutants as "homo superior,"[80] which is the same phrase that the villain Magneto stated in *The X-Men* #1 (1963), whose dialogue was written by Stan Lee and co-plotted with artist Jack Kirby.[81] Even the name "X-Men" seemed to have pulp roots in *Star Detective Magazine* (March 1937) with the lead story titled "The X-Man."[82] Another mutant story that centered on a distrust of humans was found in *Thrilling Wonder*

Stories vol. 30, #1 (April 1947), that contained a science-fiction story called "Way of the Gods" by Henry Kuttner. Kuttner depicted mutants as the "spawn of atomic fission; this strange company of mutants exiled by humanity battles against enslavement in a foreign world."[83] Another mutant story, "Children of the Atom," premiered in *Astounding Science Fiction* (November 1948) by Wilmar H. Shiras[84] and centered on a group of mutant children born to atomic weapons workers who were exposed to radiation. The mutants were genetically gifted with extreme intelligence and attended a school for gifted children,[85] which was another concept that appeared in Marvel's *X-Men*, a series that drew much of its mythos from science-fiction pulps and novels.

Ghost Rider is another Golden Age superhero who appears to have utilized imagery from the cover of *Weird Tales* (January 1924) magazine, which displayed a pale, white, and ghostly cowboy riding a specter of a horse. This "Ghost Rider" was depicted by artist R.M. Mally as a white silhouette, swinging his lasso and chasing a cowboy who was riding his horse for dear life. This was a similar visual concept to *The Ghost Rider*, created by Ray Krank and Dick Ayers for *Tim Holt* #11 (1949) for Vin Sullivan's publishing company, Magazine Enterprises.[86] Ayers depicted the Ghost Rider again at Marvel in 1967 after its trademark under Vin Sullivan had lapsed.[87]

The Suicide Squad was originally a pulp series written by Emile Tepperman that started in "Mr. Zero and The F.B.I. Suicide Squad" in *Ace G-Man Stories* (May–June 1939). This FBI task force combated domestic threats in America, including diabolical villains such as the Crime Czar and Nazis in a free-for-all murder carnival. Over two decades later, Robert Kanigher created his version of the Suicide Squad in *Brave and the Bold* #25 (1959) about four military figures called Task Force X, led by Colonel Rick Flag, who went on missions to investigate superpowered beings.[88] The concept changed once again almost two decades later when a new Suicide Squad created by John Ostrander premiered in *Legends* #3 (1987) and was instead a covert group of super prisoners forced to complete secret black ops missions for the United States government. It was this rendition that got its own movie in 2016.

DC Comics pilot Enemy Ace engaged in aviation adventures set in World War I, which was also a concept that was formerly present in the pulp magazine *G-8 and His Battle Aces* #1 (October 1933) about a World War I–era aviator written by pilot Robert Hogan. Hogan used his own experiences as well as those of "Harold O. Nevin, an Air Service squadron commander in France"[89] to infuse the storylines with realism throughout the series that lasted until 1944. This genre did not die with the pulps, as it was revisited in *Our Army at War* #151 (1965), created by Joe Kubert and Robert Kanigher. The hero was German fighter Hans von Hammer, who channeled his inner rage in a battle of strategy against Ally planes. It is considered one of DC Comics' great runs of the Silver Age due to its riveting stories and compelling artwork. Although G-8 battled against science-fiction or occult elements, both series contained thrilling action set in the wartime skies.

The Silver Age version of the Green Lantern employed science-fiction elements found in the *Grey Lensman* pulp series. *Grey Lensman* began in *Amazing Stories*

(January 1934) in an ongoing series called "Triplanetary" by Edward Smith, Ph.D. Although the initial story concerned alien breeding experiments for a galactic war, the series evolved into a saga about the Lensmen, a galactic patrol with each member deemed worthy of a lens attached to their hand, capable of transmitting energy and translating interstellar languages. Their mission in the series was to defend civilization, a concept later seen in the first appearance of the Green Lantern Corp in *Showcase* #22 (1959) by John Broome and Gil Kane. The Green Lanterns were assigned power rings chosen by the Guardians of Oa to defend their sectors of the universe; however, their links to the Grey Lensman were likely recognized and encouraged by Julius Schwartz, a former science-fiction agent in the 1930s and editor at DC Comics.

Several comic book publishers initially functioned by selling pulp magazines, then sometimes moved trademarks from their magazines to their comic books and often utilized the same artists across both media. Former military major Malcolm Wheeler-Nicholson used his world traveling experience to write a series of stories for pulp magazines and eventually created National Allied Publications in 1934 through which he created and sold the first stapled comic book with original content, *New Fun* #1 (1935).[90] He used new material from aspiring cartoonists that were less expensive than popular comic strip reprint licenses. However, it was also this direction that led writers and artists to mine plots and genres from earlier pulps to generate new stories for comic books. Wheeler-Nicholson attracted the attention of another pulp entrepreneur, Harry Donenfeld, who annexed the major's operations while publishing *Detective Comics* (1937),[91] then published the first *Action Comics* premiering Superman. The Golden Age superhero boom that followed Superman's success attracted pulp magazine publisher Martin Goodman, who then channeled his efforts in pushing original-material comic books, namely the first issue of *Marvel Comics* (1939). *Marvel Comics* was named after pulp magazine *Marvel Science Stories* #1 (August 1938), published by Postal Publications, one of many subsidiaries of what would later become Timely Comics owned by Goodman. The cover art was created by Norman Saunders and was titled "Avengers of Space," written by Robert O. Erisman. The content certainly bordered on sensationalism, depicting extraterrestrial invaders yearning for a nude female as her male counterpart was held back, shirtless, and forced to watch. Although the story wasn't very sophisticated, Goodman was certainly onto something with his terminology, because "Marvel" and "Avengers" would go on to mean much more in comic books than what was shown in this pulp magazine.[92] Goodman also hired Frank R. Paul, famous illustrator of Hugo Gernsback's *Amazing Stories* in the 1920s, to illustrate the cover to his pulp magazine *Marvel Science Stories* #2 (November 1938) and, a year later, the cover to *Marvel Comics* #1 (1939), which depicted the android Human Torch freeing himself from captivity. Goodman wasn't the only publisher who brought names from his pulp magazines to comic books. Wilford Fawcett started Fawcett Publications and put his nickname on a pulp magazine that collected war experiences in cartoons called *Captain Billy's Whiz Bang* #1 (October 1919), which was published for nearly 20 years.[93] Fawcett later published the fictional "Billy" Batson, alter ego to the very famous and successful superhero Captain Marvel in *Whiz Comics* #2 (1940). It made sense for a company's trademark to be transferred from an older magazine-style medium to a new lucrative one, which appeared to happen with both Marvels. DC Comics did something similar, but they took the name of a pulp magazine that they didn't own. *Brave and Bold* (1902–1911) was a pulp fiction magazine published by Street and Smith. Decades later, Robert Kanigher edited DC Comics' first issue of *The Brave and the Bold* (1955), which used the pulp magazine's name and started out initially as a post–Comics Code Authority series that focused mainly on knights. Knights didn't sell as well as superheroes, so the comic book series eventually became a successful Batman team-up series.

Often, pulp magazine artists also drew for comic books. One of the early 20th-century cartoonists was a highly talented African American artist by the name of Elton Fax, who illustrated pulps such as *Real Western* and *Crack Detective* beginning in the 1930s. He also created art for newspaper comic strips and comic book publishers such as Lev Gleason and Quality Comics, then later left the field for book illustration.[94] Many know Paul Reinman as the man who inked Jack Kirby in some of the early 1960s Marvel Comics such as *Avengers* #2 (1963), but he was also a talented pulp illustrator, providing interior artwork to magazines including *Adventure* vol. 105, #6 (October 1941). Jack Binder was a prolific comic book artist and was active from the late 1930s to early 1950s. He created the original Golden Age *Daredevil* for Lev Gleason and worked for Fawcett and Timely Comics. He then started the Jack Binder Studio in 1942, employing later comic greats including Carmine Infantino, Gil Kane, Kurt Schaffenberger, and Bill Ward. He and his team made comic books for various publishers, including Nedor Comics,[95] and he got his start as a pulp magazine artist producing interiors such as "Dark Invasion" in Martin Goodman's *Marvel Science Stories* #5 (1939).[96] Binder also created sharply detailed and anatomically accurate illustrations for *Astounding Science Fiction* (1941) that are in stark contrast to the cartoon style depicted in his comic books.

The comic book industry rose during the declining era of pulp magazines. As pulp magazine publishers left the medium for comic books, it became convenient to use many of the same artists, and in many cases, the same trademarks. It was also easy for comic book writers to look at pulp magazines' various super or masked proto-superheroes for inspiration. This would explain why the adventures of Golden and Silver Age superheroes such as Superman, Batman, The Fantastic Four, the Suicide Squad, Green Lantern, and the X-Men utilize tropes, plots, abilities, names, and character archetypes previously seen in pulp magazines and novels. While these proto-superheroes may not be enjoyed by most mainstream comic fans, their character traits and story elements remain popular with today's superhero comic book audience. Although pulp magazines were mined for various literary concepts by comic book writers, many comic book artists needed more visual reference than pulps could provide. So, many of them looked to classic Hollywood cinema for further inspiration.

5

Classic Hollywood Cinema and the Golden Age of Comic Books

The development of early comic books was significantly influenced by classic Hollywood cinema. While comic book writers and artists were reading pulps and newspaper comic strips, they also spent time at the movie theater absorbing movement, drama, and comedy. More importantly, there were classic Hollywood movie stars, some of whom portrayed costumed adventurers or monsters, who heavily influenced early creators' depiction of superheroes. After superheroes were established as a lucrative genre, Hollywood then began to produce serials modeled after comic books. Famous onscreen figures during this period include Douglas Fairbanks (Zorro), Conrad Veidt (Gwynplaine from *Man Who Laughs*), Bela Lugosi (Dracula), Boris Karloff (Frankenstein), Johnny Weissmuller (Tarzan), Buster Crabbe (Flash Gordon), Errol Flynn (Robin Hood), Tom Tyler (Captain Marvel), Kent Taylor (Mysterious Rider), Fred MacMurray and Kirk Alyn (Superman).

Douglas Fairbanks was born in 1883, and by the 1920s, had firmly established himself as an action movie star with tremendous athletic prowess whose portrayal of the heroes of *The Mark of Zorro* (1920) and *The Black Pirate* (1926) inspired future comic book professionals. Zorro was created by Johnston McCulley a year earlier in the pulp magazine *All-Story Weekly* (August 1919), a tale of an 1800s dark costumed crime fighter. Fairbanks's physicality brought McCulley's hero to life and prompted an onrush of *Zorro* excitement as its fandom rapidly increased,[1] gaining the attention of lovers of pop culture. Bob Kane stated that watching Douglas Fairbanks physically act out the role of *Zorro* in all its flamboyance fueled his cocreation of *Batman* (1939). "I decided to imitate my idol, Zorro—I took a running leap into the air, breaching the chasm in between, and landed on the lower pile."[2] Bob Kane also commented on *The Black Pirate* as a direct influence: "I imitated his acrobatics in all the early Batman books."[3] Both Bob Kane[4] and Bill Finger also cited Lee Falk's *The Phantom* (1936) as a source of inspiration, which swiped its origin from Douglas Fairbanks's *The Black Pirate*.[5] In both the strip and the film, a young boy witnessed his father getting killed by pirates. The young nobleman who put on his father's signet ring and swore an oath of vengeance on his father's killers, grew up to be the Black Pirate. *The Black Pirate* also influenced more creators at DC Comics. Joe Kubert noted that his *Viking Prince* (1955) panels included the hero "accelerating down to the deck of a ship, gripping his sword as it splits the ship's sail. This is the same device used by Douglas Fairbanks in the film *The Black Pirate*.... Today, movies are borrowing from us, but yesterday, we borrowed from the movies."[6] Superman creators Jerry Siegel and Joe Shuster mentioned that Douglas Fairbanks's *The Black Pirate* made a large impression on them. They clarify that his body language and action sequences influenced their creation of Superman in *Action Comics* #1 (1938). Shuster commented, "I tried to make [*Superman's*] stance the way Douglas Fairbanks looked in *The Black Pirate*." Siegel specified, "In writing the scripts I had Douglas Fairbanks very much in mind in the athletic stunts he did."[7] The famous actor, it turns out, played a role in influencing the Phantom, Batman, and Superman.

Batman's creation involved more cinematic influences. One example was the Roland West murder mystery film *The Bat Whispers* (1930), based on the 1920 Avery Hopwood and Mary Roberts Rinehart play *The Bat*. This was a film about a costumed criminal who robbed a bank then made public announcements to the police, holding the city in gripping fear in a manner that was similar to the Joker in his first appearance in *Batman* #1 (1940).[8] Bob Kane credited this film as a critical visual influence on the creation of Batman: "He wore a costume that looked a little like my early Batman's with a black robe and a bat-shaped head.... The film not only helped inspire Batman's costume but also the bat-signal, a prototype of which appeared on the wall when the Bat announced his next victim."[9] Ironically, this Bat-Man was a criminal and not a hero, but he had many of the same tricks and gimmicks as Batman, specifically how he foiled the police, hid in shadows to induce fear in others, and employed a strong flair for the theatrical. Whereas *The Bat Whispers* character was a villain, it was Conrad Veidt from the silent film *The Man Who Laughs* (1928) who played a kind, pale-skinned, and perpetually smiling sideshow freak that influenced the creation of the villain Joker by Jerry Robinson, Bill Finger, and Bob Kane.[10] Kane commented, "Conrad Veidt ... the makeup was perfect, and this inspired the Joker's grinning countenance."[11] Makeup artist Jack Pierce designed Veidt's characteristic smile as well as the classic Universal monsters. Pierce was also the makeup artist for *Dracula* (1931) starring Bela Lugosi, and helped the actor flesh out the bat-like vampire accompanied by a long black cape.[12] Bob Kane commented that Lugosi's *Dracula* was another inspiration in the creation of Batman: "The first year of Batman was heavily influenced by horror films and emulated a Dracula look."[13] This is not surprising when one analyzes Batman with his cape raised in a window, his silhouette highlighted by the moon behind him, surveying someone's home in the same manner as Dracula.[14]

Pierce also used his makeup artistry to depict more monsters that appear to have influenced comic books, including the horror film *Frankenstein* (1931). Numerous interviews by Pierce and others confirm that he developed the look and appearance of Frankenstein's monster. The makeup was carefully placed on actor Boris

Batman was confirmed by Bob Kane to have much of his presentation influenced by Bela Lugosi from the film *Dracula* (1931).

Karloff over a four-hour period to render the creature's prominent features.[15] Large, hulking, and misunderstood, Frankenstein's monster was generally drawn to female beauty, and chased away by angry, scared citizens. Both Stan Lee and Jack Kirby remarked that their creation *The Incredible Hulk* (1962) had a basis in Boris Karloff's Frankenstein's monster. Lee said Karloff's Frankenstein's monster "didn't want to hurt anybody, but he did anyway."[16] Kirby mentioned, "The Hulk was Frankenstein. Frankenstein can rip up the place."[17] Another trait shared between the two monsters was that they started gray in their first appearances and were eventually colored green.

Pierce also used his makeup skills to create the appearance of two more Universal horror films that very likely affected superhero comic books. *The Invisible Man* (1933) was based on an H.G. Wells novel (1897), and starred Claude Rains as a scientist who was made permanently invisible by a secret experiment. He found it impossible to interact with other people and so enveloped himself in bandages so they could see him. Pierce's dedication to the project was evident when a newspaper reported that he "spent one and a half hours daily wrapping and removing bandages from Claude Rains' head."[18] The Invisible Man could not control his powers and was a tragic lonely figure. He heavily resembles the appearance and tragedy of Doom Patrol's Negative Man, created for *My Greatest Adventure* #80 (1963) by Bob Haney, Arnold Drake, and Bruno Premiani. Negative Man similarly could not approach people unless wrapped up in bandages and had difficulty forming intimate relationships with others due to his freakish body. Pierce was also the makeup artist for another freakish body, *Werewolf of London* (1935), starring Henry Hull, about a wolfman with a distinctly arched widow's peak that emphasized his feral features.[19] The werewolf's appearance and hairstyle appear to be utilized by Wally Wood for his character Ani-Man, premiering in *Witzend* #1 (1966). Dave Cockrum apprenticed under Wally Wood on the comic strip character *Shattuck* (1972) for the *Overseas Weekly* before penciling the comic book *Superboy and the Legion of Super-Heroes*

#197 (1973).[20] It was on this series that Cockrum revamped team member Timberwolf's face so that it resembled both Ani-Man and the Werewolf of London.[21] After Cockrum cocreated *The All-New, All-Different X-Men* (1975), he was the first to draw Wolverine's unmasked face in *X-Men* #98 (1976) using the same facial features present in all three previous feral characters.

Johnny Weissmuller's direct connection to comics is through two newspaper strips and possibly one comic book, Hal Foster's *Tarzan*, Alex Raymond's *Jungle Jim*, and Bill Everett's *Sub-Mariner*. Weissmuller began his career as a multiple gold-medal-winning Olympic swimmer and was eventually cast as the title character in the film *Tarzan the Ape Man* (1932). Standing 6'3" tall, Weissmuller became an international sensation through the film, partially due to first fully depicting Tarzan's characteristic jungle scream.[22] His athleticism made him the perfect actor for the role and he went on to star in more than 10 Tarzan films. Incidentally, Hal Foster was the artist who drew the *Tarzan* comic at the time of Weissmuller's appearance in the 1932 *Tarzan the Ape Man* film,[23] and he doubtlessly watched the film as he drew the strip, as its appearance was consistent. Foster was also one of the cardinal newspaper comic strip artists at the time who was emulated by both the first and second generation of comic book artists. It could be rightly said that comic artists who studied Foster's *Tarzan* could have, by proxy, studied some physical aspect of Johnny Weissmuller. There is also a high probability that Weissmuller's talent and fame in the 1930s influenced Golden Age comic book artists who needed photo reference for their comics. A close-up MGM studio photo (1932) of Weissmuller's face appears as if it was swiped by Bill Everett when penciling a close-up of Sub-Mariner in his first appearance in Timely's *Marvel Comics* #1 (1939).[24] It is possible that while Everett was at comic book packager Funnies Inc. creating the Sub-Mariner, he used Weismuller as photo reference.[25] The Sub-Mariner had winged feet that allowed him to fly, and Weismuller was known for swimming at the New York Athletic Club, which had a team of swimmers called the "Winged Foot Men."[26] Weissmuller also starred in another comic-related movie, Alex Raymond's *Jungle Jim* (1934). *Jungle Jim* was initially created by Raymond to compete with Hal Foster's *Tarzan* in the hugely popular jungle action genre and it's highly probable that Raymond watched the Weismuller films. By the time the *Jungle Jim* (1948) movie was in preproduction, it became a natural fit for *Tarzan* actor Weissmuller to star in the leading role. He starred in more than 10 *Jungle Jim* movies and one syndicated TV show.[27] Both Hal Foster's and Alex Raymond's work have been studied by comic book artists since the 1930s, and Weismuller's animal magnetism and athleticism as Tarzan were likely needed to capture the essence of their respective jungle adventure comic strips.

Three influential comic strips were portrayed by actor and American gold-medal-winning Olympic swimmer Clarence Linden "Buster" Crabbe. His physical prowess matched his charisma, earning him starring roles in the comic-based serials *Tarzan the Fearless* (1933), *Flash Gordon* (1936), and *Buck Rogers* (1939). Crabbe's portrayal of Tarzan was one year after Weissmuller's first time as the character, so it's also highly probable that Hal Foster, who drew Tarzan, also watched Crabbe in the same role. In 1936, Alex Raymond was drawing the *Flash Gordon* strip and very likely watched his portrayal by Crabbe. Crabbe also portrayed Dick Calkin's *Buck Rogers* in the 1939 serial, making the actor the king of comic-strip-based action movies. *Buck Rogers* (1929) was the first science-fiction adventure comic strip that kicked off America's longtime fascination with sci-fi ray guns[28] and popularized science fiction for a mainstream audience. Crabbe was versatile with his appearance, portraying Buck Rogers with dark hair as opposed to the blond Flash Gordon.[29] These three Crabbe serials were watched by early comic book artists who, in turn, had physical reference

Don Heck confirmed that his design for Tony Stark's face in 1963 was based on actor Errol Flynn.

to draw their superheroes. EC Comics artist Angelo Torres commented, "the Buster Crabbe chapters; we grew up on those too. They were a big influence."[30]

Kent Taylor was an actor who factored into the creation of Superman, and possibly Ghost Rider. Taylor's screen presence was observed by both Golden and Silver Age comic book creators. Regarding Superman's alias, both *Superman* cocreator Joe Shuster[31] and editor Julius Schwartz admitted that Clark Kent's name was based on the first names of two actors, Clark Gable and Kent Taylor.[32] Taylor was also notable for portraying a cowboy vigilante named Benton in *The Fighting Phantom* (1933)[33] who was framed for a crime he did not commit, escaped jail, and put on a mask to evade his enemies. Benton, as the Fighting Phantom, was also referred to as "The Mysterious Rider," and fought greedy villains as a masked western hero. The concept is similar in name to *Ghost Rider* (1950), a short-lived comic series published by Vin Sullivan for Magazine Enterprises. Ghost Rider was cocreated by Dick Ayers, who brought the character to Marvel Comics 11 years after it fell out of trademark in 1967.[34] Five years later, Roy Thomas and Gary Friedrich created the iconic flaming-skull Ghost Rider in *Marvel Spotlight* #5 (1972), using a costume, according to Thomas, inspired by the 1968 Elvis Presley comeback TV special.[35] Friedrich had brought in some of his own fiery elements from his *Hell-Rider* (1971) magazine produced for Sol Brodsky's Skywald publications. Now that the *Ghost Rider* trademark was used for this new version, so, too, was the first Ghost Rider rebranded as the "Phantom Rider," which was a composite of both names, Fighting Phantom and Mysterious Rider, used to refer to Kent Taylor in 1933.

Swashbuckling movie star Errol Flynn influenced the creation of both Green Arrow and Iron Man. Pop culture lovers of the time absorbed his onscreen presence, including comic book artists who searched for reference material. Flynn's two most notable costumed adventuring films, based on early novels, were *Captain Blood* (1935) and *The Adventures of Robin Hood* (1938). In both films, he demonstrated his flair for buccaneering and was the favorite to continue Douglas Fairbanks–type films into the 1930s. The Academy Award–nominated film *Captain Blood* depicted Flynn as a dashing pirate who rebelled against King James II. This film was popular with moviegoers,[36] and the story was adapted into comic books in 1949 and again in 2009. Flynn demonstrated the same success three years later in *The Adventures of Robin Hood*. His blond goatee and green suit became iconic to mainstream audiences and mimicked by comic creators Alfred Gough, Mort Weisinger, and George Papp for the DC Comics character Green Arrow in *More Fun Comics* #73 (1941). The superhero's green costume was clearly patterned off Robin Hood, and the character eventually had a goatee in the tradition of Errol Flynn in *Green Lantern/Green Arrow* #76 (1970) penciled by Neal Adams. Adams remarked about penciling Green Arrow, "I turned him into a modern Robin Hood…. An Errol Flynn–like character with a smile and sparkle off the teeth."[37] Flynn was also confirmed as the basis for Iron Man's alter ego, Tony Stark, in his first appearance in *Tales of Suspense* #39 (1962). Don Heck, the character's cocreator and initial penciler, mentioned that although Jack Kirby designed the cover and gray Iron Man armor, it was Heck who designed Tony Stark's face from "some character I liked … an Errol Flynn type."[38] Iron Man cocreator Stan Lee also remarked, "I wanted to be like Errol Flynn. He was my hero."[39]

Actors inspired the creation of superheroes, but Hollywood later made superhero-based movies. C.C. Beck described that he patterned his cocreation Captain Marvel in *Whiz Comics* #2 (1940) after the famous actor Fred MacMurray. Beck mentioned that the actor's strength and down-to-earth demeanor inspired him to bring those characteristics into the SHAZAM-powered hero.[40] MacMurray, same as Captain Marvel, was tall, strong, and sophisticated, carrying himself with humility and grace. *Whiz Comics* starring Captain Marvel was successful enough for Republic Pictures to license a movie serial in 1941 starring Tom Tyler. Tyler's depiction in the serial, *The Adventures of Captain Marvel* (1941), was a success and is the first time a comic book superhero was featured on film.[41] Despite the serial's success, it has a somewhat notorious legacy because it prompted DC Comics to initiate a lawsuit against Fawcett, which eventually resulted in Fawcett's discontinuation of the Captain Marvel character by 1953. Tyler also notably portrayed another comic character in *The Phantom* serial (1943). *The Phantom* was produced by Columbia Pictures and many fans found that Tyler was the perfect physical rendition of this King Features Syndicate character.[42] His square jaw, good looks, and lovable yet stern countenance gave both comic characters the ideal emotional and physical tone for moviegoers.

Kirk Alyn depicted the first superhero in comic books in two movie serials produced by Columbia Pictures in both *Superman* (1948) and *Atom Man vs. Superman* (1950). Alyn was the ideal fit for Superman as the strong, dark-haired, charismatic hero. The Columbia executives felt his performance as the iconic comic book hero matched well enough to star in another comic-book-related film, *The Miraculous Blackhawk: Freedom's Champion* (1952). Blackhawk was a World War II pilot from Quality Comics' *Military Comics* #1 (1941), written by Will Eisner and illustrated by Charles Cuidera. Through the portrayal of these two characters, Kirk Alyn proved he was qualified to look the part of a comic hero in live-action serials. Despite being typecast as Superman, Alyn later became a fan favorite at comic book conventions, bringing inspiration to the next generation of fans and creators.[43]

The early superhero comic book creators gained photo reference and visual inspiration from classic Hollywood actors, some of whom portrayed costumed adventurers and monsters. The physicality of actors Fairbanks, Flynn, and MacMurray, among others, can be traced to the creation of Batman, Joker, Hulk, Sub-Mariner, Negative Man, Wolverine, Green Arrow, Iron Man, Superman, and Captain Marvel. Eventually, superheroes were licensed into their own movie serials that featured a new generation of actors such as Tom Tyler and Kirk Alyn. During this time, comic book artists and writers paid close attention, absorbing visuals from their local movie theaters, stories from pulp magazines, and panels from newspaper comic strips. However, comic book artists still needed another graphic ingredient that could solidify their ability to construct a perfect panel.

6

Classic American Illustrators Intersect with Comic Books

The concurrent histories of illustration and comic book art generally run parallel, but there are times when the two media intersect. Commercial illustrators paint detailed visuals on one canvas or panel to effectively depict the mood of a situation for an intended audience. These panels could be used for advertising, children's stories, magazines, fantasy books, adventure books, posters, and paintings. Often, comic book artists examine these media to gain inspiration, themes, characters, locations, fashion trends, design ideas, or swipes for covers or interior panels. There are also instances when a comic book artist coincidentally matches an illustrator's style because they either appeal to the same audience or have the same creative tastes. To gain that appreciation, it's first important to consider a brief history of American illustration, and then various examples of its overlap with comic books.

American illustration started in the early 1800s with Felix Octavius Carr Darley, the first illustrator to go against the British style.[1] He illustrated scenes in classic stories including *Rip Van Winkle* and *The Legend of Sleepy Hollow*. Howard Pyle continued a similar trend until the end of the 19th century illustrating *The Adventures of Robin Hood* and *The Book of Pirates*.[2] With the turn of the century came the further development of urban areas. People migrated from rural farmlands to consolidated city economies. This migration occurred as more newspaper and magazine publications established themselves due to cheaper access to printing machines,[3] creating hiring opportunities for commercial artists. Women started to follow the latest clothing trends, reproduced by artists who depicted ideal "fashion moments,"[4] with one example being Charles Dana Gibson's "Gibson Girl" (1890s).[5] Her tied-up hairstyle, dainty nose, and mildly droopy eyebrows ensnared viewers who sought to mimic her clothing. She depicted how the trendy, fashionable urban female looked and dressed. Howard Chandler Christy illustrated two fashionable lovers in his piece "A Modern-Day Motoring Couple" (1912), which featured the "Christy Girl," who depicted women's fashion in the 1910s. The 1920s was an exciting decade of glamour and escapism that J.C. Leyendecker incorporated into his piece "Couple in Boat" (1922) about two stylish sweethearts in an Arrow Collar advertisement using crosshatched strokes with oil paint. Similar fashion moments were eventually represented in comic strips and eventually comic books. The 1920s "It Girl" was depicted by comic strip artist Nell Brinkley for her Sunday strip *Sunny Sue* in the Hearst Newspapers. Brinkley's women wore the nightclub attire and sensual hairstyles of the glamorous roaring 1920s. Her imagery was summed up by comic strip historian Brian Walker: "The 'Brinkley Girl' was the Gibson Girl of the Jazz Age."[6] The "It Girls" of female fashion were represented by Jerry Siegel and Joe Shuster in various early Superman adventures, such as *Action Comics* #2 (1938), which depicted "a wealthy traveler" dressed in stylish clothing that symbolized her class and sophistication.[7] However, it wasn't just fashion; there were many genres and moods depicted by classic illustrators that either traveled along a similar creative mold or directly inspired later comic artists.

Some of the classic illustrators depicted monstrous figures, designs, and costumes that reflected similar tastes to comic book artists such as Steve Ditko, Graham Ingels, Jim Steranko, and Bruce Timm. Ditko's tastes appear to be comparable to those of Aubrey Beardsley, a British illustrator, who had a knack for art that drifted into the grotesque and weird. He lived a short life, succumbing to tuberculosis at the age of 25, but before his death, he portrayed creatures with hideously inhuman body language.[8] Tuberculosis also affected Irish illustrator Harry Clarke, considered the definitive illustrator of Edgar Allan Poe's grotesque stories in *Tales of Mystery and Imagination* (1919). His bent figures, similar to Beardsley's, pushed readers into a darker state of mind.[9] Steve Ditko entered the comic book industry in early 1950s, and was also stricken with tuberculosis.[10] His comic art for horror and suspense titles drifted toward the twisted, and this seemed to add a morbid quality to the cocreation of Spider-Man, who was portrayed in similarly distorted and unnatural poses. Some of his early grotesque art can be seen to adorn several 1950s Charlton Comics publications—for example, his electric chair cover to *Strange Suspense*

Steve Ditko first depicted Spider-Man's insect-like prowess as unnerving through the portrayal of unnatural body positions in *Amazing Fantasy* #15 (1962).

Stories #19 (1954), which fits the horror, anxiety, and tension of any Poe story. It's possible that the dread and fatigue of tuberculosis added to all three artists' commercial art presentations.

Graham Ingels's art, during his horror comics period of the early 1950s, has an aesthetic that aligned well with British illustrator Arthur Rackham, who was dubbed "The Master of the Fairy Tale" in the early 1900s. Rackham used a long, winding line to introduce ghastly elements into otherwise pristine children's stories and had a knack for merging youthful fantasy worlds with an adult sense of grisly detail.[11] He displayed this skill for depicting appalling creatures such as gnomes and witches in *Alice's Adventures in Wonderland* (1907) and the *Brothers Grimm Fairy Tales* (1917). His piece "Hansel and Gretel Meet the Witch" (1909) portrayed the villainess with a haggard face as she was hungry to devour the two children. This was done with comparable facility as Ingels, who depicted the frightful Old Witch, the character who narrated the horrifying events of his stories in the splash pages of EC Comics' *Haunt of Fear.*

In the 1960s, artist Jim Steranko made an impact on multiple industries by presenting innovative designs in book illustration, comic books, magazines, and historical texts. After depicting the adventures of *Nick Fury: Agent of S.H.I.E.L.D.* (1968), he published his own magazine, *ComixScene* (1972), utilizing his skills as a publisher, designer, illustrator, and typographer. Steranko utilized the latter three qualities for the cover of publisher Martin L. Greim's *Comic Crusader* #17 (1973). His depiction of the magazine's title juxtaposed against lady justice with various distorted figures in the foreground and Harvey Comics' "Man in Black" ominously present in the background attracted buyers. This unique visual design sense for various aspects of commercial art was also shared by Will H. Bradley, a pioneer in publishing, design, illustration, and typography in the late 1890s and early 1900s. Bradley made various advertising posters that displayed his skills, namely his "Thanksgiving Poster" from November 1895, which presented overlapping red and brown designs of the same woman twice, holding up a tray of food with a dress that filled the page in a wave-like fashion. This poster was part of a series that began Art Nouveau in America.[12] Both Bradley's[13] and Steranko's designs revolutionized their respective industries, and both innovators self-learned their crafts due to lack of access to a formal education.[14] They presented work that was sleek and polished, attracting customers to buy books whose covers they designed. They were familiar with the commercial world, and they knew what sold and what didn't, which was a critical factor to their success.

Harley Quinn was created by Paul Dini and designed by Bruce Timm for *Batman: The Animated Series*, and she made her first comic book appearance in *The Batman Adventures* #12 (1993). Although she was not intended to be a reoccurring character, her harlequin jester costume, unpredictable personality, and alluring attributes attracted fans of the Batman mythos who hoped to see more. Harley Quinn continues to maintain a strong presence in comics, animation, and film and her character's original costume is very similar to painter Gil Elvgrin's illustration

Life of the Party (1952).[15] This calendar pinup featured an enticing woman in a very similar harlequin jester costume, mischievous smile, red-and-black color palette, and curvaceous figure that also attracted the attention of many interested viewers.

Classic illustrators also directly inspired and influenced comic book artists such as Michael Kaluta, Roy Krenkel, Al Williamson, Barry Windsor-Smith, Reed Crandall, Ray Willner, Alex Ross, and Neal Adams. Michael Kaluta was inspired by illustrator Franklin Booth, who primarily worked from the 1900s to 1940s. Booth contributed to *McClure's* and *Collier's*, but is most remembered for his classical approach to art that added realism to the fantastic and otherworldly.[16] His 16 watercolor illustrations for *Flying Islands of the Night* (1913) were a revelation to comic artists including Michael Kaluta, who stated, "I wish I'd remembered to look at my copy of *Flying Islands of the Night* before tackling that particular *Dragonlance* cover: but my heart was definitely there!!! *Flying Islands of the Night* is the second amazing, illustrated book I bought for myself from the Argosy bookstore. Roy Krenkel pointed the way in 1969."[17] Roy Krenkel was an American illustrator who trained at Burne Hogarth's School of Visual Arts. Although not a superhero artist, Krenkel illustrated EC Comics anthology titles, Warren magazines, science fiction, and fantasy books. He introduced comic artists including Kaluta, Bernie Wrightson, Jeff Jones, and Al Williamson to the classic illustrators.

Comics artist Al Williamson was deeply inspired by the illustrations of Joseph Clement Coll. Williamson's early work demonstrated a propensity for illustrating proper anatomy as an assistant to Burne Hogarth on the *Tarzan* comic strip. He continued to develop this talent in his comic book art found in *Famous Funnies*, *Wonder Comics*, and *Classics Illustrated*. His appreciation for Coll became apparent when he worked on the *Secret Agent Corrigan* strip with writer Archie Goodwin from 1967 to 1980.[18] Goodwin was a comic fan turned editor of Warren's *Creepy* from 1964 to 1967 before writing strips for *Secret Agent Corrigan*.[19] One continuity in the series featured Corrigan's mortal enemy, the mysterious Dr. Seven (April 10, 1971). Dr. Seven was an Asian villain in stereotypical ancient Chinese dress, and an unfortunate by-product of the Yellow Peril caricatures of the time. This is objectionable imagery based on a fear of the Asian culture; however, there was still skill of the line to be admired in Williamson's art. Nonetheless, Dr. Seven's link to illustration was explained by Williamson who credited Roy Krenkel for introducing him to the work of Joseph Clement Coll, the original *Fu Manchu* (1913) illustrator.[20] From 1900 to 1920, Coll depicted a variety of visuals for art admirers such as the *Riddle of the 4th Dimension* (1908), *Wanderlust* (1909), and Sir Arthur Conan Doyle's *The Lost World* (1912). His career ended prematurely when he died relatively young from complications during appendicitis surgery in 1921.[21] Art historians often speculate what further works of illustrative fantasy could have been created had things gone differently.

Barry Windsor-Smith became a Pre-Raphaelite painter and fine artist after starting out at Marvel Comics in the 1960s and early 1970s. The Pre-Raphaelites were a group of artists in the 19th century who emulated Italian artists from before the 1500s Raphael era utilizing complex detail set in the natural world. One British illustrator, Robert Anning Bell, painted in the Pre-Raphaelite fashion using oil and watercolor in the 1890s and early 1900s.[22] He also made black-and-white illustrations for *The Tempest* (1901), which depicted Shakespeare's magical characters in complex compositions. Windsor-Smith also similarly depicted the fantastical world of *Conan the Barbarian* (1970) utilizing Pre-Raphaelite technique to illustrate highly detailed panels. His depictions of the Tower of the Elephant, the snake god Set, and the underground Octopus were presented in a style reminiscent of Bell's supernatural creatures in *The Tempest*. Windsor-Smith left *Conan* and comic books behind for some time to focus on his fine art career at Gorblimey Press, advancing the art form of the Pre-Raphaelites depicting scenes that arguably surpassed Bell.[23]

Comic book artist Reed Crandall was heavily influenced by illustrator Howard Pyle's paintings *Blue Skin, The True Captain Kidd*, and of other associated buccaneers that formalized the proper depiction of pirates who were active in the late 1600s. Pyle's work was compiled into *Howard Pyle's Book of Pirates* (1921), which kept the imagery active for future generations. Crandall was one of many who examined Pyle's work and swiped its imagery during his time at EC Comics. For example, Pyle's painting *Who Shall Be Captain?* (1911) was swiped by Crandall for the cover to *Piracy* #2 (1955).[24] Pyle's other work, *An Attack on a Galleon"* (1905), was traced by Crandall for the cover of *Piracy* #3 (1955).[25] Crandall was a naturally gifted illustrator, so these swipes were probably meant as an honorable homage to a creative idol. Pyle also inspired future illustrators, including poster illustrator James Montgomery Flagg and the cover illustrator of *A Princess of Mars* (1917), Frank Schoonover. Additionally, Pyle wrote and illustrated *The Merry Adventures of Robin Hood* (1883), which influenced his student N.C. Wyeth.

Comic book artist Ray Willner utilized visuals that were pioneered by illustrator N.C. Wyeth, who also was a strong influence on comic artist John Buscema.[26] Wyeth advanced beyond his teacher Howard Pyle's imagery of costumed adventurers by illustrating *Treasure Island* (1911) and *Robin Hood* (1917). Historians generally agree that Wyeth's depictions of Robin Hood shaped the 20th-century visual concept of the green hero and his merry men in their traditional hat and tights.[27] These costumes were later presented in various media, including Errol Flynn's influential film *The Adventures of Robin Hood* (1938), and in comic books by artists such as Willner and Crandall, who depicted *The Adventures of Robin Hood* (1956) for the Brown Shoe company.[28] Comic book artists who depicted the Green Arrow, such as George Papp and Neal Adams, drew the DC superhero in the classic green Wyeth-style costume. Wyeth also illustrated *Buy War Bonds* (1942), a World War II propaganda poster, which depicted Uncle Sam, whose appearance was previously standardized by James Montgomery Flagg.[29]

Comic book illustrator Alex Ross examined the patriotic artwork of James Montgomery Flagg. Flagg painted the first standardized image of Uncle Sam on a recruiting poster, *I Want You for U.S. Army* (1917), which inspired American viewers

Neal Adams's imagery of Sauron from *X-Men* #61 (1969) is visually consistent with the illustrations of the Thipdar by J. Allen St. John that were used for the cover of *At the Earth's Core* (1922).

to enlist in World War I, World War II, and the Korean War.[30] As propaganda, it helped recruit more soldiers into the armed forces, showing the world that America was a serious player on the world stage. *I Want You* and its satire poster during the Vietnam War, *I Want Out* (1971), were both discussed by Alex Ross, who illustrated *Uncle Sam* (1997) for DC's Vertigo comics line. Ross commented, "In the greatest way (Uncle Sam) was ever used…. He was the conscience and responsibility of America peering back at us."[31] Similar to Wyeth and Flagg, Ross was pushing for viewers to take Uncle Sam seriously[32] by depicting the character as homeless, despondent, beaten and weary from what he described as "our selfishness."[33]

Both comic book artist Neal Adams and classic illustrator J. Allen St. John were commissioned at different times to paint covers for various books by Edgar Rice Burroughs. Some of their artistic overlap appeared in comic books when Adams illustrated *The X-Men* #60 (1969), written by Roy Thomas, depicting the mutant team's return to the Savage Land in a team-up with Ka-Zar against the evil Sauron. Sauron was a pterodactyloid mutant who seductively mesmerized his victims to achieve his goals. This concept was in all likelihood a reference to the "Mahar" species from Burroughs's *At the Earth's Core*, which first appeared in *All-Story Weekly* (April 1914), and featured a pterodactyloid race that hypnotized their victims. The story took place in Pellucidar, an area at the center of the Earth still populated by dinosaurs and Stone Age humans. In the Burroughs continuity, the Mahar employed pterodactyl bodyguards called the Thipdar, which were illustrated by J. Allen St. John for the cover of the novel *At the Earth's Core* (1922).[34] Adam's imagery of Sauron evokes both the hypnotic concept of the Mahar and the illustrations by St. John of the Thipdar.

Although the history of classic illustration and comic book art are separate, there is imagery to suggest that a relationship exists. Some comic book artists are on record discussing illustrations that inspired them, and others created covers or panels that were identified as swipes. There are also instances when a common disease or style caused an overlap in visual tastes. Regardless, both the illustrator and comic book artist share the mutual goal of creating a dramatic visual moment that would entice a viewer. This merging of the creative arts and the commercialization of a product is inherent to the construction of superhero comic books. While superhero comic books employed the dramatic moments of illustration, the storylines of pulp magazines, the adventure of classic cinema, and the sequential art of comic strips, they also utilized the power and mystery of two real-life showmen of the Platinum Age.

Macfadden and Houdini, the Real-Life Superman and Batman

Superman and Batman were both created in the late 1930s from various pop cultural media, including classic cinema, pulp magazines, and newspaper comic strips. Their literary origins can be traced back to the late 1800s with characters Nicholas Carter and Spring-Heeled Jack. However, there were two real-life historical figures from the Platinum Age who unknowingly helped develop both of DC's premiere Golden Age superheroes. These two individuals were Bernarr Macfadden, magazine mogul, and Harry Houdini, illusionist. Macfadden was a fitness guru and publisher who established the publishing framework in which both DC Comics and Marvel Comics would later function. Houdini was the famous magician and escape artist who, with three other magicians, introduced a mystique into popular culture that established a presence in several comic books featuring superheroes, including *Batman*, *Zatanna*, *Doctor Strange*, and *Mister Miracle*.

Macfadden was one of the first publishers to introduce the topic of physical fitness and romance pulp magazines to a mainstream audience, influencing those themes in comic books. His magazine *Physical Culture* (1899) preached his doctrine of a sound mind through a healthy muscular body,[1] inspiring its many readers to exercise in a never-ending quest for the perfect physique.[2] His singular mission toward physical excellence appears rooted—same as later superheroes—in his humble origins as an orphan.[3] His financially and emotionally vulnerable beginnings likely fueled his willpower, strengthening his mind and body to overcome hardship. His eventual "superpower" was becoming a self-made media magnate whose body endured the hardship of a primitive medical system by living to the age of 87.[4] In comparison with other bodybuilding publishers of his time, Macfadden was far more successful at self-promotion. He changed his first name from Bernard to Bernarr to mimic a lion's roar and edited *Physical Culture* until 1912 while contributing several articles of his own using multiple pen names to resemble other publishers who had multiple employees on the payroll.[5] This was a strategy that Will Eisner later used in the 1930s when producing comics under the Eisner and Iger shop to help build their brand into a successful comic packager. Another Golden Age comic

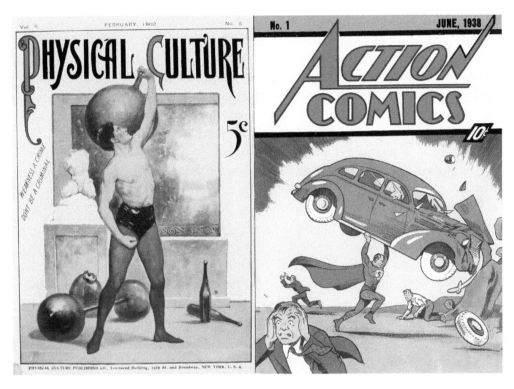

Bernarr Macfadden's *Physical Culture* magazine depicted a possible future that celebrated physical as well as mental excellence in much the same way as the man of tomorrow, Superman, in 1938.

book artist and cocreator of *Superman*, Joe Shuster, was in high school when he exercised in his local gym, striving to be as strong as the figures in Macfadden's magazines.[6] By the 1920s, Macfadden's magazines also featured advertisements by Italian immigrant and mail-order fitness instructor Angelo Siciliano, aka Charles Atlas, who followed the mogul's trend, selling the doctrine of physical perfection in various media, including early superhero comic books.[7] Atlas's advertisements generally depicted a scenario where a skinny teenager was harassed by bullies at the beach, then exercised his muscles to gain a new body so he could return to teach his tormenters some manners. Jerry Siegel, writer and cocreator of *Superman*, visited New York for the World's Fair in 1940 and met bodybuilder Charles Atlas, who was a judge in a local contest.[8] Both Macfadden's and Atlas's influence can be seen in early *Action Comics*, when Siegel and Shuster subjected Clark Kent to various scenarios of bullying from criminals before unleashing his alter ego, Superman.

Macfadden's involvement in the romance genre influenced romance comic books in a similar way. Once Macfadden gained a substantial readership, he allowed readers to send in stories for his magazines that he synthesized into a new series of first-person pulp magazines called *True Story* (1919) and *True Romances* (1923). *True Romances* sold out its first issue and demonstrated to other publishers that the romance genre was viable in this medium.[9] These romance pulp magazines influenced Joe Simon and Jack Kirby to create romance comics in the 1950s, which was corroborated by Kirby, who stated, "Macfadden was the biggest purveyor of romance in the world and was making millions at it ... except there was no romance stories in comics.... The first romance comics came from that discussion."[10]

Macfadden's publishing framework, based on selling cheap genre-specific magazines, was emulated by other publishers, eventually leading to the creation of both DC and Marvel Comics. Hugo Gernsback and Harry Donenfeld both utilized Macfadden's business formula to become genre-specific pulp magazine publishers.[11] Gernsback was the creator of the first science-fiction magazine, *Amazing Stories* (1926), which contributed to the imagination of early comic book writers, namely Jerry Siegel, who wrote a letter to its editor published in the August 1929 issue reviewing various works in "scientifiction."[12] In 1929, Gernsback went bankrupt, losing *Amazing Stories* to its new owner, Bernarr Macfadden, who is often accused by historians of forcing this transfer of ownership.[13] This led Gernsback to publish *Wonder Stories* (1930), which influenced future Marvel cocreator Jack Kirby, who cited a fondness for the magazine's rocket ships.[14] Marvel Comics publisher Martin Goodman worked with Gernsback before starting his own pulp magazine company, Red Circle, which published genre-specific titles such as *Western Supernovel Magazine* (1933) and *Marvel Science Stories* (1938).[15] Harry Donenfeld started his own publishing house and distributor with Independent News that produced genre-specific pulp magazines such as *Spicy Adventure Stories* (1934) and *Spicy Detective Stories* (1934), known for their covers containing strong sexual content. Donenfeld engaged in a Macfadden–style takeover of *Detective Comics*, a comic book that he initially co-owned with Malcolm Wheeler-Nicholson, publisher of National Allied Publications.[16] By lending printer fees, Donenfeld took advantage of Wheeler-Nicholson's low cash flow and forced him out of Detective Comics Inc. shortly before the premiere of Superman in *Action Comics* #1 (1938).

Inspired initially by *Physical Culture*, the idea for *Superman* was created and developed from science-fiction concepts that were previously presented by Gernsback's magazines, which motivated Jerry Siegel, Julius Schwartz, and Mort Weisinger to eventually join DC Comics. Their journey to DC Comics and *Superman* started when they created a series of fanzines that were inspired by Gernsback. Siegel mentioned that he created his own science-fiction fanzine, *Cosmic Stories* (1929), "a typewritten and hectographed publication."[17] Schwartz mentioned that Gernsback inspired him to cocreate *Time Traveler* (1932), a science-fiction fanzine with Mort Weisinger.[18] Weisinger read his first issue of *Amazing Stories* at age 13,[19] and went into business with Schwartz to form their own agency for science-fiction writers in 1934. Siegel and Shuster, however, enjoyed the genre's creative side and entered the comic book industry by submitting stories to Malcolm Wheeler-Nicholson's National Allied Publications in 1935. An early four-page story by the two creators, titled "Federal Men," for *New Adventure Comics* #12 (1937) depicted a futuristic federal agent named "Jor-L,"[20] one year before Superman's first appearance in *Action*

Comics #1. Jor-L's name was reused to create Jor-El, Superman's father, for the *Superman* newspaper comic strip in 1939.

Siegel also appeared to reuse material from Gernsback magazines to create the early *Superman* mythos. His concept of baby Kal-El's ship rocketing away from his home planet, Krypton, is consistent with Gernsback's cover to *Electrical Experimenter Magazine* (April 1918), featuring spaceships carrying figures away from their planet. The spaceship carrying baby Kal-El has the same design as the long red rocket on the cover of *Amazing Stories* (October 1935). The *Superman* Fleischer-animated cartoon had an episode, "The Mechanical Monsters" (1941), about large robots who chased after nearby onlookers, which appear to be inspired from the cover to Gernsback's *Science and Invention* (May 1924). While Siegel and Shuster developed Superman from pulp magazines, Weisinger left his partnership with Schwartz to be editor for *Thrilling Wonder Stories* and later edited magazines such as *Captain Future: Man of Tomorrow*, a subtitle previously used on Superman in the New York World Fair of 1939.[21] He quickly improved his science-fiction editing skills before becoming an editor at Detective Comics in 1941, overseeing *Batman* and *Superman*.[22] Schwartz finally dissolved his science-fiction agency and joined All-American Publications in 1944, which eventually merged into National Periodical Publications in 1946. These three men formed a strong foundation for the DC Universe of superheroes, which occurred as a byproduct of the physical and science-fiction themes published by Macfadden and Gernsback.

Whereas the physically fit Macfadden started the chain of events that led to the creation of *Superman* and DC Comics, it was Harry Houdini, Harry Blackstone, Sr., Leon Mandrake, and Alexander Conlin who established a mystique that manifested in superheroes such as Batman, Mister Miracle, Zatanna, and Doctor Strange, among others. Magicians were important in the late 19th and early 20th century, before the widespread use of radio and television, because they engineered special effects to establish illusions on stage that made audiences believe in the supernormal. The best magicians built their careers by suspending disbelief and creating a mystique centered on their special abilities, and some early superhero creators understood that they needed to depict a similar mystique in their comic books. The most famous magician who provided this was Harry Houdini, born Erik Weisz, who influenced the creation of Batman and Mister Miracle. Houdini's critically important year was 1899 when he met booking agent Martin Beck, who leveraged his connections in the industry to schedule highly successful vaudeville appearances that focused fans on the magician's death-defying escape acts.[23] In the following years, he impressed audiences with risky tasks such as being buried alive and escaping from the belly of a dead whale. He became famous for inventing the Chinese Water Torture Cell, an escape device where the performer is suspended upside down in a clear block filled with water. Houdini also earned his title as the "handcuff king" when he escaped from special handcuffs, keeping British onlookers in suspense for a full hour.[24] By 1907 through the 1910s, he became well-known in America and Europe for escaping from exotic places, freeing himself from straitjackets, and performing physically demanding stunts.[25] He reliably dazzled audiences by utilizing a unique combination of fear and illusion in his presentations and successfully established a mystique surrounding his name.

At the height of his fame in 1920, Houdini met and befriended Sir Arthur Conan Doyle, the famous author who created and wrote stories about the world's greatest detective, Sherlock Holmes.[26] Although Batman was later called the world's greatest detective in the fictional world of DC Comics,[27] the character holds a stronger link to Houdini through the following series of events. After the great magician died from peritonitis at age 52, his assistant and apprentice, Walter Gibson, wrote a book that cataloged the great escape artist's tricks and illusions called *Houdini's Escapes and Magic* (1930),[28] which provided a range of recipes that informed readers how he created his mystique. Gibson also later developed The Shadow's mystique and backstory in 1931 for publisher Street & Smith, and established the proto-superhero's abilities over years, utilizing various sources, including Houdini's trickery. The Shadow used darkness to scare criminals, escaped from tenuous situations, and donned disguises to infiltrate criminal organizations. These gimmicks played an important role in Bill Finger and Bob Kane's creation of *Batman* in 1939. Gibson was the common thread that linked Kane and Finger's Batman to Harry Houdini's tricks, illusions, and gimmicks, and the writer also mentored comic book artist Jim Steranko, another magician and escape artist who was also inspired by Houdini.[29] Steranko met Gibson in New York through a mutual friend, magician and *Shadow* writer Bruce Elliot, and started a "Shadow Secret Society" for fans.[30] Building a mystique meant a great deal to the young magician, who detailed his abilities in his book *Steranko's World of Escapes* (1964), which inspired comic book writer-artist Jack Kirby to create the DC Comics character and series *Mister Miracle* (1971).[31] Both *Batman* and *Mister Miracle* maintain a strong enough mystique to stay relevant in modern comics.

Harry Blackstone, Sr., was an illusionist whom Gibson also depicted as a reoccurring superhero in various Golden Age comic books. Blackstone was a natural showman who constructed devices that enabled him to portray famous illusions such as an individual's disappearance and reappearance, human levitation, and sawing an assistant in half.[32] Blackstone caught the attention of *Shadow* publisher Street and Smith, whose editor Henry Ralston included him in the comic book *Super-Magic Comics* #1 (1941), which changed to *Super-Magician Comics* with its second issue, carrying the magician's image and trademark until 1945.[33] The series utilized Gibson as the writer[34] and artists such as Charles Sultan and Jack Binder, who depicted Blackstone in a suit, using illusions such as the Hindu rope trick to save damsels in distress. Blackstone's image and trademark were licensed by another Golden Age comic book company, Vital Publications, which also hired Gibson to write the script for *Blackstone Master Magician Comics* #1–3 (1946), featuring art by Elmer Stoner.[35] This comic book portrayed Blackstone using illusion and trick photography to foil mobsters. Gibson and Stoner returned to depicting Blackstone for EC Comics in "The Stone Men of Vala" from *Blackstone, The Magician Detective Fights Crime* #1 (1947).[36] EC Comics lost the expensive license to Blackstone's name, and the series continued with issues #2–4 at Timely Comics with Gibson writing many of its stories with art by Bill Everett, Mike Sekowsky, and Allen Bellman, among others. Gibson generally depicted Blackstone utilizing scientific reasoning to defeat his adversaries rather than magic or sorcery, probably because the magician based his career on engineering illusions. This science-based approach was entertaining for its time, but the lack of a superhero costume or powers did not generate enough of a mystique for the magician to stay viable in comics.

Leon Giglio, also known as Leon Mandrake, was an illusionist whose mystique contributed to superheroes Mandrake the Magician, Zatara, Zatanna, Merlin the Magician, and the Wizard. Mandrake began his career in 1924 as a vaudeville performer who impressed his audience with fire eating, mind reading, and ventriloquism. His dark hair, moustache, top hat, tuxedo, tails, cape, and name were established as a parallel creation with Lee Falk's comic strip *Mandrake the Magician* (1934). Mandrake's artist, Phil Davis, knew the real-life magician and depicted the comic strip's lead character wearing the same tuxedo, cape, tails, and top hat.[37] As opposed to Blackstone, Mandrake demonstrated powers such as shape-changing, levitation, and teleportation, some of which were demonstrated in Falk's Sundays from March 17–24, 1935, shrinking enemies and changing their guns into snakes. It was not known to the reader whether his powers were genuine, or if the other characters from the comic strip were simply hypnotized to think it was happening. Falk was a clever writer, leaving the question of whether those powers were illusion or reality,[38] and it's likely that the uncertainty over his abilities contributed to the character's mystique and longevity. *Mandrake the Magician* continued until 2013, with historians often categorizing him as the first caped superhero in comics. Both Mandrakes appear to have been the inspiration for Fred Guardineer's own magician hero, Zatara, created for *Action Comics* #1 (1938). Zatara bore a strong resemblance to Leon Mandrake with the same cape, dark hair, tuxedo, top hat, and Italian name, Giovanni. The character demonstrated superpowers in his comic book by hypnotizing people with phrases that were written backward to control them.[39] Zatara's daughter, Zatanna, made her debut in *Hawkman* #4 (1964), replacing standard pants with fishnet stockings, which added to her sex appeal. Her creators, Gardner Fox and Murphy Anderson, depicted her with similar powers on a quest through various comic books to find her father, who had disappeared. Guardineer brought Zatara's powers to another hero, *Merlin the Magician*, starting with *National Comics* #12 (1941) for Quality Comics. Guardineer depicted Merlin using the same backward Zatara-style incantation that influenced reality,[40] making his version of the superhero another creative descendant of Mandrake. There was also another Mandrake descendant, "The Wizard," from *Top-Notch Comics* #1 (1939), a caped hero with tuxedo, top hat, and tails who used chemistry and physics to capture an enemy submarine by using precision, planning, and his secret chemical, "F22X."[41] This was another reference by

Zatara's daughter, Zatanna, first appeared in *Hawkman* #4 (1965), and her costume, top hat, and origins are linked to the illusionist Leon Mandrake.

comic book writers that a good illusion required careful analytic and practical mastery of the sciences, which could be considered a superpower by itself. However, of the various comic book derivatives of Mandrake, it was Zatanna who carried the mystique required to stay relevant in superhero comic books.

Alexander Conlin, also known as "The One Who Knows," was a mentalist whose mystique appears present in Doctor Strange, Sargon the Sorcerer, Ibis the Invincible, Kardak the Mystic, and Magar the Mystic. Alexander was born in the Midwest and became famous in the 1910s for his psychic reading act, while wearing a turban and Eastern-style robe.[42] His studies of the East resulted in books on astrology and the Higher Thought movement of the Hindus and Buddhist cultures, making him a real-life antecedent to *Chandu the Magician* (1932), a fictional character from a radio show and film. Chandu was Frank Chandler, an American who traveled eastward to India to train with a yogi. He soon returned as Chandu, wearing a turban and imbued with mystical Eastern powers such as illusion and teleportation. This origin was the same overall blueprint used for Doctor Strange, who also traveled eastward to India, trained with "The Ancient One," and returned with similar abilities. Stan Lee commented, "There was an old-time radio show that flipped me out ... it was called Chandu, the Magician,"[43] which directly inspired Doctor Strange's origin story, penciled and co-plotted by Steve Ditko in Marvel's *Strange Tales* #115 (1963). Alexander and Chandu's turban and Eastern magic are also present in the superhero Sargon the Sorcerer, created by John Wentworth and Howard Purcell. Sargon gained his abilities from an empowering ruby of life in his first appearance in *All-American Comics* #26 (1941). His magic powers were somewhat genuine, but the character enjoyed introducing doubt that he was casting illusions as a simple stage magician.[44] Another superhero from an Eastern country, wearing the characteristic turban, was Ibis the Invincible for Fawcett Comics' *Whiz Comics* #2 (1940) created by Bob Kingett. Ibis was a resurrected mummy and young prince of the 12th Egyptian dynasty who wielded the Ibistick, the source of his reality-altering power. The turban was decorative, only indicating that he was foreign by 1940s American standards. These two were both similar to the turban-wearing Kardak the Mystic from MLJ Magazines' *Top-Notch Comics* #1 (1939), who, similar to Alexander, was an American magician who traveled the world. He initially did not demonstrate any magic powers and instead used gimmicks from his stage act to foil mobsters. The character eventually gained powers, probably to increase readers' interest, but sales did not warrant continuing his storyline after three years of publication. One of the more interesting mystics with a turban and Eastern-style costume was Magar, Recreator of Souls, who first appeared in Timely Comics' *Red Raven Comics* #1 (1940). His origin was similar to the retconned Captain America, waking up after lying dormant for half a century. He used telepathy to orient "himself in this chaotic world of today,"[45] and practiced necromancy, communicating with the dead, and at times, temporarily resurrected them to aid him in his adventures. Of the five superheroes that seem to descend from Alexander Conlin, it was Doctor Strange that remained pertinent to modern popular culture due to the innovative storytelling of his creators, Lee and Ditko, who focused on world-building and character-driven storylines to construct his mystique rather than superficial gimmicks such as turbans and illusions.

Bernarr Macfadden and Harry Houdini both managed to achieve their big breakthrough in 1899 and their careers were in full swing when the 20th century arrived. They are two completely different figures in history who link to two equally different superheroes. Macfadden featured power, determination, and near immortality, promising audiences a physically powerful world of tomorrow. His success at genre-specific pulp magazine publishing was observed by figures such as Hugo Gernsback, Martin Goodman, and Harry Donenfeld who then started their own magazine companies. Goodman and Donenfeld adapted their companies to sell comic books, eventually creating Marvel and DC Comics. Gernsback inspired science-fiction fans including Jerry Siegel, Julius Schwartz, and Mort Weisinger to create and develop the "Man of Tomorrow," Superman, and other DC Comics superheroes. Houdini featured illusion, mystique, and significant risk for personal injury. He and the other three early magicians delivered wonder, awe, and otherworldly entertainment to captivate audiences before the popularity of radio and television. Comic book writers, fascinated with their mystique, created superheroes that maintain relevance in popular culture such as Batman, Mister Miracle, Zatanna, and Doctor Strange. They evolved from comic strip storytelling, pulp-era proto-superheroes, cinematic action, classic illustration, and real-life figures. By the early 1940s, Superman, the superhero genre, and the comic book medium were well-established in the pop-cultural and commercial landscape. However, courts had not yet legally accepted superheroes as their own genre, granting DC Comics another ingredient that maintained Superman as the strongest superhero at the newsstands: litigation.

PART 2

The Rise and Fall
of Superheroes

Superman's Greatest Strength: Litigation

The Golden Age of comic books started once DC Comics published Super-man in *Action Comics* #1 (1938), prompting other publishers to fill the marketplace with their own similar and competing superheroes. The last son of Krypton was always different, however, representing hope, strength, truth, and justice. Jerry Siegel and Joe Shuster created the character and the superhero genre, utilizing pre-existing themes of physical fitness and science fiction, combined with a cape and costume. That combination performed well with audiences, making *Action Comics* and the follow-up series, *Superman*, instant successes, which ensured the security of Detective Comics Inc. (DC Comics). Innovative printing and distribution strategies by Independent News Company, owned and operated by DC Comics owners Harry Donenfeld, Jack Liebowitz, and Paul Sampliner, carried these published stories to newsstands all over the country.[1] However, their security was threatened when other superhero comic books were published, and their market share was undermined by competition. This uncertainty prompted them to cancel Superman's rivals using lit-igation, maintaining their superhero's market dominance for decades. Although superheroes functioned as a genre in the Golden Age, it was in Donenfeld's favor to legally consider any of his company's characters' superpowers as a copyright, includ-ing Superman, Wonder Woman, and Batman, and then use that consideration in a legal narrative that could help prevent other companies from taking DC Comics' market share through cease-and-desist letters. DC Comics and its later parent com-pany, Warner, used this method to legally target publishers and studios such as Fox Publications, Fawcett, Republic Pictures, EC Comics, Archie, Marvel Comics, MF Enterprises, Filmation, and the American Broadcasting Company to maintain its dominance over the superhero comic book industry.

DC Comics' first target was Golden Age publisher Victor Fox, the self-proclaimed "King of Comics." As publisher of Fox Publications/Bruns Publica-tions, he too desired a profitable superhero comic book and contracted Will Eis-ner of the Eisner-Iger shop to create one for his company. So, Eisner created Wonder Man for the first issue of *Wonder Comics* (1939). Similar to Chandu, Wonder Man, also known as Fred Carson, was an American who traveled to Tibet, where an old monk bestowed upon him an Eastern ring of power. This ring gave him super abilities that were an exact replica of Superman's powers. Whereas Superman could leap one-eighth of a mile, raise tremendous weights, and run faster than an express train, Wonder Man could leap into the air, catch a bomb, and hurl it back 1,000 feet. Wonder Man's similarity to Superman was discovered by the owners of DC Comics, who initiated a copyright infringement lawsuit against Fox Publications. Once the case was brought to trial, the lawyers at DC highlighted specific stories and swipes from previous Superman adventures. Soon it became clear that it wasn't just the powers they had copied, but also various poses and panels.[2] The case was decided in court as Detective Comics Inc. versus Bruns Publications (1940). Eisner testified, and on April 29, 1940, the court ruled in favor of Detective Comics Inc., causing Fox to stop using the character. *Wonder Comics* continued for one more issue without its star character, then ceased publication.[3] DC Comics' legal victory over Fox sent a message to the industry that Superman's superpowers and the comic's panel compositions were not to be copied.

Fawcett Comics was targeted by the owners of DC Comics for two of their superheroes, Master Man and Captain Marvel. Master Man was both the main feature and title character of *Master Comics* #1 (March 1940), published before the court ruling against Fox publications. His creator and writer are unknown, but it is clear that Bill Parker edited the issue, Newt Alfred drew the interior artwork, and Harry Fiske drew the cover.[4] Master Man was blond, same as Fox's Wonder Man, wore a red-and-blue costume similar to Superman, and was gifted with super strength and super speed. An excerpt from the comic script read, "Master Man! Stronger than untamed horses! Swifter than raging winds! Braver than mighty lions! Wiser than wisdom, kind as Galahad is Master Man, the wonder of the world!"[5] Master Man gained his strength from a wise old doctor who gave him a magic capsule to ingest containing vitamins of pure energy. Despite the superhero's origin being different from Superman, and emboldened by their victory over Fox Publications, executives at DC Comics soon targeted Master Man and threatened Fawcett with a lawsuit.[6] Fawcett relented quickly, possibly due to poor financial performance, and ceased using Master Man after six issues. Master Man's reference to legendary knight of the round table Sir Galahad does point to Bill Parker as writer, who also pointed to other mythological figures as the power source of DC Comics' other target at Fawcett, Captain Marvel. About the same time as *Master Comics* #1, Fawcett also published Captain Marvel in *Whiz Comics* #2 (1940), created by Parker and C.C. Beck. Captain Marvel was young boy Billy Batson, who was given magic power of the gods to transform into his super alter ego, which had a distinctive costume, chest logo, and cape, as well as super strength, bulletproof physique, and the ability to fly. His presence in *Whiz Comics* proved highly popular with readers by garnering sales that rivaled Superman. The executives at Republic Pictures recognized an opportunity and licensed the property to produce the serial *Adventures of Captain Marvel* (1941), which attracted the attention of the owners of DC Comics. Editor Jack

Schiff confirmed this when commenting, "Donenfeld wants to make a test case of Captain Marvel."[7] His feelings on the matter were in all likelihood aggravated when newspapers of the period referred to Captain Marvel as "superman of supermen."[8] Donenfeld and his legal team sued both Fawcett Comics and Republic Pictures for copyright infringement, claiming that Captain Marvel was an intentional copy of Superman.[9] Examining this case from a technical standpoint suggests that DC Comics was partially correct about its allegations. They are different characters with Superman based on science fiction and Captain Marvel based on magic, while Batson was a young boy and Clark Kent was an adult. However, they both were tall with dark hair, wore capes, had super strength with a logo on their chest, smashed cars on their first covers, and fought villains that were bald scientists—Lex Luthor and Dr. Sivana. Both Superman and Captain Marvel also premiered in anthology titles and experienced enough success to star in their own titled comic books. *Captain Marvel Adventures* #1 (1941) was created by Joe Simon and Jack Kirby, which doubled the character's presence at the newsstand. At one point in the Detective Comics Inc. versus Fawcett Publications Inc. lawsuit, both Simon and Kirby were asked to testify. Simon testified against Fawcett Comics, staying consistent with the narrative that Superman was copied by its competition.[10] However, since the sales of *Whiz Comics* and *Captain Marvel Adventures* were still very high, it was financially feasible for the owners of Fawcett to legally defend their right to use the character. After a series of delays, National Comics Publications Inc. (DC) versus Fawcett Publications Inc. went to trial in 1948, and the court ruled in favor of Fawcett Comics. DC Comics appealed the ruling in 1951, and in 1952, a judge ruled in DC's favor.[11] By this time, the Golden Age of superhero comic books had ended. Captain Marvel was no longer as lucrative as it had previously been, and it was no longer worth the money or time to challenge the case. The two companies settled, and Fawcett ceased publishing the adventures of Captain Marvel.

Despite their early victories, DC Comics was faced with a minor legal challenge from Better Publications that forced it to acquiesce on one of its comic book titles. DC Comics published *World's Best Comics* #1 (1941), an anthology series starring superheroes including Superman, Batman, Zatara, and Robin. The comic sold well. However, Better Publications had already claimed the title in its own comic book, *Best Comics* (1939). Historian Michael Uslan commented that Better Publications sent a cease-and-desist letter to DC Comics claiming that the two similar titles would create confusion in the marketplace.[12] The owners at DC Comics probably considered this a small loss, and its legal team was probably more concerned in dealing with Fawcett, so their title was changed to *World's Finest Comics* for issue #2.

Superman stayed commercially viable in the 1950s despite the diminished popularity of superheroes during the Television Age. However, DC Comics still found a legal target in EC Comics' Superduperman caricature. EC Comics produced a variety of non-superhero genres at this point: crime, shock, horror, war, and satire. In 1952, *MAD* was created by humorist Harvey Kurtzman, known for his keen ability to

FLEXING HIS POWERFUL MUSCLES, MARVEL PULLS THE DOOR OPEN-

DC Comics' copyright infringement case against Fawcett Comics was based on swipes and similarities between Superman (1938) and Captain Marvel (1940).

challenge and satirize the status quo. The series did not sell well in its first few issues, but it found its position in the marketplace with *MAD* #4 (1953) starring Superduperman, created by Harvey Kurtzman and Wally Wood. The character was an obvious tongue-in-cheek parody of Superman that included his rivalry with "Captain Marbles," lampooning the feud between DC Comics and Fawcett. Despite it being a humorous spoof, it attracted the attention of DC Comics' owners, who threatened an infringement lawsuit against EC Comics' owner, Bill Gaines. Parody, however, is a right protected in U.S. copyright law by the doctrine of fair use, and a form of free speech. After some in-office discussion, Gaines and Kurtzman continued to publish *MAD* comics with no changes, and DC decided against initiating a formal lawsuit.[13] Harvey Kurtzman and Wally Wood apparently enjoyed this freedom since they satirized another pair of DC Comics' superheroes in "Batboy and Rubin" from *MAD* #8 (1953). The sales on these issues by Kurtzman and Wood performed well, and their tactic of "poking the lion" worked to their advantage. Ultimately, EC's humor line evaded any form of legal retaliation from DC Comics, demonstrating to the industry that the famous superhero publisher wasn't going to win every battle.

During the Silver Age, superheroes were lucrative again, prompting publishers such as Archie, Marvel, and MF Enterprises to publish titles that attracted the attention of DC Comics' owners. In 1959, President John Goldwater of Archie Comics

"Superduperman" by Harvey Kurtzman and Wally Wood challenged DC Comics by satirizing their copyright infringement case against Fawcett in *MAD* #4 (1953).

asked Joe Simon and Jack Kirby to create superheroes for a new line of comic books, resulting in *The Double Life of Private Strong* and *Adventures of the Fly*. Private Strong was a patriotic character with superhuman powers, such as harnessing lightning, super strength, and super speed. These powers were generated from experiments conducted by the hero's father in a manner similar to *Gladiator*. During this process, Strong's father died, the young boy ended up an orphan adopted by a farming couple, grew up mastering his superpowers, and donned a red-and-blue costume. Joe Simon elaborated that John Goldwater dropped *The Double Life of Private Strong* after two issues because DC Comics' lawyers had targeted them with a cease-and-desist order. They claimed that Private Strong's origin, costume, and superpowers were all too comparable to those of Superman.[14] Marvel Comics' realistic superheroes were mostly different enough from DC's roster and managed to avoid attracting unwanted attention. However, this changed when Stan Lee, Jack Kirby, and Don Heck created a new Wonder Man in *Avengers* #9 (1964). This iteration of Wonder Man was Simon Williams, an ordinary man who gained his superhuman strength and invulnerability from bombardment with ionic rays. Williams appeared as a villain but sacrificed his life and became a hero by the end of the issue. Stan Lee mentioned that when Marvel Comics began to use Wonder Man, the consequences were akin to what happened to Victor Fox in 1939. DC Comics' legal team sent Marvel a cease-and-desist letter, ordering them to immediately stop using the character. However, the letter did not state that this version of Wonder Man infringed upon Superman's copyright when they submitted their request. Instead, they stated that Wonder Man allegedly shared similarities with Wonder Woman.[15] Therefore, the character's appearance in Marvel Comics temporarily ceased until his reappearance in *Avengers* #131 (1975) when that threat was no longer substantial.

DC Comics' legal team also sent a cease-and-desist to MF Enterprises, owned and operated by Myron Fass. Fass published a character named the Bat in the third issue of his short-lived *Captain Marvel* (1966) series. He already used the *Captain Marvel* name because the trademark fell out of use after Fawcett Comics abandoned the character more than a decade earlier; however, Fass was overconfident in his usage of the Bat. To avoid litigation from DC Comics' owners, who would certainly take the small publisher to court to protect their Batman copyright and trademark, Fass had writer Carl Hubbell change the name of his Bat villain to the Ray.[16]

Two more cases in the early 1980s ended DC Comics' narrative that superpowers were a copyright and legally established superheroes as a genre: DC Comics Inc. versus Filmation Associates (1980) and Warner Bros Inc. versus American Broadcasting Companies (1983). The first case involved DC's lawsuit against Filmation for using a superhero with stretch powers in its *Super 7* television series. This character was part of an African American husband-and-wife crimefighting team, Superstretch and Microwoman. DC Comics claimed that Superstretch was too similar to their Plastic Man superhero. This lawsuit also included a complaint against two more of the series' characters, Manta and Moray, who both appeared too similar to DC Comics' Aquaman and Mera.[17] Lou Scheimer, cofounder of Filmation, described that although damages of $200,000 were awarded to DC, there was a caveat. The judge agreed that costumes, names, and appearances were legally protectable, but not superpowers. This made it not only a short-term victory for DC Comics but also a loss toward its long-term legal strategy, because it excluded all superpowers from copyright infringement.[18] The final case here came about with Warner Bros Inc. versus American Broadcasting Companies, discussing the similarities between Superman and the caped protagonist from *The Greatest American Hero* (1981). This case went through two courts and found that the two superheroes did not have sufficient overlap to constitute infringement due to two key points. The show was a legally protected parody of the superhero genre, and that the superhero genre itself was within the boundaries of fair use.[19]

The superhero genre was created at DC Comics with the introduction of Superman from physical fitness and science-fiction concepts found in various preexisting media. Although the character was copyrighted, and the name trademarked, the owners of DC Comics maintained a broad legal approach in weakening its competition. They upheld the stance that Superman's generic power set and overall costumed appearance, central to the definition of the superhero genre, was also copyrighted. This sort of legal protection also applied to their other characters, including Batman and Wonder Woman. DC Comics' legal team used these methods to establish their company's ownership of the superhero genre for decades by preventing the growth of other publishers, which helped manifest their characters as industry leaders. After alternative superheroes with other powers were introduced into comic books by other companies over several years, there was enough marketplace dilution for courts to legally establish the superhero as its own genre by the early 1980s. The main question that logically arose in the industry, during the height of DC Comics' legal maneuvers was, "What sort of super-powered origin could position itself into a comic book that could challenge Superman's market dominance?"

9

Cosmic Rays
Create Superpowers

The superhero genre appeared firmly under the control of DC Comics in the early 1950s. Lesser-known superheroes were generally phased out of competitors' comic books in favor of other genres, and DC's roster of superheroes, including Superman, Batman, and Wonder Woman, held a firm presence at newsstands. The owners of DC Comics used lawsuits and cease-and-desist letters to reduce other publishers' abilities to produce competing superhero comics. One company, Marvel Comics, was still able to introduce their superhero universe in the 1960s, avoiding DC Comics' legal radar and eliminating Superman's market dominance by adopting a science-fiction trope that started in Hugo Gernsback's pulp magazines during the Platinum Age. This key trope was relatively basic: cosmic rays and radioactivity could create superpowers, which was sufficiently different from the character origins at DC Comics, allowing a series of companies, including Marvel, to compete for the superhero market share. Cosmic-ray-based powers evolved from the initial discovery of radiation, its introduction in science fiction by Hugo Gernsback, and its presence in stories by superhero comic book creators working for companies such as Quality, Novelty Press, DC Comics, Hillman, Spark Publications, Charlton, Marvel, and Gold Key.

Henri Becquerel discovered radioactivity in 1896, and in 1900, "gamma rays" were detected by Paul Villard while studying radium.[1] After years of experimentation, it was Robert Millikan who coined the term "cosmic rays" in the 1920s after making ionization measurements underwater and in the atmosphere, identifying their source as interstellar space.[2] Gernsback paid close attention to published scientific discoveries and wrote an editorial about cosmic rays in *Science Wonder Stories* (September 1929) stating "the so-called cosmic ray, was recently discovered by Professor Milliken [*sic*] ... we suspect it is a terrific power that someday will be tapped to the benefit of humanity."[3] Gernsback's editorial implied that humans may gain great power from cosmic rays, a statement not proven by any science but still a hopeful one that prompted science-fiction writers to consider its possibilities. One famous science-fiction writer, H.G. Wells, appeared to be paying attention. The author, famous for writing *The War of the Worlds* (1898), wrote its sequel as the novel

Star-Begotten (1937). It was the story of a man who wondered if Martians had already begun to irradiate humans with cosmic rays to enhance their intelligence. The book frequently discussed human mutation from cosmic rays, as "cosmic missiles among our chromosomes would be to increase the intellectual power of the Martianized individuals very greatly."[4] Wells, as a father of science fiction, had, in a way, authenticated Gernsback's thoughts on the matter and Golden Age comic book writers utilized the idea as a novel origin for superheroes.

Quality Comics appears to have published the first cosmic-ray-powered superhero of the Golden Age in *Smash Comics* #14 (September 1940), likely written by Will Eisner and penciled by Lou Fine. The Ray was Langford Terrill, a reporter augmented by a "cosmic storm of light"[5] during a low-level space trip in a professor's "strato-balloon."[6] The hero's body was mutated into an energy-based being who could fly, cast laser beams, become invisible, and manipulate solid light constructs. The Ray continued for three years with no legal recourse from DC Comics, which likely encouraged cosmic-ray-powered figures to appear in more comic books. Joe Simon and Jack Kirby created a supervillain named Marto in *Blue Bolt* #6 (November 1940). Marto was originally a humanoid scientist who researched the secret of "cosmic rays" to increase his intelligence by speeding up the process of evolution.[7] This cosmic ray bombardment resulted in having a shriveled body but an oversize head and superpowered mind, requiring an exoskeleton to move. Kirby, an established fan of *Wonder Stories*, portrayed cosmic rays in comic books throughout his career.

DC Comics very rarely published stories concerning cosmic rays, and if so, they were generally used to power inanimate objects instead of people. One example of this was the creation of the superhero Starman by Jack Burnley for *Adventure Comics* #61 (1941). Starman was Theodore Knight, a hero with a red costume who utilized

"The Ray" from *Smash Comics* #14 (September 1940) was a normal human transformed into a superhero by cosmic rays 21 years before *The Fantastic Four* #1 (1961).

a "gravity rod" that was described in two panels as a piece of equipment that was powered by rays from the stars.[8] This series by Burnley is commonly celebrated by Golden Age fans but was an example of creators at DC Comics not taking full advantage of the cosmic-ray-powered trope. However, other comic book companies continued to do so, such as Hillman Publications. Hillman published pages written and drawn by the creator of Sub-Mariner, Bill Everett, about a cosmic-ray-powered, Nazi-killing hero named the Conqueror in *Victory Comics* #1 (August 1941). The first issue depicted the character already empowered and battling Nazis on the front lines; however, the issue's text piece explained the origin in detail. Daniel Lyons was a pilot who was wounded when his plane crashed near a scientist's laboratory. The scientist healed Lyons by exposing him to a cosmic ray lamp, which granted him superhuman strength. The script by Everett explained the motivations of the scientist: "I've been baking your body with my special cosmic ray lamp. See it there? Your body has been absorbing the energy of this ray. Your metabolism has increased tremendously already ... you will have improved a hundred percent, both physically and mentally!"[9]

Everett's explanation that cosmic rays heal, energize, and improve a person both physically and mentally was thematically the same as Gernsback's 1929 editorial, implying that he may have been one of its readers. One correction that should be made for both stories involving the Conquerer or Blue Bolt is that cosmic rays emanated from space, and man-made machines such as those present in their origins would harness "radiation" or "nuclear power." As the public began to understand the difference, comic book superheroes began to get their powers from those two sources, and the term, "cosmic rays" was reserved for outer space.

One notable radiation superhero was Atoman (1946), created by Ken Crossen and Jerry Robinson for Spark Publications. Atoman was nuclear scientist Barry Dale, who gained superpowers through exposure to nuclear materials.[10] Despite the public dread of atomic bombs, there was also a strong optimism held by Americans toward the possibilities of nuclear power. Atoman was a manifestation of this optimism as nuclear reactors were researched to eventually generate electricity in 1951. Crossen and Robinson's Atoman inspired comic book artist Steve Ditko to cocreate another radioactive superhero, Captain Atom, in *Space Adventures* #33 (1960). Ditko's inspiration from Robinson began as a child when he was a fan of his work on *Batman*. He later trained as a student under Robinson at the Cartoonist and Illustrators School in 1950.[11] When Ditko was submitting work to Charlton Comics, including the cocreation of Captain Atom with writer Joe Gill, he patterned the superhero's costume and appearance after Atoman, which included blond hair, red-and-yellow color scheme, starburst chest logo, and mask that connected down the neck to the costume. Gill and Ditko depicted Captain Adam trapped in an experimental test rocket that launched into space with him onboard.[12] The atomic warhead exploded, causing an "instant of fission" when Captain Adam was no longer "flesh, bone, and blood."[13] He reappeared at his military base, emanating radiation and ready to take instruction from both his colonel and the president as the nuclear-powered Captain Atom.

As radioactive superheroes continued to evolve at various comic book companies alongside America's innovations in nuclear energy, writers at DC Comics continued to use cosmic rays to power more inanimate objects. Bill Finger wrote about a cosmic-ray-powered hammer in *Batman* #127 (1959) with art by Sheldon Moldoff.[14] Finger's story depicted a museum curator who found the "hammer of Thor" fallen from space and energized by a radioactive meteor. He touched the hammer, absorbed its radioactive power, and was immediately hypnotized into believing he was the thunder god with a mission to steal money to pay for a temple of Odin.[15] His size and strength increased and he threw his hammer at his opponents, which he commanded to return. Batman foiled his plans, and the character was never revisited, which was a missed opportunity for DC to more fully utilize this concept that preceded Marvel Comics' Thor by three years. John Broome wrote another story for DC Comics about a cosmic-ray-powered time treadmill in *The Flash* #125 (1961) with art by Carmine Infantino. Barry Allen was depicted teaching Wally West that the treadmill could take them into the future or the past: "This treadmill is cosmic-ray powered! And it is coordinated with radiation pulses from that cosmic ray clock!"[16] However, DC Comics eventually published a story about a radiation-powered superhero, Negative Man, whose origin was revealed by writer Arnold Drake and artist Bruno Premiani in *The Doom Patrol* #106 (1966). Test pilot Larry Trainor was bathed in "radio-energy" during a flight that made superhuman structural changes to his body.[17] He was scarred to the bone and completely radioactive, and he wrapped himself in bandages to cover his acquired deformity. Drake described another unsettling ability for Negative Man, releasing a radioactive and conscious being from his body that flew free for 60 seconds. A radiation-powered human was an unusual superhero for DC Comics at this time, which appears to explain the disclaimer on its cover, "The World's Strangest Heroes!"[18]

Many of the aforementioned radiation-powered superheroes failed to maintain a strong presence at newsstands, but it was the creative group at Marvel Comics who utilized the trope well enough to eventually seize much of DC Comics' market share. This began with artist Jack Kirby, who utilized cosmic rays a second time in his career while plotting and drawing the daily newspaper comic strip *Sky Masters of the Space Force* (October 16, 1959), scripted by Dave Wood. The astronauts of the continuity were depicted on a space station, dreading the unpredictable effects of incoming cosmic ray exposure on human tissue.[19] Kirby crafted this science-fiction strip toward realism, avoiding superpowers, and instead demonstrated personality changes rather than physical mutation. However, the storyline suggested that Kirby may have saved the idea of physical mutation, in the manner of the Ray, for a later project. This appeared to manifest two years later once Martin Goodman ordered Stan Lee to create a superhero team to compete with the *Justice League of America*.[20] Both Lee and Kirby constructed the story of four astronauts gaining superpowers from incoming cosmic rays during their trip into space in *The Fantastic Four* #1 (1961).[21] The super team's origin story was a repeated science-fiction trope from previous superhero comic books, but Lee and Kirby's human approach to the characters attracted readers. They appear to have incorporated science-fiction and monster movie theatrics in *The Fantastic Four* #1, which resembled the concept of four astronauts traveling to space directly from the science-fiction classic *Destination Moon* (1950). The Thing, a misunderstood and super-strong mutated monster, seemed directly taken from the sad radioactive creature in *Day the World Ended* (1955). These factors contributed to the comic book's popularity, which holds importance as the birth issue of the Marvel Universe from which a new line of radioactive superheroes was created. Lee and Kirby maintained their monster movie approach to *The Incredible Hulk* #1 (1962), which used a gamma-ray bomb to ignite scientist Bruce Banner's cellular potential and transform him into the Hulk after running into a test area to save a young trespasser. Kirby's pages depicting the Hulk's origin were the same as the scene from the film *The Amazing Colossal Man* (1957), where a nuclear bomb accident transformed Lieutenant Colonel Glenn Manning into a similar super-strong menace. Bruce Banner changed into the Hulk depending on the day-night cycle, which was the same gimmick utilized in *The Hideous Sun Demon* (1958), a film depicting a radiated human who changed to a monster depending on whether the sun was rising or setting. Lee and Ditko applied another radiation superpowered origin to Spider-Man in *Amazing Fantasy* #15 (1962). High school student Peter Parker was bitten by a radioactive spider that crawled out of a nearby experiment. After discovering he could stick to walls with super strength, he donned his costume and became a wall-crawling superhero. Although there are radioactive spiders in monster movies of this era, it was the innovative costume, powers, and human approach to the story that eventually made Spider-Man popular enough at newsstands to be referred to as "Marvel's mascot."[22] With these innovations, Lee, Kirby, and Ditko successfully created radiation-based superheroes that could challenge Superman and DC Comics.

Although the Marvel creative team revolutionized radiation-based superheroes, Gold Key approached the topic in a standard way, which Alan Moore deconstructed two decades later. Paul Newman and Bob Fujitani created *Doctor Solar: Man of the Atom* #1 (1966), a radioactive superhero who gained his abilities from a nuclear-powered accident that was only mildly different from Jerry Robinson and Ken Crossen's *Atoman*. This origin followed physicist Dr. Phillip Solar, whose body absorbed excessive radiation during an act of atomic sabotage. His skin color turned green similar to the Hulk's and wielded the ability to store energy in a similar manner as the Ray. This origin employed more drama than Atoman, which was demonstrated in Dr. Solar's dialogue when he realized, "This rate meter says I am giving off radiation ... as if I were an atomic pile!"[23] The first two issues are generally not remembered for their story, but rather for their cover art, which was painted by Richard M. Powers. Twenty years later, Alan Moore and Dave Gibbons deconstructed the

Stan Lee and Jack Kirby set their cosmic-ray-based superheroes apart from those in other companies by also utilizing imagery and concepts from the radioactive monster films of the late 1950s.

origins of superheroes such as the Ray, Atoman, Captain Atom, and Doctor Solar in *Watchmen* (1986) when Dr. Jonathan Osterman transformed into Doctor Manhattan during a malfunctioning radiation experiment. Moore deconstructed the industry's approach to radiation-based superheroes by demonstrating its innate loss of humanity and its eventual path toward apathy.[24] By doing so, he dismantled the industry's standard approach to crafting radiation-based superheroes, which appeared to validate the revolutionary monster-based method that was presented by the three creators at Marvel Comics.

Although Gernsback hinted at the potential found in cosmic rays, the industry spent decades attempting the same failed formula of superheroes that lost their relatability through radiation-based accidents. Most of these characters in the 1940s were locked in self-limiting tropes that generally lasted a few years and lacked the humanity to find any real market presence. If a non–DC publisher tried out non-radiation-based superheroes, they held the risk of resembling a character from DC Comics and were often sent legal notices, eliminating them. When the Golden Age ended, the main superheroes that maintained a strong market share were Superman, Batman, and Wonder Woman through the early 1950s. This coincided with a change in readers' tastes as other publishers' superheroes ceased being used and other comic book genres were sold instead. As the industry mostly shifted to westerns, teen, funny animals, crime, shock, romance, war, and horror, many Golden Age superhero comic book artists also moved to different commercial fields.

10

Golden Age Comic Book Artists Leave Superheroes

Toward the end of the Golden Age, superhero escapism lost popularity with many comic book readers even though the superhero genre seemed somewhat viable but confined at DC Comics. The standard superhero with a costume, powers, code name, and mission of justice ceased to captivate audiences. Crime, westerns, romance, shock, teen, funny animal, war, and horror genres were successfully implemented at most existing publishers, but there was another trend that occurred: old artists were leaving the industry while new artists were hired to replace them. Toward the end of the 1940s, the job of a comic book artist was generally viewed as less lucrative and prestigious compared with occupations in advertising, magazine publishing, book illustration, or newspaper comic strips. Superhero comic books were on the decline, and many artists migrated to work in other commercial fields. This occurred with Golden Age comic book artists such as Mac Raboy, Lou Fine, Jack Cole, Dan Barry, Will Eisner, and Alex Schomburg. The rare instance occurred when a comic book artist such as Reed Crandall maintained their occupation but permanently left the superhero genre. However, either of the two remunerative opportunities were not available to Jerry Siegel and Joe Shuster, the two creators of the superhero genre who once boosted the comic book medium's commercial viability. Instead, they temporarily maintained a series of lesser positions in an industry that apparently grew tired of them.

Jerry Siegel and Joe Shuster's eventual exit from comic books started in 1938, when they signed their 10-year contract with Detective Comics Inc., transferring all rights of Superman for $130. Over the course of creating and developing their star character, they earned over $400,000, which adjusted for inflation, presently equates to roughly $5 million.[1] Once their contract with DC ended, both Siegel and Shuster sued for the rights to *Superman* under the advisement of attorney Albert Zugsmith, who was referred to by Bob Kane as "the worst lawyer in the world."[2] These attempted legal maneuvers unfortunately caused the two cocreators to lose all rights to *Superman*, lose their positions at DC, and have their byline removed from all *Superman* titles.[3] The pair collaborated again in 1948 on another property for Vin Sullivan's Magazine Enterprises, the same company that would later publish the original *Ghost Rider* comic book series.[4] Vin Sullivan, an editor and cover artist at DC Comics in the 1930s, understood the circumstances of helping to build a successful comic book company and then leaving to undertake another endeavor elsewhere. Siegel and Shuster pitched an idea that was almost as offbeat as Jack Cole's *Plastic Man*, with its comic book cover including the tagline, "The creators of Superman present their New HERO: Funnyman." Funnyman was comedian Larry Davis, who foiled criminals using practical jokes and comedic devices; however, the material was not well-received and sold poorly at newsstands. After six issues, the title was canceled, and Siegel and Shuster attempted to see the material in the comic strip format, which also faltered.[5] Reactions to *Funnyman* were generally poor, ranging from speculation that the loss of the rights to *Superman* ruined Siegel and Shuster's creative spark, to considering the possibility that the pair already manifested their creative peak with DC Comics. Regardless, they managed to secure the copyright to *Funnyman,* but the property did not prove profitable enough to sell in any medium, and the two creators went their separate ways.

Shuster maintained a short career in comic books after leaving *Funnyman.* He is credited with penciling various issues for Charlton such as *True Sweetheart Secrets* #8 (1952), *Wartime Romances* #18 (1953), *Crime and Justice* #20–21 (1954), and *This Magazine Is Haunted* #20 (1954)[6]; however, his wages were sparse in comparison with his previous earnings at DC Comics, causing his quality of life to suffer dramatically. He lived next to a local publisher who employed him to pencil sex cult cartoons for the *Nights of Horror* fetish pamphlets (1954) while DC Comics was generating profits from licensing his cocreation for the *Adventures of Superman* television show starring George Reeves.[7] The sex pamphlets were accused by Dr. Fredric Wertham of inspiring a series of murders by the Brooklyn Thrill Killers, which played a role in those pamphlets being appropriated and banned by the state of New York. The suffering artist eventually moved into his mother's home and worked as a deliveryman,[8] unable to draw due to failing eyesight.[9]

Jerry Siegel sustained a longer career in comic books by working on secondary titles, and eventually became as disappointed as Shuster. In 1950, William B. Ziff began a new line of comics and hired Siegel as art director,[10] hoping that his comic book line would become a financial success if they were overseen by the cocreator of *Superman.* These comic books descended from the *Amazing Stories* pulp magazines whose rights were purchased in 1938 by his company, Ziff-Davis.[11] They contained stories that are generally poorly remembered but much of the cover art impressed audiences with illustrations by Norm Saunders and Allen Anderson.[12] Siegel worked with titles that held potential but failed to meet a market demand, and the Ziff-Davis comic book line discontinued after a few short years. One notable comic book, *Amazing Adventures*, consisted of mostly forgettable material, leading the trademark to become unused after cancellation; however, the title was eventually utilized by publisher Martin Goodman for his own comic book series in 1961 and in due course became *Amazing Fantasy* (1962) and later *The Amazing Spider-Man*

(1963). Another comic from Ziff's line, called *He-Man*, also went unused for years and was later taken by the toy company Mattel to name their very popular action figure in 1981. The same pattern occurred with another Ziff-owned comic book, *G.I. Joe*, which later became a Hasbro toy line in 1964 with its own Marvel comic book series in 1982.

After Siegel's short term at Ziff-Davis, he created more characters for Charlton, returned to DC Comics, but left again for marginally known writing positions before retiring from comic books. He created *Nature Boy* (1956), with John Buscema about David Crandall, about a boy who was lost in the ocean and encountered Roman gods that gave him powers over the elements.[13] Buscema was born to Sicilian parents and enjoyed Hal Foster, Burne Hogarth, Norman Rockwell, and N.C. Wyeth.[14] His art on *Nature Boy* is considered by many to be stilted as compared with his later dynamic approach at Marvel. Siegel also created *Mr. Muscles*, with art by William Fraccio, about hero Brett Carson, who developed super strength after conquering polio.[15] Fraccio was a penciler for various Charlton titles for decades, including the first professional work of Roy Thomas. Both Thomas and Buscema later found a more successful collaboration on Marvel's *Avengers* in 1967; however, Siegel found no success with these two creations at Charlton, which could be due to the content or lack of distribution, but they do provide insight into what he thought readers would respond to: strong, powerful men. Later, Siegel's wife convinced DC co-owner Jack Liebowitz to hire her husband as a writer under Mort Weisinger for *Superman* in 1959.[16] This was a difficult period for Siegel, mainly due to Weisinger, who was known for his cruelty to writers,[17] but he managed to contribute stories to *Superman* and *The Legion of Superheroes* until 1965, while also contributing to other companies. One company he contributed to was Marvel Comics, writing adventures of the Human Torch under his pseudonym, Joe Carter, in *Strange Tales* #112–113 (1963). He also wrote stories for the *Mighty Crusaders* (1965) where he worked on another man of steel, Steel Sterling, then *The Owl* (1967), and *Tiger Girl* (1968) for Gold Key.[18] He also contributed to two titles for Fleetway's comic *LION* on "The Spider" (1966) and "Gadgetman and Gimmick-Kid" (1968).[19] In 1966, Siegel and Shuster challenged the copyright for *Superman* a second time,[20] but failed,[21] prompting Siegel to retire from comics to work as a mail sorter.[22]

Siegel and Shuster's final years involved a mild reversal of fortune, and a sentimental return to *Superman* and comic books. In 1975, they both learned that Warner Bros., who at this point owned DC Comics, started production on the first big-budget *Superman* movie. The film quickly developed a reputation as a large-scale Hollywood project with Marlon Brando attached, and a script by former *Godfather* writer, Mario Puzo.[23] The costly budget for the film, in comparison with the sparse conditions in which the *Superman* creators lived, inspired comic professionals Neal Adams and Jerry Robinson to cultivate a public relations campaign that ultimately resulted in Siegel and Shuster finally receiving their *Superman* creator byline, as well as an annual retirement pension.[24] For a number of years after, Siegel

Jerry Siegel's scriptwriting in the "Mighty Comics Group," such as that seen in *Mighty Crusaders* #4 (1966), appears to be an attempt to mimic Stan Lee's dialogue from the "Marvel Comics Group."

attended conventions and wrote a new comic for Eclipse Comics' *Destroyer Duck* #2 (1983) about a very different alien visitor from another planet. He and artist Val Mayerik created "the Starling," about an extraterrestrial who prevented a woman's rape by obliterating her offenders. The alien took advantage of her emotional vulnerability, made love to her, and then abandoned her with child. Due to her psychological devastation, she raised and tormented her half-alien child[25] in an ongoing series that depicted a darker perspective on the *Superman* narrative and appeared to incorporate the dysfunctional maternal relationship of *Mommy Dearest* (1981). This comic series halted in the middle of the storyline and was never resumed. Meanwhile, Shuster also attended comic conventions and unfortunately ran into a series of misfortunes, including a short-lived marriage and a retinal detachment surgery. He wrote a script for a potential cartoon character named *Kosmo the Whiz Kid* that went unrealized and died of congestive heart failure in 1992. Siegel suffered from ischemic heart problems from which he eventually died in 1996.[26] Both men were proud of their legacy as creators of *Superman*,[27] but also served as a sobering example of signing an unfavorable contract after experiencing one very significant mainstream success followed by a series of disappointments.

Reed Crandall was a rare instance when a highly skilled Golden Age comic book artist permanently left conventional superheroes for other genres. His career trajectory consisted of lesser-known comic book companies that mostly operated outside of mainstream superhero fandom. His professional choices not only reflect the diversity of the medium but also serve as an example of a comic book creator's lesser-remembered legacy when they are not associated with a successful and lasting superhero. Crandall was innately talented and created paintings from a young age considered to be Renaissance quality.[28] He studied illustration at the Cleveland School of Art, and forwent a lucrative career as an illustrator and instead pursued a career as a comic book artist mainly due to magazine advertisements shifting toward photography by the 1940s.[29] Crandall found work at the Eisner-Iger Shop in New York,[30] which packaged comic books for various publishers, including Quality Comics, started by former printer Busy Arnold.[31] Arnold, similar to other publishers, decided to directly hire staff artists to eliminate the need for shops and noticed Crandall's ability to deliver comic book art with high illustration quality. The artist accepted a staff position and demonstrated an illustrator's mastery over anatomy on titles including *Smash Comics* (1939) starring the Ray, *Doll Man* (1941), and *Military Comics* (1941) featuring Blackhawk.[32] He added a mild exaggeration to his realistic pencil art, which resulted in an approach to superheroes that is generally known as stylized realism. Readers typically enjoyed his ability to depict significant detail onto his cover and interior pages while experimenting with unconventional page designs such as overlaying a hero against a series of sequential panels.

Other comic book artists understood Crandall's innate talent, examined his work, and later emulated his innovations. One probable example can be seen in a story he illustrated for Quality Comics called "The Old Witch" in *Hit Comics* #10

(1941). This issue portrayed an old witch who reoccurred in the series as a narrator for various shock tales.[33] Although the plots are considered by modern readers to be fairly lackluster, a very similar Old Witch as narrator was eventually depicted by Graham Ingels as the host of EC Comics' *Haunt of Fear* (1950–1954). She introduced a horror story and finalized it with a morality tale. Later, Al Feldstein claimed to have created the narrator from "Old Witch's Tale" featured on the radio show *Lights Out* (1931)[34]; however, the similarities to Crandall's story are difficult to ignore. Besides working for Quality Comics, Crandall also penciled pages for Fiction House, which American soldiers could generally rely on for action stories starring anatomically well-endowed heroines. Fiction House was a pulp magazine publisher turned comic book company known for *Sheena, Queen of the Jungle*, created by Will Eisner and Jerry Iger. One of their titles, *Jungle Comics* (1940), allowed artists such as Lou Fine and Crandall to depict muscular heroes of the jungle that depicted the type of action originally discussed in books by Edgar Rice Burroughs. Crandall demonstrated his facility with the scenery, animal adventure, and human anatomy required in *Jungle Comics* #42 (1943), with a splash page starring Kaanga, White Lord of the Jungle and his girlfriend, Ann. His splash page was appreciated by Fiction House's editorial staff to the point that Joe Doolin traced and reused it for the cover of *Jungle Comics* #67 (1945).

Crandall's fluency with anatomy qualified him for depicting multiple genres in comic book art, which allowed him to adapt to crime and horror when the majority of publishers abandoned superheroes in the early 1950s. Quality Comics' owner, Busy Arnold, began to emphasize the crime genre in *Police Comics*, which became apparent when Plastic Man was removed from the cover after issue #102 (1950) and replaced by Private Detective Ken Shannon for the cover of #103. By issue #105, Crandall penciled a cover that introduced horror to the crime series, depicting Detective Shannon investigating a murder by a paranormal spirit in "Can a Ghost Kill?"[35] Sales improved with the addition of horror during this period, and after the detective was placed into his own series, horror imagery became a regular feature. This became apparent when Crandall depicted a zombie on the cover of issue #3, a vampire on the cover of issue #6, and a deformed killer on the cover of issue #7. Crandall also provided similar material for EC Comics, drawing pages for its publisher, Bill Gaines, who focused on adult-themed genres in science fiction, horror, and crime comic books. One memorable story that Crandall penciled during his time at EC was "Carrion Death" for *Shock SuspenStories* #9 (1953).[36] Editor Al Feldstein illustrated the cover that previewed the feature, but it was Crandall's interior art that impressed readers. A sadistic killer was stranded in the desert and encountered a series of misfortunes before being eaten alive by vultures. Crandall's rendition of this crime-turned-horror story was celebrated by later readers to the point that it was adapted for television in an episode from the *Tales from the Crypt* show airing on July 15, 1991. Crandall's unrestricted horror period at EC was short-lived due to the creation of the Comics Code Authority, which implemented the industry's rules on what constituted appropriate comic book content for newsstands. Bill Gaines adapted his line of comics to the code's regulations, and the horror and crime genres, which were at this point nonviable, were replaced with less stimulating storylines involving knights and pirates. One such series in this "New Direction" of comics was *Piracy*, which appealed to Crandall's love of classic illustrators, from which he swiped imagery from Howard Pyle's paintings "Who Shall Be Captain?" (1911) and "An Attack on a Galleon" (1905) for the covers to issues #2 and #3 (1955). After the new direction failed, Crandall provided covers and interiors for the *EC Picto-Fiction* series (1955–1956),[37] which eventually ceased along with EC Comics.

Crandall continued to pencil other non-superhero genres for lesser-known companies, despite the return of superheroes at DC Comics in 1956 and Marvel Comics in 1961. This may have been due to his artwork shifting from stylized realism to non-stylized realism with few instances of exaggerated anatomy, which generally thrived in non-superhero comic books. He joined penciler Ray Willner to illustrate *The Adventures of Robin Hood* (1956) for the Brown Shoe company.[38] The series utilized the green hero's appearance set forth by classic illustrators Howard Pyle and N.C. Wyeth, as well as actor Errol Flynn, visually outdoing other Robin Hood comic books of the period. Crandall also found work with *Classics Illustrated*, a comic book published by the Gilberton Company, whose mission was to portray great literature for kids to promote literacy.[39] He penciled *The Hunchback of Notre Dame* (1960), based on the French Gothic novel by Victor Hugo, and adapted the film *Hercules Unchained* (1960) starring Steve Reeves for Dell with both works inked by fellow EC Comics alumnus George Evans. In 1960, he started a 12-year period penciling pages for *Treasure Chest of Fun & Fact*, a Catholic comic that was started in 1946 and distributed to parochial schools.[40] The storyline that is most heavily associated with Crandall in this period was "This Godless Communism," which began in *Treasure Chest* vol. 17, #2 (September 28, 1961). The comic was a commentary on the history of communism and its growing threat to the world, which resonated with American society at the time as President John F. Kennedy was engaged in the Cold War with the Soviet Union. Communism was depicted by Crandall as a growing red octopus with its tentacles lodged into the world,[41] likely as a reference to Fred Rose's *Serio-Comic War Map* (1877), which demonstrated Russia's control during its rivalry with the Ottoman Empire. Crandall also illustrated pulp material by Edgar Rice Burroughs for book publisher Canaveral Press. Canaveral Press was founded on printing Burroughs work that was out of copyright, and eventually printed unpublished Burroughs work from his estate.[42] His illustrations impressed readers of *Tarzan and the Madman* (1964) and *John Carter of Mars* (1964). During this period, he also contributed penciled pages to Jim Warren's black-and-white *Creepy* (1964) and *Eerie* (1966) magazines, which offered a venue outside of comic books to illustrate horror stories.[43]

During Crandall's final years as a comic book artist, he returned briefly to depict caped adventurers and science fiction, but neither featured a successful and long-lasting superhero. Tower Publications hired Wally Wood to oversee a comics line where new characters and properties were to be created and sold in 1965.[44] There, Crandall penciled characters Noman and Dynamo in *T.H.U.N.D.E.R. Agents*. Crandall's illustration of NoMan's origin, depicting Doctor Dunn transferring his mind into an android body, utilized his mastery of anatomy and science fiction. His pages that portrayed the android hero in fierce combat with ape-like "sub-men" appeared to summon imagery often found in a Burroughs novel.[45] Crandall also briefly penciled the short-lived *Flash Gordon* comic book created by King Comics in 1966. Al Williamson initiated the series, maintaining the original Alex Raymond style of the 1930s comic strip, and Crandall penciled issue #6 merging Raymond's style with his own. He did manage to pencil and ink one non-superhero story for Marvel Comics titled "Where Walks the Werewolf!" for *Creatures on the Loose* #13 (1971), written by Len Wein. They depicted a blind man who had his vision restored by wolf cell transplant and went on to become a werewolf who died by falling off a cliff.[46] Crandall penciled pages for these titles while also regularly doing the same for *Treasure Chest*, which provided a regular source of income. This financial arrangement, however, changed when the company ceased publication in 1972, forcing him to get work as a security guard at a Pizza Hut warehouse. A year later, he dealt with a stroke, leaving him brain damaged and unable to draw. He lived in a facility for nine years, suffering with vascular dementia, and died of a heart attack in 1982.[47] The quantity of high-quality illustrations that he produced over decades culminates in a legacy that is generally unremembered mostly due to not being associated with an ongoing successful superhero.

Other Golden Age comic book artists such as Mac Raboy, Jack Cole, Lou Fine, Dan Barry, Will Eisner, and Alex Schomburg generally also achieved mainstream success by first working at comic book packagers, then companies such as Fawcett, Quality, Fox, Hillman, Timely, and Nedor. Despite eventually leaving the industry for other more respectable commercial avenues, most of them are still mainly remembered for contributing to superheroes. Mac Raboy was a comic book artist famous for his detailed and kinetically accurate illustration skills. He was inspired by the work of Alex Raymond's newspaper comic strips *Flash Gordon*, *Secret Agent X-9*, and *Jungle Jim*.[48] Raboy developed as an artist in the early 1940s while working at the Harry Chesler shop, one of many comic book studios at the time that packaged comic books together for sale to publishers. He later became famous for his work at Fawcett Comics, penciling *Bulletman*[49] and an often-celebrated origin of Captain Marvel Jr., which crossed over from *Master Comics* #21 (1941), through *Whiz Comics* #25, and finalized in *Master Comics* #22. These issues started the Captain Nazi story arc in which the villain crippled the young Freddy Freeman, who received power from SHAZAM to become Captain Marvel Jr. The ongoing rivalry between the young hero and Captain Nazi depicted by Raboy's pencil art is often discussed as one of the most memorable series of the Golden Age.[50] Demand for his artwork increased and editors at Fawcett used photostats of his work to maintain the pace.[51]

He eventually left Fawcett and penciled the *Green Lama* for Spark Publications in 1945 for Ken Crossen, cocreator of *Atoman*.[52] He departed the comic book industry and accepted a job penciling the *Flash Gordon* Sunday comic strip in 1946, on which he worked until his death in 1967.[53] Despite the quality of his work on *Flash Gordon*, Raboy continues to be remembered mainly for his work on *Captain Marvel Jr.*

Comic artist Jack Cole also began his comic book career penciling for the Harry Chesler shop.[54] His technique and style developed over this period, until he was directly hired by various publishers to create new properties. MLJ Magazines (*Archie*) hired Cole to create the Comet for *Pep Comics* #1 (1940),[55] a character with a uni-visor of specialized crystal that blocked his uncontrollable optic blast. Cole also changed the color of Lev Gleason's Daredevil character from yellow to red in *Silver Streak* #7 (1941).[56] Both the Comet and red Daredevil had a gimmick or name that was used by creators at Marvel two decades later for their comic book line. However, Cole's most celebrated achievement was creating Plastic Man for Quality Comics in *Police Comics* #1 (1941).[57] His artwork in this series entertained audiences with a cartoon approach to both the crime and superhero genres, and Plastic Man's jokes, physical durability, and inability to die scared and shocked criminals, while serving fans with a superhero parody that still appeals to modern readers. Few artists have been able to depict Plastic Man with as much innovation as Cole, who worked on

Mac Raboy's depiction of the superhero Captain Marvel Jr. in panels such as that seen in *Master Comics* #21 and #25 (1942) is generally more remembered and celebrated than his later art on the science-fiction comic strip *Flash Gordon*.

the character for a decade before leaving the comic book industry to be eventually hired as a cartoonist for Hugh Hefner's *Playboy*. Cole's first work for the magazine can be seen in the April 1954 issue depicting a wealthy elderly man asking his butler to have his iron lung ready after an evening out with "Miss Marlow."[58] Cole worked at *Playboy* for a few years until he tragically committed suicide on August 13, 1958, after leaving a suicide note to Hugh Hefner, implying that he was hurting someone he cared about:

> Dear Hef
>
> When you read this I shall be dead. I cannot go on living with myself + hurting those dear to me. What I do has nothing to do with you. You have been the best guy I've ever worked for in all these years. I'm only sorry I leave owing you so much, but dear Dorothy will repay you when the estate is settled. I wish you nothing but the best in the years to come. Also my best regards to Pat, Art, Ray, Joe, Etc. Etc + all the other fine folks at *Playboy*
>
> Thanks again for everything, Heffer, you're a good guy.
>
> Kindest regards,
>
> Jack[59]

It is difficult to say why exactly Cole did this, but Hefner mentioned that Cole's death probably had something to do with "sexuality … and the lack of children."[60] Cole's suicide still manages to confuse comic book fans who enjoyed his art or admired his ability to enter magazine cartooning. However, most readers continue to remember him for creating the superhero Plastic Man.

Lou Fine set a high standard for illustrating superheroes during the Golden Age. His career began in 1938 when he worked for the Eisner and Iger shop, from which his artwork appeared in comic books from various publishing companies under a range of different names.[61] Fine penciled one of the first cosmic-radiation-powered superheroes, the Ray, nearly 20 years before *The Fantastic Four*.[62] His covers to *Hit Comics*, *Jumbo Comics*, *Fantastic Comics*, and *Jungle Comics* depict heroes in battle with anatomical precision. His scenes demonstrated illustrative detail, action, and dynamism, which inspired artists such as Joe Simon to emulate his style for comic covers.[63] Fine impressed audiences with his depictions of Herculean superheroes, then departed the comic book industry toward the end of World War II to illustrate advertisements for various agencies such as J. Walter Thompson and Johnstone & Cushing.[64] This departure from comic books likely occurred because a career in advertising generally yielded more earnings than comic book art. One example from Fine during this period was his advertisement for Nabisco titled "The Mystery of the Disappearing Bridge!," which demonstrated a young man saving his sinking bus, using energy from his shredded wheat cereal.[65] Fine worked in advertising for two more decades until he passed away from a heart attack in his art studio.[66] Despite preferring not to work in comic books, his Golden Age superhero covers are still the most commonly celebrated aspect to his legacy.

Daniel Barry set a high standard in smooth line art in comic books, but he initially began inking or penciling stories for various publishers in the early 1940s such as Holyoke, Hillman, and Novelty. He eventually penciled and inked *Airboy* as well as other comics for companies including Lev Gleason and Fawcett. His predilection for inking his own pencils into a polished final work helped define the slick New York style that permeated DC Comics[67] before the 1960s Jack Kirby era at Marvel Comics.[68] Barry left the comic book industry around 1947 and worked in newspaper comic strips such as the *Tarzan* dailies for a couple of years and then the *Flash Gordon* daily starting in 1951 during the time that Mac Raboy still worked on the character's Sunday strips.[69] When Raboy died in 1967, Barry began to write, pencil, and ink the *Flash Gordon* Sundays until he retired in 1990.[70] He continued to work in his slick New York style at Continuity Comics and Dark Horse before he died in 1997. His impact was elevating the comic book industry's line art standards, but his lack of association with superheroes threatens to leave him mostly forgotten.

Will Eisner submitted his first professional comic stories to editor Jerry Iger for the comic book *Wow What a Magazine* #1–4 (1936). The comic book failed despite using pages from various artists who went on to greater success, such as Bob Kane and Bernard Baily. This failure prompted Eisner and Iger to start a comic book packaging business whose services were utilized by publishers such as Quality and Fox Comics.[71] Eisner used several pen names for various comic book stories, one of which, *Wonder Man*, caused DC Comics to sue Fox Publications. In 1940, Eisner left the comic book packager and sold his share of the ownership back to Iger to devote his time producing *The Spirit* comic insert section for the Register and Tribune Syndicate, whose owners wanted to compete with comic books.[72] This lucrative contract between Eisner and the syndicate was arranged by Busy Arnold, the publisher of Quality Comics, who co-copyrighted the feature but deferred ownership of *The Spirit*. Eisner worked on *The Spirit* newspaper insert until 1952, after he found stable work for the United States Army producing visual safety manuals for *PS: The Preventative Maintenance Monthly* (1951). Eisner worked on *PS* until 1971 and started licensing his *Spirit* comics. During the final 30 years of his career, he produced and helped pioneer the modern graphic novel format and taught at the School of Visual Arts.[73] He eventually retired and died in 2005 from complications of quadruple bypass surgery at the age of 87,[74] but lived to see comics become the serious narrative that he predicted. His work in pioneering comic storytelling started from *The Spirit* to his later graphic novels and established one of the few legacies in comic books that did not depend on an association with a superhero.

Alex Schomburg was initially a pulp magazine illustrator whose first work can be found on the cover of Better Publications' *Startling Stories* (September 1939).[75] He demonstrated a high aptitude for designing covers published by various Golden Age comic book companies such as Continental, Nedor, and Timely. His covers were noticed at newsstands for containing a hectic degree of action, sex appeal, Nazis, Japanese soldiers, explosions, and weapons of mass destruction. Publishers observed that his covers generally sold well, which kept his work in high demand. It is estimated that he penciled over 200 covers for Martin Goodman's Timely Comics,[76] but similar to other Golden Age comic book artists, Schomburg left the comic book industry with his last known comic book credit listed as *Great Love Romances #2* (1951).[77] He applied his design skills to illustrating covers and interior pages for science-fiction magazines and novels, some of which can be seen in *Son of the Stars* (1952), *Rocket to Luna* (1953), and *Mission to the Moon* (1956), among others. His clean geometric brushwork with landscapes full of crowds and machines were examples of a consistently high standard he held for *Science Fiction Plus, Galaxy, Thrilling Wonder Stories*, and *Ace Books*.[78] He retired but continued to work on cover recreations, and stayed active well into retirement before dying at age 92. Despite his beautiful work in various science-fiction media, he is still commonly celebrated for his Timely Comics' superhero covers.

By the early 1950s, whether it was due to superheroes being generally confined to DC Comics or a fading interest in the genre, many comic book publishers discovered improved sales in the crime, western, romance, shock, teen, funny animal, war, and horror genres. The most talented superhero comic book artists found other commercial fields more lucrative, leaving behind a generation of artists who resorted to sensationalizing the artwork for these other genres in ways that could attract attention at the newsstands. Teen and funny animals sold well, but there was a certain limit with how extreme that art could be depicted; however, crime, shock, horror, and war held different possibilities. To compete in a marketplace that was no longer designed to thrive on superhero theatrics, artists and writers needed to depict shocking imagery on their covers to sell at newsstands. There was one company that outperformed the others, attracting the attention of a psychiatrist who became the bogeyman of comics.

11

EC Comics versus
Fredric Wertham

In the early 1950s, EC Comics was home to comic book artists and writers Wally Wood, Al Williamson, Reed Crandall, Marie Severin, Harvey Kurtzman, and Al Feldstein, among others. These were second-generation comic book creators who entered the industry just as members of the earlier superhero generation were leaving. This group was adept at non-superhero genres geared toward realism and adult sensibilities such as crime, shock, horror, satire, and science fiction. When EC Comics was at its peak, these creators, under publisher Bill Gaines, cohesively produced groundbreaking and intelligent content that challenged the status quo of DC Comics as leader of the comic book industry. They produced titles such as *Shock SuspenStories*, *Weird Science*, *Two-Fisted Tales*, and *Tales from the Crypt* that provided social criticism and delivered high-end anthology comic books for sophisticated readers. This ended by the mid–1950s when their comic books attracted the attention of psychiatrist Fredric Wertham and Senator Estes Kefauver, both willing to demonstrate a point in moral superiority. The origin and conclusion of this confrontation started in 1944 with Bill Gaines's father and ended in the implementation of the Comics Code Authority (1954), with an aftermath that revived superhero comic books.

EC Comics, first known as Educational Comics, was founded by Max Gaines in 1944, after selling his shares in All-American Publications to DC Comics' Harry Donenfeld and Jack Liebowitz.[1] During the sale, Gaines maintained ownership of his comic series *Picture Stories* and published it under his Educational Comics banner depicting biblical and American histories.[2] His idea was to encourage children to learn through the comic book medium, which was celebrated by news outlets but failed to achieve viable sales over its three years.[3] By 1947, Gaines's company was close to $100,000 in debt when he died in a boat crash, leaving his son, Bill Gaines—a chemistry student with goals to become a teacher—hesitantly taking over the company.[4] The young Gaines made a few changes to the company, starting with the name. He changed "Educational Comics" to "Entertaining Comics" and experimented with other genres by publishing the superhero title *Moon Girl* (1947), the magician title *Blackstone the Magician Fights Crime* (1947), a crime title called *International Comics* (1947), and the western title *Gunfighter* (1948). Gaines assessed sales on these titles and used that information to adjust his publishing lineup. *Moon Girl* changed genres over its 12 issues to crime first and then romance. *Blackstone*, based on the magician, lasted for one issue, likely due to the expensive license, and then moved to Timely Comics with the second issue. *Gunfighter* ran for 10 issues. *International Comics* (1947) became *Crime Patrol* by issue #7. Despite the change in titles and genres, these comics still struggled to meet a viable position in the marketplace, and Gaines understood that it would take new talent to procure a feasible strategy.[5]

During Gaines's period of uncertainty, Al Feldstein worked as a penciler and writer at Fox Publications building a sensibility that would save EC. He penciled and wrote teen and good-girl comics such as *Junior* and *Sunny*, featuring leggy curvaceous young women, demonstrating that he understood the juvenile marketplace. Over time, he began to grow troubled by the saturation of the teen market and so applied for work at EC Comics. He was hired as an artist, then proved himself as a writer, and finally became an editor, while also suggesting to Gaines that they should try horror and shock comic books.[6] Gaines understood that EC's crime comics already contained violent endings, so the transition to horror would be a natural one thematically. This conversation between Feldstein and Gaines began EC Comics' "New Trend," so *Crime Patrol* was changed to *Crypt of Terror*, which finally became *Tales from the Crypt* (1950). Another crime title, *War Against Crime*, changed to *Vault of Horror* (1950) with its 12th issue. *Gunfighter* also changed title and genre to *Haunt of Fear* (1950) with its 15th issue. Wally Wood was penciling and inking romance titles with future science-fiction writer Harry Harrison; however, Wood was also penciling science-fiction titles at other companies.[7] Their presence is considered a factor in encouraging Bill Gaines, a fan of science-fiction pulps, namely *Astounding Stories*, to change the content of his low-selling western and romance titles. So, *Saddle Romances* was changed to *Weird Science* (1950) and *A Moon, a Girl...Romance* was changed to *Weird Fantasy* (1950). Their science-fiction comics eventually developed a fanbase for featuring Ray Bradbury stories adapted by Al Feldstein.[8] Despite the superior intellectualism found in science fiction, Gaines and Feldstein noticed that the horror comics consistently performed better, so they consolidated the two titles into one series as *Weird Science-Fantasy* by issue #23 (1954). Coinciding with the onset of the new trend, Gaines also hired writer-cartoonist Harvey Kurtzman, who added social criticism to the EC line of comics. Kurtzman first wrote and penciled the "Hey Look!" strip at Timely Comics under Martin Goodman from 1946 to 1949 and was ready to make a statement. He deconstructed the war genre with two titles, *Two-Fisted Tales* (1950) and *Frontline Combat* (1951). Rather than glorifying war, patriotism, and violence, his message was about the inhumanity of battle, and the government's tendency to take advantage of its soldiers. These issues attracted some scrutiny but are still celebrated by readers who enjoy their political commentary. Kurtzman decided to elevate his social criticism into comedic satire and worked with Bill Gaines to create *MAD* #1 (1952), recruiting the talents of

Will Elder, Wally Wood, and Jack Davis. Kurtzman used the comic to caricature all aspects of society whether it was popular culture or politics, but it was *MAD* #4 (1953) that made the comic book series a big seller.[9] Kurtzman and Wood satirized the legal battle between Detective Comics Inc. and Fawcett Publications in "Super-duperman vs. Captain Marbles."[10] The owners of DC Comics did not appreciate the humor and sent Gaines a cease-and-desist notice; however, parody was protected as fair use, and *MAD* continued uninterrupted.

By 1953, EC Comics and its bullpen produced a diverse line of non-superhero titles, with a motivated group of second-generation comic book writers and artists. There was a sophistication in their comic book line that appealed to both teenagers and adults, resulting in increased sales and profit enjoyed by Gaines. However, the crime and horror line of comic books under Feldstein were violent to the point of attracting a counterproductive form of criticism. *Crime SuspenStories* #17 (1953) vividly depicted a close-up of a man's head shot with a bullet in the same year that the cover to *Tales from the Crypt* #35 (1953) depicted a man brutally mauled in a cemetery. The cover to *Shock SuspenStories* #15 (1954) depicted a buxom woman being strangled while *Crime SuspenStories* #22 (1954) showed a similar woman on its cover, brutally decapitated with an axe.[11] Concerned parental groups took notice of their children buying these comic books at the newsstand and were justifiably upset; so they began to organize mostly under the leadership of neuropsychiatrist Fredric Wertham. Wertham had just appealed to these groups in *Ladies' Home Journal*

Shock Suspenstories #15 (1954) was an example of non-superhero genres at EC Comics depicting violent imagery to attract the attention of readers at newsstands.

(November 1953) with his article "What Parents Don't Know About Comic Books," where he revealed that his studies demonstrated a causative link between violent comic books and juvenile delinquency.

Wertham's article validated the growing anti-comic book anger in the United States, partly due to building trust with parental groups who already understood his history in child psychology. Wertham was the first psychiatrist in the United States to receive the academically celebrated National Research Council Fellowship, for writing his textbook *The Brain as an Organ* (1934), which in 538 pages described the central nervous system in anatomical, histological, physiological, and psychiatric terms. He used collected information from respected scientific journals along with new data from his own research at a New York hospital.[12] As a practitioner, he often performed psychiatric exams for New York criminal courts and acted as chief defense expert witness in 1935 for Albert Fish, aka "The Brooklyn Vampire," who had been arrested and tried for child murder. Reportedly, Fish raped, murdered, and cannibalized up to 100 children, though Wertham's main point in Fish's defense was that he followed an insane form of biblical ideology, which was responsible for his terrifying behavior. Despite Wertham's testimony, Fish was still found sane and guilty, and was eventually executed.[13] Wertham also testified in the case of Robert George Irwin, the "Easter Sunday" murderer who was granted an insanity plea to live his life in a mental institution.[14] In 1941 and later in 1950, Wertham reinterpreted the Lowenfeld Mosaic Test, a visual tool using geometric shapes that was used to diagnose mental disorders such as schizophrenia. Patients were asked to create an image based on the psychiatrist's questions, which was analyzed on a non-scoring-based system as a type of "crazy" detector,[15] and published by the *American Journal of Psychiatry.* He appeared again in another prominent case, *Brown versus the Board of Education of Topeka,* decided upon by the Supreme Court in 1954. In this case, Wertham's psychological study was used to argue that segregated schools were detrimental to children's mental health,[16] with which the court concluded that they were a violation of the equal protection clause.

These events in Wertham's career developed a significant amount of goodwill, which helped convince parental groups and legislators to organize further and intervene against the comic book industry. He used his status to play into the public fear and growing unease from families who complained to politicians that crime comic book covers were too intense for kids. However, many of these critics, including Wertham, were missing the valuable social commentary in EC's comics line. *Shock SuspenStories* #14 (1954) depicted a racist lynch mob accidentally killing their leader's daughter because it was too dark to see. *Frontline Combat* #10 (1953) depicted the tragedy of a young Korean boy watching his parents get killed as collateral wartime damage. *Weird Fantasy* #18 (1953) depicted an African American astronaut informing a racist robot society that they were not ready to be included in a galactic republic. The EC Comics line was eclectic and thought-provoking despite the harsh criticism that Wertham continued to lobby against comics. Regardless of comic books' redeeming qualities, he and other proponents of eliminating comic books gained significant social momentum, which set up the United States Senate Subcommittee on Juvenile Delinquency (USSSJD).

Both Wertham and various comic book publishers calculated their strategies carefully, understanding that the federal government could enact laws that could define which of the two sides held a decisive victory. Wertham published his book *Seduction of the Innocent* (April 1954) two days before the first of three public hearings led by Senator Estes Kefauver, in all likelihood to apply pressure on the result and sell more copies. The hearings involved testimonies of various comic book and comic strip professionals to investigate if there was indeed a link between comic books and juvenile delinquency.[17] Wertham testified using information from his book whereas Bill Gaines also testified, under the influence of Dexedrine, and did not have any satisfactory answers as to why his comics depicted women being murdered.[18] Comic book publishers watched the hearings on their televisions closely as Gaines embarrassed their professional community. They worried about a federal ban on comic books and decided to take measures to minimize the outcome. Publishers John Goldwater of Archie and Jack Liebowitz of DC Comics pushed for a self-censoring system to appease the government and avoid legal regulation.[19] These discussions formed the Comics Code Authority (CCA), a private company that was organized by executives from DC and Archie and administrated by an arbiter by the name of Charles Murphy. The CCA served as a non-federal, private, self-regulatory agency given the role of enforcing a set of rules as to what could and couldn't be included in comics, which included disallowing pro-crime, anti-police, sexual, or horror comic books. When a comic book passed inspection, their covers were given a CCA logo on the top right to demonstrate to newsstands and buyers that they were safe for kids. Having these regulations in place made newsstands less reserved about selling comics, granting the peace of mind to parents that a particular comic book's content would be suitable for children.[20] In response, most comic book publishers obediently adapted to the CCA's regulations. DC Comics and Archie were already printing material compliant with the code while Atlas adjusted its preferred genres and sterilized its content. Those who did not want to adapt their content went out of business since distributors would no longer deliver unapproved content to newsstands whose owners generally demanded that their displayed merchandise adhere to the code. However, adherence to the code also ruined comic book companies' bottom line if they depended on thrilling genres to make sales. Many publishers went out of business, but ironically, by the end of the Kefauver hearings, the senators concluded that there was no association between comic books and juvenile delinquency. Wertham was unhappy with the result because he disagreed with the findings and did not trust the CCA or private industry to police itself.[21]

The CCA was a terrible outcome for EC Comics, which noticed a slow deterioration of its brand over the next year. EC survived on genres and titles that were no longer allowed on newsstands, and their bullpen and fanbase were not positioned to suddenly start resembling DC Comics or Archie. Bill Gaines had no other option but to drop his bestselling horror and crime titles and instead focus on approved themes and code-friendly genres as part of EC's "New Direction." Those new titles were *Impact, Piracy, Valor, M.D., Incredible Science Fiction, Aces High, Extra!,* and *Psychoanalysis,* which were mostly designed to be real-world stories appreciated by mature readers. *Impact* #1 (1955) contained a short story named "Master Race" by Al Feldstein and Bernard Krigstein about a concentration camp survivor who enacted revenge on a former Nazi officer. Despite their quality, these comic books didn't sell due to Gaines's initial refusal to submit them to the CCA. Distributors, wholesalers, and newsstands refused to stock and sell these comics without a CCA logo on the top right of their covers. So, Gaines accepted the code,[22] but still struggled to regain his market share. Comic book distributors sent packages of unsold books with the CCA logo back to Gaines, demonstrating that the distributors and newsstands wanted little to do with EC Comics. There was also ongoing friction between Gaines and the CCA's administrator, Judge Murphy. Their main recorded dispute was mainly over a panel from "Judgement Day" reprinted in *Incredible Science Fiction* #33 (1956), which depicted an African American astronaut who informed a world of racist robots that they were not ready to enter the galactic republic. Gaines threatened a lawsuit, and Murphy relented, approving the story, but it didn't help sales.[23]

Harvey Kurtzman unintentionally discovered a successful method around the CCA, which Gaines unsuccessfully applied to his entire line of publications. Kurtzman resented Feldstein for overseeing the horror and crime comics that attracted the unfavorable financial situation at EC Comics, and diligently continued to edit

EC Comics published thought-provoking stories such as "Master Race" from *Impact* #1 (1955), written by Gaines and Feldstein with pencils by Bernard Krigstein, about a concentration camp survivor who enacted revenge on a former Nazi officer.

and oversee *MAD*. He had received an offer to work at a magazine and leave comic books behind. Instead, he asked Gaines to publish *MAD* as a magazine (1955) for its 24th issue. Gaines did so and discovered that magazines were not under the jurisdiction of the code, which focused exclusively on comic books. This change in medium allowed *MAD* to continue uninterrupted by the CCA's restrictions and contributed to its higher sales.[24] Gaines felt this could be the answer to EC Comics' financial problems and converted his horror, crime, romance, and shock comics into a new magazine series aimed at adult readers called *EC Picto-Fiction* (1955–1956). Gaines commissioned his bullpen artists and writers to produce black-and-white heavily typeset pages with no word balloons for four titles in the series. *Terror Illustrated* continued horror, *Confessions Illustrated* depicted romance, and *Shock Illustrated* depicted shocking morality tales. The first issue of a fourth title, *Crime Illustrated* (1955), depicted a story written by John Larner with artwork by Reed Crandall, about a man who killed his wife and brought her body out to the beach to dispose of it in the ocean. The tide was so strong that her body, which somehow appeared to be smiling, dragged him down with its weight and drowned him. Despite the provocative material, *EC Picto-Fiction* was discontinued after one to two issues after Gaines discovered many of the books were returned to him from the distributors, who hadn't delivered the magazines to newsstands. Gaines speculated that the comic storytelling was too intelligent for most readers[25]; however, it could also have been that the EC logo was no longer welcome by distributors. Another possibility was the heavily typeset format as opposed to the dialogue balloons later used by the successful black-and-white comic magazines produced by Jim Warren such as *Creepy* (1964) and *Eerie* (1966).

The failure of EC signified to Gaines that the mainstream newsstand market of 1956 was not ready for sophisticated comic magazines for adults and engendered a survivalist approach to his style of publishing. Gaines primarily focused on the financially successful *MAD* magazine edited by Harvey Kurtzman while the loss of EC's crime and horror magazines prompted Al Feldstein to work briefly at Atlas with Joe Maneely on *Yellow Claw* #1 (1956). After a dispute with Gaines regarding a percentage of *MAD*'s ownership, Kurtzman left after finishing issue #28 to join Hugh Hefner to start a more sophisticated, slick magazine named *TRUMP* (1957). *TRUMP* featured work from many of the artists at *MAD*, but it encountered a similar fate as Gaines's *EC Picto-Fiction*, ending after two issues.[26] Due to the vacancy left by Kurtzman, Feldstein returned to Gaines, becoming editor of *MAD* starting with issue #29 where he significantly improved the magazine's sales by reducing its sophistication and appealing to the juvenile market.[27] Sales continued to rise through the 1960s, giving Gaines a favorable position in selling *MAD* in 1961, which DC Comics' Independent News purchased in 1964. He sat at its board and continued to manage the magazine with no interference until his death in 1992.[28] Feldstein continued as editor until 1985, and *MAD* eventually ceased publication in 2019. From its inception, EC Comics underwent many transformations, and it was Gaines's managerial agility and the talent of Feldstein and Kurtzman that saved it.

Gaines's positive legacy is in stark contrast to Fredric Wertham's, which is generally negative after weighing the significant errors in *Seduction of the Innocent* against his later mildly redeeming work, *The World of Fanzines* (1973). Scholar Carol Tilley analyzed the data in Wertham's research papers and found significant errors, including intentional omissions that could have invalidated his claims. He selectively sampled patients with a psychological history and used anecdotal data from colleagues as real patient interviews.[29] At the time of the hearings, Senator Kefauver of the USSSJD wrote an interim report that implied a similar conclusion as Tilley. Kefauver documented that his committee did not find any data to conclude that juvenile delinquency increased with reading crime and horror comics and specifically stated that Wertham held a minority opinion on the matter, pointing to other behavioral scientists who disagreed with his position.[30] With Wertham's scientific background, he more than likely understood his own prejudice on the matter as well as his manipulation of the masses to satisfy that prejudice.

This knowledge, when weighed against his other book on popular culture, *The World of Fanzines,* yields a mildly more complex version of the same negative conclusion. Wertham wrote this book to document the teenage fascination with fan magazines or fanzines, including a list of these amateur publications and a decently researched history of science fiction, fantasy fiction, sword and sorcery, comic strips and comic books. He felt that fantasy fiction generally involved the importance of human life celebrating the human spirit as it overcame adversity. In his analysis, he highlighted fanzines around the country as an innovation in communication for the younger generation, and extended his respect to comic book fans who wrote articles in fanzines to connect with one another.[31] He commented they are a "constructive and healthy exercise of creative drives,"[32] and that science-fiction stories foster scientific invention. He also proclaimed that comic books had the benefit of revealing sociological data while also depicting the cultural history of the United States. Interestingly, Wertham also praised Will Eisner for using the comics medium as an effective teaching tool for American military instruction manuals. While Wertham's book focused on the bright side of science fiction, fantasy, and comic books, it isn't a strict apology to comic book enthusiasts. He described that those positive aspects existed in contrast to corporate periodicals whose owners censored material to appeal to the masses and maintained that comic books were commercial, morbid products generated only for profit. Based on his career before the 1950s and what he documented in his 1973 book on fanzines, it's clear that he at some points in his life cared about the psychological welfare of children. Despite being unhappy with comic book regulation occurring through private enterprise, Wertham still achieved an outcome where baby boomers were mainly exposed to child-friendly comic books such as *Archie* and Silver Age *Superman*. Many of those readers still reminisce about those simpler days that would not have occurred without Wertham and the CCA.

The negative effects of the CCA manifested through both short-term and long-term mechanisms. The short-term mechanism was the immediate elimination of struggling comic book publishers, jobs, and distributors whose supply chains were interrupted by the immediate lack of deliverable product.[33] Publishers who depended on horror and crime for their market share either stopped selling comic books or went defunct, including EC Comics, Lev Gleason, Quality, Mainline, Star, Fox, and Nedor. The CCA existed from 1954 to 2011, finally ending due to the growth of the direct market, which bypassed newsstand distributors.[34] However, the strictest years for the CCA were between 1954 and 1972. During this time, the remaining comic book companies, including DC Comics, Atlas, Archie, and Harvey, held enough market share with kid-friendly themes to stay viable. Darker storylines that appealed to an adult sensibility, including crime and horror, were no longer present on newsstands. The remaining genres were the standard superheroes, teen, funny animals, humor, and diluted forms of romance, science fiction, and westerns. Meanwhile, television was becoming more popular and affordable, offering a variety of entertaining genres, which attracted buyers away from the comic book marketplace. The CCA prevented comic book companies from adequately competing with television. It was time for the right innovator to find the correct combination of features that could help the comic book industry find a lucrative path forward.

PART 3

Flight of the Superheroes

Julius Schwartz's Silver Age

After the implementation of the Comics Code Authority (CCA) and the result-ing crash of the comic book industry, the surviving publishers needed a lucrative genre that could compete with the growing medium of variety television. The genres present in the comic book marketplace were the few remaining standard Golden Age superheroes, teen, funny animals, humor, comedy, and diluted forms of romance, science fiction, and westerns. Television threatened to diminish comic book sales by offering the same genres as well as crime, suspense, children's shows, soap operas, talk shows, and musicals. However, it was the availability of standard superheroes at DC Comics that enabled a solution. DC Comics' legal team helped discourage other companies from creating competitors to Superman, Batman, and Wonder Woman, but there was a growing sense from editor Julius Schwartz that something innova-tive could be done with science fiction. His love for the genre originated as a teen-ager with Hugo Gernsback, creator of the first wholly science-fiction-devoted pulp magazine, *Amazing Stories* (April 1926), with cover illustrations by former architect and visual futurist Frank R. Paul.[1] Schwartz enjoyed the community created when Gernsback printed the full names and addresses of readers, empowering them to correspond with one another to form science-fiction clubs. He was one of three read-ers, with Mort Weisinger and Forrest Ackerman, who met in this fashion, starting a fanzine called *The Time Traveler* (1932) and mulling on concepts they'd bring to their later publications.[2] These concepts, discussed between friends, were later used by Schwartz to update the standard formula for superheroes by making them more relatable and prompting a series of creative landmarks at DC Comics that defined the Silver Age of comic books.[3]

Schwartz cultivated his involvement in science-fiction-based comics well before the mid–1950s. While self-publishing *The Time Traveller* fanzine, Schwartz and Weisinger developed a sense for what stories sold well and they established the Solar Sales Service Agency (1934–1944), which functioned to sell manuscripts of science-fiction writers including HP Lovecraft, Ray Bradbury, and Alfred Bester.[4] He spent these years familiarizing himself with science-fiction concepts, pulp mag-azines, and publishing firms, while also helping to organize the first World Science Fiction Convention (1939). These qualifications in all likelihood played a strong role when he was eventually hired as the editor of All-American Comics in 1944, soon to merge with DC, where he wrote, plotted, and edited a series of comic books that generally had some basis in science fiction.[5] During this time, he also hired science-fiction writers for various comic books, including Bester, who wrote the Green Lantern power up chant, which continues to be regularly used.[6]

By the early 1950s, as EC Comics first printed its science-fiction series using the talents of Wally Wood and Harry Harrison, it was Schwartz who explored the genre at DC Comics in *Strange Adventures* (1950) and *Mystery in Space* (1951). These two science-fiction comic books performed reasonably well and provided a creative space for Schwartz to use tropes and concepts from his days as an agent and fan to create new characters and storylines. His close work with John Broome foreshadowed the innovation of a new breed of science-fiction superhero, including two stories in particular that introduced concepts later used in *The X-Men* and *Green Lantern*. "The Origin of Captain Comet" in *Strange Adventures* #9 (1951) used the term "mutant" to describe "a sudden, unexpected change in the natural, slow development of a species."[7] The second story concerned the character Captain Comet and his dealings with the Guardians of the Universe in *Strange Adventures* #22 (1952),[8] a label the creative team used for the Guardians of Oa in *Green Lantern* #1 (1960).

Meanwhile, DC Comics' first science-fiction superhero, Superman, overseen by editor Mort Weisinger, maintained marketplace relevance due to two changes that occurred in both television and comic books. The first was the success of the *Adventures of Superman* television series (1952–1958), starring George Reeves.[9] This show was made possible after gaining the sponsorship of Kellogg, which was available after the end of *The Adventures of Superman* radio show (1940–1951) and the interest generated by the film pilot, *Superman and the Mole Men* (1951). The second event occurred when Mort Weisinger hired science-fiction writer Otto Binder to contribute to the character's mythos in *Superman's Pal Jimmy Olsen* #1 (1954). His concepts, combined with the slick New York line[10] of Curt Swan's pencils and Ray Burnley's inks, solidified a wholesome visual standard at DC Comics of the 1950s. Binder was available to launch the successful title after his former employer, Fawcett, ceased to publish comic books after losing the copyright infringement lawsuit to DC Comics. He pioneered storylines for the Superman line of comics while introducing plots and characters that he previously used for *Captain Marvel Adventures*, such as creating Mary Marvel in 1942, then Supergirl in 1958. The world's first superhero managed to avoid becoming obsolete during the Television Age of comic books, but it was specifically the success of the television show and addition of science-fiction writer Otto Binder that made Superman, the Hercules of the DC pantheon, ready to enter the Silver Age.

Science fiction was a valid direction toward improving comic book marketplace viability, as opposed to saturating readers further with other post-comics code storylines of Knights or Robin Hood. Editors began to realize that the genre could be both thought provoking and kid-friendly, which could ideally be used to create more superheroes. DC editor Jack Schiff oversaw the first issue of a science-fiction superhero created by Joseph Samachson and Joe Certa in "The Strange Experiment of Dr. Erdel" from *Detective Comics* #225 (1955). This backup story introduced the Martian Manhunter, J'onn J'onzz, the last surviving shape-shifting Martian who fought crime on Earth.[11] His powers and origin appear inspired by Ray Bradbury's *The Martian Chronicles* (1950) about a mostly extinct race of telepathic shape-changing Martians. The character's first appearance was mildly appreciated by readers but was not considered a critical success. So, Editorial Director Irwin Donenfeld needed an editor with experience in the genre to further the superhero concept, and wisely selected Julius Schwartz.[12]

Schwartz solved the problem by retconning Golden Age superheroes such as the Flash, using 1950s-era science-fiction transformations on average human beings who accepted their powers with humility. This began with *Showcase* #4 (1956), introducing a new Flash by the name of Barry Allen, written with a stronger science-fiction origin than his 1940s counterpart. Jay Garrick, the original Flash, created by Gardner Fox and Harry Lampert, acquired speed powers when he inhaled hard water vapor during a smoking break,[13] a concept that became more absurd with time. For the 1956 retcon, Schwartz assembled the talents of Robert Kanigher, Carmine Infantino, and Joe Kubert to depict a new speed-power origin where lightning and nearby chemicals initiated a metabolic change in Barry Allen's body.[14] Gaining abilities from a more believable science-fiction event was only one aspect to the character. Schwartz required a relatable human factor and originated the character's name by combining those of two television hosts, Barry Gray and Steve Allen.[15] Under Schwartz, Barry Allen emerged as an average man who unpretentiously discovered his abilities over several issues. His shock and surprise at various aspects of his speed powers became an engrossing and reoccurring theme in the series, as he faced new science-fiction-based villains. This new approach to the superhero was validated with escalating sales, demonstrating that comic books can thrive within the narrow confines of the CCA. Under Schwartz's supervision, Gardner Fox, the original writer of the 1940s hard water inhalation origin, and Infantino elevated the series by introducing the multiverse in *Flash* #123 (1961).[16] This story started the innovative concept of Earth Two about another reality where the Golden Age comic book heroes aged in real time. The plotline utilized the growing field of quantum mechanics when the Flash vibrated quickly enough to alter his resonant frequency to match and enter Earth Two in a manner that stayed consistent with wave-particle duality. Barry Allen expressed shock and wonder while exploring Earth Two and meeting Jay Garrick, the Flash from the 1940s. This story added intriguing possibilities for writers and fans since the two versions of the same character could now interact. Readers began to understand that there were new scenarios to discover with Schwartz's inventive approach to the superhero.

Soon, science-fiction-based superpowers accepted with humility became the new formula for DC's upcoming superhero origins of the Silver Age. Schwartz oversaw the work of John Broome and Gil Kane, who applied this formula to retconning

Julius Schwartz's retcon of the Flash in *Showcase* #4 (1956) depicted relatable humans who were surprised by their new science-fiction-based powers.

a new Green Lantern, the pilot named Hal Jordan in *Showcase* #22 (1959). Although Jordan was known for being fearless, he still demonstrated humility when approaching new situations with an open mind. Kane modeled the appearance of Jordan from the famous actor Paul Newman,[17] with a costume design that was sleek, skintight, aerodynamic, and continues to be used. Broome also scripted an updated origin, which appeared consistent with science-fiction pulp magazines. Instead of using the magic lantern wielded by the Golden Age Green Lantern in *All-American Comics* #16 (1940) by Bill Finger and Martin Nodell, Schwartz oversaw Broome and Kane introducing concepts in line with the Grey Lensmen pulp series, created in 1934 by Edward Smith, Ph.D., for *Amazing Stories*. The Lensmen were a Galactic Patrol of members deemed worthy to have a power lens attached to their hand. This piece of technology transmitted energy and translated interstellar languages in the group's mission to defend civilization and stand up for truth, law, and order. These aspects of the Lensmen were present in the new *Green Lantern*,[18] who met a dying alien that gave him his light ring, establishing him as the Apollo of the DC pantheon. He channeled his ring using willpower and protected Earth as part of a galactic patrol called the Green Lantern Corps, overseen by the Guardians of the Universe. His comic book adventures as a fearless pilot in space were in keeping with the space race against the Soviet Union and the fearlessness demonstrated by heroes of the era such as John Glenn, the first American pilot and astronaut to orbit earth, in 1962.[19] That same year, Schwartz had his two retconned superheroes interact in a shared universe in two issues by writer John Broome, *Green Lantern* #13, depicted by Kane, and *Flash* #131, depicted by Infantino. Julius Schwartz commented that he encouraged team-ups and enjoyed them since he was younger, reading Street & Smith pulp magazines that included crossovers such as that of Frank and Dick Merriwell or Rafferty and Chang in *Detective Story*. Schwartz proclaimed, "Individually they were great; together they were super!"[20] Superhero team-ups such as that seen between Flash and Green Lantern are a plot device that continues to be utilized across various media.

Other creative teams began to retcon or reinvent superheroes at DC Comics after the success of Julius Schwartz's approach to his comic book line became evident.[21] Wonder Woman first appeared in *All Star Comics* #8 (1942), created by professor and polyamorous psychologist William Moulton Marston for All-American Publications. Her penciler was Harry G. Peter, whose talent was also seen during this period depicting another female hero, Invisible Scarlet O'Neil, for the cover of *Famous Funnies* #81 (1941). Marston and Peter depicted Wonder Woman as a warrior whose physical strength and quest for truth eventually earned her the position as the Athena of DC's pantheon. Despite Professor Marston's death in 1947[22] and his replacement by Robert Kanigher as writer, *Wonder Woman* maintained a stable visual continuity due to the consistent pencils of Harry Peter. Peter continued to draw the series for 16 years until he was replaced by Ross Andru and Mike Esposito in *Wonder Woman* #98 (1958). Andru and Esposito were two artists who worked together on the company's war books, and their contemporary approach to the art, with Robert Kanigher's scripts, updated the series for the Silver Age. A similar reinvention occurred with Aquaman, who was created by Mort Weisinger in *More Fun Comics* #73 (1941) as Arthur Curry, the son of an ocean explorer who gave his son the ancient Atlantean secret to breathe underwater.[23] Eighteen years later, Weisinger was editor and oversaw a retcon of the character's origin by writer Robert Bernstein and penciler Ramona Fradon for the backup section to *Adventure Comics* #260 (1959). Curry became the son of Tom Curry, a lighthouse attendant who impregnated Atlanna, a water-breathing citizen of Atlantis. Aquaman was now a hybrid mutant, instead of a boy experimented on by his father, making this updated origin similar to that of Namor, the Sub-Mariner, depicted by Bill Everett for *Marvel Comics* #1 (1939).[24] This more-believable science-fiction source of Aquaman's super strength placed him as the Neptune of DC's pantheon in the Silver Age. Weisinger also oversaw the reinvention of Green Arrow, whom he originally created in *More Fun Comics* #73 (1941) after watching the Columbia Pictures serial *The Green Archer* (1940). In the Golden Age, Green Arrow was Oliver Queen, an archaeologist who studied Native American culture and learned to use a bow and arrow while combating criminals who sought a buried treasure. Eighteen years later, Queen's origin was retconned by Jack Kirby and Ed Herron in *Adventure Comics* #256 (1959), depicting the hero as a billionaire who was stranded on an island and survived by learning to hunt with a bow and arrow.[25] Many readers consider this Silver Age origin by Kirby and Herron to be more believable, likely contributing to its continued use in various media.

Schwartz assembled these retconned and reinvented superheroes into one team, the Justice League of America (JLA), with writer Gardner Fox and penciler Mike Sekowsky in *The Brave and the Bold* #28 (1960). This issue served as a science-fiction-based reinvigoration of the Golden Age *Justice Society of America* comic book series, and featured the Flash, Wonder Woman, Martian Manhunter, Aquaman, and Green Lantern, who defeated an invasion from the giant alien monster "Starro the Conqueror" by encasing it in calcium oxide. Schwartz demonstrated that the alien invasion storyline functioned smoothly as a justification to unify superheroes into one team, which became a plot often mimicked in other superhero team-ups. He also changed the team's title to include the term "League" as a way to connect with casual readers who may have felt the term "Society" indicated "High Society"[26] because he wanted the team to emphasize compassion rather than status. This type of relatability to baby boomer youth culture was a high priority due to their considerable spending patterns, which Schwartz appealed to with the team's sidekick, Snapper Carr.[27] Carr was based on a recommendation by executive editor and television show producer Whitney Ellsworth, who recommended that Schwartz make the character resemble the actor, Edd Byrnes, who snapped his fingers in a similar way in the television show *77 Sunset Strip*.[28] Carr's innocent and hopeful disposition also epitomized an excitement about the future, inherent to many Silver Age comic books of the early 1960s. These marketable traits from the JLA team-up were successful enough to encourage the publication of an ongoing series starting with *Justice League of America* #1 (1960).

Schwartz's success at retconning Golden Age characters using science fiction led to developing more characters with the same formula. Originally, Hawkman and Hawkgirl were reincarnations of Egyptian royalty in *Flash Comics* #1 (1940) by Gardner Fox and Dennis Neville.[29] The magic-based origin that adhered to an Eastern mystique was given a Silver Age science-fiction reinvention 21 years later in *Brave and Bold* #34 (1961) with art by Joe Kubert. Schwartz and Fox conceptualized the winged duo as alien policemen from the planet Thanagar who hunted shape-shifting intergalactic criminals.[30] As opposed to magic and reincarnation, the interstellar adventures of the Silver Age Hawkman and Hawkgirl were more aligned with readers' interests in 1961, the same year that Alan Shepard became the first American astronaut to travel to space.[31] Schwartz and Fox also retconned another Golden Age hero, the Atom, a miniature masked adventurer who premiered in *All-American Comics* #19 (1940) by writer Bill O'Connor and artist Ben Flinton.[32] The character was originally Al Pratt, a trained boxer who strove to fight crime despite being short. Twenty-one years later, comic book fan Jerry Bails pitched a new version of the Atom to Schwartz, who processed the idea with Fox to debut in *Showcase* #34 (1961) with art by Gil Kane.[33] The Silver Age Atom became physicist Ray Palmer, who developed the ability to shrink using "white dwarf star matter." Palmer was named after a friend of Schwartz, who was a diminutive former editor of *Amazing Stories*.[34] Gil Kane's design of the costume was arguably sleeker than the one he made for Green Lantern, with a heroic red-and-blue pattern and atomic logo on the forehead.

Schwartz also created an original science-fiction hero and outer space adventurer, Adam Strange, whose series unknowingly helped organize the first comic book convention. Schwartz wrote Strange as a compassionate archaeologist who used a zeta beam to travel 25 trillion miles to the planet Rann, the locale of many of his adventures. The character's first name was taken from the book of Genesis, and the comic book probably retained some influence from Alex Raymond's *Flash Gordon* due to the hero's blond hair, adventures on an alien world, and his brunette girlfriend. Murphy Anderson designed the character, then Gil Kane penciled the cover of his first appearance in *Showcase* #17 (1958) with the script by Gardner Fox and interior pencils by Mike Sekowsky. Adam Strange appeared in three consecutive issues of *Showcase* before being featured regularly in *Mystery in Space* #53 (1959) when Carmine Infantino became the ongoing penciler.[35] The series is said to have reached its peak artistry with the addition of inker Murphy Anderson for issue #56. The stories by Schwartz and Fox maintained thought-provoking originality, including a plotline featuring aliens named "Eternals" in *Showcase* #17 (1958) by Fox and Sekowsky.[36] This name may have echoed to Jack Kirby, who used the same name in his later Marvel series *The Eternals* (1976). *Mystery in Space* #72 (1961) may be considered the peak of the series for two reasons. The first reason is the visuals depicted when Strange was abducted by a zeta beam into a futuristic New York cityscape, rendered with innovative architectural design, perspective, and detail by Infantino and Anderson.[37] These panoramic layouts enabled readers to escape into the fictional storylines presented in this series, which proved to regularly contain a sophisticated visual experience. That second reason was the letters page, "Rocket Mail," where comic fan GB Love commented, "I have a science-fiction club organized and if any of your readers would like to join, they can write me." Schwartz replied suggesting their name could be the same as his old club, "The Scienceers," and printed Love's address.[38] Fans read this interaction and mailed letters of enthusiasm to Love's address, which enabled him to start his *Rocket Blast* (1961) fanzine. It later merged with Jerry Bails's *Comic Collector* fanzine in 1964, consolidating both mailing lists, which in the same year helped organize the first official comic conventions, the New York Comic Art Convention and the Detroit Triple Fan Fair.[39]

Schwartz's affinity for science-fiction characters and retcons proved marketable, so he was asked to modernize more characters. By 1964, *Batman* was losing its market share under editor Jack Schiff. The science-fiction and fantasy stories depicted by Dave Wood, Bill Finger, Bob Kane, and his ghost artist Sheldon Moldoff had become dated. Irwin Donenfeld ordered that Schiff and Schwartz switch editorial duties to save *Batman* in exchange for *Mystery in Space*. Alongside Carmine Infantino, Schwartz aimed to revitalize the *Batman* series and deliver a "New Look," defined by returning the character to his relatable human roots, with a visual redesign and yellow Bat logo.[40] He eliminated Bat-Mite, Bat-Hound, and the science-fiction storylines to return the series' genre to crime and emphasize Batman's role as a detective solving mysteries. Schwartz announced his plans for the series in his first issue,

Detective Comics #327 (1964), promoting the "slicker more dramatic style of story-telling" of John Broome and Carmine Infantino. He also revealed that Bill Finger, not Bob Kane, had "written most of the classic Batman adventures of the past two decades,"[41] which damaged Kane's pride as his creative input to the title was terminated. By providing a new creative team and debunking the Golden Age myth of Kane's exaggerated legacy, Schwartz effectively brought Batman, the DC pantheon's underworld Pluto, into the Silver Age. In exchange, Schiff became editor of *Mystery in Space* with issue #92, which demonstrated an immediate reduction in quality.[42] What many considered to be Infantino's potent interior pencils were replaced by stilted efforts from Lee Elias, as the title's bright yellow banner was changed into a dull red. Fans also noticed the cover that previously depicted the proud figure of Adam Strange then displayed a flawed design with Schiff's Space Ranger on the following issue. These and other choices by Schiff caused a decline in sales of *Mystery in Space*, leading to its cancellation by issue #110 (1966). Schwartz also modernized another Golden Age character, the Spectre, who first appeared in *More Fun Comics* #52 (1940), created by Jerry Siegel and Bernard Baily. Detective Jim Corrigan was killed by criminals, placed into a barrel of cement, and deposited in a river; however, "The Voice" revived him as a spirit of vengeance.[43] Twenty-six years later, likely to pass the CCA's review committee, Schwartz directed Gardner Fox and Murphy Anderson to deemphasize the crime genre and highlight the relatability of the Spectre's human alter ego in contrast with the morbid aspects of his powers in *Showcase* #60 (1966). Their story involved a Silver Age version of Jim Corrigan, whose body contained the Spectre lying dormant for years. During a séance, the Spectre is released, anxious to find the cause of his dormancy.[44] He tracks down the demon Azmodus, ascends into the astral plane, and takes part in a celestial battle where the Spectre emerged victorious.

During the Silver Age, other editors also developed new ideas that emphasized humanity and were compliant with the CCA, including the creation of eccentric characters and unconventional superheroes. Many of these were products of brainstorming sessions held by Editorial Director Irwin Donenfeld, who previously tasked Schwartz to save a comic book series when it demonstrated reduced sales. Schwartz's success was probably a motivator for editors who needed to maintain or elevate their comic title's market share. Mort Weisinger, an old friend from their days in science-fiction fandom, probably noticed his success, spurring an expansion of the *Superman* line of comic books. This can be suspected when comparing the difference in outcomes between what he edited on *Showcase* #1, before Schwartz's success with the Flash, as compared with after. Issue #1, by writer Arnold Drake and penciler John Prentice, featured three adventures of Fireman Farrell, a character that failed to impress readers and was soon discontinued. However, after Schwartz's success with the first two Flash adventures in issues #4 and #8, Weisinger returned to the series with issue #9 introducing the concept *Superman's Girl Friend Lois Lane*, written by Jerry Coleman and penciled by Ruben Moreira. It was an attempt to spotlight

Lane and attract more female readers. Although it may have given adolescent readers an interesting relationship to ponder, the book, along with many others of the Silver Age, were generally asexual. This book was not meant to be in the romance genre, which the title implies by breaking up the term "girl friend" into two words. Along with *Superman's Pal Jimmie Olsen*, these two books contained kid-friendly situations and emphasized Superman's human characteristics through his interactions with his friends. *Lois Lane* was successful enough to earn its own title and continued successfully for 16 years, although it would have been more memorable if a woman was invited to write the character. Weisinger also expanded the *Superman* mythos by collaborating with writer Otto Binder and artist Al Plastino to further explore its science-fiction storylines and create "The Legion of Superheroes," a team of superpowered teenagers who traveled back in time for Superboy's help in *Adventure Comics* #247 (1958).[45] By setting the team in the 30th century, there was less concern with DC continuity because the Legion's adventures were often contained in the future.

Editor Jack Schiff and his successor, Jack Miller, also oversaw the creation of new unconventional heroes during the Silver Age, such as the Challengers of the Unknown, Animal Man, and Deadman. Schiff accepted a plot that Jack Kirby previously discussed with Joe Simon about four risk-takers who formed a group after a shared near-death experience. He assigned the plot to both Kirby and scriptwriter Dave Wood to create the Challengers of the Unknown for *Showcase* #6 (1957).[46] This template of characters proved successful enough with readers to earn its own title and was used again by Jack Kirby to cocreate *The Fantastic Four* (1961) with Stan Lee at Marvel. Schiff also oversaw the creation of another atypical hero, Animal Man, in *Strange Adventures* #180 (1965), with pencils by Infantino and inks by George Roussos, whose brushwork was rough compared with inkers Murphy Anderson and Joe Giella. Dave Wood wrote the script about a spaceship that crashed near a zoo and released radiation onto innocent bystander Buddy Baker,[47] giving him animal-based super abilities. The character received a costume in issue #190 and ceased to be used during this period after issue #201. *Strange Adventures* was Schiff's last remaining title, from which he retired after 25 years with the company following the cancellation of *Mystery in Space* in 1966. He was replaced by romance comics editor Jack Miller, who oversaw the creation of another character that was considered by fans to be an eccentric analogue to the Spectre. During this time, Infantino's popularity steadily elevated since his pencils were linked to many of DC Comics' successes, prompting his promotion to the role of editorial art director. Despite the increased workload, he still managed to cocreate another character, written by Arnold Drake and inked by Roussos, called Deadman for *Strange Adventures* #205 (1967). Deadman was a circus acrobat by the name of Boston Brand who was shot and killed by a sniper, only to be revived as a ghost by the spirit of the universe, Rama Kushna, who sent him back to Earth to find his murderer, known by his hooked hand.[48]

Editors Robert Kanigher, Murray Boltinoff, and George Kashdan additionally oversaw the creation of more eccentric superheroes and unpredictable team-ups such as the Metal Men, Doom Patrol, Teen Titans, and Metamorpho. Four years after the visual reinvention of *Wonder Woman*, Kanigher wrote and created the Metal Men with art team Andru and Esposito in *Showcase* #37 (1962). The Metal Men were a group of emotional robots in service to their loving master, Doc Magnus. Each character was named after a different metal with a different ability. Thick-headed Iron was super strong, the leader Gold could stretch, Lead was impervious to radiation, and Mercury melted,[49] demonstrating that their unconventional powers and repertoire incorporated a fascination with inorganic chemistry. The group's diverse interpersonal dynamic was comparable to that seen with another team, the Doom Patrol under editor Murray Boltinoff, who oversaw their creation by writers Arnold Drake and Bob Haney in *My Greatest Adventure* #80 (1963) with pencils by Bruno Premiani. This team consisted of four young deformed superpowered individuals unified under their wheelchair-using leader, Dr. Niles Caulder. Drake was a literary talent who is credited as cowriting one of the early graphic novels, *It Rhymes with Lust* (1950), and applied his acumen toward *The Doom Patrol*, which many fans consider a highly intelligent series containing both action and comedy. Premiani penciled the series using the slick New York line of the DC house style but added his distinctly unique approach to cartooning, and after an innovative five years, the characters were killed by their nemesis, Captain Zahl, in issue #121 (1968).[50] One unusual legacy of the team was its similarities to *The X-Men*, including the cover banner depicting "The Strangest Super-Heroes of All!" paralleling the banner for *The Doom Patrol* proclaiming "The World's Strangest Heroes!" Both teams were also led by a wheelchair-using professor, but the reason for this resemblance remains unknown, as the two series were initially published close to the same time. Another coincidence was that the two comic books shared the same writer. Drake left DC soon after his final issue of *The Doom Patrol* and, coincidentally, was hired by Stan Lee to write *The X-Men* from issues #47–54 (1968).

Former Drake editor Boltinoff also oversaw another unusual team-up, the formation of the Teen Titans in *The Brave and the Bold* #54 (1964), written by Haney with art by Premiani. Haney's storyline appealed to youth culture by gathering teenage sidekicks Robin, Flash, and Aqualad while depicting the generation gap between adults and teenagers in protest of one another. Adults were shown holding up signs with the phrase "Adults have rights, too" and teenagers similarly held ones that responded "Nix the curfew."[51] This was likely Haney's method of depicting protests in a manner that obeyed the CCA in a simple story where the sidekicks assemble to defeat an elderly Mr. Twister, which somehow addressed the conflict between the two generations, resulting in signs that proclaimed, "Adults we love 'em."[52] Wonder Girl joined the Teen Titans in their second appearance in *The Brave and the Bold* #60 (1965), written by Haney and edited by George Kashdan, which featured their battle with the Separated Man on "Teen Day" while utilizing the aid of local surfers. Overseen by Kashdan, Haney created another unusual character, Metamorpho, the Element Man in *The Brave and the Bold* #57 (1964), penciled by Ramona Fradon. Metamorpho was adventurer Rex Mason, who received the power to chemically change his body from exposure to a radioactive meteorite from the Egyptian Orb of Ra. The hero was popular enough to receive his own series, which parodied superheroes[53] and fully utilized Haney's imagination and Fradon's ability to both cartoon physical caricatures and illustrate anatomy.

By the end of the 1960s, the DC Universe demonstrated a new generation of superheroes, but changes in corporate ownership and narrative styles signified that the Silver Age would soon reach completion. Schwartz appeared to be a successful constant at DC, but the exit of Jack Schiff was the first of many upcoming alterations in the bullpen environment. Schiff's last credit was *Strange Adventures* #203 (1967), and a recently hired Neal Adams penciled the series from issue #206–216. Adams's well-received illustrative style was a factor in DC Comics' shift away from cartoon realism toward the stylized realism of newer artists such as Bernie Wrightson, Michael Kaluta, and Howard Chaykin. Further changes occurred in the same year when Jack Liebowitz and Irwin Donenfeld decided to sell DC Comics to Kinney National Services. This involved the complete exit of Bob Kane, who demanded compensation due to his ownership of Batman. To complete the business arrangement with Kinney, Liebowitz paid Kane $1 million and an additional $50,000 per year for 20 years. Both Kane's ghost penciler, Sheldon Moldoff, and writer, Arnold Drake, were fired at this point, possibly for demanding more benefits and health insurance.[54] So, Moldoff turned in his final pages for *Batman* #199 and *Detective Comics* #372 (1968).[55] Donenfeld unhappily departed shortly after DC's sale to Kinney was completed, whereas Liebowitz maintained his position on the board of directors. Vacancies left behind by exiting veterans were soon filled by new hires such as Denny O'Neil and Mike Friedrich. O'Neil was a 29-year-old counter-culturalist who wrote new perspectives about young adults that Schwartz previously tried to capture with Snapper Carr. O'Neil deconstructed the teenage sidekick in "Snapper Carr, Super-Traitor!" from *Justice League of America* #77 (1969) as an intensely jealous fan of the super team. In the story, Carr was convinced by the Joker, disguised as a political extremist, that superheroes were bad for normal America, and when his traitorous plans were discovered, he cursed the JLA for not being normal enough.[56] Friedrich was a writer who, similar to O'Neil, carried tendencies toward alternative culture, which was later demonstrated by his independent comic series, *Star*Reach* (1974).[57] His first published work was *The Spectre* #3 (1968), a psychedelic astral avenging story penciled by Neal Adams involving JSA member Wildcat. He soon wrote a suspense story depicting the return of the Phantom Stranger, who was on the trail of an evil cult in *Showcase* #80 (1969). The character hadn't been used since 1953, and his reappearance as well as the subject matter signaled a departure from the lighthearted super heroics of the Silver Age. *Batman* #217 (1969) also depicted a new direction for the character, written by Frank Robbins with cover art by Neal Adams and interiors by Irv Novick. The story titled "One Bullet Too Many!" featured

Neal Adams's approach to illustrating superheroes in the late 1960s shifted DC Comics' house style away from cartoon realism toward stylized realism.

Robin leaving Wayne Manor for college at Hudson University,[58] which led Batman to embark on solo adventures that returned the character to his darker roots.

The end of the Silver Age for DC Comics occurred with two events that began the Bronze Age; one was a narrative shift, and the other was a significant staff change in the bullpen, which established Schwartz's final editing position until he retired. The narrative delineation occurred when Schwartz oversaw and edited *Green Lantern/Green Arrow* #76 (1970), written by Denny O'Neil with art by Neal Adams. Adams was eager to follow in the footsteps of Gil Kane, who cocreated the ringed hero, and O'Neil was intent on critically examining the United States social system. Schwartz supervised both creators as science fiction was deemphasized while the green superheroes undertook a road trip analyzing race, pollution, and politics. The stories were memorable and signaled the beginning of social relevance in superhero comic books, but the series under this direction sold poorly. Shortly after, Mort Weisinger retired after close to 30 years, ending with *Superman* #231 (1970), and was replaced by Schwartz due to his reliability in modernizing superheroes. He edited this line of comic books until 1986, in which he became known for asking writers to emphasize character-driven storylines rather than gimmicks.[59] *Superman* was rebooted during *Crisis on Infinite Earths* (1986), a miniseries that brought an editorial change with John Byrne; however, there was one final classic Superman adventure in "Whatever happened to the Man of Tomorrow?" by artist Curt Swan and writer Alan Moore. This two-issue arc depicted the final Superman story, an imaginary tale that crossed over between *Superman* #423 (1986) and *Action Comics* #583 (1986), which brought the Schwartz-era Superman to its conclusion. Various supervillains destroyed metropolis, killed the hero's friends, and erased his powers. The character settled down, married Lois Lane, and retired to civilian life. Fans said goodbye to the old Superman as Schwartz was seen waving on the cover of the second issue, departing his position at DC as a successful editor after four decades.

Schwartz made superheroes more relatable by retconning Golden Age characters and incorporating humility and believable science fiction. His characters generally started out human and gained their powers through an accident of science that began their journey to understanding themselves and their powers. There were a couple of exceptions in the case of Batman and the Spectre, whose character identities mattered more to Schwartz over his own predilection toward science fiction. However, when one examines his work on those two superheroes closely, he still maintained a humanistic approach. The sales reports from his innovations brought him more assignments and encouraged other editors to create more relatable superheroes that generally had powers based in science fiction. By 1960, comic books demonstrated a genre that thrived within the narrow confines of the CCA and still competed with the medium of variety television, which didn't yet have the special effects to keep pace. However, the relatability of each superhero was tempered with the conformity of the Eisenhower era and much of the dialogue appeared similar. If one were to suspend disbelief, it would appear that these superheroes all spoke alike. Something was still missing and a creative team from a rival comic book company would take the relatability of the 1950s superheroes to an entirely new standard in the 1960s by featuring characters with a diverse array of flaws and imperfections.

The Birth of the Marvel Comics Group

Marvel Comics was initially built to compete with Julius Schwartz's relatable superheroes that were powered by accidents of science, after Publisher Martin Goodman directed editor Stan Lee to follow market trends and try something similar.[1] In turn, Lee utilized the talents of artists Jack Kirby and Steve Ditko to go further with Schwartz's concept by creating flawed superheroes. Their approach was more aggressive, related to the conditions in which the two organizations' fictional universes were created. Schwartz oversaw the creation of his relatable superheroes from the comfortable position of working at DC, a company that won its market share by using legal maneuvers to monopolize the genre. In comparison, Lee and the others were industry underdogs who created their imperfect superheroes in unfavorable circumstances, due to a distribution implosion. It was in this difficult environment that Goodman, Lee, Kirby, and Ditko, among others, set key milestones that established the Marvel Comics Group.

Goodman's first role in unknowingly establishing the Marvel Comics Group was the total abandonment of his distributor, Atlas News Company, which was followed by a series of significant misfortunes. Goodman created Atlas to bring his magazines and comics directly to newsstands, but he dissolved Atlas in 1956, possibly due to increasing overhead, and signed to distribute his comics through the powerful American News Company (ANC).[2] This plan failed because ANC soon became nonviable after two significant losses: losing a Justice Department antitrust lawsuit and failing to retain a lucrative contract with Dell. Goodman quickly realized his mistake, but it was too late and wasted one to two months of comic book publication. To quickly get his comics back into the marketplace, he resorted to distributing through Independent News (IND), which was owned by his primary competition, DC Comics' Harry Donenfeld and Jack Liebowitz. IND agreed to distribute eight monthly titles, drastically reducing Goodman's comic book output from its previous 80.[3] Stan Lee as editor-in-chief adapted to the new distribution schedule by converting the number into 16 bimonthly titles to create diversity and use up preexisting comics inventory, but also reducing job opportunities for many artists and writers. This event is referred to as the 1957 Atlas Implosion as the Atlas logo was eliminated from covers of the comic book line and replaced by the initial's "IND."[4] For example, *Gunsmoke Western* #42 (August 1957) had an Atlas distributor logo on the cover, which was replaced by IND on issue #43 (November 1957).[5] During this period, Lee still provided work for quick and necessary art assignments to artists such as Joe Maneely and Matt Baker, but this arrangement ended when both died soon after. Maneely died in a train incident in 1958[6] and Matt Baker from a heart attack in 1959.[7]

From Lee's perspective, Goodman, his second cousin by marriage, put the comics line under significant financial and creative strain, and he would soon understand that his circuitous intersections with Jack Kirby would prove to be a company lifeline. Lee experienced several uncertainties at the company since he was hired at 17 years old. He went to DeWitt Clinton High School, same as Bob Kane and Will Eisner, who had a flair for interacting with people.[8] His first assignment in comics was as an assistant to Joe Simon and Jack Kirby while they were producing *Captain America Comics* (1941). Lee's first creative assignment was a text insert in issue #3, scripting the first time the hero's shield was thrown as an offensive weapon.[9] This was an innovative idea, prompted after viewing the kinetics of Kirby's pages. Lee was five years younger than Kirby, who drew pictures since childhood to escape the harsh realities of Brooklyn life in the 1920s and 1930s.[10]

Kirby's prior experience in comics started when he had been hired as a strip artist by the Lincoln Newspaper Syndicate and as an "animation in-betweener" on Max Fleischer's *Popeye* cartoons.[11] In 1938, he first transitioned to penciling comic books in a wide range of genres for the Eisner and Iger shop,[12] and later found work at Fox Publications, where he met editor Joe Simon.[13] The two creators connected and started a business association under the byline "Simon and Kirby." Simon was originally an artist in newspapers and editorial cartoons,[14] and began his career in comic books in late 1930s with editor Lloyd Jacquet at Funnies Inc., which packaged *Marvel Comics* #1 (1939). Simon created the "Fiery Mask" for Timely Comics and was eventually hired by Goodman to work as editor.[15] Kirby followed Simon to Timely and penciled "Mercury" for *Red Raven Comics* #1 (1940), written by Martin A. Bursten. The plot centered on the Roman god of speed, adventuring through international and geopolitical events, dealing with Nazi Germany and Adolf Hitler.[16] Analyzing global politics came naturally to Kirby, ever since cartooning a criticism of Neville Chamberlain's gullibility regarding Hitler's intentions in 1939 for the Lincoln Newspaper Syndicate.[17] He was a natural pairing with Bursten, who later left comics for a political career.[18] Their commentary on the rise of fascism in Europe made a statement at Timely that was further emphasized when Simon and Kirby depicted their innovative new hero punching Hitler in the jaw on the cover of *Captain America Comics* #1 (1941). The red, white, and blue patriot became the superhero for Timely that Superman was for DC Comics.

However, in the early 1940s Goodman made monetary decisions that resulted in Lee's career advancement at the expense of Simon and Kirby, which also necessitated Lee to manage a series of uncertain situations at the company. The profits were high

Jack Kirby's first job for Timely Comics commented on the rise of fascism in Nazi Germany for *Red Raven Comics* #1 (1940).

from *Captain America Comics*, but Goodman withheld the sales figures from the series creators' salaries, causing Simon and Kirby to seek a better deal with competitor Harry Donenfeld to headline a similar success for Detective Comics Inc.[19] Goodman discovered their discussions with his competitor and fired them. Their exit prompted Lee's entry to management, which was announced in *Writer's Digest* (February 1942): "The comics belonging to the Red Circle group are now edited by Stan Lee, who replaces Joe Simon."[20] This was an adjustment for Lee, who needed to quickly adapt to a role that was initially meant to be temporary. He spent a short time away when he was drafted for World War II and replaced by Vince Fago but regained his position as editor in 1945. A second episode of uncertainty happened in 1950 when Goodman found it more lucrative to fire most of the staff and hire some of them back as freelancers. Lee was directed to fire friends, writers, and artists he admired,[21] and adapted the comics line accordingly. When the Comics Code Authority (CCA) was implemented in 1954, he successfully tailored the line to maintain sales, which built momentum until the 1957 Atlas Implosion. This was an unpredictable situation because he was limited in the amount of comic books that could be published, giving the business a very narrow margin of marketplace viability. There was a significant chance that the comics line would be discontinued, until Kirby and Ditko decided to work there.

When Kirby left Timely 15 years earlier for DC, he gained experience penciling and plotting top-selling comic books in various genres before returning to Lee after the Atlas Implosion. He and Simon created the Boy Commandos for *Detective Comics* and Newsboy Legion for *Star-Spangled Comics* in 1942. He was soon drafted to the front lines of World War II drawing reconnaissance maps[22] when most of his colleagues served in some form of media department. In 1945, he rejoined the Simon and Kirby team and pioneered comic book storytelling in genres including romance, horror, and crime for Crestwood Publications under the Prize imprint from the later 1940s into the early 1950s. The two creators started their very own Mainline Publications, creating various series such as *Bullseye*, *Foxhole*, *In Love*, and *Police Trap*, but their distributor, Leader News, went out of business due to losing EC Comics as an account after the implementation of the CCA.[23] Mainline failed and the Simon and Kirby team dissolved.[24] Kirby briefly returned to Lee to write and pencil Atlas's *Yellow Claw* (1956), then joined DC Comics under editor Jack Schiff, retconning Green Arrow and creating *Challengers of the Unknown* (1958) with writer Dave Wood. Schiff also arranged for Kirby and Wood to start work on the syndicated science-fiction newspaper comic strip *Sky Masters of the Space Force* (1958). However, disagreements over its royalties caused Schiff to blacklist Kirby from DC,[25] so he returned to Lee's office ready to work. Together they rekindled an old professional relationship to save Goodman's vulnerable comics line and possibly challenge DC, but they were missing a third much-needed element.

Steve Ditko's melancholy perspective on the human condition and his propensity for atmospheric storytelling added an unconventional and necessary facet to the developing Marvel Comics Group. He trained at the Johnstown Veterans Trade School, followed by the School of Visual Arts under Jerry Robinson, and published his first two comics at Ajax/Farrell and Key Publications (1953). Ditko assisted Mort Meskin at the Simon and Kirby studio in 1953, then penciled horror stories at Charlton Comics, where he had little editorial oversight, allowing him to experiment with his artistic range. He was stricken with tuberculosis, from which he finally recovered before starting work at Atlas.[26] After the Atlas implosion, he submitted more work to Charlton and expanded his craft in science-fiction and mystery titles with writer Joe Gill. After two years, Lee was ready to accept more of his work while also overseeing Kirby and other freelancers on comic books specializing in westerns, monster, teen, and science fiction. Ditko's creative momentum from his Charlton stories was palpable, and he enjoyed the opportunity to continue his innovative visual ideas into something new and special; however, he may have been aware of the stress that Lee was in, with little staff or money at his disposable. The pressure was also present in Jack Kirby who had few job choices remaining after his blacklist from DC. These three forces intersected, not knowing that they were on the verge of creating a new brand of comic book company based on imperfect superheroes.

Kirby contributed art and plots to Goodman's monster titles during his initial two years, as well as co-plotting and penciling titles with other companies, before cocreating a series of milestones that defined the Marvel Comics Group with Lee and Ditko. He reunited with previous partner Joe Simon on two titles at Archie

Comics, *Adventures of the Fly* (1959) and *The Double Life of Private Strong* (1959). *Adventures of the Fly* failed to impress readers, whereas *The Double Life of Private Strong* ceased publication after a cease-and-desist letter from DC Comics. Kirby also turned in his final strip for *Sky Masters of the Space Force* in 1961, which failed to maintain its presence in newspapers. It was at this point that Lee and Kirby created their own astronaut-themed comic book, *The Fantastic Four* (1961), about four space explorers who absorbed cosmic radiation, becoming the superheroes Invisible Girl, Mr. Fantastic, the Thing, and the Human Torch.[27] The cover stated, "for the first time in one mighty magazine," which was technically true, because it was the first time those four characters appeared anywhere. The Human Torch was retconned as a new human character named Johnny Storm, not related to the Golden Age Human Torch that was an android. Another idiosyncrasy of the cover was that there was no Marvel logo shown because the brand did not yet exist and the only logo shown was the distributor, IND, on the top left. *The Fantastic Four* fascinated readers who were initially curious of this approach to superheroes that seemed to capture the rough excitement of monster movies. Soon after, Lee and Kirby (with others) created The Incredible Hulk (1962), Thor (1962), Ant-Man (1962), and Iron Man (1963). Lee and Ditko created The Amazing Spider-Man (1962) and Doctor Strange (1963). Kirby applied boisterous and powerful figures that were part-hero and part-monster. Ditko applied an uncomfortable and morbid visceral aesthetic that dwelled in the dark. Lee appealed to his cocreators' strengths and emphasized their new characters' imperfections and anxieties. These flawed superheroes came with rogues' galleries and a mutually shared universe. To make the comic books recognizable at newsstands, Ditko envisioned a corner box logo that could portray Goodman's preferred title, "Marvel Comics Group," distinguishing the brand from its distributor, IND.[28] Increased profits from the Marvel brand of comics created an incentive for IND to allow more monthly titles. During this time, Kirby demonstrated a profound creativity and produced three or four art pages a day, which resulted in a substantial newsstand presence. For example, the September 1963 cover date featured several issues that he penciled, co-plotted, contributed to or provided cover art for, including *Avengers* #1, *X-Men* #1, *Fantastic Four* #18, *Journey into Mystery* #96, *Two-Gun Kid* #65, *Tales of Suspense* #45, *Strange Tales* #112, and *Sgt. Fury and His Howling Commandos* #3. The Marvel Method, described later in more detail, had Lee co-plot narratives with artists, which allowed them to pace out their action. Stan Lee and his brother, Larry Lieber, provided most of the dialogue and received the writer credit, whereas Kirby and Ditko were labeled as artists.[29] This was a major crediting defect in an otherwise perfect system.

A series of events led to the departure of Lee's cocreators, which appeared to start after Goodman ordered him to utilize the name of an abandoned Golden Age character.[30] Lee did so but incorporated the formula for flawed superheroes by adding blindness as the handicap with veteran co-plotter and penciler Bill Everett in *Daredevil* #1 (1964). The hero's first costume was designed by Kirby for the issue's cover, depicting an awkward yellow-and-black color scheme.[31] The character initially failed to capture readers' attention, which soon changed when Wally Wood, after leaving *MAD*, plotted subsequent issues with a redesign to a red costume.[32] Wood also visualized the character's radar sense by issue #7, when the newly red-suited Daredevil hopelessly faced the Sub-Mariner, teaching fans to never give up in the face of unbeatable odds. Despite the innovation of his work, Wood regarded the working situation with Lee as difficult and commented, "I had to make up the whole story. He was being paid for writing, and I was being paid for drawing."[33] Once Wood received a writing credit for issue #10, Lee relegated him to inker moving forward. Wood explained, "I complained about not being paid for writing, and suddenly I was inking [*Bob*] Powell."[34] Lee implied a different narrative of what occurred in the comic book's last panel: "Wally got the writing out of his system, he left it for poor Stan to finish next issue!,"[35] which demonstrated to the public that there was unhappiness with the way stories were being credited. After finishing inks on *Daredevil* #11 (1965), Wood departed Marvel to cocreate *T.H.U.N.D.E.R. Agents* for Tower Comics. Ditko also asked Lee for plotting credit on his titles and received it in late 1965. However, this ruptured his working relationship with Lee, who ceased any personal communication with him.[36] Ditko found this hurtful, and after completing roughly 10 more issues, he also left the company. His last two issues for Marvel during this period were *The Amazing Spider-Man* #38 (July 1966) and *Strange Tales* #146 (July 1966). At this point, the brand was too strong for any one creator's departure to disrupt and there were newer creators such as Roy Thomas, Gene Colan, John

Wally Wood contributed to the 1960s Marvel Comics brand by redefining the title character's costume in *Daredevil* #5 and #7 (1965).

Buscema, and John Romita, Sr., who wrote or penciled a comic book when a position was vacant. When Wood left, Romita penciled *Daredevil* #12, and later became the penciler on *The Amazing Spider-Man* #39 once Ditko withdrew his talents from the company in 1966. Jack Kirby also departed in 1970, expressing a similar dissatisfaction with how he was credited,[37] and Romita filled his vacancy on *Fantastic Four* with issue #103.

The Marvel brand continued to gain recognition as three more events solidified its market share. While DC Comics was discussing its buyout with Kinney in 1967, Goodman used the opportunity to discuss his distribution restrictions with Independent News and bargained to publish more comic books per month. As Kinney and DC established their merger, the restrictions were lifted, causing an increase in the number of popular characters starring in their own titles.[38] This new series of comics were *The Incredible Hulk, Captain America, Captain Marvel, The Invincible Iron Man, Doctor Strange, Nick Fury: Agent of S.H.I.E.L.D., Sub-Mariner,* and *Captain Savage and the Leatherneck Raiders.* The IND logo remained on the top left-hand corner of these new titles that also displayed the "Marvel Comics Group" corner box. Another merger occurred after Perfect Film & Chemical witnessed Goodman's rapidly growing circulation and purchased Marvel in 1968. IND continued to be present until 1969 when Perfect Film & Chemical started to use its own distributor, Curtis Circulation. The distributor logo changed from "IND" to "CC," as shown on *Captain Marvel* #17 (1969). The Marvel Comics Group was firmly established at this point, with its own distributor and a growing number of profitable titles.

The Marvel Comics Group was founded on the work of four men faced with the intimidating presence of Julius Schwartz's relatable superheroes, but instead disengaged from conformity in favor of characters with individual flaws and imperfections. This innovation occurred while Goodman and Lee experienced a significant economic and creative strain with the Atlas Implosion from a reduction in publishing volume, editorial challenges, and the death of two star artists. Kirby's blacklist from DC applied a creative pressure, which prompted the production of various innovative storylines and characters, while Ditko carried forth a progression of his growing artistic sensibilities. Despite the writer credit issues that alienated the brand's cocreators, Goodman, Lee, Kirby, and Ditko's circumstances intersected in a significant step to advance the superhero comic book, utilizing elements that went beyond radiation and monster movies. They used their past 10 to 20 years of experience to update old concepts and characters from a variety of sources, starting with the Golden Age.

14

Golden Age to the Marvel Age

Julius Schwartz's new relatable science-fiction superheroes were noticed by Martin Goodman when acknowledging the success of *Justice League of America* #1 (1960). There is an anecdote that he may have learned about the comic book's lucrative earnings from a golf game with DC Publisher Jack Liebowitz, but that has not been verified. Either way, Goodman was known for directing his editors to focus on genres that had already proved profitable by other publishers and likely observed that the JLA were mostly reinventions of Golden Age characters. So, he ordered Lee to create something similar,[1] and Lee would have understood to avoid any similarity to Superman and stay within the strict regulations of the Comics Code Authority. In response, Stan Lee, Jack Kirby, and Steve Ditko created the imperfect superheroes of the Marvel Comics Group alongside peripheral cocreators such as Larry Lieber, Bill Everett, Dick Ayers, Don Heck, Wally Wood, Roy Thomas, and Gene Colan, among others, who in many cases reinvented previously discarded Golden Age ideas and names. While many of these Golden Age connections are confirmed, there are several more that aren't but remain too similar to ignore.

Schwartz proved it worked to retcon Golden Age superheroes, which would have appealed to Goodman, who in the early 1950s unsuccessfully tried to republish his big three characters from Timely: the Human Torch, Sub-Mariner, and Captain America. His team had writer Hank Chapman, and pencilers Russ Heath and Carl Burgos reinstate the android Human Torch in *Young Men* #24 (1953) after the character had been unused since 1949. However, the reintroduced Human Torch was not well received by audiences, getting canceled after five issues of *Young Men* and three issues of his own title. By 1961, it seemed wise to retcon rather than reuse an unsuccessful character. So, Lee and Kirby changed his backstory from android Jim Hammond to teenager Johnny Storm, who was the brash younger brother of Susan Storm, the repressed love interest of team leader Reed Richard. The new Torch also appealed to the growing youth culture of the early 1960s, repairing cars and fraternizing with friends at the local malt shop. The Torch's opposite was the water-breathing Sub-Mariner, whose Golden Age series ended with *Sub-Mariner Comics* #32 (1949) and experienced a brief revival with *Sub-Mariner* #33 (1954). Bill Everett wrote and penciled both series but depicted him as a straightforward hero in the 1950s, elaborating on the character's mythos until issue #42, which ended from lack of sales.

Stan Lee and Jack Kirby revived the Sub-Mariner in *The Fantastic Four* #4 (1962), but instead as a misunderstood villain that entertained readers who enjoyed watching his war on the citizens of New York. *Captain America's Weird Tales* #75 (1949) ended the patriotic hero's original series, which resumed for a failed three issues of *Captain America* #76 to 78 (1954) by Don Rico and John Romita, Sr. The banner on the top of the covers depicting "Captain America … Commie Smasher" proved ineffective in attaining success. The character returned in *Avengers* #4 (1964) following John F. Kennedy's assassination, but with a story revision.[2] Lee and Kirby wrote that he was the real Captain America frozen in suspended animation in 1945, and every story until 1954 starred an imposter who was hired to be his replacement. This retcon made it possible to give the patriotic superhero a flaw, by featuring him in the 1960s as an anachronistic man out of time.

Goodman also owned more Golden Age characters for Lee's team to retcon, including Ka-Zar, the Vision, and the Falcon. Ka-Zar was created by Bob Byrd for Martin Goodman's pulp magazine line in *Ka-Zar* #1 (1936), which was adapted by Byrd and Ben Thompson for an ongoing storyline in *Marvel Comics* #1 (1939), appearing until issue #27 (1942). The story was about David Rand, a young man orphaned in the African jungle and raised by his guardian, the lion Zar.[3] Twenty-three years later, Goodman directed Lee to revive the jungle hero,[4] so he co-plotted the idea with Kirby to retcon him with a new alter ego, Kevin Plunder, and pet Zabu, the saber-toothed tiger. The new Ka-Zar premiered in "The World that Time Forgot" in *The X-Men* #10 (1965), when the team traveled to the sub-Antarctic dinosaur-laden Savage Land. By the later 1960s, newer creators followed through with reinventing Timely characters such as Roy Thomas, who was a reader of the company's comics during his childhood and retconned the Golden Age Vision, created by Simon and Kirby in *Marvel Mystery Comics* #13 (1940).[5] This issue depicted the origin of a ghostly green apparition who left his smoke dimension through the "great cold" to fight crime on Earth.[6] The Vision was a sophisticated poltergeist who grabbed a mobster and froze him with fear, then promptly disappeared in a puff of smoke. Roy Thomas revived the name and green suit, but Lee as editor wanted an android instead; so the young writer merged both concepts, retconning the character for the Silver Age in *Avengers* #57 (1968).[7] Thomas's words and John Buscema's art portrayed the new Vision as an artificial intelligence mechanism created by Ultron to infiltrate and destroy the Avengers; however, his main selling point to fans was his ongoing internal struggle to attain humanity.

In 1969, the need to retcon old Timely characters and the emerging acknowledgment of civil rights appeared to converge. Stan Lee and Gene Colan created Sam Wilson, the second African American superhero at Marvel (after the Black Panther in 1966) and friend to Captain America, in *Captain America* #117 (1969). Wilson was a social worker in Harlem who fought alongside Captain America against the Red Skull as the Falcon. The code name was used first for a Golden Age Timely superhero and lawyer, Carl Burgess, who appeared in "The Falcon" in *Daring Mystery*

Comics #5 (1940). Burgess wore a blue costume with a large yellow falcon on his chest and spent his workdays "as a brilliant young assistant district attorney."[8] Although his name sounded similar to the original Human Torch creator, Carl Burgos, there appears to be no significant relationship between the two. Falcon was created by Maurice Gutwirth, who started his career in comics in the Eisner and Iger Studio circa 1936 and his Falcon is largely forgotten, but the code name continues to persist with the character Sam Wilson.

Iron Man appears to use an origin that was initially used for a Timely super-hero, but his name and backstory seem mostly reused from a character found in another Golden Age comic book company. In his first appearance, Iron Man was dubbed "the most tragic figure on Earth" from *Tales of Suspense* #39 (1962) by Stan Lee, Don Heck, and Larry Lieber, which took place during the United States' war with North Vietnamese communists.[9] Tony Stark, industrial weapons maker and genius, traveled to Vietnam to test artillery powered by his "midget transistor" and was subsequently captured by the enemy and wounded with shrapnel embedded in his chest that slowly migrated to his flawed heart. He met Professor Yinsen, who collaborated with Stark to build the Iron Man suit to address his cardiac problems. With little time remaining, Yinsen sacrificed himself to give Stark precious extra seconds to don the suit and become Iron Man to escape.[10] Lee appears to have swiped this origin from his own Golden Age plot starring "The Destroyer" in *Mystic Comics* #6 (1941), with art by Jack Binder. In that issue, journalist Keen Marlow reported from the front lines in Nazi Germany only to be imprisoned in a concentration camp. Keen met fellow prisoner Professor Eric Schmitt, who died after giving him a special serum that enhanced his physique, allowing him to break free.[11] Destroyer didn't have armor, unlike another company's Golden Age superhero and possible Iron Man precursor, the Iron Ace from Hillman Periodicals' *Air Fighters* #2

Marvel Comics superheroes were often named after Timely Comics characters, which functioned to renew the company's trademarks. For example, the Falcon from *Daring Mystery Comics* #5 (1940) was the code name for Sam Wilson, who premiered in *Captain America* #117 (1968).

(1942). Iron Ace wore armor, and both characters' similar names employed the same lettering with attached nuts and bolts while also sharing a very similar origin story. "Captain Britain" was trapped in a Nazi prison and protected by Dr. LaFarga, who died giving him time to don his powerful magic armor. Empowered by his suit, the Iron Ace escaped and swore revenge against his Nazi captors.[12]

Iron Man's connection to Iron Ace is plausible because Goodman directed Lee to apply the Schwartz formula of retconning old superheroes to unused Golden Age trademarks and characters from other defunct comic book companies. Lee and his collaborators did so but in keeping with the Marvel style by adding flaws and imperfections. The most supported example of this pattern was Daredevil. Jack Binder and Don Rico created the original Golden Age Daredevil for Lev Gleason Publications in *Silver Streak* #6 (1940). The character, Bart Hill, was depicted with red hair and yellow costume and was labeled the "master of courage." He was branded with a hot iron while watching mobsters kill his father and rendered mute.[13] In Hill's second issue, the artist Jack Cole revised Daredevil's yellow suit into red, which was ideal for a devil-themed character; however, public interest in the character ended by 1950, prompting the hero to no longer being used and the name of the title to eventually fall out of trademark.[14] Lee later revealed that Goodman directed him to seize Daredevil's name for Marvel,[15] so he initially asked Ditko to draw the strip, and offered him the old superhero's costume, but the artist "didn't want to do it."[16] Lee remarked to Goodman's request, "So I figured I'd use the name, but I'll dream up something different for him."[17] Everett, Kirby, Ditko, and Lee collaborated on the first issue of the Silver Age Daredevil and although there were differences from the 1940s version, the similarities are clear. Marvel's Daredevil was the red-haired Matt Murdock who also lost his father, wore a yellow costume, was blind rather than mute, and was dubbed on the cover as "the man without fear." Murdock gained extrasensory abilities after radioactive elements entered his eyes and a motivation to fight crime after being orphaned when gangsters killed his father for refusing to lose his boxing match. This boxing origin for Murdock's father seemed taken from "The Poisoned Punch" in *Prize Comics* #58 (1946), which Charles Voight penciled about the boxer Moider Murdock, who was commanded to throw a fight for the mob.[18] The similarity to the Marvel story would compel any reader to consider that one of its plotters read the story in *Prize*. Murdock's original yellow costume also failed to catch audiences' attention, so Wally Wood updated it to red in issue #7.[19] Wood was a reader of the Golden Age Daredevil, sketching it as a child, and this was likely an inspiration for updating the Silver Age Daredevil costume.[20] The new Daredevil replaced the old with great success, and proved that if Schwartz can retcon Golden Age properties, then Goodman would have Lee and his colleagues do the same with other companies' characters.

Goodman was confirmed to have ordered the revival of more companies' discarded Golden Age trademarks, such as the Ghost Rider and Captain Marvel. The Ghost Rider was originally developed by Ray Krank and Dick Ayers in *Tim Holt* #11

(1949) for Vin Sullivan's publishing company, Magazine Enterprises. As an homage to Washington Irving's "The Headless Horseman," the original version involved a recently deceased Calico Kid who was resurrected after meeting the spirits of famous lawmen.[21] The character continued for five years and ceased publication in 1954. Thirteen years later, Martin Goodman directed Editor-in-Chief Stan Lee to secure the trademark at Marvel. Lee assigned Dick Ayers to draw the *Ghost Rider* (1967) and use a new origin from a script written by Gary Friedrich and Roy Thomas.[22] A similar treatment occurred with Captain Marvel, the Golden Age superhero who premiered in Fawcett's *Whiz Comics* #2 (1940). The character fell out of use by 1953 due to DC Comics' copyright infringement lawsuit,[23] and by 1966 the trademark was free to use. Goodman directed Lee to use the name for their own character in keeping with the newly branded Marvel Comics Group[24]; however, another publisher, Myron Fass, thought of the idea first with his tryout title *Captain Marvel* (1966). There are reports that Goodman used his legal team against Fass to secure the name, resulting in a transfer of funds for Captain Marvel's name to be firmly owned by Marvel Comics.[25] After Goodman secured the name, Lee and Colan created their own Captain Marvel in *Marvel Super-Heroes* #12 (1967), about a Kree soldier who infiltrated Earth and felt compassion for its citizens. The character sold well enough to star in his own series by 1968.

Lee, Kirby, and Ditko created more flawed superheroes for Marvel Comics—such as the Thing, the Hulk, Spider-Man, Cyclops, Quicksilver, Dr. Droom, Doctor Strange, Wonder Man, and Black Panther—that have unavoidable similarities to other companies' Golden Age characters, although none of the creators ever publicly confirmed a connection. The monster superheroes such as the Thing and Hulk started out as human beings transformed by accidents of science into forms that they could not control. The Thing was team pilot Ben Grimm, mutated by cosmic rays into a rocky orange monster whose first mission was to fight other monsters that were under the command of the subterranean Mole Man. The Hulk was created in a similar manner; instead, he was Dr. Bruce Banner, mutated by gamma rays into a haggard muscular behemoth. The Hulk's sidekick, Rick Jones, was similar to DC Comics' Snapper Carr and connected the series with teenage readers, but also codependently managed the Hulk's temper.[26] This dysfunctional dynamic as well as a similar Golden Age mutated and monstrous antihero was previously presented in Harry Stein and Mort Leav's "The Heap," created for Hillman Periodicals' *Air Fighters* #3 (1942). The Heap was a German World War I pilot who crashed to his death in a Polish swamp and whose desire to survive mutated him into a super-strong monster.[27] The Heap, same as the Hulk, was unpredictable and was also managed by a similar teenage sidekick, Rickie Wood, who donned the same white T-shirt and jeans worn by Rick Jones.[28]

When Spider-Man was created by Lee and Ditko in 1962, readers were impressed by his radioactive spider powers, web shooters, and innovative red-and-blue costume. His innate sense of tragedy was constructed from his pontifications as a self-doubting teenager who blamed himself for his uncle's death. Although the character's costume and anxiety were unconventional, he still had characteristics that were not original. His name and web abilities were seen before in "Tarantula," created by Mort Weisinger and Hal Sharp for *Star-Spangled Comics* #1 (1941). Tarantula crawled walls, used his web gun to capture criminals, and, in one panel, was given the nickname "Spider Man" by a radio announcer.[29] Tarantula failed to be a successful character, but the outcome may have been different had Weisinger used the name Spider Man.

The X-Men (1963) by Lee and Kirby depicted the super-powered characters Cyclops and Quicksilver, who also appear to take traits from other companies' Golden Age characters. The group's team leader, Cyclops, controlled his powerful eye laser beams by wearing a ruby quartz visor, a suppressive tool that is recognizable and specific for the Marvel Comic series. However, very similar optic blasts and visor are seen with the character, "The Comet" who debuted in *Pep Comics* #1 (1940), created by Plastic Man creator Jack Cole. In the same manner as Cyclops, the Comet wielded uncontrollable eye beams that required a special glass uni-visor to prevent him from disintegrating everything he sees.[30] One important difference in the power source of both characters is that the Comet was powered by scientific augmentation rather than mutation, but his face, visor, and powers remain the same. Cyclops often fought a fellow mutant created by Lee and Kirby named Quicksilver, who first appeared in *The X-Men* #4 (1964). His name was Pietro Maximoff, the brother of the Scarlet Witch, who eventually rehabilitated into a flawed superhero. His main power was superspeed, which was often depicted as a green or blue blur. However, neither his name nor his special ability was original. While the gypsy background and origin as a rehabilitated criminal were unique to Marvel, there was another speedster of

Some Marvel Comics' superheroes were given names that were previously used by defunct Golden Age companies, including Quicksilver from *The X-Men* #4 (1964), whose name appeared in Quality's *National Comics* #5 (1940).

the same name created by Chuck Mazoujian in *National Comics* #5 (1940), published by Quality. Mazoujian's Quicksilver was depicted as a blur in various panels, and his speed was demonstrated to run over gutters on the comic book page. His early issues depicted him as mostly always in motion, and when he stopped running, his upper body was depicted in three places at once.[31] His first comic book run ended in *National Comics* #73 (1949) and the trademark was out of use a long enough time by 1964 when Goodman secured his code name for Pietro Maximoff.

Doctor Droom, Doctor Strange, and Dr. Doom have the same origin that was present in another defunct company's Golden Age superhero. These characters were not transformed by accidents of science in the manner of many of the Silver Age heroes, but instead through training in Eastern magic. "I Am the Fantastic Dr. Droom!" was created by Stan Lee, Larry Lieber, and Jack Kirby for *Amazing Adventures* #1 (1961) about a physician who traveled to a lamasery at the top of the "snowcapped Himalayas" and learned about Eastern culture from a dying "Tibetan Lama." Once Droom passed the Lama's test, he transformed from Caucasian to Asian before departing to conquer more "diabolical forces."[32] Dr. Droom's first appearance may have made an impression on the issue's inker, Ditko, who cocreated the origin of Doctor Strange in *Strange Tales* #115 (1963) with Lee. They depicted arrogant surgeon Dr. Stephen Strange, who sought any means to repair his damaged hands. Same as Dr. Droom before him, he traveled through the Himalayas into "India, Land of Mystic Enchantment,"[33] where he transformed into a "Master of Black Magic." Another graduate of a similar Himalayan school, Dr. Doom premiered in *The Fantastic Four* #5 (1962). His origin was that of a physicist who burned his face using science to investigate black magic. After the disfiguring accident, Doom swore revenge on fellow university student Reed Richards and hiked through the snowy mountains into Tibet only to return to New York armed with "black magic and sorcery!"[34] The common thread among these three doctors who gained their magic powers in a Himalayan school appears to be the Green Lama, adapted into a comic book by creator Ken Crossen for Crestwood's *Prize Comics* #7 (1940). This superhero eventually starred in his own series by Crossen in Spark Publications' *The Green Lama* #1 (1944), with art by Mac Raboy. The Green Lama was Jethro DuMont, a wealthy playboy who traveled to Tibet and was augmented by a transformative spirit called "'Lamaism,' which granted him super strength, flight, and invulnerability."[35]

Wonder Man was created by Stan Lee, Jack Kirby, and Don Heck for *Avengers* #9 (1964) and appears to have had his name taken from two Golden Age superheroes. Marvel's Wonder Man was Simon Williams, a corrupt businessman who was bombarded by ionic rays, granting him super strength and invulnerability, which made him a strong contender against physically intimidating heroes such as Thor and Iron Man. Due to a cease-and-desist letter by DC Comics, he was killed in his first appearance, but reappeared as an ongoing flawed superhero who was eager to find his humanity in *Avengers* #131 (1975). His code name was used twice before in the Golden Age from two precursors. The first Wonder Man was created by Will Eisner for Fox Publications and appeared in *Wonder Comics* #1 (1939), whose origin resembled that of the Green Lama. This hero was Fred Carson, an American traveler who was transformed during his trip to Tibet after obtaining a power ring from an Eastern mystic who proudly declared, "Wear this ring … you will be impervious."[36] He appeared in only one issue of the comic book because a copyright lawsuit from DC Comics claimed it was too similar to Superman.[37] The code name appeared again when Pines Publishing produced its own version of the superhero, "Brad Spencer, Wonder Man," in *Complete Book of Comics and Funnies* #1 (1944), drawn by Bob Oksner, with adventures continued in *Mystery Comics* #1 (1944), that included art by Alex Schomburg. His first issue beamed him aboard "Lilith, the dark planet" to fight galactic space huns under the control of the "maniacal Dr. Voodoo."[38] Despite the uniquely hectic storylines of Pines's Wonder Man, the character was discontinued, likely from lack of sufficient sales. However, his green costume with red "W" on his chest is very similar to the costume worn by Marvel's version in 1964, suggesting that Lee's team may have known about this character.

The Black Panther is the first Black superhero in comic books, first appearing in *Fantastic Four* #52 (1966) as the African Prince T'Challa, who donned the panther suit after his father was killed by the villain Klaw. He is thought to be derived from an original African character pitched by Jack Kirby called the Coal Tiger,[39] but other influences from earlier ages likely contributed to the hero and his backstory. It's possible that Goodman wanted to trademark the name since Lee's team experimented with it in *Two-Gun Kid* #77 (1965) about a Caucasian villain named the Panther, created by Dick Ayers and Al Hartley. However, Kirby's portrayal of the Coal Tiger as an African man likely prompted the company to make a new Black Panther, but he still needed a backstory for his alter ego. The one that was used by Lee and Kirby was the same origin as another African prince who lost his father years earlier during the company's Atlas period. This was "Waku, Prince of the Bantu," portrayed by the innovative Don Rico and Jay Scott Pike in *Jungle Tales* #1 (1954), a story that Lee as editor must have known. Another set of Panthers were seen earlier, such as that found in the *Tarzan* strip, which had a "Panther Men" storyline by Bob Lubbers from October 14, 1951, to February 24, 1952. Lubbers was a comic book comic artist who worked for Golden Age publishers Centaur and Fiction House before drawing the *Tarzan* newspaper strip in 1950 after Burne Hogarth departed. The Panther Men were an African tribe that acted as villains against Tarzan, and their clothing had accompanying dark feline-themed headgear and black capes. Lubbers may have known about another Panther hero that was a previous feature at Centaur created by his colleague Paul Gustavson named "The Black Panther" for *Stars and Stripes* #3 (1941)[40] about a Caucasian man in a costume who prevented a professor's secret formula from falling into the wrong hands. Gustavson also worked at Timely when he wrote and penciled "The Angel" for *Marvel Mystery Comics* #2 (1939), adding to the possibility that Goodman may have been aware of the artist's Black Panther character from Centaur, a name that would have been available to use by 1966.

Goodman's direction to Lee to mimic Schwartz's *Justice League of America* included retconning Timely's Golden Age superheroes and available trademarks from other defunct companies. Part of the challenge was to avoid any similarity to Superman and stay within the regulations of the CCA. Lee, Kirby, Ditko, and others accomplished this task but added various flaws and imperfections to each superhero, which ranged from deformities, insecurities, anger, medical problems, and trauma. These flaws contributed to a diversity in the Marvel Comics Group that rejected the inherent conformity of characters from DC Comics. Their first deformed superhero, the Thing, was a test case of a radiation-based monstrous hero, who proved compelling enough to compete for market share, suggesting that examining the monster genre could be another golden opportunity for Marvel.

15

When Monsters
Became Superheroes

Martin Goodman understood that reinventing a Golden Age superhero, even with an entirely new costume and backstory, resulted in securing a trademark. Stan Lee understood that placing a name onto a new hero functioned well if it was accompanied by a flaw or imperfection, which he generally did when co-plotting origins with Jack Kirby and Steve Ditko. Their unique collaboration created the successful and diverse initial characters of the Marvel Comics Group whose insecurities and trauma combined well with sources of power such as scientific accidents and the occasional magical circumstance. The Thing and the Hulk exemplified powerful deformities and became tragic superheroes who incorporated qualities from the monster comic books that preceded the Marvel Comics characters. Their successful use in the medium indicated to readers that interesting superheroes can develop when creators integrate qualities from other genres. This also indicated that during the 1960s, monsters could be used to successfully build a line of comic characters that would avoid any interference from the Comics Code or similarity to Superman. So, it became a natural conclusion for Goodman, Lee, and others to continue this trend by using names or characters from their monster titles and placing them in their new line of flawed superheroes and supervillains.

Although giant monsters were featured in comics for decades, there was a much higher preponderance of them featured in Goodman's comic line, likely because of the popularity of the science-fiction movies and the availability of Jack Kirby. After the Atlas implosion of 1957, the comics line from Goodman wasn't labeled Atlas anymore; nor was it referred to as Marvel, until 1963. Those in-between years were marked by less distribution through Independent News, with fewer titles, and a significant reliance on selling comic books that featured monsters as large as *Godzilla* or *King Kong*. There were other genres of comic books in Goodman's line, but the ones that relate to the later superheroes were the monsters. In fact, it's easier to refer to this era as the company's Pre-Marvel Monster era (1959–1962) that seemed to follow the 1958 American film industry, which featured movies such as *Attack of the 50 Foot Woman, Attack of the Puppet People, Curse of the Faceless Man, The Spider,* and *Giant from the Unknown.* Other monster features of this era included *It! The Terror from*

Beyond Space, The Blob, The Colossus of New York, The Strange World of Planet X, and *The Thing That Couldn't Die*. These films, which often featured radiation and aliens, were symptoms of a rampant cultural anxiety over the side effects of the atomic bomb and foreign incursion. Martin Goodman probably understood this genre was popular and directed Lee to utilize storytellers that were adept with monsters. Before returning to Marvel, Jack Kirby wrote, penciled, and inked a monster story for DC Comics in "The Stone Sentinels of Giant Island" in *House of Mystery* #85 (1958) and depicted "Easter Island" rock monsters attacking sailors at sea.[1] His depiction of haggard large creatures set the ideal tone for the genre even if there was a lack of appreciation for these stories at DC. Once Kirby returned to Goodman's line, there was a significant increase in monster-related comic books by both himself and other creators, likely due to his presence. For example, Kirby utilized these same Stone Men in *Tales to Astonish* #16 (1961) for "THORR!" about an archaeologist who discovered sedentary statues that were alien invaders in suspended animation. One of them named Thorr awakened, soon tricked by the archaeologist who used dynamite to destroy their own island.[2] Despite Lee and Lieber getting the writing credit, it was mostly the same as Kirby's story that he wrote three years earlier for DC Comics. [*As a point of clarification on credits, Lee discussed the credits on the monster stories claiming that he "did that one, if my name was on them" and that "there were other writers like Ernie Hart and Robert Bernstein and Larry Lieber," but "those days we weren't always signing them."[3] So the credits analyzed here stem from the Grand Comics Database.*] The same Easter Island monolithic stone men also appeared as the first villains to fight the mighty Thor in his first appearance in *Journey into Mystery* #83 (1962).

Jack Kirby's depiction of extraterrestrial monsters at DC Comics, such as "The Stone Sentinels of Giant Island" from *House of Mystery* #85 (1958), was critical to creating characters at Marvel Comics, such as the first villains who fought the Mighty Thor in *Journey Into Mystery* #83 (1962).

The names of both the Thing and the Hulk were previously used to describe threatening monstrosities in the pre–Marvel monster comic books. Ditko portrayed "The Thing on Bald Mountain" in *Tales to Astonish* #7 (1960) about a sculptor who made two clay statues, one good and one evil. Lightning struck, animating them to fight one another and during the commotion, the stone monsters fell from a cliff, giving their creator a reprieve. The consistency of their bodies was similar to the stone-based creatures on the covers of *Tales to Astonish* #5–6 and #16, demonstrating a common theme, which creatively made it a natural fit to make the Thing a rocky superhero. There were also "non-rock" monsters in the series that Lee and Kirby probably drew upon to create *The Incredible Hulk* #1 (May 1962). One such monster was a previous "Hulk" featured on the cover of *Journey into Mystery* #62 (1960) by Lee, Lieber, and Kirby. This story depicted a large furry alien named Xemnu who infiltrated Earth by hypnotizing various people on his quest toward world domination. His plans, however, were thwarted when he was jettisoned into orbit around the sun, where he could no longer cause any harm. Xemnu's fur also causes historians to consider him a follow-up character to a similarly hairy Golden Age monster, the Heap, as well as a precursor to *The Incredible Hulk*. The same three creators, Lee, Lieber, and Kirby, later depicted "The Midnight Monster" in *Journey into Mystery* #79 (April 1962) about Victor, an evil scientist who swallowed a serum that made him large, strong, and hideous. His panel-by-panel transformation into a four-fingered brute was also used for the Hulk. The oversize villain was eventually chased by the military and deceived into falling into "the world's deepest hole" from which he never emerged.[4]

Dr. Doom, Diablo, and Dr. Droom also had names that first appeared as monsters. Dr. Doom's surname and cultural heritage were present in an earlier story about "VANDOOM!" in *Tales to Astonish* #17 (1961) by Lee and Kirby. This story depicted an Eastern European wax museum owner who built a new monster to attract more business. The wax creature was animated by a bolt of lightning and spent its energy defending a local village from an alien invasion.[5] This name and Eastern European background appear to be used again by Lee and Kirby for Victor "von Doom" in *The Fantastic Four* #5 (1962). Von Doom was born in the fictional Eastern European country Latveria and used both science and the occult to communicate with the dead but accidentally scarred his face in the process. Cloaked in green garb and an iron mask, he became the Fantastic Four's primary armored nemesis. Doom's mask also appeared in another story, "The Monster in the Iron Mask!" in *Tales of Suspense* #31 (1962), about an alien invader with an iron face and a green body similar to von Doom. This story was produced by Lee, Lieber, and Kirby and released with the same cover date as Dr. Doom's first appearance,[6] and appears to be an homage to the 1939 film and the 1840s novel *The Man in the Iron Mask* by Alexandre Dumas. Another enemy of the Fantastic Four whose name was seen on a preceding monster was featured in "I saw DIABLO! The Demon from the Fifth Dimension!," created by Lee, Lieber, and Kirby for *Tales of Suspense* #9 (1960). This is the story of an adventurer who used a cigarette lighter to deceive an interdimensional smoke monster into leaving Earth.[7] Diablo was also the name used by Lee and Kirby for a master alchemist in *Fantastic Four* #30 (1964), who used the Thing as a pawn against his team by promising to revert him to human form. Diablo's plans were opposed and defeated, but he occasionally returned as an irritant to various Marvel heroes. Another superhero from this period, featured briefly in the Silver Age, premiered in "I Am the Fantastic Dr. Droom!" from *Amazing Adventures* #1 (1962) by Lee, Lieber, and Kirby. The character preceded Doctor Strange as Marvel's first mystic and held four appearances in *Amazing Adventures* #1–4 and 6 before it was discontinued. He eventually returned to Marvel continuity renamed as Dr. Anthony Druid in *Weird Wonder Tales* #19 (1976)[8] and later became a reoccurring character in *The Avengers*. His name appeared originally as a giant reptilian monster in "I Saw Droom, the Living Lizard!" in *Tales to Astonish* #9 (1960) with interiors by Don Heck. Droom was abbreviated from Droomedia Rex, a reptile who was exposed to a growth formula and destroyed segments of a city. His threat was ended when the military launched him into space by rockets attached to his feet.

Therianthropic Marvel characters combined features of humans and animals, and three in particular—Gorilla Man, Spider-Man, and Werewolf by Night—used names that were featured in the company's pre–Marvel period. Gorilla Man was a short-lived Marvel-era character in *Tales to Astonish* #28 (1962) by Stan Lee, Larry Lieber, and Jack Kirby about a scientist who switched minds with a sizable ape, committed burglaries, and was eventually caged in a zoo. The same creative team revisited the character in *Tales to Astonish* #30 when Gorilla Man escaped his cage; however, despite his intellect, scientists rocketed him to outer space to test the effects of space travel on an intelligent life form. His name was used before on another "Gorilla Man" from *Men's Adventures* #26 (1954) by Robert Q. Sale. This Atlas–era monster was soldier Ken Hale, who killed the mystical Gorilla Man and inherited his curse.[9] This was the same Gorilla Man that was later a member of the 1950s Avengers in *What If?* #9 (1978) and the *Agents of Atlas* series (2006). Both Gorilla Men had opposing sources of power, magical in one and scientific in the other. Another therianthropic superhero is Marvel's most famous, the amazing Spider-Man. Although he was an innovative creation by Stan Lee and Steve Ditko in 1962, the company previously used the name during its Atlas era in a story titled "The Spider Man!," which was featured in *Uncanny Tales* #26 (1954) and penciled by Ed Winiarski. The story depicted a scientist who mutated oversize spiders and raised them with hopes that they would follow his orders to take over the world. The spiders stopped growing and the scientist waited for them to grow further until he died from "hunger and old age."[10] As a leader of the mutated spiders, he was "Spider Man" in name but with no powers, and the name lacked a hyphen. Another Atlas–era story was given a title that preceded the third therianthropic Marvel character in "Werewolf by Night," featured in *Marvel Tales* #116 (1953) by Stan Lee and Jack Abel, about a man who was frightened into helping a hostile werewolf find its victims. He later discovered that the werewolf was the father of his girlfriend, who surprised him with her own lycan-thropy, leaving his fate uncertain.[11] This story title was used by creators Roy Thomas, Mike Ploog, and Gerry Conway in "Werewolf by Night" from *Marvel Spotlight* #2 (1972), starring Jack Russell. Russell had dreams of being a werewolf, but then realized later in his first appearance that he was one, which was tragically ironic because both stories share a common trait about young men who were surprised by their intimate relationship with lycanthropy.

The X-Men depicted characters Cyclops, Colossus, and Magneto, whose names were previously used during the company's pre–Marvel monster period. Cyclops was the mutant team's repressed leader known for his uni-visor and premiered in *The X-Men* #1 (1963) by Lee and Kirby. Although Cyclops's visor and optic beam resembled the Golden Age superhero the Comet, his name appears to have been taken from another Lee and Kirby monster in a story from *Tales of Suspense* #10 (1960) titled "I Brought the Mighty Cyclops Back to Life!" This adventure featured a large one-eyed creature whose cold-induced slumber was disturbed by local explorers, prompting the Cyclops to awaken and cause significant destruction before being frozen again.[12] One of the superhero Cyclops's later teammates utilized a name that previously appeared in *Tales of Suspense* #14 (1961) by Lee, Lieber, and Kirby. "I Created the Colossus" featured a Russian statue that was possessed by an alien whose ship crashed on Earth. As the living statue, he attacked Moscow until another alien traveled to Earth and transferred his consciousness back home.[13] The name and Russian background are also present in the superhero Colossus, the mutant named Piotr Rasputin, created by Len Wein and Dave Cockrum for *Giant-Size X-Men* #1 (1975). Similar to a living statue, Rasputin was capable of transmuting his body into living

Magneto premiered as a mutant supervillain in *The X-Men* #1 (1963), but his name was previously used to describe a monstrous figure with similar powers in *Strange Tales* #84 (1961).

organic steel. His metallic body was susceptible to magnetism, a power wielded by the X-Men's primary adversary, Magneto, whose name was previously used for a monster with similar powers called "MAGNETO!" in *Strange Tales* #84 (1961) by Lee, Lieber, and Kirby. This story was about an oversize man with low intelligence who was sent into space by scientists and passed through radioactive antimatter, which granted him magnetic powers. Magneto failed to fit into human society and left Earth in a rocket to live alone on another planet.[14] His name and powers were used for the supervillain Magneto, created by Lee and Kirby in *The X-Men* #1, who felt a similar isolation as the mutant master of magnetism, waging his war for racial supremacy and eventually establishing a temporary base in outer space.

Spider-Man's rogues' gallery has members whose names were also previously used to label the company's monsters, including Electro, Sandman, Scorpion, and Molten Man. Electro's name was used at Marvel in multiple stages of its history. The supervillain that premiered in *The Amazing Spider-Man* #9 (1964) by Lee and Ditko was Max Dillon, an electrical lineman who was struck by lightning, enabling his ability to wield electricity. The name was used by a preceding monster, "Elektro!," from *Tales of Suspense* #13 (1961) by Lee, Lieber, and Kirby about an artificial intelligence who entered a robot shell to conquer Earth but failed in executing his plans when a scientist unplugged its wires to save humanity.[15] The name was also used during the Atlas era in *Captain America Comics* #78 (1954) by Lee and Romita, Sr., about a communist supervillain who wielded electric-based superpowers. The name was probably used to maintain the trademark from a previous Timely character who premiered in "Electro: The Marvel of the Age" in *Marvel Mystery Comics* #4 (1940), a robot that appears to be an homage to the real-life Electro, a machine from the 1939 World's Fair who impressed onlookers by obeying simple commands.[16] The Timely character similarly obeyed his creator Professor Zog's commands in a war on the Mafia.[17] Although Steve Dahlman was the artist responsible for this unique story, his editor on this issue was Joe Simon, who had recently departed from Fox Publications, which published a character of the same name in *Science Comics* #1 (1940). Fox's Electro was Jim Andrews, an electrical scientist who was empowered by working with a pair of giant electrodes to wage a war on crime.[18]

Marvel's Electro from *The Amazing Spider-Man* series teamed up with other villains in the Sinister Six, including Sandman and Scorpion, both of which were names used during the company's previous monster era. Lee and Ditko created the supervillain Sandman, a criminal mutated by radiation while he was standing on sand in *The Amazing Spider-Man* #4 (1963). After proving his near invincibility by counteracting Spider-Man's powers, the villain was defeated by an industrial-grade vacuum cleaner. His name was previously used in "The Sandman Cometh!" by Lee, Lieber, and Kirby in *Journey into Mystery* #70 (1961) about an alien monster made from living sand. The military failed to stop him from taking over Earth; however, a young boy defeated the sand creature with a pail of water.[19] Both Sandmen dissolved into consciously moving sand and were defeated by surprisingly mundane means. One of Sandman's partners, the Scorpion, was a villain created by Stan Lee and Steve Ditko who first appeared in *The Amazing Spider-Man* #20 (1964), wielding super strength that enabled him to wield a dangerous mechanical tail. He also appears to have been named after another pre–Marvel monster, specifically a radiated giant scorpion from "The Scorpion Strikes!" in *Journey into Mystery* #82 (1962) by Lee, Lieber, and Kirby. This beast planned to empower his species to take over Earth but was stopped by a hypnotist who thwarted his plans by implanting the suggestion of pain.[20] Another villain from Spider-Man's rogues' gallery to fit this name pattern was Molten Man, created by Lee and Ditko for *The Amazing Spider-Man* #28 (1965). This issue is known for its dense black cover that contrasted well with the red from Spider-Man's costume. The story followed smuggler Mark Raxton, who became super strong when a jar of liquid metal alloy spilled on his body, prompting him to bear a name that appears derived from "The Molten Man-Thing," created by Stan Lee and Jack Kirby for *Tales of Suspense* #7 (1960). This character was a solitary lava monster who caused local towns to evacuate due to their fear of the creature's incoming presence, which was stopped when a local man discovered a cooling blower that forced it back underground.[21]

Toward the end of the monster era, *The Fantastic Four* was Marvel Comics' only superhero comic book series from cover dates November 1961 to March 1962. The other comic books depicted non-superhero genres, including the science-fiction monster books such as *Tales of Suspense*, *Journey into Mystery*, and *Tales to Astonish*, which were published monthly while *The Fantastic Four* was bimonthly.[22] *The Fantastic Four* was an experiment that demonstrated that Lee and Kirby could adequately handle Goodman's direction to respond to DC Comics' *Justice League of America*. Their approach advanced the superhero comic book to include imperfections, Golden Age origins, reinvented characters, unused names, and monsters with a personal complexity that eclipsed Schwartz's relatable but conformist DC superheroes. This new type of superhero proved viable in the marketplace while avoiding similarities to Superman and any conflict with the Comics Code. Lee and Ditko successfully implemented this formula with *The Amazing Spider-Man* and both comic books were accompanied by a rogues' gallery that incorporated many of the same features. Their unique execution of this formula was specific to the collaboration of Stan Lee, Jack Kirby, and Steve Ditko, who initially created the diverse characters of the Marvel Comics Group to attract readers and gain market share. Their perspectives from different backgrounds connected during the evolution of the superhero comic book, due to a convergence of separate career trajectories and a short-lived shared vision to depict flawed superheroes.

16

How Lee, Kirby, and Ditko Advanced Superheroes

Martin Goodman examined his competitors, whether they were viable or defunct, and directed instructions to Stan Lee to create their own similar superheroes. Lee accepted his orders and appeared to have understood that the monstrous figures of Jack Kirby and the morbid imagery of Steve Ditko were required to create the flawed characters of the Marvel Comics Group. These three collaborated using the Marvel Method, consisting of Lee co-plotting narratives with artists, which allowed them to pace out their action that he later dialogued.[1] They utilized Golden Age origins, radiation, unused names, tropes, narratives, and monsters that were previously used in pulp magazines, cinema, comic strips, and comic books. However, Kirby, Ditko, and Lee also utilized ideas, plots, and characters from comic books that they previously worked on before intersecting to create the Marvel superheroes.

Kirby, born Jacob Kurtzberg, contributed plots, characters, and pencils toward his collaborations with Lee that were cultivated from more than 20 years of depicting genres including superheroes, romance, crime, and horror at various comic book companies. He was frustrated by his blacklist from DC Comics, which probably worsened when the company's attorneys sent a cease-and-desist letter to Archie, ending his cocreation with Joe Simon, *The Double Life of Private Strong* (1959). Kirby realized there were limited publishers to work for and he had a family to support, a fact that naturally added pressure to deliver to Lee various ideas that he previously plotted or penciled. Lee also likely understood that Kirby provided a lifeline for the company that enabled the creation of the Marvel Universe with characters such as Thor, Iron Man, Ant-Man, the Hulk, the X-Men, Fantastic Four, the Avengers, Sgt. Fury and His Howling Commandos, Spider-Man, and villains including Rama-Tut, the Lava Men, Skrulls, Impossible Man, Magneto, Sentinels, Puppet Master, M.O.D.O.K., Ringmaster, and Immortus, among many others.

It's highly probable that Kirby brought the hero Thor as well as the plot and villains used in the hero's first appearance to *Journey into Mystery* #83 (1962) despite not being credited as a writer. Kirby originally wrote and penciled "The Villain from Valhalla" for DC Comics in *Adventure Comics* #75 (1942), depicting Sandman

Lee's focus on superheroes' imperfections required the art styles of Kirby and Ditko, who depicted many of their characters as haggard and uncomfortable. Kirby image on left from *Black Magic* **#1 (1950) and Ditko image on right from** *Strange Suspense Stories* **#40 (1959).**

fighting a character named Fairy-Tales Fenton, a crime-committing metallurgist who pretended to be the thunder god.[2] Kirby revisited the character again when he wrote and penciled Thor in a story titled "The Magic Hammer" from *Tales of the Unexpected* #16 (1957), where the demigod was depicted in a few panels taking his hammer back from a thief who used it to rob banks.[3] It was here that he designed Mjölnir and tested its superior strength against a nearby tree.[4] Kirby brought the same hammer design to Marvel's first Thor appearance, and it was again thrown at a tree to demonstrate its physical supremacy.[5] Thor's first villains were "The Stone Men from Saturn," fashioned after the same monsters Kirby depicted in DC Comics' *House of Mystery* #85 (1959). The Stone Men were also from the same planet as another set of alien slavedrivers from Simon and Kirby's *Captain Marvel Adventures* #1 (1941) in which the hero was also referred to as a "thunder god."[6] The Kirby plot from *Tales of the Unexpected* #16 about Loki stealing Thor's hammer was used again in *Journey into Mystery* #92 (1963), despite the writing credit on the Marvel issue being given to Stan Lee and Robert Bernstein.[7] In keeping with their other superheroes, Lee and Kirby added a flaw that kept Marvel's Thor anxious and connected to his humanity; if he failed to maintain contact with his hammer for 60 seconds, he would turn back to his crippled alter ego, Donald Blake. Blake and Thor shared a romantic interest in nurse Jane Foster, which appears to be based on a Simon and Kirby plot previously seen in Simon and Kirby's *Young Romance* #13 (1949) that depicted a woman fantasizing about a handsome Viking lover who wore a winged helmet.[8]

Kirby also likely brought the armor and heart problems of Iron Man to Lee, who further developed the character with other cocreators. The interiors to the hero's first appearance in *Tales of Suspense* #39 (1962) were credited to Stan Lee, Larry Lieber, and Don Heck, but carried plot points previously seen in Kirby's earlier stories.[9]

Don Heck was interior penciler, and Lee and Lieber are credited as the writers, but it was Kirby who penciled the cover and designed the character's first armor.[10] In this first issue, Iron Man's alter ego, Tony Stark, developed a heart problem, which was controlled with the aid of his suit. Almost as a nod to *The Wonderful Wizard of Oz*'s Tin Man, Tony Stark's cardiac issues were the Achilles' heel of the millionaire playboy. Two years earlier, Kirby worked with Lee and Lieber on "The Thing Called Metallo!" in *Tales of Suspense* #16 (1961) about a man in an iron suit with a strikingly similar heart problem. Kirby's Metallo is considered to be linked to the first appearance of DC's Metallo in *Action Comics* #252 (1959), written by Robert Bernstein. The villain in this story had an iron body, kryptonite heart, and similar facial features to Tony Stark. Kirby reported to historian Mark Evanier that Bernstein obtained the plot from himself before presenting it to editor Mort Weisinger,[11] which suggests that Kirby conceived of Tony Stark's heart problem. In his first appearance, Stark was forced into forging weapons for communists during the Vietnam War. Wong-Chu, the story's villain, yelled at Stark, "If you design powerful new weapon for me, afterwards I have surgeon save your life!"[12] Kirby previously penciled a DC Comics story with a similar premise when he collaborated with Dave Wood for *Adventure Comics* #255 (1958) in "The War that Never Ended!" In this story, the Green Arrow was trapped by Japanese mercenaries and forced to build weapons for them while holding him captive. Major Tayako yelled, "You build giant arrow torpedoes, bombs, mines! ... Sink fleet or die! You understand?"[13] These similarities suggest that Kirby plotted a significantly higher portion of Iron Man's origin than was originally credited.

Ant-Man's powers and growth serum were likely brought to Lee by Kirby, who had already developed these ideas on several of his pre–Marvel comic books. The small hero was originally meant to premiere in an isolated science-fiction story during his first appearance from *Tales to Astonish* #27 (1962) by Lee, Lieber, and Kirby, which featured his alter ego, Dr. Henry Pym, who discovered a reducing serum that shrank him down to ant size. He found ants that were either friend or enemy and eventually grew back to human size, swearing to dispose of the dangerous formula. However, he returned as a superhero in *Tales to Astonish* #35 (1962), excited to explore the physical world from a miniaturized point of view. He soon noticed that he retained full human strength in his smaller body and developed a red costume and helmet used to communicate with ants. Although the story credited to Lee and Lieber appeared innovative, it is noteworthy to consider that Kirby experimented with a similar size-changing concept in "The Menace of the Micro-Men," from Archie Comics' *The Double Life of Private Strong* #1 (1959) concerning "Doctor Diablo," who shrank an army with hopes to invade the world.[14] Kirby depicted dynamic interactions of the shrunken Private Strong with larger objects that also appeared in his Ant-Man stories three years later. He also penciled a similar plot for "The Microscopic Army!" in *The Yellow Claw* #3 (1956), depicting the Claw's army of men that were shrunk down to ant size by a machine to "launch an invasion of America that will bring it to its knees!"[15] Kirby also wrote and drew another insect-themed story for Harvey Comics' *Black Cat Mystic* #60 (1957) in which the character drank an "Ant Extract" giving him superhuman strength to lift large objects. Kirby's first Ant-Man precursor is found during his Golden Age collaboration with Joe Simon in *Blue Bolt* #4 (1940) about "The Shrinking Serum," discovered by Dr. Bertoff to shrink the Blue Bolt to "penetrate the armed walls of the green kingdom."[16] The hero did so, finally enlarging to normal size to surprise his enemies.

It was likely Kirby who brought the gamma bomb origin to the Hulk. The credits to the character's first appearance in *The Incredible Hulk* #1 (1962) were listed as "Stan Lee + Jack Kirby,"[17] and it wasn't until issue #4 when the credits to script and art were separated. However, their depiction of the initial gamma bomb explosion that gave Hulk his powers appears to incorporate two separate preceding stories by Kirby. While huddled in the bomb shelter, Dr. Bruce Banner noticed a young man wandering out in the bomb testing site. He ran out to the adolescent's rescue, and was bombarded by the gamma bomb explosion, becoming the Incredible Hulk. This premise was already used by Kirby two years earlier in daily strips of *Sky Masters of the Space Force* (February 18–22, 1960) when military superiors tested a bomb constructed similarly to the later gamma bomb. The story's protagonist, Sky Masters, ran into the field to save a young boy and put himself at risk inside the blast radius. Masters was able to avoid injury before the bomb finally exploded as opposed to the outcome in *The Incredible Hulk*, when Banner's face appeared shocked as he was struck by gamma rays while staring at the reader, breaking the fourth wall. Kirby depicted a similar victim of a "gamma gun" who died while staring at the reader in *Captain 3D* #1 (1953),[18] demonstrating that the cause and effect of the gamma bomb were depicted separately in the above two stories.

Kirby likely brought the topic of mutants to Marvel Comics, which was the central concept to *The X-Men* #1 (1963), featuring Professor X, who trained his team of five inexperienced gifted youngsters to better deal with a cynical world. Simon and Kirby worked on a similar concept for *Black Cat Mystic* #59 (1957) in a story that also involved five mutants born with superpowers who were abducted and raised as test subjects by the government. These mutants grew tired of their isolation and used their abilities to escape from their facility to seek freedom.[19] There was a similar plotline in *Yellow Claw* #2 (1956) that was written and penciled by Kirby and dealt with a similar mutant theme about six supernormal humans born with special gifts and used by the villainous Claw to bend reality. He defined "mutant" in Jimmy Woo's dialogue balloon as "people with deviations … in either mind or body … can think the entire world into panic."[20] This definition is close to the one that Lee dialogued in the first X-Men as people who "possess an extra power … one which ordinary humans do not!"[21] Similar to the story from *Black Cat Mystic*, the mutants in *Yellow Claw* broke free by teleporting to safety. However, their species continued to be hunted by robots called Sentinels that were led by Master Mold in *The X-Men* #14 (1965), by Lee and Kirby. The Sentinels' collective artificial intelligence

Kirby's depiction of the gamma bomb origin in *The Incredible Hulk* #1 (1962) was reused from a similar situation in his newspaper comic strip *Sky Masters of the Space Force* (February 18–22, 1960).

eventually gained sentience and turned against their human inventors in a similar manner to another malignant robot created by Kirby and scriptwriter Dave Wood, in "Ultivac is Loose!" from DC's *Showcase* #7 (1957). Similar to the Sentinels, Ultivac became an enemy of his creator after gaining sentience. Lee and Kirby depicted another arch-nemesis of the X-Men, Magneto, the Master of Magnetism, as a villain that unified similarly abused and despondent mutants in *The X-Men* #1. His pre–Marvel precursor was found in Lee, Lieber, and Kirby's "The Wonder of the Ages!!! Magneto!" from *Strange Tales* #84 (1961), about a man gaining magnetic powers in space. Kirby is credited for the art only; however, his involvement with magnetic powers preceded this character in "We Were Doomed by the Metal-Eating Monster" from *My Greatest Adventure* #21 (1958).[22] This monster's magnetic rays permeated a large geographic region attracting all the metal toward it for nutritional value. It appears that the powers of mutation and magnetism piqued Kirby's interest well before cocreating *The X-Men*.

The Fantastic Four (FF) also featured a significant number of plots and characters from Kirby's pre–Marvel comic books, including the team members, group transformative experience, powers, cosmic rays, aliens, villains, the title, and time travel. Many of these topics were initially present in his cocreation with script-writer Dave Wood and Joe Simon, in the *Challengers of the Unknown* (COTU), which premiered in DC's *Showcase* #6 (1957).[23] The COTU preceded the FF by four years, but the similarities were similar enough to prompt Roy Thomas to connect the two teams: "I could see that the characters were human with more personality than most others. Part of that clearly had to do with Jack, who brought over much of the spirit of the old *Challengers of the Unknown* series, and some of it of course was Stan."[24] For example, both teams have a professor or doctor, Professor Hale in COTU (1957) and the FF's (1961) Dr. Reed Richards. Both scientists are introduced with the same pose, jacket, and pipe in hand, suggesting that Kirby had the COTU in mind[25] when he cocreated the first issue of FF with Lee.[26] Reed Richards had super-stretch powers, which was an ability wielded by "Stretcho," a character of Kirby's first fantastic foursome, the evil "Crime Carnival!" in *Adventure Comics* #84 (1943).[27] Both teams also had a strong man as a character archetype, Rocky Davis of COTU and the FF's rocky member, the Thing. They also both had an attractive blonde-haired member, Ace Morgan for COTU and the FF's Susan Storm. There was also another blonde character in COTU, June Robbins, who bore a strong resemblance to Susan Storm. Another similarity was the use of a "red" person, Red Ryan in COTU and the FF's Human Torch. Both the COTU and FF began as mundane groups who endured a near-death experience from a crash that transformed them into death-defying heroes. The COTU vowed to stay together and form a group to engage in high-intensity adventures after surviving a plane crash in an intense storm with a declaration by the team: "We should be dead.... We're living on borrowed time! ... There's no reason why we can't do it together, challenge the unknown!"[28] A similar situation occurred with the FF, who also vowed to stay together after exposure to cosmic rays that caused their spaceship to crash. The team exclaimed, "We've changed! ... We're more than just human! ... Together we have more power than any humans have ever possessed! ... We've gotta use that power to help mankind."[29] Kirby depicted the panels in both origins using similar choreography and the script by both Dave Wood on COTU and Stan Lee on FF, which expressed the same plot. Although there were no cosmic rays in COTU, they were mentioned later in Kirby and Wood's daily newspaper strip, *Sky Masters of the Space Force* (October 16, 1959), in which astronauts on a space station discussed the effects of cosmic rays on human tissue. Kirby also wrote and penciled space-related mutation in *Challengers of the Unknown* #3 (1958) when Rocky ingested a life-preserving chemical during a trip to space and, upon his return, accidentally gained superpowers. His powers resembled those of the FF, exhibiting super strength, reshaping his body, directing flame, and becoming invisible.[30]

Kirby's depiction of villains, aliens, and time travel in FF shared significant similarities to those shown in preexisting adventures of the COTU. One example from an opening midstory splash page in both *Showcase* #11 (1957)[31] and *The Fantastic*

Four #7 (1962)[32] depicted the same situation when both teams were transported by aliens from one point in their base to another using antigravity columns. Both teams also shared one identical science-fiction storyline presented first in Jack Kirby's "The Human Pets" from *Challengers of the Unknown* #1 (1958)[33] then later in Lee and Kirby's "The Infant Terrible" from *Fantastic Four* #24 (1964).[34] Both stories depicted an advanced, superior, green alien child that kidnapped the four heroes, and both children were lectured by their parents at the end of the story to return the heroes to Earth unharmed. The second story's credits listed Lee as the writer and Kirby only as the artist, despite Kirby being credited as the writer of the *Challengers* story.

Time travel was another science-fiction trope that both comic books utilized. Kirby first depicted a "time cube" that the COTU used to visit ancient Egypt to thwart the plans of the "The Wizard of Time" in *Challengers of the Unknown* #4 (1958),[35] and then he later depicted a similarly shaped time machine that the FF used to thwart Rama-Tut in ancient Egypt for *Fantastic Four* #19 (1963). In both stories, the two groups were captured by the Egyptians for slave labor, and eventually returned home. "The Wizard of Time's" distinctive round cap, flat top, goatee, collared cape, and costume design are the same that Kirby used to design Immortus for his first appearance in *The Avengers* #10 (1964).

There is a reason to consider that Kirby may have cocreated the name Fantastic Four, as well as co-plot the creation of the villains Puppet Master, the Skrulls, and the Mad Thinker. The title of *The Fantastic Four* denoted four members with "fantastic" powers, which was alluded to in Simon and Kirby's *The Double Life of Private Strong* #1 (1959). The hero's father, Professor Malcolm Strong, described his son as having "fantastic" superpowers by using other parts of his brain. It's interesting to note that Simon and Kirby demonstrated that adjective in bold for emphasis,[36] making one consider that it could have been Kirby who suggested the title for Marvel's first super team. The Puppet Master was a villain who premiered in *The Fantastic Four* #8 (1962), an issue that credited Lee as the writer and Kirby as the penciler. The last page displayed a dramatic panel[37] that was identical to one used by Simon and Kirby in Prize Comics' *Black Magic* #4 (1951)[38] of the villain falling out of a window and dropping their puppet at the heroes' feet. Kirby designed the panels to depict the inherent tragedy with which the stories concluded. He also depicted green shape-changing aliens that first appeared in *The Fantastic Four* #2 (1962) named "Skrulls" and one in issue #11 (1963) called the Impossible Man. Years before, Kirby cocreated a similar green shape-changing alien named "Space Face" in *Fighting American* #7 (1956) with script by Carl Wessler.[39] All the above panels by Kirby feature small green aliens whose powers were depicted as shape changing. Another pair of villains called the Mad Thinker and his Awesome Android were featured in *Fantastic Four* #15 (1963). The Mad Thinker was smaller and smarter than his servant, the Awesome Android, and both appear to be a combined concept repeated from Kirby's 1950s tryout strip, *Chip Hardy*. Concept art from the strip depicted a similar scientist named "Gideon Challenger," who commanded an android called "The

Child," and similar to the Awesome Android, the Child was more muscular than his diminutive master.[40]

The Avengers also contained plots, characters, and panels that were originally depicted in comic books from Kirby's pre–Marvel period. Captain America re-premiered in *The Avengers* #4 (1964) after his body was discovered by the team, frozen after roughly 20 years in suspended animation caused by defusing a bomb in an airplane that exploded and thrust him into the cold ocean. Kirby's previous patriotic hero encountered the same plane-bomb scenario in "The Ultra-Sonic Spies!" in *The Double Life of Private Strong* #2 (1959), but in this case, managed to disarm the bomb. This similarity implies that Kirby likely plotted *The Avengers* story despite not getting cowriter credit. Another similar case was the premiere of The Lava Men who appeared in *The Avengers* #5 (1964) by Lee and Kirby. Their origin and plot were the same as that depicted by Kirby in the "Volcano Men" for DC's *Tales of the Unexpected* #22 (1958). The Lava Men, under the command of their corrupt Shaman, emerged from their underground home to destroy a local village, but were challenged and convinced by the Avengers to leave. Both the Lava Men and Volcano Men were explained to be prehistoric humans who adapted their bodies to live near lava in one case and a volcano in the other,[41] eventually confronting the military only to be persuaded to return underground.

Both the Howling Commandos and M.O.D.O.K. are creations of Lee and Kirby; however, they have strong similarities to preexisting characters that Kirby created with Joe Simon during the Golden Age. One example is "The Boy Commandos" in *Detective Comics* #64 (1942) about an elite fighting force of young men combating Nazis in World War II, similar to the Young Allies that they created for Timely. Both series related to Simon's fondness for Clair W. Hayes's World War I novels about the *Boy Allies* (1915).[42] Each member of the Boy Commandos had his own unique trait and nationality that were referenced in their premiere splash page that presented their names and descriptions similar to that shown in *Sgt. Fury and His Howling Commandos* #1 (1963).[43] The plot of the Howling Commandos fighting Nazis in World War II was the same as that seen in the Boy Commandos, except the members of the later team, similar to Kirby, were 20 years older. Strangely, Kirby was not given a cowriter credit for the first issue of *Sgt. Fury and His Howling Commandos*, but there was a notable single-page gun glossary at the end of the issue where he shared a writing credit with Lee, probably because Kirby was a surviving veteran of front-line combat. Another World War II veteran, Captain America, battled the villain M.O.D.O.K., created by Stan Lee and Jack Kirby in *Tales of Suspense* #94 (1967), a character whose brain was much larger than his body to the extent that he needed an exoskeleton and hoverchair to move. Simon and Kirby appear to have created this concept first in "The Menace of Marto!" for their space fantasy series *Blue Bolt* #6 (1940). Marto, in the same manner as M.O.D.O.K., was a corrupt scientist who expanded his mind and body through cellular augmentation, but the outcome caused his brain and body sizes to diverge to the point of a wielding a gigantic head that required support mechanisms.[44]

Kirby very likely introduced the concept of Spider-Man to Marvel.[45] However, it is important to first state that Spider-Man was the joint creation of Stan Lee and Steve Ditko. Ditko designed the art, costumes, web shooters, and Peter Parker's appearance while Lee's comedic dialogue verbally registered with readers. Although Kirby drew Spider-Man's first cover for *Amazing Fantasy* #15 (1962), his actual contribution to the character was far more circuitous. It was often the case with Kirby that he designed the costume of a new character by penciling its cover, which occurred with Daredevil, Iron Man, and Immortus. Then after the cover was finished, the dialogue and interior art was added by Lee and others. Spider-Man's case was shown to be different on the back cover of *Marvelmania* #2 (1970), demonstrating an initial cover that Ditko drew that was rejected by Lee in favor of the later one by Kirby.[46] This meant that Kirby did not design the costume or the gimmicks; they were created by Ditko. However, Kirby was involved in the pre-creation of Spider-Man as an initial concept before presenting it to Lee in early 1962 from "unsold inventory ... by Joe Simon and Jack Kirby,"[47] which was followed by their usual plotting and penciling session. They generated pages that Ditko was asked to ink; however, the young artist noticed that it resembled Archie Comics' *Adventures of the Fly* by Simon and Kirby.[48] Comparing the *Adventures of the Fly* #1 (1959) with Spider-Man's debut in *Amazing Fantasy* #15 may shed light on Kirby's initial Spider Man ideas that Lee and Ditko found worth keeping. Peter Parker was an orphan raised by his Uncle Ben and was bitten by a radioactive spider that gave him powers such as wall-crawling, hyper agility, and super strength. In comparison, the Fly's alter ego was Tommy Troy, an orphan also adopted by a man named Ben, who saw a spider in its web shortly before obtaining powers such as super strength and wall-climbing from a fifth-dimensional fly.[49] The rudimentary concepts of both characters are strikingly similar. The spider web seen in *The Fly* #1 suggests that it was probably a spider-based hero that was changed into a fly in the middle of the story. There is more about that in a later chapter; however, this analysis and Ditko's commentary certainly agree with Kirby, who later claimed to bring a Spider Man to Marvel, where Lee and Ditko conceptualized it into the popular superhero.

Although Kirby delivered multiple ideas to Marvel, not all of them worked and it was Ditko who often added his own innovations to concepts to better cocreate or update superheroes with Lee. After spending the later 1950s developing his pencils and style on science-fiction, mystery, and horror anthology titles at Charlton and Atlas, Ditko undertook five main assignments at Marvel. He was responsible for the visual creation of Spider-Man in 1962, including the construction of his costume, family, workplace, and rogues' gallery.[50] In 1963, Ditko created the Marvel Comics corner box, a pivotal part of the company brand identity that became synonymous with the company's superheroes.[51] In that same year, he created and designed Doctor Strange and his multiverse,[52] then designed Iron Man's later red-and-yellow armor.[53] In 1964, Ditko also pioneered the concept of anger triggering Bruce Banner's transformation into the Hulk.[54]

To understand Ditko's approach to his five assignments, it's first important to highlight that his developing artistic sensibilities were based on analysis and function. He viewed his assignments as problems that needed to be solved to achieve an overall brand identity. So, it's not accurate to consider his contributions to the characters as entirely visual because the Marvel Method allowed him to supply former ideas and concepts, which he developed at Charlton into the plotting and storytelling stages of his Marvel stories. These stories fit into the overall development of the Marvel Comics Group. In 1966 during one of his few interviews, Ditko offered insight to his storytelling objectives, demonstrating his high regard for the art and craft of comic book design. When asked if he had any advice for aspiring artists, he responded:

> You must really understand the basics of art, perspective, composition, anatomy, drapery, light and shade, story-telling, etc. You need a solid foundation of what is right and good to build on.... You can't really draw anything well unless you understand the purpose of that drawing [*storytelling*], the best way to get the drawing across [*individual point of view, composition*], and convincingly [*perspective, anatomy, drapery, light, and shade*].[55]

Ditko also gave a rare insight into his own beginnings, as he described how he managed to teach himself the skills to learn from comic storytellers in a fashion that eventually ensured he was able to achieve his overall artistic purpose. Ditko was quoted as saying:

> Until I came under the influence of Jerry Robinson, I was self-taught, and you'd be amazed at the hours, months, and years one can spend practicing bad drawing habits. Jerry gave me a good foundation.... Practicing on a solid, proper foundation, you train your heart and mind to work like a unit while correctly broadening your knowledge and ability.... Study, draw life around you, people, drapery, and reality. Study other artists to see how they interpret reality to art.[56]

These lessons were critical to Ditko as an engineer of concepts. He was keen to point out that no artist had a claim over the wider art form itself, but merely could participate in a shared pursuit of the arts to find their own position within it. He believed that all artists should look to be as original in their work as they were in real life: "No one is an original artist; no living artist today or yesterday invented or discovered art, brushes, ink, paper, or comics. Everyone builds on what was done before or is being done."[57] His approach to comic art as an engineer of concepts makes sense in that each of his five assignments were pieces that furthered the overall identity and brand of Marvel Comics.

Ditko used his artistic discipline as a focal point toward his primary role as an engineer of concepts, which he used to cocreate Spider-Man and his universe. When asked in 1965 who created Spider-Man, Ditko replied: "Stan Lee thought the name up. I did costume, web gimmick on wrist, and the spider signal."[58] However, he elaborated on a larger creative process that took place that began when he was asked to ink a previous five-page Spider-Man story by Lee and Kirby. Ditko remarked to Lee that their original Spider-Man design resembled Simon and Kirby's previous work on *Adventures of the Fly*[59] and also included a similar magic ring that allowed the prototype hero to transform. Ditko also clarified that the Kirby Spider-Man costume was akin to previous Kirby designs, including Giant-Man or Captain America,[60] but insinuated that it lacked a sense of innovation, and understood there was a better process to address the Spider-Man problem. Lee probably wanted to avoid any legal entanglements with Archie Comics since a couple decades earlier they sent a cease-and-desist order to his publisher Goodman because Captain America's original shield closely resembled the costume of their character the Shield. This order caused Simon and Kirby to change Captain America's shield to its popular circular shape.[61] So, Lee did not want to develop Kirby's Spider-Man any further and gave the name to Ditko to visually develop a completely original and unique design for the character.[62] In response, Ditko engineered the costume, web shooters, spider signal, web swinging, wavy spider-sense lines, among others, and expressed satisfaction that his Spider-Man design worked well and met the function of the name.

Ditko also likely gained satisfaction from cocreating and visually pioneering the hero's rogues' gallery designs, including Sandman, Vulture, and Dr. Octopus, giving the series substantial variety. These characters were highlighted in the final pages of Lee and Ditko's *The Amazing Spider-Man Annual* #1 (1964)[63] while their diversity included the Burglar, Vulture, Shocker, Kraven the Hunter, Aunt May's house, the *Daily Bugle*, among others, and were all extremely important to readers' engagement of the *Spider-Man* universe. Despite creating the main character and its ancillary characters for only four years, Lee and Ditko managed to assign the series' cast a variety of appearances and psychologies, which future artists and writers continued to utilize. There are three villains, if not more, in the series' rogues' gallery that Ditko most likely introduced to Lee in their plotting discussions: Norman Osborn, Electro, and Chameleon. Norman Osborn was the evil and corrupt CEO and board director of his company, Oscorp, and the alter ego of the Green Goblin. He first appeared as a background face in *The Amazing Spider-Man* #23 (1965), depicted with his main distinguishing feature, his distinctly curly hair. Osborn's name and relation to his son, Harry Osborn, was finally revealed in *The Amazing Spider-Man* #37 (1966). Both Osborn's corporate villainy and his distinct curled hairstyle have links to Ditko's pre–Marvel period at Charlton Comics. He depicted a precursor character with the same hairstyle in *Strange Suspense Stories* #33 (1957) named descriptively as "Director of the Board." This character was an ill-tempered corporate figure who abused labor leaders and native tribesmen.[64] Ditko understood that he needed a corrupt and greedy president of a corporation for the role of Green Goblin's alter ego and appears to have used his template from Charlton. He also probably introduced an electric-based supervillain to Lee when they created Electro, who premiered in *The Amazing Spider-Man* #9 (1964). This villain could also be traced back to a similar lightning-based character in Ditko's *Strange Suspense Stories* #48 (1960) named "The Human Powerhouse," who gained his powers for a limited time to ward off an extraterrestrial attack.[65] Lee, however, likely assigned the name since it was reused from previous characters in the company. Electro's partner in the Sinister Six, the Chameleon, debuted in *The Amazing Spider-Man* #1 (1963) and was a spy who used a variety of masks to disguise his face, avoid detection, and blend into the crowd. However, Ditko apparently reused his character from *Out of This World* #6 (1957) in his short story titled "All Those Eyes," which depicted a similar faceless spy who used numerous masks to masquerade himself as other people.[66]

Ditko was also well-prepared from his years at Charlton to dramatically depict mutation in his work at Marvel, which was a common theme throughout the comic book line. Ditko depicted Spider-Man gaining powers by mutation from the bite

Some of Ditko's characters at Marvel, namely Electro in *The Amazing Spider-Man* #9 (1964), share qualities with his preexisting characters from Charlton Comics, such as the lightning-based character in *Strange Suspense Stories* #48 (1960).

of a radioactive spider, and also co-plotted another story about mutation in *Amazing Adult Fantasy* #14 (1962) with Lee. This story followed a young mutant boy who was referred to as a "mutie" by bullies and invited by a powerful telepath to a safe haven for other mutants. These were concepts that Lee probably adapted from *Odd John* (1935) with Ditko, before using them to cocreate *The X-Men* #1 (1963) with Jack Kirby. Although Kirby had a long pre–Marvel history with the topic of mutants, Ditko notably depicted mutants in comic books in the late 1950s, namely *This Magazine Is Haunted* vol. 2, #14 (1957), in his story of a "Green Man" born with chlorophyll cells for blood instead of hemoglobin and who was raised as an orphan and needed only water to survive.[67] One year later in Charlton's *Out of this World* #7 (1958), Ditko penciled a story in which radiation mutated a man using atomic fission, and as a mutant, began to question his own existence, "A Freak! I'm a Freak! Not like other people!"[68] This was the same self-hate that many mutant characters demonstrated in *The X-Men*. He also regularly depicted radiation as a trigger for mutation in Charlton's *Space War* #10 (1961) about a human transformed by an unusual radioactive accident into a cosmic supernormal being that was capable of traveling the universe at warp speeds.[69] In 1957, Ditko also penciled a story called "The Supermen" for Charlton in *Out of This World* #3 that featured the impact of radiation on men's brains, granting them telepathic powers.[70] Augmenting humans with radiation was a recurrent and ongoing theme in Ditko's comic books at Charlton. It was present in his comics well before he and Lee used the concept for Peter Parker getting his powers from the bite of a radioactive spider in *Amazing Fantasy* #15.

Doctor Strange is thought to have been conceived in Ditko's mind when he inked the Lee, Lieber, and Kirby story of "Dr. Droom" in *Amazing Adventures* #1 (1961). Similar to the problem with Kirby's Spider-Man, Ditko likely understood that there were more innovative ways to render Droom traveling to Tibet and undergoing a transformation to become a crime-fighting mystic. He succeeded in designing a superior version of that origin for Doctor Strange in *Strange Tales* #115 (1963) with Lee. Regarding the character's first appearance in issue #110, Lee remarked to his fans, "We have a new character…. Dr. Strange… 'Twas Steve's idea…. Originally decided to call him Mr. Strange … too similar to Mr. Fantastic…. We had a villain called Dr. Strange just recently … hope it won't be too confusing!"[71] Since a previous villain that was called "Dr. Strange" appeared in Lee and Kirby's *Tales of Suspense* #41 (1963), then the name probably came from Lee. However, the character was mainly Ditko's due to his specific rendition of the black magic sorcerer that was depicted with a morbid and Lovecraftian supernatural touch accompanied by design, plots, and a unique exploration of the multiverse that were very different from Lee and Kirby's approach to Droom. Much of Ditko's earlier work at Charlton naturally pointed to eventually creating a character akin to Doctor Strange. He experimented with the concept of interdimensional travel in *Strange Suspense Stories* #32 (1957) by portraying a man who walked through a mystical door into a dark dimension to steal its diamonds, leading him to be stranded.[72] Additionally, *Out of This*

World #7 (1958) featured art by Ditko depicting a man who found a time machine that transported him in a colorful swirl of visual effects to any time or place. His artistic choices in this story demonstrating "Adam" as "the universe whirled around him" are energy-based visual precursors to his representation of spells cast by Doctor Strange for Marvel.[73] Strange's distinct spell-casting hands were also previously illustrated by Ditko in *Space Adventures* #27 (1959), a story about a jailed alien sorcerer who held up his hands in the same pattern and teleported to freedom using body language that was later characteristic to Doctor Strange.[74] Ditko managed to envisage and build these ideas during the 1950s and 1960s with very little photo reference, which is assumed mainly because there was nothing else visually like it. As an engineer of concepts, he developed key storytelling graphics during his time at Charlton that were utilized for the depiction of the mystic arts. This growing skill set culminated in his portrayal of Doctor Strange observing the dimension-staggering conflict between Eternity and Dormammu in *Strange Tales* #146 (1966).

Both Iron Man and the Hulk were cleverly written as tragic figures but they both missed critical functional elements that Ditko felt compelled to address. Iron Man's original gray armor fashioned by Jack Kirby in *Tales of Suspense* #39 (1963) was considered by some as bulky and unappealing. It fit the narrative of a suit of armor with repulsor rays, but it failed to visually attract audiences in a manner similar to Daredevil's first lackluster yellow costume, which he also designed. The armor's color later changed to "untarnishable gold" in issue #40, improving the overall reader experience, but still missing a sleek functionality that was popular in many vehicles and automobiles of the 1960s. Ditko penciled and co-plotted *Tales of Suspense* #48 (1963) with Stan Lee and streamlined the armor's design, creating the polished red-and-gold color pattern of "The New Iron Man." He penciled a sequence demonstrating Tony Stark donning the new armor's various components with a splash page that revealed the final complete set. It was depicted as more flexible for improved comfort with iron-coated gloves, tennis shoes, and sleeves that wrapped around the limbs and that were stiffened by magnetic force.[75] Ditko presented the discarded fragments of the previous armor on the ground, demonstrating that the Iron Man problem was addressed. The Hulk created by Lee and Kirby had a similar problem. *The Incredible Hulk* (1962) had been canceled due to lack of sales after six issues, and Lee considered that it was worth the time to make the character viable for another attempt at an ongoing series. The original Hulk's powers solely manifested at night, making his character similar in function to a werewolf. Lee presented the problem to Ditko to address the failed character, to which he later remarked, "We had been producing Spider-Man and Dr. Strange and both features were doing okay.... Now Stan wanted me to do another character.... Our new approach was to be more of an overhaul." Ditko elaborated on "a redesign of a previous model ... there would be more emphasis on showing the psychological, social problems of Banner."[76] The Hulk's adventures were later resumed as an ongoing feature in *Tales to Astonish* #59 (1964) by Lee and Ayers with a special mention of "blood pressure" triggering Bruce

Banner's transformation into the Hulk. Ditko devoted more panels to this concept in *Tales to Astonish* #60, depicting the Hulk emerging when "strain … set off a chemical reaction in my blood cells, which causes them to change their basic atomic structure."[77] With this concept, Ditko successfully reengineered Bruce Banner's anger to be the main trigger to transform him into the Hulk, and engaged readers in a more sophisticated way than Lee and Kirby's version that functioned by a predictable day-night cycle.

Ditko and Kirby used plots and ideas from their work at previous publishers when co-plotting stories and characters with Lee. However, they were generally given only the credit of artist while Lee was credited as the writer. This occurred because Stan Lee, born Stanley Martin Lieber, used the Marvel method by discussing a plot with an artist, who penciled the story through pacing and pictures, then sometimes added dialogue or notes on the page gutters. In most cases, Lee examined their pencils, edited, and added dialogue,[78] then labeled himself a writer, and credited the artist only for the art. This method of credit ignored the contribution of new plot ideas by the artist and assigned that credit to the dialogue writer, which also created confusion among fans about who created the Marvel superheroes. In comparison, DC Comics editor Julius Schwartz sometimes edited a writer's script until it was no longer recognizable before releasing it to an artist,[79] and just called this editing. The budget was lower at Marvel, so Lee as editor eliminated the writer, whom he likely viewed as a middleman, and retained that role. Since Lee never shared co-plotting credit with the artist, some of his fans became angry and developed a false impression that he never contributed original ideas, but they ignore that Lee was co-plotting, dialoguing, and overseeing Goodman's comics line of the early 1960s while fitting their stories together into a greater Marvel Universe. He sensed which plots resonated with readers, and it can be supported with data that he contributed ideas to Marvel, Kirby, and Ditko from his experience as an editor and from comics that he previously wrote, including innovations in text inserts; letters pages; antiheroes; ice powers; journalist comic characters; hooded cults; communist villains; characters such as Mole Man, Impossible Man, Crusher Creel, Puppet Master, Baron Zemo, Black Knight, Kang, and Willie Lumpkin; Peter Parker's love triangle; and unrequited love.

As a dialogue writer, Lee was proficient at text inserts and letters pages, which contributed to the reader's experience. Lee's first published story was in *Captain America Comics* #3 (1941) for a two-page text insert used to reduce shipping costs with the post office. This text piece was not a comic but was notable for its first mention of Captain America throwing his circular shield in the manner of a frisbee. Lee wrote, "He sent his shield spinning through the air to the other end of the tent where it smacked the knife out of Haines' hand!"[80] This demonstrated an efficient usage of the shield that wasn't considered before by Simon and Kirby, who used the shield only in a defensive manner or to enhance a punch. This offensive attack was used again by Lee and Kirby in Captain America's first Silver Age Marvel appearance in *The Avengers* #4 (1964) when the shield was thrown to slice through several guns while in mid-fire.[81] Artists, writers, and filmmakers continue to depict this long-range attack in various media. Another text insert by Lee demonstrated his mastery of dialogue between different members of a team in "Marvel Get-Together" from *Marvel Mystery Comics* #25 (1941) featuring a meeting among Destroyer, Angel, Human Torch, Sub-Mariner, Toro, Ka-Zar, and Patriot. Toro was referred to as "Fire-pants" and Sub-Mariner sarcastically commented toward the Human Torch, "You're a hypocrite, but I'll come in anyway."[82] Lee demonstrated a facility with interactive dialogue early in his career, which was critical for enhancing the reader's experience in *The Avengers* (1963), depicting nicknames assigned to heroes, for example, "chrome dome" for Iron Man and "goldilocks" for Thor. Lee also depicted similar comments between members of the Fantastic Four in their first appearance when the Thing threatened Mr. Fantastic with a tree: "You don't have to make a speech, Big Shot!"[83] It was a clear pattern that Lee dialogued characters with unique voices, including his own as editor writing letters pages and interacting with his readers. He answered letters by fans on the last page of each comic book to address their concerns or share their compliments. This was usual for many editors; however, he was able to personalize his responses and develop a sense of community. The letters page in *My Own Romance* #24 (1952) demonstrated a growing intuition for this type of engagement with phrases including, "Your editors aren't so old that they can't remember their own youth and know how right you are."[84] By the 1960s, Lee's level of participation with readers was more refined, visible in the letters page from *The Amazing Spider-Man* #39 (1966) when he wrote lines such as, "Anyway, we enjoyed getting the knockdown to your group, but try to enlarge it a bit, huh? It takes a lot of those 24 cents to keep us in the latest style straitjackets!" His sense of timing through dialogue was at its peak and there was no other editor during this period who could match this level of exchange with his appreciative crowd.

Lee also created several characters with qualities that he brought to his 1960s Marvel stories featuring Ice-Man, Spider-Man, J. Jonah Jameson, and Iron Man. His first comic book story credit is creating his first superhero, "Jack Frost," illustrated by the Blue Beetle creator Charles Nicholas in *U.S.A. Comics* #1 (1941). This "King of the Cold" came from the north, fought crime, and engaged in conflict with local law enforcement. Frost's name was old-fashioned, but the character had two qualities that Lee brought to Marvel's Silver Age. His ice powers and aesthetic were present in the character Ice-Man, aka Bobby Drake, from *The X-Men* #1 (1963). Drake initially premiered as a snow-based character similar to Frost and then eventually crystallized into the modern Ice-Man by issue #8. Frost was also misunderstood by authority figures such as the military or police, causing him to become angry and antagonistic toward society. After one adventure, law enforcement decided to arrest Frost, which caused the hero to scream, "So now you would arrest me like a common criminal! ... I came to your country to help you to fight crime.... But after this sort of reception, I've changed my mind.... If I can't work with you, I'll work against you, the next time we meet, beware!"[85]

This concept of the misunderstood or flawed superhero later defined many Marvel characters, including Spider-Man, which Lee and Ditko portrayed in *The Amazing Spider-Man* #1 (1963) when local police tried to arrest him on a rooftop, wrongly accusing him of stealing secret plans.[86] Lee, not Kirby or Ditko, first demonstrated his hero's problems with law enforcement, a key factor in advancing superhero comic books in the 1960s. His questioning of authority was accompanied by an admiration for journalism that he and Harry Fisk demonstrated in "Headline Hunter Foreign Correspondent" from *Captain America Comics* #5 (1941). This brave investigator discovered the truth about the Nazis behind the front lines and reported the information to the public. It was here that Lee first expressed an interest in journalists, the newsroom, and their mission to expose injustice with his comment, "This story is respectfully dedicated to the newspapermen of all nations."[87] Lee and Ditko depicted the workplace of Peter Parker, the alter ego of the Amazing Spider-Man, in *The Daily Bugle*, a newspaper organization. As a photographer, Parker was generally close to developing news stories and regularly turned in photos to his editor and headline hunter, J. Jonah Jameson. Another journalist whom Lee created during the Golden Age was Keen Marlow, "The Destroyer," illustrated by Jack Binder in *Mystic Comics* #6 (1941). Marlow was originally captured behind enemy lines by Nazi soldiers and imprisoned with Professor Eric Schmitt, who sacrificed himself to bestow his serum that enabled Marlow to become the Destroyer.[88] Lee used the Destroyer origin in 1963 when dialoguing the first appearance of Tony Stark, whose cellmate, Professor Yinsen, was trapped by communists in North Vietnam and sacrificed himself to help Stark complete the Iron Man armor.[89]

Lee's experience in writing comic books for the Timely-Atlas era prepared him to cocreate hooded villains for Marvel such as the Secret Empire and Baron Zemo. He wrote an adventure featuring the Black Marvel in *All Winners Comics* #1 (1941) called "The Order of the Hood" about a secret society and hooded crime syndicate, "which threatened to inflict a reign of horror upon the American people."[90] This group resembles a similar group of villains created by Lee and Kirby named the Secret Empire in *Tales to Astonish* #81 (1966), a hooded terrorist group and branch of Hydra that conspired to tear down "North America, South America, and Europe."[91] Lee also cocreated the red-hooded Baron Zemo in *The Avengers* #4 (1964) and revealed his origin in issue #6. The masked Nazi was an adversary of Captain America during World War II, when during an altercation, a canister of Adhesive X spilled and fused his mask to his face, leaving him unable to remove it. Although cocreated with Kirby, this character is very similar to a previous villain created by Lee that he named "The Hooded Horror!" in *Mystic* #12 (1952). The Hooded Horror was never seen without his mask, and similar to Zemo, lamented, "If only I could take off this hood."[92] He was a calculative villain who threatened local mob bosses with certain death unless they provided him a percentage of their profits. Although both villains were feared by their enemies, they lived with the curse that their mask and face were one and the same.

Lee also featured Lilliputian characters in the Golden Age who had characteristics that he used when creating the Moloids and the Impossible Man. Lee wrote "Rockman Underground Secret Agent" in *USA Comics* #3 (1942), which also expanded on the underground mythos that was created by Basil Wolverton. The art by Charley Nicholas depicted an underground adventure with a race of "little people" called pixies who lived inside Earth. The story's hero, Rockman, traveled through caverns in his "mole-ship" and faced the pixies in combat but was quickly "overpowered by sheer weight of numbers."[93] This was the same scenario Lee wrote for the Mole Man's Moloids, also known as Mole People, who grouped together to attack and overwhelm the Thing in *Fantastic Four* #22 (1964).[94] Lee created another diminutive character, "The Imp," with artist Chad Grotkopf in *Captain America Comics* #12 (1942) about a mischievous and small cartoon-like figure who wore green clothes and annoyed his enemies.[95] He was neither a superhero nor a supervillain, but instead functioned as an unusual prankster. Lee utilized a similar concept when cocreating the Impossible Man for *The Fantastic Four* #11 (1963), who was also small and green, and manipulated his body in the manner of a typical cartoon character that defied all standards of physics. He hailed from the planet Poppup and altered his matter and size into an airplane, spider, metal, porcupine, rocket, and more. At one point in the story, Lee wrote dialogue for Susan Storm, which appeared to describe both the Imp and the Impossible man: "He looks so humorous—How can he be such a menace?"[96]

Lee in all likelihood created Crusher, aka Joseph Hogan, the wrestler who grappled with Spider-Man, as well as Crusher Creel, who became the Absorbing Man. This can be estimated because Lee wrote multiple stories that demonstrated a hero's power by having them overcome bald musclemen named "Crusher." He first used the name to denote the "World's Strongest Wrestler" when he wrote "League of Crime" in *Mystic Comics* #8 (1942) with art by Mike Sekowsky and George Klein. This story's Crusher was bald and large, and used his muscle in service of the mob to fight and lose to costumed hero the Challenger in an alleyway.[97] Lee plotted a similar character into the first Spider-Man story in *Amazing Fantasy* #15 (1962) when Parker defeated an arrogant bald wrestler named "Crusher" for extra money.[98] Lee used the same name when cocreating a similarly bald and imposing brutal figure, Crusher Creel the Absorbing Man, in *Journey into Mystery* #114 (1965), who spoke and appeared in a manner similar to the other Crushers but was empowered by Loki to fight and eventually lose to Thor.[99]

There were other Timely-Atlas stories by Lee that he likely utilized when cocreating the Puppet Master and the recurring communist villains of the early 1960s. He wrote the "The Horror of the Doll-Devil" for *Young Allies* #10 (1943) about a villain that used black magic to manipulate people's bodies with voodoo dolls.[100] Voodooism was a common trope in the 1940s and 1950s, on which Lee and Kirby added a science-fiction concept when creating "the Puppet Master," who used radioactive dolls in *The Fantastic Four* #8 (1962). The Puppet Master enjoyed using his power to keep the heroes under his control, but his plans were eventually thwarted. Another common trope of this period was depicting communist villains, which Lee did frequently, with one early example during the Atlas period in "The Last Command of Colonel Fong" from *Battle* #17 (1953), about a North Korean colonel who was as ruthless with his own men as he was with the enemy. He mercilessly killed his own soldiers and proclaimed, "We communists make our own rules!"[101] Lee's anti-communism sentiment during this time was understandable since the United States was helping South Korea against the North, and comics such as this functioned as patriotic propaganda. His sentiment was similar in the Vietnam War during the early 1960s, when he scripted Iron Man's origin in North Vietnam as well as *Journey into Mystery* #93 (1963) when Thor flew to Asia and fought against "Red Chinese" troops.[102] In this issue, the red army's scientist, Chen Lu, researched atomic machinery that empowered him to become the Radio-Active Man. Because the Comics Code was active during this period, the focus of Radio-Active Man versus Thor was on superpowered wrestling and theatrics rather than gritty realistic violence, but Lee's anti-communist remarks remained consistent. This type of propaganda in Silver Age comics parallels the use of superheroes and comic characters in the Golden Age during World War II, including Captain America, Human Torch, Sub-Mariner, Superman, Batman, Wonder Woman, and Captain Marvel.

Lee also wrote and created Atlas-era characters whose qualities appeared again when he cocreated the Marvel villains Black Knight and Kang. Lee and Joe Maneely created Sir Percy of Scandia for *Black Knight* #1 (1955), a warrior who wielded his ebony blade, forged from a meteorite, in defense of King Arthur and Merlin. The character lasted five issues and was revived by Lee and Dick Ayers as the dead ancestor of the second Black Knight, Professor Nathan Garrett, in *Tales to Astonish* #52 (1964). Garrett was unworthy to wield the ebony blade, and instead used advanced tech-based weapons as well as genetics to bio-engineer eagle's blood onto a stallion to create his flying horse.[103] Garrett initially fought Giant Man and later joined the Masters of Evil in *The Avengers* #6 (1964), but eventually died in issue #48. This character appeared briefly during the early 1960s and served a notable lesson that not all science-fiction revivals of old characters were successful. Lee and Kirby created another multigenerational villain, Rama-Tut, also known as Kang, in *Fantastic Four* #19 (1964). In his first appearance, Tut boasted about his origins, specifically mentioning that he came "from the year 3,000" and was the only one on Earth not satisfied with peace.[104] He was considered a bad seed by his people who demonstrated his restlessness and enjoyment of war as he traveled back in time to fight in numerous battles. The bad seed origin and same number of years were present in a previous Lee story called "Horror on Haunted Hill!" from *Adventures into Weird Worlds* #14 (1954) with art by Carmine Infantino and Gil Kane. A sentient tree "from the planet Saturn" was exiled to Earth because he "committed the crime of murder ... for the first time in three thousand years!"[105] This alien grew tired of his home planet's paradise and visited Earth to hurt people.

Lee demonstrated a pattern of incorporating everyday human experiences into his superhero stories, which highlighted the teenage love triangle, unrequited love, and blue-collar workers. He demonstrated a talent for teenage love in the early fifties with titles such as *Millie the Model* and, more specifically, *Homer Hooper #2–3* (1953) to mimic the teen stories that originally were presented in *Archie*. However, he captured the genre well when depicting Homer Hooper as a teenager with freckles, red hair, and a blonde girlfriend who visited the malt shop with his high school friends. Lee incorporated this teen setting into *The Amazing Spider-Man* in 1966, after Ditko departed the title and was replaced by romance artist John Romita, Sr.[106] Lee and Romita steadily transformed the neurotic series into a teen drama with a love triangle that consisted of Peter Parker, Mary Jane, Gwen Stacy, and Harry Osborn, who occupied the same roles as Archie Andrews, Veronica Lodge, Betty Cooper, and Reggie Mantle.[107] Peter was the focus of both women's curiosity while Harry was the rich friend who was unable to capture their attention. Mary Jane was the fashionable shopper while Gwen was the blonde and blue-collar daughter of a police chief. This era raised the comic book series' sales utilizing the teen genre that Lee wrote in for years. He also appealed to teenage readers by adding unreciprocated love to many of his superhero stories, a topic with which he gathered experience writing about in earlier comics such as "Love 'Em and Leave 'Em" from *Actual Confessions* #13 (1952) with art by Werner Roth. This story depicted Duncan, a womanizer who boasted about his conquests to a bartender, shortly before meeting the love of his life, Madge. He experienced a lesson in Karma when he learned that the bartender was her father, who revealed to her Duncan's sordid history. Madge left Duncan and the story concluded with him staring out a window in a panel that stated he was "not daring to give up the hope that someday she'll return."[108] Lee added similar dialogue to Cyclops in *The X-Men* #3 (1963), when he expressed his unreciprocated love for Jean Grey: "Of all the girls I've ever met, she is the one I'd give my heart to."[109] Lee applied unreciprocated love throughout much of the superhero comic book line, including *Journey into Mystery* #89 (1963), when the blonde Dr. Donald Blake languished after nurse Jane Foster: "I love Jane, but I daren't tell her! A girl so beautiful would never marry a, a weakling like me!"[110] Both stories about Blake and Grey have components that were present in a previous story scripted by Lee, "Love Story" from *My Own Romance* #27 (1953), with art by Infantino and Kane. A blonde patient fell in love with nurse "Jane Grey," who resembled Thor's nurse, Jane Foster. Though they both had the same occupation and first name, her last name was Grey, the same as Jean Grey from X-Men,[111] suggesting that Lee had a strong hand in creating both female characters. Unrequited love, although unsatisfying, often kept teenage readers engaged in Lee's scripts. Besides unrequited love, Lee placed another human element into *Fantastic Four* #11 (1963), blue-collar mailman Willie Lumpkin. This character was previously depicted in Lee's newspaper comic strip *Willie Lumpkin* (1960–1961), drawn by Archie Comics artist Dan DeCarlo, and functioned to humanize *The Fantastic Four* by reminding the heroes of everyday situations including paying their bills and the value of the elderly.

Lee accepted Martin Goodman's direction to compete with the *Justice League of America* and collaborated with Kirby and Ditko to utilize plots from previous media as well as their own experiences. It was Lee who advanced the relatability of superheroes further by shifting them toward flaws and tragedy since his stories generally dealt with "everyday problems with which the reader can identify to mix fantasy with realism."[112] He likely directed plots to give Peter Parker sinus problems or depict the Fantastic Four as late to pay their rent in a similar fashion as his favored strip writer, Milton Caniff. Those imperfections made readers relate to his dialogue more readily than other comic book writers at the time, and it's for that reason he probably gravitated toward the art styles of Kirby and Ditko, who depicted heroes as haggard and uncomfortable. However, Lee was also in all likelihood incapable of creating these compelling characters by himself and needed Kirby's two decades of experience in most genres, including his considerable knowledge in science fiction. He mentioned that Kirby was "without peer in almost every type of imaginative, far-out fantasy!"[113] He also needed Ditko's skills as a visual engineer who addressed the problems that the company needed solved to fully establish the brand. Lee described him as "an imaginative inventive perfectionist, he combines the skill of a master storyteller with the eye of a dazzling designer."[114] Lee needed these two auteurs to tell most of the story for him, while he kept the plots and dialogue focused on a common direction. He focused their different motivations in the early 1960s to tell stories with a temporary shared vision that showcased monstrous heroes with blemished faces, decrepit hands, crippled bodies, and financial problems. The comic book marketplace responded favorably to their collaboration, which proved to Lee that his approach to superheroes worked. Changing priorities terminated their unique working relationship and later creators carried their creations forward in an ongoing narrative. Many comic book professionals continued to learn more from the three Marvel cofounders as their paths diverged, notably how creators sometimes don't share credit once their superheroes become famous.

The Marvel Method's
Credit Controversy

Marvel's Silver Age advanced the qualities of the superhero comic book due to the cumulative creativity of Stan Lee, Jack Kirby, and Steve Ditko. Their work in the early 1960s changed comic book history with flawed superheroes, smart dialogue, and a shared Marvel Universe, which eventually overtook DC Comics in overall market share. When a superhero becomes successful and generates significant revenue, there can often be disagreement among its creators on what aspects they contributed. This becomes complicated in the case of the three founding fathers of Marvel Comics because Lee, as editor and writer, used the Marvel Method to generate concepts and storylines, which placed much of the responsibility of character and story creation on the artist. He described this method of comic story creation in the college magazine *Bachelor* #1 (1968):

> I discuss the plot with the artist, and we come to some agreement on what the story will be about. Then he goes home and draws the whole thing, comes back, and gives it to me or to whoever is writing it. The writer then puts in the copy right over the artist's drawings. He puts in the dialogue balloons and captions. I indicate where the balloons go on the paper and type the words on another sheet.[1]

What seemed to vary depending on the artist was how much co-plotting was done. This led to the controversy of whether the artist should also be credited as a cowriter because they cooriginated the idea and paced the plot into a sequence of panels and pages, often adding their own coordinated elements. Since Lee was both editor and final dialogue writer, he was also responsible for phrasing the credits box. He often labeled himself as the story's writer, resulting in resentment from his two cocreators. This unclear credit situation led all three creators to make claims over the years about who created what. Kirby, Ditko, and some readers accused Lee of stolen credit in various disputes over decades that have somewhat tarnished the reputation of their work. Analyzing their claims requires awareness of what the credit boxes and interviews depicted, and if there was a "share of credit," how did claims change over time? It is important to evaluate this timeline of events as a lesson in how the credit for this successful Marvel superhero franchise was shared by its contributors as it unfolded around their two most signature creations, *The Fantastic Four* by Stan Lee and Jack Kirby and *The Amazing Spider-Man* by Stan Lee and Steve Ditko.

The Fantastic Four #1 (1961) gave equal creator credit to Stan Lee and Jack Kirby.

Both comic books began with an equal share of credit that changed over time. *The Fantastic Four* #1 (1961) was created by Lee and Kirby, which the first issue stated on the top right-hand side of the first page: "Stan Lee + Jack Kirby."[2] While Lee's name appeared first, it was still evident that at least this comic book issue was created by the two men. This may have been an agreed-upon byline, but the implication was that of equal credit shared between both creators; however, their legal situations were rather different. Stan Lee was a fully employed editor-in-chief on a salary and Jack Kirby had nothing more than a work-for-hire arrangement with Marvel. However, what the credit does not reveal is who wrote the story and who drew the artwork. One year later, Spider-Man was created by Stan Lee and Steve Ditko. The credit from the hero's first appearance in *Amazing Fantasy* #15 (1962) was listed at the bottom of the first page, "Stan Lee + S. Ditko,"[3] with both men clearly and equally credited. However, the credit boxes changed over the coming months in both comic book series. *The Fantastic Four* maintained the equal Stan Lee and Jack Kirby credit for its first eight issues. Then in issue #9 (December 1962), the credit changed to "Script … Stan Lee. Art … Jack Kirby."[4] By issue #17 (1963), the credits changed again and identified Stan Lee as the person who wrote the "story" and named Jack Kirby for the story's "art."[5] One issue later, the credits changed again so the comic was described to be "written" by Stan Lee and "drawn" by Jack Kirby.[6] The first issue of *The Amazing Spider-Man* (1963) depicted a similar attribution with Stan Lee credited for the "script" and Steve Ditko credited for "art."[7] It appeared that by 1963, Lee maintained that he was the only writer on both titles. In *The Amazing Spider-Man* #3 (1963), the duties changed to "story" by Stan Lee and "art" by Steve Ditko.[8] Two issues later, this changed to "written" by Stan Lee and "drawn" by Steve Ditko.[9] Most people who read credits such as this in most media today generally think that the artist only fleshed out the writer's vision, but this was not true in the early years of Marvel. Their creative work was collaborative based on the aforementioned 1968 statement by Lee on the nature of the Marvel Method. However, the official writing credit was in the fine print, and as these series became more popular, pointed solely to Lee.

Lee and Kirby initially created Marvel through *The Fantastic Four*, and their acknowledgment of how much credit each one deserved varied over time. Once the Marvel Comics Group became a recognizable brand by the mid–1960s, news media began to pay attention to the phenomenon and interviewed Lee to discover its backstory. He and Kirby were portrayed in the *New York Herald Tribune* (January 9, 1966), demonstrating a Marvel Method plotting session where Lee was depicted as the main creator who generated ideas for Kirby to execute. Their interaction was shown as follows:

> "The Silver Surfer has been somewhere out in space since he helped the FF stop Galactus from destroying Earth," begins Lee, "Why don't we bring him back?" "Ummh," says Kirby, "Suppose Alicia, the Thing's blind girlfriend is in some kind of trouble. And the Silver Surfer comes to help her." Lee starts pacing and gesturing as he gets warmed up. "I see," says Kirby. He has kind of a high-pitched voice [...] Lee is lurching around and throwing punches now. "Right," says Kirby…. Lee sags back on his desk, limp and spent as Kirby smokes his cigar. Kirby has leaped out of the chair he was crumpled in. "Great, great." The cigar is out of his mouth and his baggy eyes are aglow.[10]

This paragraph was one of many over the years that depicted Lee as the literary genius and his collaborators as a pair of hired hands. It cannot be proven if he was a genius; however, it can be estimated that he displayed charisma when interacting with reporters. In contrast, Kirby was an artist who spent a great deal of time at the drawing board and his strength was pictorial storytelling rather than impressing journalists, which unfortunately left them focused on his "baggy" eyes. This type of report that flattered one creator over the other rightfully stirred resentment in Kirby. Lee answered more questions about his creative process during another interview in *Chicago Sun Times, Midwest* (August 28, 1966) with Roger Ebert, stating, "What we were doing was creating fairy tales for adults." Lee repeatedly used the word "we" to indicate who was creating the stories, implying a collaborative group effort. However, while Lee was quoted about the joint effort of his team, the caption next to his photo described him as the "Man behind the comic book renaissance.... Stan Lee, Editor of the Marvel Comics Group. Called 'the Homer of the Twentieth Century' by campus comic fans, he created the new breed of superheroes like Spider-Man and Fantastic Four."[11] The editor of the article contradicted Lee's collaborative statements by referring to "he" as the sole creator of the Marvel Universe with no mention of team effort in the captions. It is probable that his charisma and ability to communicate with journalists, coupled with their need to sensationalize their content, was the cause of this mischaracterization. However, these types of captions appeared frequently with him, which offended his collaborators, Kirby and Ditko.

Kirby's ex-partner, Joe Simon, depicted his impression of Lee and the topic of creator credit in the mid–1960s. Simon departed the Simon and Kirby team after the collapse of their company, Mainline Publishing Inc., amid the introduction of the Comics Code in 1954. After a couple of years in other media, he approached Crestwood publications, where Kirby and himself had previously published multiple genres of comics. He decided to create a humor-based magazine called *SICK* (1961) as an answer to *MAD* that he edited until the end of the decade.[12] A few of the pages from *SICK* #48 (1966) were used to satirize Lee in a comic strip written by Simon with art by Angelo Torres called "The New Age of Comics." Lee was depicted as the selfish editor "Sam Me" and Ditko as an artist with low self-esteem named "Dripko." In the strip, "Sam Me" exhibited a tendency to write his name as the creator on the pages of other people's stories when he directed to Dripko, "All right do the whole book over and have it on my desk in an hour—we've got twenty other books to get out today! And don't forget to sign my name on it!"[13] The meaning behind the satire was quite clear, because it appeared to depict Joe Simon's perspective on who benefited the most from the Marvel Method, which was Lee himself. Simon's opinion on Lee was not established from any interpersonal professional experience, so it was probably based on reports from Kirby, who likely experienced aggravation during the airing of *The Marvel Super-Heroes* (1966) cartoon that was produced by Grantray-Lawrence Animation. This animated show portrayed characters such as the Hulk, Iron Man, Thor, Sub-Mariner, and Captain America with a fairly low budget that mainly animated comic panels drawn by various artists from Marvel, including Kirby, but without any creator credits.

By this time, Lee may have sensed Kirby's irritation, which could have caused him to feel guilty enough to describe their work as collaborative in various public pronouncements he made over the next two years. Marvel licensed *The Fantastic Four* to Hanna-Barbera to make the property into a cartoon in 1967 with an arrangement that stated "based upon an idea by Stan Lee and Jack Kirby." This attribution demonstrated a certain degree of motivation from Goodman and Lee to share credit with Kirby and demonstrated to the public that *The Fantastic Four* comic book series was the idea of both men. In 1967, Mike Hodel interviewed both Lee and Kirby for a New York radio show on WBAI-FM and stated that Marvel's comics were "written and drawn by Stan Lee and Jack Kirby." Upon being asked about the creation of the Hulk, Lee responded by explaining that "we started that." This was another usage of "we" that indicated he also felt the Hulk was created from their collaboration. Hodel further stated that they both collaborated on the concepts and ideas for *Thor* every month. At this point, Lee corrected him and said, "Jack is the greatest mythological creator in the world," which appeared to defer the topic to Kirby as the series' main plotter. The subject of Thor versus Hercules came up, to which Kirby added, "We felt that they should contend with each other." Lee replied, "We create our own mythologies, we create our own universes." About villains such as Galactus and Ego, Lee clarified, "Jack ... is too darn imaginative ... he came up with an idea, a fellow named Ego who's a living planet ... a bio-verse." This may have appeared similar to a small confession from Lee to fans since the first appearance of Ego in *The Mighty Thor* #133 (1966) credited him with the script and Kirby only for the art. Both Hodel and Lee expressed their confusion regarding the term "bio-verse," a concept that Kirby needed to simplify for them, suggesting his superior command of science fiction. Lee also mentioned that he was impressed with his collaborator's imagination and stated, "Jack had to create a whole bunch of Inhumans.... I don't know what he's going to draw.... I put in the dialogue and captions."[14] This last point by Lee implied that Kirby initiated many of Marvel Comics' science-fiction storylines by this period, which was again alluded to a year later in the magazine *Castle of Frankenstein* #12 (1968) when Lee told an interviewer, "Kirby needs no plot at all ... he just makes up the plots for these stories. All I do is a little editing."[15] Lee further revealed some vulnerability when he stated he would "cry a little" if Kirby left and that he had "no doubt that Jack set the pace" at Marvel.[16] Lee's compliments at this point in time were consistent with the credit boxes, which changed back to a shared credit with phrases such as "Another Stan (The Man) Lee and Jack (King) Kirby Cosmic Creation!"[17] This still irritated Kirby, who was confirmed by Lee to need no plots, implying that he created most of the stories by the late 1960s and was still splitting the credit in half.

These heartfelt statements from Lee, including revised credit boxes that shared more credit, appear to be an attempt to heal Kirby's resentment. However, the comic book industry demonstrated awareness of the frustration created by the Marvel Method, suggesting that their collaborations would soon end. One sign of this industry critique was depicted in *Angel and Ape* #2 (1969) in a story called "The Most Fantastic Robbery in History," written by Sergio Aragones and Bob Oksner, penciled by Oksner, and inked by Wally Wood. The story portrayed Ape turning in completed comic pages to his "Brain Pix Comix, Inc.," editor, who bore a striking resemblance to Roy Thomas but with the name Stan Bragg. Bragg had an assistant who resembled Stan Lee. After Bragg collected the artwork, he asked Ape, "Why are you so ungrateful? When you write good stories and do good artwork, don't I sign it?"[18] This story indicated that the bullpen at DC Comics was aware of the problems that arose with

Marvel's credit boxes and echoed sentiments by Kirby, whose final 10 issues of *Fantastic Four* lacked the inspiration for which he was initially known. His growing discontent initiated his departure from Marvel Comics in 1970, two years after Perfect Film & Chemical purchased the company from Martin Goodman. This was probably a disappointment for him as he walked away from a company that he helped build.

Once Kirby left Marvel for DC Comics, he and Lee released a series of public statements that conflicted with their previous reports of a shared collaboration. Kirby expressed his frustration with Lee during an interview with the *Rocket's Blast Comic Collector* #81 (1970), when he was asked if the concept of *The Fantastic Four* was his idea:

> It was my idea. It was my idea to do it the way it was, my idea to develop it the way it was. I'm not saying that Stan had nothing to do with it. Of course he did. We talked things out. As things went on, I began to work at home, and I no longer came up to the office. I developed all the stuff at home and just sent it in. I had to come up with new ideas to help the strip sell, I was faced with the frustration of having to come up with new ideas and then having them taken from me.[19]

Kirby's frustration did not wane after their separation, probably due to Lee's rising exposure in the media, which affected the subject matter of his work at DC. This likely compounded further after several television viewers watched Lee on an episode of *To Tell the Truth* in 1971, wearing a full toupee and beard while charismatically discussing his natural ability at writing two comics a week for the past 30 years. He was still editor-in-chief at this point but was soon to become the publisher of the company. It is quite probable that Kirby saw this episode, which led to him satirize Lee as a bald man with a poorly fitting beard and toupee in *Mister Miracle* #6 (1972). Lee was characterized as "Funky Flashman," a verbose user and abuser of artistic talent, and a slave driver in this "happy ... Marvel of contrast" whose main objective was putting his "hands on the whole boodle of cash."[20] This comic book was said to have hurt Lee's feelings, but he was too busy to publicly react as he adjusted to his new role of publisher after Martin Goodman finally departed the company. Kirby may have also seen a report in a newspaper commenting on Lee's new position at Marvel that described him as the "Joe Namath" of comics, responsible for "the creation of The Fantastic Four."[21] Statements regarding Lee as the sole creator of Marvel's properties began to surface in various outlets a year into his new position, including company fanzine *FOOM!* #1 (1973), which indicated that Lee was responsible for Marvel's cultural impact in a statement that omitted Kirby as a cocreator:

> But it wasn't until 1960 that he created the Marvel Age of Comics with a new revolutionary concept that injected all-too-human personalities into the otherwise common clay of comic superheroes. Lee's technique, built upon realism and relevancy, was responsible for the comic explosion of the '60s. Lee and Marvel have since become synonymous.[22]

Lee continued this narrative of being the main creator of Marvel Comics in more interviews and statements throughout the 1970s. In 1973, Lee answered questions in Andy Warhol's *Interview* #31 (1973) about his early days in comics. He summarized his first year at Timely Comics assisting Joe Simon and Jack Kirby as "occasionally they'd let me write a story. But then the two guys who were working there quit."[23] Some readers found it peculiar that he chose not to acknowledge their names, including that of his former Marvel cocreator. His intentions became clear a year later when he formalized his narrative about the creation of *The Fantastic Four* in his book *Origins of Marvel Comics* (1974). This book served as Lee's official statement on how he created the Marvel superheroes from his own imagination, which shocked fans who remembered just a few years earlier that he shared cocreator credit with Jack Kirby. Instead, he claimed to create *The Fantastic Four* from factors relating to his wife and boss:

> At about this time I had a talk with my wife ... this time Joan was commenting about the fact that after twenty years of producing comics ... she wondered why I didn't put as much effort and creativity into the comics as I seemed to be putting into my other freelance endeavors. Martin Goodman mentioned the *Justice League of America*, why don't you create a team of superheroes? This was to be something different, something special ... to stupefy my publisher ... satisfy my wife's desire ... to prove myself.... I would create a team of superheroes.... After kicking it around with Martin and Jack for a while, I decided to call our quaint quartet The Fantastic Four.... I wrote a detailed first synopsis for Jack to follow, and the rest is history.[24]

His change in narrative toward being sole creator included information that may or may not be fully true and may have been written for reasons related to Marvel Comics' new owners. The topic of Goodman's request to mimic DC Comics was probably correct. However, the aspect regarding his wife serving as the agent of change is doubted by some readers who paid close attention and attributed the improvement in the caliber of his creations in the 1960s to the presence of Kirby and Ditko. Kirby's experience with astronaut comic strips, the *Challengers of the Unknown*, and cosmic rays made it doubtful that he only followed Lee's synopsis. However, since Goodman departed Marvel, the new owners from Perfect Film & Chemical would benefit if Lee was labeled as the sole creator. If the company satisfied Lee with his corporate position, then he could create a narrative that would legally protect them from any claims of ownership by his former cocreators. This is a legal theory held by many fans who believe Kirby's narrative of events. Besides legally protecting Perfect Film & Chemical, his primary duty as publisher involved managing the direction of Marvel from New York, as well as creating business arrangements that furthered the brand in countries including the United Kingdom, in which he oversaw Marvel Comics International. During one such trip, he was asked about his former collaborator in an interview for the British fanzine *Fantasy Advertiser International* (April 1975), where he discussed why Kirby had departed Marvel in 1970:

> I think it could be as simple as the fact that he got sick of everything he did saying "by Stan Lee and Jack Kirby." Maybe he just wanted to do his own thing and have the books saying "by Jack Kirby..." I've heard that he was tired of doing things that he never owned, to copyright

his characters, shares of his profits, and so on…. He's a good story man, and good artist, I feel he needs some control, some editing…. The trouble with Jack is that he's so imaginative, he tries to put every idea he can think of on every page…. That isn't a good story. You have to build up a mood.[25]

Lee may have been correct about Kirby needing an editor because he created several new properties for DC Comics, including the *New Gods*, *Forever People*, *Mister Miracle*, *The Demon*, *Sandman*, *Kamandi*, *Atlas*, and others that received only a lukewarm reception by readers. His failure to achieve a significant market share at DC eventually prompted his return to Marvel when he was featured in *FOOM!* #8 (1974). At this point, Kirby worked for Lee, who was his new publisher as well as his old collaborator from the 1960s and his old assistant from the 1940s. He decided to demonstrate a friendlier and more collegial tone during this interview: "Returning to Marvel Comics was like re-entering the Halls of Ivy…. Stan Lee. We shared ideas, laughs, and stubby cigars. As for all the people who make Marvel what it is, no one could respect them more than I."[26] By 1975, Lee assigned Kirby to edit, write, and draw whichever comic book series interested him. The company's narrative also officially switched toward a collaborative tone regarding Lee and Kirby in *FOOM!* #11 (1975) when an interviewer asked: "Years ago, when you and Stan first sat down and created *The Fantastic Four*, and all the other characters that were done, say, fifteen years ago, did you think they would still be around today?"[27]

Kirby was polite in his response and publicly portrayed an amicable reconciliation with Lee, discussing that he was satisfied with his return to Marvel Comics:

> Of course, I honestly think the reason I'm back is because I wanted to be back. I'm home. And being among the people of Marvel is good ground to be on…. I feel that whatever I do and put in the stories will be read sincerely by the readers and whatever comments I get will be sincere. I'm glad to be working at Marvel for that reason.[28]

At this point, both Lee and Kirby appeared to cease making polarizing statements about being Marvel Comics' main creator while their goals were aligned. After three years of peace, they collaborated on the company's first graphic novel, *Silver Surfer* (1978). They promoted the graphic novel in *FOOM!* #19, where Kirby commented on their constructive working relationship: "I've always enjoyed working with Stan—we've been a successful team. In the collaboration, something good comes out; it is the chemistry of a good team."[29] Kirby's kind words helped generate positive publicity for their book, but another creator in the industry did not hold back in publicly pointing out Lee's faults. Arnold Drake, who worked under Lee after leaving DC to write *The X-Men*, wrote a series about the publisher in *SICK* #120–124 (1978) called "Ego-Man." It was edited by Jack Sparling and described a caricature of Lee named "Stanley Boreman" of "Marble Comics" with a flailing toupee, and constantly in a state of never being able to "prove my comics genius."[30] Similar to the previous satire by Joe Simon, Drake's pages labeled him as a manipulator who robbed credit from his staff and deceived his fans.

It's not certain if Kirby read Drake's damning satire, but he felt the same way about Lee and terminated his relationship with Marvel Comics in 1978 to work in other media, including animation and toys, while Lee continued to maintain his role as the sole creator of Marvel. One of Kirby's projects was storyboarding *The New Fantastic Four* (1978) cartoon, the animated series that substituted the Human Torch with H.E.R.B.I.E. the robot due to the fiery hero's film and television rights being licensed by Universal for a potential movie. Despite there being multiple instances of Lee and Kirby publicly identified as cocreators of *The Fantastic Four*, various news media outlets with their press releases concerning the cartoon continued to make mistakes in their credits. One outlet specifically described Kirby as a "veteran comics artist ... on storyboards" whereas Lee was identified as the one "who originated the characters."[31] Fortunately for Kirby, he was the only labeled creator, as both writer and artist, for the *New Gods* and was able to contribute to the DC Comics and Kenner toy line called the *Super Powers Collection*[32] without being overshadowed by anyone.

During the 1980s, Kirby developed an adversarial relationship with Marvel, while Lee's claims of being the sole creator of its characters appeared to vary and depend on corporate events. Kirby discovered a significant amount of emotional stress when he identified stores that sold Marvel merchandise depicting characters that he cocreated. This anxiety was compounded by a long legal struggle with the company to return his 1960s original art, during a time when other artists easily obtained theirs.[33] During this period of aggravation, he was interviewed by Will Eisner in *The Spirit* #39 (1982) and claimed, "Stan Lee was not writing. I was doing the writing. It all came from my basement."[34] Lee may have read this interview since he was very familiar with both men, and omitted Kirby's name when he and Jim Shooter were interviewed in *Marvel Age* #8 (1983) when discussing how he created *The Fantastic Four*:

> My wife said to me, "Look, instead of quitting, why don't you do the books the way you'd want to do them. Just get it out of your system." So I thought, okay, I'll do a team of superheroes which he wants, but it'll be fun to try to do it a different way. They won't always win at the end, they'll fight amongst themselves, and they'll talk like real people! And that was *The Fantastic Four*.[35]

Lee may have experienced the occasional guilt at these omissions because he reversed that position in an article he wrote for *Comics Buyer's Guide* #16 (1986):

> I had the unbelievable good fortune to work with the most incredibly talented artists of our time. There was Jack Kirby with whom I co-created *The Fantastic Four*, *The Incredible Hulk*, *The Mighty Thor*, *Sgt. Fury and His Howling Commandos*, *Nick Fury, Agent of S.H.I.E.L.D.*, and *The X-Men*, just to name a few.[36]

The two creators argued with one another on August 28, 1987, when Kirby was interviewed on *Earthwatch with Robert Knight* for his 70th birthday. He made several implications of his deeper role in creating the Marvel superheroes such as "I did everything but put the words in the balloons." He also stated that all of the credit for comic book plotting, art pages, and storytelling during his 11 years at Marvel were stolen by Lee. Lee had been listening and was probably upset when he called in to the show. Their initial discussion was polite until an argument started when Lee said, "Every word of dialogue is mine, every story." Jack counter argued with, "I wrote a few lines myself [...] it was the action I was interested in." There was a moment of connection, but nothing was resolved, and they maintained their long-standing disagreement of who should be designated the primary creator of Marvel Comics.[37] However, Lee may have had other corporate events in mind that precipitated a later statement, reasserting his position as the main creator of the Marvel superheroes after the company was purchased by New World Cinema. He may have felt a need to confirm with the new owners that he was the creator with whom they should continue their alliance. This context of job insecurity may have prompted Lee to diminish Kirby's role as a cocreator in *The Village Voice* (December 8, 1987) by saying, "Jack Kirby believes he created the characters because he drew them."[38] This motive to satisfy corporate owners was similar in pattern to when he made similar statements in *Origins of Marvel Comics* (1974) shortly after Perfect Film & Chemical made him publisher.

A few years later, Kirby was featured by Fantagraphics Publisher Gary Groth in *The Comics Journal* #134 (1990), which printed an interview that immortalized his resentment toward Lee. At this point, Kirby was older, weary, and four years away from death. He was faced with financial disappointment and given no cocreator credit or residuals for his role in establishing Marvel Comics. In one passage he stated, "Stan Lee was an editor. He worked from nine to five doing business for Martin Goodman. In other words, he didn't do any writing in the office. He did Martin Goodman's business. That was his function."[39]

Kirby further stated that he entered the Marvel offices and observed Lee in tears about the state of his comics line, which was weak due to the Atlas Implosion and death of artist Joe Maneely. Kirby indicated that he created *The Fantastic Four* out of a need for stable work and a paycheck while Lee sat at his desk, editing comic books and stealing credit:

> I came in [*to the Marvel offices*] and they were moving out the furniture, they were taking desks out—and I needed the work! Stan Lee ... didn't know what to do.... I had to come up with fresh characters that nobody had seen before. I came up with the Fantastic Four. I came up with Thor.... It wasn't possible for a man like Stan Lee to come up with new things—Stan Lee is essentially an office worker.... I'm a storyteller.[40]

Kirby also discussed that he created plots and characters during the Marvel Method sessions while lamenting the lack of writer's credit, which Lee was never open to discussing. Since Lee was the editor, he maintained his influence in the office because he was the one who discussed business with the publisher. Therefore, Lee was able to control what happened to the pages that Kirby turned in, which included descriptions outside the panels that informed him how to interpret the story. Kirby claimed to have continued with this process for years because he needed the income to support his family. Not all of the details he described in this interview were true because at one point he was corrected by his wife, Roz, when he misremembered a particular detail: "I'd come in, and I'd give Stan the work, and I'd go home, and I wrote the story at home. I drew the story at home. I even lettered in the words in the balloons in pencil." Roz then clarified, "Well, you'd put them in the margins." Kirby partially recanted, "Sometimes I put them in the margins. Sometimes I put 'em in the balloons, but I wrote the entire story. I balanced the story." These small corrections created doubt about how much of the rest of the interview was exaggerated. However, Kirby's wife demonstrated support for his overall position when she said, "Jack created many characters before he even met Stan. He created almost all the characters when he was associated with Stan, and after he left Stan, he created many more characters. What has Stan created before he met Jack, and what has he created after Jack left?" Kirby also claimed that it was not Lee who created the name Fantastic Four, and that he never saw a detailed synopsis for the plot that Lee supposedly had given to him in 1961.[41] This interview reflected the emotions he held toward Marvel and Lee that he probably maintained until his death and also portrayed a tragic figure who felt exploited by the industry.

In 1989, Marvel's ownership changed again from New World Cinema to MacAndrews & Forbes Holdings.[42] Two years later, its chief executive, Ronald Perelman, made an initial public offering, placing the company on the New York Stock Exchange. That same year, in what seemed to function as a rebuttal to Kirby's interview in *The Comics Journal*, Stan Lee publicized his own retrospective in the *Fantastic Four* #358 (1991): "Here's a synopsis that I've been talking about since 1974 and this is the one I wrote when I dreamed up *The Fantastic Four* back in 1961." Two pages were shown introducing the four main characters—Reed Richards, Susan Storm, Ben Grimm, and Johnny Storm—who hijacked a spaceship to beat the communists to the stars "in the dead of night."[43] These two pages counteracted Kirby's claim of never seeing Lee's synopsis and functioned as a legal document that could protect MacAndrews & Forbes Holdings from the Kirby estate if they were to challenge the right to ownership of the characters. However, the presence of Lee's synopsis did not matter as much as whether it was written before or after discussing the idea with Kirby. Roy Thomas commented on this question in *Jack Kirby Collector* #18 (1998): "Later I saw Stan's plot for *Fantastic Four* #1, but even Stan would never claim for sure that he and Jack hadn't talked the idea over before he wrote this.... I wouldn't trust either Stan's memory or Jack's memory totally in these."[44]

The credit issue between Lee and Kirby did finally resolve, but not until well after Kirby passed away. He was found dead from heart failure at his home in 1994, and Lee attended his funeral but left before Roz could speak with him.[45] A year later, he wrote about the origin of the *Fantastic Four* in the 400th issue (1995) of the comic book series with a narrative that differed from his *Origins of Marvel Comics* (1974). He wrote that "Jack Kirby and I created the *Fantastic Four*.... Our characters would be real people (albeit superpowered) with real emotions, living in a real city [*New York*] and beset by real problems—while battling the weirdest foes of all."[46] Lee's sentiment was a response to Kirby's death, and later changed during a legal event in 2009, when he was called on to testify during the Kirby Estate versus Disney court case, which directly called into question who created what. The attorney who represented Kirby's estate, Marc Toberoff, questioned Lee about statements he made in which he explicitly described Kirby as a cocreator. Lee took back any credit he had given to Kirby in the past and protected Marvel's interests. "I tried to write these, knowing Jack would read them I tried to write them to make it look as if he and I were just doing everything together, to make him feel good."[47] By denying Kirby cocreation credit with corporate attorneys present, Lee maintained his narrative from *Origins of Marvel Comics* (1974). He was paid to protect and promote the Marvel brand, and his testimony was processed into the verdict, which decided against the Kirby estate because the artist was not an employee at Marvel but was instead paid on a work-for-hire basis. Five years later, the Kirby estate attempted to take the case to the Supreme Court, causing Disney to settle out of court to prevent any potential legal repercussions.[48] After decades, Kirby finally received cocreator credit, a settlement was made to the Kirby family, and the byline in the *Fantastic Four* comic book series now states that it was created by Stan Lee and Jack Kirby, similar to what the original byline stated in the first issue released over 60 years ago.

Steve Ditko's disagreements with Lee over the credit boxes in *The Amazing Spider-Man* were publicly discussed in the mid–1960s, much earlier than those for Kirby. Although the first Spider-Man story credited both Lee and Ditko equally, the credits in subsequent issues listed Ditko as artist and Lee as the writer. However, this changed in *The Amazing Spider-Man* #25 (1965) when Ditko started to receive plotting credit that was accompanied by Lee's announcement on the first page, "Sturdy Stevey Ditko dreamed up the plot of this tantalizing tale."[49] He explained further what circumstances led to this plotting change in the *New York Herald Tribune* (1966) while explaining his duties as writer for the comic book series:

> I don't plot Spider-Man anymore. Steve Ditko, the artist, has been doing the stories. I guess I'll leave him alone until sales start to slip. Since Spidey got so popular, Ditko thinks he's the genius of the world. We were arguing so much over plot lines I told him to start making up his own stories.... He just drops off the finished pages with notes at the margins and I fill in the dialogue.[50]

Lee had publicly demonstrated an irritation with Ditko, which was soon followed by Ditko's departure from Marvel. He worked for other companies in the later 1960s such as Charlton, Wally Wood's *Witzend*, and DC, and created characters including the Question, Blue Beetle, and Mr. A, as well as the titles *Beware the Creeper* and *The Hawk and the Dove*.[51] His withdrawal from *The Amazing Spider-Man* series and replacement by John Romita, Sr., did not diminish sales, but instead was associated with an increase over the next five years.[52] The character soon became recognized by mainstream audiences, prompting Marvel to license the character for animation. During the *Spider-Man* cartoon's later seasons under Krantz films, the credits read: "Based upon an original character created by Stan Lee." It was

Stan Lee and Steve Ditko are given equal credit for the first appearance of Spider-Man in *Amazing Fantasy* **#15 (1962).**

apparent that with Ditko absent, he would be denied the cocreator credit that Kirby received on the *Fantastic Four* cartoon.

Lee held fewer reservations about claiming to be Spider-Man's creator and wrote his account of the hero's genesis in his book *Origins of Marvel Comics* (1974), which was later given a rebuttal by both Kirby and Ditko. He wrote that he wanted a teenage character with a name that was similar to Superman and gravitated to an arachnid theme because he enjoyed *The Spider* pulp magazine as a young reader. Lee further claimed that Martin Goodman, the publisher, resisted the idea, and that he was required to convince him to approve the Spider-Man idea. He also mentioned that he first presented Spider-Man to Jack Kirby to be the series artist but claimed that that his version failed to depict him as a grounded, realistic character. He then described Kirby's Spider-Man as too heroic because it did not "deglamorize Spidey enough"[53] and failed to pass through the filter of his editorial insight, so he deferred the project to Ditko instead. However, both Kirby and Ditko refuted Lee's version of events. Kirby stated in a newspaper, *The Province* (January 18, 1977), that Lee did not originate the idea but rather he presented the Spider-Man idea to Lee from an old insect character that "was part of the unsold inventory of a company called Mainline Comics, founded in 1954 by Joe Simon and Jack Kirby."[54] Ditko corroborated both versions that Kirby penciled an initial Spider-Man design but disagreed on how he received the assignment. He also stated that he saw the art on Lee's desk and mentioned that it was too similar to Simon and Kirby's comic book for Archie Comics, *Adventures of the Fly* (1959). Ditko implied that it was the fear of litigation from Archie Comics that prompted Lee to assign the book to him to create his own visual concept.[55] Despite the different accounts by the three men, the owners of Marvel Comics would probably prefer to use Lee's narrative as the sole creator to better prepare for potential copyright infringement lawsuits from his previous cocreators and legally protect their right to sell Spider-Man comics.

When Lee was asked about Ditko in *Fantasy Advertiser International* (April 1975), he expressed bewilderment and irritation about his Spider-Man cocreator's departure from Marvel. He claimed to not understand why he left and spent substantial time discussing why he was a difficult personality who became more socially withdrawn, professionally demanding, and impossible to work with as time went on:

> With Ditko, I have less of an understanding. Steve was a very mysterious character. When he first started, he was the easiest character we ever had to work with. But … he became tougher and tougher to work with…. He'd say to me, "Gee, Stan. I don't like those plots you are writing for Spider-Man." So I'd say, "Use your own plot, I'll put the dialogue in." So he'd do his own … and I'd put dialogue in and make them conform to what I wanted…. I'd bend over backwards to accommodate him because he was so good and the strip was so successful. But it was like Chamberlain giving in to Hitler, the more I appeased him, the harder he got to work with…. Then one day he said he was leaving.[56]

Despite the publisher's apparent disapproval, Ditko returned to Marvel in 1978 upon the invitation of newly instated editor-in-chief Jim Shooter, while both Lee and Kirby claimed credit for creating Spider-Man.[57] Lee and Ditko never reconciled during this period and soon after, in 1980, Lee moved to Los Angeles and became a comic book ambassador to Hollywood. He appeared on television and narrated cartoons and was credited as the "creator of Spider-Man" on the CBC show *Beyond Reason*, which omitted Steve Ditko.[58] Ditko was very clear with the editorial team at Marvel that he would never again draw the character and continued to work on various others, including Captain Universe and his cocreation with Tom DeFalco, Speedball. The topic of Spider-Man's creation was discussed again by Kirby during his interview by Will Eisner in his magazine *Spirit* #39 (1982). "Spider-Man was discussed between Joe (Simon) and myself. Spider-Man was not a product of Marvel." Kirby elaborated further, "We had a script called the Silver Spider ... going into a magazine [*that*] folded.... I said this could become a thing called 'Spider-Man' so the idea was there when I talked to Stan."[59] A question started to manifest in fandom concerning the uncovered Simon and Kirby origins to Spider-Man, and how much of the character was truly by Ditko. This answer was suggested a few years later in *Comics Interview* #41 (1986), when Kirby clarified that Ditko developed Spider-Man and "made people interested in it."[60] By this point, all three creators agreed that Kirby drew an original Spider-Man that was assigned to Ditko to engineer into something new and interesting, but the debate continued as to who originated the name and concept.

The news media continued its trend of maintaining the Marvel Comics corporate narrative that Lee was the character's sole creator, and eventually more creators presented their accounts on the hero's origins. In 1987, Spider-Man married Mary Jane in comic books, comic strips, and television when Stan Lee officiated their wedding in Shea Stadium. The event was given coverage in local newspapers as 50,000 fans cheered for the actors portraying the two fictional newlyweds "before the New York Mets take the field."[61] During the after-wedding questions, Stan Lee was labeled by *Entertainment Tonight* as the "Spider-Man creator."[62] It seemed the media was settled on the question as to who created Spider-Man, which attracted artist Eric Stanton, who claimed that Ditko was the main creator, while claiming some credit of his own. Stanton was a former bondage artist and studio-mate with Ditko from 1958 to 1968. He was interviewed in 1988 by comics historian Greg Theakston and revealed that he helped innovate the concept of wrist web shooters:

> We worked on storyboards together, I added a few ideas. But the whole thing was created by Steve on his own.... The whole thing was Steve Ditko. I think I added the business about the webs coming out of his hands and we talked about the characters, and in turn, he helped me with my stuff.[63]

More eyewitness accounts were presented by members of the Simon and Kirby team in *The Comics Journal* #134 (February 1990). Simon admitted that his contribution to cocreating the *Fly* (1959) was from an older character that eventually became Spider-Man, which corroborated Kirby's account of the hero's origin but did not confirm that Kirby originated the idea. Simon told Gary Groth in his interview, "That is a wonderful story.... The story of the Fly ... and how it eventually became Spider-Man."[64] This is also supported by the shared themes and story concepts between the Fly and Spider-Man discussed previously. Kirby was interviewed in the same issue and issued a more extreme statement on the matter, stating, "I created Spider-Man.... I drew the first Spider-Man cover. I created the character. I created the costume.... We decided to give the book to Steve Ditko who was the right man for the job. He did a wonderful job on that."[65]

However, that statement was factually untrue because *Marvelmania #2* (1970) printed the unused first draft of the cover by Ditko that Lee rejected in favor of Kirby's second draft. The magazine's "Club News Section" stated to readers, "What you may not know is that another cover was drawn for that issue by Steve Ditko and never used."[66] Ditko issued a public statement to address Kirby's claim in Robin Snyder's *History of Comics* vol. 1, #5 (May 1990) that he received a sketch of the costume that Kirby had designed, but it appeared to have more in common with Captain America's suit rather than the final composition by Ditko. Ditko explained that "Jack's whole Spider-Man 'idea' is unexplained, non-existing, uncreated.... Almost all of the bits of this 'creation' were discarded/never used."[67] He also asserted that he himself created the costume, appearance, and movement, including crucial elements— for instance, the web shooters. He went on to describe the synopsis that Lee gave him as a summary of the Lee and Kirby conversation went mostly unused, including the penciled splash image of a Kirby-drawn Spider-Man that was similar to Giant Man, but with a web gun. Ditko also described that Kirby's "Spider-Man would be a teenager with a magic ring that could transform him into an adult hero-Spider-Man. I said it sounded similar to the Fly, which Joe Simon had co-created for Archie publications.... Kirby had penciled five pages of his Spider-Man." Ditko also clarified that he did not know who originated Spider-Man: "How much was pure Kirby, how much Lee, is for them to resolve."[68] Ditko claimed that Lee acknowledged the similarity to the Fly, called Kirby to confirm, and then gave Ditko the responsibility of developing Spider-Man. Lee hoped Ditko could add his own flair to the character to ensure it differed substantially from the Fly. "One of the first things I did was to work up a costume," Ditko elaborated, "the possible gimmicks ... a clinging power ... a hidden wrist-shooter versus a web gun and holster.... Spider theme and the webbing design."[69] Ditko also differentiated his input to the hero apart from Lee by defining which contributions came from each creator. He described that Lee's portion of the creation was the introduction of the name, as well as a one-or-two-page synopsis. Ditko clarified that he created the costume, split-face spider sense, web shooters, webs, spider tracer, and spider belt light projector.[70] This strongly emphasized that he had the most visual and kinetic input directly into Spider-Man, and that the character was a cocreation, with no one person creating him alone.

However, a question remained whether Lee or Kirby or Simon created the name *Spider-Man*, and the answer was finally revealed. Kirby previously alluded to the unused character that resulted from his discussions with Joe Simon during their time as publishers for Mainline in 1954. Simon finally offered some clarification in *The Comic Book Makers* (1990):

> In 1953 ... CC Beck, the artist ... behind ... Captain Marvel ... offered to "take a crack" at the business again, if I would come up with an idea for a new character and a script. After a lot of doodling ... I roughed up a logo, SPIDERMAN.... [*Scriptwriter Jack*] Oleck came over to my studio.... We held a script conference.... There are too many damned "Man" titles around.... I changed the title to "Silver Spider."[71]

Simon claimed that he submitted the character to Harvey Comics, which decided against publishing it, so he later submitted it to Archie in 1959 after converting it into *Adventure of the Fly* with Kirby.[72] With this statement, Simon claimed that he first created the name Spider-Man in 1953 and discussed it with C.C. Beck. However, Beck drew a villain named "Spider Man" six years earlier in *Whiz Comics* #89 (1947), written by Otto Binder for Fawcett Comics. This maligned criminal captured his prey in plastic "Webs of Crime."[73] This would more than likely be the reason why Simon did not use the name as he would not want to have any legal conflict over a protected trademark with Fawcett over the Spider-Man name. Also, it would seem that Otto Binder created the name and Beck may have submitted it to Simon. However, the name was common and used in multiple comic books. It was featured by both Atlas and DC Comics in 1954. DC published it first in *House of Mystery* #28 (July 1954), penciled by Ed Smalle, about an esoteric scientist who, searching for "the Spider Man," captured insects that he believed were reincarnated people. Atlas also published the name for their own short story penciled by Ed Winiarski a few months later in *Uncanny Tales* #26 (November 1954) about an unusual scientist who grew spiders with hopes to take over the world. Both Spider Men died in their stories, and neither company referred to them again. There was also "El Hombre Araña" in a comic from Spain called *Diamante Negro* #42 (1943) published by Ediciones Rialto, whose name directly translated into "Spider-Man." Regardless, Joe Simon's "Spider-Man" was not the first Spider-Man in comic form. That title is currently reserved for a strip that Simon routinely read,[74] Ed Wheelan's *Minute Movies* newspaper comic strip, which in the June 22, 1934, daily was titled "Spider Man." The primary point is that none of the supposed creators of Spider-Man invented the name. It had been used in comics for decades before the Marvel version that is best known today; however, between the four men discussed here, Joe Simon appeared to have uttered the name first.

Despite the new revelations made about Spider-Man's origins, Lee continued to make public statements that he was the character's creator while Ditko went about setting the record straight. Lee was referred to as Spider-Man's creator by *TIME* magazine and soon after, Ditko submitted a correction to their letters pages, which was published on December 7, 1998: "Spider-Man's existence … was a collaboration of writer-editor Stan Lee and Steve Ditko as co-creators."[75] Lee apparently responded to Ditko's statements in 1999 on his personal letterhead:

> I have always considered Steve Ditko to be Spider-Man's co-creator.... When I first told Steve my idea for a shy, teenage high-school science student who'd be bitten by a radioactive spider, thus gaining the ability to stick to walls and shoot webs, Steve took it like a duck to water.[76]

This announcement did not appear sincere to Ditko, who objected to Lee's using the term "considered" to downplay the truth of the statement. Soon after, Ditko wrote a response back to Lee, stating, "TSK!TSK! Why do some people seek the Unearned" and claiming that Stan Lee had a habit of taking credit: "You know me, I'll take any credit that isn't nailed down."[77] A series of statements from both creators were published after the *Spider-Man* film starring Tobey Maguire debuted in 2002, because there was renewed public interest in who created the character. Despite the film stating that it was "Based on the Marvel Comic Book by Stan Lee and Steve Ditko," newspapers focused on Lee, who claimed that a "fly on the wall" was his inspiration for the character. Lee explained that he went "down the list. Mosquito-Man, Beetle-Man, Fly-Man. Then I hit on Spider-Man.... That was it!"[78] The attention from Hollywood seemed to solidify in Lee's mind that he created the superhero; however, he may have softened his stance to a degree when writing his introduction to *Doctor Strange Marvel Masterworks* vol. 2 (2005): "Steve Ditko and I had come up with a winner when we created Spider-Man."[79] However, this collaborative statement by Lee appears to be negated by one he made two years later when he was asked by Jonathan Ross in his documentary *In Search of Steve Ditko* (2007) about who created Spider-Man. Lee explained that while he considered Ditko a cocreator, he still maintained the narrative that he had dreamed up "an idea for a strip called 'Spider-Man.'" He did, however, acknowledge Ditko's position of developing the character as a factor in its cocreation, but maintained that when he created the idea, he could have "give[n] it to anybody to draw."[80] The pace of the documentary seemed to shift at this point, with a resulting silence as Lee declared that Ditko was a little more than a pair of hired hands at his employment. Eight years later, Ditko explained his 1966 departure from *The Amazing Spider-Man* in an essay, "WHY I QUIT S-M, MARVEL" (2015). He noted that once he received plotting credit in *The Amazing Spider-Man* #25 (1965), Lee no longer spoke to him when he deposited his completed Spider-Man pages. He noticed that Lee's second-in-command, Sol Brodsky, accepted the pages from Ditko instead. Without that connection to Lee, and with Brodsky acting as the middleman on all communications, Ditko thought to himself, "Why should I do it? Why should I continue to do all these monthly issues, original story ideas, material, for a man who is too scared, too angry over something to even see, talk to me?"[81] Attentive fandom acknowledged Ditko's reason not to continue, and some continue to speculate or conclude that Lee did not want to engage in any discussions regarding the plot, since Ditko's credit and possible pay had been upgraded at Lee's expense. From a managerial standpoint, Lee may have been busy with other duties as editor-in-chief. However, some fans interpreted this as a passive-aggressive retaliation against Ditko for being credited for the plot. Regardless, Ditko felt ignored by Lee and departed Marvel. Both creators died within five months of each other in 2018 and the credits to the hero's comic books appeared to have been settled without any public spectacle. They read just as they did when the character was first created: "Spider-Man created by Stan Lee and Steve Ditko."[82]

Lee, Kirby, and Ditko advanced the superhero comic book by incorporating imperfections that readers could relate to, using an innovative collaboration called the Marvel Method. Their collaboration maximized their effect on readers by better utilizing panel sequences and dialogue that attracted audiences with tragic superheroes that increased the market share of Marvel Comics. The result was that the Marvel Comics Group stable of characters soon became featured in cartoons and merchandise. Their popularity engendered a resentment between the three men, who focused on how that credit should be shared, which demonstrated a historical lesson to how creators may react to an unintentionally successful superhero comic book franchise. That success probably also prompted the owners of Marvel Comics to base their narrative on who created their characters by using credits that would cause the least exposure to potential future liability. Lee likely recognized this, but also felt fulfilled that the sophistication of comic books was elevated by his flawed superheroes. The marketplace validated his approach, and he considered the possibility that the Marvel Comics Group was prepared to enter more serious media.

18

Stan Lee Expands Superheroes
Beyond Comic Books

Once the superheroes of the Marvel Comics Group established themselves as a property that steadily gained market share, Stan Lee began to consider the possibility of their entry into more serious media. They had already demonstrated a reasonable degree of success in animation with *The Marvel Super Heroes*, *Spider-Man*, and *Fantastic Four* (1966–1967). However, there was now a chance to present their tragic and entertaining stories into media for adults. From the years 1968 to 1973, Lee made a series of steps to explore this option, which established his career trajectory moving forward. In 1968, Lee used his success as editor-in-chief to establish his persona as a godfather to the Marvel superheroes, which gained popularity along with the franchise. Martin Goodman had sold Marvel to Perfect Film & Chemical in the same year and wasn't set to leave the company until 1972. So, in the time that he had, Lee used it to put himself and his superheroes in a mutually favorable position, by preparing for Goodman's departure, establishing Marvel's characters in the magazine market, and forming amicable connections with filmmakers to someday depict the superhero genre in film.

Lee demonstrated that his reputation with comic book readers and his decisions as editor-in-chief outweighed the influence of the Goodman family in a "Meet Stan Lee" feature from *Bachelor* #1 (1968). Lee was clearly the focus of the feature, connecting with fans as Marvel's premier storyteller. He discussed various aspects of managing the comic book line under publisher Martin Goodman's son, Charles Goodman (more commonly known as "Chip"), who remained mostly silent during the interview but commented on any business-related questions. Despite the apparent lack of charisma, Chip was Martin Goodman's intended heir for Marvel Comics. It was common knowledge around the office that Chip's relationship with his father was dysfunctional and satirized in *Playboy* (February 1970) by Ivan Prashker in the story "The Boss' Son." Prashker depicted Charles "Chip" Goodman as constantly bitter about his father's disapproval, with his emotional state being summed up in the line, "I at least try to please you; only, the harder I try, the more you seem to resent me."[1] Despite this, he was being groomed to think as a publisher. During the *Bachelor* interview, he was asked about Marvel Comics' sales figures, which clarified that he was in essence Lee's boss and the man who knew the numbers. His answers were fairly dry and not as captivating or witty as Lee's: "We sell about six million a month, that includes the ten titles plus the annual issues."[2] This demonstrated that Chip Goodman's priorities lay with sales as his primary focus because he was studying his father's job as the publisher to one day assume control of Marvel. It was also clear that he studied the demographics of Marvel's readers when he stated, "The majority of our readership is young children, but the growing percentage of the readership is college students and adults." Lee followed up on his statement, adding that children are attracted to "the color of the books, the action, the costumes.... Older readers ... see the little bit of philosophy, satire ... both ends of the spectrum, and everything in between." He exhibited a superior insight into younger people's tastes and maintained Marvel Comics' mission to create a more intelligent brand of comics that kids and young adults could equally enjoy.

As opposed to Chip Goodman, it was Lee's understanding about the reader's experience that allowed him to communicate in ways that were mimicked by other editors, write dialogue that rebelled against the status quo, and hire talented new creators. He elaborated on this when asked how he felt when other companies copied his style or characters, which was probably referring to DC Comics editors who failed to replicate Marvel's editorial success, or Jerry Siegel's attempt to edit and oversee the Archie superhero line, *The Mighty Crusaders*, from 1965 to 1966.[3] Siegel seemed to mimic Lee when he wrote lines in his panels such as, "Stung to the core by the sudden antagonism of the Winged Marvel, the Sinister Spider stepped in gleefully, eager to deliver the death-thrust to his weakened foe!," giving a hearty warning about "The Wicked Web of the Wily Spider!"[4] Unfortunately for Siegel and other comic book editors, no competitor matched Lee's resonance with 1960s youth. So, Lee responded to the interviewer's question, "I think we still get annoyed, but there's nothing we can do about it.... Nobody seems to have done it well yet, so as long as they don't, there is no reason for us to be upset." As opposed to other writers, he understood that commenting on social consciousness was the way to engage the interest of the youth market. He was asked by the *Bachelor* interviewer about his socially relevant messages in comic books, such as one located in *Tales to Astonish* #81 (1966) referring to the blue-skinned, Atlantean villain Krang. Krang made his skin pink in a plot against the Sub-Mariner and Lee used the opportunity to comment on race in Krang's dialogue balloon: "The color of one's skin is but a chance accident of fate! It alters nothing else about the person!" Lee explained his position on this topic: "We have our convictions ... a certain amount of influence over people.... There are certain things like brotherly love that I don't think anybody can take offense.... If they do, I don't think we should have them for our readers anyway."[5] This answer revealed another side to Stan Lee, one that valued social justice, which attracted the baby boomer generation and became a recurrent presence in his soapbox and dialogue balloons. This comment also solidified that his work did have social purpose on impressionable young minds as opposed to the Goodmans, who studied sales reports.

Lee expanded further that as a dialogue writer, he strove to add a nonconformist and rebellious streak to superheroes: "When you're college-age, the offbeat … humor that tears away a bit from the establishment is … favored…. They're rebels."[6] This observation made it clear that characters such as the Thing and Spider-Man were messengers of a social agenda. As outsiders, they decided to take a risk and "poke" the establishment even if they encountered significant risk for personal injury. This contrasted with the formal writing approach from competing comic book companies that conveyed stilted science-fiction dialogue. Compare Lee's skin color dialogue from above to a thought bubble from writer Edmond Hamilton in *Superman* #172 (1964): "Now that comet has returned … and to save helpless worlds I have to face its menace! From what I know about this comet, it may destroy! If so, for the benefit of mankind, I must appoint a successor to carry on for me!"[7] Hamilton's words appealed to young children but lacked the ability to connect with college-age rebels who often marched for social causes. It was Lee's ability to assess the tastes of younger people that enabled him to recruit talented people in an industry of aging men: "We have one new fellow, Jim Steranko, who's working on *S.H.I.E.L.D.* now. He's a fan who had joined the field, but there are few of those."[8] It appeared that Lee expressed hope for the industry that readers such as Steranko would bring their talents to maintain the company's innovative approach to making comic books. By stating a deeper connection to the youth market compared with the Goodmans, Lee was positioning himself as the next choice for publisher.

Lee also prepared Marvel for the future by reducing dependence on any single creator and selling superhero stories for adults in other media, in this case the magazine format. The *Bachelor* interview discussed the potentially disruptive scenario of what could happen if Kirby were to depart the company, to which Lee said that he was prepared because he built a structure at Marvel that would survive this event. "Fortunately, I don't think any one person is holding the whole place up. For example, Spider-Man with John Romita Sr. is one of our best-selling books. *Daredevil* with Gene Colan is doing well, and down the line, we do have others."[9] It is noteworthy that he mentioned Romita as the first example of the structure at Marvel that could stand if Kirby withdrew his services. Three years earlier, in 1965, Romita had replaced Wally Wood on *Daredevil*, and in 1966 he replaced Ditko on *The Amazing Spider-Man*. Romita had proven himself by maintaining the company's high artistic standards, and Lee appeared to notice that the penciler was the best person to implement his vision of Marvel's expansion into other media. His first attempt at tailoring superheroes toward adults was the black-and-white magazine format, which benefited from not requiring approval from the Comics Code. Lee's first published Marvel magazine was *The Spectacular Spider-Man* (1968) by himself, Romita, and inker Jim Mooney, who would become a seasoned artist for the regular *Spider-Man* series. The two-issue magazine was a test project to see whether superheroes presented in this format could generate sales in a marketplace targeted at an older demographic.[10] There seemed to be such a market since Jim Warren's adult black-and-white horror comic magazine series, *Creepy* (1964) and *Eerie* (1966), were selling well. To draw the attention of readers at the newsstand, the first issue's cover was painted by men's cover painter Harry Rosenbaum, while Romita painted the cover to the second issue. Both were large magazines, containing close to 60 pages each, and the first issue attempted to offer political commentary during the Nixon-Humphrey presidential race of 1968. The story followed the machinations of a political party nominee, Richard Raleigh, who manufactured a cyborg monster that attacked him in public places to give voters the impression that he was bullied by the city's underworld. Spider-Man uncovered the scheme and freed the creature, who soon killed Raleigh. To defend himself and the city, Spider-Man was forced to kill the creature, which further added to the mildly adult aspect of the magazine. One scene in the story had J. Jonah Jameson and two friends, Captain George Stacy and an unidentified aristocrat, comment on Republicans and Democrats. They sat together in a local men's country club and joked about Jameson's disappointed hopes for the 1964 presidential election between the failed candidate and President Lyndon B. Johnson: "Didn't you also predict a Goldwater landslide?"[11] The political references and the deaths added to the adult quality of the black-and-white magazine but still failed to attract a significant number of readers. The second issue by Lee and Romita was printed in color with hopes of capturing a superior market share compared with the first issue and involved Peter Parker's antagonism toward a more familiar enemy, Norman Osborn—the Green Goblin. Osborn was first depicted with amnesia from his previous appearance in *The Amazing Spider-Man* #40 (1966) and recovered his memory during a dream sequence, which was followed by resuming the role of the Green Goblin. Osborn soon attended a dinner with Parker and his friends, secretly threatening the lives of everyone there. He shook Parker's hand with a mischievous sneer, as Parker realized, "He's toying with me … squeezing my hand … hard enough to break my fingers."[12] Their interactions at the dinner table were effective in keeping readers curious about the outcome, which later culminated in a fight, in costume, where Spider-Man defeated the Green Goblin with "psychedelic pumpkin" bombs that induced a new episode of amnesia. Amnesia was a convenient way for the magazine to have no consequence on the continuity of *The Amazing Spider-Man* comic book series, but despite the mildly higher amount of drama, the magazine series failed to maintain marketplace viability, prompting cancellation before the release of a third issue.

Despite the initial failure of *The Spectacular Spider-Man*, the magazine market thrived by eventually featuring adult stories with Marvel characters, which along with becoming publisher, vindicated Lee's ambitions of adapting superheroes for film and television. By 1970, Romita replaced Jack Kirby on *Fantastic Four* #103 after Kirby departed the title for DC Comics. Lee was able to utilize Perfect Film & Chemical's distribution company, Curtis Circulation, to reenter the black-and-white magazine market in 1971.[13] That same year, DC Comics' Hampshire Distributors also attempted to enter the same market with two short-lived black-and-white magazines

The deaths of the villain and his henchman in the black-and-white magazine *The Spectacular Spider-Man* #1 (1968) signified an attempt by Stan Lee and John Romita to appeal toward mature audiences.

drawn and written by Jack Kirby.[14] These titles were *In the Days of the Mob* and *Spirit World*, and they served as an indication that Kirby, similar to Lee, felt that comic storytelling could be expanded to new media. However, the DC magazines halted production after one issue whereas Marvel's black-and-white magazines explored adult storylines with *Savage Tales*, *Crazy Magazine*, *Haunt of Horror*, *Dracula Lives*, *Monsters Unleashed*, *Tales of the Zombie*, *Vampire Tales*, *The Deadly Hands of Kung Fu*, *Planet of the Apes*, *The Savage Sword of Conan the Barbarian*, *Doc Savage*, *Kull and the Barbarians*, *Marvel Preview*, *Unknown Worlds of Science Fiction*, *The Rampaging Hulk*, *Howard the Duck*, and *The Tomb of Dracula*, among others. Martin Goodman departed Marvel in 1972 and Perfect Film & Chemical assigned Lee the role of publisher instead of Chip Goodman,[15] who soon departed the company as Lee oversaw the development of the Marvel brand. A year later, Lee was interviewed by Andy Warhol's *Interview* #31 (1973) for a feature titled "The Marvelous Stan Lee." One question they asked: "How many comic books do you sell?" To which Lee replied, "I would say roughly around seventy million a year."[16] This averaged out to six million a month throughout the 12-month year, which amounted to a similar number Chip Goodman quoted when he answered the same question a few years earlier. Lee, at this point, followed the company's bottom line in a manner similar to Goodman. He also mentioned that he was able to change his focus to the brand's direction rather than individual storylines due to assigning the role of editor-in-chief to Roy Thomas, another fan and protégé who entered the field under similar circumstances as Jim Steranko. Lee elaborated:

> Roy Thomas, who is our editor now, began as an English teacher in the Mid-West, and he was a real comics fan, he still is in a way…. We hired him because his letters were well written, and he seemed to have some authority. So we gave him a job or two, and we decided that he was

the one who came close to the style I was looking for. Luckily, he turned out to be very good, and I gave him the job of trying to train the other writers we hired.[17]

Thomas became a central part of the structure that Lee established to maintain the strength of the comic book line so he could study the demographics and potential new media of the marketplace. The magazine asked, "Where is your biggest market?" Lee answered Canada, United States, Europe, and Asia, then clarified with the interviewer that Marvel's readership was not merely young children, and since his black-and-white magazines were successfully out on newsstands, he seemed focused on moving superheroes into the film medium. He led into this point by explaining that comic storytelling can be appreciated by artists in other media, with personal anecdotes about two European filmmakers who stopped by to meet him to discuss Marvel Comics. "[*Alain Resnais*] came over to meet me once.... He came over here because he wanted to do a film in English, and he wanted me to write his first film."[18] At the time, Alain Resnais was a famous French filmmaker who was skilled in several aspects of producing and directing films. After his initial meeting with Lee, Resnais directed the film *Stavisky* (1974), which told the tale of the last few months of the life of con artist Serge Alexandre Stavisky. The film also explored Stavisky's childhood and youth alongside his fraudulent schemes that involved various wealthy families. Sadly, this calculative and artistic filmmaker died in 2014.[19] Lee also mentioned Italian filmmaker Federico Fellini: "Fellini came to see me once years ago... 'Hello Maestro!' and I said, 'Hello Maestro.' I wanted to talk about him and about his movies and he seemed to only want to talk about Marvel Comics.... And that was when I began to realize there are people other than little children who are reading Marvel Comics."[20] Fellini was also a screenwriter, and at the time of the Warhol interview, had just released his film *Amarcord* (1973) into theaters. His next film was *Casanova* (1976) with Donald Sutherland, which told the story of a womanizing philanderer. Fellini was older than Resnais and died long before him in 1993.[21]

However, these interactions with the two interested filmmakers appear to foreshadow Lee's interest in featuring his characters in film and television. After he was asked in the interview whether he planned to create more characters, he elaborated on these plans:

> I'd like to do other types of books. We're going to put out a regular magazine, not a comic book, called *The Haunt of Horror* ... and we're going to put out some comic books in black-and-white, in a larger size, hopefully for older readers. We want to get into television, we want to do some feature films. What I want to do is to take Marvel Comics and eventually change the name to Marvel Media. I think we should be doing some other things besides comics. [*When asked if he wanted to get into animated feature films, he replied*] We may start out that way. I'm negotiating now to do a film about Spider-Man. Eventually, we may do original stories. Eventually we may form our own production company.[22]

It was obvious that Lee's foray into media with Marvel's black-and-white magazines was merely the beginning of the superhero genre's expansion into film, animation, and television.

However, Lee's interest in producing superhero movies would encounter obstacles. In 1974, Martin Goodman expressed his frustration with Perfect Film & Chemical's refusal to assign his son, Chip Goodman, the role of publisher and created Atlas/Seaboard Comics in 1974 to compete for Marvel's market share. John Romita, Sr., discussed the mood of the situation as "pure revenge."[23] Goodman hired his son to oversee the operation and offered artists and writers better rates, benefits, returned original art, and author rights.[24] This led to a variety of submissions, which prompted other publishers to consider offering similar benefits. Onlookers at the Atlas bullpen observed Chip Goodman often photographing beautiful women for his other endeavor, *Swank* magazine, and comic book writer David Anthony Kraft mentioned that Martin Goodman's "aura" during this period was very similar to the Ray Milland character *X: The Man with the X-Ray Eyes* (1963).[25] Ultimately encountering substandard distribution, the Atlas/Seaboard Comics company went defunct in 1975. Martin Goodman retired to Florida and died in 1992[26] and Chip Goodman continued to publish the adult magazine *Swank* until he died in 1996.[27]

Lee's ambitious plans for Marvel's expansion into film and television became a reality starting in the later 1970s when he produced a variety of television projects that featured some of the Marvel superheroes, including *The Amazing Spider-Man* (1977–1979), *The Incredible Hulk* (1977–1982), *Dr. Strange* (1978), and *Captain America* (1979). Lee moved to Los Angeles to be near the Marvel Productions animation studio, where he produced cartoons including *Spider-Man and His Amazing Friends* (1981), *Defenders of the Earth* (1986), and the *X-Men: Pryde of the X-Men!* pilot (1989). He functioned as a comic book ambassador to several film producers and directors, and eventually witnessed the Marvel Comics Group with its superheroes represented in feature films and additional TV shows such as *Captain America* (1990), *Power Pack* (1991), and *Nick Fury: Agent of S.H.I.E.L.D.* (1998). Movie studios successfully adapted superheroes to film utilizing storyboards whose panels are in many instances based on comic books. Marvel's first big-budget Hollywood film success was *Blade* in 1998 followed by two sequels and a television series. This was followed by a host of successful film franchises featuring Marvel superheroes including Iron Man, Thor, Hulk, Avengers, Fantastic Four, Spider-Man, Captain America, Ant-Man, Punisher, X-Men, and Wolverine. However, there were a few more innovations for superheroes that remained to be discovered, and one specifically that was required for superheroes to have a mythologic impact on adult audiences. The genre would require long-form epics with multi-issue crossovers, a technique that was pioneered first by Jack Kirby and his interest in space gods.

Jack Kirby's Space Gods

As Stan Lee adapted superheroes to other media, Jack Kirby elevated the scope of superhero comic books with long-form space god sagas and metaseries that depicted looming intergalactic deities. Many people who knew Kirby understood that his imagination was linked to an interest in outer space. Artist and historian Jim Steranko once mentioned that Kirby had an "intuitive" rather than analytical approach to creating his comic art pages. He described that Kirby "drew from the gut" while his hands penciled the page from the top left to the bottom right, subconsciously placing new concepts and ideas to paper.[1] Through this method, Kirby pioneered multiple genres but often returned to the concept of space gods who were immortal extraterrestrials that jeopardized the status quo or ancient aliens that influenced prehistoric Earth. This subgenre of science fiction first developed prior to Kirby's work in comics, which he was influenced to incorporate into a variety of his superhero comic books from the 1940s through the 1980s.

Although later regarded by some as a historical theory, ancient aliens were originally considered a science-fiction subgenre that had been presented in popular culture since the early 1900s and eventually depicted by Kirby during the Golden Age of comic books. The first printed work on the topic appears to be *The Gods of Pegāna* (1905), written by Lord Dunsany. Dunsany created a panel of horrible gods whose chief deity, Mana-Yood-Sushai, maintained sleep by creating a lesser god who soothed him so the world could avoid an apocalypse if he were to awaken. The concept wasn't initially accepted by literary critics. *The Guardian* remarked on October 29, 1906, "Lord Dunsany's gods are a peculiar people ... in that kind of world or paradise which one sees in nightmare or under the influence of opium.... They conduct their business of godhead by the rules for nightmare."[2] However, it set a tone of extraterrestrial superbeings that lived by their own set of rules and could at any point threaten humanity's existence. This concept is thought to have gained the interest of H.P. Lovecraft, who expanded the subgenre with a tale of his own ancient aliens that visited prehistoric Earth.[3] Lovecraft portrayed them as disfigured unholy aquarian creatures in "The Call of Cthulhu," debuting in *Weird Tales* (February 1928), which focused on a psychic squid god that slept in the depths of the ocean and served as the telepathic source of all human anxiety. He added excerpts describing various deviant religions that worshipped Cthulhu with hopes of his awakening that would give rise to Armageddon. Other writers developed Lovecraft's mythos in more pulp magazines depicting other lesser demonic gods, but the material was not considered mainstream when he died in 1937. It was through reprints by business-man August Derleth in 1939 that Lovecraft's stories of space gods became part of a national discussion, prompting their entry into popular culture.[4] One likely point of entry was by the Simon and Kirby team, who referred to ancient aliens as evolved humanoid figures in "Tuk Caveboy" from *Captain America Comics* #1 (1941). The main character, Tuk, was the son of two demigods who were abandoned by their people to survive among "the beasts" of Earth, which included ape-men, rhinos, and saber-toothed tigers. The other demigods of their race were referred to as "hairless ones [*who*] departed across the long waters in a log with white wings."[5] Similar to Tarzan, Tuk was raised by an ape-man after his parents were mauled to death before starting his prehistoric journey "to the Island of the Gods," referred to as "Attilan," in order "to reclaim a lost throne."[6] This fictional island was a concept that Kirby revisited two decades later, but at its time in 1941 was implied as a place of origin for space gods that influenced early humans.

Kirby's involvement in space gods became more frequent in the late 1950s after some notable events earlier in the decade. Science-fiction writer Arthur C. Clarke wrote the first of an anthology series that began with "Sentinel of Eternity," premier-ing in *10 Story Fantasy* (spring 1951) regarding a million-year-old pyramidal device that was left on the moon by ancient aliens. The device was discovered by astronauts exploring the lunar surface whose presence ceased its ongoing signal to its creators, which indicated that intelligent life on Earth had developed. There were also recur-rent newspaper reports in 1951 that publicized the Easter Island stone heads called Moai in eastern Polynesia. One newspaper revealed that these statues were up to "40 feet high and hundreds of tons of dead weight" and "some fantastic theories have been invented to explain the transportation of these massive hulks."[7] As the Moai gained more fame, many science-fiction plots arose regarding their possible ancient alien origins. Kirby made use of this mystery by first describing the stone men of Easter Island as alien invaders in a story whose title seems partially named after Clarke's aforementioned series, "The Stone Sentinels of Giant Island" in the *House of Mystery* #85 (1959), and then again as villains in Thor's first appearance, "The Stone Men from Saturn" in *Journey into Mystery* #83 (1962).

During the 1960s, ancient aliens grew beyond fiction when they were intro-duced as plausible historical explanations for prehistoric events, which is consis-tent with Kirby's heightened participation in the subgenre. In 1960, ancient aliens were proposed as a possible reality in the French book *The Morning of the Magicians*. Written by literary editor Louis Pauwels and chemical engineer Jacques Bergier, the book discussed established physical phenomena such as Peruvian Nazca lines as possible footprints of ancient beings.[8] This, in turn, inspired Robert Charroux to write his book *100,000 Years of Man's Unknown History* (1963), the first of a series that claimed that ancient aliens were a definite reality.[9] He pointed to similarities in "gods" seen across various mythologies in ancient Celtic, Greek, and Peruvian texts as support for his arguments.[10] After a few years in circulation, Charroux's work was read by Georges Prosper Remi (Hergé), the French-speaking Belgian comic book writer and artist who depicted the concept of ancient aliens in his Tintin comic *Flight 714 to Sydney* (1966–1967). Tintin and his friends discovered signs of UFOs in underground writings, large unexplainable rotating statues, and ancient alien artifacts abandoned by old Earth civilizations in tropical caves.[11] American comic books reflected a similar interest that same year in *The Mighty Thor* #146–147 (1967) by Stan Lee and Jack Kirby, which described the origin of the Inhumans, and their homeland "Attilan," the same city first introduced in "Tuk Caveboy" in 1941. The Inhumans were described as humans whose evolution was advanced by the ancient Kree alien race during prehistoric times. They formed a colony in their technological paradise, which functioned as a refuge from surrounding savage cavemen.[12]

After depicting Attilan, Kirby became influenced by Swiss writer Erich von Däniken, who further discussed prehistoric ancient aliens in his book *Chariots of the Gods* (1968). Däniken included archeological findings such as the Easter Island Moai, Peruvian Nazca lines, England's Stonehenge, Egyptian pyramids, ruins, and statues from numerous cultures and portrayed them as constructs of ancient aliens who visited Earth many centuries ago. Despite the book encountering a significant degree of skepticism, there was a noteworthy contingent of readers who embraced this message, with one spokesperson stating, "Däniken's book swept away the cobwebs from many minds and ended confusion for hundreds of others."[13] The book was successful, later optioned into a West German documentary in 1970 that earned roughly $26 million at the box office from a minuscule budget. The same year that Däniken's book was published, the plot of "Sentinel of Eternity" was developed further by Arthur C. Clarke and Stanley Kubrick into the novel and film, *2001: A Space Odyssey* (1968). The two creators described a backstory where ancient aliens sent gene-enhancing probes to prehistoric Earth, stimulating human evolution. The aliens deposited the probe on the moon, which was later activated by nearby astronauts to send a signal to another faraway probe on Jupiter. By the end of the story, one astronaut reached the second probe and evolved into a "Star Child." The film succeeded with audiences and earned $146 million at the box office from a budget of roughly $10 million. Whether *2001: A Space Odyssey* and *Chariots of the Gods* were true or not didn't matter because the material became permanently ingrained in popular culture and the concepts of extraterrestrial menaces and ancient aliens affected Kirby's work in the 1970s through epic sagas involving the *New Gods* and *The Eternals*.

Kirby developed his first multiple-issue ongoing space god saga that spanned *The Mighty Thor* (1962–1970) at Marvel, *The New Gods* (1971–1972) at DC Comics, and *Captain Victory and the Galactic Rangers* (1981–1984) at Pacific Comics. This trilogy began in the backup title "Tales of Asgard" from *The Mighty Thor* #127–128 (1966), when Kirby depicted Ragnarök as a destructive force that upset the series' status quo by eliminating the Norse gods and giving birth to a new generation of space gods. The two issues initially depicted both Loki and Thor fighting to the death as a great upheaval resulted in the end of Asgard, with "awesome remnants of an age, a glory that is forever gone" and the birth of a "new civilization … a Golden Age … a new rebirth."[14] This new generation of space gods were depicted in the second issue's last panel as beings that were in command of great technologies, but they never reappeared in another *Thor* comic book. These characters were not published at Marvel for one of two reasons: either because Kirby withheld his ideas to keep this concept for himself[15] or Martin Goodman and/or Lee rejected the idea as they did not want to replace the profitable Thor comic book series with something new.[16] Real change was not as welcome as much as the company practice of the illusion of change due to a potential loss in revenue. Instead, Kirby continued the series, unchanged, under Lee while further designing different members of this new pantheon in the privacy of his home, where he revealed to comic book writer Marv Wolfman that he hoped to develop them into a larger story one day.[17]

Kirby considered continuing the story of his space gods with another superhero comic book publisher. A decade earlier, Kirby was blacklisted from DC when he and editor Jack Schiff were involved in a lawsuit regarding the profits of the *Sky Masters of the Space Force* newspaper strip.[18] However, the editorial structure at DC Comics changed in 1967 when Schiff retired as editor and Carmine Infantino became editorial director.[19] Infantino hoped to hire Kirby away from Lee to cripple the operations at Marvel and feature his art in a new innovative comic book. Some satirical panels in *Not Brand Echh* #11 (1968) hinted to this situation, drawn by John Verpoorten and

Kirby depicted Ragnarök in Marvel's *The Mighty Thor* #127 to 128 (1966). However, the story continued at DC Comics in *The New Gods* #1 (1971), explaining why both companies feature Thor and Loki in hand-to-hand combat.

written by Roy Thomas, who stated in a caption that Kirby slaved away for his wages at Marvel while the artist sat at his drawing board with a nearby note that said, "All is forgiven! Carmine."[20] Schiff ally Mort Weisinger also departed DC, in 1970, and there was no longer a blacklist that prevented Kirby from working there. The previous year, Kirby moved from New York to Thousand Oaks, California, for a warmer climate that could help his daughter's asthma,[21] eliminating any proximity to Lee that could prevent his departure. In 1970, he took the opportunity to leave Marvel and accepted Infantino's offer to write and draw his own metaseries of intersecting comic books titled the "Fourth World" featuring the *New Gods*, *The Forever People*, *Superman's Pal Jimmy Olsen*, and *Mister Miracle*.[22] Each of the four titles served a separate function in his overarching epic storyline. Kirby established his new pantheon of technologically advanced space beings in *New Gods*, then depicted its youth culture in *The Forever People*. He portrayed the adventures of their benevolent leader's son in *Mister Miracle* and depicted their chief villain's machinations on Earth in *Superman's Pal Jimmy Olsen*.

However, it was the splash page to *New Gods* #1 (1971) where Kirby re-depicted Ragnarök from *The Mighty Thor* #128 as the introduction to this new metaseries with Thor represented in the background with his winged helmet and hammer, dueling with another figure, which ended in the same cataclysm that created two competing planets: the benevolent New Genesis and the evil Apokolips. New Genesis was the home of the new technology-based space gods led by Highfather, an elderly bearded figure that resembled Odin (from Marvel's *The Mighty Thor*), who gained his knowledge from an ethereal being named the "Source." The fiery planet Apokolips loomed in space with ominous plans for both Earth and New Genesis and was led by the evil Darkseid. Highfather and Darkseid silently counteracted one another in a strategic cold war rather than suffer the heavy casualties of open combat because both leaders previously survived a devastating conflict that ended through a treaty sealed by the exchange of their sons, Orion and Mister Miracle.[23] Highfather never revealed to Orion the nature of his true lineage and raised him to be kind; however, the child's innate temper often required a handheld device called a motherbox for him to regain composure.[24] His violent tendences fueled his motivation to become New Genesis' greatest warrior and he utilized a weaponized version of the Source, referred to as the Astro-force, to foil Darkseid's plans in using a devastating weapon called the Anti-Life Equation. The Anti-Life Equation was the metaseries' major threat to the status quo, capable of ending the free will of all inhabitants in the entire galaxy. Orion eventually discovered his relation to Darkseid[25] and narrowly avoided death when he confronted him in *New Gods* vol. 2, #6 (1984). Orion's counterpart and Highfather's son, Scott Free, premiered in *Mister Miracle* #1 (1971) and was depicted by Kirby as a child tortured on Apokolips by Darkseid's minion, Granny Goodness. Unlike Orion, Free's tactics were to avoid confrontation by repeatedly escaping his prisons. During his final escape, he was presented with two options: follow a fellow rebel named Himon to Earth or stay on Apokolips and be corrupted by Darkseid.

Darkseid threatened the universe with the Anti-Life Equation in *New Gods* #2 (1971) and was opposed by his son, Orion, who discovered their familial relation in *New Gods* #11.

His benevolent nature prompted him to reject Darkseid to live a life of fulfillment and hope. Kirby departed the storyline, leaving the destiny of both characters unresolved after completing *The Hunger Dogs* graphic novel (1985), which depicted the destruction of New Genesis, the survival of Apokolips, and the New Gods' fortress aimlessly drifting through space.[26]

Kirby eventually depicted the conclusion to the *New Gods* saga in *Captain Victory* #11–12 (1983) at Pacific Comics.[27] The story's hero, Captain Victory, discussed his family's origins and their catastrophic war on a giant planet of unrestrained energies with beings called "Ultimates,"[28] a term that Kirby previously used to describe the New Gods in *The Hunger Dogs*.[29] More panels from the comic book demonstrated Victory's childhood in "Hellikost," a planet that represented Apokolips, where he was raised and corrupted by his wicked family members in a manner similar to DC Comics' Scott Free. It was revealed that the benevolent gods of what represented New Genesis were killed long ago, and that Victory was tormented by his royal family to the point of killing his way to freedom. During his escape, he encountered his evil grandfather, "Blackmass," a damaged disembodied spirit who was "all shadow without substance"[30] and represented DC's Darkseid. Blackmass screamed at Victory and appeared to be referring to the New Gods' Orion when he yelled, "How like your father you are! A feisty, rebellious, arrogant warrior who delighted in tearing up my dreams!"[31] Kirby depicted Blackmass as damaged and hollow after his final battle but preserved in dark unholy energy similar to the forces that kept Emperor Palpatine barely alive in *Star Wars: The Rise of Skywalker* (2019). Victory displayed satisfaction as he escaped the planet, allowing it to destroy itself in a nuclear explosion, and rode an Orion-style space sled away from the exploding debris, ready to begin a new chapter as Captain Victory. The emotional pain as well as the effort it took to discuss this difficult topic triggered a similar transformation as that of Orion into a feral and angry state, which likewise required a calming hand to maintain his gentler characteristic.[32] This story was Kirby's conclusion to the *New Gods*, which included the destruction of New Genesis and Apokolips.

Kirby's "Fourth World" metaseries failed to attract enough readers to stay viable in the marketplace, prompting cancellation within two years; however, its plots appear to have influenced creators to utilize its concepts for space operas[33] such as *Star Wars*. For example, the looming planet of Apokolips and its power craters resemble the Death Star in *Star Wars* (1977), and Obi-Wan Kenobi gained wisdom from the Force similar to Highfather from the Source in *New Gods*. Orion's blue eyes and long strawberry blond hair resembled the young Luke Skywalker,[34] with both heroes similarly powered by their respective extraterrestrial forces. Both figures also felt the obligation to fulfill their destinies by confronting their evil and corrupt fathers, Darkseid and Darth Vader. In fact, Darkseid's offer to Scott Free to stay on Apokolips was similar to Darth Vader's proposal to Luke Skywalker in *The Empire Strikes Back* (1980) to join him and succumb to the "Dark Side" of the Force: "Stay Warrior! Let me complete the destruction of Scott Free, so you may live with the majesty that is the power of Darkseid!"[35] Another similarity to *The Empire Strikes Back* was present in *The Forever People* #4 (1971), when Big Bear was depicted in a shrieking Vibro-Wave similar to the one that trapped Chewbacca on Cloud City. *The Forever People* also featured a character, Mark Moonrider, whose name sounds similar to Luke Skywalker. The links between Kirby and *Star Wars* are likely real considering that George Lucas co-owned a comic art gallery in Manhattan from the mid to late 1970s called Supersnipe[36] with partner Ed Summer, who was seen obsessing over the original art of Jack Kirby in the documentary *The World of Comic Books* (1978).[37] This would help explain why Darth Vader, who welcomed Han Solo and Princess Leia over a prepared table in *The Empire Strikes Back*, matched Dr. Doom in the same pose and intent from *Fantastic Four* #87 (1969).[38]

After the initial failure of the "Fourth World," Kirby returned to Marvel in the mid–1970s and renewed his interest in the works of Arthur C. Clarke and Erich von Däniken[39] to develop more comic book properties. This occurred after starting various titles at DC, including *Demon* and *Kamandi*, which achieved acclaim but proved less satisfying for him as compared with the *New Gods*. He worked at Marvel for three years, writing and drawing various titles, including two that focused on his interest in space gods, *2001: A Space Odyssey* and *The Eternals*. Both comics from 1976 involved prehistoric humans who were evolved by ancient aliens. Kirby's *2001: A Space Odyssey* adaptation was an oversize comic book that offered a simpler narrative and visual recreation of the Arthur C. Clarke story published as a Marvel Treasury Special. It was received well enough for Kirby to develop the property into an ongoing *2001: A Space Odyssey* comic book series that explored the alien probe's journey as it evolved various species in the galaxy. The storyline eventually changed focus to an artificial intelligence robot that was evolved by the probe and featured in his own title, *Machine Man*, and who eventually became a recurring character in the Marvel Universe.

Kirby demonstrated the concept of ancient aliens advancing human evolution in *2001: A Space Odyssey* (1976), based on the novel by Arthur C. Clarke, and *The Eternals* (1976), which was influenced by Erich von Däniken's *Chariots of the Gods.*

The Eternals was another one of Kirby's expressions of the ancient alien concept with an entirely new depiction of space giants called Celestials, who converted early prehistoric apes into three types of humanoids: Deviants, humans, and Eternals.[40] The Eternals were nearly immortal and waged war with the constantly mutating and barely humanoid Deviants, with the fate of humans constantly at risk, while all parties awaited the verdict of the Celestial judge, Arishem, who determined if Earth could continue to exist. Kirby's main inspiration for the series was displayed on the cover of *The Eternals* #2 with the caption, "More Fantastic Than *Chariots of the Gods*," which clearly indicated Erich von Däniken as the series' key influence.

Despite Kirby's initial optimism, *The Eternals* was canceled within two years and the plotline never concluded due to his departure in 1978 to start a career in animation for *The New Fantastic Four* (1978) and *Thundarr the Barbarian* (1980). However, it should be noted that *The Eternals* series reutilized and evolved space god concepts from *Superman's Pal Jimmy Olsen*, *New Gods*, *Mister Miracle*, and *Black Cat Mystic*. Kirby apparently categorized the Eternals, humans, and Deviants through what could be considered a biblical lens of angels, humans, and demons, which was the model of three previously used in the Fourth World with New Gods from New Genesis, Deviants from Apokolips, and humans from Earth. Kirby also used the same grouping of three in *Superman's Pal Jimmy Olsen* #136 (1971), discussing clones at "The Project" that were categorized into normal, step-ups, and aliens.[41] Additionally, the word "Eternal" was previously used in *Mister Miracle* #18 (1974) when Scott Free and Big Barda exchanged wedding vows: "I am Eternal with Scott Free! … I am Eternal with Barda."[42] When the Eternals were confronted with an existential threat, they could merge their minds into a collective all-powerful and space-traveling Uni-Mind in the same manner as Kirby's five aforementioned mutants from *Black Cat Mystic* #59 (1957).[43]

As Stan Lee focused on adapting superheroes to other media, it was Kirby's interest in ancient alien writers and theorists such as Arthur C. Clarke and Erich von Däniken that contributed to adapting the concept of space gods as a cosmic threat in his metaseries of superhero comic books that spanned work published by Marvel Comics, DC Comics, and Pacific Comics. His depiction of Ragnarök in *The Mighty Thor* hinted that a larger force always loomed to jeopardize a group of established heroes. Their destruction was an avenue to portray the space god Darkseid's quest for the Anti-Life Equation, which served as a greater universal menace that threatened to eliminate the free will of various heroes from his four comic book metaseries, the "Fourth World." Kirby wanted to challenge heroes with Darkseid's quest for domination, the judgment of Arishem the Celestial, or the incoming influence of ancient alien space probes that threatened to destroy the existential status quo. Despite these series' relatively quick demises, Kirby elevated comic books by depicting constantly approaching galactic threats that could narratively initiate long-form cosmic superhero crossovers, which was a technique that eventually found success with the incorporation of death by Jim Starlin.

PART 4

Modern Superheroes

20

Jim Starlin and the Death of Superheroes

As Jack Kirby expanded the scope of superhero comic books with long-form cosmic storylines presented as a metaseries, Jim Starlin increased the risk to their characters by incorporating the existential threat of death. Death was a Bronze Age trait that was more heavily introduced by comic book writers in the early 1970s.

Stan Lee wrote the death of Captain George Stacy for *The Amazing Spider-Man* #90 (1970) in "And Death Shall Come!" when debris fell toward a young boy and Captain Stacy leaped to save him at the cost of his own life.[1] The father of Gwen Stacy was created by Lee, Romita, and Heck in *The Amazing Spider-Man* #56 (1968) and originally functioned as a potential second father to Peter Parker. His relevance to the overall *Spider-Man* continuity ceased and he served a better function as a source of trauma to the story's hero. A similar event occurred with his daughter when Gerry Conway wrote "The Night Gwen Stacy Died" in *The Amazing Spider-Man* #121 (1973), when Parker's girlfriend perished from a neck fracture during an altercation with the Green Goblin.[2] Gwen Stacy was created by Lee and Ditko in *The Amazing Spider-Man* #31 (1965) as a potential love interest and competitor to Mary Jane, but the concept of a tortured Spider-Man superseded her viability, which prompted an end to her narrative purpose.[3]

The father of Namor the Sub-Mariner, Leonard McKenzie, was created by Bill Everett in *Marvel Comics* #1 (1939), but when Conway became the writer for the *Sub-Mariner* series, he wrote McKenzie's death to occur from trauma with a pipe to his head in issue #46 (1972).[4] Namor's love interest and fellow Atlantean, Lady Dorma, also created by Everett in *Marvel Comics* #1, was written as a casualty by Roy Thomas in *Sub-Mariner* #37 (1971). Her death through suffocation was depicted after her aquarium broke, depriving her of oxygen.[5] This pattern of death of ancillary characters in superhero comic books added a higher risk to their storylines, entertaining readers.

It was during this point that Kirby's "Fourth World" was canceled and Jim Starlin entered comic books, offering his originally created character Thanos as a new villain for the Marvel Comics Group. Roy Thomas understood that the ominous figure could possibly achieve what Kirby failed to do with *New Gods* and encouraged

Starlin to "show DC how to do Darkseid."[6] So, Starlin successfully wrote and penciled a long-form cosmic story arc that introduced death as a significant risk to its superheroes in a metaseries that utilized narrative topics from his early work in fanzines and his childhood enjoyment of comic books by Steve Ditko and Jack Kirby.

Starlin's origins and early fanzines foreshadowed his later contributions to superhero comic books. He grew up Catholic[7] reading the comic book work of Steve Ditko and Jack Kirby and "loved Kirby before we knew it was Kirby" as early as the 1950s.[8] He first met Ditko at his studio while the artist was drawing *The Amazing Spider-Man* #36 (1965) and studied his notebooks that depicted sketches of arms in various positions. He later joined the navy and experienced loss of lives in the aviation division during the Vietnam War, while drawing comics for fanzines when he was off duty.[9] It's in these early fanzines where he first publicly expressed his preoccupation with death that he later incorporated into his superhero stories. One example was seen in the Texas-based fanzine *Star Studded* #16 (1969), when Starlin penciled a short story named "Doomsday!" about the last man on a postapocalyptic Earth overrun by Neucromian lizards. After evading a barbaric horde, the veteran escaped into a nuclear facility, mourned the human race, and induced Armageddon by detonating the entire planet in a large-scale mercy killing.[10] Starlin portrayed death with sacrifice as an ultimately necessary method for stopping a greater evil. He developed these concepts further in "The Miracle" in *Star Studded* #18 (1972), which he both wrote and drew, starring Dr. Weird, a story that was notable for its cosmic confrontation between life and death that readers would appreciate in his later superhero comic books. The themes here were compelling as a young girl lay on her deathbed, suffering from a terminal disease. An unbiased hooded figure that embodied Death stood in a cosmic abyss, ready to receive her soul. The caped Dr. Weird, an avatar of life, flexed his muscles and took flight in a superhero costume consisting of boots, a short one-piece costume, winged chest logo, and widow's peak. A specter of the young child was then seen running along a cosmic bridge as the two opposing forces met in a mind-bending series of panels that resulted in saving her life.[11] The aesthetic was specifically Starlin's but also reminiscent of Ditko's Doctor Strange, who faced the villain Dormammu in a similar environment.[12]

The cosmic scale of life versus death such as that presented in those pages was a preview of concepts that Starlin developed further at Marvel Comics, with one example being the introduction of Dr. Weird into Marvel as Drax the Destroyer in *The Invincible Iron Man* #55 (1973). He then presented Death as a peripheral character who observed the events of a short story from *Journey into Mystery* vol. 2, #1 (1972) called "You Show Me Your Dream, I'll Show You Mine!!" This narrative was not canon but still illustrated by Starlin and scripted by Steve Skeates about a killer for hire who repeatedly dreamed about a beautiful young woman, who also dreamed about him. Unable to sleep any further, he rushed out of his home and drove in the rain, only to see her in the street. He swerved to avoid her, crashed, and died, which prompted the cosmic entity of Death, who stood in limbo, to laugh while the young woman returned to bed, dreaming no more.[13] The Death entity depicted by Starlin in this anthology title had a facial appearance that was visually in between the desiccated version from the Dr. Weird story and the bony version that he introduced into the Marvel Universe in *Captain Marvel* #26 (1973). All three versions evoked the hooded figure called "the symbol of evil," chained by Nightmare and drawn by Ditko in Doctor Strange's first appearance from *Strange Tales* #110 (1963).[14] *Captain Marvel* #26 was scripted by Mike Friedrich with plot and art by Starlin, and it depicted Marvel continuity's first portrayal of Death standing next to the demi-god Thanos shortly after Captain Marvel fought the Thing in a tense brawl. The two heroes stood puzzled, unaware that these two ominous beings would soon raise the risk of being a superhero in the Marvel Universe.

Thanos and Death are twin concepts that Starlin originated from events outside Marvel Comics, with the villain's name being a clear derivation of Thanatos, the ancient Greek personification of death. He commented on Thanos's origins, "After I got out of the service, I took a shrink class off the VA.... Thanos ... came out of that." However, when he brought Thanos to Marvel, Roy Thomas asked Starlin to outdo Darkseid,[15] which made the character a manifestation of the creator's id with a Kirby veneer. In Starlin's mythos, Thanos was a male servant to his female superior, Death, for which he felt lust. This Thanos-Death connection served Starlin's function as cosmic universal killers who endangered Marvel's superheroes.

His innate compulsion toward Death appeared outside Marvel in Mike

Starlin completed the creation of Thanos by depicting both his first murder and his consort, the cosmic entity of Death, in *Captain Marvel* # 26 (1973).

Friedrich's *Star*Reach* (1974), an independent comic consisting of creator-owned content. Starlin's art decorated the first cover with Death's cloaked visage in the background and two green seductive females in the foreground. This cover may have been designed to inspire onlooking readers to experience the same lust that Thanos felt toward his hooded companion, who was also depicted in two stories within the comic's interior pages. The first one was called the "Death Building" about Starlin himself entering the Marvel Comics office and walking by a body in the elevator who had just suffered a cosmic defeat from Death.[16] The second story involved the book of Genesis describing God's role in "The Birth of Death!" for the purpose of delivering punishment and humility to renegade angels and humans. These two stories revealed Starlin's intention that Death was a primal inevitability that would generally accompany the writer's later narratives.

Starlin utilized Thanos in a cosmic metaseries of various titles such as *The Invincible Iron Man*, *Captain Marvel*, *Warlock*, *The Avengers*, and *Marvel Two-in-One* to depict a series of events that confronted Marvel's superheroes with their mortality. His portrayal of the incoming danger of Thanos in Marvel Comics was direct and physical as compared with Kirby's philosophical approach of Darkseid's Anti-Life Equation in DC Comics. An example was seen during Thanos's arrival on Earth, which was recounted in *Captain Marvel* #32 (1974) when he murdered the innocent bystanders Arthur Douglas and his wife to maintain secrecy. Their demise was swift and brutal, sending a message to readers that he wasted no time in managing obstacles regardless of the consequences. Douglas's death prompted Thanos's grandfather Kronos to resurrect him into the newly powered Drax the Destroyer with the same appearance and role as Starlin's earlier creation Dr. Weird, the avatar of life.[17] In another cosmic Starlin tale, the Matriarch of the Universal Church of Truth was severely weakened due to the lethal machinations of Adam Warlock's future self, the Magus, in *Warlock* #10 (1975). She noticed Warlock in the darkness asking, "Is that you, Death?" She lay in his arms and perished with mistress Death's face in the background hissing, "Die!"[18] Starlin used these events to enhance the sorrow and trauma of his storylines, which reminded the reader that superheroes were not capable of saving everyone. *Avengers Annual* #7 (1977) depicted Adam Warlock helpless to save Gamora, who was in severe pain and dying from being crushed by the Mad Titan, Thanos, who also later mentally destroyed Pip the Troll.[19] Starlin's narratives emphasized the powerlessness of superheroes, as evidenced by Thanos's use of his soul-gem-powered spaceship, *Sanctuary*, that was used to induce a nearby sun to explode, wiping out a solar system of planets in a scene that appeared to be an homage to *Star Wars* (1977). The character Moondragon was depicted with her eyes widened in shock as she telepathically sensed "millions of voices dying all at once."[20] As the catastrophic and callous "stellar genocide" continued, Adam Warlock confronted Thanos, but was killed in battle while Death presided over his body. Thanos triumphantly boasted, "So Die, Adam Warlock. My mistress awaits you."[21] He was shown taking Warlock's soul gem to "appease Death" and pontificated that for a "chosen hero ... life abandoned him casually," which suggested that death was a routine and anticlimactic event for the villain. However, Warlock's spirit was revived by the soul gem and killed Thanos by freezing him in "solid granite,"[22] delivering the conclusion that in a high-risk fictional narrative, anyone, including the main villain, could die.

Death was a plot device that Starlin continued to use in cosmic storylines while submitting his work to publishers that offered better contracts for his work. The legal aspect to publishing changed when the Copyright Act of 1976 became effective in 1978, prompting him to submit his next cosmic epic, the "Metamorphosis Odyssey," to the creator-owned side of Marvel Comics under editor Archie Goodwin in *Epic Illustrated* #1 (1980), a magazine conceived by Rick Marschall.[23] The contracts formulated for *Epic Illustrated* were drafted so that Marvel "bought first printing rights only and allowed creators to retain their copyrights."[24] Retaining the copyrights attracted the attention of creators such as Starlin, whose history in the magazine *Star*Reach* suggested that he preferred the option of payment for reprint rights. There was also another advantage: the Marvel Universe offered the opportunity to utilize established characters for new stories, but the company practice of the impermanent illusion of change prevented any true advancement from the status quo. However, in his own fictional universe, Starlin could depict the death of any character that maximized his narrative purpose. He also used more advanced techniques in paint and illustration to construct his 14-chapter limited series for "Metamorphosis Odyssey," which he acquired from a recent career in book cover illustration.[25] The story was about Vanth Dreadstar, an antisocial survivor whose energy sword empowered him to work with an elder god, Aknaton, to locate the "Infinity Horn" and destroy a great intergalactic evil, the Zygoteans. The series was well-received by readers who enjoyed its science fiction and adventure while newspapers described it as a "beautiful ... visual delight."[26] The story ended in *Epic Illustrated* #9 (1981), when the Infinity Horn was finally used to destroy the incoming armies of the Zygoteans and the Milky Way and its billions of inhabitants in a galactic mercy killing.[27] Furious at the casualties, Dreadstar killed his ally Aknaton in a fit of rage, and the antihero was depicted in Starlin's final pages, grieving as he stared at a new universe wondering if the same outcome needed to occur again.

As Starlin's comic books depicted intergalactic death for an eager audience, the industry's payment structure was also changing. Direct-market comic stores were in growing demand of more content. Distributors needed more product, and independent comic publishers supplied creator-owned graphic novels.[28] Starlin utilized this growing industry and signed a contract with Eclipse Comics to publish a sequel to "Metamorphosis Odyssey." *The Price* (1981) depicted the demonic origin of Darklock, a cybernetic wizard who killed enemies and allies on his quest for greater power. The story ended as he acknowledged the people that he sacrificed to one day fight a greater incoming evil. The graphic nature of the story was compatible with direct-market comic stores that sold the material to older clientele who enjoyed adult-themed graphic novels. Independent comic book publishers used this model to seize market share, which prompted executives at DC and Marvel Comics to adapt by creating royalty programs for their comic books. Editor-in-Chief Jim Shooter, Vice President Michael Hobson, and Mike Friedrich also coordinated with Starlin to formulate a new contract for creators who contributed to their graphic novel line.[29] Creators received a nonrefundable cash advance against future royalties from their books, which prompted Starlin to sign a contract for two more graphic novels. One was the sequel to both the "Metamorphosis Odyssey" and *The Price* titled *Dreadstar* (1982) about the antihero domesticated and married in a remote village. He met Darklock, who warned him too late of an oncoming greater evil, as his wife and village were murdered. They decided to leave the idyllic paradise and embark on a mission of revenge against two intergalactic armies, the Monarchy and the Instrumentality.[30] *Dreadstar* continued as a series for Epic's comics line, and then moved to First Comics, continuing the saga into the 1990s.

Starlin's second graphic novel under Marvel's new contract was *The Death of Captain Marvel* (1982), a story that offered the creator an opportunity to exorcise the emotional difficulties of his father's death.[31] He submitted the idea of the cosmic hero dying of cancer. Shooter responded, "A superhero dying of a disease. Holy cow.... I don't think anyone's ever done that. Let's do it."[32] In its final pages, the spirit of a dead Captain Marvel encountered the specter of Thanos and the entity of Death. He yielded to both, took their hands, and accepted his mortality as all three stepped into a light that symbolized the afterlife.[33] Starlin suspended disbelief for readers who accepted that superheroes could have souls and that it was important to acknowledge their passing in a deep and meaningful way. This was accomplished with a minimal portrayal of fight scenes and its vulnerable depiction of the human condition, with Shooter commenting, "I was amazed ... he brought some real human stuff into the superhero genre."[34]

The royalty program at DC Comics offered Starlin more lucrative opportunities to write stories about Batman that utilized death in the late 1980s. One example was the morbid 1988 miniseries with art by Bernie Wrightson, *Batman: The Cult*, in which the hero was kidnapped, drugged, and brainwashed by a charismatic cult leader. Under his influence, Batman found himself using a gun to shoot a man as part of a massacre during "an underworlder's raid on a Mafia Don's house."[35] Wrightson's visual history with horror proved the correct artistic choice, depicting the Dark Knight confused and surrounded by hundreds of corpses while witnessing the leader bathing in a pool of blood. The positive impact of this miniseries on readers proved that Batman was a superhero whose comic book was compatible with Starlin's predilection toward writing about death. Another example was "Ten Nights of the Beast," a four-part story that began in *Batman* #417 (1988) about a Soviet assassin and member of an extreme wing of the KGB sent to the United States to kill nine key members of the Star Wars missile-defense program. The KGBeast was depicted killing hundreds of people before Batman eventually managed to lock him in a sewer, leaving him to die. In an almost Ayn Randian fashion, Batman declared, "There's no reason for me to risk my life, coming in there after you. Sometimes you have to ignore the rules."[36] Starlin also wrote of another death that still has repercussions in DC's continuity, the death of Jason Todd/Robin in *Batman* #428 (1988). He commented publicly, "I'd wanted to kill Robin ever since I started writing Batman. He worked fine in the '40s…. I found Batman much more interesting as a loner, I've always seen Batman as almost a sociopath."[37] Starlin fulfilled his desire to end Robin's presence in the comic series after a public vote-in telethon confirmed that readers wanted the same thing. So, he wrote a scene where the Joker used a crowbar to violently beat the teenager unconscious, then left him to die in an explosion.

Starlin also depicted cosmic narratives at DC Comics that utilized death and annihilation. One example was another miniseries with art by Bernie Wrightson, *The Weird* (1988), about an energy being from another dimension whose people were consumed by an enemy race, the Macrolatts. The Weird escaped the genocide through a portal and helped members of the Justice League defend Earth from their influence while killing the Macrolatts in the process. Weird's molecular structure became unstable, causing him to explode in space shortly after commenting that he lived "a good and exciting life."[38] Significantly more deaths occurred in *Cosmic Odyssey* (1988), a four-issue limited series written by Starlin and penciled by Mike Mignola about various DC heroes, including the New Gods separating into teams to find the Anti-Life Equation. Starlin demonstrated intergalactic casualties that were similar in scope to the "Metamorphosis Odyssey." An extinction-level event occurred at the planet Xanshi, which was exterminated due to Green Lantern's overconfidence, causing the hero to contemplate suicide. An entire dimension was also vaporized when Dr. Fate cauterized a multidimensional wound that was infected with antilife.[39] Similar to Starlin's stories at Marvel, the DC superheroes were portrayed as unable to prevent any of these deaths, including that of Forager from the New Gods, who sacrificed himself during his mission with Batman. Orion laughed at the sacrifice, which continued a callous trend in the warrior who earlier murdered a group of mind-controlled Thanagarians, despite pleas from Superman.[40] The heroes realized that they were capable only of minimizing death, which served as a reminder to newspaper critics who commented that Starlin's realism was "entering heroes' lives … with less simple-minded heroism."[41]

He returned to Marvel in 1990 and revived Thanos for a series of galactic conflicts that depicted the character's interest in Death and the Infinity Stones for a superhero metaseries that extended for more than two decades. The character was resurrected in *Silver Surfer* #34 (1990) and journeyed across the universe during *The Thanos Quest* (1990) to recover each Infinity Stone from various guardians and assemble them during *The Infinity Gauntlet* (1991). Thanos's goal was to activate the power of the stones to terminate half of the universe and appease mistress Death.[42] Starlin used this opportunity to restore Warlock, Pip, Drax, and Gamora for this larger-scale adventure that fulfilled Thanos's promise of existentially ending half of

Marvel's superheroes. The remaining superheroes united and eventually reversed the deaths that Thanos caused, which allowed Starlin to tell his story and still maintain the company's illusion of change. The villain's return demonstrated profitable sales at the marketplace, and the series was officially declared successful.[43] Starlin continued his cosmic metaseries describing Thanos's ambitions for power in titles including *Infinity War* (1992), *Infinity Watch* (1992), *Infinity Crusade* (1993), *Infinity Abyss* (2002), *Marvel: The End* (2003), *Infinity Revelation* (2014), *Infinity Relativity* (2015), *Infinity Finale* (2016), *Infinity Siblings* (2018), *Infinity Conflict* (2019), *Infinity Ending* (2019), and their associated crossovers. His usage of Thanos successfully achieved Kirby's dream of raising the scope and risk of superhero adventures in a cosmic metaseries of intersecting comic books.

Kirby's New Gods eventually became a point of focus for Starlin after creating a few miniseries that depicted death in occult fiction and science fiction. *Breed* (1994) was published by Malibu Comics about a boy named Raymond Stoner who was originally conceived by demons in a house full of bones and blood-soaked ancient symbols.[44] Stoner later realized that he was a half-demon, half-human creature and could augment his body to counter these demons from hell, whose threat was eventually neutralized after a substantial number of casualties. Starlin also added another demonic entity into a six-issue limited series for DC Comics named *Hardcore Station* (1998), about a cosmic dictator named Synnar whose deal with a "Nameless" supernatural entity gave him great physical power. Synnar schemed with the greedy Entreplaneteurs to destroy a planet for its energy, which resulted in the death

Thanos threatened the status quo of the Marvel Universe by bringing death to 50 percent of its superheroes in *The Infinity Gauntlet* (1991).

of three billion people. This genocide attracted the attention of the Justice League of America, which included Superman and Orion, who defeated Synnar in a battle with significant collateral damage.[45]

Starlin continued this storyline into the miniseries *Mystery in Space* (2006), which began with the death of Captain Comet and his immediate resurrection into a clone who discovered a sequence of clues to identify who killed him. The new Comet encountered the Eternal Light Corporation (ELC), whose religious idealism and greed was responsible for murdering his friend and starting a space war that resulted in the suffocation and death of numerous sectors of an extraterrestrial metropolitan city.[46] He gained the alliance of the Weird and defeated the ELC by bombing the walls of their containment unit, sending their leader and his followers out into the vacuum of space. The last panel of the story depicted Orion from the New Gods in his space sled, suggesting to readers that a new saga was to follow.

Starlin had grown frustrated by various writers who portrayed the New Gods but failed to reach the potential that Kirby originally hoped to have. Disheartened by these "mixed results," Starlin decided that he was "cleaning house."[47] He made an agreement with DC Comics to write and pencil the *Death of the New Gods* (2007), which he felt was "half honoring Jack Kirby, half mercy killing."[48] Mercy killing was a well-established theme of his stories by this point. The first few pages startled readers when the Black Racer lay in a hospital bed with his heart torn out. More violent killings appeared to target members of New Genesis and Apokolips, with one notable scene that depicted Mr. Miracle kneeling over Big Barda's bloody corpse. Superman investigated the murders, hoping to stop each New God from successively dying, eventually revealing that the Source killed the New Gods and merged New Genesis and Apokolips into a new planet. By the end of the story, the last son of Krypton flew home questioning if he could have saved them by doing anything differently, while acknowledging his own powerlessness.

Starlin's stories worked well with audiences because they utilized previously established techniques in comic book storytelling, with new dramatic innovations. Although Kirby's long-form philosophical approach with the *New Gods* failed to capture market share, it influenced Starlin, who added a significant amount of death, which increased a superhero's exposure to risk and notified readers that they were reading serious literature. He depicted superheroes as helpless to save everyone since their jobs put them in situations where they could only minimize death, but not fully prevent it. His creation and usage of Thanos as an intergalactic killer maximized these factors and successfully fulfilled Kirby's dream of creating a cosmic metaseries of intersecting comic books for older readers. However, there were some readers who tired of Bronze Age death and demanded superhero sentiment of the Golden and Silver Ages, but without the dated art and script styles. To maintain further viability, superhero comic books needed a writer and artist who could revitalize the genre and medium for a new generation.

John Byrne and the Modernization
of Superheroes

Shortly after Jim Starlin incorporated death into his cosmic storylines, another group of comic creators were eager to revitalize the work of Jerry Siegel, Joe Shuster, Bob Kane, Bill Finger, Julius Schwartz, Stan Lee, Jack Kirby, and Steve Ditko for the next generation of readers. John Byrne was the most successful of his generation to do so, partly due to an early childhood enjoyment of *Superman* and Kirby's art. He commented that his "journey into comics began with the George Reeves *Superman* series ... when I was about 6 years old" and "Super Comics ... featured a ... Batman story [*that*] hooked me for life."[1] The young Byrne soon enjoyed the action and suspense of Lee and Kirby's *The Fantastic Four* #5 (1962)[2] featuring the first appearance of Doctor Doom. He quickly noticed that "it was so different from DC, DC was bland to be kind.... I was eleven and I was a sensitive child."[3] He eventually found some success cartooning his own comics for his school newspaper at the Alberta College of Art and Design in Calgary, Canada.[4] His depiction of Frankenstein was published by Marvel in "FOOM fan art gallery" in *FOOM!* #5 (1974),[5] and he illustrated a horror story called "The Castle" in Skywald's *Nightmare* #20 (1974).[6] Positive reception to his early publications encouraged him to work as a freelance artist for Charlton Comics professionally publishing "Rog-2000" in *E-Man* #6 (1975) with scriptwriter Nicola Cuti.[7] Byrne's skill at visual storytelling was used at Marvel, where he drew a significant quantity of issues and characters, including *FOOM!*, *The Champions*, *Marvel Team-Up*, *Marvel Preview*, *The Uncanny X-Men*, and *Fantastic Four*. Byrne's aesthetic seemed to combine the cartoon realism of Jack Kirby and the stylized realism of Neal Adams, which manifested into a remarkable visual appeal that sold in high numbers at the marketplace. As Golden Age artists such as Kirby and Siegel aged out of the comic book industry, Byrne revitalized their characters for a new generation, contributing to the growth of the superhero genre's fanbase, as well as his and Marvel's success in the 1980s.

Byrne's early career at Marvel Comics, in some ways, was patterned after Kirby. For instance, the number of comic books that Byrne penciled per month rivaled a similar number from Kirby's period in the early 1960s. Regarding the cover date of September 1963, Kirby penciled and co-plotted *The X-Men* #1, *The Avengers* #1,

Fantastic Four #18, and *Sgt. Fury and His Howling Commandos* #3.[8] Byrne was determined to catch up to him. In describing Kirby's high output per month, he said, "I thought he was doing three monthly books ... so I figured I have to do three monthly books."[9] Although Byrne spoke in jest, his sense of competition was apparent and during his peak at Marvel, he penciled a similar number of monthly comic books. By the early 1980s, his command of both writing and penciling pages at a considerable rate made him an heir to Kirby's legacy at Marvel Comics. For the cover date of July 1980, Byrne wrote and/or penciled four issues: *The Uncanny X-Men* #135, *Captain America* #247, *The Amazing Spider-Man* #206, and the *Fantastic Four* #220.[10] However, Kirby was the cocreator of those respective four issues, whereas Byrne was a writer of one issue. While Byrne did not create as many characters and series as Jack Kirby, he still had a specific aesthetic, heightened skill, and the discipline to produce quality comic books in high numbers. He positioned himself, similar to Kirby, as the talented, productive artist who shaped the overall house style at Marvel Comics of the early 1980s. Before Byrne was Marvel's premier superhero artist, he penciled a memorable double-page spread that celebrated "Kirby's Kosmic Konsciousness" in *FOOM!* #11 (1975). At this point, Byrne was both an artist struggling to get recognized and a fan of the Marvel cocreator. He illustrated Kirby's distinctive eyes, upper face, cigar in hand, with head partially open and characters including Silver Surfer, Thor, Thing, and Captain America jumping out.[11] Although Byrne's penciling style was close to established, he still drew the image in the boxy cartoon realism that Kirby was known to utilize. Byrne also paid homage to Kirby when he penciled the cover of the same *FOOM!* issue that celebrated Kirby's return to Marvel adorned in a red cape and costume, large K on the chest, and classic cigar shedding Kirby crackle. In a sense, Byrne's welcoming Kirby back to Marvel was a watershed moment, as one career was showing signs of winding down, while the other was just starting.

Kirby's work continued to be featured in Byrne's early pencils, which delivered the material in a new way for the next generation of readers. Byrne's drawing style was noticed while at *FOOM!* and soon after was featured in the pages of *Iron Fist*, on which he collaborated with *X-Men* writer Chris Claremont. Similar to later artists, Mike Zeck and Gene Day, Byrne honed his skills on the martial arts action genre and mastered the ability to sequentially move anatomy in panels, taking the reader through all angles of physical combat. He revisited the technique of the one-page nine-panel action sequence in *Iron Fist* #7 (1976), which was originally used by Kirby in *Fighting America* #3 (1954),[12] *Two-Gun Kid* #62 (1963),[13] and *Tales of Suspense* #85 (1967).[14] Byrne also utilized Kirby's imagery in "The Fate of the Phoenix!" from *The Uncanny X-Men* #137 (1980), which was a best-seller that used two of the senior artist's sequences. Byrne depicted the same architecture and setting for the blue area of the moon that Kirby drew in *The Fantastic Four* #13 (1963) when the team fought the Red Ghost and his super monkeys. Another sequence by Byrne depicted Wolverine stumbling into the Watcher's house. The Watcher became so offended by his presence that he hurled the mutant through a dinosaur swamp in Earth's ancient past and then through exploding volcanoes of the future before casting him out. This treatment of Wolverine was originally depicted by Kirby when the Watcher did the same to the Red Ghost in *The Fantastic Four* #13.[15] Their angles and panel construction were mostly identical. Many new readers had not before seen this older material, which Byrne used to capture the imagination of the next generation of readers.

Marvel's lucrative royalty plan was newly available during the 1980s when Byrne continued to emulate various works by Kirby, which contributed to a brief professional disagreement. Byrne referenced the Simon and Kirby cover to *Captain America Comics* #1 (1941), which featured Captain America punching Hitler in the jaw as German guards unsuccessfully tried to shoot him on the splash page of *Captain America* #255 (1981). He used the same design with the addition of the Red Skull on a viewing screen in the background to utilize its nostalgia to bring new readers to the origins of the hero and included a sequence depicting FDR giving him his characteristic round shield. Byrne's usage of Kirby's imagery sold well during a time at Marvel when there was a lucrative royalty program. The program was originated by Paul Levitz at DC Comics, which prompted executives at Cadence Publishing, formerly known as Perfect Film & Chemical, to compete with DC and release a memo by Vice President Michael Hobson to Marvel's staff on December 22, 1981, announcing a similar incentive plan. Every comic that sold more than 100,000 copies would result in a profit-share percentage to the contributors. Editor-in-Chief Jim Shooter explained that these royalty programs were a positive move toward creator rights, but critics noted the company's failure to compensate the cocreators of the original characters due to their original work-for-hire agreement.[16] This explained why

John Byrne often renewed Jack Kirby's characters, plots, and story arcs for a new generation. One example is the Blue Area of the Moon depicted by Kirby in *Fantastic Four* #13 (1963) and Byrne in *X-Men* #137 (1980).

Silver Age artists such as Kirby felt frustration from never receiving royalties from his creations,[17] which was compounded by not being able to receive his original art from 1960s Marvel in the same manner as other artists.[18] The return of original art was a process originated by Roy Thomas back in the 1970s,[19] and it soon became a standard procedure until the Marvel legal team demanded special conditions for Kirby's artwork. This situation prompted Kirby to publicly express that that he had been deprived of creator credit while cocreating the Marvel Universe with Stan Lee.[20] In *Comics Scene* #2 (1981), Byrne responded to Kirby's statement in an editorial: "When a comic pro creates a new character or any other such merchandisable commodity, it belongs wholly and solely to the company."[21] He described himself as a "company man" as well as "a cog in the machine which was Marvel Comics."[22] He also mentioned that the creators of *Superman* no longer had any rights to the character since they sold it, especially since it was no longer remotely close to the original version they had created. This was a polarizing stance for Byrne to take; however, the system worked in his favor as he received royalties for penciling and writing *Fantastic Four* while creating original stories that utilized many Kirby storytelling techniques. One example can be found in *Fantastic Four* #244 (1982), in which Byrne depicted the Human Torch unsuccessfully chasing Nova into the atmosphere because his flame burned out, which was a clear acknowledgment that flying excessively high exerted too much strain.[23] Kirby first pioneered the Torch's strain in a panel with similar layout in *The Fantastic Four* #5 (1962), when the hero chased Doom, who used a faster jet pack.[24] Another similar homage occurred in *Fantastic Four* #258 (1983) when Dr. Doom's young ward Kristoff suggested that Magneto rivaled him. Doom, whom Byrne depicted as infuriated by the comment, held up the boy in the air and screamed, "No One Rivals DOOM! No one!"[25] The exchange of words in this conversation was the same as the one between Dr. Doom and Gustav Hauptmann in *Fantastic Four* #85 (1969) when Lee and Kirby depicted the lackey asserting that Doom's brilliance "rivals that of the Red Skull himself!" Kirby portrayed Doom's body immediately stiffened as he grabbed the scientist against the wall and screamed, "Doctor Doom has no rivals!! None!"[26] These two scenes demonstrated Doom's indignation at having a rival, and Byrne solidified the Kirby homage by having Gustav's brother Gert Hauptmann killed in the same issue. As these homages continued, Steve Gerber and Jack Kirby responded to Marvel's legal team and John Byrne's editorial by creating the miniseries *Destroyer Duck* (1982) to raise funds for a court case. Gerber engaged in his own legal dispute with Marvel over the ownership of *Howard the Duck* and needed money for legal fees. He wrote a miniseries about a Howard-like duck who was kidnapped by the company Godcorp and the hero, Destroyer Duck, fought its employees to retrieve his little friend. Gerber approached Kirby to draw the series, and since he was also upset at Marvel, he agreed to do it for free.[27] Kirby penciled Gerber's story and depicted John Byrne as the "cog" otherwise known as "Cogburn ... machismo posturing, the overblown ego, and the company men mentality ... never question what the company tells them."[28]

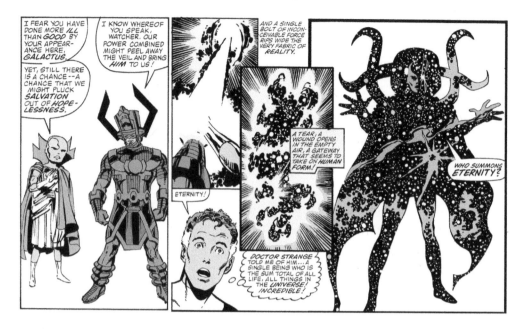

Cosmic creations of Lee, Kirby, and Ditko were revitalized for modern readers of the 1980s during John Byrne's celebrated "The Trial of Reed Richards" storyline in *Fantastic Four* #262 (1984).

Gerber later mentioned that "Byrne and I have shaken hands and made up since then," but confirmed that Cogburn was in fact based on Byrne, as "it was inspired by an interview he gave in some fan magazine."[29] This was an interesting interaction between Kirby and Byrne, who were likened to two ships passing in the night toward very different destinies.

Byrne continued to write and pencil successful original stories at DC Comics that also revitalized their older characters and panel designs that were first created by Kirby and Siegel. By 1985, he became one of the most financially prosperous artists to have worked at Marvel and was relied upon for effective storytelling with various series, such as *The Uncanny X-Men*, *Fantastic Four*, *The Incredible Hulk*, *Alpha Flight*, and other fan favorites. He added his own science-fiction stories into his superhero books that demonstrated nostalgia toward the past while also advancing the writing and artistic detail for a new generation with a fan reception that was rarely rivaled in the industry. Byrne's approach to comics demonstrated significant viability in the marketplace and comic stores ran advertisements in newspapers offering "John Byrne" comics to attract buyers.[30] With the financial incentive of the royalty program, Marvel and DC paid him "ten million [*dollars*] over 20 years"[31] as he wrote his own stories and utilized Kirby and Siegel's cocreations and designs.

Byrne's notable career at DC began when he departed Marvel to revitalize *Superman* in 1986. *Superman* had been under the consecutive creative control of Siegel, Shuster, Weisinger, and then Schwartz, and at this point began to reduce in sales, prompting DC to hire Byrne to attract new readers and regain market share. He modernized *Superman* by elevating its science-fiction aspect but at the same time using his artistic acumen and dialogue to make the character more relatable. Sales on the title significantly improved, causing him to earn "a couple million dollars,"[32] and he decided to provide Kirby's "Fourth World" a similar treatment in *Legends* #1–6. Byrne succeeded in updating the *New Gods* and *Superman* for a new generation that felt the older material appeared too dated and admitted that "during the fourth world stuff was when I felt I was most doing Kirby."[33] He eventually returned to Marvel to write and pencil the *West Coast Avengers* and changed the series' name. In *Avengers West Coast* #51 (1989), he depicted the Scarlet Witch having a nervous breakdown after watching her husband, the Vision, get dismantled and discovering that their kids were not real. His storyline became a critical aspect to the Emmy Award–winning series *WandaVision* (2021) on Disney plus. In the series, Byrne utilized a panel and story concept that was originally pioneered by Kirby when depicting Agatha Harkness menacingly petting her cat to examine Wanda's two sons.[34] Harkness held the cat with her left arm, petting it with her right, modeled from Kirby's similar panel of the witch in *Fantastic Four* #94 (1970), who was created by Lee and Kirby to be a nanny for Susan Richard's newborn son, Franklin.[35]

Byrne also wrote and drew another Kirby creation called *OMAC* (1991), a black-and-white four-part limited series. OMAC stood for One Man Army Corps, a concept Kirby created for DC Comics in *OMAC* #1 (1974). Kirby's concept was about a future where a Global Peace Agency polices the world using a satellite named Brother Eye to grant power to a 98-pound weakling, Buddy Blank, who became a futuristic super soldier. The series lasted eight issues, but Byrne successfully revitalized the character for new readers while also employing Kirby's visuals in his own penciling style.[36] Readers who were familiar with the older version recognized the homage when Byrne depicted flashbacks of Kirby's sex robot factory.[37] Byrne also wrote his own science-fiction story for the series and depicted OMAC going back in time to kill Hitler, which created an innovative fictional time experiment.

Throughout his career, Byrne returned to Kirby's characters while also creating his own lucrative superheroes, such as *Alpha Flight* and *Next Men*. He was asked if he would rather write and draw his own creations as opposed to Kirby's characters. Byrne confirmed he "would rather work on a Jack Kirby."[38] Byrne continued to do so when he wrote and drew *X-Men: The Hidden Years* with inker Tom Palmer (1999–2001). The original X-Men by Lee and Kirby didn't sell as well as their other team titles, which prompted Marvel editors to stop publishing new stories after issue #66 and instead reprint old adventures during the late 1960s from #67–93. Byrne addressed this apparent gap in the team's narrative by writing and penciling new stories of the original Lee and Kirby X-Men team with his new series. He also paid attention to the few early 1970s appearances of the original X-Men team and narratively planned for up to a hundred issues. Unfortunately, it was the "least selling X-Book," inducing its cancellation after 22 issues.[39]

Byrne succeeded in modernizing the super-heroics of the Golden and Silver

Ages in the 1980s for a new generation of readers. His creative ability to assist Marvel and DC to acquire more market share also served as two lessons in modern superhero comic books: old artists needed to be replaced by new ones to maintain a comic series' viability in the marketplace and an artist can increase their own professional value in the industry by successfully doing so. Through the work of Starlin, Byrne, and other creators who followed their trends, the superhero comic book encountered death and revitalization to stay relevant. However, during the 1980s, a writer from England deconstructed American superheroes and unintentionally provided a conclusion in the development of the superhero genre.

Alan Moore and Deconstructing the Superheroes

During the mid–1980s, writers and artists had followed the Starlin or Byrne models of either depicting death or revitalizing superhero comic books. Marv Wolfman and George Perez succeeded in combining the two approaches in *Crisis on Infinite Earths* (1985) by portraying Golden or Silver Age characters emotionally break down as their friends, such as Supergirl and the Flash, were killed. This approach was compatible with direct-market specialty shops that focused on superheroes for mature consumers.[1] Depicting superheroes as emotionally damaged characters had become the ultimate expression of Stan Lee's flawed superhero philosophy. Frank Miller achieved this in *The Dark Knight Returns* (1986) by deconstructing Batman into a questionable fascist. An aged Batman faced his mortality and decided to adapt his methods to a grisly violent Gotham by assembling an army of skinheads to remake society.[2] Although Miller's use of caption boxes, panel angles, and sequences advanced the visual language of comic storytelling,[3] it was actually the 12-issue maxi-series *Watchmen* (1986–1987) by Alan Moore and Dave Gibbons that deconstructed superheroes by breaking character archetypes into their basic components and following through on the disastrous conclusions of realistically depicting the genre, which helped establish a dark trend in the comic book industry.[4]

The origin of *Watchmen* began during Alan Moore's youth in Northampton, England, while growing up on American Silver Age classics such as Lee and Kirby's *Fantastic Four*, Mort Weisinger's *Superman*, Julius Schwartz's *The Flash*,[5] and Steve Ditko's "The Question."[6] As a British native, Moore was able to examine the American superhero genre from an outsider's perspective and identify its hypocrisies. His first famous example of this was writing scripts for Marvelman, a character first created in 1954 England based on Fawcett's Captain Marvel. Moore depicted the hero in *Warrior* magazine (1982) and later as "Miracleman" in American reprints but unconventionally portrayed the hero as emotionally underdeveloped due to an overreliance on transforming to his super-powered self. This quality was expressed further with the character's sidekick, Kid Marvelman, whose abuse of his powers corrupted him into becoming a sociopathic mass murderer. The corruption of power obviated

Alan Moore depicted the arrested development of alter egos who escape into their role as a powerful superhero in *Miracleman* #15 (1988).

one of the three essential qualities that are required to define a superhero, which was the selfless and pro-social sense of mission to help others, while still maintaining the other two qualities of having a costume/code name and super ability. By incorporating the real-life belief that power corrupts, Moore provided an initial insight into a deconstruction of the genre, that superheroes cannot exist in the real world, rendering the quest for their realism as meaningless.

After writing the stories of Marvelman, Moore was likely motivated at this point to expand his deconstruction of the American superhero to several archetypes and the opportunity to do so was present when DC Comics purchased the rights to the Question, as well as the rest of the Charlton Action Heroes line in 1983.[7] This line also included Captain Atom, the Blue Beetle, Nightshade, the Peacemaker, and Thunderbolt, and their transfer of rights prompted Moore to write a comic that could successfully reboot them[8] while also utilizing characteristics from MLJ Magazine's Golden Age superhero the Shield.[9] Giordano read Moore's script and felt its despondent nature rendered the Charlton heroes unusable and asked the writer to rename them into original characters.[10] After a considerable rewrite, Moore created *Watchmen*, a limited series that depicted an alternate timeline of real-world events such as World War II, the Vietnam War, and the Cold War. He deconstructed each character as a different American superhero archetype inspired from characters of both the Golden and Silver Ages and realistically depicted them as innately detached, colonialist, self-defeating, violently moral, obsolete, and fetishistic fantasies. Moore depicted these intrinsic flaws in the series' six main superheroes: Doctor Manhattan, Comedian, Ozymandias, Rorschach, Nite Owl, and Silk Spectre.

Doctor Manhattan was the one character from the series with actual superpowers that resulted in his emotional detachment from the rest of humanity. Originally a nuclear scientist, he was involved in a lab accident involving intrinsic fields that disintegrated him, only to eventually reassemble his atoms through his newfound mastery over quantum nuclear energy.[11] This gaining of power through a relatable science-fiction event was a clear influence from the American Silver Age of comics. However, he differed from those types of heroes due to his failure to maintain a mission to protect the innocent. Moore's script followed through on a more logical conclusion: the character's loss of empathy. This occurred when Doctor Manhattan realized he also gained the ability to view his past, present, and future in the same moment, which elevated his consciousness but left him emotionally isolated from other humans who couldn't relate to him. Instead of compassion for mankind, Doctor Manhattan's apathy came with a sense of pointlessness toward the human struggle. Any attempt to fight crime proved to be nonfunctional because when he used a small fraction of his powers against mobsters, then innocent bystanders were traumatized after watching his enemies' heads explode. He chafed at the idea of the military giving him a costume with a gaudy atomic logo, and instead carved his forehead with the main symbol of his respect, a proton and electron, which symbolized that "matter" mattered more to him than people. He grew self-involved and focused mainly on his science experiments rather than helping others. However, he continued to follow military orders such as President Nixon's request to intervene in North Vietnam and proceeded to obliterate the Vietcong but committed obvious international human rights violations that were ignored by the media.[12] Through Doctor Manhattan, Moore revealed that any superhero with omnipotent powers, such as Superman, Wonder Man, and Thor, would lose their humanity, become abused by politicians, and feel uncaringly alone.

Although Doctor Manhattan served as a criticism of many Silver Age American

Alan Moore depicted that genuine superpowers in the real world would likely be accompanied by apathy toward the human condition in *Watchmen* #4 (1986).

superheroes, Moore directly based him on the Charlton Action Hero Captain Atom, created by Steve Ditko and Joe Gill for *Space Adventures* #33 (1960). Captain Atom was similarly disintegrated in a nuclear explosion and reassembled into a servant for the military, and happily accepted the gaudy costume and logo handed to him by President Eisenhower, who declared him a deterrent of war. Doctor Manhattan is also naturally linked to a Golden Age superhero that inspired Captain Atom's costume and origins, *Atoman* (1946) by Jerry Robinson and Ken Crossen.[13] Atoman and Captain Atom were both founded on the optimistic notion that America's grasp of nuclear power would be a benefit to mankind. However, Moore's representation of Doctor Manhattan deconstructed this as a naive notion and concludes that their powers would be weapons under hegemonic control used to bring terror and imbalance to the world's political ecosystem.

Moore deconstructed patriotic superheroes through his use of the Comedian as a sociopathic special-operations solider who was sent on missions that furthered the colonialist goals of the American government. He was originally a street vigilante who displayed violent tendencies that included the attempted rape of one of his teammates,[14] and was identified as an ideal personality to serve the country's interests in matters of foreign warfare. He donned a red, white, and blue costume but found no redemption as a patriotic superhero because he reveled in war crimes such as using a flame thrower on unarmed soldiers in North Vietnam[15] and callously shooting a local Vietnamese woman who was pregnant with his child.[16] After he defeated the North Vietnamese army with Doctor Manhattan, he reported back to the United States and violently subdued protestors in a metropolitan city and proudly proclaimed that he was the American Dream.[17] He enforced peace through extreme violence and generally appeared to understand the hypocrisy of his secret government assignments and his country's geopolitical need for power. Whether it was capitalism, democracy, or communism, he was depicted as understanding that the point of his assignments was to perpetuate the United States' global control under the guise of a positive cause. Moore suggested this when he wrote the dialogue of Doctor Manhattan stating, "As I come to understand Vietnam and what it implies about the human condition, I also realize that few humans will permit themselves such an understanding. Blake's [*aka Comedian*] different. He understands perfectly … and he doesn't care."[18]

Although the Comedian appeared to be a criticism of superheroes such as Captain America, his sense of mission was based on the Silver Age Charlton Action Hero the Peacemaker, created by Joe Gill and Pat Boyette for *Fightin' 5* #40 (1966). The Peacemaker, however, was a neutral figure who lived in Switzerland, so the Comedian's patriotism was based on his Golden Age counterpart, the Shield from MLJ Magazines. The Shield was created by Irv Novick and Harry Shorten for *Pep Comics* #1 (1940) and was described as a "G-Man" who wore his bulletproof uniform, swearing "his life to shielding the U.S. Government and its people from any harm."[19] Initially, Alan Moore wrote the series starting with "the Shield being found dead in the

The Comedian served as Moore's critique of the patriotic superhero who, in reality, would likely need to be a sociopath to enforce America's interests at all costs in *Watchmen* #4 (1986).

harbor,"[20] but instead incorporated the singularly focused Peacemaker to create the Comedian. During World War II, patriotic heroes represented the hope and honor of the armed forces. That viewpoint changed with Moore's description of the Comedian, whose antisocial behavior was ultimately a critique of Captain America, The Shield, Fighting American, and General Glory, among others, whose duty was problematically enforcing America's interest and culture at all costs without regard for anyone else.

Ozymandias was a hero known for his blond hair, Eastern roots, and martial arts skills whose physical and mental perfection was depicted by Moore as qualities that would inevitably lead to becoming a dangerous supervillain. He was labeled as the "world's smartest man"[21] who thought heavily on the world's problems such as famine and impending nuclear war with the Soviet Union and decided to murder a few million people to save billions. He did so by strategically killing various people in the story's narrative to manipulate the direction of its events as well as falsify an alien invasion by using secret technology that terminated the inhabitants of New York City.[22] His false alien attack united the countries of the world, causing them to cease using nuclear weapons. This utilitarian approach to save the world appeared to be a logical extension of the pro-social mission followed by mentally perfect heroes such as Batman, Mister Fantastic, and Tony Stark, but also established that this journey resulted in becoming the supervillain and mass murderer of the story.

Alan Moore noted that he liked "the idea of this character using the full 100% of his brain and sort of having complete physical and mental control" when describing that Ozymandias's origin grew "directly out of the Peter Cannon, Thunderbolt character."[23] Pete Morisi created *Peter Cannon … Thunderbolt* #1 (1966) as a hero raised in a Himalayan lamasery and trained "to activate and harness that unused portion of the brain."[24] Ozymandias is also linked to another Golden Age superhero, Lev Gleason's Daredevil,[25] from which Morisi created a similar suit design, half green and half red that was split down the middle for Thunderbolt. Although Ozymandias, similar to Thunderbolt, was calculative enough to make the world a better place, he found that his journey morally degraded his soul, leading humanity's smartest man to defeat himself.

Extreme morality proved to be its own menace with the hero Rorschach, who was described by Moore as an "extremely right-wing"[26] masked vigilante whose code of ethics justified hurting people, which made him incompatible with the civilized world. He was raised by a prostitute[27] and later witnessed the depravity of a child predator,[28] which led to an uncompromising sense of right and wrong along with an intolerance for the gray areas of human behavior. This morality was motivated by a sense of vengeance to the criminals of the city, causing him to brutally enforce his black-and-white standards on what he referred to as "vermin," "whores," "politicians," and "communists," which never appeared to calm his anger.[29] This cruel war on crime by Rorschach failed to instill any sense of hope into local citizens, who dreaded watching him enter a room because they feared for their own lives. This character represented Moore's criticism of brutal vigilantes such as Moon Knight, Green Arrow, and the Punisher, but was directly inspired by two similarly disguised Ayn Randian characters created by Steve Ditko.

Ditko used comic books as a creative outlet for his leanings toward Rand's objectivist philosophy through "The Question,"[30] who premiered in *Blue Beetle* #1 (1967), and his character Mr. A,[31] who first appeared in Wally Wood's *Witzend* #3 (1967). In *Witzend* #3 (1967), Mr. A confronted the serial killer Angel, who struggled to keep from falling off a building, but the merciless Mr. A let him fall to his death and explained, "I have no mercy or compassion for aggressors.... To have any sympathy for a killer is an insult to their victims."[32] The Question stated something similar in *Blue Beetle* #4 (1967) when two murderers on the verge of drowning started begging for their lives: "You're both crazy if you think I'd risk my neck to save the likes of you! As far as I'm concerned, you're just so much sewage! And you deserve to be right where you are!" Moore responded to this line of thinking by demonstrating the innate problem of the masked street-level vigilante who held no accountability and an addiction to violence as incompatible with the peaceful new world established by Ozymandias's genocidal scheme. The never-compromising Rorschach viewed the world's smartest man's murder of New York as a crime against humanity and intended to reveal to the public what exactly happened. Despite it being the moral thing to do, it would also return various countries to the brink of nuclear war. Rorschach did not care about the consequences and, similar to an inflexible rabid dog, had to be put down by Doctor Manhattan to make the world a better place, confirming to the reader that superhero morality had no place in a better world.[33]

As opposed to the Question, the two Nite Owl characters in *Watchmen* were depicted as well-intended vigilantes. However, their kindness rendered themselves obsolete and unable to sustain the role of a useful superhero. This code name was used for two characters in *Watchmen*, the 1940s adventurer Hollis T. Mason and the 1960s inventor Daniel Dreiberg. The first Nite Owl was a retired Irish cop who donned the Nite Owl costume to fight crime in the city and used his "left hook that floored Captain Axis,"[34] but his good-heartedness made him painfully naive about human nature. One situation by Moore depicted him as too excited from a recent photo opportunity with his friends to notice his teammate and love interest, Silk Spectre, being brutalized by the Comedian in the next room.[35] After a few years of fighting crime, he retired from working as a superhero and was depicted spending the rest of his life living above his repair shop, displaying a sign that appeared to describe himself, "obsolete models a specialty."[36] He enjoyed telling stories of his earlier days as an adventurer to the second Nite Owl, which added to the tragedy of his final moments that were portrayed after he opened his front door to a gang who pretended to be trick-or-treaters that proceeded to club him to death.[37] Through these examples, Moore demonstrated that he was too trusting to be a useful superhero.

The second Nite Owl was written by Moore to be the privileged son of a dead banker who spent his inheritance inventing gadgets to fight crime but lacking the conviction to continue helping people. He spent many evenings listening to the first Nite Owl's old crime-fighting stories, which inspired him to assume the same code name and use his money and technical skill to build his own Owl-themed devices as well as a flying airship that transported him to places in the city that required his help. Moore depicted Drieberg's sense of independence and industriousness beginning "as a kid ... I read about Pegasus, flying carpets, then later about birds and planes. Finally, I mastered in Aeronautics and zoology at Harvard."[38] His inventive approach to crime fighting proved to be useful; however, he grew discouraged that his sense of rugged individualism was challenged after observing the Comedian dressed in red, white, and blue, brutalizing protestors as he lamented the end of the American Dream.[39] He eventually became too afraid to continue and departed the role of Nite Owl when the United States government outlawed costumed adventuring,[40] leaving him despondent and impotent.[41] He eventually returned to wearing his costume and discovered Ozymandias's plan to improve the world's safety by committing genocide but realized that morality could be sacrificed to save the most people. Moore depicted Drieberg's personal journey as an individualist whose personal failings led toward ineffectuality and despondency, and a final realization that morality was optional.

Moore based both Nite Owls on Golden and Silver Age versions of the Blue Beetle. The first Blue Beetle was created by Charles Nicholas Wojtkoski for Fox Publications' *Mystery Men Comics* #1 (1939). Similar to the first Nite Owl, he was a police officer who decided that the law was insufficient to deter crime and used a disguise to fight criminals as a masked mystery man.[42] Moore explained that "Nite-Owl and ... Blue Beetle were equivalent. Because there was a pre-existing, original Blue Beetle in the Charlton cosmology ... it might be nice to have an original Nite-Owl."[43] The second Nite Owl was based on the Silver Age Blue Beetle created by Steve Ditko for *Captain Atom* #83 (1966), who was also a scientist and engineer and who embarked on his own journey of rugged individualism "after months of labor, hours of testing, practice with my equipment, and a crash physical training program."[44] He was depicted as having beetle-themed devices, bug-shaped personal aircraft, and an unwavering sense that "man is not helpless! Man can set a goal and achieve it."[45] In a manner similar to Mr. A and the Question, Ditko wrote his personal philosophy as the dialogue of the Blue Beetle: "Whatever it takes to achieve anything worthwhile! It can only be done by struggling to succeed!"[46] Similar to Ayn Rand, Ditko was writing for individualism against collectivism as Blue Beetle, but with Nite Owl, Moore criticized that optimistic viewpoint depicted in some street-level superheroes such as Spider-Man, Nightwing, and Robin as naive and leading to eventual disappointment.

Silk Spectre was a code name given to two costumed crime fighters: Sally Jupiter and her daughter, Laurie, whom Moore appears to present as a criticism toward the objectification of female superheroes. Sally Jupiter joined the other Golden Age masked vigilantes to further her modeling career and achieve success as a celebrity by hiring her agent to stage her crime-fighting victories. In *Watchmen*, she used vanity to process the Comedian's sexual assault, which led her to reconnect with him and become pregnant with her daughter, Laurie. In her later years, her self-esteem depended on other men's lust, which was evident when she was depicted as proudly holding up an eight-page Tijuana Bible pornographic comic starring herself, and describing it as flattering.[47] Her shallow role as the earlier team's sex symbol was a commentary by Moore on the "Phantom Lady … my favorite sort of costume heroines anyway."[48] Phantom Lady was created by Arthur Petty for *Police Comics* #1 (1941), and in the same manner as Silk Spectre, Phantom Lady wore a revealing yellow costume and high heels. Eventually, Quality Comics ceased their use of the character, which led to Fox Publications publishing the title in the late 1940s. Fox increased the sexual appeal of the heroine in *Phantom Lady* #13 (1947) with a more revealing blue costume by "good girl" artist Matt Baker. With these influences, the character of Sally Jupiter in *Watchmen* satirized the problematic nature of female superheroes such as Wonder Woman, Supergirl, and Ms. Marvel, who were often fetishized into sexual objects.

Laurie Jupiter, however, rebelled against the "good girl" stereotype. As the second Silk Spectre, she physically trained over time into a fierce physical force. She despised her mother's tendency to objectify herself, stating, "I just don't know how you can stand being degraded like this…. Don't you care how people see you?"[49] Despite being underage, her mother still expected her to wear a similar revealing costume for her teammates, to which she remarked, "Ten years running round in a stupid costume because my stupid mother wanted me to!"[50] Laurie's analogue at Charlton Comics was the deadly and underaged Nightshade, created by Steve Ditko and Dave Kaler in *Captain Atom* #82 (1966), who formed a team with her love interest, Captain Atom, to serve the government's interests. Her character ceased after a few issues at Charlton, causing her character to be arrested in development as a product of her times. In *Watchmen*, Alan Moore advanced Laurie Jupiter beyond the initial teenage infatuation with her nuclear-powered boyfriend by having her abandon her relationship with Doctor Manhattan and seek a genuine human connection with old friend Dan Drieberg, the second Nite Owl. No longer impressed with superpowers, she asked Doctor Manhattan, "Pain ... fears ... life.... Ordinary people.... All the things that happen to them.... Doesn't that move you more than a bunch of rubble?"[51] Her grief brought meaning to *Watchmen* when she realized the Comedian was her father, who previously returned to Sally Jupiter for a consenting sexual encounter. She emotionally resolved the combined hypocrisy and passion of her conception, which inspired Doctor Manhattan to aid humanity, demonstrating that the human condition transcended the vigilante methods of her colleagues.

Alan Moore examined these Charlton characters from the past and deconstructed them in *Watchmen* to portray how unsatisfactory they would be in the real world. His superheroes demonstrated that the power, patriotism, physical sensuality, violence, humility, individualism, and hyper intelligence inherent in the genre were logically nonfunctional due to the inherent loss of humanity, compassion, and selfless mission to help others. By removing the most important aspect of superheroes, the pro-social mission, Moore invalidated the superhero genre as a realistic impossibility, and defined selfish superpowered narcissists as the new normal. This invalidation of the superhero genre caused some cultural historians to call *Watchmen* the series that broke the superhero. Superhero readers absorbed this message en masse and *Watchmen* proved to be an enormous success.[52] One newspaper reported, "People are picking it up out of curiosity and finding they are enjoying it. It's intelligently written ... what the TV generation can relate to."[53] DC Comics editor Mike Carlin described *Watchmen* as a "really watershed" comic.[54]

Its success became a strong part of Alan Moore's disappointment in the comic book industry. Before its release, he commented, "DC owns it for the time they're publishing it, and then it reverts to Dave and me, so we can make all the money from the Slurpee cups."[55] However, DC Comics never stopped publishing it because readers continued to buy copies and trade paperback reprints. Moore grew angry and decided to cease all future projects with DC Comics in 1989 as he stated, "You have managed to successfully swindle me, and so I will never work for you again."[56] He became just as disappointed in the system as his various characters in the *Watchmen* series became with the world in which they lived. His concept that superheroes are a fundamentally broken genre continues to make an impression on readers. When DC Comics published prequels to *Watchmen* in 2012, Moore commented, "They are still apparently dependent on ideas that I had twenty-five years ago."[57] Moore regrets this and observed that the superhero genre is forever damaged, and although styles or media changed over the years, it still maintains all the qualities present in comic trends that finalized in *Watchmen*. His notions about the invalidation of the genre were the last original idea used in the development of superheroes in comic books. He expressed that superhero comics of today are "not aimed at children anymore." He fondly remembers that 1960s Superman stories stimulated a child's imagination, but after he critiqued the genre for a mature readership, this "coincided with the emotional age of the mass audience coming the other way." Many comic writers continue to mimic this approach and now appeal to an audience of "12-year-old boys of 50 years ago."[58] The success of comic books such as Garth Ennis's *The Boys* (2006), and its associated Amazon Prime series, demonstrates that many fans consider a selfish superhero more believable and interesting than the Silver Age Superman, who was generous and wholesome.

The Origin of the Superhero Graphic Novel

The superhero graphic novel format evolved alongside comic books over the course of the 20th century. Comic books are short periodicals devoted solely to comics, which generally carry comic strip reprints or original material, often presented as a series, generally for a younger age group. They are usually a little over 20 pages in length, often depicting ongoing storylines with a specific set of characters. Graphic novels tend to be longer, provide more serious content for adults, and often demonstrate an artistic statement within one self-contained long-form sequential-pictorial book.

Starting with *The Passion of a Man* (1918), graphic novels eventually became a refined visual art form that settled into its current commercial format established in the 1980s. The term "novela grafica" had already been used to identify comic books in Latin America as early as the 1950s, but the terminology refined over time. The phrase "graphic novel" was first introduced to American comic readers as an "artistically serious 'comic book strip'" by historian Richard Kyle in 1964.[1] Kyle also later determined that a comic miniseries aimed toward adults that tell a story could be collected into a single book called a graphic novel.[2] Overall, three distinct phases appear to have contributed to the overall formation of the modern superhero graphic novel; the early Experimental phase; the second, Cinematic phase; and the third and final Commercial phase of the early 1980s and beyond. At that final point, the format was economically viable, ready to be replicated, and sold directly to the market. By 1986, the three big miniseries turned graphic novels were *MAUS*, *Watchmen*, and *The Dark Knight Returns*, but it's the key early pioneers that made their format possible. They were works by Frans Masereel, Milt Gross, Lynd Ward, Gayle Hoskins, Matt Baker, Georges Prosper Remi (Hergé), Arnold Drake, Bill Gaines, Gil Kane, Burne Hogarth, Jim Steranko, Don McGregor, George Metzger, Richard Corben, Howard Chaykin, Will Eisner, Jack Kirby, Stan Lee, Jim Starlin, and José Luis García-López.

Frans Masereel was a Belgian artist known for contributing to graphic novel development using woodcuts to stamp ink onto one panel per page in sequential stories with no dialogue. Similar to the comic pamphlets of the 1600s, he expressed his personal political beliefs in self-contained adult-themed visual narratives. His first work, published in Switzerland, *The Passion of a Man* (1918), was a commentary about the inhumanity of industrial capitalism, using 25 panels to describe the sad fate of a worker who was executed for leading a revolt against his employer. This story was received with significant acclaim and the author became famous in Europe for telling stories through woodcuts that resonated with his audience by discussing the struggles of the period.[3] His work pioneered the representation of mature political themes into graphic novels and influenced American woodcut artist Lynd Ward when he traveled to Germany.[4] Inspired by Masereel,[5] Ward created the first wordless graphic novel in the United States with *God's Man* (1929) utilizing expressive black-and-white contrasts to depict an artist who made a deal with the devil for a magic brush that made him miserably successful. The anti-capitalist message in the early woodcut movement became the central theme to another Ward story, *The Wild Pilgrimage* (1932), about a man who left his factory only to discover a world of hate, lust, injustice, and occasional kindness. In the end, he returned to his factory life as part of a workers' revolt that led to his death.

The right wing of the Belgian political spectrum found expression in Hergé's initial Tintin strip continuities that were collected into complete story albums.[6] His first three graphic novels, *Tintin in the Land of Soviets* (1929), *Tintin in the Congo* (1930) and *Tintin in America* (1931), were about the boy reporter and his dog, Snowy, that were designed to encourage capitalism and colonialism, and are correctly criticized today for their racist imagery. Hergé's work did evolve, however, to well-researched and stimulating adventure stories such as *The Blue Lotus* (1934), which, similar to Milton Caniff in his respective strip, *Terry and the Pirates*, discussed the Japanese invasion of Manchuria as well as potential dangers found in opium dens.[7] The story was recolored and partly redrawn in 1946, then presented as a "masterpiece" graphic novel in the genre of adventure and mystery.[8]

Wordless graphic novels compel the artist to use exaggerated visual expression to carry the story. This was the case with Milt Gross's *He Done Her Wrong* (1930), described by early reviewers as "the first American comic novel."[9] Similar to silent film director Ernst Lubitsch, Gross cartooned hyperbolic body language to depict drama, tragedy, and comedy, both efficiently and emotionally. The story was about a brawny country hero who fell in love with a lounge singer and confronted a wily mustached villain. Gross utilized the presence and absence of blacks on white paper using chiaroscuro, a style from the Renaissance highlighting direction of shadows.

Some argue that the photorealistic illustrator and graduate of the School of the Art Institute of Chicago Gayle Hoskins created an early form of the graphic novel in 1931. Hoskins depicted a western about "A Cowboy's Day" over 27 consecutive covers of Street and Smith's *Western Story Magazine* from January 3, 1931, to July 4, 1931. Each cover was photo-realistically illustrated with a caption to help the reader understand the events of this biweekly adventure. The first cover signaled to the reader, "This is Slim.... Follow his pictured adventures every week."[10] During the

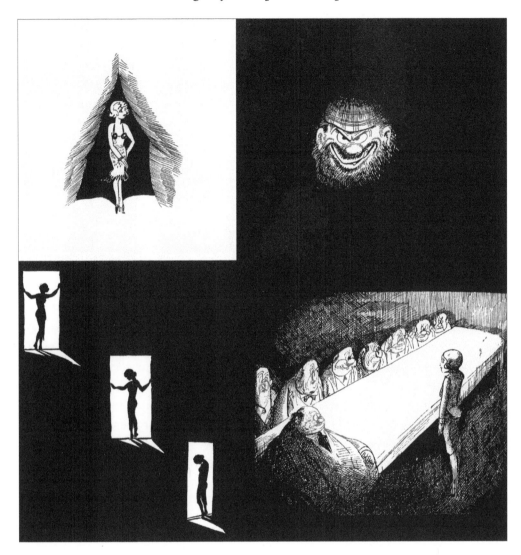

Milt Gross cartooned hyperbolic body language to depict drama and tragedy in *He Done Her Wrong* (1930).

continuity, Slim saddled up his horse, followed a trail, and saved a cowgirl from "rustlers."

The Cinematic phase of graphic novels started as the medium began to be experienced in the style of motion pictures on paper. That likely began with *It Rhymes with Lust* (1950), written by Arnold Drake and Leslie Waller. Dubbed a "picture novel," the story followed reporter Hal Weber, who struggled to thwart former lover Rust Masson from achieving criminal and political control over a local town. *It Rhymes with Lust* was published by St. John Publications and is known for its story regarding greed and lust, which was accentuated by Matt Baker's pencils and Ray Osrin's inks.[11] Reading it is similar to enjoying a black-and-white film from the period.

Non-superhero genres were explored in the early 1950s and with EC Comics decreasing publication, Bill Gaines published *EC: Picto-Fiction* from 1955 to 1956 as an attempt to sell similar shocking stories in a magazine format. His stable of artists still included shock endings but they utilized various cinematic storytelling techniques in black-and-white magazines that contained sophisticated half-text and half-illustration narratives aimed at adults. Talents such as Jack Kamen, Joe Orlando, Wallace Wood, Reed Crandall, and Johnny Craig contributed anthology stories in the romance, crime, and horror genres. These were more comparable to pulp magazines with typeset text but with more images. Although the *EC: Picto-Fiction* line failed to capture market share, these stories influenced later graphic novelist and Warren Magazine editor Archie Goodwin, who described the *Crime Illustrated* stories as "especially good"[12] and said that he "liked"[13] the romance stories aimed toward female readers in *Confessions Illustrated*.

Creepy magazine creator Russ Jones departed Warren magazines to produce Ballantine Books' *Dracula* (1966) original graphic novel with illustrations by Alden McWilliams and script adapted from Bram Stoker's original novel (1897) by Otto Binder and Craig Tennis.[14] Jones arranged a foreword by popular horror British actor Christopher Lee and, probably in exchange, produced *Christopher Lee's Treasury of Terror* (1966) for Pyramid Books. The *Dracula* graphic novel strongly favored the appearance of Christopher Lee as the evil vampire, and the dark imagery was compatible with the tone and pacing of the script. The isolation of Jonathan Harker in Dracula's castle and Dracula's eventual travel to London were depicted in a manner that captured the story's desolation and despair.

Archie Goodwin scripted *His Name Is … Savage* (1968), which was plotted and illustrated by Gil Kane, who sought to depart the conventional comic book industry when he created this graphic novel, an action-thriller with cold war themes modeled after the Lee Marvin film *Point Blank* (1967).[15] A retired cyborg general kidnapped the president and manipulated the United Nations to start World War III. Kane's pacing matched the storytelling techniques in films of this era. One example depicted three panels devoted to a pistol breaking through a man's teeth,[16] and five panels were devoted to the nuance of Savage's hand dropping a cigarette to roll on a table as the dialogue continued.[17] Unfortunately, this graphic novel suffered from lack of distribution, and if it had been released in the 1980s, it probably would have succeeded due to the willingness of direct-market comic book shops to sell adult-oriented stories. Kane also signed a contract with Bantam Books to produce the warrior fantasy graphic novel *Blackmark* (1971). This 119-page story was placed into a customary paperback format that utilized captions and word balloons dialogued by Archie Goodwin.[18] The story was about a child who was chosen by fate to witness an invading army murder his parents. He became a slave and was strengthened by the experience into a fearsome warrior sharing a similar origin to Robert E. Howard's "Conan the Cimmerian" (1932). Kane interposed text and imagery to maximize the impact of the story, but the book failed to attract readers and Bantam abandoned the project, causing its sequel to be published much later in *Marvel Preview* #17 (1979).[19] Kane expressed an interest in the sword and sorcery genre again when he illustrated Robert E. Howard's *The Valley of the Worm* (1934) in Marvel's *Supernatural Thrillers* #3 (1973), depicting a barbaric warrior in battle with a large serpent. This issue was not a graphic novel; however, Richard Corben adapted the story into *Bloodstar* (1976), published as a stand-alone book with each page illustrated and painted. Its dust jacket described *Bloodstar* as "a graphic novel, which combines all the imagination and visual power of comic strip art with the richness of the traditional novel."

After Hal Foster departed Edgar Rice Burroughs's *Tarzan* comic strip in 1937, Burne Hogarth became the regular artist until 1950. More than two decades later, he illustrated the graphic novel *Tarzan of the Apes* (1972), of which he commented, "Tarzan is the paradigm of a certain image … that cannot be perverted. What we are seeing is the coming to life of a mythic figure in a new time."[20] This graphic novel included Edgar Rice Burroughs's text and over 100 pages of illustrations penciled, inked, and colored by Hogarth depicting a considerable amount of detail and dynamic anatomy that exemplified the artist's skill with stylized realism. Four years later, Hogarth finished his second graphic novel, *Jungle Tales of Tarzan* (1976), where he penciled and inked 160 pages of four loosely connected Tarzan stories written by Burroughs. There was no color, but the black-and-white inks emphasized Tarzan's physique and jungle background, which was presented with unconventional page designs.

Crime pulp magazine writer Raymond Chandler wrote hard-boiled detective fiction such as *The Big Sleep* (1939) and *The Long Goodbye* (1953) patterned after the works of Carroll John Daly and Dashiel Hammett. Chandler's stories were read by comic book artist and book cover illustrator Jim Steranko, who studied the cinematography of the film *The Big Sleep* (1946) as well as the body language of actor Humphrey Bogart. Steranko also analyzed the imagery "in those Warner Brothers films … black cars … speeding along with tommy gun muzzles sticking out their windows, spraying death over gangland streets"[21] and illustrated his "visual novel" for Pyramid Books, *Chandler: Red Tide* (1976). It was an homage to hard-boiled detective fiction rendered in the film noir style and has been argued by some to be the first modern graphic novel due to each page's unique approach of depicting two columns of illustration with text underneath, crafted in a sequence that Steranko stated "readers would be very comfortable with."[22]

George Metzger's *Beyond Time and Again* was an underground serial comic strip that started in 1967[23] and was collected by Richard Kyle and Denis Wheary into "hardcover book form in 1976 with the subtitle 'a graphic novel' on its title page."[24] Some argue that a limited series cannot be collected into one graphic novel, but Richard Kyle, who previously defined and popularized the term "graphic novel,"[25] applied that label to Metzger's hardcover collection, so this label can be applied to other collected miniseries that tell one story. Metzger's subject matter aligned with counterculture comics of the late 1960s, depicting the main protagonist traveling through time, which led him to the far future as the last man on Earth right before its extinction from a nearby supernova. He was soon drugged and forced to impregnate every local woman before traveling back to the past.

Mainstream readers were attracted to Marvel's first graphic novel by the briefly reunited team of Stan Lee and Jack Kirby, titled *The Silver Surfer: The Ultimate Cosmic Experience* (1978). Their reunion was solidified further with Kirby's pencils embellished by longtime *Fantastic Four* inker Joe Sinnott. Lee and Kirby revisited the Silver Surfer's first mission to Earth, but in an alternate universe where the Fantastic Four did not exist. Instead of encountering Alicia Masters, the Surfer conversed with a woman who resembled his love interest, Shalla-Bal. This encounter activated his compassion, prompting the Surfer to reject Galactus, who attempted to seduce him using Ardina, a female construct with artificial intelligence. Ardina was destroyed, Earth was spared, and the Surfer guided Galactus to a different planet.

The science-fiction and swashbuckling genres were combined by Don McGregor and Paul Gulacy for their postapocalyptic adventure *Sabre* (1978), published by Eclipse Enterprises. Don McGregor's experience writing the Marvel series *Jungle Action featuring The Black Panther* (1973–1976) was utilized well with *Sabre*, which included an interracial romance and intricate panel construction that depicted a disturbing future landscape destroyed by a biological agent. Gulacy's innovative page designs and highly detailed black-and-white action sequences expertly contrasts with the conclusion to McGregor's story.

Will Eisner was an early reader of both Frans Masereel and Lynd Ward,[26] and advanced the graphic novel format when illustrating *A Contract with God* (1978) eight years after his 16-year-old daughter died from leukemia.[27] It has received some criticism for not being a true graphic novel; however, it does fit the key criteria. It is one long-form story of four situations centered on the same Bronx tenement and portrayed realistic and mature themes such as death, seduction, poverty, racism, and the human struggle to survive. Eisner introduced the reader to his childhood New York neighborhood by focusing on the fictional setting of 55 Dropsie Avenue, which he continued to depict in *A Life Force* (1988) and *Dropsie Avenue* (1995).

Howard Chaykin demonstrated an advanced aptitude with the science-fiction genre in his graphic novelization of Alfred Bester's *The Stars My Destination* (1956) for publisher Byron Preiss in 1979. Chaykin depicted a future dystopia featuring antihero Gully Foyle, the lone survivor of the spaceship *Nomad*, who sought revenge in a story that ended with a significant space-time explosion as Foyle propelled through the past and present, narrowly escaping a PyrE proto-matter detonation. Chaykin's kaleidoscopic illustrations were compatible with Bester's cerebral concepts, which demonstrated that the artist utilized various techniques from his own practice as well as from his tutelage under Gil Kane, Wallace Wood, and Neal Adams. He applied himself as a graphic novelist a second time when he provided the artwork for Michael Moorcock's *The Swords of Heaven, The Flowers of Hell* (1979) for publisher Heavy Metal. Moorcock purposefully sought Chaykin because he had demonstrated a superiority to other sequential illustrators at the time.[28] Chaykin's mastery of composition, magical landscapes, and anatomy was well received by readers of the fantasy genre.

Don McGregor and Marshall Rogers produced the graphic novel *Detectives Inc.: A Remembrance of Threatening Green* (1980), which depicted a fascinating visual perspective on a murder mystery. The introductory double splash page was presented in a horizontal movie screen aspect ratio, containing unconventional lettering and vertical panels, which established the emotional isolation of the detectives' client.[29] The lesbian romance at the center of the murder mystery was brave and ahead of its time, and the words of McGregor, combined with the innovative graphics by Rogers, portrayed an unconventional crime story that guided readers through a series of emotions.

The Commercial phase appears to begin when the big two comic corporations, Marvel and DC, considered that the graphic novel format could be a viable source of revenue. The art form matured to the point of making this self-contained storytelling style available to the public in established bookstores as well as newly risen comic book stores. Editor-in-Chief Jim Shooter acknowledged the successful Tintin-style European comic albums and sensed opportunity in the domestic marketplace. He convinced executives at Marvel to publish stories in the graphic novel format that could be sold through the direct market.[30] This corporate interest revitalized the medium with legal contracts that also benefited the creators. Marvel published Jim Starlin's *The Death of Captain Marvel* (1982), about the cosmic hero dying from cancer due to an on-the-job superhero work hazard. The industry acknowledged the success of this new graphic novel line when after a few months, *The Death of Captain Marvel* had already sold "80,000 copies at $5.95 each" at comic book stores and big bookstore chains. The legal contracts, production, and its success established a formula in which Marvel was then able to publish the *Marvel Graphic Novel* series

Jim Starlin brought humanity to the superhero genre in *The Death of Captain Marvel* (1982) by depicting the hero's struggle with cancer.

because there were enough consumers willing to pay for them. Newspapers commented, "Maybe Jim Shooter will have his way and something will come of Marvel's plan for adult comic books."[31]

With this newly discovered market support, DC Comics published their first graphic novel, *Star Raiders* (1983), written by Elliot S. Maggin and penciled by José Luis García-López. This story contained high-quality illustrations depicting material from Atari's 1979 cartridge video game with glowing colors that expressed an early 1980s aesthetic. Although based on a short-lived licensed product, readers enjoyed the visuals of an evil insectoid race in combat with a group of rebels. Warner Communications owned both Atari and DC Comics and combined their licenses with hopes to achieve a successful corporate synergy. However, this graphic novel failed to save Atari, contributing to its game console division to be sold in 1984.[32] The *DC Graphic Novel* line lasted only a few years, probably due to their lack of portraying established superheroes, which also appeared to curse Julius Schwartz, who edited his own parallel science-fiction graphic novel series that lasted only one year longer. However, creators at DC Comics discovered more success with superhero graphic novels such as *The Dark Knight Returns* (1986), *Arkham Asylum: A Serious House on Serious Earth* (1989), and *Kingdom Come* (1996).

Graphic novels have a unique history and are differentiated from comic books by their higher number of pages, serious content for adults, and self-contained stories that usually provide an artistic statement. Newsstands carried comic books and other serialized periodicals, but graphic novels would need to be sold in bookstores or gift shops or distributed in libraries. The graphic novels published during the Experimental phase (1842–1949) were by creators who used unique methods and art styles to tell their stories and were rarely given meaningful distribution. They were able to receive exposure in larger metropolitan areas, but the access was limited nationwide.[33] The graphic novels of the Cinematic Phase (1950–1981) had more distribution and were generally presented as well-crafted narratives that exhibited the influence of Hollywood films. A milestone in terminology occurred in this phase when Richard Kyle defined that a miniseries could be collected into a graphic novel. The graphic novels sold during the Commercial Phase (1982–present) are in a format of superior paper quality and validated by mainstream publishers that generally use marketable genres and topics such as superheroes to sell to bookstores and comic book stores that provided market support to predictably generate revenue. It is during this time that miniseries such as *MAUS*, *Watchmen*, and *The Dark Knight Returns* were collected into reprint graphic novels that continue to sell well while the graphic novel went on to become an established format for presenting longer-form superhero stories.

PART 5

Diversity and Aftermath

24

Women in 20th-Century
Comic Books

There have been a diverse population of contributors to superhero comic books, including women and African Americans. I met Trina Robbins at the Cartoon Art Museum in 2018 when she was presenting "Women in Comics" with fellow historian Nicky Wheeler-Nicholson, and I introduced myself to her to learn more about the topic. I was aware of two of her achievements with costumed heroines in comics: co-designing Vampirella and being the first woman to draw *Wonder Woman*; however, I immediately became enthralled by her knowledge, speaking style, sincerity, and devout research into the history of women in comic books. I invited her for an interview on *the Comic Book Historians Podcast*, and the effect on me was profound.[1] I found her research fascinating and compiled a portion of the interview responses into this edited timeline on the "her-story" of women comic creators and female comic characters.

Trina Robbins: In 1896, there was a magazine called *Truth*. I happened to know from my research that Grace Drayton had drawn for *Truth* and that possibly Nell Brinkley had also drawn for it. I found some copies that were $5 each and bought them to bring them home. I looked through them and found that there was a comic strip by Rose O'Neill called *The Old Subscriber Calls* from 1896 and that is accepted generally as the earliest known comic strip by an American woman cartoonist.

Gladys Parker had a passion for fashion and the first strip she drew was in the 1920s called *Flapper Fanny*. But after that she drew *Mopsy*, who was her main character and whom she identified with the most; she also was the spitting image of Mopsy. She looked exactly like her character, which is something that women in comics tend to do that men do not. She drew it from 1937 until 1966 and died the year after that. She also, throughout the 1930s, was a very successful fashion designer and had a line of clothing of beautiful high-end dresses at high-end department stores. By 1940, she moved to Hollywood and was designing clothes for movie stars like Barbara Stanwyck and Hedy Lamarr. Of all the women whom I have written about, she's the one I wish I could have had lunch with.

Lily Renée was once a talented Jewish teenager in Vienna before the Nazis marched in 1938 and she escaped to England in 1939, having to leave her parents behind, not knowing if they were dead or alive. Her parents knew she was in England but did not know where. They escaped to America and located her in England, so she then took a ship to join them in New York. They all wound up living hand to mouth with a bunch of other refugees in a tenement building. She later got a job for Fiction House drawing comics and she's wonderful. She's so great.

Starting in 1940, Dale Messick, who drew *Brenda Starr*, dyed her hair a really bright shade of orange to match her character's hair. She basically didn't turn the character into herself, she turned herself into the character, and she always dressed to kill. Surely you know Brenda Starr was very fashionable.

In 1941, Tarpe Mills, a creative woman, made *Miss Fury*, a comic that featured a female heroine dressed in a black leopard outfit working in South America against the Nazis. One of the more fascinating things is how women will turn themselves into the main characters of the strip, because Tarpe Mills looked exactly like Miss Fury, and she even gave Miss Fury a pet cat that was identical to Tarpe Mills's cat. Tarpe Mills had a white Persian cat named Peri-Purr and Miss Fury also had a white Persian cat named Peri-Purr.

During World War II, the comic books had been very male, and by that I mean they'd been doing very male superhero stuff. The guys were off fighting the war and suddenly in every industry in the factories, everywhere, women stepped in to take the jobs that the men had left behind. They were doing things that women had never done before, such as building planes and ships and in many cases flying the planes and driving trucks and buses, and the same thing happened in the comics industry.

Suddenly women were drawing for the comic books and what they drew was very different from what the men drew, which was so interesting. They were drawing heroines, beautiful, smart, competent women who fought the Nazis, and who could take care of themselves. They didn't need to be rescued by some guy, which before that, the role of women in comics were as superheroes' girlfriends who got tied up. Many women worked for Fiction House and signed their names on their work. Lily Renée's work is usually signed L. Renée and Fran Hopper simply signed "Fran Hopper." Maybe sometimes they would use an initial. I think Barbara Hall called herself B. Hall. There was no secret about the fact that they were women. Pauline Loth, well, of course, she drew for the girls' magazine *Miss America*. Everyone knew that it was Pauline Loth. Fiction House published comics during the war that had more women cartoonists than any other company. Everyone was publishing women cartoonists, including all the comic book companies, because the guys were away fighting. They still published more than any of the others and theirs were the best. These women were great.

Starting in 1944 with the first *Miss America* magazine, which as you know was a girls' magazine that also had comics in it. You also had *Patsy Walker* originating in 1944 drawn by Pauline Loth and also by Christopher Rule, who, in my opinion, is one of the greatest cartoonists who ever lived. Then in '45, Ruth Atkinson drew the first year of *Patsy Walker* comic books. Originally *Patsy Walker* was in *Miss America* magazine as just one comic in the magazine and by '45 she was so successful that they did *Patsy Walker* comic books. That was when they started *Millie the Model* comics and Ruth Atkinson drew the first year of *Patsy Walker* as well as the first *Millie the Model* comic book in 1945. There would be three *Patsy Walker* stories drawn by her and one *Patsy Walker* story contributed by Fran Hopper. That was practically an all-woman deal there.

Around 1945, guys came back from the war, and they wanted their old jobs back. That's exactly what happened, but they were still the Timely teen titles from the late forties and fifties. I loved them, and they were drawn by guys at that point, but they were still vibrant, alive, exciting, and about teenage girls. That continued but it started falling apart in the sixties, just about when Marvel started its superhero renaissance, and they just devoted themselves to the superheroes and threw the girl titles under the bus because the superheroes were doing so well.

Timely Comics was very girl-friendly. There was a story that Ruth Atkinson did in 1945 about allowing girls to wear pants to high school because in those days the rule was you had to wear skirts. The girls all spoke up and said something like, "We are here for the liberation of all women."[2] They really said that, wore pants to school, and broke the rules. At this time, I had read comics and wasn't just the geeky girl in the corner who reads comics; everyone my age, all the kids, read comics. My girlfriends read comics, and we would trade comics, and I knew what the girls read because I had read them, and I knew that really what I was trying to prove was that, of course, girls read comics. When you give girls comics they like to read, girls will read comics, but if all you give them is muscular guys with big chests punching each other out, then they won't be interested.

Romance comics started right after the war, I believe, with Joe Simon and Jack Kirby. I believe their first romance comic book was *Young Romance*, starting in 1947. They were just back home from the war, they were veterans, and the teen comics were doing great, which were also about teenage girls. The love magazines did really well, but those were for women in their 20s. Even late teens, maybe 18 or 19, were reading the romance magazines and they said, "Well, why don't we do a comic?" The first one was an enormous success and, of course, what happens when one book is a success is other people start copying it. So, all of the other comic publishers had their romance titles. The teen girls became a little older or were reading the romance comics. They were younger girls who had just been reading about funny animals and teen comics; the teen comics still did very well in the fifties.

Comparing *Katy Keene* and *Torchy* in the 1940s and 1950s highlights the divide of how women are portrayed. *Torchy* was drawn with the intent to be sexy to sex-crazed readers whereas *Katy Keene* was classy, sophisticated, and geared toward an innocent female perspective. Al Feldstein's *Sunny* in 1947 for Fox and Quality's *Candy* had a similar polarization, and then in the nineties you have *Lady Death* versus the real girl comics. There are always going to be guys who do comics specifically for other guys, and *Torchy* was not really done for girls. *Torchy* was a pinup comic done for guys for fetish reasons; I mean, Bill Ward was totally a fetish artist. He couldn't help himself, that's just what he drew. So, he had to draw those legs with the super-high-heeled shoes and the seams on the stockings. It was what he did, and this was not for teenage girls. Bill Woggon was extremely unique, taking designs that had been sent to him by readers. I can tell you that I am in a class that is all seniors, and we got into a discussion, men and women. We brought up the comics we had liked as kids and somebody said *Katy Keene*. Then all of the women went, "Oh yes, *Katy Keene*." You know people, girls loved it. Girls loved it, and one woman even said, "They should bring it back."

As soon as I could discover comics, I was buying. I loved jungle comics. I was a huge *Sheena* fan. I was into jungle comics. My mother was a little alarmed because, you know, the girls were kind of sexy, but by today's standards, they're just pretty girls. You've seen "bad girl" comics and how horrendous they are.

In the 1950s, women in comics appear at EC Comics; Marie Severin was the colorist and that was it. Severin was born in Long Island, New York, and started coloring comics for the EC line where her brother, John, also worked as an artist. She was known for coloring any excessive blood as dark blue to reduce the gore of the line and utilized a limited color scheme with excellence.

By 1966, I was still living in Los Angeles when someone showed me the *East*

Comics such as Bill Woggon's *Katy Keene* #9 (1953) depicted women with class and sophistication as compared with Bill Ward's *Torchy* #5 (1950), which focused on sexualization and fetish.

Village Other. Every major city and college town, at that point, had one underground newspaper. In LA, ours was the *L.A. Free Press,* and I hung out with the *L.A. Free Press* crowd; I even did one four-panel comic for them. Then someone showed me the *East Village Other* and the comics were "Underground," but that term didn't exist yet. I called them hip comics. We talked about our counterculture rather than short-haired superheroes punching each other out. You know, it was something I could have never forgotten. There was this one full-page comic called *Gentles Tripout,* signed Panzika, and it was totally, totally psychedelic. It didn't really have a story or anything. It was just very psychedelic, and I thought, this is what I want to do. Two years later when I was in New York, I met Panzika, who turned out to be a woman. So, a woman was really my first major comics influence. Almost immediately, I was published in the *East Village Other.*

By the 1970s, so many of us had become feminists, and the traditional love comics were just something to laugh at because the stories they told had nothing to do with our lives. You know, girl meets guy and is afraid he doesn't love her for some reason or other and then it turns out he really does love her. I mean really these were simple, simple stories and so cliché.... Well, they had also become much more cliché by the seventies. The love comics that still existed are incredibly clichéd if you compare them with the earlier love comics, which sometimes were absolutely brilliant. The underground comics scene was a new art form, and that period of time was very revolutionary. The idea that you could do comics that were not Spider-Man or Batman, that were counterculture. It was a brand-new art form, and it was very exciting, vigorous, and very alive. There were comic books coming out of San Francisco; it was like the Mecca of underground comics, and I call it a migration of underground cartoonists from New York to San Francisco starting 1969 through 1971.

It Ain't Me Babe was the first in those days, and we didn't call it feminism yet; we called it women's liberation. *It Ain't Me Babe* was the first women's liberation newspaper in America. It came out of Berkeley, of course, and I saw maybe the first or second issue, and contacted them, then wound up drawing for them. Roughly every three weeks, we would have paste-up night, and I would do little spot illustrations right there for the articles. I also drew the comic for the back page and did covers, too. Women's liberation happened around the same time as women's liberation underground comics. It was still a very small group of people, just me and one other woman, Willie Mendes. The comics suddenly took a turn, I would say around 1969, for the extremely misogynistic and you have to understand that there was no comics code in underground comics. These guys could draw whatever they wanted and what was coming out of their ideas was an amazing hatred for women containing vicious, violent, misogyny. I had gotten turned on to what we called women's liberation, and I think even if I haven't gotten turned on to women's liberation, I would still react the same way because it was horrifying. I objected to it, and the guys were extremely threatened by women's liberation. My God, they were so threatened it was ridiculous, so basically, I was shut out. I mean, there was a boy's club, and I was definitely shut out.

I hate to pick on Crumb because he was a brilliant artist and a brilliant cartoonist. He kind of became the god of underground comics, and what he did was sacrosanct. If you dared to criticize him, you were burned at the stake in the marketplace. He always said, "Well, I'm being honest, and this is what is in my head. I'm just showing it on a slate," but that doesn't really make it okay. Racists are honest, too.

Wimmen's Comix had started in 1972, and two weeks after we started it, we discovered that there were these two women in Southern California who were also doing an all-woman book, but theirs had a much more outrageous title than ours. It was called *Tits and Clits*. We didn't know about each other and yet here within two weeks of meeting (two different groups of women from either side of California), we're producing these all-women comics.

I would go back to New York periodically because there were fantastic airline deals in those days where you could book a round trip for $199, and I would stay with friends often. I occasionally stayed with Flo Steinberg, who was a very dear friend and did her own underground comic, *Big Apple Comics*, in 1975. Then Denis Kitchen published a few magazines under Curtis Circulation for Marvel, *The Comix Book,* which was the mainstream Marvel underground magazine. This was kind of a conflicted category. I had some "Panthea" comics that were in there because they were paying $100 a page, which was incredible for us underground cartoonists. We were happy to get $25 a page if we even got paid. Panthea's mother's plane crashes, and she, as a baby girl, is the only survivor. She's brought up by a lion and becomes his mate. They have a daughter who is part lion, part woman, named Panthea.

Nineteen seventy-two was sort of the birth of autobiographical graphic novels in *Wimmen's Comix* by Aline Kominsky. Women love to share confidences, and they put themselves in their stories a lot. I contributed to *Tits and Clits* underground comics in 1977, and the comic discussed underground sexuality from a woman's perspective whereas the guys didn't want to talk about women's sexuality. It was the same thing with *Wimmen's Comix*. I mean, we dealt with subjects that the guys would not be the least bit interested in talking about. We talked about menstruation—the first issue had a comic called "A Teenage Abortion," which at the time was still illegal. Ron Turner was the publisher of Last Gasp comics, and he had published *It Ain't Me Babe* Comics, which was the first all-woman comic book. I produced that one. I completely take credit for that because I completely thought it up and produced it.

I did *Misty Comics* in the eighties under Jim Shooter for Marvel's Star comics line. Misty was an offshoot of *Millie the Model* because she was Millie's niece and that was continuity that got it into Marvel Comics. Later during the eighties and the nineties, it was all guys, and the women were reduced to being add-on characters. The super teams would be like three guys and a girl or four guys and a girl while the 1980s and the direct market became a funnel for mainly boys reading superhero comics. At that time, only superhero comics were put out and girls were almost edged out off to the side when there were many previous decades that women were attracted to comics. Then by the 1990s, you had those horrible bad-girl comics like *Lady Death* and these horrible hyper-sexualized soft-core porn characters.

At present, the awareness and involvement in women in comics has grown. There is a cultural acknowledgment that women have as much to contribute and as much to gain from the industry by bringing awareness to the women that did so in the past. This logic also applies to the representation of African American comic book characters and creators.

African Americans
in 20th-Century Comic Books

I came upon Professor William Foster III, an esteemed historian who specializes in African American representation in comics, while watching two documentaries, *Comic Book Superheroes Unmasked* (2003) for the History Channel and *Superheroes: A Never-Ending Battle* (2013). After the latter, I began to catch wind of another side to comics history through the African American experience. I read his book *Looking for a Face like Mine* (2005), concerning Black representation in comics, which I found really moving and a tremendous asset to any historian. He has since also written a second volume called *Dreaming of a Face Like Ours* (2010), and I was excited that he accepted my offer for an interview on the *Comic Book Historians Podcast*.[1] I found his research fascinating and compiled one section of the interview into this edited chapter discussing the timeline of Black characters in comics and getting his impression of each milestone.

William Foster III: Local New York life with its racially diverse set of children were present in *The Yellow Kid* (1896). Basically, if you look at the neighborhood photographs, you can't tell somebody's Irish by looking, unless he's got one of those little white pipes in his mouth…. Or the Jewish kid has a yarmulke, and the Black kid, obviously a little more obvious for him, you can tell. Sometimes, you couldn't even tell if the girls were girls because they'd be wearing pants like the boys. It was like the *Our Gang* (1922–1944) kind of theory; the idea is that these are just kids coming from different places, speaking differently, but getting along. Now, the adults can't do it, but the kids can. In fact, *Our Gang* made that main town, the center team, kind of an American team. Because in a district of a big city, you're living next door to somebody, you know exactly what's going on there. You know when there's a funeral. You know when there's a wedding. You know when there's an argument all because the walls are paper thin. Here you understood that everybody was the same and that our experiences are pretty much the same. We're all going through the same thing.

Now, you're moving to the 1920s, 1930s, and comic books have taken on a place of their own. Consider *Best Comics* #1 (1939) "The Red Mask." The first Black hero in a comic book eight years before *All-Negro Comics* came out. No one knows who definitely wrote or drew it; sometimes it's credited to George West and sometimes to

Kerry McRoberts, but when the people found out that he was a Black superhero, they tried to put out another one where he turned White. Then that just disappeared off the face of the Earth.

Now let's talk about George Herriman, who came out of Louisiana, probably near New Orleans. Of all the places in this country, that place is notorious for race-fixing that takes place on a regular level, but if your skin was White, it didn't matter what you were. So, people said, he was trying to act like he wasn't Black. I suppose he kept his hair short, and he always wore a hat. But then, you had people who would say, "Well, you're crazy. He took it off whenever he felt like it."[2] He was a darker-skinned guy, but it sheds some light on the kind of sickness about race that we have in this country; about how you can't be too dark. However, I don't feel like he was trying to hide who he was. I love *Krazy Kat* (1913) and was introduced to it when I was a kid—the animated *Krazy Kat*, which was made by the same people who made *Popeye*. I decided something similar about *Superman* and *Batman*, because I love their books, but noticed that the Black race was not represented in them. That doesn't mean that I didn't love their books.

Little Lulu (1935), when she appeared in ads in *The Saturday Evening Post*, there was a lot of anti–Black imagery in *Little Lulu* and only once or twice in her animated cartoons. I was stunned by that because it was *The Saturday Evening Post*! Now let's talk about the flipside to that, Jackie Ormes, the first female African American cartoonist. She cartooned the *Torchy Brown* (1937) newspaper comic strip, and they're syndicated going until 1940, and then there's a later run. It was an interesting period of time, and she was very prolific in that; how she portrayed the character, an environmentalist, a nurse. I can tell you, from my family, when they left the South, there was nothing that would bring them back, but she had an appreciation, there was a call, and a calling, and that's what she did. So, she's a creator much to be truly admired.

Let's talk about Will Eisner's Ebony character from *The Spirit* (1940). I'll start with my conversation with Will Eisner at San Diego Comic-Con. So, I had said, "Mr. Eisner, I'm a big fan of your work," and I talked to him about Ebony. I said, "What do you think about how people felt about Ebony?" He paused for a second and it was obvious that's the first time in a while that he'd been asked. He said, "Well, depends on when you ask me. Sometimes, people have said that it was a great idea to be inclusive, and other people said how dare you have a despicable image of us?" He went on to talk about how he got awards from the NAACP at one point, and he said, "In another point, they completely condemned it." That's interesting to me, because he also had a Black police officer who was in more than one strip, in more than one comic. He had another one where Ebony got turned down by a Black girl and decided he's going to go back to school to get rid of his southern accent because he didn't want to be recognized as a minstrel. So, if I was drawing characters, I would be really careful about who I painted.

Hank Ketcham, the creator of the American comic strip *Dennis the Menace*, came out with a Black character, Jackson (1970), two years after Charles Schulz introduced the Black character Franklin in *Peanuts* (1968). Ketcham did not receive the same reaction as Charles Schulz because people came after him with guns and knives. He was in Europe at the time, and he got a wire saying, "Get back over here. They're crashing in the offices, destroying property." His response was this: "Wait a minute, every cartoon character is a caricature of somebody. Find somebody who looks like Mr. Wilson with his big ass. How about Dennis' father who has a nose like a nose cone, or Dennis himself who looked like a tramp with a load in his pants. That's what I'm doing." He continued, "I can't make anybody less sensitive than they are, when they see an image that they think is really negative." So, in the case of Ebony, I didn't feel insulted. An example of processing these sorts of racial depictions is the old TV show *I Spy* (1965) with Robert Culp and Bill Cosby. I want you to think about a typical episode. They're getting into a car, who's driving? Is it Cosby or is it Culp? If it's Cosby, is he the servant? If it's Culp, it's because he's the master, or does it not make a difference? There's got to be artistic freedom on one side, and you have to be telling the story on the other side. Think about a character like *Spawn* (1992), who was a Black guy when he was alive but now the skin's burned off. However, people still think of him as a Black superhero. I have a friend who says, "No, I don't want no dead guy as a superhero." So, it depends on your point of view.

In 1945, in *World's Finest Comics* #17, there's a tribute to African Americans serving in World War II called "Johnny Everyman." Then a couple of years after that, *All-Negro Comics* (1947) by Orrin Evans with African Americans having control over their own imagery. Orrin Evans was a reporter, and he was more than just a reporter because he was the guy who created the Negro journalism organization. He was not afraid to get into a cop's face, which even then, at that point in time, would have been horrendously dangerous. He said that he got tired of seeing comic strips that didn't have people like him. So, when the paper he was working for went out of business, he got a bunch of guys who he knew could do the job, and they put out their own book. He was told and pressed that he couldn't sell this book. He sold this for 15 cents while every other comic book was selling for 12, which was a major thing to do. In full color, he did the book and not only the cover but also the inside. He produced a diverse array of Black characters, including a great African king, a Black detective, and Black fairies, while taking the story to wherever he could. I think that was amazing, but unfortunately it only lasted one issue. Other comic makers considered that maybe they ought to try this, so you get *Negro Heroes* (1947) by the publishers of *Parents Magazine,* and then you have *Lobo* (1965), the first comic book that features a Black man as a main character.

Batman #57 (1950), "Batman and Robin Stand Up for Sportsmanship," was probably Jack Schiff's assertion that racial wars weaken our country, which was an interesting thing. EC Comics made a statement in 1953 with their "Judgment Day" story. A Black astronaut has made contact with a robot planet and there's one color robot versus another. There is this kind of bigotry going on, and then the astronaut says, "You guys aren't quite ready yet." I love that story and it's surprising to me how well-known it has become.

There were a lot of discussions around race in the sixties starting to manifest, and by 1964-ish, you have war genre comics that discussed race, including *Our Army at War, Star Spangled War Stories*, and *Sgt. Fury and His Howling Commandos*. Really early in the run of *Sgt. Fury and His Howling Commandos*, they had a guy who joined their commando unit. They had an Englishman, they had an Italian American, they had a Jewish guy, they had a Black guy, they had a southern guy, and then they had Sgt. Fury, who was from New York City. There was also this racist guy in one issue who they brought into the barracks where they say, "Here, you'll be sleeping next to this guy." The racist responds, "I'm not sleeping next to a Black guy," and they call them out on it. They said, "You're a bigot and we work as a team. If we don't, we all die." Sure enough, this guy, because he wants to be a hero and he's struggling to fight when they're right in front of the Germans, gets wounded in battle and needs a blood transfusion from his fellow Black squad member, which was an amazing lesson. Marvel felt that they could do it. DC, maybe not so much, and Marvel ran with it.

Black representation shows up in a significant way in pop culture of the 1970s, almost like an explosion, including *Inner City Romance* (1972) by Guy Colwell, *Super Soul Comics* (1972) by Richard "Grass" Green, *Luke Cage* (1972) at Marvel, and Don McGregor's *Jungle Action* (1973) series with Black Panther. The counterculture was taking over. When you see a major trend come in or a major wave coming through, it's making money and everyone else wants to make money, too. So, you try things out, you start seeing a lot more women manifest themselves in the comic book world. Not just as superheroes, but as policemen, or police chiefs in some cases, head of government agencies, and politicians. So, the seventies adds that diversity to comic books, although sometimes it's clumsy. Ask anybody you know about Luke Cage, when the last time was that they had a Black guy say, "Sweet Christmas"? Also, there was another phase, too, that every Black superhero had to have Black in front of his name [e.g., *Black Lightning or Black Goliath*]. And that had to be a joke. Even now, it's still kind of a joke. But I understand what that was; it was important to declare if one was Black. If this is the only way you can say it, that's fine. I've known Don McGregor for a long time and read his *Jungle Action* series. The title makes some people pause, but he was always trying to treat each character as a human being and that's what happened with Black Panther for a long time. People didn't know how to deal with him, so he was kind of a background character. Is he a monarch of a country? Is he a superhero? How is he a person? At one point, I think he had a job as a teacher in a high school, so they couldn't really decide what they wanted to do with his character. I was reading the book on a regular basis, but I couldn't read any more because I couldn't tell where it was going.

The creation of Storm in 1975 by Len Wein and Dave Cockrum was notable because she became their strong female Black leader. She has blue eyes, but still, is an African princess. I think it's important because there was no one like her before.

She had an African mother and an African American father, who both died, and she was forced to be a thief in Cairo as a young kid. Chris Claremont added elements to her story and then she became Kitty's godmother, so, she has different hats she wears. I was surprised to see how much she called the professor on ethical issues, and I thought that was important to have somebody like that because if you're an all-powerful person, what's going to stop you? As we saw in Jean Grey's character, with no one more powerful than Phoenix, what happens? Wonder Woman had a Black sister, Nubia. It's interesting that when they did the amalgamation comics and combined the Marvel and DC heroes, Storm combined with Wonder Woman and became an Amazon, which tells you how powerful an image that she had. It was a natural fit and they didn't have to explain that to anybody.

There are a couple of things that happened in 1978. *Sabre*, by Don McGregor, was basically one of the earlier modern graphic novels and portrayed a strong Black

Storm was created in *Giant-Size X-Men* #1 (1975) by Len Wein and Dave Cockrum and eventually became the team's first female Black leader under writer Chris Claremont.

adventurer. However, in the same year, there was also Bill Mantlo's *Spider-Man* story about a poorly made character, the Hypno-Hustler. Sabre, if you look at him, is basically inspired by Jimi Hendrix; there's no question, and he spoke lyrically. He didn't give a straightforward line, and it's obviously postapocalyptic. He used his instinct, his natural ability, which we've always thought was kind of a sixties thing, and had a gun but it's not the first thing he reached for because he knew how to use a sword. No doubt, the people who are after him have a hierarchy that they respect more than anything else. They think of him as an animal, so he's like an outsider, but he's an outsider that you admire because he's moving as naturally as he can. Hypno-Hustler was voted the worst supervillain in all of Marvel history, and I don't know who voted that, but my vote would've counted on that, too. Once again, that character was an example of somebody trying to take advantage of a trend, the disco era with that very corny and badly assembled costume.

Bertram Fitzgerald published his *Golden Legacy* (1966–1976) series, then his *Fast Willie Jackson* (1976) with the Archie-type art by Gus Lemoine. He started *Golden Legacy* for the same reason that brother Evans started *All-Negro Comics*, because he got tired of not seeing Black people in comics. So, he dedicated an entire series to that. He was told by Black and White people alike, "It will never sell." No one would sell him a subscription list so he couldn't sell at newsstands where comic books were sold, but he was clever and inventive. He went to grocery stores, got advertising from different groceries, then sold them there, and he started doing very well. He also submitted to the Urban League and got support because those books were amazing. He had to go and find his own printer, and a guy was stealing his designs then selling them off the books, prompting Fitzgerald to take the guy to court. While he was at the courtroom, he had a heart attack, went to the hospital, came back out, and still won the case. So, what he was looking for in *Fast Willie Jackson* was a book that he wanted for young people, and it was so different from *Golden Legacy*. He said, "How can I tell if they're reading this?" So, they held a contest in the letters to the editor page, and said, "If you can come up with a good ending for this story, we'll use your story." He said they got an amazing number of letters coming back to them and it was an important thing for him to try out.

In the eighties, there were a few comics that featured African Americans like *Daddy Cool* in 1984, but it's not as much as the seventies and the nineties. It's almost like there's less of these in some way. I think it had to do with the economic conditions of the country at that time and the political feeling on what was happening from the Reagan years. *Daddy Cool* was deep, printed by the same people who did *Player* magazine. It was a large-sized format, and they reduced it later, into a paperback size, but the person who reduced it wasn't paying attention, so the page count was all off. Despite the production errors, it was an amazing story, and he became very popular.

The nineties was a really interesting time because Black comics came back strong. There was a thing in the early nineties when cards were a big deal and even

Marvel hopped on the bandwagon with their Marvel Comics cards. There was a huge card industry and Revlon, which bought Marvel, also bought a card company. During this period, there were the 1990 *Miss Black America Trading Cards*, the 1992 *Civil Rights Movement Task Cards*, and the 1993 *African American History Cards*.

As far as Milestone Comics (1993), there's a great story about Dwayne McDuffie, when he initially went to Marvel. He said, "Give me control of your worst-selling book, and I bet you, I'll turn it around," and that's exactly what he did. The worst-selling book was the aftermath of all the fights with superheroes and gods, and warriors, and demons and stuff. There's always a mess in the city. Who is the company that came through for cleaning? *Damage Control* (1988). I was stunned by his work, as well as his imprint for DC Comics named Milestone Comics, which achieved and didn't achieve what they wanted. The main difficulty for African American comic book publishers was distribution. If you don't have any distribution, it's never the same, even if you're online. So, DC said, "We'll cover that for you." But then, as you should have suspected, you knew who Daddy Warbucks is, right? The character from *Little Orphan Annie*. Daddy Warbucks may look like a sympathetic old guy, but he never was going to let go of the reins because he doesn't care what you think. So, DC was always saying, "Well, no, you can't put that stuff in." Milestone would say, "Wait a minute. Our contract clearly says that." DC would reiterate, "Now, well, we say no." So, it became that Dwayne McDuffie wrote the lightning character *Static* (1993), who had a girlfriend and they decided they want to have sex; that's the story. Okay, now here's the thing, DC didn't want them to show a condom, and McDuffie said, "Wait a minute, if I had put her butt in a prominent image on the front cover, you would've made twice as many copies." The condom was subtly placed, and it wasn't like they were brandishing while putting them on because they were on the side table. But without discussing it with McDuffie first, DC put an extra cover on top of it, and when you opened it up, you saw the real cover. McDuffie said that was pretty much it for him. They wanted editorial control over their line, which should've been made clear to everybody. I get the feeling it wasn't, but then, how often does that come true with a partner?

There are some other nineties milestones like *Barry Crockett Motown Man* (1999), then there's *Still I Rise: A Cartoon History of African Americans* (1997), which chronicles the history of Black Americans starting in 1619. Personal computers gave people the tools to write; you can have a program that could draw, and if you had the internet, you could distribute. You don't have to wait in line. Back then, there were basically two to maybe five comic companies, and you knew they only took what they wanted. They hired guys to write what they wanted them to write. But now, independent creators were assembling such as the Independent Black Comic Book Producers, which has become an important network, and in fact, it mirrors a network that was in place when the Black Pullman porters and Black press somewhat cooperated. Certain towns wouldn't take Black papers, and the Pullman would grab a bunch and throw them off when they knew somebody would pick them up. So, they defeated to an extent that kind of thing, where you're not going to get the news in many places. That was the same thing with Black comics. When people realized that they could cooperate with somebody else other than the big guys, and still get their job done, and be creative—that was what the nineties were about.

A few things happened in 2003: first, the creation of a Black Captain America, Isaiah Bradley, and its commentary on the government experimenting on African Americans. Also, in the same year, Thunder, Black Lightning's daughter, was created. The second-generation superhero had been kicked around a little bit but not really done, but then, you find that they do it, and it's an African American family. Of course, now we had it as a TV show, and it was amazing because they could have done any number of ways with that since the characters have been around for a little bit. The Tuskegee Experiment, where Black prisoners were told they were given a cure for syphilis and gonorrhea, and in fact, they were not, is still unknown by a lot of people. They were given nothing, not even penicillin. The goal of the experiment was to see what would happen; the results would be that syphilis would be in the human body for 30 years, and they all died horribly. So, someone said, "What happens if the super-soldier serum, given to Captain America, was tried out on Black people first?" and that Captain America is the benefit of having abused some Black guys to first see how it was going to work. The fact that they made it a part of the continuity of Captain America's origin for all time stuns me beyond words. I think that's amazing, because I'm a DC kid, and how many years did I have to put up with imaginary stories, or stories that could've happened? It just seemed like a copout but that's what they did. They said, "Nope, this is how we're always going to play it." I'm not saying that everybody else was a coward, but somebody took a chance. It does not always have to be pretty and in the light. Sometimes, it's in the dark, and we can still do some good stuff with it.

The Death of the 20th-Century Comic Book Greats

Later ages of superhero comic books utilize plots, techniques, and tropes that build upon on the work of the previous century's giants to advance the art form. As fans enjoy the properties created by the comic book pioneers, the torch is passed from one generation to the next as the lives of the preceding creators pass. These 20th-century comic book greats maintained an overall approach and aesthetic to the visual medium of comics that mark more than half a century of consumer tastes and culture. These old professionals were generally children of the Great Depression who survived World War II and left behind a considerable portfolio in comics. Even though some were indeed treasured while they were here, many were not. They contributed to the development of superhero comic books and sadly died in various ways. These comic book greats include Dick Ayers, John Broome, John Buscema, Gene Colan, Vince Colletta, Steve Ditko, Gardner Fox, Archie Goodwin, Don Heck, Carmine Infantino, Harvey Kurtzman, Jack Kirby, Gil Kane, Harvey Kurtzman, Stan Lee, Sheldon Mayer, Jerry Robinson, Julius Schwartz, Marie Severin, Joe Simon, Joe Sinnott, Al Williamson, and Wally Wood.

Dick Ayers was born in New York and studied under Burne Hogarth in what became the School of Visual Arts in 1947. He was known for inking Jack Kirby on many early Marvel Silver Age comics, including *The Fantastic Four* (1962) and *Tales to Astonish* (1962). He also penciled *Sgt Fury and His Howling Commandos* (1964) for 10 years and then freelanced for various companies for the next few decades. Ayers wrote and drew his autobiography, *The Dick Ayers Story: An Illustrated Autobiography* (2005), and was inducted into the Eisner Hall of Fame in 2007. He passed away at the age of 90 in 2014[1] and is generally known as an early contributor to the birth of the Marvel Universe.

John Broome was a writer for science-fiction pulp magazines and was hired by agent Julius Schwartz to write scripts for DC Comics' superheroes during the Golden Age. He was a writer for both *Strange Adventures* and *Mystery in Space* in the early 1950s and was the main writer for Silver Age heroes *Flash* and *Green Lantern*. He cocreated Professor Zoom, Abra Kadabra, and Wally West, among others, with Carmine Infantino and submitted his final scripts to DC Comics in 1969, retiring to live in East Asia, where he died in 1999.

John Buscema penciled art pages for various Marvel series, including *The Amazing Spider-Man* and *Silver Surfer*. Over the decades he worked on *Conan the Barbarian* (1973), *Tarzan* (1977), and *Nova* (1976), among many others. After Kirby left Marvel Comics in 1970, Buscema's four decades of work helped maintain the company's house style. Due to his high speed and considerable work ethic, he produced enough art to appear on comics, T-shirts, coffee mugs, calendars, and trade paperbacks. He died shortly after being diagnosed with stomach cancer in 2002, and his last published comic was *Superman: Blood of My Ancestors* (2002), initially started by Gil Kane, who had passed away just before him.[2] His art quality and quantity maintained its high standard until the end of his life.

Gene Colan demonstrated his unique approach to illustration in genres such as western, horror, superheroes, and crime, among others. His first comic book publication was for Fiction House on *Wings Comics* (1944) and he is known for cocreating two African American superheroes, the Falcon (1969) and Blade (1973). His art on *Tales to Astonish* (1965), *Daredevil* (1966), *Doctor Strange* (1968), *Tomb of Dracula* (1972), and *Howard the Duck* (1976) is commonly celebrated. After a lengthy career in several comic book companies, he was inducted into the Will Eisner Hall of Fame (2005). He won another Eisner in 2010 for his 40-page *Captain America* #601 (2009) and in 2011 died from complications of cancer and liver disease.[3] His pencils portrayed an unusual mastery over shadow and texture that baffled many inkers.

Vince Colletta was a Sicilian immigrant who entered comics in the early 1950s. He worked on romance comics such as *Intimate Love*, *Daring Love*, and *Stories of Romance*, then later became known for inking over Jack Kirby's pencils for *The Mighty Thor* during the 1960s. He was art director at DC Comics in the 1970s and was known to be reliable to editors for always turning in his inking assignments on time. His ability to finish an assignment at a moment's notice was coupled with a tendency to erase pencils to meet a deadline. He departed comic books for screenwriting toward the end of his life and suffered a heart attack, then died in 1991 shortly after discovering he had cancer.[4] His work ethic, high volume of pages, and history in romance comics leave behind a legacy to be remembered.

Steve Ditko departed Charlton's failed Action Heroes line for DC Comics, cocreating *Beware the Creeper* (1968) and *The Hawk and the Dove* (1968) with Steve Skeates. In the early 1970s, he worked mainly for Charlton and other small publishers, then created *Destructor* (1975) with Archie Goodwin for Atlas/Seaboard, *Stalker* (1975) with Paul Levitz, as well as *Shade, The Changing Man* (1977). He returned to Marvel but refused to further contribute any pages toward his cocreations *The Amazing Spider-Man* or *Doctor Strange*, but instead penciled *Machine Man* (1979), *Captain Universe* (1980), *The Micronauts* (1982), and *Rom* (1984). Additionally, he created The Mocker in *Silver Star* #2 (1983), as well as Speedball (1988) with Tom DeFalco, and Squirrel Girl with Will Murray (1991). He also penciled *Magnus* (1992) and *Solar: Man of the Atom* (1992) for Valiant Comics. Ditko was always diligent about answering fan letters and writing essays published by his friend Robin Snyder up until his death of a heart attack in 2018.[5] He died the way he lived, on his own terms.

Gardner Fox was a lawyer, novelist, and writer for science-fiction pulp magazines during the difficult era of the Great Depression, which bridged his career writing comic books. He wrote and cocreated the batarang, batgyro, Sandman, Hawkman, the Justice Society of America, the Justice League of America, and the DC Multiverse, among others, and was an important writer for the "New Look" Batman. He was known for being one of Julius Schwartz's main writers during the Silver Age and departed DC Comics in 1968 when the company was undergoing a change in ownership and editorial structure. He briefly worked in the comic magazine market of the early 1970s and died of pneumonia in 1986.

Archie Goodwin joined Marvel in the late 1960s after leaving Warren Magazines, then was hired by DC Comics to briefly edit *Detective Comics*. He returned to Marvel and cocreated Luke Cage (1972) and Spider-Woman (1977), then became the company's editor-in-chief in 1976. He was heavily involved in Marvel's *Star Wars* (1977) comics and edited the creator-owned *Epic Illustrated* (1980) line of magazines and comic books, then returned to DC Comics in 1989 overseeing a series of Batman-related publications. He died at age 60 from cancer in 1998[6] and is arguably the most-liked creator in comics history.

Don Heck was born in Centereach, New York, and started work at Harvey Comics in 1949. After some time in production, he drew his first comic in *War Fury* #1 (1952) for the publisher Comic Media, then freelanced in various genres for Quality Comics, Hillman, Toby Press, and Atlas Comics. For Marvel, he cocreated Iron Man (1962), Black Widow (1964), Mandarin (1964), Hawkeye (1964), and Wonder Man (1964) and penciled *Tales of Suspense* (1962), *The Avengers* (1964), *The X-Men* (1967), and *The Champions* (1975), among others. He also penciled various assignments for DC Comics, such as *House of Secrets* (1970) and *Wonder Woman* (1973), then contributed to various independent comics up through the early 1990s and died of lung cancer in 1995.[7] His early contributions to Marvel are critically important but generally overlooked.

Carmine Infantino was promoted to DC Comics publisher, then later worked with Stan Lee to co-publish the company's first superhero crossover, *Superman vs. the Amazing Spider-Man* (1976), and was a story consultant on the first *Superman* (1978) film starring Christopher Reeve. Warner Bros. replaced Infantino as publisher in 1976 with Jenette Kahn, prompting his return to the industry as a freelance comic book artist. He created the character Paladin with Jim Shooter for *Daredevil* #150 (1978) and penciled pages for Marvel and DC on series such as *Star Wars*, *The Flash*, *Red Tornado*, and *Justice League of America*, among others. He was a teacher at the School of Visual Arts and unsuccessfully sued DC Comics in 2004 for ownership of various characters such as Captain Boomerang, Abra Kadabra, and Wally West, among others. He died in 2013 at the age of 87 of natural causes.

Gil Kane entered the comics industry in 1941 and was published in MLJ Magazine's *Pep Comics*,[8] Timely's *Young Allies Comics*, and DC's *Adventure Comics*. After cocreating the Silver Age Green Lantern, he served as a premier cover artist for Marvel in the 1970s and later illustrated the newspaper comic strip *Star Hawks* (1977). He designed characters for animation companies Hanna-Barbera and Ruby-Spears, then returned to superheroes at DC Comics in the 1980s. He contributed original art to comic book companies such as Topps, Malibu, Darkhorse, and Awesome Entertainment in the 1990s. For more than a decade, he was treated for lymphoma and still penciled art pages through chemotherapy-radiation treatments, dying in 2000 at the age of 73.[9] He is one of the few pencilers whose art improved with age.

Jack Kirby rightfully benefited from DC Comics' merchandising royalty deal with Paul Levitz and Jenette Kahn over the Kenner *Super Powers* collection that focused on his New Gods. He later signed a negotiated form with Marvel's legal department for return to him of roughly 2,000 original art pages. Kirby made several convention appearances in the late 1980s and early 1990s, then died of heart failure in 1994.[10] His name began to be listed as the cocreator of several Marvel properties soon after Disney legally settled with his estate in 2014, and he is rightfully celebrated as the most abundant creator of superhero comic books.

Harvey Kurtzman maintained his innate talent as a humorist after leaving *MAD*. He cut his association with Gaines to work on the short-lived magazine *Trump* for Hugh Hefner, then moved on to *Humbug* for a short time in the late 1950s before leaving for Jim Warren's *Help!* Magazine, on which he worked from 1960 until 1965, mentoring young talents such as Terry Gilliam and Gloria Steinem. Finding glamour in slick magazines, Kurtzman dedicated himself to Hugh Hefner's *Little Annie Fanny* strip for *Playboy* from 1962 to 1988, during which he reconciled with Bill Gaines, then wrote *From Aargh! to Zap! Harvey Kurtzman's Visual History of the Comics* (1991). He spent his final years being treated for Parkinson's disease and cancer, dying in 1993,[11] but never forgot to find a clever laugh in everyday situations.

Stan Lee worked for Marvel as publisher and then in 1981 moved to Los Angeles to promote the company's superheroes' transition to film and animation. He returned to comics for occasional projects, such as cocreating *The Savage She-Hulk* (1980), writing the *Silver Surfer* one-shot (1982) with John Byrne, *Silver Surfer: Parable* (1988) with Moebius, and *Silver Surfer: The Enslavers* (1990) with Keith Pollard. During the 1990s, he resigned from Marvel but continued to receive a million-dollar annual salary as chairman emeritus. He created *Ravage 2099* (1992) and *Stripperella* (2003), which featured celebrities Pamela Anderson and Mark Hamill. He later co-started Stan Lee Media (1998), which filed for bankruptcy in 2001 and managed to secure a payout from the successful Marvel film franchise through a lawsuit that started in 2002 and resolved in 2005. He started the company POW! Entertainment (2001) and contributed to various pop culture properties such as the reality television show *Who Wants to Be a Superhero?* (2006). He realized his

60-year mission to encourage the superhero genre's successful transfer to film and television and appeared in a series of memorable cameos in most of the productions to date in the Marvel Cinematic Universe. Lee's final two years were filled with some degree of notoriety, which involved questionable elder abuse allegations, and he passed away in 2018 from cardiopulmonary failure at the age of 95.[12] He is considered by some to be the most over-credited creator and under-credited editor in comic book history.

Sheldon Mayer was born in Harlem, New York, and worked for the Fleischer Animation studios in 1934, then later found work at Malcolm Wheeler-Nicholson's National Allied Publications in the mid–1930s. He edited comics at Dell, the McClure Syndicate, and All-American Publications in 1939, where he oversaw and encouraged the creation of *Wonder Woman*, *Flash*, *Green Lantern*, and *Justice Society of America,* and departed his role as editor to cartoon his own strip, *Scribbly the Boy Cartoonist.* He also worked on the teen humor comic book *Sugar and Spike* (1956) for DC Comics, then toward the end of his career, wrote comic book scripts in the 1970s and died of cancer in 1991.[13] As an editor, he was known for always having an open mind for the intricacies of storytelling.

Jerry Robinson illustrated newspaper comic strip *Still Life* (1963) for 32 years as well as covers for *Playbill* magazine starting in the 1950s. He also served as the National Cartoonist Society's president from 1967 to 1969 and utilized that position in a public relations campaign on behalf of Siegel and Shuster to acquire creator credit for *Superman* in 1975. He also founded the Cartoonists & Writers Syndicate in 1978 and managed it for decades, before dying in his sleep in 2011 at age 89.[14] Despite being heavily active in comics after illustrating *Batman* in the 1940s, he is still generally remembered for cocreating the Joker.

Julius Schwartz retired from DC in 1986 after editing the *Superman* comics for 15 years and adapted stories for the company's failing science-fiction graphic novel line until 1987. He retained the role of editor emeritus and continued to attend conventions until 2003. He died suddenly in 2004 at the age of 88 after being hospitalized for pneumonia.[15] His legacy changed into notoriety after death, when various women in the comic book industry came forth with sexual misconduct allegations.[16]

Marie Severin started work at Marvel Comics in the production department in 1959 and became an artist on *Doctor Strange* (1967), cocreating the Living Tribunal with Stan Lee. She penciled titles such as *Not Brand Echh* (1967), *The Incredible Hulk* (1967), *Sub-Mariner* (1969), and colored *Iron Man* (1976), among others, then cocreated Spider-Woman (1977). She worked in Marvel's Special Projects division handling licensed non-comic products and eventually won both the Eisner and Harvey Awards. She died of a hemorrhagic stroke at the age of 89 in 2018[17] and was famous for her caricatures that depicted staffers' intricacies.

Joe Simon demonstrated a strong aptitude for penciling, inking, writing, lettering, and editing comic books. After departing his partnership with Jack Kirby in

1955, Simon worked outside comics[18] and eventually created and edited the satirical magazine *Sick* (1960) for a decade and contributed to Harvey Thriller comics such as *Spyman* (1966) with George Tuska and Jim Steranko. Simon created *Brother Power the Geek* (1968) and *Prez* (1973) for DC Comics, where he reunited with Jack Kirby on one issue of *Sandman* (1974). He died in 2011 at the age of 98 after a "brief illness"[19] and always understood both the creative and legal aspects of the comic book business.

Joe Sinnott penciled comics for Dell before regularly inking Kirby on the *Fantastic Four* (1965). After Kirby departed Marvel in 1970, he continued to ink over various pencilers for a wide array of comic books, including *The X-Men*, *The Avengers*, *The Mighty Thor*, and *Captain America*, among others, from 1965 to 1992, maintaining the visual polish of the company. He departed comic books to ink *The Amazing Spider-Man* newspaper strip until 2019[20] and professionally drew comics until the very end when he died in 2020 at the age of 93.

Al Williamson was born in New York and raised in Colombia, where he read comic strips as a child. He moved back to America, where he trained under Burne Hogarth and assisted him on *Tarzan* comic strips (1940s), then later illustrated the *Secret Agent Corrigan* strip with writer Archie Goodwin from 1967 to 1980. In 1980, he began illustrating the *Star Wars* newspaper comic strip, then became an inker for Marvel in the 1990s. He returned to illustrating *Flash Gordon* for a two-issue limited series for Marvel Comics and penciled the cover for *Space Cowboy* (2001). He eventually retired from comics and developed Alzheimer's, of which he died from complications in 2010 at age 79.[21] His friends frequently comment that his charm was outmatched only by his skill.

Wally Wood's contributions to *T.H.U.N.D.E.R. Agents* ended in 1969 as he began to produce comic strips for the military newspaper *The Overseas Weekly*, where he presented adult-oriented characters Sally Forth, Shattuck, and Cannon. He returned to depicting superheroes at DC Comics in the mid–1970s and inked the pencils of artists such as Kirby, Ditko, and Simonson. He cocreated Power Girl in *All Star Comics* #58 (1976) and later resumed portraying his character Sally Forth in a pornographic comic book. He was known to have suffered from a stroke in one eye in addition to starting dialysis, which all likely played a factor one fateful night when Wood was alone in his apartment in 1981 and died from a self-inflicted gunshot wound.[22] The one constant in his tumultuous life was his ability to always make something beautiful.

As old comic books become digitized in the new millennium, it becomes more obvious to newer generations that there is an almost endless amount of comic book history to discover. Truthfully, the list of contributors extends well beyond what is written here, but hopefully this history gives a head start for newcomers who are looking to gain an appreciation for the development of the superhero genre. Through hard work, blood, sweat, and tears, these men and women used pencil and ink to fashion the comic book art form. Many grew up during the era of the Great

We will forever be grateful for the work of the 20th-century greats and their unique contributions to the history of superhero comic books. Image from *The Death of Captain Marvel* (1982).

Depression and World War II while surviving the great challenges of the comic book industry and leaving behind an incredible trail of stories, cartoons, and illustrations before their deaths. We will forever be grateful for the work they did and the unique contributions each of them made to the history of superhero comic books.

Epilogue

The success of *Watchmen* was followed by Dark and Extreme Age trends that suggested the superhero comic book ceased any further significant development. Once the genre was deconstructed in 1986, superhero comic books that appeared afterward generally utilized the plot devices that were pioneered in the previous ages. Titles such as *Kingdom Come*, *The Invisibles*, and *The Boys* deconstructed superheroes in a fashion similar to Moore. The Extreme Age of the 1990s still followed the same trends, but the decade was mostly defined by the overall direction of the industry to exaggerate, rather than innovate, the predefined qualities of the superhero comic book to maximize sales to collectors. The heroes were depicted using many of the same plot devices and personality traits during this era, but in titles such as *X-Force*, *X-Men*, *Superman*, and *DC versus Marvel*, among others, mainly emphasized larger muscles, breasts, guns, crossovers, and gimmicks. This was not a viable long-term strategy and contributed to a boom-and-bust comic book economy, as the marketplace suffered and the superhero genre demonstrated no significant innovation.

The industry required a lifeline that could revitalize the significance of the superhero genre because the comic book medium now also needed to compete with the internet for market share. This coincided with the advancement of computer graphics that allowed the depiction of superpowers on film, resulting in the expansion of the genre to other visual media in the Movie Age. Successful films such as *Blade* (1998), *X-Men* (2000), and *The Avengers* (2012) demonstrated that superheroes were a viable commodity of the film industry. This also altered the function of new superhero comic books and graphic novels to serve dual roles, as entertainment for readers as well as pitches for a Hollywood production. This synergy with film and television maintains the relevancy of the comic book medium, as it continues to express multiple genres, identities, and fantasies in creative verbal and pictorial ways. Although the superhero genre is depicted using plots and tropes pioneered in the last century, the execution of the stories and art demonstrates a constant sense of modernization that evokes a similar satisfaction to incoming readers as Byrne's modernization created for comic fans of the 1980s. Snyder and Capullo's *Batman*, Jeff Lemire's *Moon Knight*, Matt Fraction's *Hawkeye*, and Jonathan Hickman's *Fantastic Four* are some examples of clever creators making older characters relevant to a newer generation.

There are also renewed calls for more diverse representation in comics in a fashion first envisioned by Schwartz, O'Neil, and Adams, which also follows Stan Lee's mission to depict the world outside one's window. Examples abound of this recent trend, such as *Ms. Marvel*, which now features a young Pakistani Muslim female; *Werewolf by Night* features a teenage Hopi American; Superman's son, Jonathan Kent, revealed himself as bisexual; Ghost Rider is Latin American; Thor is female; Captain America is African American; the recent comic book reboot of *Shang Chi: Master of Kung Fu* was done with an Asian team of comic creators; and the television show *Batwoman* stars an African American female. This pattern helps serve underrepresented populations while also portraying an ideal world where all groups of people are truly equal, possibly signaling that we might be in the beginnings of the next age, one in which superhero comic books, video games, films, and television shows, featuring diversity like never before, are presented to audiences with cross-platform tie-ins. For superheroes, the journey continues...

Chapter Notes

Introduction

1. Peter Coogan, *Superhero: The Secret Origin of a Genre* (Austin: MonkeyBrain Books, 2006), 30.

2. Stan Lee, "Marvel Comic Group," *Sub-Mariner Comics* #31 (New York: Marvel, 1949), 13.

3. Stephen Lee and Sidney Lee, *Dictionary of National Biography* vol. 48 (London: Smith, Elder, & Co., 1896), 47.

4. Robert Beerbohm, Doug Wheeler, and Leonardo De Sá, "Töpffer in America," in *Comic Art Magazine* #3 (M. Todd Hignite & Daniel Zimmer, 2003), 28–47.

5. Ada Darling, "Obadiah Oldbuck, Hero of Long Ago, Now Character Doll," in *Dunkirk Evening Observer* (Ogden Newspapers, 4 June 1941), 11.

6. "Comic books published by Cupples & Leon," *My Comic Shop* (Lone Star Comics, 1996-2021), https://www.mycomicshop.com/search?pl=Cupples%20%26%20Leon.

7. Stacy Haslem, "Getting Serious About Comics," *Great Falls Tribune* (Gannett, 30 March 2003), 5P.

8. Carlin, Karasik, Walker, Crouch, and Hammer, *Masters of American Comics* (Hammer Museum, 2005), 173.

9. Greg Sadowski, *Action! Mystery! Thrills! Great Comic Book Covers 1936-1945* (Seattle: Fantagraphics, 2012), 186.

10. Ron Goulart, "Famous Funnies," *Comic Book Encyclopedia* (New York: Harper Entertainment, 2004), 163.

11. Contributor, "Famous Funnies a Carnival of Comics," in *Grand Comics Database*, https://www.comics.org/issue/75/.

12. Ron Goulart, "The Funnies," *Comic Book Encyclopedia* (New York: Harper Entertainment, 2004), 144.

13. M.C. Gaines, "Narrative Illustration: The Story of Comics," *Print* (Santa Barbara: William Edwin Rudge, 1942), 36.

14. Alan Cowsill, Alex Irvine, Matthew K. Manning, Michael McAvennie, Melanie Scott, and Daniel Wallace, *DC Comics Year by Year: A Visual Chronicle* (London: Dorling Kindersley, 2010), 13.

15. Coogan, *Superhero: The Secret Origin of a Genre*, 30.

16. Anthony Wall, *The Comic Strip Hero* (BBC, 1981), *2:40*.

17. Bill Everett, "The Sub-Mariner," *Marvel Comics* #1 (Timely Comics, 1939), 28.

18. Bob Kane and Bill Finger, "The Case of the Chemical Syndicate," *Detective Comics* #27 (DC Comics, 1939), 6.

19. Jerry Siegel and Joe Shuster, "Superman Champions Universal Peace," *Superman* #2 (DC Comics, 1939), 20.

20. Whitney Ellsworth, discovered by Ken Quattro, *Editorial Taboos* (DC Comics, 1941), 1–2.

21. Kurt Mitchell and Roy Thomas, *American Comic Book Chronicles: 1940–1944* (Raleigh: Two-Morrows, 2019), 125.

22. Rick Brough, "Horror Comics Censored," *The Daily Utah Chronicle* (Salt Lake City: University of Utah, 8 November 1976), 7.

23. Amy Nyberg, *Seal of Approval: The Origins and History of the Comics Code*, vol. 1 (Jackson: University Press of Mississippi, 1998), 61–63.

24. Digby Diehl, *Tales from the Crypt: The Official Archives* (New York: St. Martin's Press, 1996), 148–149.

25. Paul Sassiene, *The Comic Book: The One Essential Guide for Comic Book Fans Everywhere* (Edison: Chartwell Books, 1994), 69.

26. Eric Nash, "Julius Schwartz: Comic-book editor revived superhero genre," *Pittsburgh Post-Gazette* (John Robinson Block, 14 February 2004), B-5.

27. Robert Genter, "With Great Power Comes Great Responsibility: Cold War Culture and the Birth of Marvel Comics," *The Journal of Popular Culture* (Wiley-Blackwell, 2007), 953.

28. Judith Duke, *Children's Books and Magazines: A Market Study* (White Plains: Knowledge Industry Publications, 1979), 119–120, 185.

29. Nicholas von Hoffman, "When fear turns to exultation," *The Windsor Star* (Postmedia Network, 15 October 1970), 13.

30. Jim Beard, Keith Dallas, and Jason Sacks, *American Comic Book Chronicles: 1970s* (Raleigh: TwoMorrows, 2014), 25.

31. Scott Williams, "Gerry Conway: Everything but the Gwen Stacy Sink," *Back Issue!* #44 (Raleigh: TwoMorrows, 2010), 12–13.

32. David Andelman, "Today's Comics Feature

Black Characters as Heroes," *The Palm Beach Post* (Gannett, 4 October 1970), E2.

33. Roy Thomas and John Buscema, "Come on in … the Revolution's Fine!," *The Avengers* #83 (Marvel, 1970), cover.

34. Kim Thompson, "Marvel Focuses on Direct Sales," *The Comics Journal* #59 (Seattle: Fantagraphics, 1980), 11–12.

35. Lori Groller, "The Amazing Comic Book Industry," *The Morning Call* (Tribune Publishing, 18 November 1985), D1–D2.

36. Tom Heintjes, "Charlton Goes Down for the Count," *The Comics Journal* #103 (Seattle: Fantagraphics, 1985), 10–11.

37. Mike Dodd, "Comic books go modern but maintain values," *Battle Creek Enquirer* (Gannett, 30 September 1984), A-10.

38. Dan Taylor, "Zapping the POWers that be," *The Press Democrat* (Sonoma Media Investments, 10 February 1984), 1D.

39. D.R. Martin, "Upgraded comic book illustrates the dark side of superheroism," *Star Tribune* (Star Tribune Media Company, 17 January 1988), 11F.

40. Editorial, "Opponents overreact to threat of obscenity," *Angus-Leader* (Gannett, 11 February 1988), 8A.

41. Sara Williams and Lane Crockett, "Cash in on comics," *News-Press* (News-Press & Gazette Company, 15 December 1991), 1F.

42. Beth Ann Krier, "Drawing on the Cool Factor," *The Los Angeles Times* (Los Angeles Times Communications, 15 April 1992), E1.

43. Tim Tesconi, "Superman comic book's super price," *The Press Democrat* (Sonoma Media Investments, 1 December 1992), B1.

44. Walter Pierce, "'Blade' defies comic book-based movie stereotype," *The Daily Advertiser* (Gannett, 4 September 1998), 3.

45. Nico Lang, "Marvel is ruining superhero movies: Corporate synergy is a poor substitute for artistic vision," *Salon* (Richmond and Schoentrup, 2016), https://www.salon.com/2016/05/18/marvel_is_ruining_superhero_movies_corporate_synergy_is_a_poor_substitute_for_artistic_vision/.

46. Sandy Cohen, "Hollywood animates San Diego's Comic-Con," *Austin American-Statesman* (Gannett, 21 July 2010), D2.

Chapter 1

1. Stephen Lee and Sidney Lee, *Dictionary of National Biography,* vol. 48 (London: Smith, Elder, & Co., 1896), 47.

2. Kate Loveman, *Romantic Echoes in the Victorian Era* (Farnham: Ashgate, 2008), 100.

3. Beerbohm, Wheeler, and De Sá, "Töpffer in America," 28–47.

4. W.G. Rogers, "A Family Is a Family," *Tucson Daily Citizen* (Gannett, 30 September 1967), 6.

5. Brian Walker, "100 Years of King Features Syndicate—Part One," *Public Opinion* (Gannett, 15 November 2015), 2.

6. Ian Gordon, *Comic Strips and Consumer Culture* (Washington, D.C., Smithsonian Institution, 1998), 31–32.

7. John Goodspeed, "Comic strip books, past and present," *The Star-Democrat* (Adams Publishing Group, 19 January 1996), 4D.

8. Robert C. Harvey, *The Art of the Funnies: An Aesthetic History* (Jackson: University Press of Mississippi, 1994), 7.

9. Leonard Lyons, "The Lyons Den," *The Bangor Daily News* (Bangor Publishing Company, 7 July 1949), 15.

10. Brian Walker, *The Comics* (HNA, 2002), 26.

11. R.C. Harvey, "OUTCAULT, GODDARD, THE COMICS, AND THE YELLOW KID," *The Comics Journal* (Fantagraphics, 2016), https://www.tcj.com/outcault-goddard-the-comics-and-the-yellow-kid/.

12. Philip Love, "April `71-`72 is Diamond Jubilee for Comics," *The Columbia Record* (Knight-Ridder, 21 April 1971), 2-C.

13. Otto Dekom, "266 German Kids on Public View," *The News Journal Papers* (Gannett, 14 November 1979), 30.

14. Allan Holtz, *American Newspaper Comics: An Encyclopedic Reference Guide* (Ann Arbor: The University of Michigan Press, 2012), 183.

15. James Stuart Blackton and Albert E. Smith, *Hooligan Assists the Magician* (Thomas A. Edison, 1900), 0:00–1:41.

16. Thomas Andrae and Jerry Siegel, "Of Superman and Kids with Dreams," *NEMO: The Classics Comics Library* #2 (Seattle: Fantagraphics, 1983), 6–19.

17. John Canemaker, *Winsor McCay: His Life and Art* (New York: Harry N. Abrams, 2005), 175.

18. Jim Vadeboncoeur, Jr., "About Winsor McCay," *Little Nemo in Slumberland So Many Splendid Sundays* (Palo Alto: Sunday Press Books, 2014), 1.

19. John Canemaker, *Winsor McCay: His Life and Art* (New York: Harry N. Abrams, 2005), 164, 168.

20. Harvey, "Thematic Choruses of Bud Fisher and George McManus," *The Art of the Funnies: An Aesthetic History*, 37.

21. "Fisher Is Original Hard-Boiled Egg," *Edmonton Journal* (Postmedia Network, 24 April 1926), 3.

22. Star Co. v. Wheeler Syndicate (Supreme Court, New York Special Term, 1915), 91 Misc. 640.

23. Fisher v. Star Co. (United States Court of Appeals New York, 1921), 231 NY 414.

24. Arthur Berger, "Krazy Kat's Creator," *St. Lous Post-Dispatch* (Lee Enterprises, 2 November 1971), 3A.

25. Gilbert Seldes, "The Krazy Kat That Walks by Himself," *The Comic Art of George Herriman* (New York: Harry N. Abrams, 2004), 17.

26. "The Amazing Spider-Man monthly sales," (Comichron, 2021), https://www.comichron.com/titlespotlights/amazingspiderman.html.

27. Patrick McDonnel, Karen O'Connell, and Georgia Riley De Havenon, *Krazy Kat: The Comic Art of George Herriman* (New York: Abradale Press, 1986), 214.

28. *Ibid.*, 217.

29. *Ibid.*, 165.

30. Jeet Heer, "The Most Musical of Cartoonists, Cliff Sterrett," *Polly and Her Pals 1913–1927* (IDW, 2010), 11–15.

31. M. Thomas Inge, *Comics as Culture* (Jackson: University Press of Mississippi, 1990), 82.

Chapter 2

1. "New York News Publisher, Joseph M. Patterson, Dies," *Great Falls Tribune* (United Press International, 27 May 1946), 1, 6.

2. John Serbell, "Dick Tracy: 50 Golden Years," *The Oklahoma Times* (Oklahoma Publishing Company, 1 December 1981), 10.

3. "William R. Hearst Dies; Founder of Modern Era of Journalism, Was 88," *Binghamton Press* (Gannett, 14 August 1951), 26.

4. Bruce Smith, "'Annie' again," *Daily News* (Tribune Publishing, 9 May 1982), C11.

5. Harold Gray, *Little Orphan Annie* vol. 1 (San Diego: IDW, 2008), 36.

6. *Ibid.*, 37.

7. *Ibid.*, 194.

8. *Ibid.*

9. "Linlee School Notes," *The Lexington Herald* (The McClatchy Company, 18 March 1934), 8.

10. Jackie Harper, "Spiderman's a Big Man on Campus," The Honolulu Advertiser (Black Press, 29 April 1968), D7.

11. Harold Gray, *Little Orphan Annie* vol. 4 (San Diego: IDW, 2009), 88.

12. *Ibid.*, 88.

13. Steve Ditko, *The Mr. A Collection* (Seattle: Fantagraphics, 1985), 20.

14. Gray, *Little Orphan Annie* vol. 1, 368.

15. *Ibid.*, 316.

16. Harold Gray, *Little Orphan Annie* vol. 2 (San Diego: IDW, 2009), 160.

17. *Ibid.*, 168.

18. *Ibid.*, 169.

19. Serbell, "Dick Tracy: 50 Golden Years," 10.

20. Brian Walker, *The Comics* (New York: Harry N. Abrams, 2004), 226.

21. Chester Gould, *Dick Tracy Dailies & Sundays 1938–1939* (San Diego: IDW, 2008), 6 October 1938.

22. Chester Gould, *Dick Tracy Dailies & Sundays 1931–1933* (San Diego: IDW, 2016), 18.

23. Gould, *Dick Tracy Dailies & Sundays 1938–1939*, 22 January 1938.

24. Chester Gould, *Dick Tracy Dailies & Sundays 1935–1936* (San Diego: IDW, 2013), 19 March 1935.

25. Chester Gould, *Dick Tracy Dailies & Sundays 1933–1935* (San Diego: IDW, 2009), 11 November 1934.

26. Chester Gould, *Dick Tracy Dailies & Sundays 1936–1938* (San Diego: IDW, 2013), 3 February 1937.

27. *Ibid.*, 19 November 1937.

28. *Ibid.*, 9 January 1938.

29. Curt Swan, *Superman's Girl Friend Lois Lane* (DC Comics, 1970), cover.

30. Gould, *Dick Tracy Dailies & Sundays 1935–1936*, 29 January 1935.

31. J.A. Lewis and M. Cuppari, "The polygraph: The truth lies within," *Journal of Psychiatry and Law* 27, no. 37 (Elsevier, 2009): 85-92.

32. Gould, *Dick Tracy Dailies & Sundays 1931–1933*, 20 November 1932.

33. Kane and Finger, "The Case of the Chemical Syndicate," *Detective Comics* #27, 6.

34. Jerry Siegel and Joe Shuster, "Superman Champions Universal Peace," *Superman* #2 (DC Comics, 1939), 20.

35. Gould, *Dick Tracy Dailies & Sundays 1933–1935* (San Diego: IDW, 2009), 16 March 1934.

36. Gould, *Dick Tracy Dailies & Sundays 1938–1939* (San Diego: IDW, 2008), 21 March 1938.

37. Stan Lee, "Meet Stan Lee," *Bachelor* #1 (Chasan, 1968), 33.

38. Gary Groth and Jack Kirby, "Jack Kirby Interview with Gary Groth," *The Comics Journal* #134 (Fantagraphics, 1990), 63.

39. John Romita and Roy Thomas, *Alter Ego* vol. 3 #9 (TwoMorrows, 2013), 7.

40. Jim Amash and Carmine Infantino, *Carmine Infantino, Penciler-Publisher-Provocateur* (Raleigh: TwoMorrows, 2010), 9.

41. Stan Lee, *Comic Book Greats with Bob Kane* (Excelsior Productions, 1992), 34:00.

42. Andrew Welsh-Huggins, "Rembrandt of the comics," *Daily Press* (Tribune Publishing, 28 October 2007), G3.

43. "Joseph Medill Patterson, Playwright, Is a Millionaire Socialist," *The Kansas City Times* (McClatchy, 5 May 1911), 2.

44. "About Caniff and a Guy Named Steve," *The Charlotte News* (Chatham Asset Management, 11 January 1947), 11A.

45. Bob Kane and Tom Andrae, *Batman & Me* (Forestville: Eclipse Books, 1989), 30.

46. Lee, "Meet Stan Lee," *Bachelor* #1, 33.

47. Milton Caniff, *The Complete Terry and the Pirates* vol. 1 (San Diego: IDW, 2007), 328.

48. *Ibid.*, 96.

49. Bob Kane, Bill Finger, and Jerry Robinson, *Batman* #1 (Detective Comics, 1940), 45.

50. Milton Caniff, *The Complete Terry and the Pirates* vol. 2 (San Diego: IDW, 2007), 227.

51. Tom DeFalco, "John Romita," *Comics Creators on Spider-Man* (Titan, Books 2004), 36.

52. Milton Caniff, *The Complete Terry and the Pirates* vol. 3 (San Diego: IDW, 2008), 64.

53. Milton Caniff, *The Complete Terry and the Pirates* vol. 4 (San Diego: IDW, 2008), 155.

54. Jon B. Cooke, "John Romita on Milton Caniff," *Comic Book Creator* #21 (TwoMorrows, 2019), 24.

55. Caniff, *The Complete Terry and the Pirates* vol. 3, 161.

56. Carmine Infantino and Gardner Fox, *Flash* #150 (DC Comics, 1965), 4.

57. Mort Meskin, *More Fun* #85 (DC Comics, 1942), 46.

58. Caniff, *The Complete Terry and the Pirates* vol. 4, 252.

59. Bruce Canwell, "The Protean Illustrator," *Scorchy Smith and the Art of Noel Sickles* (San Diego: IDW, 2008), 47.

60. Caniff, *The Complete Terry and the Pirates* vol. 4, 258.

61. Cooke, "John Romita on Milton Caniff," *Comic Book Creator* #21, 23.

62. "'Steve Canyon' Out and 'Cathy' Strip Begins," *Victoria Advocate* (M. Roberts Media, 5 June 1988), 1.

63. Milton Caniff, *Steve Canyon* vol. 1 (San Diego: IDW, 2012), 24.

64. James Gardner, "The Man Who Made Marvel," *The Winchester Sun* (Boone Newspapers, 24 November 2018), A9.

65. Caniff, *Steve Canyon* vol. 1, 162.

66. "Now Introducing the One-And-Only Popeye the Sailorman," *The World* (Lee Enterprises, 17 October 1936), 5.

67. Lee, *Comic Book Greats with Bob Kane*, 27:00.

68. EC Segar, *Popeye* vol. 1 (Seattle: Fantagraphics, 2006), 117.

69. *Ibid.*, 122.

70. EC Segar, *Popeye* vol. 2 (Seattle: Fantagraphics, 2007), 23.

71. *Ibid.*, 65.

72. Chris Claremont and John Byrne, *The Uncanny X-Men* #133 (Marvel, 1980), 4.

73. Chris Claremont and Dave Cockrum, *The Uncanny X-Men* #96 (Marvel, 1975), 13.

74. Segar, *Popeye* vol. 1, 157.

75. EC Segar, *Popeye* vol. 3 (Seattle: Fantagraphics, 2008), 13.

76. *Ibid.*, 24.

77. *Ibid.*, 27.

78. Segar, *Popeye* vol. 2, 108.

79. *Ibid.*, 153.

80. *Ibid.*, 92.

81. *Ibid.*, 30.

82. Chris Claremont and Frank Miller, *Wolverine* #1 (Marvel, 1982), 1.

Chapter 3

1. Gray, *Little Orphan Annie* vol. 1, 80.

2. Gould, *Dick Tracy Dailies & Sundays 1931–1933* vol. 1, 21 October 1931.

3. *Ibid.*, Oct. 2, 1932.

4. Gould, *Dick Tracy Dailies & Sundays 1933–1935* vol. 2, 30 July 1933.

5. Andrae and Siegel, "Of Superman and Kids with Dreams," *NEMO: The Classics Comics Library* #2, 6–19.

6. Burne Hogarth, *Tarzan and the City of Gold* (London: Titan, 2014), 149.

7. E.C. Segar, *Popeye* (Seattle: Fantagraphics, 2007), 48.

8. Caniff, *Terry and the Pirates* vol. 2, 229.

9. Bob Kane, "A Preference for Newspaper Strips," *Batman: The Dailies 1943–1946* (Princeton: Kitchen Sink Press, 2007), vol. II 5.

10. Bob Kane, Bill Finger, and Jerry Robinson, "Robin the Boy Wonder," *Detective Comics* #38 (DC Comics, 1940), 3.

11. Joe Desris, "Tracy's Influence," *Batman: The Sunday Classics 1943–1946* (Princeton: Kitchen Sink Press, 2007), 208.

12. Joe Desris, "A History of the 1940s Batman Newspaper Strip Part 2," *Batman: The Dailies 1943–1946* vol. II (Princeton: Kitchen Sink Press, 2007), 14.

13. Kane and Andrae, *Batman & Me*, 41.

14. Lee Falk and Ray Moore, *The Phantom vol.1 1936–1937* (New Castle: Hermes Press, 2010), 138.

15. Gary Groth and Carmine Infantino, "The Carmine Infantino Interview," *TCJ.com* (Seattle: Fantagraphics, 2010), https://www.tcj.com/the-carmine-infantino-interview/.

16. Amash and Infantino, *Carmine Infantino, Penciler-Publisher-Provocateur*, 9.

17. Tim Skelly and Jack Kirby, "My School Was Alex Raymond and Milton Caniff," *The Nostalgia Journal* #27 (Seattle: Fantagraphics, 1976), 17.

18. RC Harvey and Murphy Anderson, *The Life and Art of Murphy Anderson* (Raleigh: TwoMorrows, 2003), 18.

19. Andrae and Siegel, "Of Superman and Kids with Dreams," *NEMO: The Classics Comics Library* #2, 6–19.

20. *Ibid.*, 6–19.

21. Groth and Kirby, "Jack Kirby Interview with Gary Groth," *The Comics Journal* #134, 62.

22. Mark Evanier, "Introduction," *Jack Kirby's The Demon* (DC Comics, 2008), 4.

23. Groth and Kirby, "Jack Kirby Interview with Gary Groth," *The Comics Journal* #134, 63.

24. Stan Lee and Jack Kirby, "Meet the Skrulls from Outer Space," *Fantastic Four* #2 (Marvel, 1962), 6.

25. Stephen Baxter, *War of the Worlds: Fresh Perspectives on the H.G. Wells Classic* (Dallas: Benbella, 2005), 186–187.

26. Dick Calkins, *Buck Rogers in the 25th Century* vol. 1 (New Castle: Hermes Press, 2009), 204.

27. Roy Thomas, "Introduction," *Marvel Masterworks Captain Marvel* vol. 2 (New York: Marvel, 2007), 2.

28. Laura Hudson, "Real-life heroes and villains of Marvel Comics," *The Los Angeles Times* (Los Angeles Times Communications, 14 October 2012), E6.

29. Gray, *Little Orphan Annie* vol. 1, 284.

Chapter 4

1. Coogan, *Superhero: The Secret Origin of a Genre*, 30.

2. Quentin Reynolds, "From Nick Carter to the Slicks," *The Evening Sun* (Gannett, 1956), 20.

3. Jess Nevins, *The Evolution of the Costumed Avenger: The 4,000-Year History of the Superhero* (Westport: Praeger, 2017), 119.

4. Jerome Siegel, *Amazing Stories* (Gernsback Publications, August 1929), 474–475.

5. Andrae and Siegel, "Of Superman and Kids with Dreams," *NEMO: The Classics Comics Library* #2, 6–19.

6. Phil Seuling, "Jim Steranko & Gardner Fox at the 1971 Comic Art Convention Luncheon," *1972 Comic Art Convention Programme* (Seuling, 1972), 70–78.

7. Jerry Belcher, "Shazam! Comic Books Turn 50," *The Charlotte Observer* (The McClatchy Company, 25 July 1984), 3D.

8. Isidor Feinstein, "A Huge Hero," *Courier-Post* (Gannett, 29 May 1930), 8.

9. Philip Wylie, *Gladiator Annotated* (New York: Independently Published, 2021), 5.

10. Jerry Siegel and Joe Shuster, "Superman," *Action Comics* #1 (DC Comics, 1938), 1.

11. Larry Tye, *Superman: The High-Flying History of America's Most Enduring Hero* (New York: Random House, 2012), 33.

12. Edwin Balmer and Philip Wylie, "When World's Collide," *The Friend Sentinel* (Seward Independent, 24 January 1935), 6.

13. Al Williamson and Peter Poplaski, "Introduction to Alex Raymond," *Flash Gordon: Mongo, the Planet of Doom* (Northampton: Kitchen Sink Press, 1990), 5.

14. Robert Worth, "Savage Man Is Taught Modern Man's Manners," *The Charlotte News* (Chatham Asset Management, 27 November 1932), 6B.

15. Lester Dent, *The Man of Bronze* (Canada: pgdpcanada, 2017), 10.

16. Will Murray, *Writings in Bronze—Kindle* (Grand Rapids: Altus Press, 2011), 413.

17. Joe Simon and Jack Kirby, *The Double Life of Private Strong* #1 (Archie, 1959), 4.

18. Alan Moore and Chris Sprouse, *Tom Strong* #1 (America's Best Comics, 1999), 15.

19. Dent, *The Man of Bronze*, 6, cover.

20. *Ibid.*, 108.

21. *Ibid.*, 9.

22. Lester Dent, *Fortress of Solitude* (Canada: pgdpcanada, 2017), 8.

23. Wayne Boring and Stan Kaye, *Superman* #58 (DC Comics, 1949), 39.

24. Dent, *Fortress of Solitude*, 102.

25. Lester Dent, *Brand of the Werewolf* (Canada: pgdpcanada, 2017), 14.

26. *Ibid.*, 28.

27. Bob Kane, Bill Finger, Gardner Fox, and Sheldon Moldoff, *Detective Comics* #33 (DC Comics, 1939), 3.

28. Dent, *The Man of Bronze*, 23.

29. Dent, *The Man of Bronze*, 120.

30. Kane, Finger, Fox, and Moldoff, *Detective Comics* #33, 3.

31. Dent, *The Man of Bronze*, 125.

32. Dent, *Fortress of Solitude*, 23.

33. Dent, *The Man of Bronze*, 17.

34. Kane, Finger, Fox, and Moldoff, *Detective Comics* #33, 11.

35. Lester Dent, *The Sargasso Ogre* (Canada: pgdpcanada, 2021), 111.

36. Will Murray, "The Shadowy Origins of Batman," *The Shadow by Maxwell Grant* (Vista: The Sanctum Books/Nostalgia Ventures, 2007), 71.

37. Lester Dent, *The Thousand-Headed Man* (Canada: pgdpcanada, 2017), 87.

38. Will Murray, "The Retrospective Stan Lee," *Alter Ego* #150 (TwoMorrows, 2018), 8.

39. Dent, *The Man of Bronze*, 6.

40. Stan Lee and Jack Kirby, *Fantastic Four* #2 (Marvel, 1962), 11.

41. Dent, *The Man of Bronze*, 7.

42. *Ibid.*, 5.

43. *Ibid.*, 38.

44. Bob Kane, Gardner Fox, and Sheldon Moldoff, *Detective Comics* #31 (DC Comics, 1939), 4.

45. Bruce Hamilton, "A Talk with Artist-Writer-Editor Jack Kirby," *Jack Kirby Collector* vol. 4 (Raleigh: TwoMorrows, 2004), 188.

46. JS Mackley, *Spring-Heeled Jack: The Terror of London (1886)* (London: Independently Published, 2020), i.

47. "Spring-Heeled Jack," *Southern Kansas Journal* (Severy, Kan, 3 October 1884), 3.

48. JS Mackley, *Spring-Heeled Jack: Articles and Short Fiction (1838–1897)* (London: Independently Published, 2020), i.

49. Jim Steranko, *The Steranko History of Comics* #1 (Reading: Supergraphics, 1970), 45.

50. Will Murray, "Maxwell Grant's Shadow Theodore Tinsley Interviewed by Will Murray," *The Shadow: Cyro* (San Antonio: Sanctum Books, 2012), 123.

51. JS Mackley, *Spring-Heeled Jack (1904)* (London: Independently Published, 2020), 9.

52. Theodore Tinsley, *Partners of Peril* (Blackmask Online, 2001), 51, 40, 26.

53. Mackley, *Spring-Heeled Jack (1904)*, 9.

54. Kane and Finger, "The Case of the Chemical Syndicate," *Detective Comics* #27, 5.

55. Mackley, *Spring-Heeled Jack (1904)*, 15.

56. *Ibid.*, 11.

57. *Ibid.*, 27.

58. *Ibid.*, 14.

59. Bob Kane and Bill Finger, *Detective Comics* #28 (DC Comics, 1939), 2.

60. *Ibid.*, 6.

61. Kane and Finger, *Detective Comics* #27, 8.

62. Kane, Finger, Fox, and Moldoff, *Detective Comics* #33, 2.

63. Bob Kane and Bill Finger, *Detective Comics* #29 (DC Comics, 1939), 11.

64. Kane and Finger, *Detective Comics* #27, 8.

65. Mackley, *Spring-Heeled Jack (1904)*, 28–30.

66. Kane and Finger, *Detective Comics* #27, 8.

67. Mackley, *Spring-Heeled Jack (1904)*, 29.

68. Baroness Orczy, "An Adventure of the

Scarlet Pimpernel," *Tampa Bay Times* (Poynter Institute, 27 December 1925), 34.

69. Frank L. Packard, "The Adventures of Jimmie Dale," *The Journal* (White Family, 20 April 1921), 7.

70. Ron Goulart, "Introduction," *The Phantom: The Complete Newspaper Dailies* vol. 1 (New Castle: Hermes Press, 2010), 5–6.

71. Anthony Tollin, "Spotlight on The Shadow," *The Shadow #1: The Golden Vulture and Crime Insured*. (Encinitas: Nostalgia Ventures, June 2006), 4–5.

72. Steranko, *The Steranko History of Comics #1*, 45.

73. Philip Schweier, "Shedding Light on the Shadow," *Back Issue! #89* (TwoMorrows, 2016), 8.

74. Murray, "The Shadowy Origins of Batman," *The Shadow by Maxwell Grant*, 71.

75. Lew Merrill, "Batman," *Spicy Mystery Stories* (Culture Publications, February 1936), 16.

76. Steranko, *The Steranko History of Comics #1*, 45.

77. Joe Simon and Louis Cazeneuve, "The Red Raven," *Red Raven Comics #1* (Timely, 1940), 8.

78. Nils Sonderland, "The Angel from Hell," *Marvel Tales #6* (Western Fiction Publishing, 1938), 10.

79. "Variation on the Visitor from Mars," *Fort Worth Star-Telegram* (The McClatchy Co., 6 September 1936), 7.

80. Olaf Stapledon, *Odd John & Sirius* (Dover Publications, 1972), 121.

81. Stan Lee and Jack Kirby, *The X-Men #1* (Marvel, 1963), 11.

82. NV Romero, "The X-Man," *Star Detective Magazine* vol. 2, #1 (Western Fiction Publishing Co., March 1937), 6.

83. Henry Kuttner, "Way of the Gods," *Thrilling Wonder Stories* vol. 30, #1 (A Thrilling Publication, 1947), 11.

84. Wilmar Shiras, "Children of the Atom," *Astounding Science Fiction* (Street & Smith Publications, 1948), 40.

85. Mickey Friedman, "Recycled Science Fiction," *The San Francisco Examiner* (Clint Reilly Communications, 31 July 1978), 18.

86. Raymond Krank and Dick Ayers, "The Ghost Rider!," *Tim Holt #11* (Magazine Enterprises, 1949), 10.

87. Dick Ayers, Gary Friedrich, and Roy Thomas, "Origin of the Ghost Rider," *The Ghost Rider #1* (Marvel, 1967), 1.

88. Robert Kanigher and Ross Andru, "Suicide Squad," *Brave and the Bold #25* (DC Comics, 1959), 6.

89. Sidney Bradd, "Robert J. Hogan," *Ageofaces.net* (Age of Aces, 2019), https://www.ageofaces.net/authors-artists/robert-j-hogan/.

90. Ron Goulart, *Ron Goulart's Great History of Comic Books* (Chicago: Contemporary Books, 1986), 55.

91. Nicky Wheeler-Nicholson, *DC Comics Before Superman* (New Castle: Hermes Press, 2018), 12, 15.

92. Robert Erisman, "Avengers of Space," *Marvel Science Stories #1* (Postal Publications, August 1938), 98.

93. Neal Gendler, "Whiz Bang Days named in honor of Capt. Billy," *Star Tribune* (Star Tribune Media Company, 7 July 1983), 13.

94. Ken Quattro, "Elton Clay Fox & George Dewey Lipscomb," *Invisible Men: The Trailblazing Black Artists of Comic Books* (YoeBooks/IDW, 2020), 103–114.

95. Jim Steranko, *The Steranko History of Comics #2* (Reading: Supergraphics, 1972), 29–37.

96. Frederick Arnold Kummer, Jr., "Dark Invasion," *Marvel Science Stories #5* (Western Fiction Pub. Co., August 1939), 6.

Chapter 5

1. Tracey Goessel, *The First King of Hollywood* (Chicago: Chicago Review Press, 2016), 2.

2. Kane and Andrae, *Batman & Me*, 9.

3. *Ibid.*, 38.

4. *Ibid.*, 38, 41.

5. Les Daniels and Chip Kidd, *Batman: The Complete History* (San Francisco: Chronicle Books, 1999), 23.

6. Joe Kubert, "Introduction," *The Viking Prince* (DC Comics, 2010), 5.

7. Anthony Wall, *The Comic Strip Hero* (BBC, 1981), 2:40.

8. Reviewer "'The Bat Whispers' at State this Week," *The News and Observer* (The McClatchy Company, 23 November 1930), 7.

9. Kane and Andrae, *Batman & Me*, 38.

10. Lee, *Comic Book Greats with Bob Kane*, 11:38.

11. Kane and Andrae, *Batman & Me*, 107.

12. Arthur Lennig, *The Immortal Count: The Life and Films of Bela Lugosi* (Lexington: The University Press of Kentucky, 2003), 144.

13. Kane and Andrae, *Batman & Me*, 41.

14. Kane and Finger, *Detective Comics #29*, 5.

15. Paul Harrison, "Screen Chats," Shamokin News-Dispatch (Sample News Group, 27 November 1939), 9.

16. Stephen Lynch, "Boris Karloff inspired creation of the Hulk," *The Post-Star* (Lee Enterprises, 20 June 2003), D6.

17. Groth and Kirby, "Jack Kirby Interview with Gary Groth," *The Comics Journal #134*, 82.

18. Reporter, "Zipper Saves Time of Invisible Man," *Democrat and Chronicle* (Gannett, 5 November 1939), 9D.

19. Lyle Rooks, "Genius in a Rouge Box," *Oakland Tribune* (Digital First Media, 29 November 1935), 9.

20. Gary Groth, *Wallace Wood Presents Shattuck Original Art Edition* (Seattle: Fantagraphics, 2016), 40.

21. *Ibid.*

22. "Johnny Weissmuller Buried," *The Courier-News* (Gannett, 23 January 1984), A-3.

23. Linda Rosenkrantz, "Rare and very vine: *Tarzan of the Apes* on page and screen," *Lancaster New Era* (LNP Media Group, 2003), A6.

24. Everett, "The Sub-Mariner," *Marvel Comics* #1, 34.

25. Roy Thomas, "Bill Everett & Joe Kubert Interviewed by Gil Kane & Neal Adams," *Alter Ego* #22 (TwoMorrows, August 2003), 7.

26. Brad Ricca, "Salvador Dali's Sub-Mariner," *Comics Beat* (Comicsbeat.com, 2015), https://www.comicsbeat.com/unassuming-barber-shop-salvador-dalis-sub-mariner/.

27. John Scott, "Ex-Tarzan talks, wears, Clothes as 'Jungle Jim,'" *The Los Angeles Times* (Los Angeles Times Communications, 16 December 1948), 47.

28. Jack Cluett, "Jest Among Ourselves," *Brooklyn Daily Eagle* (Brooklyn Daily Eagle, 22 September 1936), 17.

29. David Kaufman, "'Buster Crabbe' says July 4th at Clear Lake Happiest He's Had Since He Was Kid," *Globe-Gazette* (Lee Enterprises, 5 July 1941), 2.

30. SC Ringgenberg, "The Angelo Torres Interview," *The EC Artists Part 2* (Seattle: Fantagraphics, Books 2016), 157.

31. Dennis Dooley, "He can blow out 50 birthday candles with one puff!," *Great Falls Tribune* (Gannett, 17 January 1988), 6F.

32. Julius Schwartz and Brian M. Thomsen, *Man of Two Worlds* (New York: Harper Entertainment, 2000), 142.

33. John Cones, *Motion Picture Biographies: The Hollywood Spin on Historical Figures* (New York: Algora Publishing, 2015), 37.

34. Will Murray, "Marvel's Founding Father—MARTIN GOODMAN," *Alter Ego* #165 (TwoMorrows, 2020), 30.

35. Beard, Dallas, and Sacks, *American Comic Book Chronicles: 1970s*, 65.

36. Tony Thomas, Rudy Behlmer, and Clifford McCarty, *The Films of Errol Flynn* (Secaucus: Citadel Press, 1969), 31.

37. Joe Strike, "Comic Chameleons," *Daily News* (Tribune Publishing, 13 August 2006), 2.

38. John Coates, *Don Heck, A Work of Art* (Raleigh: TwoMorrows, 2014), 41.

39. Chip Carter and Jonathan Carter, "Spider-Man creator Stan Lee opens up," *Florida Today* (Gannett, 6 January 1996), 2D.

40. C.C. Beck, *Fawcett Companion: The Best of FCA* (Raleigh: TwoMorrows, 2001), 28–29.

41. William Cline, "Adventures of Captain Marvel in 1941 pioneered a completely new type of screen champion—the SuperHero," *In the Nick of Time* (Jefferson: McFarland & Co., 1984), 20.

42. Mark Voger, "The Ghost Who Walks," *Ashbury Park Press* (Gannett, 2 June 1996), E6.

43. "Superman joins nostalgia craze," *Johnson City Press* (Six Rivers Media, 5 July 1972), 22.

Chapter 6

1. Hervey Allen, *Israfel: The Life and Times of Edgar Allan Poe* (New York: Farrar & Rinehart, 1934), 224.

2. Charles David Abbott, "Howard Pyle," *Dictionary of American Biography* (New York: Scribner, 1935), 287–290.

3. Martyn Lyons, *Books: A Living History* (London: Thames & Hudson, 2011), 193–196.

4. Jeff A. Menges, *101 Great Illustrators from the Golden Age* (Mineola: Dover Publications, 2016), xii.

5. Allan Mazur, "U.S. trends in feminine beauty and over-adaptation," *Journal of Sex Research* #22 (Routledge, August 1984): 287.

6. Walker, *The Comics*, 147.

7. Jerry Siegel and Joe Shuster, *Action Comics* #2 (Detective Comics, 1938), 9.

8. James Saxon Childers, "1890 Dandy Left Wealth of Beauty," *The Birmingham News* (Advance Publications, 9 December 1934), 4.

9. Margie Fishman, "POE-Etic License," *The News Journal* (Gannett, 16 September 2012), F2.

10. Andy Webster, "Steve Ditko, 90, artist, co-creator of Spider-Man," *Republican and Herald* (Times-Shamrock, 8 July 2018), A10.

11. Humphrey Carpenter, Mari Prichard, *The Oxford Companion to Children's Literature* (Oxford: Oxford University Press, 1984), 440.

12. Clarence Hornung, *Will Bradley's Graphic Art* (Mineola: Dover, 2017), vi, viii.

13. *Ibid.*, v.

14. James Romberger, *Steranko: The Self-Created Man* (Silver Spring: Ground Zero Books, 2018), 9.

15. Charles G. Martignette and Louis K. Meisel, *Gil Elvgren: All His Glamorous American Pin-Ups* (Cologne: Taschen, 2003), 129.

16. Jeff A. Menges, *101 Great Illustrators from the Golden Age*, 28–29.

17. Alex Grand, *Comic Book Historians Group* (Facebook, 18 August 2018), https://www.facebook.com/groups/1604914006455533/search/?q=kaluta%20alex%20grand%20booth.

18. Mark Schulz, *Secret Agent Corrigan vol. 1: 1967–1969* (San Diego: IDW, 2013), 5–8.

19. Rick Veitch, *Secret Agent Corrigan vol. 4: 1974–1977* (San Diego: IDW, 2013), 5–7.

20. Al Williamson and Mark Schultz, *Joseph Clement Coll: The Art of Adventure* (Santa Cruz: Flesk Publications, 2003), ix.

21. *Ibid.*, xii.

22. Emily James, *Who's Who: An Annual Biographical Dictionary* vol. 59 (A&C Black, 1907), 130.

23. M. Dean, *The Studio* (Holland: Dragon's Dream, 1979), 104.

24. Howard Pyle, *Howard Pyle's Book of Pirates* (New York: Harper & Brothers, 1921), 105.

25. *Ibid.*, v.

26. J. David Spurlock, *John Buscema Sketchbook* (Lebanon: Vanguard, 2001), 27, 60–61.

27. "Pyle, Wyeth Gave Robin Hood Fame," *The Morning News* (The Morning News, 10 July 1946), 5.

28. Joseph Procopio, *The Lost Art of Ray Willner* (Silver Spring: Lost Art Books, 2014), 5.

29. Edward J. Sozanski, "No Pirates but some interesting Wyeth's," *The Philadelphia Inquirer* (The Philadelphia Foundation, 20 July 2001), W28.

30. "Patriotism in Art," *The Ogden-Standard-Examiner* (Ogden, 3 July 1964), 13.

31. "In times of crisis, America looks for a hero—and our patriotic patriarch is once again reporting for duty," *The Palm Beach Post* (Gannett, 24 September 2001), 3E.

32. Alex Ross and Steve Darnall, *Uncle Sam* (Vertigo, 1997), 1–2.

33. "In times of crisis, America looks for a hero—and our patriotic patriarch is once again reporting for duty," *The Palm Beach Post*, 3E.

34. Stephen D. Korshak, *The Paintings of J. Allen St. John Grand Master of Fantasy* (Vanguard, 2009), 89.

Chapter 7

1. "Are You Strong? If Not, Why Not?" *Belfast News-Letter* (JPI Media, 22 February 1899), 4.

2. "Macfadden Wins the Day," *The Central New Jersey Home News* (Gannett, 9 February 1907), 1.

3. Tim O'Connor, "Holy Homicide! It's the True Detectives!," *The Kansas City Times* (McClatchy, 20 May 1986), B7.

4. Joe Schwarcz, "Bernarr's ideas on exercise and whole grains were OK. But wood chewing?" *The Gazette* (Postmedia Network, 23 October 2005), IN6.

5. Jim Beckerman, "The strange, true story of kooky bodybuilding star, Bernarr Macfadden," *The Herald News* (Shaw Media, 3 June 2019), 6A.

6. Gerard Jones, *Men of Tomorrow: Geeks, Gangsters, and the Birth of the Comic Book* (New York: Basic Books, 2004), 70, 179.

7. Mary Cross, *A Century of American Icons: 100 Products and Slogans from the 20th-Century Consumer Culture* (Westport: Greenwood Press, 2002), 76–78.

8. "Program for Today at the World's Fair," *The New York Times* (The New York Times Company, 3 July 1940), 14.

9. Tim O'Connor, "Holy Homicide! It's the True Detectives!," *The Kansas City Times* (McClatchy, 20 May 1986), B7.

10. Will Eisner and Jack Kirby, "Jack Kirby," *Will Eisner's Spirit Magazine* #39 (Kitchen Sink, 1982), 24.

11. Jones, *Men of Tomorrow: Geeks, Gangsters, and the Birth of the Comic Book*, 70.

12. Jerome Siegel, *Amazing Stories* (Gernsback Publications, August 1929), 474–475.

13. Lester Del Rey, *The World of Science Fiction: 1926–1976: The History of a Subculture* (New York: Ballantine Books, 1979), 47.

14. Groth and Kirby, "Jack Kirby Interview with Gary Groth," *The Comics Journal* #134, 97.

15. Blake Bell and Dr. Michael J. Vassallo, *The Secret History of Marvel Comics* (Fantagraphics, 2013), 12.

16. Wheeler-Nicholson, *DC Comics Before Superman*, 9, 11.

17. Andrae and Siegel, "Of Superman and Kids with Dreams," *NEMO: The Classics Comics Library* #2, 6–19.

18. Schwartz and Thomsen, *Man of Two Worlds*, 8, 13.

19. John Peel, "Julius Schwartz," *Comics Feature* (New Media, 8 July 1984), 32–41.

20. Jerry Siegel and Joe Shuster, "Federal Men," *New Adventure Comics* #12 (DC Comics, 1937), 60.

21. Guy H. Lillian III, "Mort Weisinger: The Man Who Wouldn't Be Superman," *The Amazing World of DC Comics* #7 (DC Comics, 1975), 2–8.

22. Barbara Carlson, "Editor Hated Superman," *Hartford Courant* (Tribune Publishing, 7 February 1972), 7.

23. William Lindsay Gresham, *Houdini: The Man Who Walked Through Walls* (New York: Henry Holt & Company, 1959), 82–83.

24. "Takes London by Surprise," *Appleton Post* (Gannett, 21 April 1904), 2.

25. "Harry Houdini's Stunt," *The Times-Tribune* (Shamrock Communications, 7 August 1926), 6.

26. William Kalush and Larry Sloman, *The Secret Life of Houdini: The Making of America's First Superhero* (New York: Simon & Schuster, 2006), 375.

27. Curt Swan, *Superman's Girl Friend Lois Lane* (DC Comics, 1970), cover.

28. Ann Ehrenburg, "Who knows what magic lurks in the hearts of men?" *Fort Worth Star-Telegram* (The McClatchy Company, 3 September 1978), 24a.

29. Alex Grand and Jim Steranko, "The Steranko Experience," *Comic Book Historians YouTube Channel* (CBH, 2018), 09:21.

30. Tom Hennessy, "Pulps Arise from Dust of the Past," *Detroit Free Press* (Gannett, 9 November 1975), 13A.

31. Mark Evanier, *Kirby: King of Comics* (New York: Abrams, 2017), 185.

32. Anthony Slide, *The Encyclopedia of Vaudeville* (Jackson: University Press of Mississippi, 2012), 52.

33. "Super-Magician Comics vol. 1, #2," *Grand Comics Database*, https://www.comics.org/issue/1654/.

34. J. Randolph Cox, *Man of Magic and Mystery* (Metuchen: Scarecrow Press, 1988), 230.

35. Clarkkent54321, *Blackstone Master Magician Comics* (Comic Book Plus, 2012), https://comicbookplus.com/?dlid=29511.

36. "Blackstone #1," *Grand Comics Database*, https://www.comics.org/issue/6183/.

37. Chuck Davis, "What's in a name?" *The Vancouver Sun* (Postmedia Network, 11 April 2005), 15.

38. Lee Falk and Phil Davis, *Mandrake the Magician* (London: Titan, 2016), 28–29.

39. Fred Guardineer, "Zatara Master Magician," *Action Comics* #1 (DC Comics, 1938), 25.

40. Fred Guardineer, "Merlin the Magician," *National Comics* #12 (Quality Comics, 1941), 59.

41. Edd Ashe, "The Wizard," *Top Notch Comics* #1 (Archie, 1939), 12.

42. James Randi, *Conjuring* (New York: St. Martin's Press, 1992), 230.

43. Stan Lee, *Origins of Marvel Comics* (New York: Fireside, 1974), 223.

44. John B. Wentworth and Howard Purcell, "Sargon the Sorcerer," *All-American Comics* #26 (All American Publications, 1941), 40.

45. "Re-Creator of Souls," *Red Raven Comics* #1 (Timely, 1940), 47.

Chapter 8

1. Wheeler-Nicholson, *DC Comics Before Superman*, 9, 11.

2. Bob Andelman, *Will Eisner: A Spirited Life* (Milwaukie: M Press, 2005), 44–45.

3. "Superman Comic Strip Is Winner in Court Action," *Honolulu Star-Bulletin* (Black Press, 23 May 1940), 6.

4. Mitchell and Thomas, *American Comic Book Chronicles: 1940–1944*, 54.

5. Newt Alfred, "Master Man," *Master Comics* #1 (Fawcett Comics, 1940), 2.

6. Mike Benton, *Superhero Comics of the Golden Age: The Illustrated History* (Dallas: Taylor Publishing Company, 1992), 172.

7. Joe Simon and Jim Simon, *Comic Book Makers* (Lebanon: Vanguard, 2003), 54.

8. "Captain Marvel Serial to Begin," *The Honolulu Advertiser* (Black Press, 28 September 1941), 10.

9. "National Comics Publications v. Fawcett Publications," 93F Supp.349, *Court Listener* (S.D.N.Y., 1950), https://archive.ph/20140906072002/https://www.courtlistener.com/nysd/b79w/national-comics-publications-v-fawcett-publication/.

10. Simon and Simon, *Comic Book Makers*, 55.

11. *Ibid.*, 54–55.

12. Michael Uslan, *Superman: The World's Finest Comics Archives* vol. 1 (New York: DC Comics, 2004), 7.

13. Bill Schelly, *Harvey Kurtzman: The Man Who Created MAD and Revolutionized Humor in America* (Seattle: Fantagraphics, 2015), 260.

14. Simon and Simon, *Comic Book Makers*, 182.

15. Stan Lee, *The Comics Journal* #42 (Seattle: Fantagraphics, 1978), 54.

16. Mike Howlett, *The Weird World of Eerie Publications* (Port Townsend: Feral House, 2010), 282.

17. Lou Scheimer and Andy Mangels, *Lou Scheimer: Creating the Filmation Generation* (Raleigh: TwoMorrows, 2012), 158.

18. *Ibid.*, 171–172.

19. *Warner Bros. Inc. v. American Broadcasting Companies Inc.*, 720 F.2d 231–248 (2d Cir., 1983).

Chapter 9

1. Marjorie C. Malley, *Radioactivity: A History of a Mysterious Science* (Oxford: Oxford University Press, 2011), 78–79.

2. H. Geiger, Lord Rutherford, E. Regener, FA Lindemann, CTR Wilson, and J. Chadwick, "Discussion on Ultra-Penetrating Rays," *Proceedings of the Royal Society of London* (The Royal Society Publishing, 1931), 331–349.

3. Hugo Gernsback, "Hidden Wonders," *Science Wonder Stories* (Gernsback Publications, September 1929), 293.

4. H.G. Wells, *Star Begotten* (Freeditorial, 1937), 43.

5. "Smash Comics 14," (Quality, 1940), https://dc.fandom.com/wiki/Smash_Comics_Vol_1_14.

6. Lou Fine and Will Eisner, *Smash Comics* #14 (Quality, 1940), 34.

7. Jack Kirby and Joe Simon, *Blue Bolt* #6 (Novelty Press, 1940), 4.

8. Jack Burnley, *Adventure Comics* #61 (Detective Comics, 1940), 5.

9. Gilbert James, *Victory Comics* #1 (Hillman Comics, 1941), 32–33.

10. Jerry Robinson and Ken Crossen, *Atoman Comics* #1 (Spark Publications, 1946), 12.

11. Blake Bell, *Strange and Stranger: The World of Steve Ditko* (Seattle: Fantagraphics, 2008), 15, 20.

12. "Space Adventures 33" (Charlton, 1960), https://dc.fandom.com/wiki/Space_Adventures_Vol_2_33.

13. Steve Ditko and Joe Gill, *Space Adventures* #33 (Charlton, 1960), 20.

14. "Batman 127," (DC Comics, 1959), https://dc.fandom.com/wiki/Batman_Vol_1_127.

15. Bill Finger and Sheldon Moldoff, *Batman* #127 (DC Comics, 1959), 31.

16. John Broome and Carmine Infantino, *The Flash* #125 (DC Comics, 1961), 4.

17. Arnold Drake and Bruno Premiani, *Doom Patrol* #106 (DC Comics, 1966), 21.

18. *Ibid.*, cover.

19. Jack Kirby, Dave Wood, Wood Wallace, and Dick Ayers, *Sky Masters of the Space Force: The Complete Dailies* (New Castle: Hermes Press, 2017), 127.

20. Lee, *Origins of Marvel Comics*, 16–18.

21. Stan Lee and Jack Kirby, *Fantastic Four* #1 (Marvel Comics, 1961), 10.

22. Kathy Barberich, "Bullard alumnus draws on his talent at cartoon school," *The Fresno Bee* (The McClatchy Company, 6 January 1994), C8.

23. Bob Fujitani and Paul Newman, *Doctor Solar: Man of the Atom* #1 (Gold Key, 1962), 14.

24. Alan Moore and David Gibbons, "Watchmaker," *Watchmen* #4 (DC Comics, 1986), 12, 14.

Chapter 10

1. Larry Tye, *Superman: The High-Flying History of America's Most Enduring Hero*, 119.

2. Mark Evanier, *Set the TiVo!* (News From Me, July 27, 2020), https://www.newsfromme.com/2020/07/27/set-the-tivo-80/.

3. Jones, *Men of Tomorrow: Geeks, Gangsters, and the Birth of the Comic Book*, 244, 251–252.

4. Matthew Price, "'Superman' creators' forgotten character is examined," *The Daily Oklahoman* (Gannett, 28 May 2010), 10D.

5. *Ibid.*, 10D.

6. "Joe Shuster," *Grand Comics Database*, https://www.comics.org/checklist/name/Joe%20Shuster/?page=3.

7. Craig Yoe, *Secret Identity* (Abrams, 2009), 17–34.

8. Victoria Graham, "Originators of Superman Destitute," *Lansing State Journal* (Gannett, 25 November 1975), D-3.

9. Newsmakers, "Superman Turns into Santa for Two," *The Los Angeles Times* (Los Angeles Times Communications, 24 December 1975), 5.

10. Marschal Rothe, "Superman Originator, Publisher Visit Miami," *The Miami Herald* (Chatham Asset Management, 15 November 1950), 11-A.

11. Jerome Siegel, *Amazing Stories* (Gernsback Publications, August 1929), 474–475.

12. "Ziff-Davis," *Grand Comics Database*, https://www.comics.org/publisher/212/.

13. "Jerry Siegel," *Grand Comics Database*, https://www.comics.org/checklist/name/Jerry%20Siegel/?page=7.

14. J. David Spurlock, *John Buscema Sketchbook*, 27, 60–61.

15. Loftypilot and Josemas, *Mr. Muscles #22* (Comic Book Plus, 2012), https://comicbookplus.com/?dlid=26518.

16. Jones, *Men of Tomorrow: Geeks, Gangsters, and the Birth of the Comic Book*, 283.

17. Hendre Weisinger, *Comic Book Historians Podcast* (YouTube, 2020), https://youtu.be/Ed9858EOwPg?t=1474.

18. "Jerry Siegel," *Grand Comics Database*, https://www.comics.org/checklist/name/Jerry%20Siegel/?page=7-9.

19. "Jerry Siegel," *Grand Comics Database*, https://www.comics.org/checklist/name/Jerry%20Siegel/?page=7-9.

20. Larry Tye, *Superman: The High Flying History of America's Most Enduring Hero*, 272.

21. *Ibid.*, 272.

22. "Only things super are fond memories," *Fort Worth-Star Telegram* (The McClatchy Company, 25 November 1975), 13A.

23. Alexander Walker, "Day that scared the 'Godfather,'" *Evening Standard* (Evgeny Lebedev, 19 May 1975), 12.

24. David Vida, "Superman comes to the rescue of his creators," *The Press Democrat* (Sonoma Media Investments, 28 December 1975), 1.

25. Jerry Siegel and Val Mayerik, "The Starling," *Destroyer Duck #2* (Eclipse, 1983), 26–29.

26. Brad Ricca, *Super Boys* (New York: St. Martin's Press, 2013), 285–296.

27. "Superman co-creator dies," *The Leader-Post* (Postmedia Network, 1 February 1996), D7.

28. Roger Hill, *Reed Crandall: Illustrator of the Comics* (Raleigh: TwoMorrows, 2017), 9–17.

29. Tom Alstiel, Jean Grow, and Marcel Jennings, *Advertising Creative* (Thousand Oaks: SAGE Publications, 2018), 156.

30. Jon B. Cooke, "Reed Crandall," *The T.H.U.N.D.E.R. Agents Companion* (Raleigh: TwoMorrows, 2001), 67.

31. Steranko, *The Steranko History of Comics #2*, 92.

32. "Reed Crandall, Classic Draftsman, Dead at 65," *The Comics Journal #77* (Fantagraphics, November 1982), 12.

33. Reed Crandall, "Old Witch," *Hit Comics #10* (Quality, 1941), 55.

34. SC Ringgenberg, "An Interview with Al Feldstein," *The Comics Journal #177* (Fantagraphics, 1995), 79.

35. "Police Comics," *Grand Comics Database*, https://www.comics.org/series/226/covers/?page=3.

36. "Shock SuspenStories #9," *Grand Comics Database*, https://www.comics.org/issue/10579/.

37. "Reed Crandall, Classic Draftsman, Dead at 65," *The Comics Journal #77* (Fantagraphics, November 1982), 13.

38. Joseph Procopio, *The Lost Art of Ray Willner*, 5.

39. Michael Sawyer, "Albert Lewis Kanter and the Classics: The Man Behind the Gilberton Company," *The Journal of Popular Culture* 20 (Wiley-Blackwell, 1987): 1–18.

40. Virginia Rohan, "Spreading the Word," *The Record* (Gannett, 19 October 2008), F3.

41. Reed Crandall, *Treasure Chest of Fun and Fact* vol. 17, #8 (George A. Pflaum, 1960), 23.

42. Richard Lupoff, "SF Recollections," *Time Binders: Preserving Fannish History* (Timebinders, 1995), https://fanac.org/timebinders/lupoff.html.

43. Reed Crandall and Archie Goodwin, "The Coffin of Dracula," *Creepy #27* (Warren, 1969), 20.

44. Len Brown, "Foreword," *T.H.U.N.D.E.R. Agents Archives #6* (DC Comics, 2005), 7–10.

45. Reed Crandall, *T.H.U.N.D.E.R. Agents #1* (Tower, 1965), 20, 26.

46. Len Wein and Reed Crandall, *Creatures on the Loose #13* (Marvel, 1971), 31.

47. Steve Stiles, *A Look at EC Great, Reed Crandall* (SteveStiles, 2005), www.stevestiles.com/reedc.htm.

48. Marguerite Cotto, "Flash Gordon," *The Guide to United States Popular Culture* (GSU Popular Press, 2001), 283.

49. Drew Friedman, *Heroes of the Comics: Portraits of the Pioneering Legends of the Comic Books* (Seattle: Fantagraphics, 2014), 82.

50. Mac Raboy, *Master Comics #22* (Fawcett, 1942), 13.

51. Roger Hill, *Mac Raboy: Master of Comics* (Raleigh: TwoMorrows, 2019), 37.

52. Mac Raboy, *Green Lama* #1 (Spark Publications, 1944), 1.

53. "Deaths Elsewhere," *Chicago Tribune* (Tribune Publishing, 24 December 1967), 7.

54. Steranko, *The Steranko History of Comics* #2, 87.

55. *Ibid.*, 88.

56. Jack Cole, *Silver Streak Comics* #7 (Lev Gleason, 1941), 12.

57. Steranko, *The Steranko History of Comics* #2, 88.

58. Jack Cole, *Playboy* #5 (Playboy Enterprises, 1954), 25.

59. Jack Cole, *Comic Book Historians* (CBH, 2019), https://comicbookhistorians.com/jack-coles-suicide-note-to-hugh-hefner-1958/.

60. Mark Hamill, "Interview with Hugh Hefner," *Comic Book: The Movie* (Miramax, 2003), 18:08.

61. Alan Woollcombe, "Will Eisner," *The Independent* (Evgeny Lebedev, 6 January 2005), 43.

62. "Smash Comics #14," *Grand Comics Database*, https://www.comics.org/issue/1018/.

63. Simon and Simon, *Comic Book Makers*, 34.

64. Steven Brower, *Comics Ad Men* (Seattle: Fantagraphics, 2019), 11.

65. Lou Fine, "The Mystery of the Disappearing Bridge!," *Nabisco* (Nabisco, 1953), https://allthingsger.blogspot.com/2015/04/mixed-messages.html.

66. Will Eisner, "Interview with Gill Fox," *Will Eisner's Shop Talk* (Milwaukie: Dark Horse, 2001), 179.

67. Matt Silvie, "Dan Barry Dead at 73," *The Comics Journal* #194 (Fantagraphics, 1997), 29.

68. Canwell, "The Protean Illustrator," *Scorchy Smith and the Art of Noel Sickles*, 47.

69. Dave Schreiner, "Flash Gordon vs. The Reluctant Collaborators of Manhattan Isle," *Flash Gordon Dailies: Dan Barry—The City of Ice, 1951–1953* (Titan Comics, 2016), 8.

70. Jim Keefe, *Jimkeefe.com* (jimkeefe.com, 2021), https://www.jimkeefe.com/archives/4750#:~:text=1990%3A%20Dan%20Barry%20quits%20after,is%20called%20in%20to%20assist.

71. Louise Rough and Geoff Boucher, "Will Eisner, 87 and Pioneer of Graphic Novels," *The Los Angeles Times* (Los Angeles Times Communications, 5 January 2005), B8.

72. Alan Woollcombe, "Will Eisner," *The Independent* (Evgeny Lebedev, 6 January 2005), 43.

73. Ann Eisner, "Preface," *Will Eisner: The Best of the Preventive Maintenance Monthly* (Abrams, 2011), 8–9.

74. "Comics pioneer dies at age 87," *St. Cloud Times* (Gannett, 5 January 2005), 3A.

75. "Meet Our Science Fiction Family—Alex Schomburg," *Thrilling Wonder Stories* (Better Publications, June 1939), 87.

76. Jess Harold and John Rhett Thomas, *Marvel 80 for 80* (New York: Marvel, 2019), 14.

77. "Alex Schomburg," *Grand Comics Database*, https://www.comics.org/checklist/283/.

78. "Alex Schomburg Dies at Age 92," *The Comics Journal* #204 (Fantagraphics, 1998), 22.

Chapter 11

1. Jones, *Men of Tomorrow: Geeks, Gangsters, and the Birth of the Comic Book*, 164, 223.

2. Harold Keenan, "Comics Can Be Helpful," *The Courier-News* (Gannett, 22 July 1948), 14.

3. Editorial, "Prizes Won in Contest," *The Bennington Evening Banner* (Vermont News and Media, 12 October 1945), 3.

4. Diehl, *Tales from the Crypt: The Official Archives*, 18.

5. Gary Groth and Dwight Decker, "An Interview with William M. Gaines," *The Comics Journal* #81 (Fantagraphics, 1983), 56.

6. SC Ringgenberg, "An Interview with Al Feldstein," *The Comics Journal* #177 (Fantagraphics, 1995), 79.

7. Diehl, *Tales from the Crypt: The Official Archives*, 54.

8. Ringgenberg, "An Interview with Al Feldstein," *The Comics Journal* #177, 81.

9. JPC James, "Harvey Kurtzman Interview: 1965," *The Comics Journal* #153 (Fantagraphics, 1992), 50.

10. Groth and Decker, "An Interview with William M. Gaines," *The Comics Journal* #81, 79.

11. Sigrid Arne, "Loose Morals, Murder and Thievery Portrayed," *The Daily Argus-Leader* (Gannett, 17 October 1954), 2A.

12. Fredric Wertham, *The Brain as an Organ* (New York: Macmillan, 1934), 1–538.

13. "Fish Is Mentally Ill, Psychiatrist Testifies at Trial," *Record-Journal* (White Family, 29 March 1935), 11.

14. GB Lal, "New Mental Disease is Key to Easter Murders," *The Knoxville Journal* (Gannett, 9 April 1937), 19.

15. _____, "Explore Your Mind, With Baby's Blocks," *The San Francisco Examiner* (Clint Reilly Communications, 5 March 1944), 7.

16. Bart Beaty, *Fredric Wertham and the Critique of Mass Culture* (Jackson: University Press of Mississippi, 2005), 135–136.

17. "Publisher Denies Comic Book Harmful," *Dayton Daily News* (Cox, 22 April 1954), 6.

18. Groth and Decker, "An Interview with William M. Gaines," *The Comics Journal* #81, 64–65.

19. "Comic Book 'Czar' May Be Named," *The Tampa Tribune* (Tampa Media Group, 21 August 1954), 1.

20. Virginia Irwin, "New Czar of the Comic Book Industry," *St. Louis Post-Dispatch* (Lee Enterprises, 10 November 1954), 3F.

21. Less Barry, "The Barry Patch," *St. Albans Daily Messenger* (O'Rourke Media Group, 7 April 1955), 4.

22. Ringgenberg, "An Interview with Al Feldstein," *The Comics Journal* #177 (Fantagraphics, 1995), 83.

23. *Ibid.*, 84–85.

24. James, "Harvey Kurtzman Interview: 1965," *The Comics Journal* #153, 52.

25. Rich Hauser, "Bill Gaines: Vintage 1969," *Tales of Terror!* (Seattle: Fantagraphics Books and Gemstone Publishing, 2000), 176–85.

26. James, "Harvey Kurtzman Interview: 1965," *The Comics Journal* #153, 52.

27. Ringgenberg, "An Interview with Al Feldstein," *The Comics Journal* #177, 85.

28. Groth and Decker, "An Interview with William M. Gaines," *The Comics Journal* #81, 84.

29. Carol L. Tilley, "Seducing the Innocent: Fredric Wertham and the Falsifications That Helped Condemn Comics," *Information & Culture: A Journal of History* 47, no. 4 (2012): 383–413.

30. Estes Kefauver, "Comic Books and Juvenile Delinquency," *Committee on the Judiciary* (Senate Committee on the Judiciary Juvenile Delinquency, 1955–6), http://www.thecomicbooks.com/1955senateinterim.html.

31. Fredric Wertham, *The World of Fanzines* (Southern Illinois University Press, 1973), 35.

32. *Ibid.*, 33–61.

33. Karen McPherson, "Don't be afraid to let children read graphic novels. They're real books, too," *The Windsor-Star* (Postmedia Network, 14 March 2020), C12.

34. Mike Dodd, "Comic books go modern but maintain values," *Battle Creek Enquirer* (Gannett, 30 September 1984), A-10.

Chapter 12

1. Clark Kinnaird, "Great Prophet in Christmas Cards," *Kenosha News* (Lee Enterprises, 17 December 1965), 40.

2. Schwartz and Thomsen, *Man of Two Worlds*, 8, 13.

3. Eric Nash, "Julius Schwartz Comic-book editor revived superhero genre," *Pittsburgh Post-Gazette* (John Robinson Block, 14 February 2004), B-5.

4. Andrew A. Smith, "Julius Schwartz, a man of many worlds," *The Leaf-Chronicle* (Gannett, 14 February 2004), C7.

5. *Ibid.*

6. Alfred Bester, "The School for Vandals," *Green Lantern* #9 (All-American Comics, 1943), 12.

7. Julius Schwartz and John Broome, "The Origin of Captain Comet," *Strange Adventures* #9 (DC Comics, 1951), 6.

8. Julius Schwartz and John Broome, "The Guardians of the Clockwork Universe!," *Strange Adventures* #22 (DC Comics, 1951), 2.

9. Barba Vancheri, "A Super Club," *Pittsburgh Post-Gazette* (Block Communications, 13 June 2013), W-23.

10. Jim Keefe, *Jimkeefe.com* (jimkeefe.com, 2021), https://www.jimkeefe.com/archives/4750#:~:text=1990%3A%20Dan%20Barry%20quits%20after,is%20called%20in%20to%20assist.

11. Jack Miller, Joseph Samachson, and Joe Certa, "Manhunter from Mars," *Detective Comics* #225 (DC Comics, 1955), 25.

12. Paul Kupperberg, "Foreword," *The Flash Archives* vol. 1 (New York: DC Comics, 1996), 5–7.

13. Gardner Fox and Harry Lampert, *Flash Comics* #1 (All-American Comics, 1940), 2.

14. Schwartz and Thomsen, *Man of Two Worlds*, 87.

15. Carmine Infantino and J. David Spurlock, *Amazing World of Carmine Infantino* (Lebanon: Vanguard Publications, 2001), 51.

16. Gardner Fox and Carmine Infantino, "The Flash of Two Worlds," *The Flash* #123 (DC Comics, 1961), 4.

17. Gary Groth, "Gil Kane," *The Comics Journal* #186 (Fantagraphics, 1996), 79.

18. John Broome and Gil Kane, "S.O.S. Green Lantern," *Showcase* #22 (DC Comics, 1959), 4.

19. Associated Press, "People Throughout the Free World Anxiously Followed Glenn's Flight," *Johnson City Press* (Six Rivers Media, 1962), 1.

20. Schwartz and Thomsen, *Man of Two Worlds*, 89.

21. Eric Nash, "Julius Schwartz Comic-book editor revived superhero genre," *Pittsburgh Post-Gazette* (John Robinson Block, 14 February 2004), B-5.

22. Obituary, "Dr. Marston Dies," *The Daily Times* (Jones Media, 20 May 1947), 1.

23. Paul Norris and Mort Weisinger, "Aquaman," *Millennium Edition More Fun Comics* #73 (DC Comics, 2001), 60.

24. Robert Bernstein and Ramona Fradon, "How Aquaman Got His Powers!," *Adventure Comics* #260 (DC Comics, 1959), 17.

25. Jack Kirby and Ed Herron, "The Green Arrow," *Adventure Comics* #256 (DC Comics, 1959), 25.

26. Schwartz and Thomsen, *Man of Two Worlds*, 95.

27. Michael Eury, *The Justice League Companion: A Historical and Speculative Overview of the Silver Age Justice League of America* (Raleigh: Two-Morrows, 2005), 14.

28. Will Murray, "Three Easy Pieces Starring Julius Schwartz," *Alter Ego* vol. 3, #38 (TwoMorrows, 2004), 27.

29. Dennis Neville and Gardner Fox, "The Hawkman," *Flash Comics* #1 (All American Comics, 1940), 22.

30. Joe Kubert and Gardner Fox, *Hawkman* #1 (DC Comics, 1964), 3.

31. Alvin B. Webb, "Spaceman Shepard Safe, Survives Shot," *Daily Herald-Telephone* (Daily Herald Media, 5 May 1961), 1.

32. Bill O'Connor and Ben Flinton, "Introducing the Mighty Atom," *All-American Comics* #19 (All-American Comics, 1940), 9.

33. Roy Thomas, "Splitting the Atom," *Alter Ego* vol. 3, #2 (TwoMorrows, 1999), 8–13.

34. Schwartz and Thomsen, *Man of Two Worlds*, 88.

35. Jim Amash, "Foreword," *The Adam Strange Archives* vol. 1, 5–8.

36. Gardner Fox and Mike Sekowsky, "Secret of the Eternal City," *Showcase* #17 (DC Comics, 1958), 1.

37. Gardner Fox and Carmine Infantino, "The Multiple Menace Weapon!," *Mystery In Space* #72 (DC Comics, 1961), 2.

38. GB Love, "Wonders of Space via Rocket Mail," *Mystery in Space* #72 (DC Comics, 1961), 19.

39. J. Ballman, *The 1964 New York Comicon: The True Story Behind the World's First Comic Convention* (Totalmojo Productions, 2016), 9–41.

40. Michael Eury, "The Man Who Redesigned Batman," *The Batcave Companion* (Raleigh: Two-Morrows, 2009), 15–27.

41. Julius Schwartz, "Batman's Hot-Line," *Detective Comics* #327 (DC Comics, 1964), 20.

42. "Mystery in Space 82," *Grand Comics Database*, https://www.comics.org/issue/18428/.

43. Jerry Siegel and Bernard Baily, "The Spectre!," *More Fun Comics* #52 (DC Comics, 1940), 9.

44. Gardner Fox and Murphy Anderson, "The Spectre: War That Shook the Universe," *Showcase* #60 (DC Comics, 1966), 4.

45. Irvine and Dolan, *DC Comics Year by Year: A Visual Chronicle*, 89.

46. Dan Wallace, "Challengers of the Unknown," *The DC Comics Encyclopedia* (London: Dorling Kindersley, 2008), 77.

47. Carmine Infantino and Dave Wood, "I was the Man with Animal Powers," *Strange Adventures* #180 (DC Comics, 1965), 2.

48. Carmine Infantino and Arnold Drake, *Strange Adventures* #205 (DC Comics, 1967), 13.

49. Robert Kanigher, Ross Andru, and Mike Esposito, "Metal Men," *Showcase* #37 (DC Comics, 1962), 4.

50. Arnold Drake and Bruno Premiani, *Doom Patrol* #121 (DC Comics, 1968), 28.

51. Bob Haney and Bruno Premiani, *The Brave and the Bold* #54 (DC Comics, 1964), 2.

52. *Ibid.*, 25.

53. Gerard Jones and Will Jacobs, *The Comic Book Heroes* (New York: Prima Lifestyles, 1996), 76–77.

54. Mike W. Barr, "The Madames & the Girls, The DC Writers Purge of 1968," *Comic Book Artist Collection* vol. 2 (Raleigh: TwoMorrows, 2002), 57.

55. Amash and Infantino, *Carmine Infantino, Penciler-Publisher-Provocateur*, 103.

56. Dennis O'Neil and Dick Dillin, "Snapper Carr—Super-Traitor!," *Justice League of America* #77 (DC Comics, 1969), 4.

57. Richard Arndt, *Star Reach Companion* (Raleigh: TwoMorrows, 2013), 15–19.

58. Frank Robbins and Novick, Irv, "One Bullet Too Many!," *Batman* #217 (DC Comics, 1969), 3.

59. Schwartz and Thomsen, *Man of Two Worlds*, 131–135.

Chapter 13

1. Danny Fingeroth, *A Marvelous Life: The Amazing Story of Stan Lee* (New York: St. Martin's Publishing Group, 2019), 87.

2. Bill Schelly, *American Comic Book Chronicles 1950s* (Raleigh: TwoMorrows, 2013), 41.

3. Andrew A. Smith, "Insane bombshell in comics distribution world," *The Missoulian* (Lee Enterprises, June 21, 2020), C9.

4. Fingeroth, *A Marvelous Life: The Amazing Story of Stan Lee*, 65.

5. "Gunsmoke Western," *Grand Comics Database*, https://www.comics.org/series/1123/covers/?page=1.

6. Michael Vassallo, "Joe Maneely: Adventure Comics," *Marvel Masterworks Atlas Era Black Knight/Yellow Claw* (Marvel, 2009), 244.

7. Keith M. Booker, "Baker, Matt," *Comics Through Time* (Santa Barbara: Greenwood, 2014), 26.

8. Fingeroth, *A Marvelous Life: The Amazing Story of Stan Lee*, 21.

9. *Ibid.*, 26.

10. Evanier, *Kirby: King of Comics*, 19.

11. *Ibid.*, 35–37.

12. *Ibid.*, 40.

13. *Ibid.*, 42, 44.

14. Simon and Simon, *The Comic Book Makers*, 24–25.

15. *Ibid.*, 26–28.

16. Martin Burstein and Jack Kirby, "Mercury," *Red Raven Comics* #1 (Timely, 1940), 28.

17. Evanier, *Kirby: King of Comics*, 35–37.

18. Simon and Simon, *The Comic Book Makers*, 154–156.

19. Fingeroth, *A Marvelous Life*, 27–28.

20. *Writer's Digest* (Active Interest Media, February 1942), 22.

21. Fingeroth, *A Marvelous Life: The Amazing Story of Stan Lee*, 55.

22. Ronin Ro, *Tales to Astonish: Jack Kirby, Stan Lee, and the American Comic Book Revolution* (New York: Bloomsbury 2004), 35.

23. Simon and Simon, *Comic Book Makers*, 137, 148.

24. Ro, *Tales to Astonish: Jack Kirby, Stan Lee and the American Comic Book Revolution*, 54.

25. Cavna, Michael, "Trump's proposed 'Space Force' has its pop-culture roots in a little-known comic," *The Bellingham Herald* (The McClatchy Company, 28 June 2018), 15T.

26. Bell, *Strange and Stranger: The World of Steve Ditko*, 15–40.

27. "Issue Checklist for Creator Jack Kirby," *Grand Comics Database*, https://www.comics.org/checklist/2/?page=5-9.

28. Stan Lee, "Fantastic Fan Page 4," *Fantastic Four* #18 (Marvel, 1963), 29.

29. Gary Groth, "Editorial," *The Comics Journal* #75 (Fantagraphics, 1982), 4.

30. Will Murray, "Daredevil vs. The Avengers," *Alter Ego* #118 (TwoMorrows, 2013), 3–4.

31. Mark Evanier, "The Jack FAQ," (News From ME, 2013), 4.

32. Stan Lee and Wally Wood, *Daredevil* #5 (Marvel, 1964), 1.

33. Mark Evanier, "The Man Without Peer," *The Life and Legend of Wallace Wood* vol. 1 (Seattle: Fantagraphics, 2017), 248.

34. *Ibid.*, 248.

35. Stan Lee and Wally Wood, *Daredevil* #11 (Marvel, 1965), 20.

36. Steve Ditko, "Why I Quit S-M," *FPS* #9 (Robin Snyder, 2015), 1–4.

37. Bruce Hamilton, "A Talk with Artist-Writer-Editor Jack Kirby," *The Collected Jack Kirby Collector* vol. 4 (Raleigh: TwoMorrows, 2004), 188.

38. John Wells, *American Comic Book Chronicles 1965–1969* (Raleigh: TwoMorrows, 2014), 192–193.

Chatper 14

1. Fingeroth, *A Marvelous Life: The Amazing Story of Stan Lee*, 87.

2. "Marvel," *Grand Comics Database*, https://www.comics.org/publisher/78/?, 7, 14, 50, 53, 82, 107.

3. Bob Byrd and Ben Thompson, "Adventures of Ka-Zar the Great," *Marvel Comics* #1 (Timely, 1939), 53.

4. Murray, "Marvel's Founding Father—MARTIN GOODMAN," *Alter Ego* #165, 29.

5. Karen Walker, "Shattered Dreams: Vision and the Scarlet Witch," *Back Issue!* #45 (TwoMorrows, December 2010), 61.

6. Jack Kirby and Joe Simon, "The Vision," *Marvel Mystery Comics* #13 (Timely, 1940), 23.

7. Karen Walker, "Shattered Dreams: Vision and the Scarlet Witch," *Back Issue!* #45 (TwoMorrows, December 2010), 61.

8. Maurice Gutwirth, "The Falcon," *Daring Mystery Comics* #5 (Timely, 1940), 57.

9. Stan Lee, Larry Lieber, and Don Heck, "Iron Man Is Born!," *Tales of Suspense* #39 (Marvel, 1963), 3.

10. *Ibid.*, 6.

11. Stan Lee and Jack Binder, *Mystic Comics* #6 (Marvel, 1941), 7.

12. Fred Kida, "The Origin of the Iron Ace," *Air Fighters* #2 (Hillman, 1942), 32.

13. Don Rico and Jack Binder, "The Daredevil, Master of Courage," *Silver Streak* #6 (Lev Gleason, 1940), 6.

14. Steve Ditko, "Martin Goodman/Stan Lee," *Avenging Mind* (Bellingham: Snyder & Ditko, 2008), 26–27.

15. Will Murray, "Daredevil vs. The Avengers," *Alter Ego* #118 (TwoMorrows, 2013), 3–4.

16. Ditko, "Martin Goodman/Stan Lee," *Avenging Mind*, 27.

17. Murray, "Daredevil vs. The Avengers," *Alter Ego* #118, 3–4.

18. Charles Voight, "Boom Boom Brannigan," *Prize Comics* #58 (Feature, 1946), 38.

19. Wally Wood, "In Mortal Combat with … Sub-Mariner!," *Daredevil* #7 (Marvel, 1965), 5.

20. Bhob Steward and J. Michael Catron, *The Life and Legend of Wallace Wood* (Seattle: Fantagraphics, 2016), 27.

21. Barry Pearl, *F.F.F.: A Life in Comics!* (Barry's Pearls of Comic Book Wisdom, 26 July 2015), https://forbushman.blogspot.com/2015/07/the-original-ghost-rider-volume-1-with.html.

22. Murray, "Marvel's Founding Father—MARTIN GOODMAN," *Alter Ego* #165, 30.

23. Simon and Simon, *Comic Book Makers*, 54–55.

24. Murray, "Marvel's Founding Father—MARTIN GOODMAN," *Alter Ego* #165, 30.

25. Graeme McMillan, "'Captain Marvel' and 'Shazam!' Share a Complicated Past," *The Hollywood Reporter* (Penske Media Corporation, 5 April 2019), https://www.hollywoodreporter.com/movies/movie-news/captain-marvel-shazam-share-a-strange-past-1199825/.

26. Stan Lee and Jack Kirby, *The Incredible Hulk* #1 (Marvel, 1962), 5–6.

27. Harry Stein and Mort Leav, *Air Fighters* #3 (Hillman, 1942), 15.

28. Bill Woolfolk and Carmine Infantino, "Enter: Rickie Wood," *Airboy* #32 (Hillman, 1946), 22.

29. Hal Sharp and Mort Weisinger, *Star Spangled Comics* #1 (DC Comics, 1941), 33.

30. Jack Cole, "The Coming of the Comet," *Pep Comics* #1 (MLJ, 1940), 12.

31. Chuck Mazoujian, "Presenting Quicksilver," *National Comics* #5 (Quality, 1940), 38.

32. Stan Lee, Larry Lieber, and Jack Kirby, "I am the Fantastic Dr. Droom!," *Amazing Adventures* #1 (Marvel, 1961), 25.

33. Stan Lee and Steve Ditko, "The Origin of Dr. Strange," *Strange Tales* #115 (Marvel, 1963), 20.

34. Stan Lee and Jack Kirby, "Prisoners of Doctor Doom!," *The Fantastic Four* #5 (Marvel, 1962), 4.

35. Ken Crossen and Mac Raboy, *Green Lama* #1 (Spark, 1944), 2.

36. Will Eisner, "The Wonder Man," *Wonder Comics* #1 (Fox Publications, 1939), 1.

37. "Superman Comic Strip Is Winner in Court Action," *Honolulu Star-Bulletin* (Black Press, 23 May 1940), 6.

38. Alex Schomburg, "Lilith the Dark Planet," *Mystery Comics* #1 (Pines, 1944), 1.

39. John Morrow, "Key 1960s Moments," *Jack Kirby Collector* #60 (TwoMorrows, 2013), 69.

40. Paul Gustavson, "The Black Panther," *Stars and Stripes* #3 (Centaur, 1941), 25.

Chapter 15

1. Jack Kirby, "The Stone Sentinels of Giant Island," *House of Mystery* #85 (DC Comics, 1958), 23.

2. Stan Lee and Larry Lieber, "Here Comes … Thorr the Unbelievable," *Tales to Astonish* #16 (Marvel, 1960), 1.

3. Murray, "The Retrospective Stan Lee," *Alter Ego* #150, 7–8.

4. Stan Lee, Larry Lieber, and Jack Kirby, "The Midnight Monster!," *Journey into Mystery* #79 (Marvel, 1962), 9.

5. Stan Lee and Jack Kirby, "VanDoom, The Man Who Made a Creature!," *Tales to Astonish* #17 (Marvel, 1960), 1.

6. Stan Lee, Larry Lieber, and Jack Kirby, "The Monster in the Iron Mask!," *Tales of Suspense* #31 (Marvel, 1962), 1.

7. _____, "I saw Diablo! The Demon from the 5th Dimension!," *Tales of Suspense* #9 (Marvel, 1960), 1.

8. _____, "I Am Dr. Druid!," *Weird Wonder Tales* #19 (Marvel, 1976), 1.

9. Robert Q. Sale, "Gorilla Man," *Men's Adventures* #26 (Marvel, 1954), 25.

10. Ed Winiarski, "The Spider Man!," *Uncanny Tales* #26 (Marvel, 1954), 8.

11. Jack Abel, "Werewolf by Night," *Marvel Tales* #116 (Marvel, 1953), 8.

12. Stan Lee and Jack Kirby, "I Brought the Mighty Cyclops Back to Life!," *Tales of Suspense* #10 (Marvel, 1960), 1.

13. Stan Lee, Larry Lieber, and Jack Kirby, "I Created the Colossus," *Tales of Suspense* #14 (Marvel, 1961), 1.

14. _____, "The Wonder of the Ages!!! Magneto!," *Strange Tales* #84 (Marvel, 1961), 1.

15. _____, "Elektro! He Held a World In His Iron Grip," *Tales of Suspense* #13 (Marvel, 1961), 1.

16. George R. Dempster, "One of the star attractions at the New York World's Fair," *The Knoxville Journal* (Gannett, 9 August 1940), 1.

17. Steve Dahlman, "Electro: The Marvel of the Age," *Marvel Mystery Comics* #4 (Timely, 1940), 41.

18. Robert Webb, "The Origin of Electro," *Science Comics* #1 (Fox Publications, 1940), 9.

19. Stan Lee, Larry Lieber, and Jack Kirby, "The Sandman Cometh," *Journey into Mystery* #70 (Marvel, 1961), 1.

20. _____, "The Scorpion Strikes!," *Journey into Mystery* #82 (Marvel, 1962), 1.

21. _____, "I Fought the Molten Man-Thing," *Tales of Suspense* #7 (Marvel, 1960), 22.

22. "Marvel" *Grand Comics Database*, https://www.comics.org/publisher/78/?sort=year&page=4.

Chapter 16

1. Gary Groth, "Editorial," *The Comics Journal* #75 (Fantagraphics, 1982), 4.

2. Jack Kirby and Joe Simon, "The Villain from Valhalla!," *Adventure Comics* #75 (DC Comics, 1942), 54–63.

3. Jack Kirby, *Tales of the Unexpected* #16 (DC Comics, 1957), 4.

4. *Ibid.*, 4.

5. *Ibid.*

6. Joe Simon and Jack Kirby, "The Monsters of Saturn," *Captain Marvel Adventures* #1 (Fawcett, 1941), 33.

7. "Journey into Mystery #92," *Grand Comics Database*, https://www.comics.org/issue/17671/.

8. Jack Kirby, "Sailor's Girl!," *Young Romance* #13 (Prize, 1949), 5.

9. Lee, Lieber, Heck, "Iron Man Is Born!," *Tales of Suspense* #39, 1.

10. Coates, *Don Heck, A Work of Art*, 41.

11. Mark Evanier, "Jack F.A.Q.s," *Jack Kirby Collector* #45 (TwoMorrows, 2006), 31–32.

12. Lee, Lieber, Heck, "Iron Man Is Born!," *Tales of Suspense* #39, 5.

13. Dave Wood and Jack Kirby, "The War That Never Ended," *Adventure Comics* #255 (DC Comics, 1958), 20.

14. Joe Simon and Jack Kirby, "The Menace of the Micro-Men!," *The Double Life of Private Strong* #2 (Archie, 1959), 25.

15. Jack Kirby, "The Microscopic Army!," *Yellow Claw* #3 (Marvel, 1956), 1.

16. Joe Simon and Jack Kirby, "The Shrinking Serum," *Blue Bolt* #1 (Novelty Press, 1940), 1.

17. Lee and Kirby, *The Incredible Hulk* #1, 1.

18. Joe Simon, Jack Kirby, and Mort Meskin, "The Man From the World of D," *Captain 3-D* #1 (Harvey, 1953), 4.

19. Joe Simon and Jack Kirby, "Today I Am A-?," *Black Cat Mystic* #59 (Harvey, 1957), 1.

20. Jack Kirby, "Concentrate on Chaos!," *Yellow Claw* #2 (Marvel, 1956), 4.

21. Lee and Kirby, *The X-Men* #1, 8.

22. Jack Kirby, "We Were Doomed by the Metal-Eating Monster," *My Greatest Adventure* #21 (DC Comics, 1958), 1.

23. M. Keith Booker, "Challengers of the Unknown," *Comics Through Time* vol. 2 (Santa Barbara: Greenwood, 2014), 513.

24. George Olshevsky and Roy Thomas, "Conversation with Roy Thomas," *Collectors Dream* #5 (G&T Enterprises, 1978), 38.

25. Dave Wood and Jack Kirby, "Ultivac is Loose!," *Showcase* #7 (DC Comics, 1957), 3.

26. Lee and Kirby, "The Fantastic Four!," *The Fantastic Four* #1, 9.

27. Jack Kirby, "Crime Carnival!," *Adventure Comics* #84 (DC Comics, 1943), 1.

28. Dave Wood and Jack Kirby, "The Secrets of the Sorcerer's Box!," *Showcase* #6 (DC Comics, 1957), 3.

29. Lee and Kirby, "The Fantastic Four!," *The Fantastic Four* #1, 13.

30. Jack Kirby, "Menace of the Invisible Challenger," *Challengers of the Unknown* #3 (DC Comics, 1958), 22.

31. Dave Wood and Jack Kirby, "The Day the Earth Blew Up!," *Showcase* #11 (DC Comics, 1957), 11.

32. Stan Lee and Jack Kirby, "Prisoners of Kurrgo, Master of Planet X," *The Fantastic Four* #7 (Marvel, 1962), 15.

33. Jack Kirby, "The Human Pets," *Challengers of the Unknown* #1 (DC Comics, 1958), 29.

34. Stan Lee and Jack Kirby, "The Infant Terrible," *The Fantastic Four* #24 (Marvel, 1964), 22–23.

35. Jack Kirby, "The Wizard of Time," *Challengers of the Unknown* #4 (DC Comics, 1958), 5.

36. Joe Simon and Jack Kirby, "The Double Life of Private Strong," *The Double Life of Private Strong* #1 (Archie, 1959), 3.

37. Stan Lee and Jack Kirby, "Prisoners of the Puppet Master," *The Fantastic Four* #8 (Marvel, 1962), 23.

38. Jack Kirby, "Voodoo on Tenth Avenue!," *Black Magic* #4 (Prize, 1951), 9.

39. Carl Wessler and Jack Kirby, "About Space-Face," *Fighting American* #7 (Prize, 1955), 19–20.

40. Jack Kirby, *Chip Hardy* (Unpublished, 1950s), https://kirbymuseum.org/blogs/effect/2018/09/08/looking-for-the-awesome-16/.

41. Jack Kirby, "Invasion of the Volcano Men," *Tales of the Unexpected* #22 (DC Comics, 1958), 27.

42. Simon and Simon, *The Comic Book Makers*, 45.

43. Joe Simon and Jack Kirby, "The Boy Commandos," *Detective Comics* #64 (DC Comics, 1942), 15.

44. Joe Simon and Jack Kirby, "The Menace of Marto!," *Blue Bolt* #6 (Novelty 1940), 3–4.

45. Groth and Kirby, "Jack Kirby Interview with Gary Groth," *The Comics Journal* #134, 82.

46. Mark Evanier, *Marvelmania* #2 (Dimensional Industries, 1970), Backcover.

47. Michael Walsh, "Extra! Read all about Spider-Man!," *The Province* (Pacific Newspaper Group, 18 January 1977), 21.

48. Steve Ditko, "A Mini-History 13," *The Comics!* vol. 14, #8 (Robin Snyder, 2003), 1.

49. Joe Simon and Jack Kirby, "The Strange New World of the Fly," *Adventures of the Fly* #1 (Archie, 1959), 1.

50. Greg Theakston, "The Road to Spider-Man," *Steve Ditko Reader* #1 (New York: Pure Imagination, 2002), 15.

51. Stan Lee, "Fantastic Fan Page 4," *Fantastic Four* #18 (Marvel, 1963), 29.

52. Stan Lee, *The Comic Reader* #16 (Bails, 1963), 3.

53. Stan Lee and Steve Ditko, *Tales of Suspense* #48 (Marvel, 1963), 10.

54. Steve Ditko, *The Complete Four-Page Series and Other Essays* (Bellingham: Snyder & Ditko, 2020), 68.

55. Robert Greene, "Steve Ditko Interview," *Rapport* #2 (Rapport,1966), 12.

56. *Ibid.*, 12.

57. *Ibid.*

58. Gary Martin, "Steve Ditko Interview," *The Comic Fan* #2 (The Comic Fan, 1965), https://ditkocultist.wordpress.com/2012/03/05/steve-ditko-interview-the-comic-fan-2-1965/.

59. Steve Ditko, "A Mini-History 13," *The Comics!* vol. 14, #8, 1.

60. Steve Ditko, "An Insider's Part of Comics History: Jack Kirby's Spider-Man," *Avenging World* (Bellingham: Snyder & Ditko, 2002), 57–60.

61. Simon and Simon, *Comic Book Makers*, 52.

62. Ditko, "An Insider's Part of Comics History: Jack Kirby's Spider-Man," *Avenging World*, 57–60.

63. Stan Lee and Steve Ditko, "Supporting Cast Pin-Ups," *The Amazing Spider-Man Annual* #1 (Marvel, 1964), 42–70.

64. Steve Ditko and Joe Gill, "Director of the Board," *Strange Suspense Stories* #33 (Charlton, 1957), 10–15.

65. _____, "The Human Powerhouse," *Strange Suspense Stories* #48 (Charlton, 1960), 1.

66. _____, "All Those Eyes," *Out of this World* #6 (Charlton, 1957), 1.

67. _____, "The Green Man," *This Magazine Is Haunted* vol 2, #14 (Charlton, 1957), 11.

68. _____, "The Most Terrible Fate," *Out of this World* #7 (Charlton, 1958), 11.

69. _____, "The Comeback," *Space War* #10 (Charlton, 1961), 30.

70. Steve Ditko and Jack Oleck, "The Supermen," *Out of this World* #3 (Charlton, 1957), 1.

71. Stan Lee, *The Comic Reader* #16 (Bails, 1963), 3.

72. Steve Ditko, "A World of His Own," *Strange Suspense Stories* #32 (Charlton, 1957), 1.

73. Steve Ditko and Joe Gill, "Journey to Paradise," *Out of this World* #7 (Charlton, 1958), 6.

74. _____, "The Wrong Planet," *Space Adventures* #27 (Charlton, 1959), 15.

75. Stan Lee and Steve Ditko, *Tales of Suspense* #48 (Marvel, 1963), 10.

76. Ditko, *The Complete Four-Page Series and Other Essays*, 70–72.

77. Stan Lee and Steve Ditko, *Tales to Astonish* #60 (Marvel, 1964), 18.

78. Lee, "Meet Stan Lee" *Bachelor* #1, 35.

79. Schwartz and Thomsen, *Man of Two Worlds*, 94–95.

80. Stan Lee, "Captain America Foils the Traitor's Revenge," *Captain America Comics* #3 (Marvel, 1941), 37.

81. Stan Lee and Jack Kirby, "Captain America Joins ... The Avengers," *Avengers* #4 (Marvel, 1964), 13.

82. Stan Lee, "Marvel Get-Together," *Marvel Mystery Comics* #25 (Marvel, 1941), 34.

83. Lee and Kirby, "The Fantastic Four!," *The Fantastic Four* #1, 12–13.

84. Stan Lee, "Heart to Heart Talk," *My Own Romance* #24 (Marvel, 1952), 14.

85. Stan Lee and Nicholas Charley, "Jack Frost," *USA Comics* #1 (Timely, 1941), 64.

86. Stan Lee and Steve Ditko, "Spider-Man vs. the Chameleon," *The Amazing Spider-Man* #1 (Marvel, 1963), 21.

87. Stan Lee and Harry Fisk, "Headline Hunter Foreign Correspondent," *Captain America Comics* #5 (Marvel, 1941), 49.

88. Stan Lee and Jack Binder, "The Destroyer," *Mystic Comics* #6 (Marvel, 1941), 7.

89. Lee, Lieber, and Heck, "Iron Man Is Born!," *Tales of Suspense* #39, 6.

90. Stan Lee, Al Avison, and Al Gabriele, "The Order of the Hood," *All Winners Comics* #1 (Timely, 1941), 15.

91. Stan Lee, Jack Kirby, and Bill Everett, "The Stage is Set!," *Tales to Astonish* #81 (Marvel, 1966), 15.

92. Stan Lee, Carmine Infantino, and Gil Kane, "The Hooded Horror!," *Mystic* #12 (Marvel, 1952), 5.

93. Stan Lee and Charley Nicholas, "Rockman Underground Secret Agent," *USA Comics* #3 (Marvel, 1941), 44.

94. Stan Lee and Jack Kirby, "The Return of the Mole Man!," *Fantastic Four* #22 (Marvel, 1964), 17, 20.

95. Stan Lee and Chad Grotkopf, "The Imp," *Captain America Comics* #12 (Marvel, 1942), 42.

96. Stan Lee and Jack Kirby, "The Impossible Man," *The Fantastic Four* #11 (Marvel, 1963), 12.

97. Stan Lee, Mike Sekowsky, and George Klein, "League of Crime," *Mystic Comics* #8 (Marvel, 1942), 56.

98. Stan Lee and Steve Ditko, "Spider-Man!," *Amazing Fantasy* #15 (Marvel, 1962), 5.

99. Stan Lee and Jack Kirby, "The Stronger I Am, the Sooner I Die!," *Journey into Mystery* #114 (Marvel, 1965), 4.

100. Stan Lee, "The Horror of the Doll-Devil," *Young Allies* #10 (Marvel, 1943), 4.

101. Stan Lee and Werner Roth, "The Last Command of Colonel Fong," *Battle* #17 (Marvel, 1953), 1.

102. Stan Lee and Jack Kirby, "The Mysterious Radio-Active Man!," *Journey into Mystery* #93 (Marvel, 1963), 4.

103. Stan Lee and Dick Ayers, "The Black Knight Strikes!," *Tales to Astonish* #52 (Marvel, 1964), 4.

104. Stan Lee and Jack Kirby, "Prisoners of the Pharaoh!," *Fantastic Four* #19 (Marvel, 1964), 10.

105. Stan Lee, Carmine Infantino, and Gil Kane, "Horror into Haunted Hill!," *Adventures into Weird Worlds* #14 (Marvel, 1954), 1.

106. "John Romita," *Grand Comics Database*, https://www.comics.org/credit/name/John%20Romita/sort/chrono/.

107. Stan Lee and John Romita, Sr., "In the Clutches of … The Kingpin!," *The Amazing Spider-Man* #51 (Marvel, 1967), 10.

108. Stan Lee and Werner Roth, "Love 'em and Leave 'em," *Action Confessions* #13 (Marvel, 1952), 10.

109. Stan Lee and Jack Kirby, "Beware the Blob!," *The X-Men* #3 (Marvel, 1964), 4.

110. Stan Lee and Jack Kirby, "The Thunder God and the Thug!," *Journey into Mystery* #89 (Marvel, 1963), 3.

111. Stan Lee, Carmine Infantino, and Gil Kane, "Love Story," *My Own Romance* #27 (Marvel, 1953), 14.

112. Jerry Flemmons, "Batman's Back and All's Right with the World," *Fort Worth Star-Telegram* (McClatchy Company, 19 January 1966), 2.

113. Stan Lee, "Hi, Marvelites!," *Fantasy Masterpieces* #1 (Marvel, 1965), inside cover.

114. *Ibid.*

Chapter 17

1. Lee, "Meet Stan Lee," *Bachelor* #1, 35.

2. Lee and Kirby, "The Fantastic Four!," *The Fantastic Four* #1, 1.

3. Lee and Ditko, "Spider-Man!," *Amazing Fantasy* #15, 1.

4. Stan Lee and Jack Kirby, "The End of the Fantastic Four!," *The Fantastic Four* #9 (Marvel, 1962), 1.

5. _____, "Defeated by Doctor Doom!," *Fantastic Four* #17 (Marvel, 1963), 1.

6. _____, "A Skrull Walks Among Us!," *Fantastic Four* #18, 1.

7. Lee and Ditko, "Spider-Man," *The Amazing Spider-Man* #1, 1.

8. Stan Lee and Steve Ditko, "Spider-Man vs. Doctor Octopus," *The Amazing Spider-Man* #3 (Marvel, 1963), 1.

9. _____, "Marked for Destruction by Dr. Doom!," *The Amazing Spider-Man* #5 (Marvel, 1963), 1.

10. Nat Freedland, "Super Heroes with Super Problems," *New York Herald Tribune* (Reid Family, 9 January 1966), Sunday Magazine Section.

11. Roger Ebert, "A Comeback (Sock!), For Comic Books (Pop!)," *Chicago Sun-Times Sunday Supplement, MIDWEST* (Sun-Times Investment Holdings, 28 August 1966), 22, 27.

12. Simon and Simon, *Comic Book Makers*, 160–162.

13. Joe Simon and Angelo Torres, "The New Age of Comics," *Sick* #48 (Crestwood, 1966), 25.

14. Danny Fingeroth and Roy Thomas, "Will Success Spoil Spider-Man?" *The Stan Lee Universe* (Raleigh: Twomorrows, 2011), 161-169.

15. Ted White and Stan Lee, "A Conversation with the Man Behind Marvel Comics, Stan Lee," *Castle of Frankenstein Magazine* #12 (Gothic Castle Publishing, 1968), 60.

16. Lee, "Meet Stan Lee," *Bachelor* #1, 33, 35.

17. Stan Lee and Jack Kirby, "Shall Earth Endure?," *Fantastic Four* #77 (Marvel, 1968), 1.

18. Sergio Aragonés, Bob Oksner, and Wally Wood, "Most Fantastic Robbery in History!," *Angel and Ape* #2 (DC Comics, 1969), 7.

19. Hamilton, "A Talk with Artist-Writer-Editor Jack Kirby," *The Collected Jack Kirby Collector* vol. 4, 188.

20. Jack Kirby, "Funky Flashman!," *Mister Miracle* #6 (DC Comics, 1972), 23.

21. Jim Panyard, "King of the Comic Books," *The News Journal* (Ogden Newspapers, 20 November 1972), 23.

22. "The Foom Connection," *FOOM!* #1 (Marvel, 1973), 3.

23. Delfina Rattazzi and Stan Lee, "The Marvelous Stan Lee," *Andy Warhol Interview* #31 (Jason Nikic, 1973), 36.

24. Lee, *Origins of Marvel Comics*, 16–18.

25. Charles Murry and Stan Lee, *Fantasy Advertiser International* (Fantasy Advertiser International, April 1975), https://forbushman.blogspot.com/2017/06/a-serious-interview-with-stan-lee-april.html.

26. "Joe Simon and Jack Kirby: 'By Their Works Shall Ye Know Them,'" *FOOM!* #8 (Marvel, 1974), 16.

27. "Kirby Speaks!," *FOOM!* #11 (Marvel, 1975), 6.

28. *Ibid.*, 7.

29. "Another FOOMtastic Preview Feature!," *FOOM!* #19 (Marvel, 1977), 7.

30. Arnold Drake and Jack Sparling, "Ego-Man," *SICK* #120 (Charlton, 1978), 6.

31. Megan Powell, "A Child's Garden of Television," *Contra Costa Times* (Digital First Media, 22 October 1978), 2.

32. Evanier, *Kirby: King of Comics*, 209, 212.

33. Fred Van Lente and Ryan Dunlavey, *The Comic Book History of Comics* (San Diego: IDW, 2012), 157–160.

34. Eisner and Kirby, "Jack Kirby," *Will Eisner's Spirit Magazine* #39, 38.

35. Stan Lee and Jim Shooter, "Stan Lee and Jim Shooter," *Marvel Age* #8 (Marvel, 1983), 12.

36. Stan Lee, "Twenty Five Years? I Don't Believe It!," *The Comic Book Price Guide* #16 (Overstreet, 1986), A-82.

37. Robert Knight, "Jack Kirby's 70th Birthday," *Earthwatch* (WBAI, 28 August 1987), https://kirbymuseum.org/blogs/effect/2012/06/29/1987-august-28-jack-kirby-interview-partial/.

38. Janet Bode, "A Comic Book Artist KO'D," *The Village Voice* (Brian Calle, 8 December 1987), 34.

39. Groth and Kirby, "Jack Kirby Interview with Gary Groth," *The Comics Journal* #134, 80.

40. *Ibid.*, 81.

41. *Ibid.*

42. "Coleman agrees to buyout," *Fort Worth Star-Telegram* (The McClatchy Company, 27 March 1989), 7.

43. Stan Lee, "Hi, Heroes!," *Fantastic Four* #358 (Marvel, 1991), 41.

44. Jim Amash, "Roy Thomas Interview," *Jack Kirby Collector* #18 (TwoMorrows, 1998), 21.

45. Evanier, *Kirby: King of Comics*, 221.

46. Stan Lee, "Introduction," *Fantastic Four* #400 (Marvel, 1995), 2.

47. Evanier, *Kirby: King of Comics*, 228.

48. Ryan Faughnder, "Comic book artist's heirs settle Marvel dispute," *Los Angeles Times* (Los Angeles Times Communications, 2014), B5.

49. Stan Lee and Steve Ditko, "Captured by J. Jonah Jameson!," *The Amazing Spider-Man* #25 (Marvel, 1965), 1.

50. Nat Freedland, "Super Heroes with Super Problems," *New York Herald Tribune* (Reid Family, 9 January 1966), Sunday Magazine Section.

51. "Issue Checklist for Creator Steve Ditko," *Grand Comics Database*, https://www.comics.org/checklist/19/?page=5.

52. "The Amazing Spider-Man monthly sales," (Comichron, 2021), https://www.comichron.com/titlespotlights/amazingspiderman.html.

53. Lee, *Origins of Marvel Comics*, 135.

54. Michael Walsh, "Extra! Read all about Spider-Man!," *The Province* (Pacific Newspaper Group, 18 January 1977), 21.

55. Steve Ditko, "A Mini-History #13," *The Comics!* vol. 14, #8 (Bellingham: Snyder & Ditko, 2003), 1.

56. Charles Murry and Stan Lee, *Fantasy Advertiser International* (Fantasy Advertiser International April 1975), https://forbushman.blogspot.com/2017/06/a-serious-interview-with-stan-lee-april.html.

57. Jim Shooter, Alex Grand, and Jim Thompson, "Jim Shooter Biographical Interview," *Comic Book Historians YouTube* (CBH, 2021), 6:47:06.

58. Paul Soles, *Beyond Reason* (CBC, 1980), https://youtu.be/NJOdRLChhw8?t=81.

59. Will Eisner and Jack Kirby, "Jack Kirby," *Will Eisner's Spirit Magazine* #39 (Kitchen Sink, 1982), 38.

60. Mark Borax and Jack Kirby, "Jack Kirby," *David Anthony Kraft's Comics Interview* #41 (Fictioneer, 1986), 45.

61. Phillip Morago, "Comics shop caught up in Spider-Man wedding," *Hartford Courant* (Tribune Publishing, May 20, 1987), B2.

62. John Tesh, "Spider-Man's Wedding—Shea Stadium 1987," *Entertainment Tonight* (ViacomCBS, 1987), https://youtu.be/UQwslg6lat8?t=281.

63. Greg Theakston, "The Road to Spider-Man," *Steve Ditko Reader* #1 (Pure Imagination, 2002), 16.

64. Groth and Simon, "Joe Simon Interviewed by Gary Groth," *The Comics Journal* #134, 106.

65. *Ibid.*, 82.

66. Evanier, *Marvelmania* #2, 15.

67. Ditko, "An Insider's Part of Comics History: Jack Kirby's Spider-Man," *Avenging World*, 58.

68. *Ibid.*, 57.

69. *Ibid.*

70. Steve Ditko, "Tsk! Tsk!: Whatever Happened to Common Sense?," *Avenging World* (Bellingham: Snyder & Ditko, 2002), 68.

71. Simon and Simon, *Comic Book Makers*, 173–174.

72. *Ibid.*, 176–177.

73. Otto Binder and CC Beck, "Captain Marvel and the Webs of Crime," *Whiz Comics* #89 (Fawcett, 1947), 2.

74. Simon and Simon, *Comic Book Makers*, 16.

75. Steve Ditko, "Spider-Man's Co-Creators," *TIME* (Time USA, December 7, 1998), 38.

76. Stan Lee, "To Whom It May Concern," *Stan Lee Media* (Stan Lee Media, 18 August 1999), https://www.tcj.com/steve-ditko-1927-2018/.

77. Ditko, "Tsk! Tsk!: Why Do Some People Seek the Unearned?," *Avenging World*, 88.

78. Anthony Breznican, "Superhero creator sees no reason to call it quits," *The Sault Star* (Postmedia, 3 May 2002), C2.

79. Stan Lee, "Introduction," *Doctor Strange Marvel Masterworks* vol. 2 (New York: Marvel, 2005), vi.

80. Jonathan Ross, *In Search of Steve Ditko* (BBC, 2007), 49:57

81. Ditko, "Why I Quit S-M, Marvel," 2.

82. Credits, *The Amazing Spider-Man* (Marvel, 2021), 1.

Chapter 18

1. Ivan Prashker, "The Boss's Son," *Playboy* (Playboy Enterprises, February 1970), 195.

2. Lee, "Meet Stan Lee," *Bachelor* #1, 16.

3. Michael Eury, *The Krypton Companion* (Raleigh: TwoMorrows, 2006), 48.

4. Jerry Siegel and Paul Reinman, "The Fly-Man's Partners in Peril," *Fly Man* #31 (Archie, 1965), 27.

5. Lee, "Meet Stan Lee," *Bachelor* #1, 17.

6. *Ibid.*, 33.

7. Curt Swan and Edmond Hamilton, "The New Superman!," *Superman* #172 (DC Comics, 1964), 3.

8. Lee, "Meet Stan Lee," *Bachelor* #1, 16.

9. *Ibid.*, 35.

10. Steve Saffel, "A Not-So-Spectacular Experiment," *Spider-Man the Icon: The Life and Times of a Pop Culture Phenomenon* (Titan, 2007), 31.

11. Stan Lee and John Romita, Sr., "Lo, This Monster!," *The Spectacular Spider-Man* #1 (Marvel, 1968), 28.

12. Stan Lee and John Romita, Sr., "The Goblin Lives!," *The Spectacular Spider-Man* #2 (Marvel, 1968), 30.

13. "Savage Tales #1," *Grand Comics Database*, https://www.comics.org/issue/24237/.

14. McAvennie, "1970s," *DC Comics Year by Year: A Visual Chronicle*, 147.

15. Les Daniels, "The Changing of the Guard," *MARVEL: Five Fabulous Decades of the World's Greatest Comics* (Harry N. Abrams, 1991), 155–156.

16. Rattazzi and Lee, "The Marvelous Stan Lee," *Andy Warhol Interview* #31, 36.

17. *Ibid.*, 44.

18. *Ibid.*

19. Tim Page, "Alain Resnais" *The Independent* (Independent Digital News & Media, 4 March 2014), 53.

20. Rattazzi and Lee, "The Marvelous Stan Lee," *Andy Warhol Interview* #31, 36.

21. Daniel J. Wakin, "Italian Film Director Federico Fellini Dies," *Albuquerque Journal* (Journal Publishing Company, 1 November 1993), A2.

22. Rattazzi and Lee, "The Marvelous Stan Lee," *Andy Warhol Interview* #31, 44.

23. John Romita, Sr., "Fifty Years on the 'A' List," *Alter Ego* vol. 3, #9 (TwoMorrows, 2001), 35.

24. Howard Chaykin, Alex Grand, and Jim Thompson, *Comic Book Historians Presents ... Howard Chaykin, Dark Prince of Comics* (Sacramento: Comic Book Historians, 2021), 36–37.

25. David Anthony Kraft, Alex Grand, and Jim Thompson, "David Anthony Kraft Interview," *Comic Book Historians Podcast* (Comic Book Historians, 2019), 13:00.

26. The Associated Press, "Martin Goodman, 84, Marvel Comics Founder," *Newsday* (Newsday Media, 12 June 1992), 43.

27. Charles Goodman, A Publisher, 55," *The New York Times*, (New York Times, 3 March 1996), 40.

Chapter 19

1. Jim Steranko, "Jack Kirby Panel," *Dallas Fantasy Fair* (CBH, 2018), https://youtu.be/vmCElMOv1lg?t=479.

2. "New Books," *The Guardian* (Guardian Media Group, 29 October 1906), 5.

3. Michael Dirda, "Boo! The best ghost stories you haven't heard yet," *The Fresno Bee* (The McClatchy Company, 29 October 2017), 10C.

4. "Powers of Darkness," *Chicago Daily Tribune* (Tribune Publishing, 27 April 1945), 14.

5. Joe Simon and Jack Kirby, "Tuk Caveboy," *Captain America Comics* #1 (Marvel, 1941), 59.

6. *Ibid.*

7. "If Only the Statues Could Speak!," *The Minneapolis Star* (Star Tribune Media Company, 9 September 1952), 10.

8. Lawrence Guillot, "The New Thing in Paris is 'Fantastic Realism,'" *The Kansas City Star* (McClatchy, 29 November 1964), 6D.

9. Jason Colavito, *The Cult of Alien Gods: H.P. Lovecraft and Extraterrestrial Pop Culture* (Amherst: Prometheus Books, 2005), 138.

10. Robert Charroux, *Lost Worlds: Scientific Secrets of the Ancients* (United Kingdom: Fontana, 1974), 97.

11. Hergé, *Flight 714 to Sydney* (New York: Little, Brown, 1975), 43.

12. Stan Lee and Jack Kirby, "The Reason Why!," *The Mighty Thor* #147 (Marvel, 1967), 21.

13. "Chariots of the Gods: Your Letters," *The Sydney Morning Herald* (Fairfax Media, 10 August 1969), 49.

14. Stan Lee and Jack Kirby, "Aftermath," *The Mighty Thor* #128 (Marvel, 1966), 20–21.

15. Evanier, *Kirby: King of Comics*, 180.

16. Jon B. Cooke, "The Cosmic Code Authority Speaks! Talking with Jim Starlin, Alan Weiss and Al Milgrom on those trippy '70s Marvel Comics," *Comic Book Artist* #18 (TwoMorrows, 2002), 26–27.

17. Marv Wolfman, "A Visit with Jack Kirby," *New Gods* #1 (DC Comics, 1971), 30.

18. Michael Cavna, "Trump's proposed 'Space Force' has its pop culture roots in a little known comic," *The Miami Herald* (The McClatchy Company, 29 June 2018), 4G.

19. Staff Report, "Legendary Comic Artist to

Attend Superman Fest," *The Paducah Sun* (Paxton Media Group, 2 May 2010), 2A.

20. Roy Thomas and John Verpoorten, "Auntie Goose Rhymes Dept.," *Not Brand Echh* #11 (Marvel, 1968), 48.

21. John Morrow and Lisa Kirby, "The Kid from Left Field," *Jack Kirby Collector* #20 (TwoMorrows, 1998), 4.

22. Ro, *Tales to Astonish: Jack Kirby, Stan Lee, and the American Comic Book Revolution*, 148.

23. Jack Kirby, *The New Gods* #7 (DC Comics, 1971), 22.

24. Jack Kirby, *The New Gods* #5 (DC Comics, 1971), 20.

25. Jack Kirby, *The New Gods* vol. 2, #6 (DC Comics, 1984), 44.

26. Jack Kirby, *The Hunger Dogs* (DC Comics, 1985), 59–60.

27. John Morrow, "The Captain Victory Connection," *The Collected Jack Kirby Collector* vol. 1 (Raleigh: TwoMorrows, 2004), 105.

28. Jack Kirby, *Captain Victory and the Galactic Rangers* #11 (Pacific, 1983), 5.

29. Jack Kirby, *The Hunger Dogs* (DC Comics, 1985), 26.

30. Jack Kirby, *Captain Victory and the Galactic Rangers* #12 (Pacific, 1983), 5.

31. *Ibid.*

32. Kirby, *Captain Victory and the Galactic Rangers* #11, 7.

33. Cooke, "The Cosmic Code Authority Speaks! Talking with Jim Starlin, Alan Weiss and Al Milgrom on those trippy '70s Marvel Comics," *Comic Book Artist* #18, 26.

34. Jack Kirby, *The New Gods* #2 (DC Comics, 1971), 22.

35. Jack Kirby, *Mister Miracle* #9 (DC Comics, 1972), 25.

36. JW Rinszler, "George Lucas and Comic Books: An Early Link," *STAR WARS BLOG* (StarWars.com 2013), https://www.starwars.com/news/george-lucas-and-comic-books-an-early-link.

37. John Siuntres, *The World of Comic Books* (Behind the Scene, 1978), https://youtu.be/Wsykqt5D8yg?t=452.

38. Stan Lee and Jack Kirby, "The Power and the Pride!," *Fantastic Four* #87 (Marvel, 1969), 14.

39. Groth and Kirby, "Jack Kirby Interview with Gary Groth," *The Comics Journal* #134, 97.

40. Jack Kirby, *The Eternals* #1 (Marvel, 1976), 10.

41. Jack Kirby, *Superman's Pal Jimmy Olsen* #136 (DC Comics, 1971), 20.

42. Jack Kirby, *Mister Miracle* #18 (DC Comics, 1974), 19.

43. Joe Simon and Jack Kirby, "Today I am A—?," *Black Cat Mystic* #59 (Harvey, 1957), 7.

Chapter 20

1. Stan Lee and Gil Kane, "And Death Shall Come!," *The Amazing Spider-Man* #90 (Marvel, 1970), 20.

2. Gerry Conway and Gil Kane, "The Night Gwen Stacy Died," *The Amazing Spider-Man* #121 (Marvel, 1973), 18.

3. Sean Howe, *Marvel Comics: The Untold Story* (New York: Harper Perennial, 2013), 136.

4. Gerry Conway and Gene Colan, "Even the Noble Die!," *Sub-Mariner* #46 (Marvel, 1972), 22.

5. Roy Thomas, Ross Andru, and Mike Esposito, "The Way to Dusty Death!," *Sub-Mariner* #37 (Marvel, 1971), 20.

6. Cooke, "The Cosmic Code Authority Speaks! Talking with Jim Starlin, Alan Weiss, and Al Milgrom on those trippy '70s Marvel Comics," *Comic Book Artist* #18, 26.

7. Pierre Comtois, *Marvel Comics in the 1970s: An Issue-by-Issue Field Guide to a Pop Culture Phenomenon* (Raleigh: TwoMorrows, 2011), 195.

8. Cooke, "The Cosmic Code Authority Speaks! Talking with Jim Starlin, Alan Weiss, and Al Milgrom on those trippy '70s Marvel Comics," *Comic Book Artist* #18, 16.

9. Jim Starlin, *The Art of Jim Starlin: A Life in Words and Pictures* (Aftershock Comics, 2018), 18–22.

10. Jim Starlin and Larry Herndon, "Doomsday!," *Star-Studded* #16 (Texas Trio, 1969), 8.

11. Jim Starlin, "The Miracle," *Star-Studded* #18 (Texas Trio, 1972), 2.

12. Stan Lee and Steve Ditko, "The End—At Last!," *Strange Tales* #146 (Marvel, 1966), 15.

13. Jim Starlin and Steve Skeates, "You Show Me Your Dream—I'll Show you Mine!!," *Journey into Mystery* vol. 2, #1 (Marvel, 1972), 31.

14. Steve Ditko and Stan Lee, "Dr. Strange, Master of Black Magic," *Strange Tales* #110 (Marvel, 1963), 28.

15. Cooke, "The Cosmic Code Authority Speaks! Talking with Jim Starlin, Alan Weiss, and Al Milgrom on those trippy '70s Marvel Comics," *Comic Book Artist* #18, 26.

16. Jim Starlin, "Death Building," *Star*Reach* #1 (Star*Reach, 1974), 7.

17. Jim Starlin and Mike Friedrich, "Thanos the Insane God!," *Captain Marvel* #32 (Marvel, 1974), 19.

18. Jim Starlin and Marv Wolfman, "How Strange My Destiny!," *Warlock* #10 (Marvel, 1975), 9.

19. Jim Starlin, "The Final Threat," *Avengers Annual* #7 (Marvel, 1977), 3, 26.

20. *Ibid.*, 7.

21. *Ibid.*, 29.

22. Jim Starlin, "Death Watch," *Marvel Two-in-One Annual* #2 (Marvel, 1977), 33.

23. Steve Ringgenberg, "Archie Goodwin," *The Comics Journal* #78 (Fantagraphics, 1982), 76.

24. Robert Greenberger, "Marvel Introduces New Contracts," *Comics Scene* #2 (Starlog Presents, 1982), 18.

25. Starlin, *The Art of Jim Starlin: A Life in Words and Pictures*, 117.

26. Keith Roysdon, "Newsstands full of SF publications," *Muncie Evening Press* (Gannett, 18 April 1981), T-8.

27. Jim Starlin, "Doomsday!," *Epic Illustrated* #9 (Marvel 1981), 13.

28. Dan Taylor, "Zapping the POWers that be," *The Press Democrat* (Sonoma Media Investments, 10 February 1984), 1D.

29. Greenberger, "Marvel Introduces New Contracts," *Comics Scene* #2, 18.

30. Jim Starlin, *Dreadstar* (Marvel, 1982), 30.

31. Cooke, "The Cosmic Code Authority Speaks! Talking with Jim Starlin, Alan Weiss and Al Milgrom on those trippy '70s Marvel Comics," *Comic Book Artist* #18, 26.

32. Grand, Thompson, and Shooter, "Jim Shooter Biographical Interview," *Comic Book Historians YouTube* (CBH, 2021), https://youtu.be/FBh709_dLNs?t=14594.

33. Jim Starlin, *The Death of Captain Marvel* (Marvel, 1982), 63.

34. Grand, Thompson, and Shooter, "Jim Shooter Biographical Interview," *Comic Book Historians YouTube* (CBH, 2021), https://youtu.be/FBh709_dLNs?t=14744.

35. Jim Starlin and Bernie Wrightson, *Batman: The Cult* #2 (DC Comics, 1988), 5.

36. Jim Starlin and Jim Aparo, "Ten Nights of the Beast: Part 4," *Batman* #420 (DC Comics, 1988), 21.

37. Jim Starlin, "The Rise and Fall of Robin," *The Palm Beach Post* (Gannett, 3 November 1988), 11D.

38. Jim Starlin and Bernie Wrightson, *The Weird* (DC Comics, 1988), 37.

39. Jim Starlin and Mike Mignola, *Cosmic Odyssey* #4 (DC Comics, 1988), 24.

40. *Ibid.*, 40.

41. Jenny Vogt, "Realism now entering heroes' lives and stories," *The Palm Beach Post* (Gannett, 3 November 1988), 11D.

42. Jim Starlin and George Perez, *Infinity Gauntlet* #1 (Marvel, 1991), 26.

43. "Comic Book News," *Tampa Bay Times* (Poynter Institute, 10 April 1992), 44.

44. Jim Starlin, *'Breed* #1 (Malibu, 1994), 9.

45. Jim Starlin, *Hardcore Station* #6 (DC Comics, 1998), 16.

46. Jim Starlin, Ron Lim, and Shane Davis, "Ultimatum!," *Mystery in Space* #7 (DC Comics, 2007), 8.

47. Andrew Smith, "October brings death to comics," *Casper Star-Tribune* (Lee Enterprises, 3 October 2007), A9.

48. Jim Starlin, "Death of the New Gods," *Comic Vine* (Whiskey Media, 2021), https://comicvine.gamespot.com/death-of-the-new-gods/4045-48489/.

Chapter 21

1. John Byrne, *Byrne Robotics* (ByrneRobotics.com, 2005), http://www.byrnerobotics.com/forum/forum_posts.asp?TID=5806&KW=Bromwich.

2. John Byrne and Roger Stern, "Avengers Assemble!," *The Avengers* #233 (Marvel, 1983), 23.

3. John Byrne, Walt Simonson, and Chris Ryall, *Jack Kirby Panel* (NYCC, 2017), 4:40.

4. Jon B. Cooke, "Drawing with a Ballpoint Pen," *Modern Masters Vol. Seven: John Byrne* (Raleigh: TwoMorrows, 2006), 18.

5. John Byrne and Duffy Vohland, "Foom Fan Art Gallery," *FOOM!* #5 (Marvel, 1974), 21.

6. ———, "The Castle," *Nightmare* #20 (Skywald, 1974), 51.

7. Nicola Cuti and John Byrne, "ROG-2000 in That Was No Lady," *E-Man* #6 (Charlton Comics, 1975), 22.

8. "Issue Checklist for Creator Jack Kirby," *Grand Comics Database*, https://www.comics.org/checklist/name/Jack%20Kirby/?page=25.

9. Byrne, Simonson, and Ryall, *Jack Kirby Panel* (NYCC, 2017), 54:30.

10. "Issue Checklist for Creator John Byrne," *Grand Comics Database*, https://www.comics.org/checklist/name/John%20Byrne/?sort=publication_date&page=7.

11. John Byrne, "Kirby's Kosmic Konsciousness," *FOOM!* #11 (Marvel, 1975), 16.

12. Joe Simon and Jack Kirby, *Fighting American* #3 (Prize, 1954), 15.

13. Jack Kirby and Stan Lee, "Gunman at Large!," *Two-Gun Kid* #62 (Marvel, 1963), 12.

14. Stan Lee and Jack Kirby, "The Blitzkrieg of Batroc!," *Tales of Suspense* #85 (Marvel, 1966), 20.

15. Chris Claremont and John Byrne, "The Fate of the Phoenix!," *The Uncanny X-Men* #137 (Marvel, 1980), 20.

16. Comics Reporter, "DC Rocks Industry with Royalty Program," *Comics Scene* #2 (Starlog Presents, 1982), 7.

17. Howard Zimmerman, "KIRBY takes on Comics," *Comics Scene* #2 (Starlog Presents, 1982), 25.

18. Mark Borax and Jack Kirby, "Jack Kirby," *David Anthony Kraft's Comics Interview* #41 (Fictioneer, 1986), 54.

19. Starlin, *The Art of Jim Starlin: A Life in Words and Pictures*, 175.

20. Will Eisner and Jack Kirby, "Jack Kirby," *Will Eisner's Shop Talk* (Darkhorse, 2001), 221.

21. John Byrne, "On Creator's Rights," *Comics Scene* #2 (Starlog Presents, 1982), 56–57.

22. *Ibid.*

23. John Byrne, "Beginnings and Endings," *Fantastic Four* #244 (Marvel, 1982), 14.

24. Lee and Kirby, "Prisoners of Doctor Doom!," *The Fantastic Four* #5, 23.

25. John Byrne, "Interlude," *Fantastic Four* #258 (Marvel, 1983), 13.

26. Stan Lee and Jack Kirby, "Within this Tortured Land," *Fantastic Four* #85 (Marvel, 1969), 7.

27. Howard Zimmerman, "KIRBY takes on Comics," *Comics Scene* #2 (Starlog Presents, 1982), 25.

28. Steve Gerber and Jack Kirby, "Spineless," *Destroyer Duck* #4 (Eclipse, 1983), 6.

29. Steve Gerber and John Morrow, "The Other Duck Man," *The Collected Jack Kirby Collector* vol. 2 (Raleigh: TwoMorrows, 2004), 74.

30. "Komico: Comics Comics Comics," *The Gazette* (Postmedia Network, 24 July 1982), D16.

31. John Byrne, *Marv Wolfman vs Marvel Enterprises* (1999), https://ohdannyboy.blogspot.com/2012/09/when-i-am-working-for-marvel-i-am-loyal.html.

32. *Ibid.*

33. Byrne, Simonson, and Ryall, *Jack Kirby Panel*, 23:30.

34. John Byrne, "I sing of arms and heroes… ," *Avengers West Coast* #51 (Marvel, 1989), 4.

35. Stan Lee and Jack Kirby, "The Return of the Frightful Four!," *Fantastic Four* #94 (Marvel, 1969), 5.

36. Jack Kirby, "OMAC," *OMAC* #1 (DC Comics, 1974), 2.

37. John Byrne, *OMAC* #1 (DC Comics, 1991), 40.

38. Byrne, *Marv Wolfman vs Marvel Enterprises*, https://ohdannyboy.blogspot.com/2012/09/when-i-am-working-for-marvel-i-am-loyal.html.

39. John Byrne, "Why was HIDDEN YEARS cancelled?," *Byrne Robotics* (ByrneRobotics.com, 2013), https://web.archive.org/web/20130126025406/http://www.byrnerobotics.com/FAQ/listing.asp?ID=2&T1=Questions+about+Comic+Book+Projects#54.

Chapter 22

1. Andrew Friedenthal, "Monitoring the Past: DC Comics' Crisis on Infinite Earths and the Narrativization of Comic Book History," *Interdisciplinary Comic Studies* (ImageTexT, 2011), https://web.archive.org/web/20180315212451/http://www.english.ufl.edu/imagetext/archives/v6_2/friedenthal/.

2. Frank Miller, *The Dark Knight Returns* #4 (DC Comics, 1986), 48.

3. Don Watson, "Shazam! The hero breaks down," *The Observer* (Guardian Media Group, 2 November 1986), 57.

4. David Marchese and Alan Moore, "Alan Moore on Why Superhero Fans Need to Grow Up, Brexit, and His Massive New Novel," *New York Vulture* (VoxMedia, 12 September 2016), https://www.vulture.com/2016/09/alan-moore-jerusalem-comics-writer.html.

5. George Khoury, *The Extraordinary Works of Alan Moore* (TwoMorrows, 2003), 24–25.

6. Jonathan Ross, *In Search of Steve Ditko* (BBC, 2007), 36:35.

7. Michael Eury, *Dick Giordano: Changing Comics, One Day at a Time* (Raleigh: TwoMorrows, 2003), 117.

8. *Ibid.*, 124.

9. Jon B. Cooke, "Toasting Absent Heroes," *Comic Book Artist* #9 (TwoMorrows, 2000), 101–102.

10. *Ibid.*, 102.

11. Moore and Gibbons, "Watchmaker," *Watchmen* #4, 8–10.

12. *Ibid.*, 19–20.

13. Bell, *The World of Steve Ditko*, 15, 20.

14. Alan Moore and Dave Gibbons, "Absent Friends," *Watchmen* #2 (DC Comics, 1986), 6.

15. Moore and Gibbons, *Watchmen* #4, 19.

16. Moore and Gibbons, *Watchmen* #2, 15.

17. *Ibid.*, 18.

18. Moore and Gibbons, *Watchmen* #4, 19.

19. Harry Shorten and Irv Novick, "The SHIELD," *PEP Comics* #1 (Archie, 1940), 1.

20. Cooke, *Comic Book Artist* #9, 101.

21. Alan Moore and Dave Gibbons, "At Midnight, All the Agents…," *Watchmen* #1 (DC Comics, 1986), 17.

22. Alan Moore and Dave Gibbons, "A Stronger Loving World," *Watchmen* #12 (DC Comics, 1986), 1.

23. Cooke, *Comic Book Artist* #9, 103.

24. Pete Morisi, *Peter Cannon … Thunderbolt* #1 (Charlton, 1966), 7.

25. Glen D. Johnson, "Pete Morisi, Man of Thunderbolt," *Comic Book Artist* #9 (TwoMorrows, 2000), 62–63.

26. Cooke, *Comic Book Artist* #9, 100.

27. Alan Moore and Dave Gibbons, "The Abyss Gazes Also," *Watchmen* #6 (DC Comics, 1986), 30.

28. Moore and Gibbons, *Watchmen* #6, 24.

29. Moore and Gibbons, *Watchmen* #1, 1.

30. Cooke, *Comic Book Artist* #9, 103.

31. Ross, *In Search of Steve Ditko* (BBC, 2007), 36:35.

32. Steve Ditko, "Mr. A," *Witzend* vol. 1 (Fantagraphics, 2014), 87.

33. Moore and Gibbons, *Watchmen* #12, 24.

34. Moore and Gibbons, *Watchmen* #1, 9.

35. Moore and Gibbons, *Watchmen* #2, 5.

36. Moore and Gibbons, *Watchmen* #1, 9.

37. Alan Moore and Dave Gibbons, "Old Ghosts," *Watchmen* #8 (DC Comics 1986), 28.

38. Moore and Gibbons, *Watchmen* #7, 5.

39. Moore and Gibbons, *Watchmen* #2, 18.

40. Moore and Gibbons, *Watchmen* #1, 13.

41. Alan Moore and Dave Gibbons, "A Brother to Dragons," *Watchmen* #7 (DC Comics 1986), 15.

42. Charles Nicholas, "The Armored Truck Robbery," *Mystery Men Comics* #2 (Fox Publications, 1939), 47.

43. Cooke, *Comic Book Artist* #9, 103.

44. Steve Ditko, "The End is a Beginning!," *Blue Beetle* #2 (Charlton, 1967), 12.

45. Steve Ditko, "Faces the Destroyer of Heroes," *Blue Beetle* #5 (Charlton, 1968), 3.

46. *Ibid.*, 18.

47. Moore and Gibbons, *Watchmen* #2, 4.

48. Cooke, *Comic Book Artist* #9, 103.

49. Moore and Gibbons, *Watchmen* #2, 8.

50. Moore and Gibbons, *Watchmen* #1, 25.

51. Alan Moore and Dave Gibbons, "The Darkness of Mere Being," *Watchmen* #9 (DC Comics, 1986), 16.

52. Gene Armstrong, "Comics with Kick,"

Arizona Daily Star (Lee Enterprises, 5 December 1987), 11.

53. Anna Byrd David, "Comic book format draws readers to graphic novels," *The Albuquerque Tribune* (EW Scripps Company, 12 January 1988), B5.

54. Stella Babirz, "Drawn and quartered," *The Age* (Nine Entertainment, 6 February 1999), 10.

55. Alan Moore, "Alan Moore on (Just About), Everything!," *The Comics Journal* #106 (Fantagraphics, 1986), 38.

56. Dave Itzkoff, "The Vendetta Behind 'V for Vendetta,'" *The New York Times* (The New York Times Company, 12 March 2006), 1.

57. Matthew Price, "'Watchmen' prequels announced," *The Daily Oklahoman* (Gannett, 3 February 2012), 11D.

58. Marchese, *New York Vulture* (Vox Media, Sep. 12, 2016), https://www.vulture.com/2016/09/alan-moore-jerusalem-comics-writer.html.

Chapter 23

1. Richard Kyle, "Richard Kyle's WONDERWORLD," *K-A CAPA alpha 02* (K-A CAPA alpha, November 1964), 31.

2. Paul Levitz, "Will Eisner and the Secret History of the Graphic Novel," *New York Vulture* (VoxMedia, 10 November 2015), https://www.vulture.com/2015/10/will-eisner-graphic-novels-paul-levitz.html#.

3. George Walker, "The Passion of a Man," *Graphic Witness* (Richmond Hill: Firefly, 2007), 19–21.

4. Madeleine Schwartz, "Lynd Ward's America," *The New Yorker* (Condé Nast, 2010), https://www.newyorker.com/books/page-turner/lynd-wards-america.

5. Walker, "The Passion of a Man," *Graphic Witness*, 27.

6. Pierre Assouline, *Hergé, the Man Who Created Tintin* (Oxford: Oxford University Press, 2009), 26–29.

7. *Ibid.*, 48–55.

8. Suzanne Curley, "Comic-book hero's good deeds reap rich rewards for reader," *Fort Worth Star-Telegram* (The McClatchy Company, 15 August 1984), 3B.

9. Greenwald, Seymour, "He Done Her Wrong," *The Morning Call* (Alden, 10 January 1931), 18.

10. Gayle Hoskins, "A Cowboy's Day," *Western Story Magazine* (Street & Smith, 1931), cover.

11. Arnold Drake, Leslie Waller, and Matt Baker, *It Rhymes with Lust* (Milwaukie: Darkhorse, 2007), 136.

12. Roger Hill, "Introduction," *Crime Illustrated* (Gemstone, 2006), 1.

13. _____, "Introduction," *Confessions Illustrated* (Gemstone, 2006), 1.

14. J. David Spurlock, "Horror & Dracula: Ancient Transylvanian Lore to Modern Graphic Novel," *Dracula* (Vanguard, 2021), 10–11.

15. Daniel Herman, *Gil Kane: The Art of Comics* (New Castle: Hermes Press, 2002), 69–74.

16. Gil Kane, *His Name Is … Savage* (Adventure House Press, 1968), 14.

17. *Ibid.*, 33.

18. Groth, "Gil Kane," *The Comics Journal* #186, 87.

19. *Ibid.*, 89.

20. Dane Lanken, "The return of Tarzan as seen by Hogarth," *The Gazette* (Postmedia Network, 18 November 1972), 53.

21. Siuntres, *The World of Comic Books*, https://youtu.be/3Vmq8DSkb_4?t=6.

22. Daniel Robert Epstein, "The First Graphic Novel? Steranko's Take," *Newsarama/GamesRadar* (Imaginova, 2003), https://web.archive.org/web/20051224054554/http://newsarama.com/forums/showthread.php?s=&threadid=4576#.

23. "Beyond Time and Again," *Fantagraphics.com* (Fantagraphics, 2016), https://www.fantagraphics.com/products/beyond-time-and-again.

24. Paul Levitz, "Will Eisner and the Secret History of the Graphic Novel," *New York Vulture* (VoxMedia, November 10, 2015), https://www.vulture.com/2015/10/will-eisner-graphic-novels-paul-levitz.html#.

25. Kyle, "Richard Kyle's WONDERWORLD," *K-A CAPA alpha 02*, 31.

26. Gail De Vos, "A Contract with God," *Encyclopedia of Comic Books and Graphic Novels* (Westport: Greenwood, 2010), 117.

27. Michael Schumacher, *Will Eisner: A Dreamer's Life in Comics* (New York: Bloomsbury Publishing, 2010), 196–197.

28. Michael Moorcock, "Introduction," *The Swords of Heaven, The Flowers of Hell* (New York: Heavy Metal, 1979), 1–2.

29. Don McGregor and Marshall Rogers, *Detectives, Inc.* (Staten Island: Eclipse, 1980), 2–3.

30. Alex Grand, Jim Thompson, and Jim Shooter, "Jim Shooter Biographical Interview," *Comic Book Historians YouTube* (CBH, 2021), https://youtu.be/FBh709_dLNs?t=14515.

31. Marc Kirkeby, "Flash! Batman Neurotic, Superman to See Shrink!," *Daily News* (Tribune Publishing, 12 September 1982), 26.

32. James Peltz, "Warner sells Atari to Tramiel's Company," *Fort Worth Star-Telegram* (The McClatchy Company, 3 July 1984), D1.

33. Alexis C. Madrigal, "A Golden Age of Books? There Were Only 500 Real Bookstores in 1931," *The Atlantic* (Emerson Collective, June 8, 2012), https://www.theatlantic.com/technology/archive/2012/06/a-golden-age-of-books-there-were-only-500-real-bookstores-in-1931/258309/.

Chapter 24

1. Alex Grand, Jim Thompson, "Trina Robbins Superstar," *Comic Book Historians Podcast* (2019), Episodes 34, 41.

2. *Ibid.*, the quotes in this chapter are from Robbins's personal communication and research.

Chapter 25

1. Alex Grand, Jim Thompson, "Professor William H. Foster III & African Americans in Comics," *Comic Book Historians Podcast* (2021), Episodes 100, 101.

2. *Ibid.*, the quotes in this chapter are from Professor Foster's personal communication and research.

Chapter 26

1. "Richard B. Ayers," *The Journal News* (Gannett, 8 May 2014), 16A.

2. Florentino Flórez, *Big John Buscema* (IDW, 2012), 291–292.

3. Matt Moore and Ula Ilnytzky, "Comic book artist Gene Colan dies," *The Times and Democrat* (Lee Enterprises, 27 June 2011), A7.

4. Robert Bryant, *The Thin Black Line* (Raleigh: TwoMorrows, 2010), 115.

5. Aaron Couch and Andy Lewis, "Steve Ditko, Spider-Man Co-Creator and Legendary Comics Artist, Dies at 90," *The Hollywood Reporter* (Penske Media Corporation, 2018), https://www.hollywoodreporter.com/movies/movie-news/steve-ditko-dead-spider-man-creator-was-90-1125489/.

6. Mike Antonucci, "Sci-fi's quiet gurus were among media heroes lost in 1998," *The Indianapolis News* (Tegna, 31 December 1998), D1.

7. Page X, "One Heck of an Artist," *The Central New Jersey Home News* (Gannett, 21 April 1995), 3.

8. Daniel Herman, *Gil Kane: The Art of Comics* (New Castle: Hermes Press, 2002), 25.

9. *Ibid.*, 133–137.

10. Evanier, *Kirby: King of Comics*, 217–225.

11. Schelly, *Harvey Kurtzman: The Man Who Created MAD and Revolutionized Humor in America*, 573–576.

12. Fingeroth, *A Marvelous Life*, 340–341.

13. Jon B. Cooke, "A Sheldon Mayer Timeline," *Comic Book Artist* #11 (TwoMorrows, 2001), 10B–11B.

14. Dennis Hevesi, "Jerry Robinson, Godfather of a Comic-Book Villain, Dies at 89," *The New York Times* (The New York Times Compaany, 9 December 2011), 28.

15. J. Michael Catron, "Julius Schwartz, 1915–2004," *The Comics Journal* #259 (Fantagraphics, 2004), 23–24.

16. Michael Dean, "Two Sides of Julie the Ladies' Man," *The Comics Journal* #259 (Fantagraphics, 2004), 22.

17. "Marie Severin Comics Hall of Famer, 89," *The Philadelphia Inquirer* (The Philadelphia Foundation, 5 September 2018), B4.

18. Skelly and Kirby, "My School was Alex Raymond and Milton Caniff," *The Nostalgia Journal* #27, 17.

19. Matt Moore, "Joe Simon, co-creator of Captain America," *The Herald-News* (Shaw Media, 16 December 2011), C7.

20. Steve Ringgenberg, "Joe Sinnott: 1926–2020," *The Comics Journal* (Fantagraphics, 2020), https://www.tcj.com/joe-sinnott-1926-2020/.

21. Steve Holland, "Al Williamson obituary," *The Guardian* (Scott Trust Limited, 2013), https://www.theguardian.com/books/2010/jul/14/al-williamson-obituary.

22. Steve Starger and J. David Spurlock, "The End," *Wally's World* (Lebanon: Vanguard, 2007), 210–215.

Bibliography

Abbott, Charles David. "Howard Pyle." *Dictionary of American Biography*. New York: Scribner's, 1935.

Abel, Jack. "Werewolf by Night." *Marvel Tales* #116. Marvel, 1953.

Active Interest Media. *Writer's Digest*. Active Interest Media, 1942.

Ad. "Komico: Comics, Comics, Comics." *The Gazette*. Postmedia Network, 24 July 1982.

Alan. "Alan Moore on Why Superhero Fans Need to Grow Up, Brexit, and His Massive New Novel." *New York Vulture*. VoxMedia, 2016. https://www.vulture.com/2016/09/alan-moore-jerusalem-comics-writer.html.

Alfred, Newt. "Master Man." *Master Comics* #1. Fawcett Comics, 1940.

Allen, Hervey. *Israfel: The Life and Times of Edgar Allan Poe*. New York: Farrar & Rinehart, 1934.

Alstiel, Tom, Jean Grow and Marcel Jennings. *Advertising Creative*. Thousand Oaks, California: SAGE Publications, 2018.

Amash, Jim. "Foreword." *The Adam Strange Archives*: Volume 1. DC Comics, 2003.

———. "Roy Thomas Interview." *Jack Kirby Collector* #18. TwoMorrows, 1998.

Amash, Jim, and Carmine Infantino. *Carmine Infantino, Penciler-Publisher-Provocateur*. North Carolina: TwoMorrows, 2010.

Andelman, Bob. *Will Eisner: A Spirited Life*. New Orleans: M Press, 2005.

Andelman, David. "Today's Comics Feature Black Characters as Heroes." *The Palm Beach Post*. Gannett, 10 April 1970.

Andrae, Thomas. *The Phantom: The Complete Sundays: Volume 1 (1939–1942)*. New Castle: Hermes Press, 2012.

Andrae, Thomas, and Jerry Siegel. "Of Superman and Kids with Dreams." *NEMO: The Classics Comics Library* #2. Fantagraphics, 1983.

Antonucci, Mike. "Sci-fi's quiet gurus were among media heroes lost in 1998." *The Indianapolis News*. The Indianapolis News, 1998.

Aragonés, Sergio, Bob Oksner, and Wally Wood. "Most Fantastic Robbery in History!" *Angel and Ape* #2. DC Comics, 1969.

Armstrong, Gene. "Comics with Kick." *Arizona Daily Star*. Lee Enterprises, 12 May 1987.

Arndt, Richard. *Star Reach Companion*. Raleigh: TwoMorrows, 2013.

Arne, Sigrid. "Loose Morals, Murder and Thievery Portrayed." *The Daily Argus-Leader*. Gannett, 17 October 1954.

Ashe, Edd. "The Wizard." *Top Notch Comics* #1. Archie, 1939.

The Associated Press. "Martin Goodman, 84, Marvel Comics Founder." *Newsday*. Newsday Media, 12 June 1992.

The Associated Press. "People Throughout the Free World Anxiously Followed Glenn's Flight." *Johnson City Press*. Tennessee: Six Rivers Media, 1962.

Assouline, Pierre. *Hergé, the Man Who Created Tintin*. Oxford: Oxford University Press, 2009.

Ayers, Dick. *The Dick Ayers Story*, vol. 2. Columbia: Mecca Comics Group, 2005.

Ayers, Dick, Gary Friedrich, and Roy Thomas. "Origin of The Ghost Rider." *The Ghost Rider #1*. Marvel, 1967.

Babirz, Stella. "Drawn and Quartered." *The Age*. Nine Entertainment, 6 February 1999.

Baker, Matt. "Scoundrels and Scandals." *Phantom Lady* #14. Fox Publications, 1947.

Ballman, J. *The 1964 New York Comicon: The True Story Behind the World's First Comic Convention*. Bethesda: Totalmojo Productions, 2016.

Balmer, Edwin, and Philip Wylie. "When World's Collide." *The Friend Sentinel*. Seward Independent, 24 January 1935.

Barberich, Kathy. "Bullard alumnus draws on his talent at cartoon school." *The Fresno Bee*. The McClatchy Company, 1994.

Barr, Mike W. "The Madames & the Girls, The DC Writers Purge of 1968." *Comic Book Artist Collection*, vol. 2. Raleigh: TwoMorrows, 2002.

Barry, Less. "The Barry Patch." *St. Albans Daily Messenger*. O'Rourke Media Group, 7 April 1955.

Baxter, Stephen. *War of the Worlds: Fresh Perspectives on the H.G. Wells Classic*. Dallas: Benbella, 2005.

Beard, Jim, Keith Dallas, and Jason Sacks. *American Comic Book Chronicles: 1970s*. Raleigh: TwoMorrows, 2014.

Beaty, Bart. *Fredric Wertham and the Critique of Mass Culture*. Jackson: University Press of Mississippi, 2005.

Beck, CC. *Fawcett Companion: The Best of FCA*. Raleigh: TwoMorrows, 2001.

Beckerman, Jim. "The strange, true story of kooky bodybuilding star, Bernarr Macfadden." *The Herald News*. South Illinois: Shaw Media, 2019.

Beerbohm, Robert, Doug Wheeler, and Leonardo De Sá. "Töpffer in America." *Comic Art Magazine* #3, 2003.

Belcher, Jerry. "Shazam! Comic Books Turn 50." *The Charlotte Observer*. Sacramento: The McClatchy Company, 25 July 1984.

Bell, Blake. *Strange and Stranger: The World of Steve Ditko*. Seattle: Fantagraphics, 2008.

Bell, Blake, and Dr. Michael J. Vassallo. *The Secret History of Marvel Comics*. Seattle: Fantagraphics, 2013.

Benton, Mike. *Superhero Comics of the Golden Age: The Illustrated History*. Dallas: Taylor Publishing Company, 1992.

Berger, Arthur. "Krazy Kat's Creator." *St. Lous Post-Dispatch*. Davenport: Lee Enterprises, 2 November 1971.

Bernstein, Robert, and Ramona Fradon. "How Aquaman Got His Powers!" *Adventure Comics* #260. DC Comics, 1959.

Bester, Alfred. "The School for Vandals." *Green Lantern* #9. All-American Comics Publications, 1943.

Better Publications. "Meet Our Science Fiction Family—Alex Schomburg." *Thrilling Wonder Stories*. Better Publications, 1939.

Binder, Otto, and CC. Beck. "Captain Marvel and the Webs of Crime." *Whiz Comics* #89. Fawcett, 1947.

Black Press. "'Captain Marvel' Serial to Begin." *The Honolulu Advertiser*. Black Press, 1941.

———. "Superman Comic Strip Is Winner in Court Action." *Honolulu Star-Bulletin*. Black Press, 1940.

Blackton, James Stuart, and Albert E. Smith. *Hooligan Assists the Magician*. West Orange: Thomas A. Edison, 1900.

Bode, Janet. "A Comic Book Artist KO'D." *The Village Voice*, 12 December 1987.

Booker, Keith M. "Baker, Matt." *Comics Through Time: A History of Icons, Idols, and Ideas*, vols. 1–4. Westport: Greenwood, 2014.

Borax, Mark, and Jack Kirby. "Jack Kirby." *David Anthony Kraft's Comics Interview* #41. Fictioneer Books, 1986.

Boring, Wayne, and Stan Kaye. *Superman* #58. DC Comics, 1949.

Boucher, Geoff. "Alex Toth, 77; Maverick Artist Drew Comic Books." *The Los Angeles Times*. Los Angeles Times Communications, 2006.

Boyd, Alex. "The Once and Future King!" *FOOM!* #11. Marvel, 1975.

Bradd, Sidney. "Robert J. Hogan." *Ageofaces.net*. Age of Aces Books, 2019. https://www.ageofaces.net/authors-artists/robert-j-hogan/.

Breznican, Anthony. "Superhero creator sees no reason to call it quits." *The Sault Star*. Postmedia, 3 April 2002.

Broome, John, and Carmine Infantino. *The Flash* #125. DC Comics, 1961.

Broome, John, and Gil Kane. "S.O.S. Green Lantern." *Showcase* #22. DC Comics, 1959.

Brough, Rick. "Horror Comics Censored." *The Daily Utah Chronicle*. University of Utah, 8 November 1976.

Brower, Steven. *Comics Ad Men*. Seattle: Fantagraphics, 2019.

Brown, Len. "Foreword." *T.H.U.N.D.E.R. Agents Archives* #6. DC Comics, 2005.

Bryant, Robert. *The Thin Black Line*. Raleigh: TwoMorrows, 2010.

Burnley, Jack. *Adventure Comics* #61. Detective Comics, 1940.

Burstein, Martin, and Jack Kirby. "Mercury." *Red Raven Comics* #1. Timely, 1940.

Buscema, John. "Story Search Results." *Grand Comics Database*, 2021. https://www.comics.org/credit/name/John%20Buscema/sort/chrono/.

Byrd, Bob, and Ben Thompson. "Adventures of Ka-Zar the Great." *Marvel Comics* #1. Timely, 1939.

Byrne, John. "Beginnings and Endings." *Fantastic Four* #244. Marvel, 1982.

———. *Byrne Robotics*. Byrne Robotics.com, 2005. http://www.byrnerobotics.com/forum/forum_posts.asp?TID=5806&KW=Bromwich.

———. "I sing of arms and heroes...." *Avengers West Coast* #51. Marvel, 1989.

———. "Interlude." *Fantastic Four* #258. Marvel, 1983.

———. "Kirby's Kosmic Konsciousness." *FOOM!* #11. Marvel, 1975.

———. *Marv Wolfman vs Marvel Enterprises*. 1999. https://ohdannyboy.blogspot.com/2012/09/when-i-am-working-for-marvel-i-am-loyal.html.

———. *OMAC* #1. DC Comics, 1991.

———. "On Creator's Rights." *Comics Scene* #2. Starlog Presents, 1982.

_____. "Why was HIDDEN YEARS cancelled?" *Byrne Robotics,* 2013. https://web.archive.org/web/20130126025406/http://www.byrnerobotics.com/FAQ/listing.asp?ID=2&T1=Questions+about+Comic+Book+Projects#54.

Byrne, John, and Duffy Vohland. "The Castle." *Nightmare* #20, Skywald. 1974.

_____. "Foom Fan Art Gallery." *FOOM!* #5. Marvel, 1974.

Byrne, John, and Roger Stern. "Avengers Assemble!" *The Avengers* #233. Marvel, 1983.

Calkins, Dick. *Buck Rogers in the 25th Century,* vol. 1. New Castle: Hermes Press, 2009.

Canemaker, John. *Winsor McCay: His Life and Art.* New York: Harry N. Abrams, 2005.

Caniff, Milton. *The Complete Terry and the Pirates,* vol. 1. San Diego: IDW, 2007.

_____. *The Complete Terry and the Pirates,* vol. 2. San Diego: IDW, 2007.

_____. *The Complete Terry and the Pirates,* vol. 3. San Diego: IDW, 2008.

_____. *The Complete Terry and the Pirates,* vol. 4. San Diego: IDW, 2008.

_____. "Dickie Dare." *Chillicothe Gazette.* Gannett, 9 May 1934.

Canwell, Bruce. "The Protean Illustrator." *Scorchy Smith and the Art of Noel Sickles.* IDW, 2008.

Carlin, John, Paul Karasik, Brian Walker, Tom De Haven, Cynthia Burlingham, Stanley Crouch, Jules Feiffer, et al. *Masters of American Comics.* New Haven, Connecticut: Yale University Press, 2005.

Carlson, Barbara. "Editor Hated Superman." *Hartford Courant.* Tribune Publishing, 7 February 1972.

Carlson, Michael. "Frank Frazetta." *The Independent.* Evgeny Lebedev, 20 July 2010.

Carpenter, Humphrey, and Mari Prichard. *The Oxford Companion to Children's Literature.* Oxford: Oxford University Press, 1984.

Carter, Chip, and Jonathan Carter. "Spider-Man creator Stan Lee opens up." *Florida Today.* 6 January 1996.

Catron, J. Michael. "Julius Schwartz, 1915–2004." *The Comics Journal* #259. Fantagraphics, 2004.

Cavna, Michael. "Trump's proposed 'Space Force' has its pop-culture roots in a little-known comic." *The Bellingham Herald.* The McClatchy Company, 28 June 2018.

Charroux, Robert. *Lost Worlds: Scientific Secrets of the Ancients.* London: Souvenir Press, 1973.

Chatham Asset Management. "About Caniff and a Guy Named Steve." *The Charlotte News.* 1947.

Childers, James Saxon. "1890 Dandy Left Wealth of Beauty." *The Birmingham News.* Advance Publications, 1934.

Claremont, Chris, and Frank Miller. *Wolverine* #1. Marvel, 1982.

Claremont, Chris, and John Byrne. "The Fate of the Phoenix!" *The Uncanny X-Men* #137. Marvel, 1980.

_____. *The Uncanny X-Men* #133. Marvel, 1980.

Clark, Noelene. "New Marvel world ready for fall debut." *The Los Angeles Times.* Los Angeles Times Communications, 2015.

Clarkkent54321. *Blackstone Master Magician Comics.* Comic Book Plus. Harare, Zimbabwe: Vital Publications, 2012. https://comicbookplus.com/?dlid=29511.

Cline, William. "Adventures of Captain Marvel in 1941 pioneered a completely new type of screen champion—the SuperHero." *In the Nick of Time.* Jefferson: McFarland, 1984.

Cluett, Jack. "Jest Among Ourselves." *Brooklyn Daily Eagle,* 22 September 1936.

Coates, John. *Don Heck: A Work of Art.* Raleigh: TwoMorrows, 2014.

Cohen, Sandy. "Hollywood animates San Diego's Comic-Con." *Austin American-Statesman,* 21 July 2010.

Colavito, Jason. *The Cult of Alien Gods: H.P. Lovecraft and Extraterrestrial Pop Culture.* Amherst: Prometheus Books, 2005.

Cole, Jack. "The Coming of the Comet." *Pep Comics* #1. MLJ Magazines, 1940.

_____. *Playboy* #5. Playboy Enterprises, 1954.

_____. *Silver Streak Comics* #7. Lev Gleason, 1941.

Comichron. "The Amazing Spider-Man monthly sales." 2021. https://www.comichron.com/titlespotlights/amazingspiderman.html.

Comics Reporter. "DC Rocks Industry with Royalty Program." *Comics Scene* #2. Starlog Presents, 1982.

Comtois, Pierre. *Marvel Comics in the 1970s: An Issue-by-issue Field Guide to a Pop Culture Phenomenon.* Raleigh: TwoMorrows, 2011.

Cones, John. *Motion Picture Biographies: The Hollywood Spin on Historical Figures.* New York: Algora Publishing, 2015.

Contributor. "Famous Funnies a Carnival of Comics." *Grand Comics Database.* Eastern Color, 1933. https://www.comics.org/issue/75/.

Conway, Gerry, and Gene Colan. "Even the Noble Die!" *Sub-Mariner* #46. Marvel, 1972.

Conway, Gerry, and Gil Kane. "The Night Gwen Stacy Died." *The Amazing Spider-Man* #121. Marvel, 1973.

Conway, Gerry, Roy Thomas, and Gray Morrow. "...Man-Thing!" *Savage Tales* #1. Marvel, 1971.

Coogan, Peter. *Superhero: The Secret Origin of a Genre.* Austin: MonkeyBrain Books, 2006.

Cooke, Jon B. "The Cosmic Code Authority Speaks! Talking with Jim Starlin, Alan Weiss and Al Milgrom on those trippy '70s Marvel Comics." *Comic Book Artist* #18. TwoMorrows, 2002.

_____. "Drawing with a Ballpoint Pen." *Modern Masters Vol. Seven: John Byrne.* TwoMorrows, 2006.

_____. "John Romita on Milton Caniff." *Comic Book Creator* #21. TwoMorrows, 2019.

_____. "Reed Crandall." *The T.H.U.N.D.E.R. Agents Companion.* TwoMorrows, 2001.

_____. "A Sheldon Mayer Timeline." *Comic Book Artist* #11. TwoMorrows, 2001.

_____. "Toasting Absent Heroes." *Comic Book Artist* #9. TwoMorrows, 2000.

Cotto, Marguerite. "Flash Gordon." *The Guide to United States Popular Culture*. Atlanta: Georgia State University Popular Press, 2001.

Couch, Aaron, and Andy Lewis. "Steve Ditko, Spider-Man Co-Creator and Legendary Comics Artist, Dies at 90." *The Hollywood Reporter*. Penske Media Corporation, 2018. https://www.hollywoodreporter.com/movies/movie-news/steve-ditko-dead-spider-man-creator-was-90-1125489/.

Cox. "Publisher Denies Comic Book Harmful." *Dayton Daily News*, 1954.

Cox, J. Randolph. *Man of Magic and Mystery*. Lanham: Scarecrow Press, 1988.

Crandall, Reed. "Old Witch." *Hit Comics* #10. Quality, 1941.

_____. *T.H.U.N.D.E.R. Agents* #1. Tower, 1965.

_____. *Treasure Chest of Fun and Fact*, vol. 17, #8. George A. Pflaum, 1960.

Crandall, Reed, and Archie Goodwin. "The Coffin of Dracula." *Creepy* #27. Warren, 1969.

Cross, Mary. *A Century of American Icons: 100 Products and Slogans from the 20th-Century Consumer Culture*. Westport: Greenwood Press, 2002.

Crossen, Ken, and Mac Raboy. *Green Lama* #1. Spark, 1944.

Curley, Suzanne. "Comic-book hero's good deeds reap rich rewards for reader." *Fort Worth Star-Telegram*. The McClatchy Company, 1984.

Cuti, Nicola, and John Byrne. "ROG-2000 in That Was No Lady." *E-Man* #6. 1975.

Dahlman, Steve. "Electro: The Marvel of the Age." *Marvel Mystery Comics* #4. Timely, 1940.

Daniels, Les. "The Changing of the Guard." *MARVEL: Five Fabulous Decades of the World's Greatest Comics*. Harry N. Abrams, 1991.

Daniels, Les, and Chip Kidd. *Batman: The Complete History*. Chronicle Books, 1999.

Darling, Ada. "Obadiah Oldbuck, Hero of Long Ago, Now Character Doll." *Dunkirk Evening Observer*. Ogden Newspapers, 1941.

David, Anna Byrd. "Comic Book format draws readers to graphic novels." *The Albuquerque Tribune*, 12 January 1988.

Davis, Chuck. "What's in a name?" *The Vancouver Sun*. Postmedia Network, 11 April 2005.

DC Fandom. "Batman #127." *DC Database*. DC Comics, 1959. https://dc.fandom.com/wiki/Batman_Vol_1_127.

_____. "Smash Comics #14." *DC Database*. DC Comics, 1940. https://dc.fandom.com/wiki/Smash_Comics_Vol_1_14.

_____. "Space Adventures Vol 2 33." *DC Database*. Charlton, 1960. https://dc.fandom.com/wiki/Space_Adventures_Vol_2_33.

Dean, M. *The Studio*. Lewes: Dragon's Dream, 1979.

Dean, Michael. "Two Sides of Julie the Ladies' Man." *The Comics Journal* #259. Fantagraphics, 2004.

Decker, David, and Gary Groth. "An interview with William M. Gaines." *The Comics Journal*, 1983.

DeFalco, Tom. "John Romita." *Comics Creators on Spider-Man*. London: Titan Books, 2004.

Dekom, Otto. "266 German Kids on Public View." *The News Journal Papers*, 14 November 1979.

Del Rey, Lester. *The World of Science Fiction: 1926–1976: The History of a Subculture*. New York: Ballantine Books, 1979.

Dempster, George R. "One of the star attractions at the New York World's Fair." *The Knoxville Journal*. Gannett, 1940.

Dent, Lester. *Brand of the Werewolf*. Canada: pgdpcanada 1933 reprint, 2017.

_____. *Fortress of Solitude*. Canada: pgdpcanada 1938 reprint, 2017.

_____. *The Man of Bronze*. Canada: pgdpcanada 1933 reprint, 2017.

_____. *The Thousand-Headed Man*. Canada: pgdpcanada 1934 reprint, 2017.

Desris, Joe. "A History of the 1940s Batman Newspaper Strip Part 2." *Batman: The Dailies 1943–1946*, vol. 2. Princeton: Kitchen Sink Press, 2007.

_____. "Tracy's Influence." *Batman: The Sunday Classics 1943–1946*. Princeton: Kitchen Sink Press, 2007.

De Vos, Gail. "A Contract with God." *Encyclopedia of Comic Books and Graphic Novels*. Westport: Greenwood, 2010.

Diehl, Digby. *Tales from the Crypt: The Official Archives*. New York: St. Martin's Press, 1996.

Dirda, Michael. "Boo! The best ghost stories you haven't heard yet." *The Fresno Bee*. The McClatchy Company, 2017.

Ditko, Steve. "The End is a Beginning!" *Blue Beetle* #2. Charlton, 1967.

_____. "Faces the Destroyer of Heroes." *Blue Beetle* #5. Charlton, 1968.

_____. "An Insider's Part of Comics History: Jack Kirby's Spider-Man." *Avenging World*. Snyder & Ditko, 2002.

_____. "Martin Goodman/Stan Lee." *Avenging Mind*. Bellingham: Snyder & Ditko, 2008.

_____. "A Mini-History 13." *The Comics!* 14, no. 8. Robin Snyder, 2003.

_____. *The Mr. A Collection*. Seattle: Fantagraphics, 1985.

_____. "Mr. A." *Witzend*, vol. 1. Seattle: Fantagraphics, 2014.

_____. "Spider-Man's Co-Creators." *TIME.* Time USA, 7 December 1998.

_____. "Tsk! Tsk! Why Do Some People Seek the Unearned?" *Avenging World.* Snyder & Ditko, 2002.

_____. "Why I Quit S-M, Marvel." *Robin Snyder and Steve Ditko,* 2015.

_____. "A World of His Own." *Strange Suspense Stories* #32. Charlton, 1957.

Ditko, Steve ,and Jack Oleck. "The Supermen." *Out of this World* #3. Charlton, 1957.

Ditko, Steve, and Joe Gill. "All Those Eyes." *Out of this World* #6. Charlton, 1957.

_____. "The Comeback." *Space War* #10. Charlton, 1961.

_____. "Director of the Board." *Strange Suspense Stories* #33. Charlton, 1957.

_____. "The Green Man." *This Magazine Is Haunted,* vol. 2, no. 14. Charlton, 1957.

_____. "The Human Powerhouse." *Strange Suspense Stories* #48. Charlton, 1960.

_____. "Introducing Captain Atom." *Space Adventures* #33. Charlton, 1960.

_____. "Journey to Paradise." *Out of this World* #7. Charlton, 1958.

_____. "The Most Terrible Fate." *Out of this World* #7. Charlton, 1958.

_____. "The Space Prowlers." *Space Adventures* #37. Charlton, 1960.

_____. "The Wrong Planet." *Space Adventures* #27. Charlton, 1959.

Ditko, Steve, and Stephen Skeates. *The Complete Four-Page Series and Other Essays.* Suffolk: Snyder & Ditko, 2020.

_____. "The Question?" *Blue Beetle* #4. Charlton, 1967.

Dodd, Mike. "Comic books go modern but maintain values." *Battle Creek Enquirer.* 30 September 1984.

Dooley, Dennis. "He can blow out 50 birthday candles with one puff!" *Great Falls Tribune.* 17 January 1988.

Drake, Arnold, and Bruno Premiani. *Doom Patrol* #106. DC Comics, 1966.

_____. *Doom Patrol* #121. DC Comics, 1968.

Drake, Arnold, and Jack Sparling. "Ego-Man." *SICK* #120. Charlton, 1978.

Drake, Arnold, Leslie Waller, and Matt Baker. *It Rhymes with Lust.* Milwaukee: Darkhorse, 2007.

Duke, Judith S. *Children's books and magazines: A market study.* White Plains: Knowledge Industry Publications, 1979.

Editorial. "Opponents overreact to threat of obscenity." *Angus-Leader,* 11 February 1988.

_____. "Prizes Won in Contest." *The Bennington Evening Banner.* Vermont News and Media, 12 October 1945.

Ehrenburg, Ann. "Who knows what magic lurks in the hearts of men?" *Fort Worth Star-Telegram.* The McClatchy Company, 3 September 1978.

Eisner, Ann. "Preface." *Will Eisner: The Best of The Preventive Maintenance Monthly.* Abrams, 2011.

Eisner, Will. "Interview with Gill Fox." *Will Eisner's Shop Talk.* Dark Horse, 2001.

_____. "The Wonder Man." *Wonder Comics* #1. Fox 1939.

Eisner, Will, and Jack Kirby. "Jack Kirby." *Will Eisner's Spirit Magazine.* Princeton: Kitchen Sink Press, 1982.

_____. "Jack Kirby." *Will Eisner's Shop Talk.* Darkhorse, 2001.

Ellsworth, Whitney. *Editorial Taboos,* discovered by Quattro, Ken. DC Comics, 1941.

Epstein, Daniel Robert. "The First Graphic Novel? Steranko's Take." *Newsarama/GamesRadar.* Imaginova, 2003. https://web.archive.org/web/20051224054554/http://newsarama.com/forums/showthread.php?s=&threadid=4576#.

Erisman, Robert. "Avengers of Space." *Marvel Science Stories* #1. Postal Publications, 1938.

Eury, Michael. *Dick Giordano: Changing Comics, One Day at a Time.* Raleigh: TwoMorrows, 2003.

_____. *The Justice League Companion: A Historical and Speculative Overview of the Silver Age Justice League of America.* Raleigh: TwoMorrows, 2005.

_____. *The Krypton Companion.* Raleigh: TwoMorrows, 2006.

_____. "The Man Who Redesigned Batman." *The Batcave Companion.* TwoMorrows, 2009.

Evanier, Mark. "Introduction." *Jack Kirby's The Demon.* DC Comics, 2008.

_____. "Jack F.A.Q.s." *Jack Kirby Collector* #45. TwoMorrows, 2006.

_____. "The Jack FAQ." *News From ME,* 2013.

_____. *Kirby: King of Comics.* New York: Abrams, 2017.

_____. "The Man Without Peer." *The Life and Legend of Wallace Wood,* vol. 1. Seattle: Fantagraphics, 2017.

_____. *Marvelmania* #2. Dimensional Industries, 1970.

Everett, Bill. "The Sub-Mariner." *Marvel Comics* #1. Timely Comics, 1939.

Evert, Roger. "A Comeback (Sock!) For Comic Books (Pop!)." *Chicago Sun-Times Sunday Supplement, MIDWEST.* Sun-Times Investment Holdings, 28 December 1966.

Fairfax Media. "Chariots of the Gods: Your Letters." *The Sydney Morning Herald,* 1969.

Falk, Lee, and Phil Davis. *Mandrake the Magician.* London: Titan, 2016.

Falk, Lee, and Ray Moore. *The Phantom, Vol. One 1936–1937.* New Castle: Hermes Press, 2010.

Fantagraphics. "Beyond Time and Again." *Fantagraphics.com,* 2016. https://www.fantagraphics.com/products/beyond-time-and-again.

_____. "Reed Crandall, Classic Draftsman, Dead at 65." *The Comics Journal* #77. Fantagraphics, 1982.

Faughnder, Ryan. "Comic book artist's heirs settle Marvel dispute." *Los Angeles Times.* Los Angeles Times Communications, 2014.

Feinstein, Isidor. "A Huge Hero." *Courier-Post*, 29 May 1930.

Fine, Lou. "The Mystery of the Disappearing Bridge!" *Nabisco*. Nabisco, 1953. https://allthingsger.blogspot.com/2015/04/mixed-messages.html.

Fine, Lou, and Will Eisner. *Smash Comics* #14. Quality, 1940.

Finger, Bill, and Sheldon Moldoff. *Batman* #127. DC Comics, 1959.

Fingeroth, Danny. *A Marvelous Life: The Amazing Story of Stan Lee.* New York: St. Martin's Publishing Group, 2019.

Fisher v. Star Co. 231 N.Y. 414. *United States Court of Appeals New York*, 1921.

Fishman, Margie. "POE-Etic License." *The News Journal*, 16 September, 2012.

Flemmons, Jerry. "Batman's Back and All's Right with the World." *Fort Worth Star-Telegram*. McClatchy Company, 1966.

Fleskes, John. *Joseph Clement Coll: The Art of Adventure.* Santa Cruz: Flesk Publications, 2003.

Flórez, Florentino. *Big John Buscema.* San Diego: IDW, 2012.

FOOM. "Another FOOM-tastic Preview Feature!" *FOOM!* #19. Marvel, 1977.

———. "Joe Simon and Jack Kirby: 'By Their Works Shall Ye Know Them.'" *FOOM!* #8. Marvel, 1974.

———. "Kirby Speaks!" *FOOM!* #11. Marvel, 1975.

Fox, Gardner, and Carmine Infantino. "The Flash of Two Worlds." *The Flash.* DC Comics, 1961.

———. "The Multiple Menace Weapon!" *Mystery in Space* #72. DC Comics, 1961.

Fox, Gardner, and Harry Lampert. *Flash Comics* #1. All-American Comics, 1940.

Fox, Gardner, and Mike Sekowsky. "Secret of the Eternal City." *Showcase* #17. DC Comics, 1958.

Fox, Gardner, and Murphy Anderson. "The Spectre: War that Shook the Universe." *Showcase* #60. DC Comics, 1966.

Fox, Gardner, Bob Kane, and Sheldon Moldoff. *Detective Comics* #31. DC Comics, 1939.

Fox, Gardner, and Bob Kane. *Detective Comics* #29. DC Comics, 1939.

Freedland, Nat. "Super Heroes with Super Problems." *New York Herald Tribune.* Reid Family, 9 January 1966.

Friedenthal, Andrew. "Monitoring the Past: DC Comics' Crisis on Infinite Earths and the Narrativization of Comic Book History." *Interdisciplinary Comic Studies.* ImageText, 2011. https://web.archive.org/web/20180315212451/http://www.english.ufl.edu/imagetext/archives/v6_2/friedenthal/.

Friedman, Drew. *Heroes of the Comics: Portraits of the Pioneering Legends of the Comic Books.* Seattle: Fantagraphics, 2014.

Friedman, Mickey. "Recycled Science Fiction." *The San Francisco Examiner.* Clint Reilly Communications, 1978.

Fujitani, Bob, and Paul Newman. *Doctor Solar: Man of the Atom.* Gold Key, 1962.

Gaines, MC. *Narrative Illustration: The Story of the Comics.* EC Comics, 1942.

Gannett. "Comics pioneer dies at age 87." *St. Cloud Times,* 2005.

———. "Johnny Weissmuller buried." *The Courier-News,* 1984.

———. "Macfadden Wins the Day." *The Central New Jersey Home News,* 1907.

———. "Richard B. Ayers." *The Journal News,* 2014.

———. "Takes London by Surprise." *Appleton Post,* 1904.

Gardner, James. "The Man Who Made Marvel." *The Winchester Sun.* Boone Newspapers, 24 November 2018.

Geiger, H., Lord Rutherford, E. Regener, F.A. Lindemann, C.T.R. Wilson, and J. Chadwick, et al. "Discussion on Ultra-Penetrating Rays." In *Proceedings of the Royal Society of London.* London: The Royal Society Publishing, 1931.

Gendler, Neal. "Whiz Bang Days named in honor of Capt. Billy." *Star Tribune.* Star Tribune Media Company, 7 July 1983.

Genter, Robert. "'With great power comes great responsibility': Cold War culture and the birth of Marvel Comics." *The Journal of Popular Culture* 40, no. 6. 2007.

Gerber, Steve and Jack Kirby. "Spineless." *Destroyer Duck* #4. Eclipse, 1983.

Gerber, Steve, and John Morrow. "The Other Duck Man." *The Collected Jack Kirby Collector,* vol. 2. Raleigh: TwoMorrows, 2004.

Gernsback, Hugo. "Hidden Wonders." *Science Wonder Stories.* Gernsback Publications, 1929.

Gill, Joe, and Pat Boyette. "Introducing: The Peacemaker." *Fightin' Five 40.* Charlton, 1966.

Gill, Joe, and Steve Ditko. *Space War* #10. Charlton Comics, 1961.

Goessel, Tracey. *The First King of Hollywood.* Chicago: Chicago Review Press, 2016.

Goodspeed, John. "Comic strip books, past and present." *The Star-Democrat.* Adams Publishing Group, 1996.

Gordon, Ian. *Comic Strips and Consumer Culture.* Washington, D.C.: Smithsonian Institution, 1998.

Goulart, Ron. "Famous Funnies." *Comic Book Encyclopedia.* New York: Harper Entertainment, 2004.

———. "Introduction." *The Phantom: The Complete Newspaper Dailies: Volume One.* New Castle: Hermes Press, 2010.

———. *Ron Goulart's Great History of Comic Books.* Chicago: Contemporary Books, 1986.

Gould, Chester. *Dick Tracy Dailies & Sundays 1931–1933*. San Diego: IDW, 2016.

_____. *Dick Tracy Dailies & Sundays 1933–1935*. San Diego: IDW, 2009.

_____. *Dick Tracy Dailies & Sundays 1936–1938*. San Diego: IDW, 2013.

_____. *Dick Tracy Dailies & Sundays 1938–1939*. San Diego: IDW, 2008.

Graham, Victoria. "Originators of Superman Destitute." *Lansing State Journal*. 25 November 1975.

Grand, Alex. "Marvel Precursors." *Jack Kirby Collector* #78. TwoMorrows, 2020.

Grand, Alex, and Bill Field. *Comic Book Historians Presents. Neal Adams: Master Illustrator*. Sacramento: Comic Book Historians, 2021.

Grand, Alex, and Jim Thompson. *Comic Book Historians Presents. David Anthony Kraft: Mad Genius Comics Journalist*. Sacramento: Comic Book Historians, 2022.

_____*Comic Book Historians Presents. Frank Thorne the Blue, Wizard of the Comic Arts*. Sacramento: Comic Book Historians, 2021.

_____. *Comic Book Historians Presents. Howard Chaykin, Dark Prince of Comics*. Sacramento: Comic Book Historians, 2021.

_____. "You Need Somebody to Give You a Sense Of that History." *Alter Ego* #173. January 2022.

Grand Comics Database. "Blackstone #1." *Grand Comics Database*, 2021. https://www.comics.org/issue/6183/.

_____. "Frank Frazetta." *Grand Comics Database*, 2021. https://www.comics.org/searchNew/?q=frazetta.

_____. "Gunsmoke Western." *Grand Comics Database*, 2021. https://www.comics.org/series/1123/covers/?page=1.

_____. "Issue Checklist for Creator John Romita." *Grand Comics Database*, 2021. https://www.comics.org/checklist/7146/?page=3-5.

_____. "John Romita." *Grand Comics Database*, 2021. https://www.comics.org/credit/name/John%20Romita/sort/chrono/.

_____. "Journey into Mystery #92." *Grand Comics Database*, 2021. https://www.comics.org/issue/17671/

_____. "Marvel." *Grand Comics Database*, 2021. https://www.comics.org/publisher/78/?sort=year&page=4.

_____. "Mystery in Space 82." *Grand Comics Database*, 2021. https://www.comics.org/issue/18428/.

_____. "Savage Tales #1." *Grand Comics Database*, 2021. https://www.comics.org/issue/24237/.

_____. "Shock SuspenStories #9." *Grand Comics Database*, 2021. https://www.comics.org/issue/10579/.

_____. "Super-Magician Comics." *Grand Comics Database*, vol. 1, no. 2, 2021. https://www.comics.org/issue/1654/.

_____. "Tales of Suspense #39." *Grand Comics Database*, 2021. https://www.comics.org/issue/17575/.

_____. "Tales of Suspense." *Grand Comics Database*, 2021. https://www.comics.org/series/1442/covers/.

Gray, Harold. *Little Orphan Annie*, vol. 1. San Diego: IDW, 2008.

_____. *Little Orphan Annie*, vol. 2. San Diego: IDW, 2009.

_____. *Little Orphan Annie*, vol. 4. San Diego: IDW, 2009.

Greenberger, Robert. "Marvel Introduces New Contracts." *Comics Scene* #2. Starlog Presents, 1982.

Greene, Robert. "Steve Ditko Interview." *Rapport* #2, 1966.

Greenwald, Seymour. "He Done Her Wrong." *The Morning Call*, 10 January 1931.

Gresham, William Lindsay. *Houdini: The Man Who Walked Through Walls*. New York: Henry Holt & Company, 1959.

Groller, Lori. "The Amazing Comic Book Industry." *The Morning Call*. Tribune Publishing, 18 November 1985.

Groth, Gary. "Editorial." *The Comics Journal* #75. Fantagraphics, 1982.

_____. "Gil Kane." *The Comics Journal* #186. Fantagraphics, 1996.

_____. "Jack Kirby Interview with Gary Groth." *The Comics Journal*, 1990.

_____. *Wallace Wood Presents Shattuck: Original Art Edition*. Seattle: Fantagraphics, 2016.

Groth, Gary, and Dwight Decker. "An Interview with William M. Gaines." *The Comics Journal* #81. Fantagraphics, 1983.

Groth, Gary, and Joe Simon. "Joe Simon Interviewed by Gary Groth." *The Comics Journal* #134. Fantagraphics, 1990.

Guardian Media Group. "New Books." *The Guardian*. Guardian Media Group, 1906.

Guardineer, Fred. "Merlin the Magician." *National Comics* #12. Quality Comics, 1941.

_____. "Zatara Master Magician." *Action Comics* #1. DC Comics, 1938.

Guillot, Lawrence. "The New Thing in Paris is Fantastic Realism." *The Kansas City Star*. McClatchy, 29 November 1964.

Gustavson, Paul. "The Black Panther." *Stars and Stripes* #3. Centaur, 1941.

Hall, Ed. "Steel yourself for return of Man of Bronze." *The Atlanta Constitution*. Cox Enterprises, 27 July 2007.

Hamill, Mark. "Interview with Hugh Hefner." *Comic Book: The Movie*. Miramax, 2003.

Hamilton, Bruce. "A Talk with Artist-Writer-Editor Jack Kirby." *The Collected Jack Kirby Collector*, vol. 4. Raleigh: TwoMorrows, 2004.

Haney, Bob, and Bruno Premiani. *The Brave and the Bold* #54. DC Comics, 1964.

Harold, Jess, and John Rhett Thomas. *Marvel 80 for 80*. Marvel, 2019.

Harper, Jackie. "Spiderman's a Big Man on Campus." *The Honolulu Advertiser,* 29 April 1968.

Harrison, Paul. "Screen Chats." *Shamokin News-Dispatch.* Sample News Group, 27 November 1939.

Harvey, RC. *The Art of the Funnies: An Aesthetic History.* Jackson: University Press of Mississippi, 1994.

Harvey, RC, and Murphy Anderson. *The Life and Art of Murphy Anderson.* Raleigh: TwoMorrows, 2003.

———. "Outcault, Goddard, the Comics, and *The Yellow Kid*." *The Comics Journal,* 2016. https://www.tcj.com/outcault-goddard-the-comics-and-the-yellow-kid/.

Haslem, Stacy. "Getting Serious About Comics" *Great Falls Tribune,* 30 March 2003.

Hauser, Rich. "Bill Gaines: Vintage 1969." *Tales of Terror!* Fantagraphics Books and Gemstone Publishing, 2000.

Heer, Jeet. "The Most Musical of Cartoonists, Cliff Sterrett." *Polly and Her Pals 1913–1927.* San Diego: IDW 2010.

Heintjes, Tom. "Charlton Goes Down for the Count." *The Comics Journal* #103. Fantagraphics, 1985.

Hennessy, Tom. "Pulps Arise from Dust of the Past." *Detroit Free Press,* 9 November 1975.

Hergé. *Flight 714 to Sydney.* Little Brown, 1975.

Herman, Daniel. *Gil Kane: The Art of Comics.* New Castle: Hermes Press, 2002.

Hevesi, Dennis. "Jerry Robinson, Godfather of a Comic-Book Villain, Dies at 89." *The New York Times,* 9 December 2011.

Hill, Roger. "Introduction." *Crime Illustrated.* Gemstone, 2006.

———. *Mac Raboy: Master of Comics.* Raleigh: TwoMorrows, 2019.

———. *Reed Crandall: Illustrator of the Comics.* Raleigh: TwoMorrows, 2017.

Hodel, Mike. "Will Success Spoil Spider-Man?" *WBAI FM.* Pacifica Foundation, 1967. https://kirbymuseum.org/blogs/effect/2020/04/11/1967-hodel/

Hogarth, Burne. *Tarzan and the City of Gold.* London: Titan, 2014.

Holland, Steve. "Al Williamson obituary." *The Guardian.* Scott Trust Limited, 2013. https://www.theguardian.com/books/2010/jul/14/al-williamson-obituary.

Holtz, Allan. *American Newspaper Comics: An Encyclopedic Reference Guide.* Ann Arbor: The University of Michigan Press, 2012.

Hornung, Clarence. *Will Bradley's Graphic Art.* New York: Dover, 2017.

Hoskins, Gayle. "A Cowboy's Day." *Western Story Magazine.* Street & Smith, 1931.

Howe, Sean. *Marvel Comics: The Untold Story.* New York: Harper Perennial, 2013.

Howlett, Mike. *The Weird World of Eerie Publications.* Washington: Feral House, 2010.

Hudson, Laura. "Real-life heroes and villains of Marvel Comics." *The Los Angeles Times,* 2012.

"In times of crisis, America looks for a hero—and our patriotic patriarch is once again reporting for duty." *The Palm Beach Post,* 24 September 2001.

Infantino, Carmine, and Arnold Drake. *Strange Adventures* #205. DC Comics, 1967.

Infantino, Carmine, and Dave Wood. "I was the Man with Animal Powers." *Strange Adventures* #180. DC Comics, 1965.

Infantino, Carmine, and Gardner Fox. *The Flash* #150. DC Comics, 1965.

Infantino, Carmine, and J. David Spurlock. *Amazing World of Carmine Infantino.* Okemos: Vanguard Publications, 2001.

Inge, M. Thomas. *Comics as Culture.* Jackson: University Press of Mississippi, 1990.

Irvine, Alex, and Hannah Dolan. *DC Comics Year by Year: A Visual Chronicle.* London: Dorling Kindersley, 2010.

Irwin, Virginia. "New Czar of the Comic Book Industry." *St. Louis Post-Dispatch,* 10 November 1954.

Itzkoff, Dave. "The Vendetta Behind 'V for Vendetta.'" *The New York Times.* The New York Times Company, 2006.

James, Emily. *Who's who: An Annual Biographical Dictionary,* Vol. 59. A&C Black, 1907.

James, Gilbert. *Victory Comics* #1. Victory Comics, 1941.

James, J.P.C. "Harvey Kurtzman Interview: 1965." *The Comics Journal* #153. Fantagraphics, 1992.

Johnson, Glen D. "Pete Morisi, Man of Thunderbolt." *Comic Book Artist* #9. TwoMorrows, 2000.

Jones, Gerard. *Men of Tomorrow: Geeks, Gangsters, and the Birth of the Comic Book.* New York: Basic Books, 2004.

Jones, Gerard, and Will Jacobs. *The Comic Book Heroes.* Louisiana: Prima Lifestyles, 1996.

JPI Media. "Are You Strong? If Not, Why Not?" *Belfast News-Letter,* 1899.

Kalush, William, and Larry Sloman. *The Secret Life of Houdini: The Making of America's First Superhero.* New York: Simon & Schuster, 2006.

Kane, Bob. "A Preference for Newspaper Strips." *Batman: The Dailies 1943–1946,* vol. 2. Kitchen Sink Press, 2007.

Kane, Bob, and Bill Finger. "The Case of the Chemical Syndicate." *Detective Comics* #27. DC Comics, 1939.

———. *Detective Comics* #29. DC Comics, 1939.

Kane, Bob, and Tom Andrae. *Batman & Me.* Rolla, Missouri: Eclipse Books, 1989.

Kane, Bob, Bill Finger, and Jerry Robinson. *Batman* #1. Detective Comics, 1940.

_____. "Robin the Boy Wonder." *Detective Comics* #38. DC Comics, 1940.

Kane, Bob, Bill Finger, Gardner Fox and Sheldon Moldoff. *Detective Comics* #33. DC Comics, 1939.

Kane, Gil. *His Name Is ... Savage.* Maryland: Adventure House Press, 1968.

Kanigher, Robert, and Ross Andru. "Suicide Squad." *Brave and the Bold* #25. DC Comics, 1959.

Kanigher, Robert, Ross Andru and Mike Esposito. "Metal Men." *Showcase* #37. DC Comics, 1962.

Kaufman, David. "'Buster Crabbe' says July 4th at Clear Lake Happiest He's Had Since He Was Kid." *Globe-Gazette.* Lee Enterprises, 5 July 1941.

Kaye, Phyllis L. "They Die on Mars." *Fantastic Science Fiction.* Super Science Fiction Publishers, August 1952.

Keef, Jim. *Jimkeefe.com,* 2021. https://www.jimkeefe.com/archives/4750#:~:text=1990%3A%20Dan%20 Barry%20quits%20after,is%20called%20in%20to%20assist.

Keenan, Harol. "Comics Can Be Helpful." *The Courier-News,* 22 July 1948.

Kefauver, Estes. "Comic Books and Juvenile Delinquency." *Committee on the Judiciary.* Senate Committee on the Judiciary Juvenile Delinquency, 1955–1956.

Kevin, Patrick. *Comics Down Under Blog.* Blogger, 24 September 2020.

Khoury, George. *The Extraordinary Works of Alan Moore.* Raleigh: TwoMorrows, 2003.

Kida, Fred. "The Origin of the Iron Ace." *Air Fighters* #2. Hillman, 1942.

Kinnaird, Clark. "Great Prophet in Christmas Cards." *Kenosha News,* 17 December 1965.

Kirby, Jack. *Captain Victory and the Galactic Rangers* #12. Pacific, 1983.

_____. *Chip Hardy.* Tryout Strip. 1950. https://kirbymuseum.org/blogs/effect/2018/09/08/ looking-for-the-awesome-16/.

_____. "Concentrate on Chaos!" *Yellow Claw* #2. Marvel, 1956.

_____. "Crime Carnival!" *Adventure Comics* #84. DC Comics, 1943.

_____. *The Eternals* #1. Marvel, 1976.

_____. *Forever People* #1. DC Comics, 1971.

_____. "Funky Flashman!" *Mister Miracle* #6. DC Comics, 1972.

_____. "The Human Pets." *Challengers of the Unknown* #1. DC Comics, 1958.

_____. *The Hunger Dogs.* DC Comics, 1985.

_____. "Invasion of the Volcano Men." *Tales of the Unexpected* #22. DC Comics, 1958.

_____. "Menace of the Invisible Challenger." *Challengers of the Unknown.* DC Comics, 1958.

_____. "The Microscopic Army!" *Yellow Claw* #3. Marvel, 1956.

_____. *Mister Miracle* #18. DC Comics, 1974.

_____. *Mister Miracle* #9. DC Comics, 1972.

_____. *The New Gods* #1. DC Comics, 1971.

_____. *The New Gods* #11. DC Comics, 1971.

_____. *The New Gods* #2. DC Comics, 1971.

_____. *The New Gods* #5. DC Comics, 1971.

_____. *The New Gods* #7. DC Comics, 1971.

_____. *The New Gods,* vol. 2, #6. DC Comics, 1984.

_____. "OMAC." *OMAC* #1. DC Comics, 1974

_____. "Sailor's Girl!" *Young Romance* #13. Prize, 1949.

_____. "The Stone Sentinels of Giant Island." *House of Mystery* #85. DC Comics, 1958.

_____. *Superman's Pal Jimmy Olsen* #136. DC Comics, 1971.

_____. *Tales of the Unexpected* #16. DC Comics, 1957.

_____. "Today I Am A-?" *Black Cat Mystic* #59. Harvey, 1957.

_____. "Voodoo on Tenth Avenue!" *Black Magic* #4. Prize, 1951.

_____. "We Were Doomed by the Metal-Eating Monster." *My Greatest Adventure* #21. DC Comics, 1958.

_____. "The Wizard of Time." *Challengers of the Unknown* #4. DC Comics, 1958.

Kirby, Jack, and Ed Herron. "The Green Arrow." *Adventure Comics* #256. DC Comics, 1959.

Kirby, Jack, and Joe Simon. *Blue Bolt* #6. Novelty Press, 1940.

_____. *Captain Marvel Adventures* #1. Fawcett, 1942.

_____. "The Villain from Valhalla!" *Adventure Comics* #75. DC Comics, 1942.

_____. "The Vision." *Marvel Mystery Comics* #13. Timely, 1940.

Kirby, Jack, and Martin A. Bursten. "Mercury in the 20th Century." *Red Raven Comics* #1. Timely, 1940.

Kirby, Jack, and Stan Lee. "Gunman at Large!" *Two-Gun Kid* #62. Marvel, 1963.

Kirby, Jack, Dave Wood, Wood Wallace, and Dick Ayers. *Sky Masters of the Space Force: The Complete Dailies.* New Castle: Hermes Press, 2017.

Kirby, Jack, Stan Lee, and Larry Lieber. *Journey into Mystery* #83. Marvel, 1962.

Kirkeby, Marc. "Flash! Batman Neurotic, Superman to See Shrink!" *Daily News.* Tribune Publishing, 12 September 1982.

Knight, Robert. "Jack Kirby's 70th Birthday." *Earthwatch,* 28 August 1987. https://kirbymuseum.org/blogs/ effect/2012/06/29/1987-august-28-jack-kirby-interview-partial/.

Korshak, Stephen D. *The Paintings of J. Allen St. John: Grand Master of Fantasy.* Somerset: Vanguard, 2009.

Kraft, David Anthony, Alex Grand, and Jim Thompson. "David Anthony Kraft Interview." *Comic Book Historians Podcast*. Comic Book Historians, 2019.

Krank, Raymond, and Dick Ayers. "The Ghost Rider!" *Tim Holt* #11. Magazine Enterprises, 1949.

Krier, Beth Ann. "Drawing on the Cool Factor." *The Los Angeles Times*. Los Angeles Times Communications, 1992.

Kubert, Joe, and Gardner Fox. *Hawkman* #1. DC Comics, 1964.

———. "Introduction." *The Viking Prince*. DC Comics, 2010.

Kummer, Frederick Arnold, Jr. "Dark Invasion." *Marvel Science Stories* #5. Western Fiction Publishing Co., 1939.

Kupperberg, Paul. "Foreword." *The Flash Archives,* vol. 1. DC Comics, 1996.

Kuttner, Henry. "Way of the Gods." *Thrilling Wonder Stories* vol. 30, #1. A Thrilling Publication, 1947.

Kyle, Richard. "Richard Kyle's WONDERWORLD." *K-A CAPA alpha* #02, 1964.

Lal, GB. "Explore Your Mind, With Baby's Blocks." *The San Francisco Examiner*. Clint Reilly Communications, 1944.

———. "New Mental Disease is Key to Easter Murders." *The Knoxville Journal,* 9 April 1937.

Lang, Nico. "Marvel is ruining superhero movies: Corporate synergy is a poor substitute for artistic vision." *Salon*. Oakland: Richmond and Schoentrup, 2016. https://www.salon.com/2016/05/18/marvel_is_ruining_superhero_movies_corporate_synergy_is_a_poor_substitute_for_artistic_vision/.

Lanken, Dane. "The return of Tarzan as seen by Hogarth." *The Gazette*. Postmedia Network, 18 November 1972.

Lea, Charlton. *Spring-Heeled Jack (1904) (The Spring-Heeled Jack Library)*. Kindle, Independent, 2020.

Lee, Sidney. *Dictionary of National Biography: Pocock-Puckering,* vol. XLVI. London: Smith, Elder & Company, 1896.

Lee, Stan. "Captain America Foils the Traitor's Revenge." *Captain America Comics* #3. Marvel, 1941.

———. *Comic Book Greats with Bob Kane*. Missouri: Excelsior Productions, 1992.

———. "*The Comic Reader* #16. Bails, 1963.

———. *The Comics Journal* #42. Fantagraphics, 1978.

———. "Fantastic Fan Page 4." *Fantastic Four* #18. Marvel, 1963.

———. "Heart to Heart Talk." *My Own Romance* #24. Marvel, 1954.

———. "Hi, Heroes!" *Fantastic Four* #358. Marvel, 1991.

———. "Hi, Marvelites!" *Fantasy Masterpieces* #1. Marvel, 1965.

———. "The Horror of the Doll-Devil." *Young Allies* #10. Marvel, 1943.

———. "Introduction." *Doctor Strange Marvel Masterworks,* vol. 2. Marvel, 2005.

———. "Introduction." *Fantastic Four* #400. Marvel, 1995.

———. "Marvel Comic Group." *Sub-Mariner Comics* #31. Marvel, 1949.

———. "Marvel Get-Together." *Marvel Mystery Comics* #25. Marvel, 1941.

———. "Meet Stan Lee." *Bachelor* #1. Chasan, 1968.

———. "Nostalgic Note." *Marvel Super-Heroes* #14. Marvel, 1968.

———. *Origins of Marvel Comics*. New York: Fireside, 1974.

———. "To Whom It May Concern." *Stan Lee Media,* 18 August 1999. https://www.tcj.com/steve-ditko-1927-2018/.

———. "Twenty Five Years? I Don't Believe It!" *The Comic Book Price Guide* #16. Overstreet, 1986.

———. "Unsolved Mysteries." *Young Allies Comics*. Timely, 1941.

Lee, Stan, Al Avison, and Al Gabriele. "The Order of the Hood." *All Winners Comics* #1. Timely, 1941.

Lee, Stan, and Chad Grotkopf. "The Imp." *Captain America Comics* #12. Marvel, 1942

Lee, Stan, and Charley Nicholas. "Jack Frost." *USA Comics* #1. Timely, 1941.

———. "Rockman Underground Secret Agent." *USA Comics* #3. Marvel, 1941.

Lee, Stan, and Dick Ayers. "The Black Knight Strikes!" *Tales to Astonish* #52. Marvel, 1964.

Lee, Stan, and Gene Colan. "Story Conference." *Daredevil Annual* #1. Marvel, 1967.

Lee, Stan, and Gil Kane. "And Death Shall Come!" *The Amazing Spider-Man* #90. Marvel, 1970.

Lee, Stan, and Harry Fisk. "Headline Hunter Foreign Correspondent." *Captain America Comics* #5. Marvel, 1941.

Lee, Stan, and Jack Binder. "The Destroyer." *Mystic Comics* #6. Marvel, 1941.

Lee, Stan, and Jack Kirby. "Aftermath." *The Mighty Thor* #128. Marvel, 1966.

———. "Beware the Blob!" *X-Men* #3. Marvel, 1964.

———. "The Blitzkrieg of Batroc!" *Tales of Suspense* #85. Marvel, 1966.

———. "Captain America Joins … The Avengers." *The Avengers* #4. Marvel, 1964.

———. "Defeated by Doctor Doom!" *Fantastic Four* #17. Marvel, 1963.

———. "The End of the Fantastic Four!" *The Fantastic Four* #9. Marvel, 1962.

———. "Everett, Bill: The Stage is set!" *Tales to Astonish* #81. 1966.

———. *Fantastic Four* #1. Marvel Comics, 1961.

———. *Fantastic Four* #2. Marvel, 1962.

———. "The Fantastic Four!" *The Fantastic Four* #1. Marvel, 1961.

_____. *Fantastic Four* #77. Marvel, 1968.

_____. "I Brought the Mighty Cyclops Back to Life!" *Tales of Suspense* #10. Marvel, 1960.

_____. "The Impossible Man." *Fantastic Four* #11. Marvel, 1963.

_____. *The Incredible Hulk* #1. Marvel, 1962.

_____. "The Infant Terrible." *Fantastic Four* #24. Marvel, 1964.

_____. "The Mysterious Radio-Active Man!" *Journey into Mystery* #93. Marvel, 1963.

_____. "The Power and the Pride!" *Fantastic Four* #87. Marvel, 1969.

_____. "Prisoners of Doctor Doom!" *The Fantastic Four* #5. Marvel, 1962.

_____. "Prisoners of Kurrgo, Master of Planet X." *The Fantastic Four* #7. Marvel, 1962.

_____. "Prisoners of the Pharaoh!" *Fantastic Four* #19. Marvel, 1964.

_____. "Prisoners of the Puppet Master." *The Fantastic Four* #8. Marvel, 1962.

_____. "The Reason Why!" *The Mighty Thor* #147. Marvel, 1967.

_____. "The Return of the Frightful Four!" *Fantastic Four* #94. Marvel, 1969.

_____. "The Return of the Mole Man!" *Fantastic Four* #22. Marvel, 1964.

_____. "A Skrull Walks Among Us!" *Fantastic Four* #18. Marvel, 1963.

_____. *Strange Tales* #135. Marvel Comics, 1965.

_____. "The Stronger I Am, the Sooner I Die!" *Journey into Mystery* #114. Marvel, 1965.

_____. "The Thunder God and the Thug!" *Journey into Mystery* #89. Marvel, 1963.

_____Van Doom, The Man Who Made a Creature!" *Tales to Astonish* #17. Marvel, 1960.

_____. "Within this Tortured Land." *Fantastic Four* #85. Marvel, 1969.

_____. *The X-Men* #1. Marvel, 1963.

Lee, Stan, and Jim Shooter. "Stan Lee and Jim Shooter." *Marvel Age* #8. Marvel, 1983.

Lee, Stan, and John Romita, Sr. "The Goblin Lives!" *The Spectacular Spider-Man* #2. Marvel, 1968.

_____. "In the Clutches of … The Kingpin!" *The Amazing Spider-Man* #51. Marvel, 1967.

_____. "Lo, This Monster!" *The Spectacular Spider-Man*. Marvel, 1968.

Lee, Stan, and Steve Ditko. "Captured by J. Jonah Jameson!" *The Amazing Spider-Man* #25. Marvel, 1965.

_____. "The End—At Last!" *Strange Tales* #146. Marvel, 1966.

_____. "Marked for Destruction by Dr. Doom!" *The Amazing Spider-Man* #5. Marvel, 1963.

_____. "The Origin of Dr. Strange." *Strange Tales* #115. Marvel, 1963.

_____. "Spider-Man vs. Doctor Octopus." *The Amazing Spider-Man* #3. Marvel, 1963.

_____. "Spider-Man vs. the Chameleon." *The Amazing Spider-Man* #1. Marvel, 1963.

_____. "Spider-Man!" *Amazing Fantasy* #15. Marvel, 1962.

_____. "Supporting Cast Pin-Ups." *The Amazing Spider-Man Annual* #1. Marvel, 1964.

_____. *Tales of Suspense* #48. Marvel, 1963.

_____. *Tales to Astonish* #60. Marvel 1964.

Lee, Stan, and Wally Wood. *Daredevil* #5. Marvel, 1964.

_____. *Daredevil* #11. Marvel, 1965.

Lee, Stan, and Werner Roth. "The Last Command of Colonel Fong." *Battle* #17. Marvel, 1953.

_____. "Love 'em and Leave 'em." *Action Confessions* #13. Marvel, 1952.

Lee, Stan, Carmine Infantino, and Gil Kane. "The Hooded Horror!" *Mystic* #12. Marvel, 1952.

_____. "Horror into Haunted Hill!" *Adventures into Weird Worlds* #14. Marvel, 1954.

_____. "Love Story." *My Own Romance* #27. Marvel, 1953.

Lee, Stan, Jack Kirby and Larry Lieber. "Here Comes … Thorr the Unbelievable." *Tales to Astonish* #16. Marvel, 1960.

Lee, Stan, Larry Lieber, and Don Heck. "Iron Man is Born!" *Tales of Suspense* #39. Marvel, 1963.

Lee, Stan, Larry Lieber, and Jack Kirby. "Elektro! He Held a World in His Iron Grip." *Tales of Suspense* #13. Marvel, 1961.

_____. "I Am Dr. Druid!" *Weird Wonder Tales* #19. Marvel, 1976.

_____. "I am the Fantastic Dr. Droom!" *Amazing Adventures* #1. Marvel, 1961.

_____. "I Created the Colossus." *Tales of Suspense* #14. Marvel, 1961.

_____. "I Fought the Molten Man-Thing." *Tales of Suspense* #7. Marvel, 1960.

_____. "I saw Diablo! The Demon from the 5th Dimension!" Tales of Suspense #9. Marvel, 1960.

_____. "The Midnight Monster!" *Journey into Mystery* #79. Marvel, April 1962.

_____. "The Monster in the Iron Mask!" *Tales of Suspense* #31. Marvel, 1962.

_____. "The Sandman Cometh." *Journey into Mystery* #70. Marvel, 1961.

_____. "The Scorpion Strikes!" *Journey into Mystery* #82. Marvel, 1962.

_____. "The Wonder of the Ages!!! Magneto!" *Strange Tales* #84. Marvel, 1961.

Lee, Stan, Mike Sekowsky, and George Klein. "League of Crime." *Mystic Comics* #8. Marvel, 1942.

Lee, Stephen, and Sidney Lee. *Dictionary of National Biography*, volume 48. London: Smith, Elder, & Co., 1896.

Lee Enterprises. "Now Introducing the One-and-Only Popeye the Sailorman." *The World*. Lee Enterprises, 1936.

Lennig, Arthur. *The Immortal Count: The Life and Films of Bela Lugosi*. Lexington: The University Press of Kentucky, 2003.

Levitz, Paul. "Will Eisner and the Secret History of the Graphic Novel." *New York Vulture*. VoxMedia, 10 November 2015. https://www.vulture.com/2015/10/will-eisner-graphic-novels-paul-levitz.html#.
_____*Will Eisner: Champion of the Graphic Novel*. New York: Abrams, 2015.
Lewis, Jerry A., and Michelle Cuppari. "The polygraph: The truth lies within." *The Journal of Psychiatry & Law*, 2009.
Lillian III, Guy H. "Mort Weisinger: The Man Who Wouldn't Be Superman." *The Amazing World of DC Comics* #7. DC Comics, 1975.
Loftypilot/Josemas. *Mr. Muscles* #22. Comic Book Plus, 2012. https://comicbookplus.com/?dlid=26518.
Love, G.B. "Wonders of Space via Rocket Mail." *Mystery in Space* #72. DC Comics, 1961.
Love, Philip. "April '71–'72 is Diamond Jubilee for Comics." *The Columbia Record*. Knight-Ridder, 21 April 1971.
Loveman, Kate. *Romantic Echoes in the Victorian Era*. Farnham: Ashgate, 2008.
Lupoff, Richard. "SF Recollections." *Time Binders: Preserving Fannish History*. Timebinders, 1995. https://fanac.org/timebinders/lupoff.html.
Lynch, Stephen. "Boris Karloff inspired creation of the Hulk." *The Post-Star*. Lee Enterprises, 20 June 2003.
Lyons, Leonard. "The Lyons Den." *The Bangor Daily News*. Bangor Publishing Company, 7 July 1949.
Lyons, Martyn. *Books: A Living History*. London: Thames & Hudson, 2011.
M. Roberts Media. "'Steve Canyon' Out; 'Cathy' Strip Begins." *Victoria Advocate*. M. Roberts Media, 1988.
Mackley, JS. "Introduction" *Spring-Heeled Jack: Articles and Short Fiction 1838–1897*. Independently Published, 2020.
_____. *Spring-Heeled Jack (1904)*. Independently Published, 2020.
_____. *Spring-Heeled Jack: The Terror of London (1886) Book 1*. Independent, 2020.
Madrigal, Alexis C. "A Golden Age of Books? There Were Only 500 Real Bookstores in 1931." *The Atlantic*. Emerson Collective, 8 June 2012.
Malley, Marjorie C. *Radioactivity: A History of a Mysterious Science*. Oxford: Oxford University Press, 2011.
Marchese, David. "Alan Moore on Why Superhero Fans Need to Grow Up, Brexit, and His Massive New Novel." *New York Vulture*. Vox Media, 12 September 2016. https://www.vulture.com/2016/09/alan-moore-jerusalem-comics-writer.html.
Martignette, Charles G., and Louis K. Meisel. *Gil Elvgren: All His Glamorous American Pin-ups*. Los Angeles: Taschen America, 2003.
Martin, DR. "Upgraded Comic Book Illustrates the Dark side of Superheroism." *Star Tribune*. Star Tribune Media Company, 17 January 1988.
Martin, Gary. "Steve Ditko Interview." *The Comic Fan* #2. 1965. https://ditkocultist.wordpress.com/2012/03/05/steve-ditko-interview-the-comic-fan-2-1965/.
Marvel. "The Foom Connection." *FOOM!* #1. Marvel, 1973.
Marvel Credits. *The Amazing Spider-Man*. Marvel, 2021.
Mason, Bill. "Any Idea in Any Form." *Witzend* vol. Seattle: Fantagraphics, 2014.
Maurice, Gutwirth. "The Falcon." *Daring Mystery Comics* #5. Timely, 1940.
Mazoujian, Chuck. "Presenting Quicksilver." *National Comics* #5. Quality, 1940.
Mazur, Allan. "U.S. trends in feminine beauty and over-adaptation" *Journal of Sex Research* 2. Routledge, 1984.
McAvennie, Michael. "1970s." *DC Comics Year by Year: A Visual Chronicle*. Dorling Kindersley, 2010.
McClatchy. "Joseph Medill Patterson, Playwright, is a Millionaire Socialist." *The Kansas City Times*, Kansas City Star, 1911.
The McClatchy Company. "Coleman agrees to buyout." *Fort Worth Star-Telegram*. The McClatchy Company, 1989.
_____. "Linlee School Notes." *The Lexington Herald*. The McClatchy Company, 1934.
_____. "Only things super are fond memories." *Fort Worth-Star Telegram*. The McClatchy Company, 1975.
Mcgaffin, William. "Fight Against Sex and Violence in Comic books is Near a Test Point." *The Kansas City Times*. Kansas City Star, 1955.
McGregor, Don, and Marshall Rogers. *Detectives, Inc.* Eclipse, 1980.
McMillan, Graeme. "'Captain Marvel' and 'Shazam!' Share a Complicated Past." *The Hollywood Reporter*. Penske Media Corporation, 2019. https://www.hollywoodreporter.com/movies/movie-news/captain-marvel-shazam-share-a-strange-past-1199825/.
McPherson, Karen. "Don't be afraid to let children read graphic novels. They're real books, too." *The Windsor-Star*. Postmedia Network, 2020.
Menges, Jeff A. *101 Great Illustrators from the Golden Age*. New York: Dover Publications, 2016.
Merrill, Lew. "Batman." *Spicy Mystery Stories*. Culture Publications, 1936.
Meskin, Mort. *More Fun* #85. DC Comics, 1942.
Miller, Frank. *The Dark Knight Returns* #4. DC Comics, 1986.
Mitchell, Kurt, and Roy Thomas. *American Comic Book Chronicles: 1940–1944*. Raleigh: TwoMorrows, 2019.
Moorcock, Michael. "Introduction." *The Swords of Heaven, The Flowers of Hell*. Heavy Metal, 1979.
Moore, Alan. "Alan Moore On (Just About) Everything!" *The Comics Journal* #106. Fantagraphics, 1986.

Moore, Alan, and Chris Sprouse. *Tom Strong* #1. America's Best Comics, 1999.

Moore, Alan, and Dave Gibbons. "Absent Friends." *Watchmen* #2. DC Comics, 1986.

_____. "The Abyss Gazes Also." *Watchmen* #6. DC Comics, 1986.

_____. "At Midnight, All the Agents." *Watchmen* #1. DC Comics, 1986.

_____. "A Brother to Dragons." *Watchmen* #7. DC Comics, 1986.

_____. "The Darkness of Mere Being." *Watchmen* #9. DC Comics, 1986.

_____. "Old Ghosts." *Watchmen* #8. DC Comics, 1986.

_____. "A Stronger Loving World." *Watchmen* #12. DC Comics, 1986.

_____. "Watchmaker." *Watchmen* #4. DC Comics, 1986.

Moore, Matt. "Joe Simon, co-creator of Captain America." *The Herald-News*. Shaw Media, 27 June 2011.

Moore, Matt, and Ula Ilnytzky. "Comic book artist Gene Colan dies." *The Times and Democrat*. Lee Enterprises, 16 December 2011.

Morago, Phillip. "Comics shop caught up in Spider-Man wedding." *Hartford Courant*. Tribune Publishing, 20 May 1987.

Morisi, Pete. *Peter Cannon … Thunderbolt*. Charlton, 1966.

The Morning News. "Pyle, Wyeth Gave Robin Hood Fame" *The Morning News*, 1946.

Morrow, John. "The Captain Victory Connection." *The Collected Jack Kirby Collector Vol. 1*. Raleigh: TwoMorrows, 2004.

_____. "Key 1960s Moments." *Jack Kirby Collector* #60. TwoMorrows, 2013.

Morrow, John, and Lisa Kirby. "The Kid from Left Field." *Jack Kirby Collector* #20. TwoMorrows, 1998.

Mougin, Lou. *Secondary Superheroes of Golden Age Comics*, McFarland & Co., 2020.

Murray, Will. "Daredevil vs. The Avengers." *Alter Ego* #118. TwoMorrows, 2013.

_____. "Journey into Strange Tales of Suspense to Astonish." *Comic Book Marketplace* #72. Gemstone, 1999.

_____. "Marvel's Founding Father—MARTIN GOODMAN." *Alter Ego* #165. TwoMorrows, 2020.

_____. "Maxwell Grant's Shadow Theodore Tinsley Interviewed by Will Murray." *The Shadow*. Cyro, Sanctum Books, 2012.

_____. "The Retrospective Stan Lee." *Alter Ego* #150. TwoMorrows, 2018.

_____. "The Shadowy Origins of Batman." *The Shadow by Maxwell Grant*. The Sanctum Books/Nostalgia Ventures, 2007.

_____. "Three Easy Pieces Starring Julius Schwartz." *Alter Ego* 3, #38. TwoMorrows, 2004.

_____. *Writings in Bronze*. Kindle, Altus Press, 2011.

Murry, Charles, and Stan Lee. *Fantasy Advertiser International*. April 1975. https://forbushman.blogspot.com/2017/06/a-serious-interview-with-stan-lee-april.html.

My Comic Shop. "Comic books published by Cupples & Leon." *Mycomicshop.com*. Lone Star Comics, 2021. https://www.mycomicshop.com/search?pl=Cupples%20%26%20Leon.

NA. "Oldest Color Comic Becomes Newest Daily Strip as Creator of Hans and Fritz Returns to Easel." *The Pittsburgh Press*. Block Communications, 1933.

_____. "Variation on the Visitor from Mars." *Fort Worth Star-Telegram*. The McClatchy Co., 6 September 1936.

Nash, Eric. "Julius Schwartz Comic-book editor revived superhero genre." *Pittsburgh Post-Gazette*. John Robinson Block, 14 February 2004.

National Comics Publications v. Fawcett Publications, 93F Supp.349. *Court Listener*, 1950. https://archive.ph/20140906072002/https://www.courtlistener.com/nysd/b79w/national-comics-publications-v-fawcett-publication/.

Neville, Dennis, and Gardner Fox. "The Hawkman." *Flash Comics* #1. All American Comics, 1940.

Nevins, Jess. *The Evolution of the Costumed Avenger: The 4,000-Year History of the Superhero*. Westport: Praeger, 2017.

"New York News Publisher, M. Joseph and Dies Patterson." *Great Falls Tribune*. Boca Raton: United Press International, 1946.

The New York Times Company. "Program For Today at the World's Fair." *The New York Times*. The New York Times Company, 1940.

Newsmakers. "Superman Turns into Santa for Two." *The Los Angeles Times*. Los Angeles Times Communications, 24 December 1975.

Nicholas, Charles. "The Armored Truck Robbery." *Mystery Men Comics* #2. Fox Publications, 1939.

Norris, Paul, and Mort Weisinger. "Aquaman." *Millennium Edition More Fun Comics* #73. DC Comics, 2001.

Nyberg, Amy. *Seal of Approval: The Origins and History of the Comics Code*, vol. 1. Jackson: University Press of Mississippi, 1998.

Obituary. "Dr. Marston Dies." *The Daily Times*. Jones Media, 20 May 1947.

O'Connor, Bill, and Ben Flinton. "Introducing the Mighty Atom." *All-American Comics* #19. All-American Comics, 1940.

O'Connor, Tim. "Holy Homicide! It's the True Detectives!" *The Kansas City Times*. McClatchy, 20 May 1986.

Ogden. "Patriotism in Art." *The Ogden-Standard-Examiner*. Ogden, 1964.

Olshevsky, George, and Roy Thomas. "Conversation with Roy Thomas." *Collectors Dream #5*. G&T Enterprises, 1978.

O'Neil, Dennis, and Dick Dillin. "Snapper Carr–Super-Traitor!" *Justice League of America #77*. DC Comics, 1969.

Orczy, Baroness. "An Adventure of the Scarlet Pimpernel." *Tampa Bay Times*. Poynter Institute, 27 December 1925.

Packard, Frank L. "The Adventures of Jimmie Dale." *The Journal*. White Family, 20 April 1921.

Page, Tim. "Alain Resnais." *The Independent*. Independent Digital News & Media, 4 March 2014.

Page X. "One Heck of an Artist." *The Central New Jersey Home News,* 21 April 1995.

Panyard, Jim. "King of the Comic Books." *The News Journal*. Ogden Newspapers, 20 November 1972. https://comicsdownunder.blogspot.com/?view=classic.

Pearl, Barry. *F.F.F.: A Life in Comics!* Barry's Pearls of Comic Book Wisdom. 26 July 2015. https://forbushman.blogspot.com/2015/07/the-original-ghost-rider-volume-1-with.html.

Peddy, Arthur. "The Coming of the Phantom Lady." *Police Comics #1*. Quality, 1941.

Peel, John. "Julius Schwartz." *Comics Feature*. New Media, 8 July 1984.

Peltz, James. "Warner sells Atari to Tramiel's Company." *Fort Worth Star-Telegram*. The McClatchy Company, 1984.

The Philadelphia Foundation. "Bernarr MacFadden, Physical Culturist, Dies." *The Philadelphia Inquirer*. The Philadelphia Foundation, 1955.

———. "Marie Severin Comics Hall of Famer, #89." *The Philadelphia Inquirer*. The Philadelphia Foundation, 2018.

Pierce Walter. "*Blade*' defies comic book-based movie stereotype." *The Daily Advertiser*, 1998.

Police Comics. *Grand Comics Database*. Quality Comics 1941 Series, 2021. https://www.comics.org/series/226/covers/?page=3.

Postmedia Network. "Fisher is Original Hard-Boiled Egg." *Edmonton Journal*. Postmedia Network., 1926.

———. "Science Fiction Tops" *Saskatoon Star-Phoenix*. Post Media, 1961.

———. "Superman co-creator dies." *The Leader-Post*. Postmedia Network, 1996.

Powell, Megan. "A Child's Garden of Television." *Contra Costa Times*. Digital First Media, 1978.

Poynter Institute. "Comic Book News." *Tampa Bay Times*. Poynter Institute, 1992.

Prashker, Ivan. "The Boss's Son." *Playboy*. Playboy Enterprises, 1970.

Price, Matthew. "'Superman' creators' forgotten character is examined." *The Daily Oklahoman*, 2010.

———. "'Watchmen' prequels announced." *The Daily Oklahoman*, 3 February 2012.

Procopio, Joseph. *The Lost Art of Ray Willner*. Covington: Lost Art Books, 2014.

Pyle, Howard. *Howard Pyle's Book of Pirates*. New York: Harper & Brothers, 1921.

Quality Comics. *Grand Comics Database*, 2021. https://www.comics.org/publisher/67/.

Quattro, Ken. "Elton Clay Fox & George Dewey Lipscomb." *Invisible Men: The Trailblazing Black Artists of Comic Books*. San Diego: IDW, 2020.

Raboy, Mac. *Green Lama #1*. Spark Publications, 1944.

———. *Master Comics #22*. Fawcett, 1942.

Randi, James. *Conjuring*. New York: St. Martin's Press, 1992.

Raphael, Jordan, and Tom Spurgeon. *Stan Lee and the Rise and Fall of the American Comic Book*. Chicago: Chicago Review Press, 2004.

Rattazzi, Delfina, and Stan Lee. "The Marvelous Stan Lee." *Andy Warhol Interview #30*. Jason Nikic, 1973.

Reporter. "Zipper Saves Time of Invisible Man." *Democrat and Chronicle,* 5 November 1939.

Reviewer. "'The Bat Whispers' at State this Week." *The News and Observer*. The McClatchy Company, 23 November 1930.

Reynolds, Quentin. "From Nick Carter to the Slicks." *The Evening Sun,* 1956.

Ricca, Brad. "Salvador Dali's Sub-Mariner." *Comics Beat*. Comicsbeat.com, 2015.

———. *Super Boys*. New York: St. Martin's Press, 2013.

Rico, Don, and Jack Binder. "The Daredevil, Master of Courage." *Silver Streak #6*. Lev Gleason, 1940.

Ringgenberg, Steve. "Archie Goodwin." *The Comics Journal #78*. Fantagraphics, 1982.

———. "An Interview with Al Feldstein." *The Comics Journal #177*. Fantagraphics, 1995.

———. "Joe Sinnott: 1926–2020." *The Comics Journal*. Fantagraphics, 2020. https://www.tcj.com/joe-sinnott-1926-2020/.

Rinszler, JW. "George Lucas and Comic Books: An Early Link." *STAR WARS BLOG*. StarWars.com, 2013. https://www.starwars.com/news/george-lucas-and-comic-books-an-early-link.

Ro, Ronin. *Tales to Astonish: Jack Kirby, Stan Lee, and the American Comic Book Revolution*. London: Bloomsbury, 2004.

Robbins, Frank, and Irv Novick. "One Bullet Too Many!" *Batman #217*. DC Comics, 1969.

Robinson, Jerry, and Ken Crossen. "The Making of The Mightiest Man!" *Atoman Comics #1*. Spark, 1946.

Rogers, WG. "A Family is a Family." *Tucson Daily Citizen*, 30 September 1967.

Rohan, Virginia. "Spreading the Word." *The Record*. Gannett, 2008.

Romberger, James. *Steranko: The Self-Created Man*. Maryland: Ground Zero Books, 2018.

Romero, NV. "The X-Man." *Star Detective Magazine* 2, no. 1. Western Fiction Publishing Co., 1937.

Romita, John, Sr. "Fifty Years on the 'A' List." *Alter Ego* 3, #9. TwoMorrows, 2001.

Romita, John, Sr., and Roy Thomas. *Alter Ego* 3, #9. TwoMorrows, 2013.

Rooks, Lyle. "Genius in a Rouge Box." *Oakland Tribune*. Digital First Media, 29 September 1935.

Rosenkrantz, Linda. "Rare and very vine: *Tarzan of the Apes* on page and screen." *Lancaster New Era*. LNP Media Group, 2003.

Ross, Alex, and Steve Darnall. *Uncle Sam*. New York: Vertigo, 1997.

Ross, Jonathan. *In Search of Steve Ditko*. BBC, 2007.

Rothe, Marschal. "Superman Originator, Publisher Visit Miami." *The Miami Herald*. Chatham Asset Management, 1950.

Rough, Louise, and Geoff Boucher. "Will Eisner, 87; Pioneer of Graphic Novels." *The Los Angeles Times*. Los Angeles Times Communications, 2005.

Roysdon, Keith. "Newsstands full of SF publications." *Muncie Evening Press*, 18 April 1981.

Sacks, Jason, Keith Dallas, and Dave Dykema. *American Comic Book Chronicles: The 1970s*. Raleigh: Two-Morrows Publishing, 2014.

Sadowski, Greg. *Action! Mystery! Thrills! Great Comic Book Covers 1936–1945*. Seattle: Fantagraphics, 2012.

Saffel, Steve. "A Not-So-Spectacular Experiment." *Spider-Man the Icon: The Life and Times of a Pop Culture Phenomenon*. London: Titan, 2007.

Sale, Robert Q. "Gorilla Man." *Men's Adventures* #26. Marvel, 1954.

Samachson, Joseph, and Joe Certa. "Manhunter from Mars." *Detective Comics* #225. DC Comics, 1955.

Sassiene, Paul. *The Comic Book: The One Essential Guide for Comic Book Fans Everywhere*. New York: Chartwell Books, 1994.

Sawyer, Michael. "Albert Lewis Kanter and the Classics: The Man Behind the Gilberton Company." *The Journal of Popular Culture* 20. Wiley-Blackwell, 1987.

Scheimer, Lou, and Andy Mangels. *Lou Scheimer: Creating the Filmation Generation*, Raleigh: TwoMorrows, 2012.

Schelly, Bill. *American Comic Book Chronicles 1950s*. Raleigh: TwoMorrows, 2013.

———. "Creepy Beginnings." *James Warren Empire of Monsters*. Seattle: Fantagraphics, 2019.

———. *Harvey Kurtzman: The Man Who Created MAD and Revolutionized Humor in America*. Seattle: Fantagraphics, 2015.

Schomburg, Alex. "Issue Checklist for Creator Alex Schomburg (b. 1905)." *Grand Comics Database*, 2021. https://www.comics.org/checklist/283/.

———. "Lilith the Dark Planet." *Mystery Comics* #1. Pines, 1944.

Schreiner, Dave. "Flash Gordon vs. The Reluctant Collaborators of Manhattan Isle." *Flash Gordon Dailies: Dan Barry Volume 1—The City of Ice, 1951–1953*. London: Titan Comics, 2016.

Schulz, Mark. *Secret Agent Corrigan Volume One: 1967–1969*. San Diego: IDW Publishing, 2013.

Schumacher, Michael. *Will Eisner: A Dreamer's Life in Comics*, London: Bloomsbury Publishing, 2010.

Schwarcz, Joe. "Bernarr's ideas on exercise and whole grains were OK. But wood chewing?" *The Gazette*. Postmedia Network, 2005.

Schwartz, Julius. "Batman's Hot-Line." *Detective Comics* #327. DC Comics, 1964.

Schwartz, Julius, and Brian M. Thomsen. *Man of Two Worlds*. Sydney: Harper Entertainment, 2000.

Schwartz, Julius, and John Broome. "The Guardians of the Clockwork Universe!" *Strange Adventures* #22. DC Comics, 1951.

———. "The Origin of Captain Comet." *Strange Adventures* #9. DC Comics, 1951.

Schwartz, Madeleine. "Lynd Ward's America." *The New Yorker*. Condé Nast, 2010. https://www.newyorker.com/books/page-turner/lynd-wards-america.

Schweier, Philip. "Shedding Light on the Shadow." *Back Issue!* #89. TwoMorrows Publishing, 2016.

Scott, John. "Ex-Tarzan talks, wears clothes as 'Jungle Jim.'" *The Los Angeles Times*. Los Angeles Times Communications, 16 December 1948.

Segar, EC. *Popeye,* vol. 1. Seattle: Fantagraphics, 2006.

———. *Popeye,* vol. 2. Seattle: Fantagraphics, 2007.

———. *Popeye,* vol. 3. Seattle: Fantagraphics, 2008.

———. *Popeye*. New York: King Features, 31 October 1930.

Seldes, Gilbert. "The Krazy Kat That Walks by Himself." *The Comic Art of George Herriman*. New York: Harry N. Abrams, 2004.

Serbell, John. "Dick Tracy: 50 Golden Years." *The Oklahoma Times*, 1 December 1981.

Seuling, Phil. "Jim Steranko & Gardner Fox at the 1971 Comic Art Convention Luncheon." *1972 Comic Art Convention Programme*. Seuling, 1972.

Severy, Kan. "Spring-Heeled Jack." *Southern Kansas Journal*. 1884.

Shamrock Communications. "Harry Houdini's Stunt." *The Times-Tribune*. Shamrock Communications, 1926.

Sharp, Hal, and Mort Weisinger. *Star Spangled Comics* #1. DC Comics, 1941.

Shiras, Wilmar. "Children of the Atom." *Astounding Science Fiction*. Street & Smith Publications, 1948.

Shorten, Harry, and Chuck Winter. "Mystic." *Top-Notch Comics* #1. MLJ Magazines, 1939.

Shorten, Harry, and Irv Novick. "The SHIELD." *PEP Comics* #1. Archie, 1940.

Shuster, Joe. "Issue Checklist for Creator Joe Shuster." *Grand Comics Database,* 2021. https://www.comics. org/checklist/name/Joe%20Shuster/?page=3.

Siegel, Jerome. *Amazing Stories.* New York: Gernsback Publications, 1929.

Siegel, Jerry. "Issue Checklist for Creator Jerry Siegel." *Grand Comics Database,* 2021. https://www.comics. org/checklist/name/Jerry%20Siegel/?page=7.

Siegel, Jerry, and Bernard Baily. "The Spectre!" *More Fun Comics* #52. DC Comics, 1940.

Siegel, Jerry, and Joe Shuster. *Action Comics* #2. Detective Comics, 1938.

_____. "Federal Men." *New Adventure Comics* #12. DC Comics, 1937.

_____. "Superman Champions Universal Peace." *Superman* #2. DC Comics, 1939.

_____. "Superman." *Action Comics* #1. DC Comics, 1938.

Siegel, Jerry, and Paul Reinman. "The Fly-Man's Partners in Peril." *Fly Man* #31. Archie, 1965.

Siegel, Jerry, and Val Mayerik. "The Starling." *Destroyer Duck* #2. Eclipse, 1983.

Silvie, Matt. "Dan Barry Dead at 73." *The Comics Journal* #194. Fantagraphics, 1997.

Simon, Joe, and Angelo Torres. "The New Age of Comics." *Sick 48.* Crestwood, 1966.

Simon, Joe, and Gary Groth. *Joe Simon Interviewed by Gary Groth.* Seattle: Fantagraphics, 1990.

Simon, Joe, and Jack Kirby. "The Boy Commandos." *Detective Comics* #64. DC Comics, 1942.

_____. "Captain America and the Ringmaster of Death." *Captain America Comics* #5. Timely, 1941.

_____. "The Double Life of Private Strong." *The Double Life of Private Strong* #1. Archie, 1959.

_____. *The Double Life of Private Strong.* Archie, 1959.

_____. *Fighting American* #3. Prize, 1954.

_____. "The Menace of Marto!" *Blue Bolt* #6. Novelty Press, 1940.

_____. "The Menace of the Micro-Men!" *The Double Life of Private Strong* #2. Archie, 1959.

_____. "The Monsters of Saturn." *Captain Marvel Adventures* #1. Fawcett, 1941.

_____. "The Shrinking Serum." *Blue Bolt* #1, Novelty Press, 1940.

_____. "The Strange New World of The Fly." *Adventures of the Fly* #1. Archie, 1959.

_____. "Today I Am A--?" *Black Cat Mystic* #59. Harvey, 1957.

_____. "Tuk Caveboy in Stories from the Dark Ages." *Captain America Comics* #1. Marvel, 1941.

_____. "Tuk Caveboy." *Captain America Comics* #1. Marvel, 1941.

Simon, Joe, and Jim Simon. *The Comic Book Makers.* Culver City, California: Vanguard Productions, 2003.

Simon, Joe, and Louis Cazeneuve. "The Red Raven." *Red Raven Comics* #1. Timely, 1940.

Simon, Joe, Jack Kirby, and Mort Meskin. "The Man from the World of 'D.'" *Captain 3-D 1.* Harvey, 1953.

Simonson, Walt, and Chris Ryall. *Jack Kirby Panel.* New York: NYCC, 2017.

Siuntres, John. *The World of Comic Books.* Dallas: Behind the Scene, 1978. https://youtu. be/3Vmq8DSkb_4?t=6.

Six Rivers Media. "Superman joins nostalgia craze." *Johnson City Press.* Six Rivers Media, 1972.

Skeates, Steven. "The Silver Age Sage." *A Tribute to the Silver Age of DC.* 2009. http://www.wtv-zone.com/ silverager/interviews/skeates_1.shtml.

Skelly, Tim, and Jack Kirby. "My School was Alex Raymond and Milton Caniff." *The Nostalgia Journal* 27. Fantagraphics, 1976.

Slide, Anthony. *The Encyclopedia of Vaudeville.* Jackson: University Press of Mississippi, 2012.

Smash Comics #14. *Grand Comics Database,* 2021. https://www.comics.org/issue/1018/.

Smith, Andrew A. "Insane bombshell in Comics distribution world." *The Missoulian.* Lee Enterprises, 2020.

_____. "Julius Schwartz, a man of many worlds." *The Leaf-Chronicle,* 14 February 2004.

_____. "October brings death to comics." *Casper Star-Tribune.* Lee Enterprises, 3 October 2007.

Smith, Bruce. "'Annie' again." *Daily News.* Tribune Publishing, 9 May 1982.

Soles, Paul. *Beyond Reason.* CBC, 1980. https://youtu.be/NJOdRLChhw8?t=81.

Sonderland, Nils. "The Angel from Hell." *Marvel Tales* #6. Western Fiction Publishing, 1938.

Sozanski, Edward J. "No Pirates but some interesting Wyeth's." *The Philadelphia Inquirer.* The Philadelphia Foundation, 2001.

Spurlock, J David. "Horror & Dracula: Ancient Transylvanian Lore to Modern Graphic Novel." *Dracula.* Lebanon: Vanguard, 2021.

_____. *John Buscema Sketchbook.* Lebanon: Vanguard, 2001.

Staff Report. "Legendary Comic Artist to Attend Superman Fest." *The Paducah Sun.* Paxton Media Group, 2010.

Stapledon, Olaf. *Odd John & Sirius.* New York: Dover Publications, 1972.

Star Co. V. Wheeler Syndicate, 91. Misc. 640. *Supreme Court, New York Special Term.* Star Co. V. Wheeler Syndicate, 1915.

Star Tribune Media Company. "If Only the Statues Could Speak!" *The Minneapolis Star.* Star Tribune Media Company, 1952.

Starger, Steve, and J. David Spurlock. "The End." *Wally's World.* Lebanon: Vanguard, 2007.

Starlin, Jim. *The Art of Jim Starlin: A Life in Words and Pictures.* Sherman Oaks: Aftershock Comics, 2018.

_____. *Breed* #1. Malibu, 1994.

_____. "Death Building." *Star*Reach* #1, 1974.

_____. *The Death of Captain Marvel*. Marvel, 1982.

_____. "Death of the New Gods." *Comic Vine*. Whiskey Media, 2021. https://comicvine.gamespot.com/death-of-the-new-gods/4045-48489/.

_____. "Death Watch." *Marvel Two-in-One Annual* #2. Marvel, 1977.

_____. "Doomsday!" *Epic Illustrated* #9. Marvel, 1981.

_____. *Dreadstar*. Marvel, 1982.

_____. "The Final Threat." *Avengers Annual* #7. Marvel, 1977.

_____. *Hardcore Station* #6. DC Comics, 1998.

_____. "The Miracle." *Star-Studded* #18. Texas Trio, 1972.

_____. "The Rise and Fall of Robin." *The Palm Beach Post*, 3 November 1988.

Starlin, Jim, and Bernie Wrightson. *Batman: The Cult* #2. DC Comics, 1988.

_____. *The Weird*. DC Comics, 1988.

Starlin, Jim, and George Perez. *Infinity Gauntlet* #1. Marvel, 1991.

Starlin, Jim, and Jim Aparo. "Ten Nights of the Beast Part 4." *Batman* #420. DC Comics, 1988.

Starlin, Jim, and Larry Herndon. "Doomsday!" *Star-Studded* #16. Texas Trio, 1969.

Starlin, Jim, and Marv Wolfman. "How Strange My Destiny!" *Warlock* #10. Marvel, 1975.

Starlin, Jim, and Mike Friedrich. "Thanos the Insane God!" *Captain Marvel* #32. Marvel, 1974.

Starlin, Jim, and Mike Mignola. *Cosmic Odyssey* #4. DC Comics, 1988.

Starlin, Jim, and Steve Skeates. "You Show Me Your Dream—I'll Show You Mine!!" *Journey into Mystery* vol. 2, #1, 1972.

Starlin, Jim, Ron Lim, and Shane Davis. "Ultimatum!" *Mystery in Space* #7. DC Comics, 2007.

Stein, Harry, and Mort Leav. *Air Fighters* #3. Hillman, 1942.

Steranko, Jim. "Jack Kirby Panel." *Dallas Fantasy Fair*. Comic Book Historians, 2018. https://youtu.be/vmCElMOvIlg?t=47.

_____. *The Steranko—History of Comics* #1. Supergraphics, 1970.

_____. *The Steranko—History of Comics* #2. Supergraphics, 1972.

Steranko, Jim, and Alex Grand. "The Steranko Experience." *Comic Book Historians YouTube Channel*, 2018.

Steward, Bhob, and J. Michael Catron. *The Life and Legend of Wallace Wood*. Seattle: Fantagraphics, 2016.

Strike, Joe. "Comic Chameleons." *Daily News*. Tribune Publishing, 13 August 2006.

Swan, Curt. *Superman's Girl Friend Lois Lane*. DC Comics, 1970.

Swan, Curt, and Edmond Hammilton. "The New Superman!" *Superman* #172. 1964.

Tampa Media Group. "Comic Book 'Czar' May Be Named." *The Tampa Tribune*. Tampa Media Group, 1954.

Taylor, Dan. "Zapping the POWers that be." *The Press Democrat*. Sonoma Media Investments, 10 February 1984.

Tesconi, Tim. "Superman comic book's super price." *The Press Democrat*. Santa Rosa: Sonoma Media Investments, 1992.

Tesh, John. "Spider-Man's Wedding—Shea Stadium 1987." *Entertainment Tonight*. ViacomCBS, 1987.

Theakston, Greg. "The Road to Spider-Man." *Steve Ditko Reader* #1. Pure Imagination, 2002.

Thomas, Roy. "Bill Everett & Joe Kubert Interviewed by Gil Kane & Neal Adams." *Alter Ego* #22. TwoMorrows, 2003.

_____. "Introduction." *Marvel Masterworks Captain Marvel*, vol. 2. Marvel, 2007.

_____. "Splitting the Atom." *Alter Ego* 3, #2. TwoMorrows, 1999.

Thomas, Roy, and John Buscema. "Come on in … the Revolution's Fine!" *The Avengers* #83. Marvel, 1970.

Thomas, Roy, and John Verpoorten. "Auntie Goose Rhymes Dept." *Not Brand Echh* #11. Marvel, 1968.

Thomas, Roy, Ross Andru, and Mike Esposito. "The Way to Dusty Death!" *Sub-Mariner* #37. Marvel, 1971.

Thomas, Tony, Rudy Behlmer, and Clifford McCarty. *The Films of Errol Flynn*. Secaucus: Citadel Press, 1969.

Thompson, Kim. "Marvel Focuses on Direct Sales." *The Comics Journal* #59. Fantagraphics, 1980.

Tilley, Carol L. "Seducing the Innocent: Fredric Wertham and the Falsifications That Helped Condemn Comics." *Information & Culture: A Journal of History* 47, no. 4. University of Texas Press, 2012.

Timely. "Re-Creator of Souls." *Red Raven Comics* #1. Timely, 1940.

Tollin, Anthony. "Spotlight on The Shadow." *The Shadow #1: The Golden Vulture and Crime Insured*. Nostalgia Ventures, 2006.

Tribune Publishing. "Deaths Elsewhere." *Chicago Tribune*. Tribune Publishing, 1967.

_____. "Powers of Darkness." *Chicago Daily Tribune*. Tribune Publishing, 1945.

Tye, Larry. *Superman: The High Flying History of America's Most Enduring Hero*. New York: Random House, 2013.

Uncredited. "Sleuths in Skirts." *Showcase* #9. DC Comics, 1956.

Uslan, Michael. *Superman: The World's Finest Comics Archives*, vol. 1. New York: DC Comics, 2004.

Vadeboncoeur, Jim, Jr. "About Winsor McCay." *Little Nemo in Slumberland: So Many Splendid Sundays*. Palo Alto: Sunday Press Books, 2014.

Vancheri, Barba. "A Super Club." *Pittsburgh Post-Gazette*. Block Communications, 13 June 2013.

Van Lente, Fred, and Ryan Dunlavey. *The Comic Book History of Comics.* San Diego: IDW, 2012.

Vassallo, Michael. "Joe Maneely: Adventure Comics." *Marvel Masterworks: Atlas Era Black Knight/Yellow Claw.* New York: Marvel, 2009.

Veitch, Rick. *Secret Agent Corrigan Volume Four: 1974–1977.* San Diego: IDW Publishing, 2013.

Vidal, David. "Superman comes to the rescue of his creators." *The Press Democrat.* Sonoma Media Investments, 1975.

Voger, Mark. "The Ghost Who Walks." *Ashbury Park Press,* 1996.

Vogt, Jenny. "Realism now entering heroes' lives and stories." *The Palm Beach Post,* 3 November 1988.

Voight, Charles. "Boom Brannigan." *Prize Comics* #58. 1946.

Von Hoffman, Nicholas. "When fear turns to exultation." *The Windsor Star.* Postmedia Network, 15 October 1970.

Von Maurer, Bill. "At the Earth's Core turns up dirt, dinosaurs." *The Miami News.* Cox Enterprises, 15 September 1976.

Wakin, Daniel J. "Italian Film Director Federico Fellini Dies." *Albuquerque Journal.* Journal Publishing Company, 1993.

Walker, Alexander. "Day that scared the 'Godfather." *Evening Standard.* Evgeny Lebedev, 19 May 1975.

Walker, Brian. *The Comics.* New York: Harry N. Abrams, 2002.

———. *The Comics.* New York: Harry N. Abrams, 2004.

———. "100 Years of King Features Syndicate—Part One." *Public Opinion,* 15 December 2015.

Walker, George. "The Passion of a Man." *Graphic Witness.* Firefly, 2007.

Walker, Karen. "Shattered Dreams: Vision and the Scarlet Witch." *Back Issue!* #45. TwoMorrows, 2010.

Wall, Anthony. *The Comic Strip Hero.* BBC, 1981.

Wallace, Dan. "Challengers of the Unknown." *The DC Comics Encyclopedia.* Dorling Kindersley, 2008.

Wallace, Daniel, Alan Cowsill, Alex Irvine, Matthew K. Manning, and Michael McAvennie. *DC Comics Year by Year: A Visual Chronicle.* New York: Dorling Kindersley, 2010.

Walsh, Michael. "Extra! Read all about Spider-Man!" *The Province.* Pacific Newspaper Group, 1977.

Warner Bros. Inc. v. American Broadcasting Companies Inc., 720 F.2d 231–248, 2d Cir., 1983.

Watson, Don. "Shazam! The hero breaks down." *The Observer.* Guardian Media Group, 2 November 1986.

Webb, Alvin B. "Spaceman Shepard Safe, Survives Shot." *Daily Herald-Telephone.* Daily Herald Media, 1961.

Webb, Robert. "The Origin of Electro." *Science Comics* #1. Fox Publications, 1940.

Webster, Andy. "Steve Ditko, 90, artist, co-creator of Spider-Man." *Republican and Herald.* Times-Shamrock, 2018.

Wein, Len, and Reed Crandall. *Creatures on the Loose* #13. Marvel, 1971.

Weinberg, Robert. "The Green Lama." *Pulp Classics* #14. Weinberg, 1976.

Weisinger, Hendre. *Comic Book Historians Podcast.* YouTube, 2020.

Wells, H.G. *Star Begotten.* Freeditorial, 1937.

Wells, John. *American Comic Book Chronicles 1965–1969.* Raleigh: TwoMorrows, 2014.

Welsh-Huggins, Andrew. "Rembrandt of the comics." *Daily Press.* Tribune Publishing, 28 October 2007.

Wentworth, John B., and Howard Purcell. "Sargon the Sorcerer." *All-American Comics* #26. All American Publications, 1941.

Wertham, Fredric. *The Brain as an Organ.* New York: Macmillan, 1934.

———. *The World of Fanzines.* Carbondale: Southern Illinois University Press, 1973.

Wessler, Carl, and Jack Kirby. "About Space-Face." *Fighting American* #7. Prize, 1955.

Wheeler-Nicholson, Nicky. *DC Comics Before Superman.* New Castle: Hermes Press, 2018.

White, Ted, and Stan Lee. "A Conversation with the Man Behind Marvel Comics, Stan Lee." *Castle of Frankenstein Magazine* #12. Gothic Castle Publishing, 1968.

White Family. "Fish is Mentally Ill, Psychiatrist Testifies at Trial." *Record-Journal.* White Family, 1935.

"William R. Hearst Dies; Founder of Modern Era of Journalism, Was 88." *Binghamton Press,* 14 August 1951.

Williams, Sara, and Lane Crockett. "Cash in on comics." *News-Press.* News-Press & Gazette Company, 15 December 1991.

Williams, Scott. "Gerry Conway: Everything but the Gwen Stacy Sink." *Back Issue!* #44. TwoMorrows Publishing, 2010.

Williamson, Al, and Mark Schultz. *Joseph Clement Coll: The Art of Adventure.* Santa Cruz: Flesk Publications, 2003.

Williamson, Al, and Peter Poplaski. "Introduction to Alex Raymond." *Flash Gordon: Mongo, the Planet of Doom.* Princeton: Kitchen Sink Press, 1990.

Winiarski, Ed. "The Spider Man!" *Uncanny Tales* #26. Marvel, 1954.

Wolfman, Marv. "A visit with Jack Kirby." *New Gods* #1. DC Comics, 1971.

Wood, Dave, and Jack Kirby. "The Day the Earth Blew Up!" *Showcase* #11. DC Comics, 1957.

———. "The Secrets of the Sorcerer's Box!" *Showcase* #6. DC Comics, 1957.

———. "Ultivac is Loose!" *Showcase* #7. DC Comics, 1957.

———. "The War That Never Ended." *Adventure Comics* #255. DC Comics, 1958.

Wood, Wally. "In Mortal Combat with … Sub-Mariner!" *Daredevil* #7. Marvel, 1965.

Woolfolk, Bill, and Carmine Infantino. "Enter: Rickie Wood." *Airboy* #32. Hillman, 1946.

Woollcombe, Alan. "Will Eisner." *The Independent*. Evgeny Lebedev, 2005.

Worth, Robert. "Savage Man is Taught Modern Man's Manners." *The Charlotte News*. Chatham Asset Management, 1932.

Wylie, Philip. *Gladiator Annotated*. Independently Published, 2021.

Yoe, Craig. *Secret Identity*. New York: Abrams, 2009.

Ziff-Davis. *Grand Comics Database*, 2021. https://www.comics.org/publisher/212/.

Zimmerman, Howard. "KIRBY takes on Comics." *Comics Scene* #2. Starlog Presents, 1982.

Interviews

Grand, Alex. *Bob McLeod Con Interview*. Comic Book Historians, 2021. https://youtu.be/Mt_BdKLXo9I.

———. *Bud Plant Biographical Interview*. Comic Book Historians, 2021. https://youtu.be/f12umtFZKwQ.

———. *Mike Royer, Inker of the Greats*. Comic Book Historians, 2018. https://youtu.be/cqFNC7QZmZM.

———. *The Steranko Experience*. Comic Book Historians, 2018. https://youtu.be/MyLfgrsyL-g.

Grand, Alex, and Bill Field. *Neal Adams Biographical Interview*. Comic Book Historians, 2021. https://youtu.be/kd4O_GiGhro.

Grand, Alex, and Filippo Marzo. *Jerry Ordway Power Hour Interview*. Comic Book Historians, 2021. https://youtu.be/f_o_Qpb85e4.

Grand, Alex, and Jim Thompson. *Carl Potts Biographical Interview*. Comic Book Historians, 2020. https://youtu.be/4HH6AQslPmM.

———. *Danny Fingeroth Biographical Interview*. Comic Book Historians, 2019. https://youtu.be/ER7sOR8TNGs.

———. *David Anthony Kraft Biographical Interview*. Comic Book Historians, 2020. https://youtu.be/eDlj2HjpzFs.

———. *Don McGregor Biographical Interview*. Comic Book Historians, 2021. https://youtu.be/WJux2Hw-ukM.

———. *Erik Larsen Biographical Interview*. Comic Book Historians, 2020. https://youtu.be/nSq8E5f0HA4.

———. *Frank Thorne Interview*. Comic Book Historians, 2021. https://youtu.be/k01GM7BB5h8.

———. *Gary Groth Biographical Interview*. Comic Book Historians, 2021. https://youtu.be/K7q6620dO20.

———. *Howard Chaykin Biographical Interview*. Comic Book Historians, 2021. https://youtu.be/W3tasvv_tb0.

———. *Jim Shooter Biographical Interview*. Comic Book Historians, 2021. https://youtu.be/FBh709_dLNs.

———. *Joe Staton Biographical Interview*. Comic Book Historians, 2020. https://youtu.be/41TUgNexSHo.

———. *Josef Rubinstein Biographical Interview*. Comic Book Historians, 2019. https://youtu.be/l-a7c7NQKT8.

———. *Lev Gleason: American Daredevil Interview with Brett Dakin*. Comic Book Historians, 2020. https://youtu.be/9rC_pM1LC7M.

———. *Mark Chiarello Biographical Interview*. Comic Book Historians, 2019. https://youtu.be/Ndbx2QSm8kQ.

———. *Mort Weisinger's Legacy with Hendre Weisinger*. Comic Book Historians, 2020. https://youtu.be/Ed9858EOwPg.

———. *Paul Levitz Biographical Interview*. Comic Book Historians, 2019. https://youtu.be/MD9Mt-FUDcY.

———. *Professor William H. Foster III & African Americans in Comics*. Comic Book Historians, 2021. https://youtu.be/ycxvn8uoW6I.

———. *Rick Marschall Biographical Interview*. Comic Book Historians, 2018. https://youtu.be/xiJjrNyB1b8.

———. *Robert Beerbohm's Comic Store Wars Interview*. Comic Book Historians, 2018. https://youtu.be/AecPQuQzUf8.

———. *Ron Frenz Biographical Interview*. Comic Book Historians, 2018. https://youtu.be/BJlow_oVPXE.

———. *Roy Thomas Power Hour Marvel Age Interview*. Comic Book Historians, 2021. https://youtu.be/_NBP2EYHyac.

———. *Steve Geppi Biographical Interview*. Comic Book Historians, 2020. https://youtu.be/_iekEvSvdjc.

———. *Tim Sale Biographical Interview*. Comic Book Historians, 2019. https://youtu.be/myfXsJqaAvVA.

———. *Tom Brevoort Biographical Interview*. Comic Book Historians, 2021. https://youtu.be/blLPFG-xbsg.

———. *Tom DeFalco Biographical Interview*. Comic Book Historians, 2020. https://youtu.be/985b1FFeqUQ.

———. *Tom Orzechowski Biographical Interview*. Comic Book Historians, 2017. https://youtu.be/AsLkUVho7qM.

———. *Tom Palmer Biographical Interview*. Comic Book Historians, 2021. https://youtu.be/XiDs65zCIo4.

———. *Trina Robbins Biographical Interview*. Comic Book Historians, 2019. https://youtu.be/Xmr3nIADcRQ.

Index

Page numbers in **bold italics** indicate pages with illustrations

Milton Keynes UK
Ingram Content Group UK Ltd.
UKHW020656150624
444068UK00006B/51

9 781476 690391